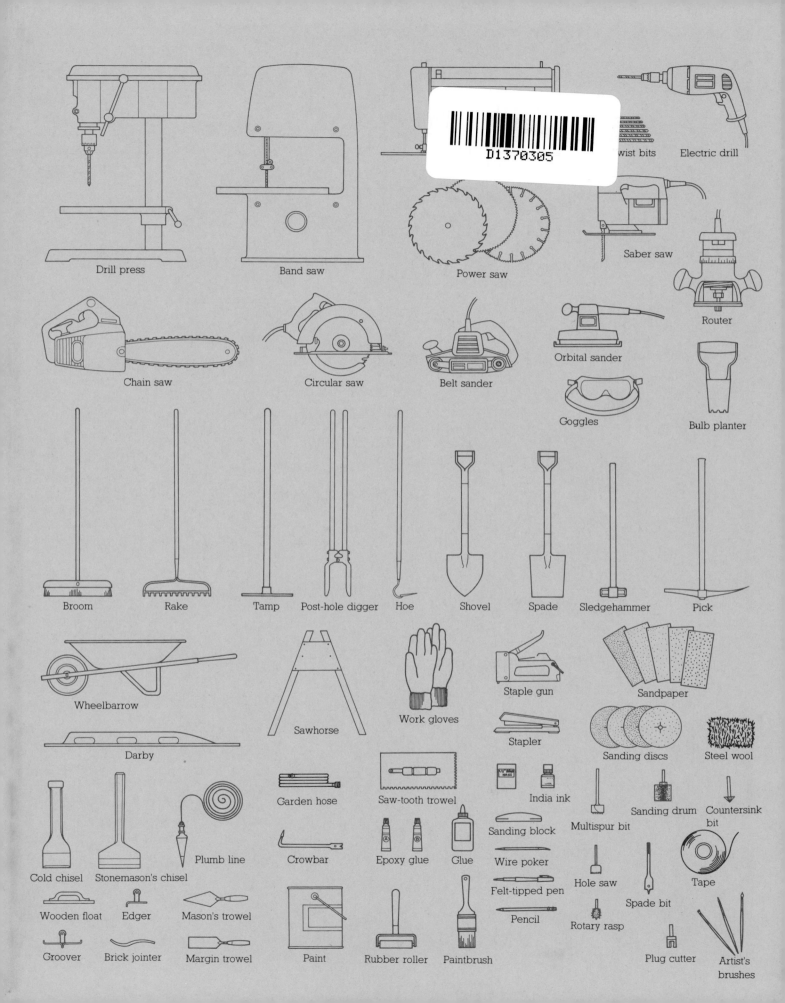

Drill press

Band saw

Power saw

Twist bits

Electric drill

Saber saw

Router

Chain saw

Circular saw

Belt sander

Orbital sander

Goggles

Bulb planter

Broom

Rake

Tamp

Post-hole digger

Hoe

Shovel

Spade

Sledgehammer

Pick

Wheelbarrow

Darby

Sawhorse

Work gloves

Staple gun

Stapler

Sandpaper

Sanding discs

Steel wool

Cold chisel

Stonemason's chisel

Plumb line

Garden hose

Crowbar

Saw-tooth trowel

Epoxy glue

Glue

India ink

Sanding block

Wire poker

Felt-tipped pen

Pencil

Multispur bit

Hole saw

Spade bit

Rotary rasp

Sanding drum

Countersink bit

Tape

Wooden float

Edger

Mason's trowel

Paint

Rubber roller

Paintbrush

Plug cutter

Artist's brushes

Groover

Brick jointer

Margin trowel

Reader's Digest

101 DO-IT-YOURSELF PROJECTS

Reader's Digest

101 DO-IT-YOURSELF PROJECTS

The Reader's Digest Association, Inc.
Pleasantville, New York
The Reader's Digest Association (Canada) Ltd.
Montreal

101 DO-IT-YOURSELF PROJECTS

The credits and acknowledgments that appear on the facing page and page 378 are hereby made a part of this copyright page.

Printed in the United States of America

Library of Congress Cataloging in Publication Data
Main entry under title:

101 do-it-yourself projects.

At head of title: Reader's digest.
Includes index.
1. Handicraft. 2. Do-it-yourself work. I. Reader's
Digest. II. Title: One hundred one do-it-yourself
projects. III. Title: One hundred and one do-it-yourself
projects.
TT157.A14 1983   684   82-61581
ISBN 0-89577-163-2

Staff

Project Editor
Wade A. Hoyt

Project Art Director
Joel Musler

Art Production Editor
Karen Mastropietro

Associate Editors
Valentin Chu
James Dwyer
Sally French
Robert V. Huber

Copy Editor
Elaine Pearlmutter

Art Associates
Gordon Chapman
Morris Karol
Edward R. Lipinski
Robert Steimle

Art Production Associate
Lisa Grant

Art Assistant
Carol Waters

Editorial Assistant
Barbara Flinn-Dunn

Group Art Director
David Trooper

Group Editor
Norman Mack

Contributors

Chief Woodworking Consultant
Joseph Dross

Contributing Consultants
Andrew Beason
Robert G. Beason
William Blanco
Frances Cohen
Karli R. Dwyer
Wendy Everett
Mario Ferro
Maurice Fraser
Thomas D. Garcia
Gene Hamilton
Katie Hamilton
Harry Lawton
Leonard G. Lee
Paul Lewis
Andres Mannik
Kenneth J. McGahren, RA
Barbara Murphy
Sam Posey
Bernard Price
Rudd Rowen
Robert Solomon
Henry Walthert
John Maury Warde

Contributing Artists
Dominic Colacchio
Michael Goodman
John A. Lind Assoc.
Peter McGinn
Bob McMahon
Max Menikoff
Ken Rice
Gerhard Richter
Jim Silks
Ray Skibinski
Robert K. Steimle
Russell J. von Sauers

Contributing Writers
David Hebb
Mort Schultz
Daniel Weiss

Contributing Photographers
Joseph Barnell
Wayne Bukevicz
Ernest Coppolino
Ellen Greisedieck
Gene Hamilton
William Sonntag

Cover photo:
Joseph Barnell.
Tools courtesy of
the Garrett Wade Co., Inc.

The editors are grateful
for the assistance
provided by
the following:

Tools and Equipment
Black & Decker Inc.
Fine Tools Shops
Garrett Wade Co., Inc.
General Products Co., Inc.
Heatilator, Inc., Div. of HON Industries
Rockwell International, Power Tools Div.
Shenandoah Mfg. Co., Inc.
Sony Corp. of America

Technical Advice
Boise Cascade Corp.
Brick Institute of America
California Redwood Assn.
Canadian Hardwood Plywood Assn.
Clay Brick Assn. of Canada
Lee Valley Tools, Ltd.
Mason & Sullivan Co.
Portland Cement Assn.
Shopsmith, Inc.

Materials
American Olean Tile
The Bartley Collection, Ltd.
California Redwood Assn.
Cohasset Colonials
E. I. du Pont de Nemours & Co.
Emperor Clock Co.
Heath Co.
Hunt Mfg. Co.
Lighting Products Div., McGraw-Edison Co.
L & M Surco Mfg., Inc.
Ralph Wilson Plastics Co.
Sears, Roebuck and Co.

Special thanks to Mr. and Mrs. David
Sposato for permission to photograph their
kitchen and to Pat Cooper for allowing us to
photograph her flagstone patio.

ABOUT THIS BOOK

101 Do-it-yourself Projects is designed for the person who enjoys making things. It is a book that will work hard for you. It is not meant to be read cover to cover while curled up in front of a roaring fire, as you might do with a good novel. Instead, start by browsing through the color gallery of the 101 projects, which begins on page 8. When you come across a particular project that appeals to you, turn to the plans to get some sense of how much skill and time are required. You can get a rough idea from the tools pictured on the opening page of each project. If there are a few simple hand tools, you can safely assume that the project is not complicated. If the column of tools is packed with expensive specialized tools, you can be sure that the project is for an experienced craftsman.

This book is not intended for someone who has never used a saw or hammered a nail. However, if you are already a do-it-yourselfer, you will find projects of varying degrees of difficulty, ranging from such relatively simple projects as a spice rack to challenging pieces of cabinetry for the highly experienced craftsman. The list that follows classifies all of the 101 projects into three categories, depending on both the skill and time required to finish each. *Apprentice* projects, suitable for anyone with even a little do-it-yourself experience, will not take much time and are easy to build. *Journeyman* projects

are for the builder who has advanced beyond the novice rank. *Craftsman* projects are the most difficult and time-consuming and may require tools not found in the ordinary workshop.

Apprentice projects: Coat tree, Pegged coffee table, Foyer bench, Window seat, Breakfast bar, Spice rack, Hanging storage rack, Cork message board, Knife storage block, Globe lamp, Stenciled blanket chest, Mission-style headboard, Reading lamp, Jewelry box, Kitchen or bar stool, Freestanding fireplace, Folding screen, Inlaid checker or chess board, Acrylic chess set, Picture frame, Outdoor table and bench, Outdoor lighting fixture, Deck or patio planter, Basket-weave garden fence, Trellis, Rock garden, PVC canvas chair, PVC bicycle rack, Bird feeder, Birdhouse, A-frame doghouse, Picket fence and gate, Compost bin, Window greenhouse, Log tote and cradle, Metal jewelry, Playground set, Children's workbench and tool caddy, Modular dollhouses, Rocker and seesaw, Grandfather clock kit, Low bed and trundle bed kits, Butler's table kit.

Journeyman projects: Plywood desk, Shaker plant stand, Early American bookcase, Vinyl-covered couch, Modular couch, Serving cart, Mobile work island, Peninsula work center, Cafe table and chairs, Menu-planning center, Butcher-block table, Storage bins, Bathroom vanity, Early American night table, Old-world workbench, Room divider, Sewing center, Built-in bookcase, Prep and serve center, Mobile dry bar, Chinese boxes wall unit, Picnic or patio table, Tie garden, Concrete driveway, patio, or walk, Potting cart, Garden fountain, Refuse

locker, Brick driveway, patio, or walk, Flagstone patio, Brick-and-wood steps, Concrete steps, Glass-house terrarium, Steel wine rack, Downhill racer, Candle-powered boats, Bunk beds, Jungle gym, Chest of drawers kit.

Craftsman projects: Rolltop desk, Jointed hardwood bookcase, Trestle coffee table, Dining table, TV and stereo cabinet, Cherry end table, Kitchen base cabinet, Kitchen wall cabinet, Kitchen cupboard, Chest of drawers, Platform bed, Cabinet headboard unit, Entertainment center, Built-in fireplace, Greenhouse, Storage shed, Wooden deck, Brick screening wall, Brick barbecue, Stained-glass lamp.

It is the hope of the editors that the beginner will be able to advance from *Apprentice* to *Journeyman* and even *Craftsman* projects as his skills and confidence increase with the use of this book. Before starting any project, be sure to price the materials and any special tools that are required for the job. Also see pages 44–45, which show how to change our plans to suit varying tastes and needs. And do not overlook the *Index of construction techniques* (p.379), which serves as a cross-reference to the entire book.

—The Editors

CONTENTS

WARNING!

Many of the 101 projects require the use of potentially dangerous power tools. For clarity, most of the illustrations do not show the protective guards that are supplied with these tools, but you should always operate such tools with their guards in place, carefully following all of the manufacturer's operating instructions and safety advice.

GALLERY OF 101 DO-IT-YOURSELF PROJECTS

On the following 36 pages you will find color illustrations of all 101 projects that were designed for this book. Each illustration is accompanied by a brief description of the project and the page number on which it begins.

As you browse through this gallery, keep in mind that the projects are intended to appeal to various tastes and levels of skill. Some of them are for beginners who are just learning carpentry and other do-it-yourself skills, others are for highly ambitious and experienced craftsmen. However, the vast majority are for practiced do-it-yourselfers who are not yet so bold as to think of themselves as craftsmen. Whatever your level of expertise, you will find something here for you. You may want to start with the simpler projects and, as your ability increases, move on to more demanding ones.

There is not room in this book to repeat the directions for every procedure in every project. If, for example, you are working on a project where you must cut dadoes, and no specific instructions are given for cutting them, you will find this procedure—and many others—cross-referenced in the *Index of construction techniques*, which begins on page 379. Here you will be directed to another project where the operation of cutting dadoes is explained in step-by-step detail. Therefore, it is important to remember that whenever a project does not explain every construction technique, you will be able to locate instructions by turning to this special index.

Because tastes and furnishing styles differ, information on varying our plans has been included (pp.44–45) so that, for example, you can use the plans for an Early American bookcase to make a modern bookcase. You will also find useful advice on buying lumber, plywood, and hardwood (pp.46–47) and instructions on how to use the grids found in many projects to make full-size patterns (p.48).

ROLLTOP DESK / p.52

This is an ambitious project and well worth the effort. When you are finished, you will have created a piece of furniture that should remain beautiful and useful for a lifetime. Lumber-core plywood is used throughout except for the hardwood handles and trim—and of course the tambour, or rolltop, which is made from thirty ¾-in. hardwood slats glued to a canvas backing. All exposed edges are veneered to match the plywood.

PLYWOOD DESK / p.49

Here is proof that an attractive design can be simple and inexpensive to build. A single panel of ¾-in. plywood yields all major parts of the desk except the drawer bottom, which is ⅛-in. Masonite. The top of the desk shown here is covered with white plastic laminate, and the sides are veneered in walnut to match the scheme of the room for which the piece was built. You could use any other veneers without changing our plans.

SHAKER PLANT STAND /p.58

The religious creed of the austere Shaker sect included a reverence for good, unornamented workmanship. This clean and graceful design is true to the Shaker code. Because of its very simplicity, the joinery must be precise—a single careless joint will make the whole piece look sloppy. Plans call for the use of hand tools—a drill is the only power tool needed, and even it could be replaced by an old-fashioned brace and bit.

COAT TREE /p.60

Oak and brass work well together in this traditional piece. The gracefully curved feet are joined to the beveled body with hardwood dowels. Plans include instructions on making a doweling jig to ensure that the dowel holes are identically spaced.

EARLY AMERICAN BOOKCASE /p.62

Plans for this knotty pine bookcase, with its six adjustable shelves, are easily adapted to suit your needs. The freestanding piece shown here calls for mitered moldings at the top and base. If the moldings are cut straight and applied only to the front, the piece becomes one unit of a wall-to-wall bookcase. If the moldings are eliminated altogether, the bookcase is not only cheaper and easier to make, but its clean lines will also harmonize with modern furnishings.

PEGGED COFFEE TABLE /p.76

Rugged, rustic, and easy to build—provided that you begin with straight 4 x 4 lumber and heavy-duty tools—this table is held together entirely by hardwood dowels and glue. The project includes plans for such variations as square and rectangular tables, benches, and stools so that you can completely furnish a playroom, patio, or outdoor dining area.

FOYER BENCH /p.86

A little extra storage space is always welcome, especially in the places where this traditional Early American bench is designed to go. It is a charming and convenient addition to an entryway or stair landing, and the hinged seat lifts up to reveal a chest for linens, toys, outdoor gear, or whatever else you may wish to store.

JOINTED HARDWOOD BOOKCASE /p.68

Time-honored techniques of joinery and hand workmanship go into this modern design, the softly flowing lines crafted from solid cherry and ash. Of special interest to the woodworker is the separate plinth, its mitered corners reinforced by splines and its entire structure strengthened by laminated corner blocks so that it will be sturdy enough to stand up under a full load of books. The back of the bookcase rests directly on the back piece of the plinth, but the other three edges fit into 1-in. rabbets in the plinth sides and front. The plinth and bookcase units are not glued together or joined in any way—a standard cabinetry device to avoid the problems that would result from joining two pieces of wood whose grains run in opposite directions. The project includes instructions on edge-joining: gluing two or more narrow boards together to make one wide one.

DINING TABLE /p.80

The sharply defined figure of African zebrawood lends a dramatic flair to this extension-leaf table. It is an expensive material, however, and difficult to work with. You could build the table from almost any hardwood without altering the basic design. The top and leaves are of lumber-core plywood with hardwood edging, and the legs and aprons are of matching hardwood stock. The table is 35½ in. wide and 56 in. long when the leaves are in their storage position. Each leaf adds 22½ in. to the length so that when the table is fully extended the overall length is nearly 8½ ft.

VINYL-COVERED COUCH /p.88

When you have completed this project, you will possess more than a comfortable and attractive couch—you will have acquired the skill of building upholstered furniture out of plywood, polyurethane foam, and vinyl fabric. You can then apply the techniques that you used for this couch to the design and construction of matching chairs.

CHERRY END TABLE /p.108

SERVING CART /p.112

The sculptured beauty of this delicate-looking table is the result of careful hand shaping. Its sturdiness is due to equally careful mortise-and-tenon joinery and a precisely fitted shelf. Plans include a pattern for the tapered legs and instructions on installing the top with slotted screw blocks, which allow the wood to expand and contract with changes in humidity.

Serve your guests in style from a rolling cart of red oak and glass—or use the piece as an elegant portable stand for plants, a TV set, or a microwave oven. Each plate-glass shelf rests on a latticelike frame of interlocking ½-in. oak strips. The center shelf is adjustable.

MODULAR COUCH /p.94

Three units—a sofa and two chairs—make a versatile living room set that is easy to build. The frames are made of plywood, covered with red oak tongue-and-groove flooring and trimmed with strips of red oak lumber. Casters enable you to move all the units easily despite their weight. Plans include step-by-step instructions for making cushions to fit the seats, backs, and arms of all three pieces.

WINDOW SEAT/p.106

A bay window without a seat just begs for the addition of this cozy built-in bench. A hinged lid in the seat provides extra storage space as well. Plans tell how to build a seat of this design into a bay or bow window of any size.

TRESTLE COFFEE TABLE/p.72

The same designer who created the cherry end table on the opposite page gave us this graceful coffee table of solid birch. Like that project—and like the jointed hardwood bookcase shown on page 10—this piece is intended for the craftsman who takes pleasure in working intimately with wood. The tapered top, feet, and stretcher are shaped with a rasp, plane, chisel, and spokeshave. The top is of special interest on several counts. It is made by edge-joining five narrow boards with a board of dark heartwood in the center. This straight, dark stripe contrasts with the tapered shape and heightens the illusion of thinness at both ends, created by rounding the undersides slightly. Rabbeted buttons, which secure the top to the base and fit into grooves in the crosspieces, allow the wood to adjust to changes in humidity. Plans include instructions for making mortise-and-tenon joints.

TV AND STEREO CABINET/p.100

When you want your stereo or TV set out of the way, just close the doors of this rich walnut cabinet and all you will see is a fine piece of furniture. The doors of the left-hand section open to reveal three shelves wide enough to house most stereo components. The right-hand section is divided into six compartments that are just the right height for storing records upright. Instructions for building the pullout tray for the TV set are included in the *Entertainment center* project, which begins on page 206.

KITCHEN CABINETS/pp.115, 120

Nowhere in the house is space at more of a premium than in the kitchen. Glassware, crockery, pots and pans, utensils, spices, canned foods, packaged goods—all must go somewhere and still leave room for appliances, plumbing, and work surfaces. Each kitchen is unique, so the modular cabinets that are the basis of most kitchen designs should be custom fitted. In these two projects detailed plans are given for the cabinets shown at the left, and methods are discussed for adapting the plans to available space, as in the kitchen above. Below are some possible variations.

VARIATIONS

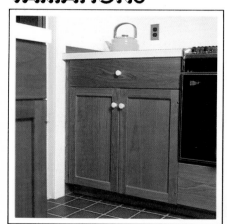

A base cabinet with a single wide drawer and two flush-mounted doors nestles between the wall and a built-in electric range. The drawer is deep enough for cooking utensils; the cabinet space beneath holds pots and pans.

Two units—an open-faced wall cabinet and a base cabinet with two wide doors—give the impression of a one-piece hutch. Note the short backsplash attached to the counter top, preventing liquids from running down the wall.

This clever double-hinged door makes the most of a space that might otherwise be wasted. A piano hinge joins the two panels, which swing together to the left on flush-mounted pivot hinges to reveal L-shaped corner shelves where canned goods are stored.

KITCHEN CUPBOARD /p. 124

Although this compact cupboard is only 30 in. wide, its double doors conceal more than 45 ft. of usable shelf space, ranging in depth from 3⅝ to 16 in. The secret is in the two swing-out units, which are connected to the center divider by piano hinges. Each has a full set of shelves, and behind each is another set of shelves built into the back of the cupboard proper.

BREAKFAST BAR /p. 136

Within the mahogany frame of this convenient counter, ceramic tiles form an attractive surface that is easy to wipe clean. The bar makes a pleasant place for an informal breakfast, an ideal buffet, or an extra work space. It is fixed to the wall, so there are no legs to get in the way.

PENINSULA WORK CENTER /p. 132

You can divide a large kitchen to make a separate dining area with this peninsula work center, or you can replace an existing wall with this unit to make the separation between the rooms less distinct. The two lower cabinets for this project were bought ready-made, then screwed together (one faces the kitchen, the other the dining area) and covered with a single counter. The upper unit was custom-built and fitted with sliding glass doors.

MOBILE WORK ISLAND /p. 128

Locking casters and a 1½-in. butcher-block top make this cabinet on wheels a handy item in any kitchen. It provides extra work space and can be easily moved to wherever needed, from kitchen to dining room to patio. In addition, the unit features two adjustable shelves and a built-in dispenser that holds a roll of 30 plastic garbage bags.

CAFE TABLE AND CHAIRS /p.139

Oak tongue-and-groove flooring and plywood form the two layers of this small table's round top, and the laminated edge is covered with birch-veneer tape. The rest of the table and its matching chairs are made of poplar. Plans include patterns for the table's tapered feet and braces, as well as the chairs' subtly curved back posts. legs, and side rails.

MENU-PLANNING CENTER /p.144

Although designed for the kitchen, this wall-mounted unit can be a useful addition to almost any room in the house. Behind its fold-down door are assorted shelves and compartments in which to organize recipes, bills, receipts, lists, letters, and other paperwork. The door itself becomes a writing surface when open. The menu-planning center is made of mahogany with brass fittings.

SPICE RACK /p.148

Recycle your empty vitamin bottles to make a striking set of spice containers, and store them in plain sight with this cleverly designed rack of interlocking oak strips. Yokelike slots are cut in the crosspieces to fit the narrow necks of the bottles so that each bottle slides effortlessly in and out of its assigned spot. Plans are easily adapted to make a rack wider or longer than shown in order to accommodate more bottles.

HANGING STORAGE RACK /p.156

Add a little open storage space for attractive crockery and kitchen implements by suspending these slatted maple shelves on brass chains from the ceiling, the bottom of a cabinet, or in some other spot that is going to waste. This simple project can be built with hand tools, although a power drill and circular saw will make the job even easier. Any hardwood can be used in place of the maple, but softwood is not recommended.

BUTCHER-BLOCK TABLE /p.150

Strips of 1½-in. walnut alternate with traditional maple to give this butcher-block table top an unusual and dramatic appearance. The trestle base is made entirely of maple, and the whole piece is finished with antiquing oil for a long-lasting luster. Complete instructions are given for constructing butcher blocks, from selecting the stock to cutting, planing, and joining the pieces.

STORAGE BINS /p.152

You can store more than 1½ pecks of dry food, such as rice, macaroni, peas, or beans, in each of this handsome cabinet's drawer bins (nearly half a bushel in the lower bins). The cabinet shell is made entirely of cherry-veneer plywood with solid cherry edging, although you could use some other hardwood. The bins are also of cherry plywood with mahogany plywood bottoms; their sloping fronts are solid cherry frames—made with mortise-and-tenon joints—that surround clear glass panels. Plans tell how to make a simple jig for cutting the 80½° angles needed to create the raked front.

CORK MESSAGE BOARD/p.158

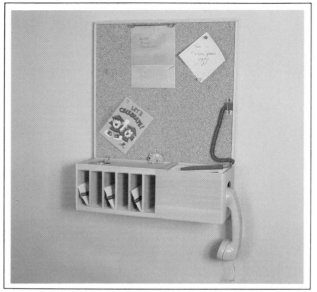

More than a mere bulletin board for shopping lists and other general items, this handy message center has a pigeonhole for each family member's notes and mail, a built-in paper roll and permanently attached pen, and even a place to hang the phone receiver while you write.

KNIFE STORAGE BLOCK/p.160

Every kitchen needs a safe and convenient place to store knives so that their cutting edges will not be dulled by contact with each other. This relatively simple project gives you such a place—and the piece is good-looking as well. All the parts can be cut from a 38-in.-long board of ⅝ x 12 hard maple.

BATHROOM VANITY/p.162

The distinctive look of copper, brass, and marble combines with the rich tones of walnut in this elegantly paneled vanity. The sink is made from a 12-in. copper mixing bowl, and the marblelike surface in which it rests is actually man-made Corian, a material that is almost as easy to cut and shape as wood. Standard brass fixtures complete the work surface. The walnut cabinet has panels of ½-in. stock planed to a thickness of ¼ in. Plans tell how to use walnut plywood as a substitute. Variations include a double sink and a vanity designed for a standard-size bathroom sink.

EARLY AMERICAN NIGHT TABLE/p.166

This traditional night table with its graceful lines fits right into almost any bedroom decor. Ours was made of inexpensive pine, then given a walnut finish to match an existing bedroom set. The same plans could be used for a hardwood table.

GLOBE LAMP/p.168

Modern geometric styling is easy to achieve, using prewired globe fixtures for these lamps. The bases are boxes made of ½-in. particle board covered with plastic laminate—you could use cork, mirror tile, or any other covering just as well. Plans include a smaller variation, with a simple spherical light bulb in place of a globe, and a formula for determining the size of any base from the circumference of an available globe fixture.

CHEST OF DRAWERS/p.170

The trick of constructing this stackable chest of drawers is to make identical dovetail joints in all units. When they are properly done—plans for the project tell you how—the dovetails look like butterfly joints holding the sections together. In fact, the interchangeable sections are not joined to each other but are held in alignment by pegs. New sections can be added or old ones removed to meet the needs of the moment. Plans include instructions for installing drawers with self-aligning dovetailed hardwood guides.

READING LAMP/p.190

Ample reading light, focused exactly where you want it, is the main feature of this wall-mounted bedside lamp of copper and maple. The housing swings from side to side, the head swivels two ways, and the 19-in. arm telescopes out to a total length of 25 in. Plans include patterns for the parts of the copper shade and instructions for shaping and soldering them.

MISSION-STYLE HEADBOARD/p.188

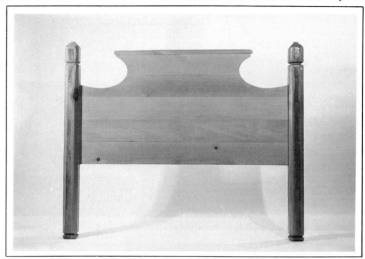

Clean lines and simple ornamentation were hallmarks of the wooden furniture that originated in the Spanish missions of the Old Southwest. The style is clearly reflected in this headboard of pine and cedar, designed to fit a standard double bed. Plans tell how to adapt the headboard's dimensions for beds of different sizes.

STENCILED BLANKET CHEST/p.176

White birds and blue tulips decorate this colorful chest of painted pine. Its design was inspired by the brides' chests in which young Pennsylvania Dutch girls of more than a century ago accumulated handmade clothing, household goods, and other treasures for their future weddings. Plans tell how to make and use templates for routing the decorative grooves in the front and side panels.

PLATFORM BED/p.180

A challenging project, this queen-size platform bed features a distinctive sunburst headboard, veneered in walnut and oak to match the woods used in the bed. Four large drawers of birch plywood with oak facings give plenty of storage space beneath the overhanging platform. Plans include dado patterns for the tongue-and-groove joints of the bed frame and drawers, as well as complete instructions on cutting and applying the wedge-shaped veneer pieces for the headboard.

CABINET HEADBOARD UNIT/p.185

This handsome unit, designed as an alternative to the sunburst headboard for the platform bed shown above, can be easily adapted for use with any queen-size bed. Like the platform bed, it is made mostly of walnut and oak, with oak-faced drawers of birch plywood, and its basic joinery is tongue and groove. Plans include dado patterns for all joints and instructions for installing the sliding doors on runners.

JEWELRY BOX / p.192

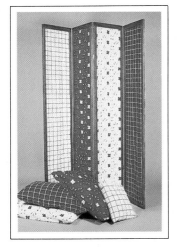

Though it has the look of translucent marble, the man-made Corian used for the body of this box can be cut and shaped with the same woodworking tools that are used for the teak interior. The top tips back at the touch of a finger to display your valuables, neatly sorted into seven compartments of various sizes.

OLD-WORLD WORKBENCH / p.194

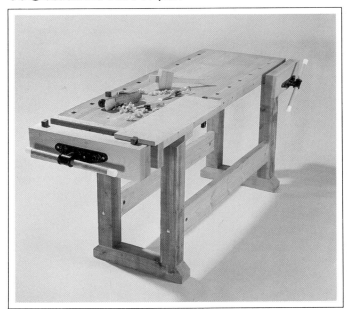

A good workbench is the heart of a woodworking shop. This one, modeled after a Scandinavian design, features a hard maple top, two built-in vises, and a flexible system of bench dogs capable of handling large panels or small blocks. The sturdy underframe is made of mortised-and-tenoned pine lumber.

FOLDING SCREEN / p.236

Versatility best describes this screen, useful for closing off a work area, temporarily dividing a room, or performing many other similar services. Its fabric panels are stretched between removable dowels so that they can be changed to suit the mood of the moment. Almost any wood can be used for the frames—these are made of red oak with a teak stain and a tung oil finish.

ENTERTAINMENT CENTER /p.206

Stereo, tape deck, turntable, TV set, VCR—there is room in this handsome unit for all of these home entertainment components and more. A demanding project, the entertainment center features pivoting pullout trays in the lower cabinets and adjustable shelves in the upper section.

SEWING CENTER /p.202

This wall-mounted cabinet has two personalities. Closed, it offers a handy assortment of needles, thread, and other emergency repair items. Open, it becomes a worktable for more ambitious needlework; there is plenty of room behind the fold-down door for a portable sewing machine, patterns, materials, and other supplies.

PREP AND SERVE CENTER/p.220

Prepare a simple meal or appetizers on this versatile oak unit, place the prepared food on its shelves—together with the china and stemware you will need—and then wheel the entire meal to the table. Or use the unit as a portable bar. The drop leaf will shield the contents of one shelf when it is down and will double the work surface when it is raised. The entire piece can be easily disassembled for storage.

KITCHEN OR BAR STOOL/p.218

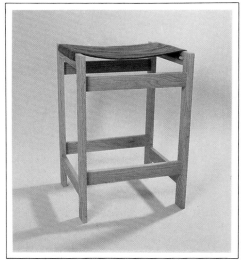

Lightweight and comfortable, this contemporary oak stool with its corduroy sling seat is ideal for use either in the kitchen or at the bar. If you plan to use it in the kitchen, build it 26 in. high as shown. If you prefer to use it as a bar stool, adjust the legs to suit the height of your bar.

BUILT-IN BOOKCASE/p.214

A wall-to-wall bookcase adds dignity and elegance to a room. The built-in bookcase shown here has a hutchlike design. The deep lower section has three compartments, the center one divided by a shelf that can be used for flat objects like scrapbooks. The high area under the shelf can be used for storing records or large books. The outer compartments have doors and can also be equipped with shelves. There is room for stereo components, a television set, or video recorder on top of the lower compartments. The upper section of the bookcase consists of shallow shelves that are ideal for books and knickknacks. The bookcase is constructed of birch plywood and pine. Tongue-and-groove knotty pine floorboards give the unit a warm, country look. Some parts are painted and others are varnished.

MOBILE DRY BAR /p.224

If you like to give parties, you can build this mobile dry bar and serve your guests in style. When the party is over, store your supplies in the cabinet underneath the bar, fold down the hinged top to reduce its size by two-thirds, and roll the entire unit into an out-of-the-way corner.

FREESTANDING FIREPLACE /p.234

Want to get back to basics and heat your home with wood? If so, you can install a woodburning stove or the freestanding fireplace shown here. The unit is sold already assembled (you need only screw on the legs), but you will have to install the stovepipe and chimney and build a heat-resistant platform and wall shield to reduce the hazard of fire. The platform is made of asbestos sandwiched between tile and plywood. The copper-covered shield is positioned 1½ in. from the wall.

BUILT-IN FIREPLACE /p.228

The roar of an open fire is tamed to produce useful heat in this Advantage fireplace with its glass doors, cold air intake, and heat-circulating ducts. Heatilator supplies the basic elements of the fireplace in several kits, but the builder must install them and construct the hearth and the enclosing walls. Although this is an ambitious project for a do-it-yourselfer, it is a rewarding one that will give many years of pleasure to your family.

For this installation the fireplace was set at a 63° angle to one wall, rather than the usual 45°, so that it could fit into a corner with one wall that was less than 4 ft. long. The oak mantel opens out to cover the top of the built-in log bin. Matching oak facing is used around the tile hearth, and the heat vents are disguised by oak molding and decorative brass trivets that match the brass trim on the fireplace. Plans include instructions for installing the fireplace, hearth, chimney, and roof termination.

ACRYLIC CHESS SET/p.240

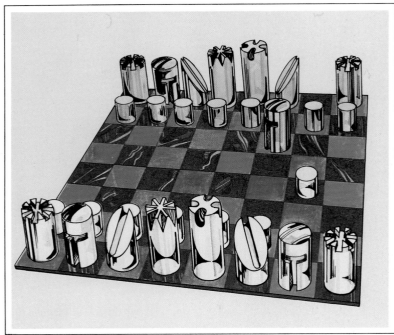

Light refraction is the reason that each of these highly stylized chessmen is identifiable at a glance. The pieces and pawns are all made of clear acrylic rod, a material that seems to absorb and glow with passing rays of light. The symbols of rank are created with a minimum of filing and polishing. One set is soaked in black dye, resulting in a rich amber color, while the other set remains clear. The board is a piece of black acrylic; steel wool is used to lighten alternate squares.

CHINESE BOXES WALL UNIT/p.244

This striking piece is surprisingly easy to build, whether made of inexpensive pine lumber, as used here, or a more elegant hardwood. The corners of all four boxes are made with double rabbet joints, and the spacers between the boxes are inserted into blind dadoes. The wall unit can be equally serviceable as a room divider. Plans include cutting patterns for all the rabbets and dadoes.

ROOM DIVIDER /p.198

An open-faced record compartment, a storage cabinet with translucent doors, and a cabinet open on both sides are just three of the possible features that make this room divider useful and versatile. The basic structure—two ladderlike floor-to-ceiling frames joined by stretchers—is made of 5/4 red oak lumber. The cabinets are red oak plywood with solid trim, and the doors are smoked acrylic plastic. The cabinet units rest on adjustable shelf supports and can be easily removed if you want to relocate the room divider.

INLAID CHECKER OR CHESS BOARD /p.238

Each square of this distinctive game board is made by gluing together a dozen small oak floor tiles. All the tiles of one square are aligned with the end grain showing, and all the tiles of the next square have the side grain up. Because end grain absorbs more liquid than side grain does, one application of oil stain serves to color both the dark and the light squares.

PICTURE FRAME /p.242

A print should be protected by glass, and its frame must allow for the thickness of the glass as well as the mat that keeps the glass from touching the print. Plans tell how to construct a frame, how to cut the mat, and how to mount the picture with tape. The instructions can be used to make any style frame.

PICNIC OR PATIO TABLE /p.247

Eight people can sit comfortably at this octagonal table with its four matching benches. Not only do the benches complement the table's distinctive design, but they are also free of the usual problems that come with picnic benches: they do not easily tip over, and they allow people to come and go without disturbing everyone else. The legs and braces are bolted to the table and bench tops for easy disassembly.

DECK OR PATIO PLANTER /p.256

This ingenious project is nothing but notched 1 x 4's, which can be arranged in a number of ways to hold potted plants or enclose an inexpensive sheet-metal planting box. Plans include patterns for square, rectangular, and L-shaped planters. By cutting the notches at an angle, you could also make a planter to match the design of the picnic table above.

OUTDOOR LIGHTING FIXTURE /p.254

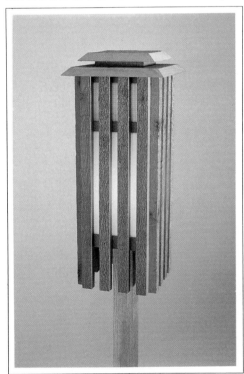

Like a cage of fireflies, this cedar lamp will cast a soft glow over your patio or doorstep, or along your driveway or garden path. Construction is simple and the plans are easily adapted so that you can make several matching lights at once. A 6-ft. length of 1 x 12 yields all the wood for each fixture; the plastic diffusion panels come from a fluorescent light.

OUTDOOR TABLE AND BENCH /p.252

Whether built with the 2 x 2 slats running in one direction or arranged in a herringbone pattern (like that used for the bench at the rear of the picture), this striking set of low-slung occasional pieces is handy for the lawn, deck, patio, or poolside. Our table and bench are made of pressure-treated pine, covered with a coat of latex paint. Redwood, cedar, or another outdoor wood can be used.

WOODEN DECK /p.301

The tiered design of this redwood deck makes it ideal for a gently sloping yard but by no means limits it to such a site. Plans for this ambitious project are adaptable and include instructions for seating the posts firmly so that the deck will be level whether the land is or not. The 3-ft.-square modules that compose the floor can be assembled indoors in advance when the weather is bad. Note the outthrust joists, which form "shelves" for planting boxes.

GREENHOUSE / p. 258

The Lucite used in this project is not only shatter-resistant, but it also has better insulating properties than glass. The interior is finished with redwood tongue-and-groove paneling. You can build the greenhouse on an existing patio or deck (as this one was), or you can start from scratch and build a foundation.

REFUSE LOCKER / p.298

Among life's irksome details, trash cans rate high. You cannot really do without them, but they are unsightly at best and often attract dogs, raccoons, and assorted varmints. While we do not promise that this refuse locker will make trash fun, it is an easy and inexpensive way to make two 32-gal. cans less of a problem. The frame is pine lumber in standard sizes; the floor, hinged lid, and sliding doors are ¾-in. plywood; and the exterior is prefinished siding with the look of split cedar. You could also use siding to match your house.

TIE GARDEN / p.264

A pink-flowered azalea and other evergreen shrubs overlook a bed of pachysandra in this terraced garden. Lower tiers hold seasonal flowers—marigolds among red tulips, and Johnny-jump-ups backed by white zonal geraniums. The 6 x 6 ties that separate the levels are held in place by ½-in. steel rods, and the short crossties that border the stepping stones are secured with 20d nails. Plans tell how to design a tie garden to suit your own landscaping needs.

ROCK GARDEN /p.272

Daffodils, tulips, hyacinths, and other bright bulbs are the springtime highlight of this doorstep garden. Later on the flowers of summer— including black-eyed Susans and New England asters— will take over. Plans feature a suggested layout for this 14- x 20-ft. plot as well as tips on designing and building your own rock garden, whether the plot is on level ground, a gentle slope, or a rocky hillside.

BASKET-WEAVE GARDEN FENCE /p.266

Interwoven 1 x 8's make a fence that is strong for its weight and that screens a garden area without cutting off all light and air. Plans include instructions on setting 4 x 4 posts in several kinds of soil. Variations on the basic post-and-rail construction are shown, such as board-on-board, grape-stake, and louvered fencing.

TRELLIS / p.270

Honeysuckle vines, morning glories, Virginia creepers, climbing roses, and espaliered fruit trees are among the plants that grow more happily with a solid trellis for support. This one is 5 ft. high and 6 ft. wide and is secured to firmly seated 4 x 4 posts. Variations include an open ladder-work design and an A-frame trellis that doubles as a shady shelter.

BIRDHOUSE /p.284

House-hunting bluebirds will find that this cedar and pine nesting box is made cozily to order for raising a family—especially if you mount it on a 5- to 10-ft. post in an open field. (They are not apt to nest in any place as busy as a suburban yard, however.) Plans tell how to adapt this design to suit the needs of many kinds of birds, from wrens to wood ducks, as well as how to build a log nesting box for such woodland species as chickadees, titmice, nuthatches, and owls.

BIRD FEEDER /p.282

This tufted titmouse finds a meal of seeds to its liking. Downy woodpeckers and other meat eaters will be attracted by the suet on the other side of this redwood bird feeder—the floor is tilted slightly so that seeds slide into the proper trough. The roof of the feeder is easily removed so that the seed supply can be replenished.

STORAGE SHED /p.278

Cedar shingles cover the walls of this handy outbuilding, while the shallow gambrel roof is protected by asphalt shingling. The floor space of about 88 sq. ft. allows plenty of room for your yard and garden tools or for a small workshop if you prefer. The roof is slightly higher than 8 ft. at the center, and the door measures 3 x 6 ft. Plans include instructions on laying a floor of paving stone—although you might want a wood, concrete, or plain dirt floor instead.

PVC AND CANVAS CHAIR /p.274

A-FRAME DOGHOUSE /p.286

Your dog will be as appreciative as this one is when you give him a two-room A-frame house built to his own specifications. The small front room acts as a windbreak so that Fido will be warmer in the winter. A floor made of slats keeps him off the damp ground, prevents him from digging inside the house, and allows dirt to fall through. The roof is hinged so that you can clean his private den when necessary—or reach him if he is sick or hurt. Plans tell how to adapt the design for dogs of various sizes.

Although intended for plumbing, PVC (polyvinyl chloride) pipe has many other virtues. It is easy to cut with a hacksaw and to join with standard fittings—the ends need not be squared, mitered, or threaded. It is lightweight, sturdy, and weatherproof and can yield attractive outdoor furniture like this sling chair. Plans give complete instructions on how to work with PVC pipe and also include patterns for the canvas seat and back.

PVC BICYCLE RACK /p.276

When you buy a factory-made bicycle rack, chances are that the wheel slots will be a single size—too narrow for the thick tires and wide forks of many children's bikes and too wide to give proper support to a slender 10-speed racer or touring model. The slots will also be so close together that tangled handlebars become a problem. In this project you will learn how to create your own rack to the dimensions you need, using only PVC pipe and elbow fittings.

POTTING CART/p.288

Gardening will be a pleasure with this handsome oak potting cart. The trough at the top is ideal for containing soil, and the slatted shelf is for storing gardening supplies. You can wheel the cart anywhere you need it, indoors or out. You can also transform it into a serving cart by covering the trough with a removable top.

COMPOST BIN/p.292

Most compost bins are crude receptacles built of scrap wood or chicken wire. They are efficient but unsightly. This one is made of redwood, which is both attractive and rot-resistant. You can build it either as a solid unit or with one removable end.

GARDEN FOUNTAIN/p.296

The gentle sound of cool water trickling down rocks into a pool below can be totally relaxing. You can build such a fountain in your own garden and put unwanted rocks to good use. Our fountain has a high back wall, built of rocks and mortar, rising above a well and basin. An electric pump circulates the water.

WINDOW GREENHOUSE/p.294

If you enjoy growing plants, either for ornament or food, and have a sunny window you would like to devote to them, our greenhouse will bring nature right to your window. Since the greenhouse is built entirely of transparent acrylic, it is nearly invisible; only the plants can be seen. The project is relatively easy to build—just a few basic tools are needed. Adding louver covers and an electric heating cable can extend the growing season through the winter.

PICKET FENCE AND GATE/p.290

Nothing evokes the nostalgia of a charming country home like a white picket fence. If you share such memories, you can build your own picket fence by following the directions for this project. The fence is made of 4 x 4's for the corner and gate posts, 1 x 3's for the pickets themselves, and 2 x 4's for the remaining parts. Plans include directions for laying out the fence, building and leveling it, and making the gate.

BRICK SCREENING WALL / p.310

A carport is enclosed, but not entombed, by this three-sided wall. Not only does the latticed design let light and air through, but it is also less expensive than a solid wall, requiring fewer bricks and a smaller footing. This project is actually a crash course in bricklaying; concrete and mortar recipes are included, as are illustrations of such techniques as cutting bricks, throwing and clipping mortar, buttering bricks, pointing joints, and aligning courses with a taut line and level.

BRICK DRIVEWAY, PATIO, OR WALK / p.306

Only the bricks around the edges of this 50-ft. driveway are set in mortar. The rest are on a 2-in. bed of sand on top of a 4-in. gravel base. This flexible (mortarless) method can be used without the gravel base for fairly level patios and paths. Plans include several brickwork patterns.

BRICK-AND-WOOD STEPS / p.317

Here is a practical and distinctive way to extend a brick walkway up a slope. Narrow redwood steps with 3½-in. risers alternate with deeper ones of redwood and brick whose risers are 7½ in. high. The bricks, like those of the driveway shown at the left, are mortarless; in this project they are enclosed on four sides by redwood.

BRICK BARBECUE / p.314

Cookouts are more fun with a well-designed barbecue. This one has built-in rods to support two grill racks—one for hot coals and the other for food—and a damper door at the right height for tending the fire, shoveling out coals, and cleaning up afterward. Plans are for a freestanding barbecue on a concrete foundation; they can be easily adapted to make it a part of a wall or patio as shown here.

CONCRETE DRIVEWAY, PATIO, OR WALK / p.268

Like most of the projects on these two pages, this one is more than step-by-step instructions for making something specific. Plans tell how to build the 30-ft. driveway shown here and also how to apply the same techniques to other concrete work. Among the questions answered: What wood is best for concrete forms? When is the best time to pour concrete? How do you ensure proper drainage?

CONCRETE STEPS / p.320

The trick of making concrete steps is to pour one step at a time, overlapping the one below by at least 2 in., then letting it set, but not cure, before pouring the next step. The same wooden form can be used for each step. Plans tell how to figure out, from the height and pitch of a slope, how many steps are needed and what size they should be.

FLAGSTONE PATIO / p.308

Random rectangular flagstones are generally available in multiples of 6 in. (12 x 12 in., 12 x 18 in., 18 x 36 in., and so on, up to 42 in. square). Plans for this project tell you how to use this bit of information, predesigning your patio on paper rather than shifting heavy stones from place to place. You will also learn how to save time, money, and aggravation when the stones, sand, and other materials are delivered.

Note: Building codes and other ordinances may apply to the projects on these two pages. Consult with local authorities before beginning work.

STAINED-GLASS LAMP/ p.323

It is easier than it looks to make a Tiffany lamp the same way Louis Tiffany did nearly a century ago. The method, known as the copper foil technique, involves edging pieces of glass with foil, then soldering them together. The procedure is explained and illustrated in this project, as are the uses of such glazier's tools as glass cutters, grozing pliers, breaking pliers, and cut-running pliers. Plans include patterns for the charming lamp shown here, combining yellow, green, purple, and magenta glass.

STEEL WINE RACK/ p.332

Slender steel rods are bent in the shape of W's, then joined like latticework and attached to an upright frame of heavier steel to create this striking lightweight wine rack. All joints are secured by brazing with nickel-silver filler, using a Mapp gas torch for the heat source—propane and butane do not burn hot enough to do the job. The rack is painted mat black to resemble wrought iron.

GLASS-HOUSE TERRARIUM/ p.328

Tropical plants thrive in the closed environment of this glass house while hardier plants grow and flower in the chimney and side pots. The hinged roof sections give easy access to the interior; so the house is practical for starting seeds or cuttings. Or, by leaving the roof open, you can turn the piece into an unusual planter. Plans call for the same glazing techniques used for the stained-glass lamp.

LOG TOTE AND CRADLE/p.330

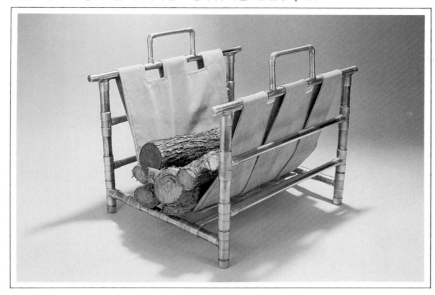

Handsome, handy, and easy to assemble, this project is made entirely of copper tubing and fittings, plus a canvas sling. The joints are sweat-soldered as they would be for plumbing; but because they need not be watertight, the job is less demanding. The sling is large enough to carry a reasonable load of firewood, and the pipes to which its handles are attached fit into U-shaped rests on top of the cradle legs; so the wood stays neatly stacked until you put it in the fire. Plans include a sewing pattern for the canvas sling.

METAL JEWELRY/p.334

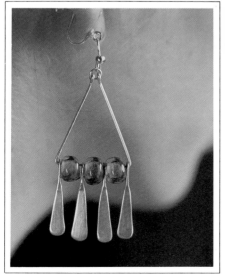

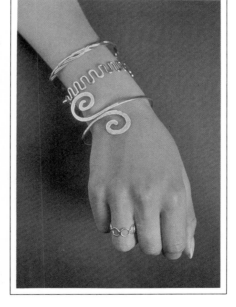

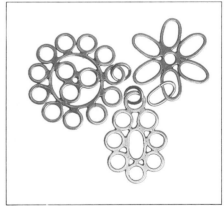

The satisfaction of designing your own jewelry is heightened when you compare the cost of the raw materials with the price of similar creations in stores. These earrings, bangles, and pendants are made from silver wire, jump rings (standard fasteners), and findings, plus a few glass beads and some bits of silver tubing. The rings require sheet silver and bezel wire (for the bands that surround the stones) and the stones themselves. Plans include instructions on all required metalworking techniques.

CHILD'S WORKBENCH AND TOOL CADDY / p.340

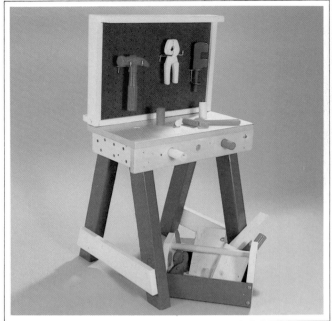

Your very young carpenter will enjoy using a plastic hammer or a wooden mallet to pound colored pegs through holes of various sizes that are drilled into the top and front of this workbench. The plans are easy to adapt to the needs of an older child, who will enjoy using real tools to make real projects. The bench includes a pegboard panel for tool storage backed by a blackboard with a chalk ledge. The tool caddy is light and sturdy—just the thing to carry toy tools to a make-believe emergency.

MODULAR DOLLHOUSES / p.344

Apartment houses, Tudor mansions, sprawling ranch houses—whatever your young architect dreams up—can be created on the spot. Interchangeable open-back boxes, each slightly under a foot square, fit snugly together, and all are capable of receiving roof modules. False front panels of ⅛-in. hardboard, painted to resemble your house or any other, are easily attached to any box by means of Velcro fasteners.

PLAYGROUND SET / p.337

A series of notched planks and a few straight boards are all it takes to make this giant Tinkertoy set—the more parts you make, the more versatile the set becomes. Plans are given for constructing a slide tower, a seesaw, and a pretend pickup truck. All are fun to assemble, play on, and then reassemble for a different game. Once your children get the hang of it, they are bound to devise even more imaginative innovations.

ROCKER AND SEESAW / p.358

Here are two action toys in one. Young children will delight in riding the rocking boat, and older kids can simply fit the spine of the 8-ft. seesaw board into slots in the rocker to create their own backyard seesaw. The project is easy to build from ½-in. plywood and 1-in. pine or other softwood, using standard hand tools.

CANDLE-POWERED BOATS / p.350

Tiny steam engines drive these boats. Water in a copper coil is heated by a candle flame until it is forced out as an underwater jet of steam and more water is sucked in. Plans include a simple design—merely a floating engine—and a more elaborate model.

JUNGLE GYM / p.360

This all-around playground is complete with swings, a slide, monkey bars, a climbing rope, and a fireman's pole. The two-story structure at its heart has ladders for walls and 2 x 6 ridgepoles to support a canvas roof. It is all held together with nuts and bolts for easy disassembly in case you ever want to move it to another spot.

DOWNHILL RACER / p.346

Sam Posey was only six years old when he built his first wooden racer. Although he went on to become a world-class driver of grown-up racing cars, he never abandoned his early love for gravity-powered go-carts and even gave his autobiography the same title as his first racer: *The Mudge Pond Express*. When we went to him for advice in designing a car that would be both fun and safe for children to use, he gave us more than we asked for—he created this racer, based on the same aerodynamic principles that help modern racing cars hug the road, making them easier to handle and brake.

BUNK BEDS / p.354

Here is a simple variation on the standard bunk-bed design that gives headroom to the children in both beds and incorporates desk space as well. The beds and desk are made of ¾-in. lumber-core plywood, the posts are of 5/4 hardwood lumber, and the ladder rungs and guardrail are standard dowels. Plans include a limited-space arrangement in which the beds are laid out in the usual parallel fashion.

CHEST OF DRAWERS KIT/ p.374

The original of this block-front chest was built by a master cabinetmaker more than 200 years ago, when the elaborate Chippendale style was in its heyday. The kit from the Bartley Collection provides an accurate reproduction, complete with solid brass drawer hardware.

BUTLER'S TABLE KIT/ p.372

Even if you do not employ a butler to carry in supper for two on the inlaid top, this mahogany butler's table from the Heath Company can add a touch of elegance to your living room.

GRANDFATHER CLOCK KIT/ p.366

You can buy the kit for this 6-ft. grandfather clock case from the Emperor Clock Company with or without the clockworks. If you take the complete package, you have your choice of traditional faces: either the moving moon dial shown here, which reflects the phases of the moon, or a stationary *tempus fugit* design.

LOW BED AND TRUNDLE BED KITS/ p.369

Two kits are required to make this space-saving bedroom set: one for the twin-size low bed and another for the trundle bed that fits neatly beneath it. The low bed is adapted to receive box springs (the holes in the footrail, through which a rope mattress support was strung, are faithfully reproduced nonetheless). Both kits are available from Cohasset Colonials, which also sells coverlets and a foam mattress for the trundle bed.

Note: The four projects on this page are made from kits in which the wooden parts are precut and shaped, ready for final fitting and assembly. All necessary hardware and finishing materials are provided but few if any tools.

VARIATIONS ON OUR PLANS

If you were to complete all of the 101 projects in this book, you would have built 10 tables, 4 bookcases, 3 beds, and a pair each of desks, couches, bars, fireplaces, driveways, and TV/stereo cabinets. The reason for this seeming duplication is variety. Each of those 10 tables has a distinct shape, size, or style and serves a different purpose. By making simple changes in our plans, you can create even more variations. For example, if you were to build the *Early American bookcase* (pp.62–67) without its decorative molding, it would be easier and cheaper to make. In addition, it would have the clean, uncluttered lines that go well with modern or contemporary furnishings.

Transforming a modern design into an Early American one is more difficult but still possible. To convert the *Plywood desk* (pp.49–51), for instance, it would be necessary to make a number of changes. First, the cutouts in the sides should be altered to something similar to those on our *Early American night table* (pp.166–167). The drawer front should also be changed to resemble the one on the night table and the desk top made larger than the sides so that it overlaps them. Then

fluted edging should be applied to the edges of the desk top as was done for the shelves of the *Entertainment center* (pp.206–213). Finally, the front must be made taller so that there is no gap between it and the repositioned desk top.

Our *Picnic or patio table* (pp.247–251) would be easier to build and more conventional in appearance if the top were round rather than octagonal and the benches built to match. The bench tops could each be made from three straight slats about 48 in. long. You should attach supports to the slats, draw and cut curves on the front and back edges to match the round table, and then add the legs.

The choice of building materials and finishing techniques can radically alter the appearance of a project. Choosing different woods, stains, laminates, or fabrics to blend with your home's decor is an obvious way to change many of our furniture projects. Such substitutions can even be applied to large projects, like the *Built-in fireplace* (pp.228–233). It was enclosed with gypsum wallboard, painted to match the surrounding walls, but you could just as easily enclose it with paneling to contrast with the walls. Wood,

brick, or fieldstone paneling are only three of many choices.

Where room permitted, we have suggested alterations in the projects themselves under the subhead "Variations." Of course, these represent just a few of the many possibilities; your imagination and daring are the only limitations. If different construction techniques are required for a variation, you will be able to find many of them cross-referenced in the *Index of construction techniques* (p.379).

Because careful planning is necessary if you decide to deviate from our plans, start by sketching out your variations to see how they look in three dimensions. Then carefully lay out each altered part on graph paper and calculate its dimensions. Make a new parts list, like the ones included in our plans, and be certain that instructions are available for any additional construction techniques that may be required.

If you follow the old adages "Plan ahead" and "Measure twice, cut once," you should be on safe ground. Changing our plans can add scores of challenging new projects to the 101 that are already on these pages.

Early American bookcase as shown in our plans (left) and altered for a contemporary look (right).

Plywood desk featured in our plans (left) and altered to fit into a home with Early American furnishings (right).

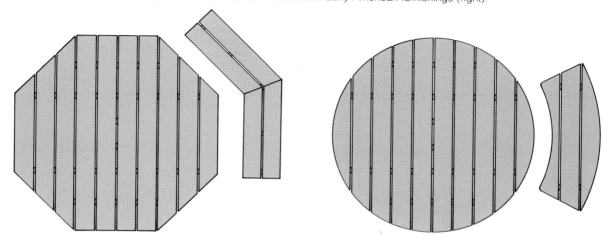

Octagonal picnic table with angled benches as it appears in our plans (left) and an easier-to-build round version (right).

Built-in fireplace can be enclosed with wallboard (left) or with rustic fieldstone paneling (right).

HOW TO BUY WOOD

When you walk into a lumberyard, you enter a confusing world of special grades, sizes, and classifications. Until you become familiar with the terminology used, nothing describing lumber seems to mean quite what it says.

The difference between hardwood and softwood, for example, has little to do with the hardness of the wood. It is true that most softwood is easier to cut and to shape than most hardwood and that softwood generally receives nails and screws more willingly. But it is also true that some softwoods, such as larch and yellow pine, are harder—which is to say, the fibers are more dense—than such hardwoods as poplar and balsa.

Hardwood comes from flowering trees and its fibers are long and stiff, containing vessels that carry fluids up and down the trunk of the living tree. Softwood comes from conifers, which have no such vessels (fluids ooze from one cell to another), and its fibers are shorter and more flexible. In practical terms, softwood tends to splinter under stress and hardwood is more likely to split. Because of the tendency to splinter, few softwoods can be worked with great precision or finished to a hard, smooth surface. Moreover, softwood swells and shrinks with changes in humidity more than hardwood does, so joints become unstable. Hardwood is better suited for intricate joinery and softwood for hammer-and-nail construction.

The average retail lumber dealer is actually a specialist in softwoods, such as pine, fir, redwood, cedar, and spruce, milled to standard sizes. He may also carry some premilled hardwoods, such as cherry, white oak, poplar, and perhaps even walnut and hard maple, but the prices will probably be quite high and the selection limited. Dealers who handle lumber for boats are the exception—they will have a good selection of premilled hardwoods, particularly teak and mahogany, although the prices will still be high. For the lowest cost and widest selection, seek out a dealer or distributor who specializes in hardwood. If you stick to local woods, you can probably buy quality lumber at bargain prices directly from a local lumber mill.

The lumber from a hardwood dealer will probably not be premilled—which is to say, the surface will be rough-cut and uneven, the way it comes from the big blade that reduces trees to boards—and it will almost certainly not be jointed, which means widths will be random and the edges of the boards will be irregular and perhaps still covered with bark. The

only way you can be sure of getting the wood you want is to pick out each board yourself. (For an idea of the way a board will look when finished, brush water or paint thinner on the rough surface.) After you have selected your lumber, you can have it milled, usually for a small fee, and ripped on one side to give you even edges to work with.

When buying hardwood or softwood, look for lumber that has been properly dried and is not warped. Test for dryness by smelling the wood and by touching it with your face, wrist, or the back of your hand. It may take some practice, but once you have learned the odor and feel of moist wood, the method is dependable.

You have a right to expect high-grade

lumber that is not warped; with lower grades you take your chances. There is no law about this, so it is always best to pick out wood yourself. As a rule of thumb, long, wide boards are safer to order than short, narrow ones.

The commonest mistake people make in buying lumber is to order higher grades than they really need. Bear in mind that "No. 1 common" white pine, for example, may cost three or four times the price of "No. 3 common," yet the wood between knotholes may be just as good—it may even be "clear," the costliest grade of all. If half the wood ordered goes to waste, you will still save money with the lower grade, and you can use the scrap in a number of ways.

Grades of lumber

Grades of softwood

Select grade	Description	Waste	Suitable for
A (clear)	Nearly free from blemishes; not warped; highly sandable	None	Staining; natural finishes over large surfaces
B	A few small blemishes; probably not warped	Little	Staining; natural finishes
C	Some sizable blemishes; sandable; perhaps slight warpage	Some	Painting on large surfaces
D	Many blemishes; probable warpage	Much	Painting

Common grade	Description	Waste	Suitable for
No. 1	Defects minimal; knots sound and tight; not warped; virtually waterproof	None	Construction in long lengths with thin, narrow boards; knotty paneling
No. 2	Some defects; knots sound and tight; little or no warpage	Little	Construction in long lengths with wide or thick boards; knotty paneling
No. 3	Occasional knotholes or loose knots; few other defects; possible warpage	Some	Construction in medium to short lengths; heavy timbers
No. 4	Many knotholes and other defects; probable warpage; perhaps some decay	Much	Construction in short pieces; filler

Grades of hardwood

Grade	Approximate waste
Firsts and seconds (FAS)	Less than 15%
No. 1 common and select	Up to 33%
No. 2 common and sound wormy	Up to 50%
Nos. 3a common and 3b common	Up to 75%

Different systems are used to grade softwood and hardwood for quality, based on the way the woods are likely to be used.

Softwood is divided into two categories: *select* and *common*. Select lumber has a good appearance and can be expected to take a finish well; it is further divided into four grades—A to D—based on the number and kinds of blemishes in a board. Common lumber has defects, such as knots, that detract from its looks, but it is suitable for construction; its four grades are numbered

1 to 4 to reflect the size, quantity, and severity of the defects.

Hardwood is graded according to the percentage of usable wood that you can expect to cut from a board. This judgment is highly subjective and, depending on your relationship with the dealer and your own bargaining talent, may be open to board-by-board debate when buying rough-cut lumber. The grading does not apply to premilled hardwood, which should all be usable and is priced at the highest rate.

Sizes and prices of lumber

The sizes of a board are given by thickness, width, and length, in that order. The thickness and width of premilled lumber are *nominal* dimensions—they refer to the size of the wood before it is seasoned, milled, and ripped. The *actual* dimensions are always smaller. Length is not affected; if anything, a board will be an inch or so longer than specified.

The thickness of rough-cut lumber is often not given in inches, but in quarter-inches, and the numbers are fairly precise. Thus, a rough-cut board 1 inch thick is called 4/4 lumber. When 4/4 hardwood is milled, it should be $^{13}/_{16}$ inches thick; 4/4 softwood varies more and will probably be a little thinner after milling.

Prices are figured by the *board foot*. This is a measure of volume, based on nominal dimensions. A board foot is equal to a square foot of lumber that is 1 inch thick. (For instance, a 2-foot-long 1 x 12 is 2 board feet; so are a 2-foot-long 2 x 6, a 3-foot-long 2 x 4, a 4-foot-long 2 x 3, and an 8-foot-long 1 x 3.)

Dealers may quote prices for premilled lumber in terms of *running feet*. This is simply a translation of board-foot prices into the cost per foot of a given sized board. It is wise to do the math yourself before accepting such quotations. When you buy hardwood in random widths, each board should be graded, measured, and priced individually.

Standard premilled lumber sizes

Nominal	Actual ✲
1"	$^3/_4$"
5/4"†	$1^1/_8$"
2"	$1^1/_2$"
3"	$2^1/_2$"
4"	$3^1/_2$"
6"	$5^1/_2$"
8"	$7^3/_8$"
10"	$9^3/_8$"
12"	$11^3/_8$"

✲ Thickness may vary by $^1/_{16}$", width by as much as $^1/_8$".
†Thickness only .

Buying plywood

Plywood is made by laminating an odd number of wooden layers with their grains running across each other to form panels in which the grains of both faces run lengthwise. The center layer, or core, may be veneer, in which case the plywood is called *veneer core*, or the core may be pieces of solid wood, in which case the plywood is *lumber core*.

The size of a panel is specified by thickness, width, and length, in that order, and the dimensions should be accurate within $^1/_{32}$ inch. Standard thicknesses are available in increments of $^1/_8$ inch to a maximum of $^3/_4$ inch. (Thicker plywood is made but is generally available only by special order.) A standard panel is 4 feet wide and 8 feet long, and most dealers sell plywood only in that size. Some may carry 7- and 10-foot lengths as well, and a few have 5- and 6-foot widths, but in general you are safer if you plan your projects in terms of 4- x 8-foot panels. Before you order a piece of plywood smaller than the standard size, find out if you will be paying for an entire panel.

The corners of a plywood panel should be very nearly square, but do not count on absolute squareness. Industry standards allow a tolerance of $^3/_{32}$ inch between the two corner-to-corner measurements; if true corners are important to a project, plan on cutting a little off the edges of a panel to achieve them. This is a good idea anyway, as panels often have damaged edges when you buy them.

Like solid lumber, plywood has two major categories: *construction plywood*, which is usually made of softwood veneer (the commonest is Douglas fir) and *decorative plywood*, which is usually of hardwood veneer. Panels in both categories may be specified *interior* or *exterior*, depending on the weather resistance of the glue used to join the layers.

Further grading differs for the two categories, although both systems are based on the quality of the outermost veneers. The face and back veneers are graded, and the two grades affect the price of a panel. When you order plywood, you must specify the grades of both sides, giving the face (best) grade first.

The highest grade of construction plywood is N, or *natural*; it means that the veneer is smooth and evenly matched,

suitable to receive a natural finish. Other grades are lettered A to D, in descending order of quality. There is a special grade between B and C called *plug-face*, or *C-plugged*, in which the small knotholes and other defects allowable in Grade C have been filled with synthetic material to make a solid, paintable surface, although it cannot be sanded as smooth as Grade B veneer can.

The highest decorative plywood grade is A, or *premium*. Lower grades are numbered and named as follows: 1, *good*; 2, *sound*; 3, *utility*; and 4, *backing*. In addition, there is a *specialty grade* (SP), which includes such decorative veneers as bird's-eye maple and wormy chestnut.

Several organizations exist to oversee the grading standards of plywood. Some, such as the American Plywood Association (APA) and the Douglas Fir Plywood Association (DFPA), concern themselves only with construction plywood. Others, such as the Hardwood Plywood Manufacturers Association (HPMA), deal only with decorative plywood. Look for their stamps on the back (poorer side) of a plywood panel before you buy it.

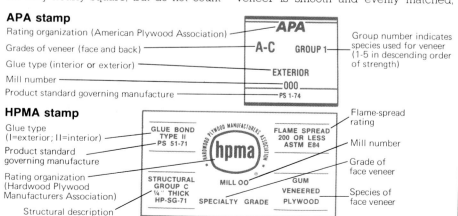

APA stamp
- Rating organization (American Plywood Association)
- Grades of veneer (face and back)
- Glue type (interior or exterior)
- Mill number
- Product standard governing manufacture

APA
A-C GROUP 1
EXTERIOR
000
PS 1-74

Group number indicates species used for veneer (1-5 in descending order of strength)

HPMA stamp
- Glue type (I=exterior; II=interior)
- Product standard governing manufacture
- Rating organization (Hardwood Plywood Manufacturers Association)
- Structural description

GLUE BOND TYPE II PS 51-71
HARDWOOD PLYWOOD MANUFACTURERS ASSOCIATION
hpma
STRUCTURAL GROUP C $^1/_4$" THICK HP-SG-71
MILL OO
SPECIALTY GRADE
FLAME SPREAD 200 OR LESS ASTM E84
GUM VENEERED PLYWOOD

- Flame-spread rating
- Mill number
- Grade of face veneer
- Species of face veneer

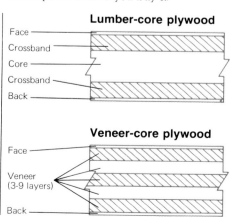

Lumber-core plywood
- Face
- Crossband
- Core
- Crossband
- Back

Veneer-core plywood
- Face
- Veneer (3-9 layers)
- Back

HOW TO MAKE A PATTERN

Some of the projects in this book require you to cut wood or other materials into curves or irregular shapes. Patterns are supplied to guide you in cutting. Because many of these patterns are too large to be reproduced full size, they have been reduced and printed on a grid. The patterns can easily be enlarged and transferred to the material being cut.

Enlarging the pattern: With each reduced pattern is a caption giving the actual size of the squares on the grid. Using a framing square, lightly draw a grid on a large piece of paper with the same number of squares as the grid in the book. Make each square of the new grid the size given in the caption. Number the squares across the bottoms of both grids and letter them down the sides.

Make a dot at each point on the large grid where the design touches a line on the small grid. Once this is done, use a pencil to connect the dots. Use a straight-edge to copy the straight lines.

Transferring the pattern: After you have enlarged the pattern, you must transfer it to the wood or other material being cut. One way is to cut the pattern out and temporarily secure it to the wood with pushpins or tape, and then cut the wood following the edges of the cutout pattern. Or you can put the uncut pattern over the wood and trace over the design with a tracing wheel (available in sewing supply stores) to etch the design lightly into the wood.

You can also put transfer paper (sold in art supply stores) under the pattern and trace it. Transfer paper is easier to clean off than carbon paper and is less likely to smudge. When tracing, tape the pattern securely to the wood.

Enlarge any pattern in this book by recopying it on a larger grid. For example, a reduced pattern for our *Stained-glass lamp* project is shown at left. An enlarged (but still not full-size) pattern is shown below. Each square on the grid of the reduced pattern equals 1 in. on the full-size pattern. To make the enlargement, lightly draw a grid with the same number of squares on a large sheet of paper, making each square 1 in. wide and 1 in. high. Starting at any square, such as B–9, mark the large grid with a dot wherever a line in the reduced design intersects a line in the corresponding square. Connect all the dots to draw the full-size pattern.

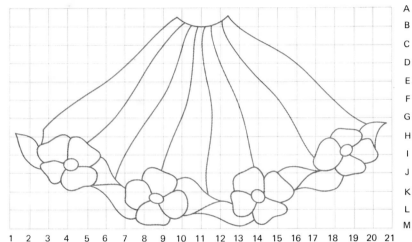

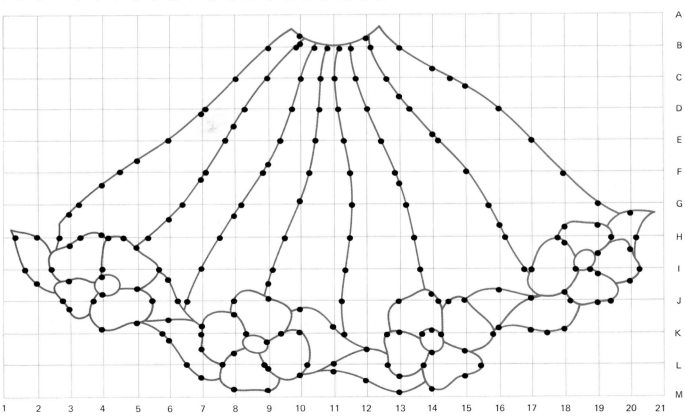

PLYWOOD DESK

Simple in design and inexpensive, this plywood desk is made from a single 4- x 8-foot panel. Plywood is available with many hardwood veneers; it can also be covered with plastic laminate (see *Index*, p.379), which is well suited for a work surface. Since you have many options for the materials and colors of the desk, you could use one wood veneer or one laminate throughout, mix wood veneers, or mix a wood veneer and plastic.

When you cut plywood with a power saw, the better side of the wood must be kept face down so that it does not splinter as the teeth of the saw pass through it. If you use a handsaw, whose teeth cut on the downward stroke, cut the wood with the good side facing up.

When the desk is completed, cover the exposed edges of the plywood with strips of the same laminate or veneer that covers the faces of the panels.

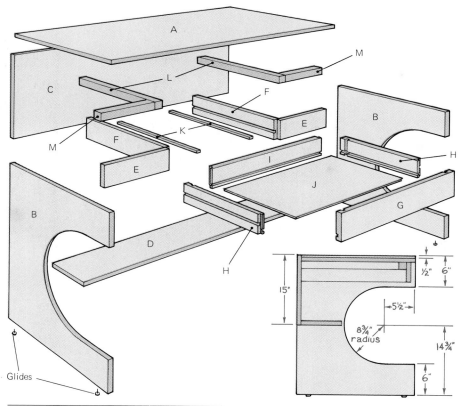

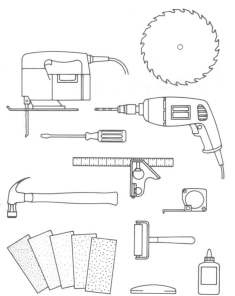

Parts list

Part	Name	Quantity	Thickness	Width	Length	Material
A	Top	1	¾"	23³⁄₁₆"	48"	Plywood
B	Side	2	¾"	23¹⁵⁄₁₆"	29½"	Plywood
C	Back	1	¾"	15"	48"	Plywood
D	Shelf	1	¾"	8"	48"	Plywood
E	Front	2	¾"	4"	12"	Plywood
F	Drawer support	2	¾"	4"	21³⁄₁₆"	Plywood
G	Drawer front	1	¾"	4"	23⅞"	Plywood
H	Drawer side	2	¾"	3¼"	23"	Plywood
I	Drawer back	1	¾"	3¼"	21¾"	Plywood
J	Drawer bottom	1	⅛"	21½"	21¾"	Masonite
K	Drawer slide	2	½"	¾"	23⅞"	Maple (or any hardwood)
L	Drawer glue block	2	1½"	1½"	21³⁄₁₆"	Maple (or any hardwood)
M	Front glue block	2	1½"	1½"	10¼"	Maple (or any hardwood)

Tools and materials: Radial arm saw with a dado head and a fine-tooth blade. Saber saw. Electric drill with 2" Screwmate drill bit. Steel tape rule, combination square, pencil. Clamps. Screwdriver, hammer, rubber roller. Sanding block, No. 100 sandpaper. Wood glue, contact cement. A candle stub. Veneer tape ¾" wide. Wood (see above). Four nail-in metal or plastic glides. Four doz. 2" No. 10 flathead wood screws.

Plywood desk

You can cut all plywood pieces required for this project from a standard 4- x 8-ft. panel of ¾-in. plywood. Use a steel tape rule to measure off the widths of parts A, B, C, D, E, F, H, and I across the plywood panel. Be sure to add the kerf (the thickness of the cut made by your saw blade) to each measurement. Make a short test cut in the upper right-hand corner of the panel and measure its width. (Or measure, mark, and cut one piece at a time, using the dimensions in the chart on page 49; and always cut just outside the pencil line on the plywood.) Use the framing square to draw cutting lines across the plywood. Measure off the lengths of parts B, E, F, G, H, and I, and use the square to mark off their edges. Use a compass, yardstick, or string and nail to draw the circular part of B (see *Index*, p.379). Use a saber saw for the curves.

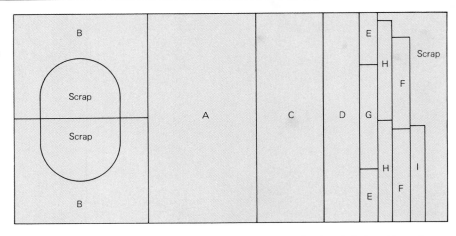

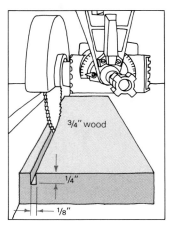

1. To make dado cuts for the drawer bottom on the four sides of the drawer (G, H, and I), fit the radial arm saw with a ⅛-in. dado head. Position the dado head ½ in. above the saw table. Cut through a piece of scrap wood ¾ in. thick, then measure the cut; it should be ⅛ in. wide and ¼ in. deep. Make adjustments, if necessary, until part J fits snugly into the cut. Then cut dadoes along the length of the drawer sides (H), back (I), and front (G) ¼ in. from the bottom edges of each part.

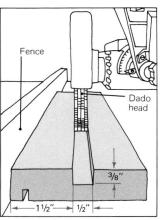

2. Adjust the dado head for a ½-in.-wide cut. Position the blade ⅜ in. above the saw table. Cut another piece of scrap wood and measure the cut, adjusting the blade, if necessary, so that the cut is exactly ½ in. wide and ⅜ in. deep. Then cut dadoes along the length of the two drawer sides (H) on the faces opposite the ⅛-in. dadoes cut in Step 1, positioned 1½ in. from the lower edges. Make identical cuts on the inner faces of the drawer supports (F).

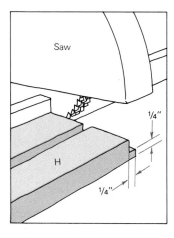

3. Cutting away a section ¼ in. wide and ½ in. deep from the front ends of the drawer sides (H) and both ends of the drawer back (I) will create tongues ¼ in. thick. To do so, lower the dado head to ¼ in. above the table. Make a mark ¼ in. from each end of I and from the front ends of parts H. Lay each drawer side flat on the table with the ⅛-in. dadoes you have already cut facing down; then cut away the ¼ in. between your marks and the ends of the parts. Lay the drawer back on the table, its ⅛-in. dado facing down, and cut ¼-in. sections from both ends, making two tongues.

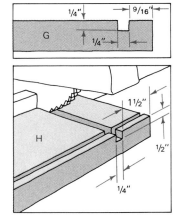

4. Set the dado head to make a ¼-in.-wide cut and raise it to ½ in. above the saw table. Cut through a piece of ¾-in. scrap wood. If the tongues you made in Step 3 do not fit snugly into this dado, adjust the saw to make a dado that will fit snugly. Then cut two vertical dadoes on the inner face of the drawer front (G) ⁹⁄₁₆ in. from each end. Also cut one vertical dado ¼ in. wide and ½ in. deep on the inner face of each drawer side (H) 1½ in. from the back ends.

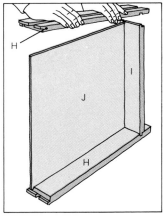

5. To check that the drawer assembly fits snugly, slip together one side and the back, and slide in the bottom (J). Then add the other side and the front. If they do not fit snugly, make adjustments before you go any further. Sand dadoes that are too tight; discard parts that are too loose and cut replacements. When everything fits properly, pull the pieces apart and reassemble them in the same sequence, this time gluing all joints as you go.

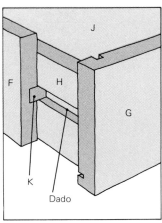

6. Fit the hardwood slides (K) into the dadoes in the drawer supports (F). They should fit snugly. If they are too tight, sand the dadoes. If they are too loose, cut new slides. When the slides fit properly, glue them in place. After the glue dries, place the supports beside the drawer to see if the drawer sits well on the slides and can move easily along them; if not, sand down the slides. Rub a candle over the slides and along the dadoes to lubricate them.

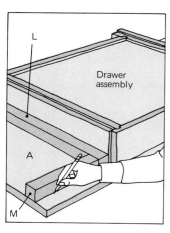

7. Place the desk top (A) upside down. Place the supports and slides into the sides of the drawer, leaving a slight clearance on each side; then position this assembly carefully on the desk top. Place two glue blocks (L) beside the supports, and place the other blocks (M) perpendicular to them. Mark the positions of the four glue blocks carefully on the desk top.

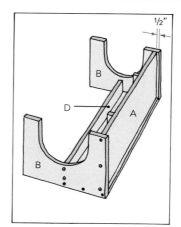

11. Prop the desk top (A) between the sides so that its top surface is vertical and ½ in. below the top edges of the back and sides. Drill three holes through each side and into the top, using the Screwmate bit. Attach the top with six screws. Turn the desk upright and drill six more holes through the back of the desk and into the top, and insert screws. Put the shelf (D) in place, its bottom flush with the bottom edge of the back, and attach it to the sides in the same way as the top, using two screws on each end and six along the back.

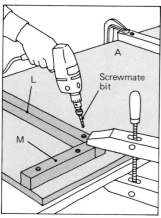

8. Remove the drawer and supports from the desk top. Align the glue blocks on the marks you just drew. Use a 2-in. No. 10 Screwmate bit to drill countersink, clearance, and pilot holes simultaneously through each block and into the desk top. Drill holes for two screws into each glue block about 2 in. from each end.

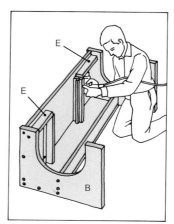

12. Put the fronts (E) in place so that they rest against the glue blocks (M) and the sides (B) of the desk. Use the Screwmate bit to drill a hole through each side into the centers of the edges of the front pieces. Drill one hole through the center of each glue block M into each front piece. Place glue on the outside edges of the front pieces and over the faces of the glue blocks. Insert 2-in. screws into pilot holes.

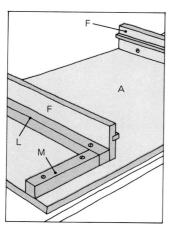

9. Spread glue on the bottom of each block, then screw all four of them to the desk top with 2-in. No. 10 flathead wood screws. Put the drawer supports (F) in place beside the glue blocks. Use the Screwmate bit to drill holes through each drawer support into the glue blocks about 4 in. from each end.

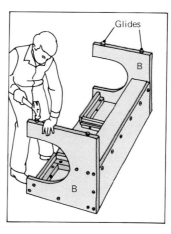

13. Turn the desk onto its top, and hammer two glides into the bottom edge of each side (B) about 3 in. from the front and back corners.

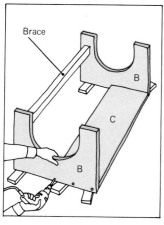

10. Lay the desk sides (B) on their back edges (so the U's face upward) with the back (C) between them. Align the edges and corners, and prop up the sides so they are perpendicular to the back, then nail a temporary brace between the sides. Drill three holes through each side into the back, using the Screwmate bit. Apply glue to the edges of the back and assemble the parts with 2-in. screws. Remove brace.

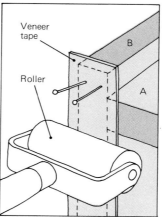

14. Cover the cut edges of the plywood wherever they are exposed with ¾-in. veneer tape that matches the faces of the plywood. Measure the exposed edges, cut strips of tape to the proper length, cover them with contact cement, and let cement become tacky. Carefully position the tape and press it in place with a rubber roller. If necessary, sand the tape down to the width of the plywood with No. 100 paper. Be careful not to damage the veneer on the faces of the plywood. Stain and finish the veneer (see *Index*, p.379).

51

ROLLTOP DESK

For the person who hates to clear off a desk, who wants to leave everything where it is overnight yet still have the clutter hidden, a rolltop desk is a godsend. The tambour hides everything! Our design, a modern interpretation of the 19th-century design, goes well with contemporary or traditional furnishings.

Lumber-core plywood is used for most of the desk, supplemented by solid hardwood stock walnut, maple, oak, or cherry. The edges of the plywood are covered with a matching veneer tape.

The need for extreme accuracy in measuring and cutting cannot be stressed too strongly. With one exception, all the construction is ambitious but straightforward—that exception is the tambour, which is made up of thirty ¾-inch-wide hardwood slats. A scant ¼-inch tongue at

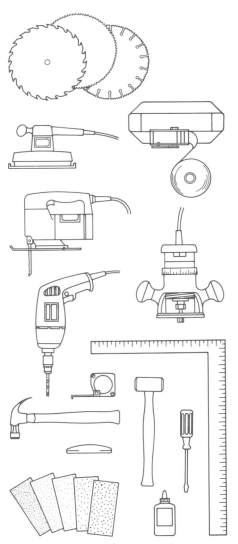

Parts list

Part	Name	Quantity	Thickness	Width	Length	Material
Tambour case						
A	Side	2	¾″	15½″	30¼″	Plywood
B	Back	2	¼″	14⅝″	56″	Plywood
C	Top	1	¾″	11½″	56″	Plywood
D	Rail	1	¾″	⅞″	55½″	Plywood
Cubbyhole unit						
E	Top	1	¾″	10″	55½″	Plywood
F	Shelf	1	½″	9¾″	28¾″	Plywood
G	Shelf	4	½″	9¾″	10¼″	Plywood
H	Side	2	½″	9¾″	12¼″	Plywood
I	Back	1	¼″	12¼″	55½″	Plywood
J	Divider	2	½″	9¾″	12¼″	Plywood
K	Divider	5	½″	9¾″	3⅞″	Plywood
L	Divider	2	½″	9¾″	8¼″	Plywood
M	Cleat	1	¾″	¾″	55½″	1 x 6 hardwood
Tambour						
N	Handle	1	1½″	1⁵⁄₁₆″	56″	2 x 8 hardwood
O	Slat	30	¾″	¾″	56″	1 x 6 hardwood
P	Retaining strip	1	¼″	1″	55½″	1 x 6 hardwood
Q	Backing	1	—	23⅝″	55½″	Canvas
Desk-top unit						
R	Top	1	¾″	29¼″	60″	Plywood
S	Bottom	1	¾″	29¼″	59″	Plywood
T	Side	2	¾″	5½″	29¼″	Plywood
U	Back	1	¼″	4¾″ ✳	59¼″ ✳	Plywood
V	Partition	2	¾″	4½″	29″	Plywood
W	Horizontal trim	2	¾″	¾″	60″	1 x 6 hardwood
X	Side trim	2	¾″	¾″	5½″	1 x 6 hardwood
Y	Partition trim	2	¾″	¾″	4¼″	1 x 6 hardwood
Z	Spline	2	⅛″	¾″	29¼″	1 x 6 hardwood
Base units						
AA	Top	2	¾″	16″	26¼″	Plywood
BB	Bottom	2	¾″	16″	25½″	Plywood
CC	Front	2	¾″	3¾″	16″	Plywood
DD	Side	4	¾″	24½″	27½″	Plywood
EE	Back	2	¼″	16¼″ ✳	24⅛″ ✳	Plywood
FF	Pin	8	¼″ dia.	—	¾″	Hardwood dowel

✳Measurement is approximate; cut to fit during construction.

Tools and materials: Radial arm or table saw with carbide-tipped or planing blade and dado head. Saber saw. Router with ¼″ straight bit and ⅝″ cove bit. Drill with ¼″ twist bit. Hammer, mallet, screwdriver. Two web clamps. Framing square, steel tape rule. Orbital sander and sanding block with Nos. 100, 150, and 220 sandpaper. Hide or resin glue, adhesive sponge. Wood stain, varnish, paste wax. Candle stub. 1⅔ yd. of canvas at least 26″ wide. Veneer tape. Lumber-core plywood: one panel ¼″ x 4′ x 8′, 1½ panels ½″ x 4′ x 8′, three panels ¾″ x 4′ x 8′. A ⅛″ x 4′ x 8′ panel of tempered hardboard. Six 5′ lengths of 1 x 6 hardwood boards, one 5′ length of 2 x 8 hardwood board. One ¼″ dowel. Four ¼″ dowel centers. Nine pairs of drawer slides (metal or hardwood). A 55½″ length of weather stripping. Four ½″ No. 6 brass wood screws, four 1½″ No. 10 brass wood screws, 1″ box nails.

each end of each slat allows the tambour to slide up and down in ¼-inch grooves that have been routed in the sides of the tambour case (see diagram, p.55). Where the grooves curve, they will have to be widened a bit to accommodate the width of the slats as they make the turn.

The tambour slats should be finished and waxed before they are glued to the canvas backing; it would be impossible to finish them once they are glued down. However, do not finish the bottoms of the slats; these must accept the glue.

The finish you choose depends on the hardwood you select for the desk. For light woods, such as oak or maple, you may want to apply a stain, followed by varnish and wax. But darker woods may need no more than light sanding and tung oil. (For finishing details, see the *Index,* p.379.)

You may find it easier to finish the individual sections of the desk—the tambour and case, desk-top unit, base units, drawers, and cubbyhole unit—before assembly. If so, take extra care during assembly that you do not mar the finish. Build the cubbyhole unit after the tambour case has been built and fitted to the desk top in order to be sure that the cubbyhole unit fits perfectly within the case.

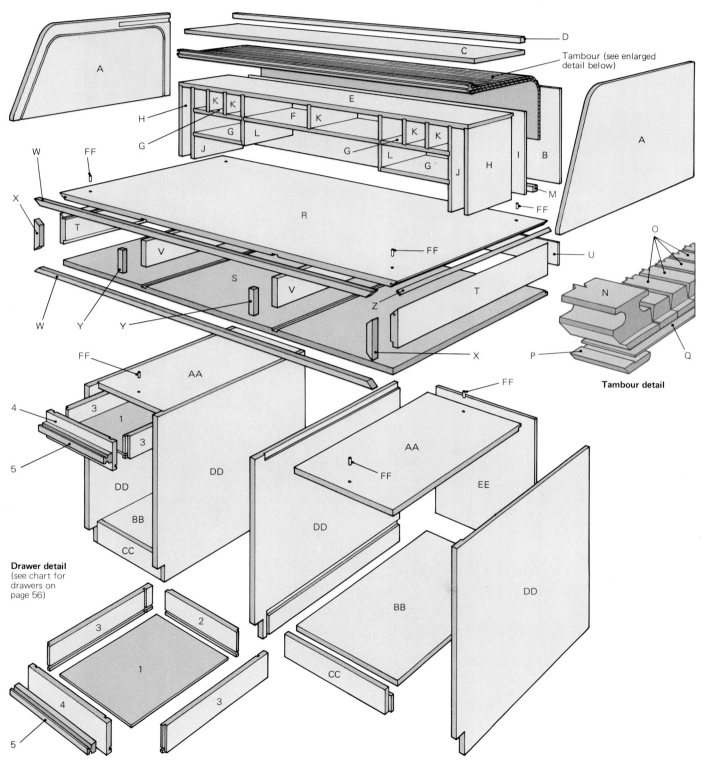

Tambour (see enlarged detail below)

Tambour detail

Drawer detail
(see chart for drawers on page 56)

Tambour and case

Cut 30 slats (O), ¾ inch square and 56 inches long, from 1 x 6 hardwood boards. Set the table saw blade at a 10° angle and position the fence so that the blade will cut a 10° bevel, ending ¼ inch above the base of each slat. Cut a rabbet ½ inch deep and ¼ inch wide into each end of each slat. Finish the slats.

Build a frame of scrap lumber with inside dimensions of 25 x 56 inches. Stretch the canvas tightly over a piece of scrap plywood; check that the frame is square, then nail the frame through the canvas and to the plywood. Apply hide or resin glue to a third of the canvas and put down 10 slats. Clamp the slats against one end of the frame, holding them down on the canvas with weights. When the glue has dried, put down 10 more slats, then the final 10.

Cut slats for the tambour handle (N) and drawer handles by ripping a 2 x 8 hardwood board into 1½- x 1⁵⁄₁₆-inch strips. Bevel as shown. Use a ⅝-inch cove router bit to cut grooves in the handles to a depth of ½ inch in two passes, removing ¼ inch of wood at each pass. Cut the tambour handle 56 inches long and cut a rabbet in each end to match the slats. Glue the handle to the canvas. When the glue dries, trim the canvas to the tambour edges.

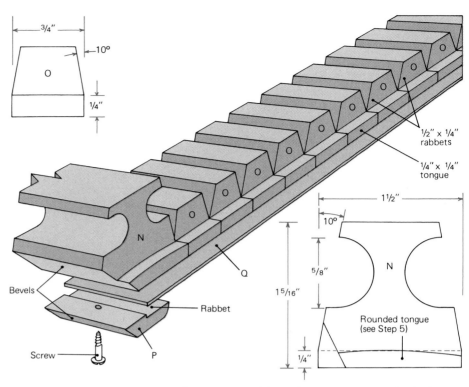

Tambour detail shows canvas (Q) sandwiched between handle (N) and retaining strip (P). Bevel front edge of strip to match the bevel on handle. Cut a shallow rabbet in the retaining strip to accommodate the thickness of the canvas. Finish the lower side of the strip, then glue it to the canvas. Drill pilot holes and screw parts N and P together.

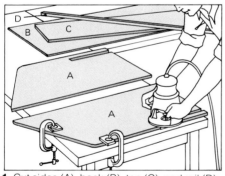

1. Cut sides (A), back (B), top (C), and rail (D) to size. Following the diagram at top of opposite page, cut a ¼- x ¾-in. blind dado in each side for top and ⅛- x ⅜-in. rabbet for back.

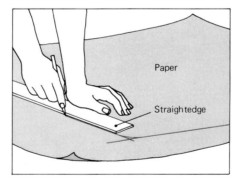

2. Make a paper pattern for cutting tambour grooves with a router and template guide (see illustration, opposite page), allowing clearance needed by your guide (see *Index*, p.379).

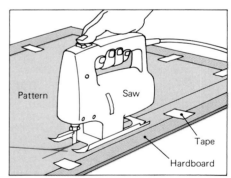

3. Cut a hardboard template from the pattern, using a saber saw. A 2-in. radius is needed on the curves so that the tambour will not bind. Be sure the curves flow smoothly.

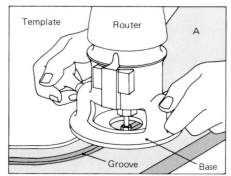

4. Use a ¼-in. straight router bit to cut ¼-in.-deep grooves in sides. Widen the grooves at the curves by making a second pass with the router after shifting the template slightly.

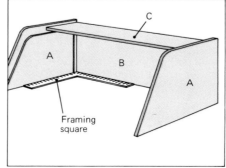

5. Round the tongues on the handle (N) so that it will travel smoothly in the grooves. Glue top to sides. Glue back to sides and top, making sure the assembly is square.

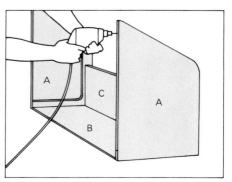

6. Nail back to sides and top. Glue rail (D) to sides and top. Drill ¼-in. holes ¼ in. deep in the bottom edges of the sides 2 in. from back corners, 3 in. from front.

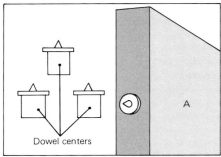

7. Purchase four ¼-in. dowel centers to insert into the holes drilled in Step 6. These will be used in Steps 23–26 to mark the positions of the dowel holes in the desk top.

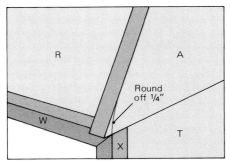

8. After completing desk-top unit (below), position tambour case on desk top (R). Round off front corners of case flush with top. Apply veneer tape to exposed plywood edges.

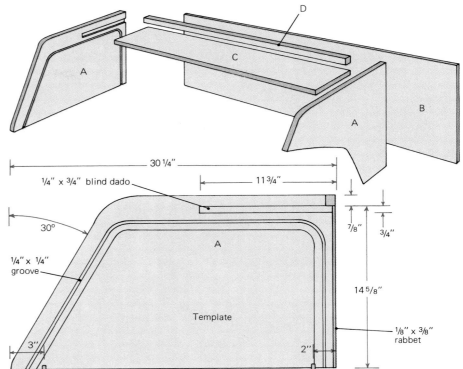

Drawings show assembly of parts for tambour case (top) and dimensions and locations for dowel holes, dado, and rabbet (bottom). The template for cutting the grooves in the sides (A) must be made to conform to the thickness of the template guide for your router (see *Index*, p.379). Use a 2-in. radius for the curves of the grooves.

Desk-top unit

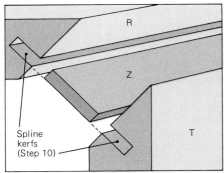

9. Cut parts R–Z to size (see chart, p.52), but do not cut the back (U) yet. Grain must run the length of splines (Z). Cut 45° bevels in top (R) and sides (T) as shown.

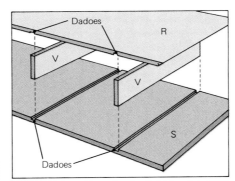

10. Cut ⅛-in.-wide spline kerfs ⅜ in. deep into the top and sides. Cut dadoes ¼ in. deep and ¾ in. wide into the bottom (S) and top (R) for partitions (V).

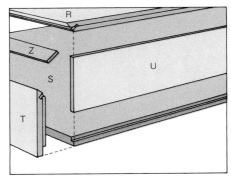

11. Cut a ¼- x ¾-in. rabbet into the bottom edges of the sides (T) to accept the bottom (S). Cut a ⅜- x ¼-in. rabbet into the back edges of parts R, S, and T for back (U).

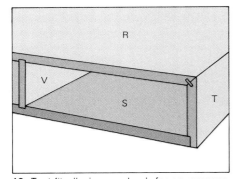

12. Test-fit all pieces, check for squareness, make adjustments; assemble with glue. Glue splines (Z) to top and sides (T); glue partitions (V) to top. Glue bottom to parts T and V.

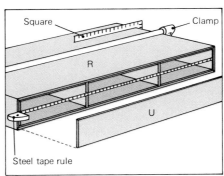

13. Clamp assembly, making certain front is square, and brace it diagonally with scrap wood. Measure opening inside rabbets, then cut back (U) to fit opening exactly.

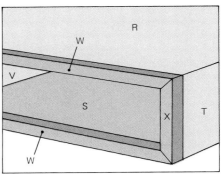

14. Glue the back to parts R, S, T, and V. Check that assembly is still square and nail back piece in place. Test-fit the trim (W, X, and Y); then glue trim in position.

Base units

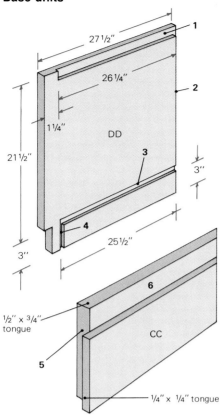

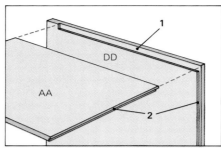

15. Cut base parts (AA–DD and FF) to the sizes given in the chart on page 52. Cut a ¼- x ¾-in. blind rabbet (1) into each side (DD) for the tops (AA). Cut a ⅜- x ¼-in. rabbet (2) in the sides and tops (AA) for the backs (EE).

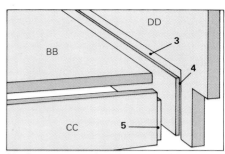

16. Cut a ¼- x ¾-in. blind dado (3) into the sides for the bottoms (BB). Cut a ¼- x ¼-in. dado (4) in the sides for the fronts (CC). Cut a ¼- x ½-in. rabbet (5) at each end of the fronts (CC) to make ¼- x ¼-in. tongues.

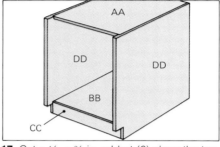

17. Cut a ¼- x ¾-in. rabbet (6) along the top of each front (CC). Test-fit pieces and make any necessary adjustments. Glue the fronts to the bottoms; then glue these and their tops (AA) into dadoes in sides.

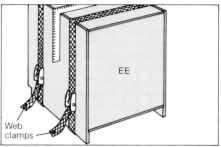

18. Clamp each base assembly with web clamps. Square the fronts with a framing square and prop up with diagonal braces. Measure openings and cut backs (EE) to fit. Glue and nail backs in place.

Drawers

Cut the drawer fronts from ¾-inch plywood, the sides and backs from ½-inch plywood, and the bottoms from ⅛-inch hardboard (see chart at right). Cut dadoes and rabbets into the backs, sides, and fronts, following the drawings below. The drawer handles were shaped at the same time as the tambour handle (p.54) and must now be cut to length. For general instructions on drawer construction, see the *Index,* p.379.

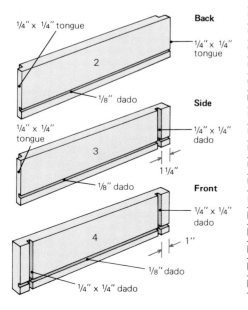

Parts list

Part	Name	Quantity	Thickness	Width	Length	Material
Side desk-top drawers (2)						
S1	Bottom	2	⅛"	15½"	23⅛"	Hardboard
S2	Back	2	½"	3½"	15½"	Plywood
S3	Side	4	½"	3½"	23⅞"	Plywood
S4	Front	2	¾"	4"	17"	Plywood
S5	Handle	2	1½"	1⁵⁄₁₆"	17"	2 x 8 hardwood
Center desk-top drawer (1)						
C1	Bottom	1	⅛"	21½"	23⅛"	Hardboard
C2	Back	1	½"	3½"	21½"	Plywood
C3	Side	2	½"	3½"	23⅞"	Plywood
C4	Front	1	¾"	4"	23"	Plywood
C5	Handle	1	1½"	1⁵⁄₁₆"	23"	2 x 8 hardwood
Upper drawers for base units (4)						
U1	Bottom	4	⅛"	14"	23⅛"	Hardboard
U2	Back	4	½"	3½"	14"	Plywood
U3	Side	8	½"	3½"	23⅞"	Plywood
U4	Front	4	¾"	4"	15½"	Plywood
U5	Handle	4	1½"	1⁵⁄₁₆"	15½"	2 x 8 hardwood
Lower drawers for base units (2)						
L1	Bottom	2	⅛"	14"	23⅛"	Hardboard
L2	Back	2	½"	11½"	14"	Plywood
L3	Side	4	½"	11½"	23⅞"	Plywood
L4	Front	2	¾"	12"	15½"	Plywood
L5	Handle	2	1½"	1⁵⁄₁₆"	15½"	2 x 8 hardwood

Cubbyhole unit

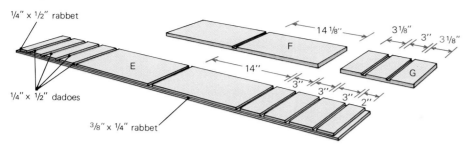

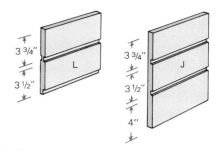

19. Cut the top (E), the shelves (F and G), the sides (H), the back (I), the dividers (J, K, and L), and the cleat (M) to size (see chart, p.52). Cut dadoes and rabbets ¼ in. deep and ½ in.

wide into the top (E) for parts H, J, K, and L. Cut a rabbet ⅜ in. deep and ¼ in. wide into the top for the back (I). Cut ⅛- x ½-in. dadoes into the shelves for dividers K.

20. Cut ⅛- x ½-in. dadoes and rabbets into dividers L to receive the shelves (F and G). Cut ⅛- x ½-in. dadoes into dividers J for shelves G. Set pieces aside.

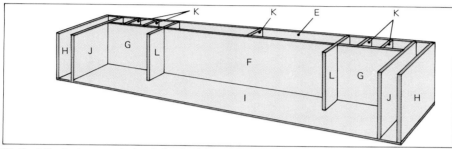

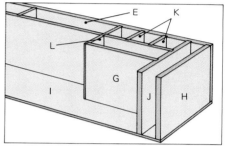

21. Test-fit all pieces and check the fit of the unit within the tambour case. Then glue and nail top (E) to sides (H). Glue back (I) to top and sides; square assembly, then nail. Glue

parts L, F, and center divider K to each other and to top. Glue remaining dividers K to top, and upper shelves G to dividers K and L. Then glue dividers J to top and upper shelves G.

22. Glue remaining shelves G to dividers J and L. Square up assembly, draw center lines of parts F, G, J, K, and L on the back (I). Then nail through I into F, G, J, K, and L.

Final assembly

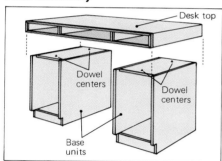

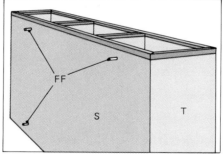

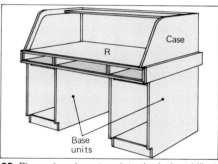

23. Drill ¼-in. holes ½ in. deep in the center of the base tops (AA) near the front and back edges. Place dowel centers in the holes. Set base units against a wall, 23 in. apart, and carefully center desk-top unit over bases.

24. Press down on desk-top unit, then remove it; dowel centers will make marks on underside of desk-top unit. Drill ¼-in. holes ¼ in. deep at these marks. Insert ¼- x ¾-in. pins (FF) into holes and set desk-top unit on bases.

25. Place dowel centers into the holes drilled in the tambour case in Step 6. Lightly position the case on desk top (R). When it is in the proper position, press down firmly on the case so the dowel centers mark the top below.

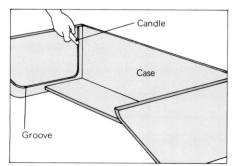

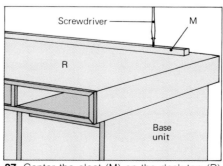

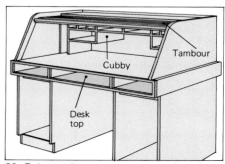

26. Remove the case and the dowel centers. At the marks drill four ¼-in. holes ½ in. deep and insert ¾-in.-long pins. On a clean surface invert the tambour case and rub a candle stub in the tambour grooves.

27. Center the cleat (M) on the desk top (R) 2½ in. from the rear edge of the top. Tape or clamp the cleat in place, drill four ⁷⁄₆₄-in. pilot holes 1½ in. deep, and attach the cleat to the top with No. 10 brass screws.

28. Rub candle wax on tongues of tambour. Carefully feed tambour into its case from the front. Lower the case over the pins (FF) in the desk top. Position the cubbyhole unit so that its back touches the cleat (M).

SHAKER PLANT STAND

The Shakers were members of an austere religious sect that flourished in the 19th century. Among other things, the Shakers made their own furniture, distinguished for its clean, simple designs, careful workmanship, and great beauty. Because this Shaker-style plant stand can be constructed with a few simple hand tools, it is a good project for a beginner.

To build the plant stand, first cut all the wood to length using a backsaw, then cut the braces to the correct width using a ripsaw. Cut out the notches for the braces with a backsaw and enlarge them for a perfect fit with a file. Join the side sections together with a doweled joint. To make this operation simpler, construct a doweling jig of scrap wood to guide you. If you work carefully, the joint will be nearly invisible, yet very strong. The graceful arc of the feet is merely a semicircle. Draw it with a compass and cut it out with a coping saw. Since the stand may be subject to spilled water, it needs a durable finish. Sand and stain it, then apply several coats of tung oil, rubbing it down with 000 steel wool and dusting it thoroughly between coats.

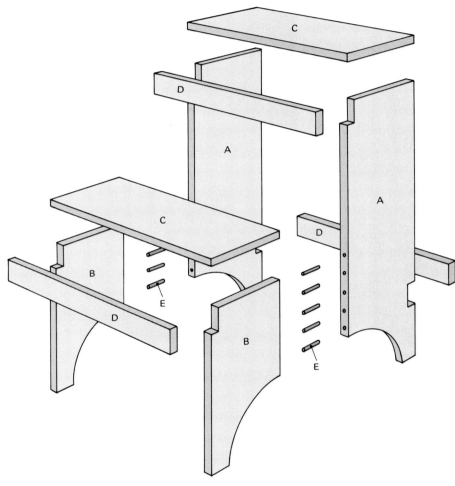

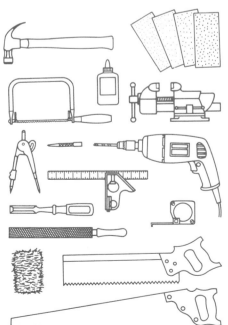

Parts list

Part	Name	Quantity	Thickness	Width	Length	Material
A	Tall side section	2	¾"	5½"	25"	1 × 6 cherry or pine
B	Short side section	2	¾"	5½"	12½"	1 × 6 cherry or pine
C	Shelf	2	¾"	5½"	16"	1 × 6 cherry or pine
D	Brace	3	¾"	1¾"	16"	1 × 6 cherry or pine
E	Dowel	10	⅜" dia.	—	1"	Hardwood dowel

Tools and materials: Backsaw, ripsaw, coping saw. Drill with ⅜" bit. Vise, coarse file or wood rasp. Wood chisel, hammer, nail set. Try square or combination square, steel tape rule, compass, pencil. Nos. 100 and 150 sandpaper, carpenter's glue, wood putty, wood stain, tung oil, 000 steel wool, soft cloths. A 12' length of 1 × 6 cherry or clear pine. A ⅜" hardwood dowel 1' long, scrap wood. 4d finishing nails.

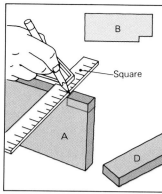

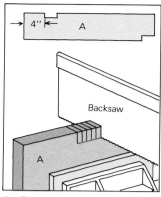

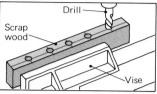

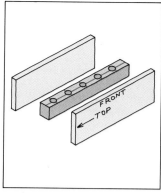

1. Cut wood as indicated in chart. Trace outlines of braces (D) onto side sections (A and B). Braces should be positioned at the top front corners of each side section and 4 in. above bottom rear corners of tall side sections (A). Use a square to extend outlines around side sections.

2. To form notches for front braces, use a backsaw to cut just inside the outlines at corners of side sections. Cut notches for back brace by making several parallel cuts about ¼ in. apart and removing wood with chisel. Test-fit braces. File down notches until braces fit snugly.

3. Cut a piece of scrap wood ¾ in. × 1 in. × 9 in. to make a doweling jig. Using a square, draw lines across thickness of scrap wood every 1½ in., then draw line down center of thickness. Holding drill perfectly perpendicular to scrap wood, drill ⅜-in. holes where lines cross.

4. Cut another two pieces of scrap wood, each about 2½ in. × 9 in., and nail them to the sides of the doweling jig that do not have holes. Label one side of the completed jig "front" and label the other side "back." Choose either end to be the top of the jig and mark "top" on both sides.

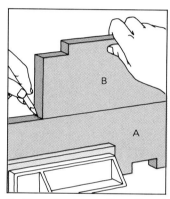

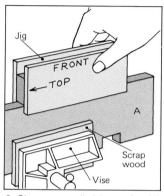

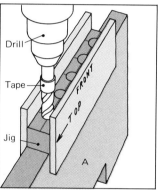

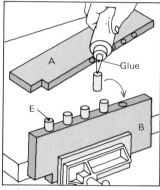

5. Place the side sections (A and B) next to each other with their bottoms aligned. Draw a line on each tall side section (A) to indicate where the upper edge of each short side section (B) will meet it. Label the top, front, and back of each side section for later identification.

6. Clamp one tall side section (A) into a vise, buffering it with scrap wood to protect its surface from the rough jaws of the vise. Fit the jig over the edge of the side section, aligning it with the line drawn in Step 5 and aligning the front and top of the jig with the front and top of the side section.

7. Drill through the holes in the jig and into the edge of the side section to a depth of ½ in. To judge correct depth, attach a piece of tape to drill bit 1½ in. above its point; stop drilling when tape reaches top of hole in jig. Repeat the drilling operation on the other tall side section.

8. Drill holes into edges of short side sections (B), being careful to align top and front of jig with tops and fronts of side sections. Test-fit the dowels (E) and check the depths of all holes for uniformity. Apply glue to the ends of the dowels and slip them into the holes in the short side sections.

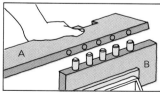

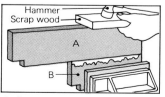

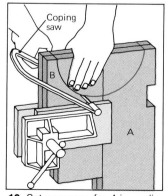

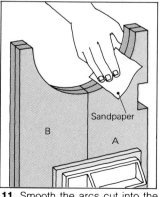

9. Run a generous bead of glue over edges of short and tall side sections and over tops of dowels. Fit holes in tall side sections over dowels in short side sections. Tap pairs of side sections together with a hammer buffered with scrap wood. Wipe off excess glue with a damp cloth. Let dry.

10. Set compass for 4-in. radius. Place its point at bottom of one side where A and B meet. Draw a semicircle. Then clamp the two sides together in vise buffered with scrap wood, and cut out semicircle with a coping saw, working from one end to middle and from other end to middle.

11. Smooth the arcs cut into the two sides with No. 100 sandpaper until both arcs are identical. Connect the two sides by gluing and nailing the lower front brace (D) into place. Add the upper front brace and back brace. Square up sides and then glue and nail on shelves (C).

12. Set all nailheads with nail set and hammer. Fill nail holes and any imperfections in joints with putty. When putty is dry, sand entire stand with No. 100, then No. 150 sandpaper. Apply stain, remove excess after a few minutes, and let dry. Apply several coats of tung oil.

COAT TREE

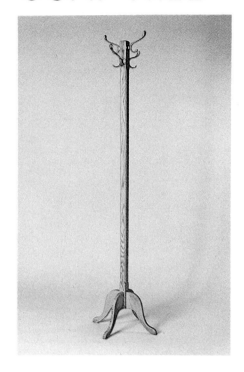

Oak and brass work well together to produce this traditional coat tree, a useful addition to any entry or hallway. Its gracefully curved feet and elegantly beveled body give the coat tree the look of a fine antique, but it is easy to construct with a few simple hand tools.

The main body of the coat tree is 1½ inches square. If you cannot find this stock in a 5-foot length, make the main body (A) by ripsawing a ¾-inch-thick board into two pieces 1½ inches wide and gluing them together with the grains matching. (You can have the board ripped at the lumberyard if you prefer.) Clamp the pieces together until the glue is dry, then smooth the sides of the laminated piece (A) with a jack plane. Adjust the plane for a very fine cut and plane with the grain to avoid chipping. Begin on the sides with the glue and then plane the other sides to the same width. Finish the job with a bench plane or large jack plane. Even if you use a solid 1½-inch-square piece of oak, you should plane it smooth if its surface is at all rough.

Shape the feet, bevel the body, and assemble the coat tree as described in the step-by-step directions. Finish the piece by sanding and staining it, then rubbing it with tung oil. (For directions on ripsawing and finishing furniture, see the *Index,* p.379.)

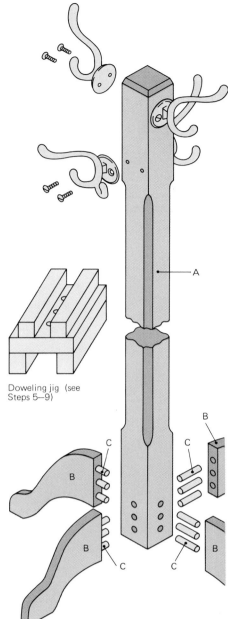

Doweling jig (see Steps 5–9)

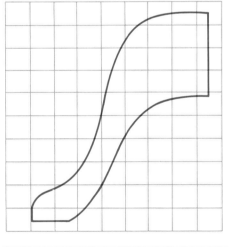

Transfer this pattern for the feet (B) to a 9- x 10-in. piece of cardboard, enlarging each square to 1 in. Cut out the outline of the foot from the cardboard to serve as a sawing pattern (see p.48).

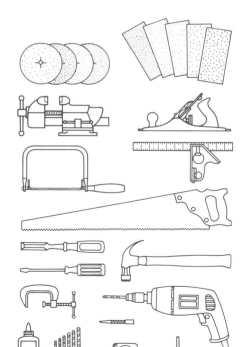

Parts list

Part	Name	Quantity	Thickness	Width	Length	Material
A	Main body	1	1½"	1½"	5'	2 x 2 red oak
B	Foot	4	¾"	Cut to pattern		1 x 6 red oak
C	Dowel	12	⅜" dia.	—	1"	Hardwood dowel

Tools and materials: Electric drill with rotary rasp or sanding drum, sanding disc, and twist bits. Coping saw, handsaw. Block plane, jack plane, bench plane or large jack plane. Vise, four 3" C-clamps. Combination square, steel tape rule. Screwdriver, ½" chisel, hammer, nail set. White glue, Nos.

150 and 220 sandpaper, stain, tung oil, soft cloths. Cardboard. A 4' length of 1 x 6 red oak board, a 5' length of 2 x 2 red oak (or 5' length of 1 x 4 red oak board). Two plain brass hooks, two brass hooks with double hat hooks (order from specialty hardware supplier).

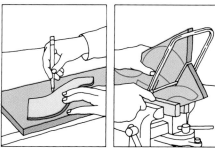

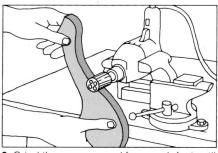

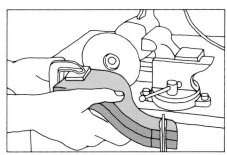

1. Cut out a cardboard pattern for the foot (previous page) and trace outline of pattern onto an oak board for each of the four feet (B). Use a coping saw to cut out feet, cutting close to, but outside of, outline. Clamp an electric drill with a rotary rasp into a vise.

2. Grind the excess wood from each foot until its edges are even with the pencil marks. Clamp two feet together and grind them until they are uniform. Repeat with other two feet, then compare them with first two. All legs should match, even if they differ from pattern.

3. Replace the rotary rasp with a sanding disc and sand the feet in the same way you ground them in Step 2, smoothing them to their final contours. Again, be sure that all the feet match exactly. Finish the sanding by hand. Prepare main body (A) as described in text.

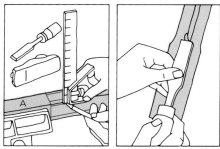

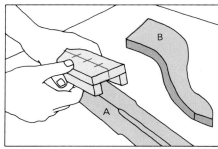

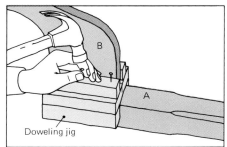

4. Draw lines around the main body (A) 6 in. from each end. Use a combination square as shown to draw rules between these lines and ⅛ in. from each edge of the body. Plane off corners between lines and rules to create 45° bevels. Finish ends of bevels with a chisel.

5. Make a 4-in.-long doweling jig from three pieces of scrap wood nailed together to form a trough (see the detail on previous page). It should fit snugly over main body. Draw a line along center of top of jig, and mark dowel locations along this line at 1-in. intervals.

6. Place one foot (B) on the center line of the jig and draw lines parallel with its sides. Be sure that the foot is aligned with the center of the jig, then nail scrap wood along these lines to sandwich foot into place. Remove foot and label one end of jig as the bottom.

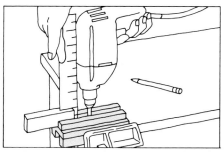

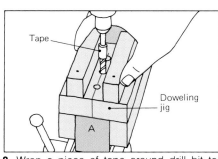

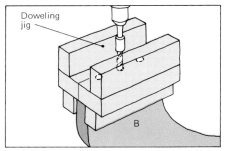

7. Use a nail set to indent the dowel marks made on the jig in Step 5. Carefully drill ⅜-in. holes through the jig at each mark, keeping the drill vertical with a combination square. Place the jig over the main body (A) so that its bottom is even with bottom of main body.

8. Wrap a piece of tape around drill bit to serve as a depth gauge, but before beginning to drill, seat bit against main body to keep holes in jig from being reamed out by repeated use. Drill 1-in.-deep dowel holes through guide holes in jig into main body.

9. Drill the dowel holes into the other three sides of the main body, then place the jig over each foot, in turn, with the marked end of the jig aligned with the bottom of the foot, and drill dowel holes into the foot. Cut twelve 1-in.-long pieces of dowel (C) from dowel stock.

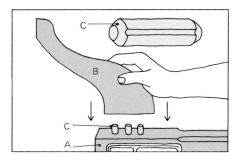

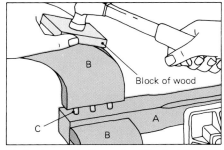

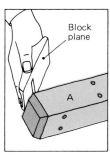

10. Taper dowel ends with sandpaper to make them easier to insert, and use a knife to cut narrow grooves along dowels to prevent air pockets from forming in holes. Test-fit each foot and mark best fits. Coat dowels with glue and insert them into main body.

11. Apply glue to the parts of the feet that will fit against the main body, and assemble the joints. You may have to tap the feet with a block of wood and a hammer to fully seat them against main body. Wipe away excess glue with a damp cloth. Lay tree aside to dry.

12. Mark locations for large brass hooks 5 in. from top of main body and for small hooks 1½ in. from top. Drill ³⁄₃₂-in. pilot holes for screws. Use block plane to make a ⅛-in. bevel at top of main body, cutting across grain. Screw on hooks. Sand and finish piece.

EARLY AMERICAN BOOKCASE

This Early American bookcase is versatile enough to blend with almost any decor. If you eliminate the decorative molding, the bookcase is not only easier to build, but it will also fit in with most modern or traditional furnishings. As shown, the bookcase is 7 feet high, 30 inches wide, and about 12 inches deep, but its design can be varied to suit your needs. The bookcase can also be used as a unit in wall-to-wall bookcases.

If you plan to build wall-to-wall bookcases, omit the molding supports where the sides of two units meet, since the moldings will get sufficient support from the adjoining sides. You can also omit the mitered joints and the side sections of the crown and baseboard moldings.

Construction: Begin the construction of the bookcase by cutting and assembling the shell. Cut the two sides (A), bottom (B), and top (C) of the shell from three 8-foot-long 1 x 12's. The top and bottom pieces fit into dadoes in the sides of the shell. The plywood back (E) is fitted into rabbets in the sides. (Directions are given in Steps 4–8 for cutting dadoes and rabbets with a circular saw. To find directions for cutting dadoes by other methods, see the *Index,* p.379.)

Before you assemble the shell, you must drill holes for the shelf supports at uniform 2-inch intervals. It is very important to space the holes properly, otherwise the shelves will not hang evenly. To avoid problems, use a homemade template as described in Step 9.

After the top, bottom, and sides are assembled, use the actual dimensions of the shell as a guide for cutting the shelves (D), the plywood back (E), the moldings (F–K), and the molding supports (L). Cut the shelves from two 8-foot-long 1 x 12 boards. Make each shelf 3/16 inch shorter than the interior width of the assembled shell and test-fit the first shelf before cutting the other five.

If you do not wish to use the exact moldings shown on the following page, you can substitute other moldings, but be sure to use moldings of the same width as those indicated in the chart, or adjust the measurements accordingly. Cut the shelf molding (F) from two 8-foot lengths. Cut the other molding and molding supports from 7-foot lengths of the appropriate material. Order extra molding to allow for possible errors in mitering. You may want to substitute simple 3-inch baseboard molding for the crown moldings (J and K), as the latter require an extra-deep miter box in order to be cut.

Never apply clamps directly to the surface of wood or they may leave unsightly marks. Always cushion the clamp by placing bits of scrap wood between the clamp and the good wood.

Before applying stain to the finished bookcase, test it on a piece of scrap wood. The longer you leave the stain on the wood before wiping off the excess, the darker the wood will become, so experiment on scrap wood in order to get the shade you prefer on the finished unit.

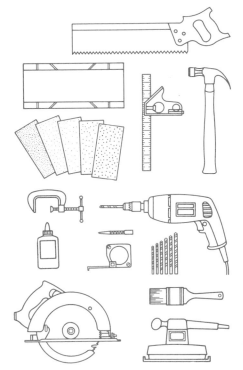

Parts list

Part	Name	Quantity	Thickness	Width	Length	Material
A	Side	2	3/4″	11½″	82″	1 x 12 knotty pine
B	Bottom	1	3/4″	11¼″	29″	1 x 12 knotty pine
C	Top	1	3/4″	11¼″	29″	1 x 12 knotty pine
D	Shelf	6	3/4″	10⅛″ ✳	28⁵⁄₁₆″ ✳	1 x 12 knotty pine
E	Back	1	¼″	29¼″ ✳	78½″ ✳	Birch plywood
F	Shelf molding	6	—	⅞″	26⅞″ ✳	Pine
G	Front baseboard molding	1	—	3½″	30½″ ✳	Pine
H	Side baseboard molding	2	—	3½″	11½″ ✳	Pine
I	Fluted molding	2	—	1½″	77″ ✳	Pine
J	Front crown molding	1	—	3″	30½″ ✳	Pine
K	Side crown molding	2	—	3″	11½″ ✳	Pine
L	Molding support	2	3/4″	3/4″	77″ ✳	1 x 1 pine

✳Measurements are approximate. Parts D–L should be measured against the assembled bookcase shell before cutting.

Tools and materials: Circular saw with adjustable blade depth or table saw or radial arm saw. Electric drill with set of twist bits. Backsaw, deep miter box. Orbital sander (optional). Combination square, framing square, steel tape rule, pencil. Four 5″ C-clamps. Hammer, nail set. Paintbrush. Wood putty. Nos. 80, 100, 150, and 220 sandpaper, 0000 steel wool, oil stain, satin finish polyurethane, turpentine, paste wax, carpenter's glue. Tack cloth, soft cloths. Wood and molding (see above) and 3″ x 82″ scrap of ¼″ pegboard. Box of 3/4″ 19-gauge wire brads. 3d, 4d, and 6d finishing nails, 3d common nails. Twenty-four metal shelf rests.

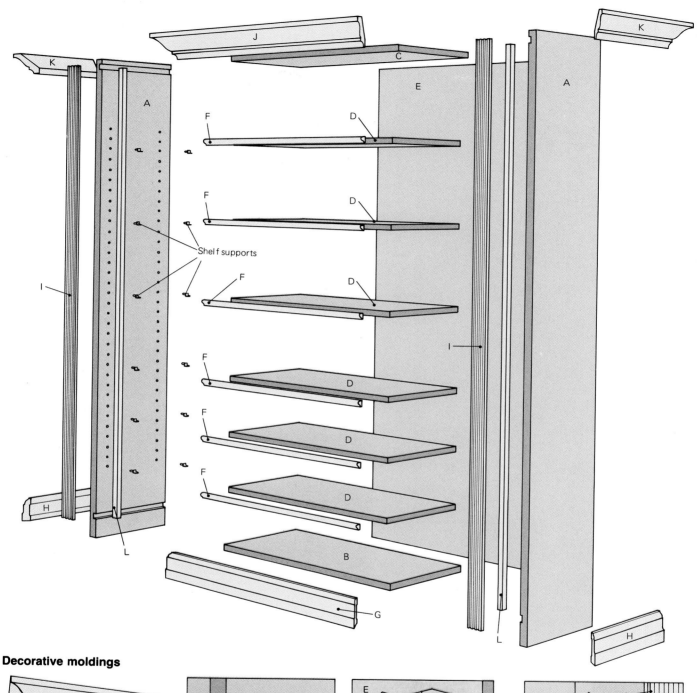

Decorative moldings

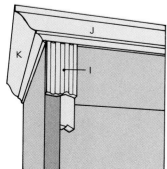

The fluted moldings (I) on the front edges of the bookcase meet the flared crown moldings (J and K) at the top corners.

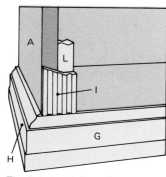

The fluted moldings (I) also meet baseboard moldings (G and H) and are attached to bookcase sides (A) and supports (L).

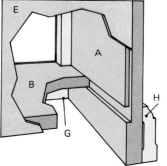

The bookcase back (E) fits into the rabbets cut into bookcase sides (A); it is flush with lower edge of bookcase bottom (B).

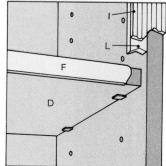

Each shelf (D) is faced with 7/8-in. pine molding (F) that fits with a small clearance against supports (L) at each side.

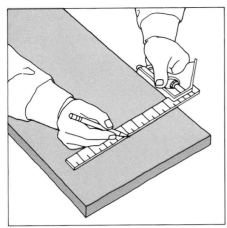

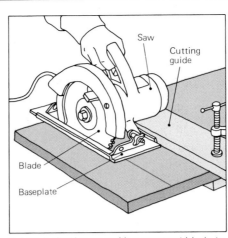

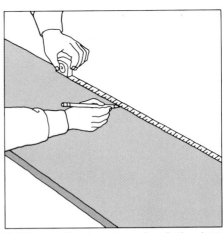

1. Cut ¼ in. from width of lumber for bookcase bottom (B) and top (C) using a circular saw with a rip blade and a guide (see Step 2). Use a combination square and pencil to draw a squared-off line for first crosscut near ends of this lumber and lumber for sides (A).

2. Use a circular saw with a crosscut blade to cut along the line. Clamp a straight strip of wood to the piece being sawed to act as a cutting guide; the distance between guide and cutting line must equal the distance between the saw's baseplate and blade.

3. Following the dimensions given in the chart, measure the correct distance from the squared end of the board to the next cut, then use combination square to draw a line for the next crosscut and cut along it. Label each piece as you cut it for easy identification.

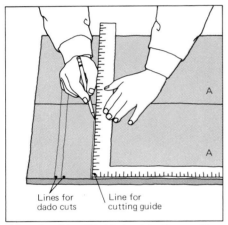

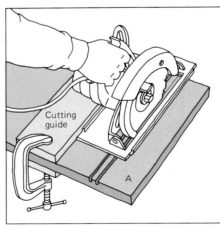

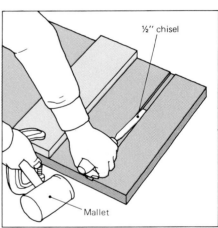

4. Lay the sides (A) side by side. Draw cutting lines for the bottom dadoes across both sides 2¾ in. and 3½ in. from one end. Set the blade of the circular saw to cut to a depth of ¼ in. and cut dadoes between the pairs of cutting lines into one side at a time (Steps 5 and 6).

5. Clamp a scrap-wood cutting guide to each side (A), in turn, so that when the baseplate of the saw butts against the guide, the saw blade is just inside one rule. Cut along the rule. Move the guide and cut along the other rule. Make several parallel cuts between these two.

6. Remove the waste wood with the saw or with a chisel and mallet. Measure and mark off cutting lines for the top dadoes ¾ in. and 1½ in. from the opposite ends of the side pieces. Cut ¼-in.-deep dadoes between these pairs of cutting lines as you did for bottom dadoes.

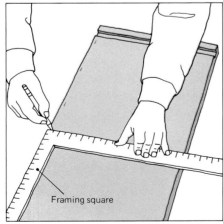

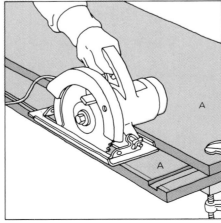

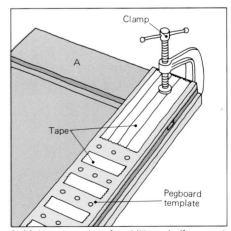

7. Use a framing square and a pencil to mark off points along the inside of the two bookcase sides (A) ¼ in. from the back edges. Draw rules through these points from top dado to bottom dado to serve as cutting lines for the rabbets the plywood back (E) will fit into.

8. Set the circular saw blade for a ⅜-in.-deep cut. Clamp one side (A) on top of the other to serve as a cutting guide and cut along the rule. Reposition the cutting guide and cut the remaining wood from the edge. Repeat this process to cut the rabbet on the other side.

9. Make a template for drilling shelf-support holes by cutting a scrap of ¼-in. pegboard 3 in. wide by 82 in. long with a row of holes at its exact center. Clamp template to the front inside edge of one bookcase side (A). Block alternate rows of holes with tape.

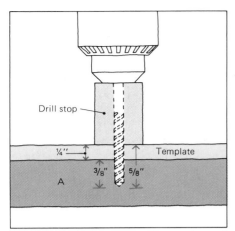

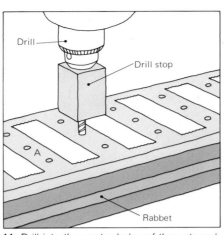

10. Make a drill stop by cutting a piece of scrap wood so that when the drill goes through it, ⅝ in. of the drill protrudes, excluding its point. This will allow the drill to pass through the ¼-in. template and bore exactly ⅜ in. into the side (A).

11. Drill into the center holes of the untaped rows in the template. Slide the template to the back edge of the side (A) and drill into the same holes. Move the template, with the same side facing up and its ends pointing in the same direction, to the second side.

12. Bore shelf-support holes into the second side (A) as you did into the first. Sand the inner portions of the sides, bottom (B), and top (C) with Nos. 80, 100, and then 150 sandpaper. Lay out the sides, inner portions up, and apply glue to the dadoes.

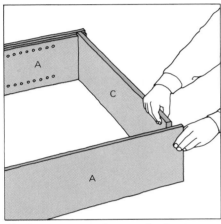

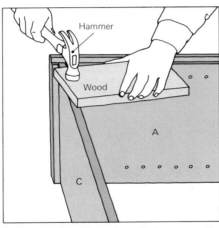

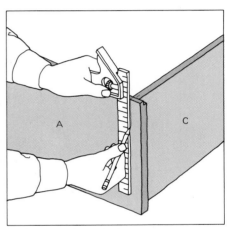

13. Be sure to apply enough glue to completely cover the bottoms and sides of the dadoes, then fit the bookcase bottom (B) and top (C) into the dadoes of one side (A) and then the other. (Position the bookcase shell with the rabbets facing up.)

14. Before glue dries, wipe off all excess with a damp cloth. Align the top and bottom of the bookcase with the back edges of the dadoes by tapping them gently near the joints with a hammer that is buffered with a piece of wood, as shown, or with a mallet.

15. Mark the center of the top and bottom dado joints on the outside of the bookcase sides. Use a combination square and pencil to extend each mark along each side, forming rules that can be used to guide the proper placement of the reinforcing nails.

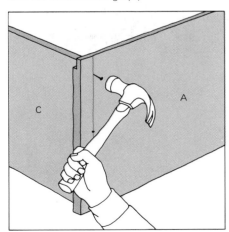

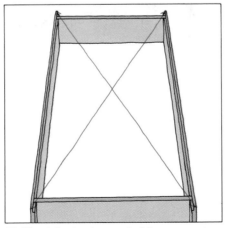

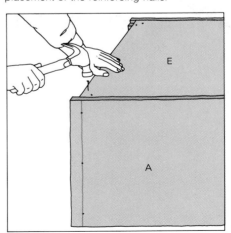

16. Nail the bookcase sides (A) to the bookcase bottom (B) and top (C) with 6d finishing nails. Use about three nails for each joint and drive them in along the guide rules that were drawn in Step 15. Use a nail set and hammer to set all the nails.

17. Check the bookcase shell for squareness by measuring its front from the upper lefthand corner to the lower right and the upper right to the lower left. If the two measurements are not identical, the bookcase is not square. Adjust the squareness before the glue dries.

18. Get exact measurements for the bookcase back (E) from the shell, cut the plywood accordingly, and sand one side with Nos. 80, 100, and then 150 paper. Position back over shell, sanded side down, and nail each of its corners to shell with two 3d nails.

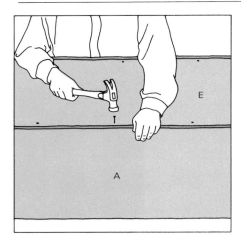

19. Drive more nails through the back into the sides, bottom, and top of the bookcase. Use one nail about every 8 in. If the bookcase sides bow out, pull them inward as you drive the nails home along the center portions of the sides. Do not set the nails.

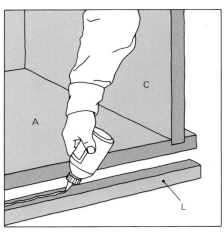

20. Measure and cut the molding supports (L), and then glue and nail them to the inside front edges of the bookcase sides (A). These will support the thin fluted moldings that run down the front of the bookcase. Use 3d finishing nails and set them.

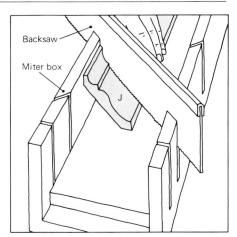

21. Clamp a length of crown molding (J) into a deep miter box with the top of the molding facing down. Angle the molding, as shown, with its bottom flush against the side of the box and its top against the floor of the box. Make a 45° miter cut with a backsaw.

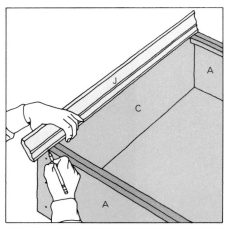

22. Place the cut piece of crown molding against the top of the bookcase shell, with the shorter cut corner of the molding against one front top corner of the shell. Mark the molding for the second miter cut where it meets the other side of the bookcase shell.

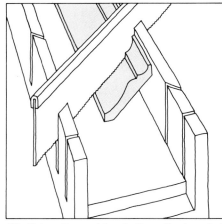

23. Return the molding to the miter box, but this time place it against the opposite side of the box with the cutting mark against a saw slot that runs in the opposite direction from the first. Hold the molding firmly in place and make the second miter cut.

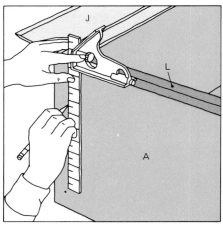

24. Glue and nail the mitered molding to the top of the bookcase with 4d finishing nails, but do not drive the nails all the way in. Use a combination square to draw rules on the sides of the bookcase to extend the bottom line of the front molding (J) along the sides (A).

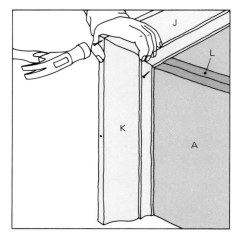

25. Measure the side crown moldings (K) against the bookcase and cut miters in one side. Cut the opposite side flush with the back of the bookcase. Rub glue into the mitered edges and position the side moldings on the bookcase and nail them on.

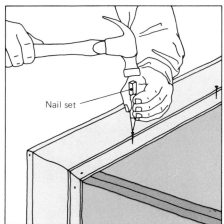

26. Align the mitered joints and carefully wipe off all the excess glue with a well-dampened cloth. (The stain will not penetrate the glue, so it is important to remove all the excess.) Drive all the nails home and use a nail set and hammer to set them.

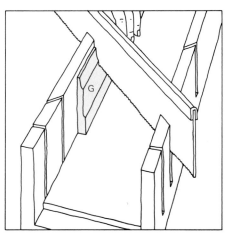

27. Measure, mark, cut, and attach the front and side baseboard moldings (G and H) as you did the crown moldings in Steps 21–26, but when cutting the miters in the baseboard moldings, hold each molding flush against the side of the miter box, as shown here.

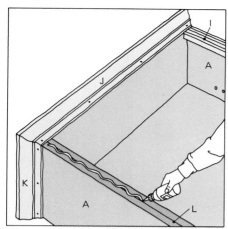

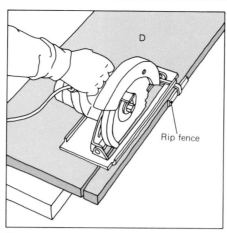

Rip fence

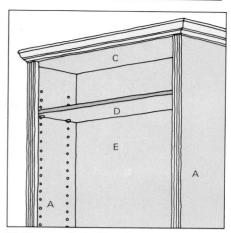

28. Measure the fluted moldings (I) against the sides of the bookcase and cut them. Glue them to the sides and molding supports, and wipe off the excess glue with a damp cloth. Nail the moldings down with ¾-in. 19-gauge wire brads. Set the brads.

29. In order to fit properly, the shelves (D) must be narrower than the boards they are cut from. Use a circular saw with a rip blade and rip fence to cut the boards to a width of 10⅛ in. Set fence for amount of wood to be removed and cut along length of each shelf.

30. Measure the inside width of the bookcase and cut the first shelf ³⁄₁₆ in. shorter than the measurement you get. Test-fit shelf by placing it into position. It should fit in easily without forcing. Adjust your measurements, if necessary, and cut the other five shelves.

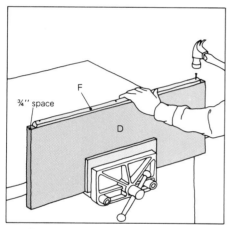

¾″ space

Putty knife

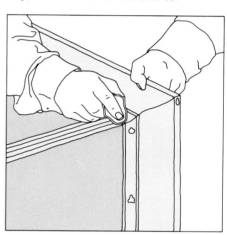

31. Clamp each shelf to the workbench, in turn, with the front edge up. Measure the shelf molding (F) against the shelf, leaving ¾ in. on each side. Cut the molding, and glue and nail it to the shelf with 4d finishing nails. Set the nails with a nail set.

32. Fill all the holes left by these nails with putty. Use your finger or a small putty knife to work the putty firmly into the holes. Leave the putty a little higher than the surface of the wood; it will shrink as it dries, and if it is still too high, you can sand it down.

33. When the putty is dry, sand the bookcase and shelves with Nos. 80, 100, and then 150 sandpaper. When sanding moldings, use No. 100, then No. 150 paper and bend it around your finger. When sanding near mitered joints, sand away from joints along molding.

34. Brush the sanded bookcase and shelves with a tack cloth to remove the sawdust created by the sanding. Use a small brush to paint on the stain. Let the stain sit for 10 min., and then wipe off the excess with a clean, soft cloth. Let the stain dry for 24 hr.

35. So that the first coat of polyurethane penetrates more deeply, brush on a coat of sealer made up of 70% satin polyurethane and 30% turpentine. Wipe off the excess after 10 min. After 4 hr. brush on a coat of full-strength polyurethane. Let it dry for 24 hr.

36. Sand all surfaces lightly with No. 220 sandpaper, then remove the sawdust with a tack cloth. Brush on another coat of full-strength polyurethane and let it dry for 24 hr. Apply paste wax with 0000 steel wool using medium pressure. Buff with a soft cloth.

JOINTED HARDWOOD BOOKCASE

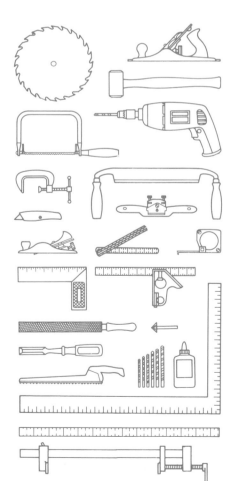

The softly flowing lines and sturdy jointed construction of this hardwood bookcase can be achieved only by careful workmanship, fitting and shaping each part to blend with the whole. It is a job for an experienced craftsman.

The care begins with the selection of wood. The sides are of richly textured cherry, noted for its graceful figuring, and the horizontal members are of light-colored ash, straight grained and durable. These hardwoods are seldom found at reasonable prices in the widths needed for the project; therefore, it is necessary to edge-join narrower boards (see opposite page). Choose the boards carefully so that the colors and figures will blend; to bring up the figure of unplaned wood so that you can see it, brush a little paint thinner on the surface.

The lumber you buy will probably not be fully dressed; you will have to square the edges on a jointer or table saw (see *Index,* p.379). In any case, the faces of the boards must be planed flat before edge-joining and planed again afterward for a good, flush surface. Buy rough lumber at least ¼ inch thicker than specified in the chart below; buy dressed lumber at least ⅛ inch thicker.

The joinery looks deceptively simple. The shelves are glued into dadoes in the sides with no attempt to conceal the joints. This means that the dadoes must be precisely cut to the thickness of the shelves—

there is no tolerance for error. In this project instructions are given for fitting these and the several tongue-and-groove joints when using a dado head on a radial arm or table saw. The job can also be done patiently by hand with a backsaw and chisel (see *Index,* p.379).

All edges and corners are rounded and shaped by hand. This is a matter of esthetic judgment, based in part on the figure and quality of the wood you are using. A spokeshave and drawknife are the tools of choice, but you can use a rasp, plane, Surform tool, and sandpaper to good effect. Note that the edge of the plinth front (H) is 3/16 inch below the upper face of the bottom piece (E) and that both corners are rounded where they meet. This is a traditional way of turning a possible defect into a design advantage. The shelf unit is not joined to the plinth; if the two surfaces were flush, the crack between them would always show. In this way, the crack is concealed at the bottom of a graceful ripple.

Because the weight of a full bookcase will tend to force the joints of the plinth apart, the mitered joints are reinforced with splines, and laminated corner blocks are glued all around.

Finishing: To bring out the warmth of the wood, rub in several coats of tung oil, allowing plenty of drying time. Protect the surface with hand-rubbed wax or a satin polyurethane finish (see *Index,* p.379).

Parts list

Part	Name	Quantity	Thickness	Width	Length	Material
A	Side	2	¾"	12"✳	44½"	Cherry
B	Top shelf	1	¾"	7¾"	24⅞"	Ash
C	Middle shelf	1	¾"	9⅜"	24⅞"	Ash
D	Bottom shelf	1	¾"	11⅜"	24⅞"	Ash
E	Bottom	1	1³⁄₁₆"	11¾"	25⅛"	Ash
F	Top	1	1¼"	10"	27¼"	Ash
G	Back	1	¼"	25⅛"✳	44⅜"✳	A–2 cherry plywood
H	Plinth front	1	1¼"	4"	29"	Ash
I	Plinth side	2	1¼"	4"	14"✳	Ash
J	Plinth back	1	1¼"	3"	26⅝"	Ash
K	Plinth spacer	1	1¼"	3"✳	10⅝"✳	Ash
L	Spline	6	⁵⁄₁₆"	1½"	2"	Ash
M	Corner block laminate	28	¾"	1¼"	1¼"	Ash

✳Measurement is approximate; cut to fit during construction.

Tools and materials: Drill with twist bits and countersink. Table saw or radial arm saw with combination blade, dado head, and splining jig. Band, saber, or coping saw. Several 6" C-clamps and 6' bar or pipe clamps, quick-action clamps (optional). Smooth plane, jack plane, block plane. Rasp, spokeshave, drawknife, and/or Surform tool. Wooden mallet, ¼" and ⅜" straight chisels. Try square, combination square, framing square, steel ruler, steel tape rule, wooden extension rule, knife, pencil. Nos. 60, 80, 120, and 220 sandpaper. Paraffin or beeswax, carpenter's glue. Wood (see above). One 2¼" No. 10 flathead wood screw, ¾" No. 6 panhead wood screws.

Edge-joining boards

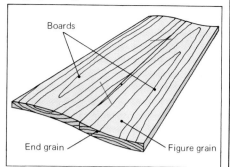

Boards

End grain

Figure grain

Choosing boards. First, look at the end grain. As a board ages, it will tend to cup in the opposite direction from the arch of the annual rings. To minimize the effect of this warpage, lay boards side by side so that the direction of the arch alternates. Align boards so that their figures blend into an attractive pattern. Use a pencil to make a few slanting lines across each joint to guide in realignment. Saw boards to approximate length.

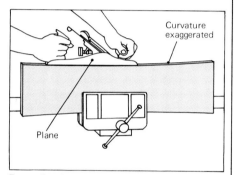

Curvature exaggerated

Plane

Preparing boards. Plane to within 1/8 in. of final thickness. Plane edges smooth and square. The boards will eventually shrink a little more across the ends than across the middle; to prevent the wood from splitting at the ends when this happens, plane both edges of joint slightly concave—the center of the joint should be separated by a gap that you can squeeze shut with your hands (less than 1/64 in.).

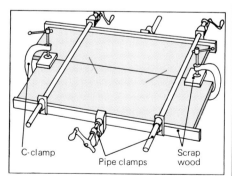

C-clamp

Pipe clamps

Scrap wood

Gluing and clamping. Apply all clamps before gluing; mark positons and order of application. Then unclamp and apply a thin, even coat of glue to both edges of joint. Reclamp quickly, tightening firmly but not forcing out all glue. First, use C-clamps to align faces of boards at both ends. Then apply bar or pipe clamp across center, forcing faces of boards into alignment, if necessary, as you tighten. Remaining clamps should alternate top and bottom.

Exploded view shows how parts fit together. All joints are glued except those securing the back (G) to the shelf unit, which are secured with 3/4-in. No. 6 panhead wood screws (Step 18); use a 5/64-in. bit for pilot holes. The shelf unit is not joined to the plinth but rests on the plinth back (J) and spacer (K) and inside the rabbets of the plinth front (H) and sides (I)—if a plinth side were glued to a side (A) of the shelf unit, the fact that the grains run in opposite directions would cause stress, and probably splitting, in the shelf side. The corner blocks (M) that reinforce the joints of the plinth are intentionally laminated with the wood grains running in alternate directions, ensuring that no joint is compromised by the sole presence of end grain. The front joints of the plinth are further reinforced by splines (L) 5/16 in. thick; order ash stock planed to thickness, or cut a strip to thickness on a table saw, then dado slots to fit (Step 15). There is little danger of the shelf unit slipping backward on the plinth, but if you wish to ensure its security, drill and countersink a 3/16-in. hole up through the front part of the plinth spacer (K) and drive a 2 1/4-in. No. 10 wood screw through it; drill a 7/64-in. pilot hole in the bottom. You can also glue two slotted blocks onto the plinth back (J) to receive additional, smaller screws (see *Index*, p.379, for instructions).

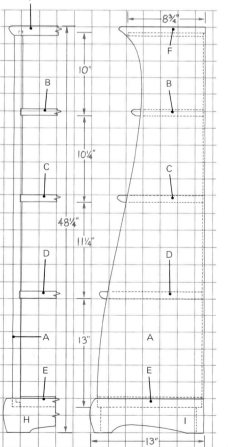

Tongues

F

G

B

C

A

D

A

E

I

K   J

M

H

I

L

After joining boards for sides (A), shelves (B, C, and D), bottom (E), and top (F), cut all stock to final length, and plane to final thickness. Rip shelves, top, and bottom to width. Use 2-in. grid (see p.48) to make full-size patterns for sides (A), plinth front (H), and plinth sides (I) and to guide in shaping the protruding edges of the top and shelves (Step 4). To make the pattern for the plinth front, duplicate the section shown and its mirror image; connect the lines for the cutout portion with an arc that rises to the same height as the cutouts in the sides.

Trace patterns onto side pieces (A). Before cutting the long S curve, use a table saw or radial arm saw to make a square cut from the top edge of each piece, 8 3/4 in. from the back, for the front of the tongues. Then rough-cut the pieces individually with a band saw, saber saw, or coping saw. Clamp them back to back, and shape them simultaneously to the line with a rasp, drawknife, or spokeshave. Cut rabbets into the top outer edges of the sides, leaving tongues 1/2 in. thick and 1/2 in. deep. Cut the dadoes for the shelves 1/4 in. deep, marking the width of each dado from the thickness of the shelf that will fit into it. (Measurements between shelf dadoes are given from bottom edge to bottom edge; to achieve dado cuts that match the thickness of the wood, make test cuts in scrap wood, inserting paper washers between dado heads as necessary.) To ensure that the shelves will be level, lay the side pieces side by side and mark across both at once.

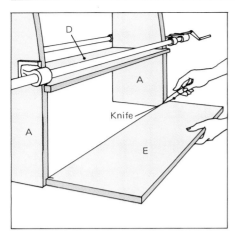

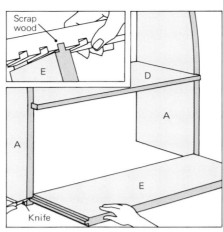

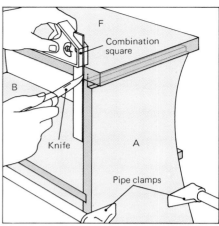

1. Clamp sides (A) and shelves (B, C, and D) together with all joints square. Center bottom (E) against front edge; use a sharp knife to mark points where bottom meets sides. Rabbet both ends of E to these marks, leaving tongues centered and ½ in. thick.

2. With a sharp knife mark position and thickness of tongues on front and back of sides (A). Make test cuts in scrap wood to set dado heads to exact width and depth needed; then cut dadoes in sides to receive tongues of bottom. Reassemble unit with bottom in place.

3. Position top (F) so its back is flush and overhang is equal on sides. Mark width of tongues on back of top and mark front of tongues on underside. Cut dadoes to receive tongues (see Step 2). Dadoes do not go all the way through; finish blind ends with a chisel.

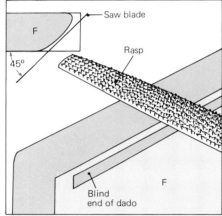

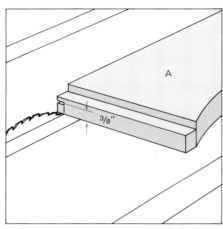

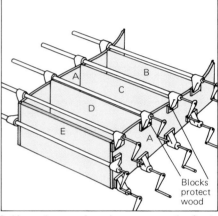

4. With top in place, sketch rounded patterns on edges of top (F) and shelves (B, C, and D). Disassemble unit and shape edges; use table saw set at 45° to remove the main body of wood from lower edge. Finish shaping with jack plane, rasp, and No. 60 sandpaper.

5. Cut ¼-in. rabbets ⅜ in. deep in back of sides (A) and top (F) to receive ¼-in. plywood back. Sand all interior surfaces with No. 80 sandpaper, then with No. 120, and finally No. 220. Assemble shelves, bottom, and sides without glue, applying all clamps.

6. Use a bar or pipe clamp across the front and back of each shelf and the bottom, and apply another across center of bottom to prevent buckling. Mark placement of clamps and disassemble. Apply glue to dadoes and reclamp quickly. Let glue dry.

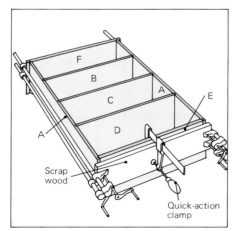

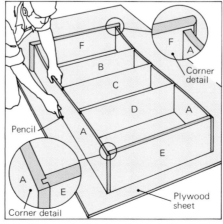

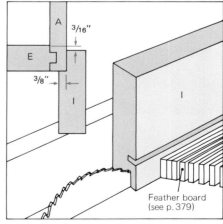

7. Before gluing top (F) to its tongues, cut a piece of scrap the same length as top to overhang the bottom and equalize the pressure of clamping. Apply glue to dadoes and clamp top in place, using two bar or pipe clamps on each end, running to scrap on bottom.

8. To find most attractive figure for back (G) lay shelf unit on plywood sheet. Trace outline of unit, and cut plywood to outline. Then fit back precisely within rabbets on sides and top. Sand back with Nos. 80, 120, and 220 sandpaper; do not secure it to unit.

9. Rip stock for plinth front (H) and sides (I), and plane to width. Cut each piece 3–4 in. longer than specified. Cut rabbets ⅜ in. deep along one face of each piece to receive shelf unit; to find width of rabbets, deduct ³⁄₁₆ in. from thickness of bottom (E).

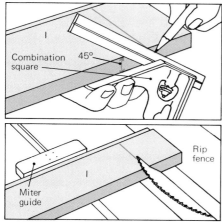

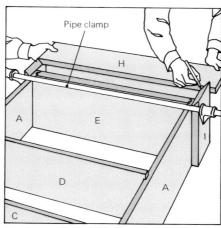

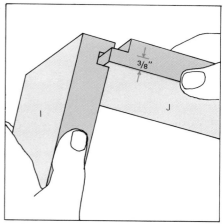

10. Cut 45° bevels on front end of each plinth side (I) and one end of front (H). For accurate cuts, scribe edge of wood first with combination square; set table saw to 45° and cut ⅟₁₆ in. too long, then shave to line, adjusting blade if needed. Check cuts with square.

11. Clamp plinth sides (I) to shelf unit so beveled ends align with front of unit. Fit plinth front (H) by holding beveled end against one side bevel and marking other end; cut overlong, then shave a little at a time until both mitered joints fit snugly. Cut sides to length.

12. Rip and plane stock for plinth back (J) and spacer (K) to width of unrabbeted portion of sides. Cut plinth back to length. Rabbet both rear corners, leaving tongues ⅜ in. thick. Mark and cut dadoes in plinth sides (I) to fit. (See Steps 1 and 2.)

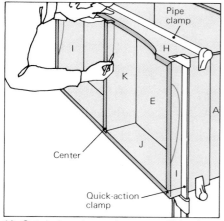

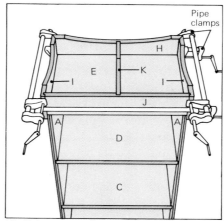

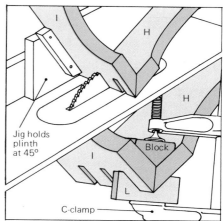

13. Cut dadoes to receive spacer ¼ in. deep across center of inner faces of plinth front and back. Clamp plinth pieces in place around shelf unit and cut spacer to fit between dadoes. Scribe and rough-cut cutouts on plinth front and sides and front end of spacer.

14. Rub wax on front corners of shelf unit. Then, after establishing clamping procedure with a dry run, apply a thin coat of glue to all mitered ends and clamp plinth together around shelf unit. (Put back and spacer in place for clamping, but do not glue them.)

15. Dado three slots across each mitered corner, using scrap wood to set width and depth of saw. Cut splines (L) square to length of slots. Apply glue. Use a C-clamp to force each into its slot. When glue dries, saw splines parallel to wood surface; plane flush.

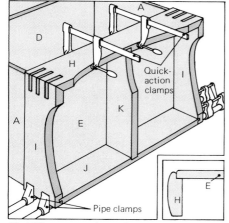

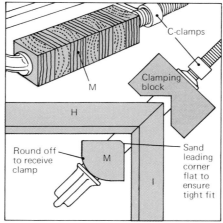

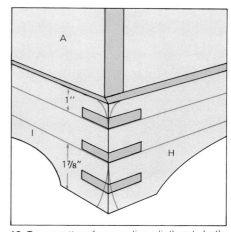

16. With rasp and sandpaper, shape inner edges of plinth sides and front, finish shaping cutout sections, and round front edge of bottom piece (E). Clamp plinth to unit, gluing tongues of back (J) into their dadoes. When dry, glue and clamp spacer (K) in place.

17. Glue corner block laminates (M) in stacks, alternating grain direction. Saw to lengths needed. Glue and clamp into joints of plinth. When glue is dry, begin shaping plinth. First, rule lines along face of front (H) and sides (I) 1 in. from top edge and 1⅞ in. from bottom.

18. Trace pattern for rounding plinth onto both faces of front corners and onto rear edge. Plane to desired shape. Complete shaping all edges with No. 80 sandpaper, then sand with Nos. 120 and 220. Finish shelf unit, plinth, and back, then screw back in place.

TRESTLE COFFEE TABLE

Subtle shaping brings out the beauty of the birchwood in this coffee table with a trestle base. The top is made of five edge-glued boards. The narrow center board is darker than the others and is 1⁵⁄₁₆ inches wide; the other four boards measure between 4 inches and 5½ inches each—enough to add up to the total width of 20½ inches. Buy the lumber dressed to the thicknesses given below, and rip the boards using a straightedge to ensure that they are square (see *Index,* p.379). Order from 25% to 30% more than the amount specified, and spend time matching the boards in different ways before you begin

cutting those for the top to the final length.

Measurements given in the chart for the feet (A), crosspieces (C), lower stretcher (D), and top (F) are for the boards before they are shaped. The step-by-step directions show how to cut tapers and shape curves. Templates for these shapes (pp.73 and 75) should be enlarged according to the directions on page 48. Be sure to cut all the joints (p.73) before shaping the parts.

The top is screwed to the base with movable buttons, allowing the wood to contract and expand with changes in humidity while being held fast.

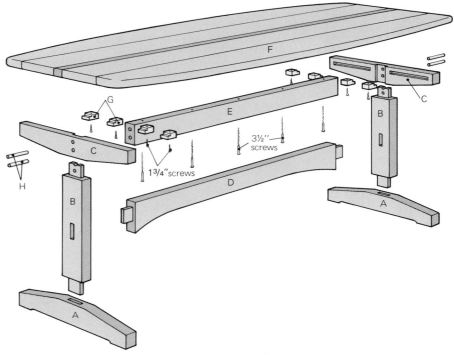

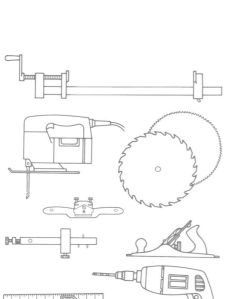

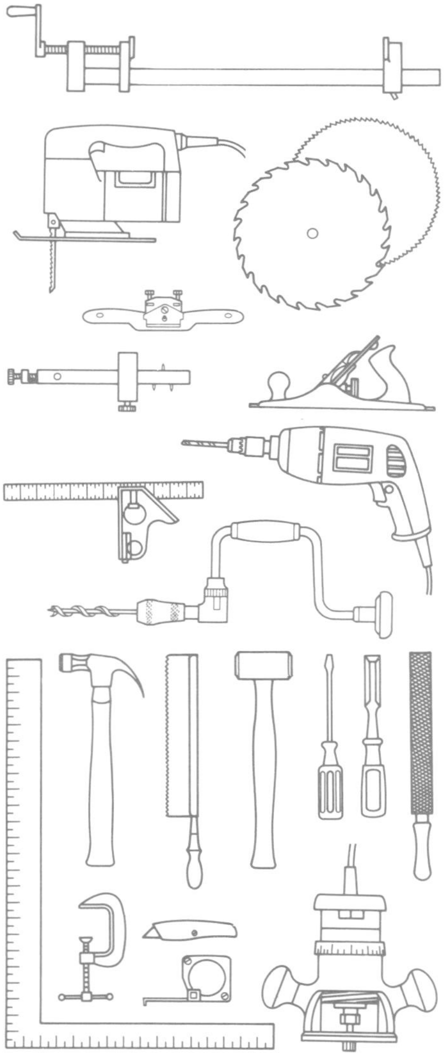

Parts list

Part	Name	Quantity	Thickness	Width	Length	Material
A	Foot	2	1¾″	2¾″	16″	Birch
B	Leg	2	1¼″	3″	15″	Birch
C	Crosspiece	2	1¼″	2½″	14″	Birch
D	Lower stretcher	1	1¼″	3⅞″	32½″	Birch
E	Upper stretcher	1	1⅜″	2½″	29⅞″	Birch
F	Top	1	1¼″	20½″	50″	Birch
G	Button	8	1″	1¼″	⅞″	Birch
H	Dowel	4	½″ dia.	—	2⁵⁄₁₆″	Dowel

Tools and materials: Table saw with combination blade, dado head, tenoning jig. Crosscut tray (optional). Band, saber, or coping saw. Dovetail saw. Router with ⅜″ straight bit. Drill with ⁹⁄₆₄″, ¹³⁄₆₄″, ²⁵⁄₆₄″ straight bits and ½″ brad-point bit. Brace with ⅜″ auger bit and depth gauge. Drill press and large hand screw (optional). Four 3′ bar clamps, four 6″ C-clamps. Smooth plane, fore or jack plane. Rasp, spokeshave or Surform, cabinet scraper, 1″ bevel-edged chisel, ⅜″ mortise chisel. Framing square, combination square, steel tape rule, mortise gauge, knife. Wooden mallet, standard screwdriver, stubby screwdriver, hammer. Carpenter's glue, wax paper. Nos. 80, 120, and 220 sandpaper. Tung oil, 0000 steel wool, hard wax, cloths. Wood (see above). Eight 1¾″ and five 3½″ No. 10 flathead wood screws.

Mortise-and-tenon joints

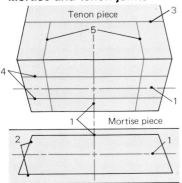

Tenon piece
Mortise piece

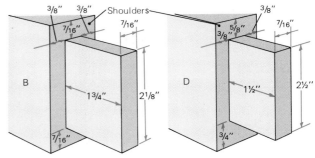

Shoulders

B   1 3/4"   2 1/8"   7/16"   3/8"   3/8"   7/16"

D   1 1/2"   2 1/2"   5/8"   3/8"   3/8"   7/16"   3/4"

Cut and fit mortises and tenons prior to shaping parts. To lay out joints on legs (B), lower stretcher (D), feet (A), and crosspieces (C), mark in numbered order as at left.
1. Mark center lines.
2. Hold each piece that will have a tenon against its mortise piece (see captions at right for placement). Match center lines, and outline tenon pieces on mortise pieces.
3. Mark shoulder line of each tenon.
4. Use a mortise gauge to mark the thickness of each tenon on the end and sides of the tenon piece.
5. Mark the length of each tenon. Mark mortises in Steps 7 and 10.

Cut this tenon on both ends of legs (B). Mortises are centered in the feet (A) and the crosspieces (C).

For tenons on lower stretcher (D), measure 4 in. from shoulders of top tenons on legs to top of D in Step 2.

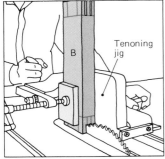

Tenoning jig

B

Cutting the tenons: 6. Use a tenoning jig on the table saw, and set the blade so that it cuts a scant 1/16 in. below the shoulder lines. On each tenon on both legs (B) cut one face; then reverse the work in the jig and cut the other face. Make all similar cuts before resetting the jig to make the next cut.

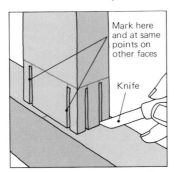

Mark here and at same points on other faces

Knife

7. Before sawing the waste at the shoulders, center each tenon piece over its mortise piece. Hold a knife against the inner surface made by each saw cut and use it to mark the dimensions of each tenon on its mortise piece These lines will later be extended (Step 10) to mark the outlines of the mortises.

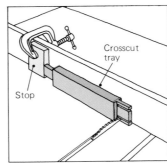

Crosscut tray
Stop

8. Clamp a scrap of wood to the crosscut tray as a stop; position it so that the saw will cut a scant 1/16 in. from the shoulder lines. Adjust the blade height, and cut off all the waste, turning each leg and holding it against the stop. If you do not have a crosscut tray, saw off the waste with a dovetail saw or other fine-tooth saw.

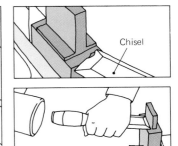

Chisel

9. Trim each joint to the shoulder line with a narrow chisel, held with its beveled side up. Take paring cuts (do not use the mallet), working from one side, then the other. Trim along the long edge with your widest chisel and a wooden mallet. Follow the same procedure for the through tenons on the lower stretcher (D).

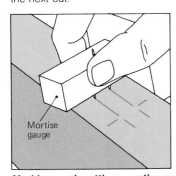

Mortise gauge

Marking and cutting mortises: 10. Set mortise gauge by marks made in Step 7; mark sides of each mortise. Using a combination square, mark the ends. Mark through mortises on each leg (B) the same way, and square markings around to opposite face. Have mortise gauge bear on same edge of each piece.

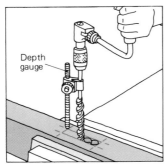

Depth gauge

11. Using a brace and 3/8-in. auger bit, set depth gauge so that the bit will bore a scant amount deeper than each tenon's length. Drill on center line, making several holes. For each through mortise, bit should just pierce opposite surface. Turn work over and drill from that point or from center line.

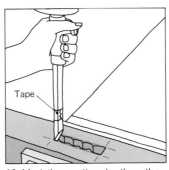

Tape

12. Mark the mortise depth on the mortise chisel by wrapping it with tape to match the length of each tenon. Use the chisel and a mallet to chop out the waste at the ends and in the bottom of the mortises. Work inward from both faces of the legs toward the center of the through mortises to clean their ends.

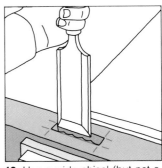

D

13. Use a wide chisel (but not a mallet) to take paring cuts that will smooth the sides of each mortise. Pare off 1/32 in. from both sides to allow the tenons an easy fit; keep trying the pieces so that the joints will not be loose. Work from both faces of each through mortise so that the edges will not splinter.

Scale drawings of trestle base parts

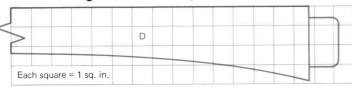

D

Each square = 1 sq. in.

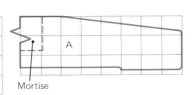

A

Mortise
Mortise

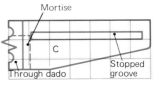

Mortise
C
Through dado
Stopped groove

Each scale drawing represents half a member; the opposite half is identical. (Enlarge according to instructions on page 48.)

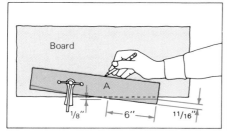

14. Measure 6 in. from each end on top edge of each foot (A). Draw a diagonal line from that point to form a triangle with an 1¹¹/₁₆-in. base (see scale drawing, p.73). To construct a jig, clamp one foot to a squared board that is a third longer than the foot so that the taper line is parallel to the board's edge and overhangs it by ⅛ in. Outline the foot on the board, then unclamp it.

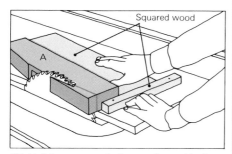

15. Nail two squared pieces of wood to the board along the side and back lines. Place each foot in this jig and saw along the taper; reverse each foot to saw the taper on the other end of the foot. Use the same jig for cutting each crosspiece (C); remove a triangle 1 in. at the base and 5 in. along the lower edge of each part C.

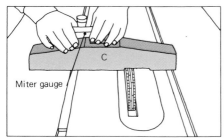

16. Shape the underside of each foot by setting the dado head at ⁵/₃₂ in. high and making repeated crosscuts using the miter gauge. Or you can use a Surform tool to remove and shape the wood.

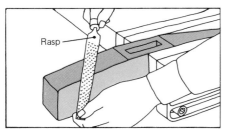

17. Round all corners and edges of feet and crosspieces with a rasp. Make one pass at 45°, and rasp off additional facets above and below until apparently round. Then finish the rounding off with Nos. 80, 120, and 220 sandpaper. Rasp and sand the underside of each foot.

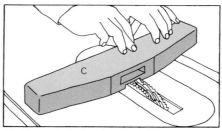

18. Use a dado head in the table saw, or a router and a straight bit, to cut a through dado in each crosspiece (C). Make it ³/₁₆ in. deep and 1⅜ in. wide. To cut the stopped grooves in the crosspieces, use a ⅜-in. straight bit in the router.

19. Enlarge the scale drawing on page 73 to make a template for the lower stretcher (D); transfer shape to wood. Cut the curve with a band saw, saber saw, or coping saw. Refine the shape with a rasp using its curved side. Rasp and sand the edges round as in Step 17.

20. Mark a center line the length of the upper stretcher (E) on its bottom surface. Along that line mark the positions of the five screws that will secure the table top to the stretcher—one in the center, one 1½ in. from each end, and the other two halfway between. Drill shank holes with ¹³/₆₄-in. bit, and counterbore with ²⁵/₆₄-in. bit.

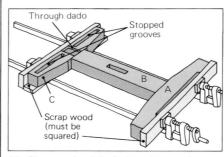

21. Glue one leg into foot and crosspiece for each end. Lay the pieces on two bar clamps with scrap wood protecting the surfaces and a scrap piece on one side of the crosspiece to make it lie evenly on the clamps. Spread glue on all surfaces of the tenons except the ends. Tighten clamps. Check that each side of the assembly is the same height; tighten clamp on longer side. Repeat for other end of base.

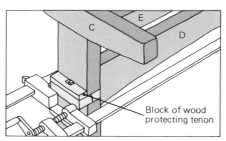

22. Cut two blocks of wood ¾ in. x 3 in. x 3 in., and in each make a channel to accommodate the through tenons. Tape these over the through tenons to protect them. Dry-fit the base; trim joints for fit. Spread glue on tenon surfaces that will be inside mortises. Place clamps parallel to lower stretcher with handles at opposite ends. Drop the upper stretcher (E) into its dado, but glue it later. Check diagonally for squareness (see *Index,* p.379).

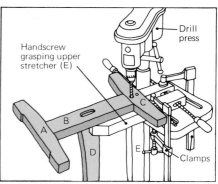

23. Clamp each leg assembly to a drill press table as shown, and drill holes for dowels (H) in each crosspiece with a ½-in. brad-point bit. Make holes 2¼ in. deep and center them ⅝ in. from top and bottom of crosspiece. Or use an electric drill with drill guide so hole is straight. Chamfer entering end of each dowel. Spread glue onto dowels and drive them into holes with a mallet. Saw ends almost flush and plane flat.

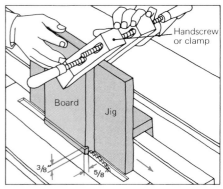

24. To make buttons (G), square and plane a board to 1 in. thick, 5–6 in. wide, and about 1 ft. long. Use the table saw to cut a cross-grained rabbet at both ends of the board ⅝ in. deep and ⅜ in. wide. Make the ⅝-in. cut into the thickness of the board; then stand the board on end in tenoning jig and make a ⅜-in. cut. (Rabbet can also be cut with a router.)

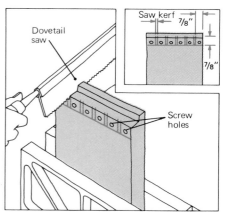

25. Scribe lines, as shown, on top of boards. To drill screw holes, clamp a scrap of wood tightly to underside and use a ¹³/₆₄-in. bit. Drill through to scrap; counterbore with ²⁵/₆₄-in. bit. Use table saw or dovetail saw to cut along right margin of each button to the ⅞-in. line. Saw along that line to separate buttons.

The table top

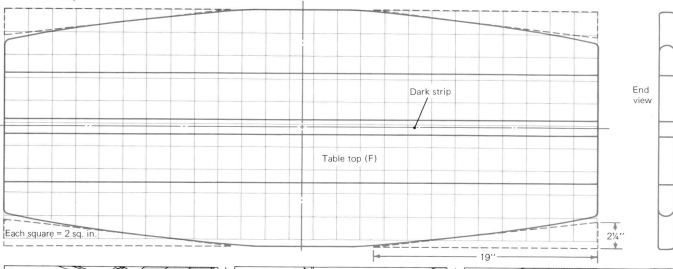

Dark strip

Table top (F)

End view

Each square = 2 sq. in.

2¼″

19″

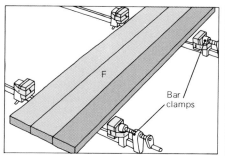

F

Bar clamps

26. Check board for squareness; plane if necessary. Leave board from which you will cut center strip its full width until Step 28 to make planing easier. Tape scrap wood to jaws of four bar clamps; place two clamps on work surface with wax paper across bars. Do a dry assembly to check procedure. Apply glue to one edge of dark center board and to two boards flanking that side. Join and rest boards on clamps.

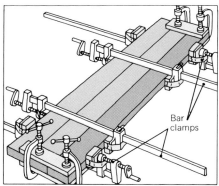

Bar clamps

27. Place C-clamps directly over the glued edges at each end, protecting table top (F) with scraps of wood rubbed with paraffin. Tighten C-clamps to bring edges flush. Check with hand along the length of joint that all edges are flush; pound with wooden mallet to align them. Add bar clamps across top; tighten bar clamps.
28. Remove clamps after 2–4 hr., and saw center board to final width. Check for squareness and plane the sawed edge. Glue together the other two boards, as in Steps 26 and 27, then glue them to the first three boards.

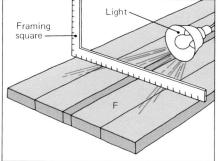

Framing square

Light

F

29. Scrape glue from surfaces. Beam a strong light across top, and move a framing square the length of the surface to check that it is level. Make pencil marks on high spots—where light does not show through.
30. Plane down these high spots with a fore or jack plane, moving it in the same direction as the grain. Use a smooth plane to remove any remaining rough spots.

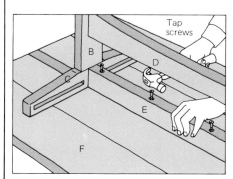

Tap screws

B

C

D

E

F

31. Center base on underside of table and draw its outline. Insert a 3½-in. screw in each hole in the upper stretcher, then tap screws to mark their positions on underside of table. Drill pilot holes 1 in. deep using a ⁹⁄₆₄-in. bit. (Wrap the bit with tape to serve as a depth gauge.)
32. Make a template for shaping the table top from scale drawing at top of page. Construct a jig similar to the one used to taper the feet and crosspieces (Steps 14 and 15). Saw off triangles that are 2¼ in. at the base and 19 in. along the table-top edge. Tape the cutoff pieces back in place while sawing triangles from the other end.

Spokeshave

33. If remaining waste is wide enough, saw it off with a dovetail saw; otherwise use a smooth plane. Enlarge the scale drawing at top right. Transfer the curve to the ends of the table top. Use a spokeshave or a Surform tool, followed by a rasp, to shape the curve. Continue rounding along the side edges, but gradually decrease the curve toward the center so that only the corners of the vertical surface are rounded.

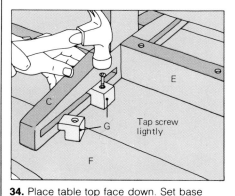

C

E

G

F

Tap screw lightly

34. Place table top face down. Set base onto outline made in Step 31. Place buttons in grooves in each crosspiece. Insert a 1¾-in. screw in each hole; tap it to mark its position. Remove base and buttons. Drill pilot holes ¾ in. deep with a ⁹⁄₆₄-in. bit.
35. Insert 3½-in. screws in upper stretcher and tighten with a stubby screwdriver. Screw buttons in place. Sand table with Nos. 80, 120, and 220 sandpaper. Wet top with a cloth and let dry overnight. Resand with used No. 220 paper. Apply three or more coats of tung oil; rub each section hard until warm, then wipe dry immediately. Let sit overnight, and remove residue with 0000 steel wool. Wax if desired.

PEGGED COFFEE TABLE

Pegged construction and heavy 4 x 4 lumber give a rustic look to this sturdy coffee table. It can be built in a number of shapes to suit your needs. No nails or screws are used in its assembly; the rugged table is held together by dowels and glue, adding to its primitive charm.

Construction: The table is relatively simple to assemble if the parts are aligned and glued together first, then drilled and doweled. If you attempt to drill all the holes first, then apply glue and insert the dowels, the operation becomes much more difficult.

When you insert a tight-fitting dowel into a hole, it will displace most of the glue, which not only creates a big cleanup job but also makes the joint weaker than it might be. Lumberyards that cater to advanced woodworkers often carry dowels that have spiral grooves on their outer surfaces. Such dowels displace less glue and produce stronger joints than smooth dowels. If you cannot find dowels that have spiral grooves, you can cut straight grooves into smooth dowels.

Common construction-grade lumber is often flawed by excessive knots, splits, and warping. Minor imperfections add to the rustic charm of this piece, but if the lumber available locally has too many imperfections, you may have to special-order select grades.

Seriously warped lumber cannot be forced into alignment during the construction of this table as it can, for instance, during the construction of a redwood deck. Because of the half-inch spacing between the slats of the table top, the lumber used should not curve more than ⅛ inch along the length of the longest pieces. Once the pieces are pegged and glued, they will not warp further.

As time passes, the 4 x 4 lumber will shrink more than the hardwood dowels will. This is why the dowels are cut shorter than the holes they are forced into. If they were not shorter, the dowels would begin to protrude from the surface of the table over the years. The caps on the table top hide this expansion space.

A reversible ⅜- or ½-inch drill is needed to make the deep peg holes through the table top and into the table's base. You will need to reverse the drill periodically to clear debris from the holes. A ¾-inch auger bit (normally used in a hand brace) does the best job of drilling such deep holes. You can fit it into a ⅜-inch or larger electric drill by cutting off the tapered end of the auger bit's shank. Secure the bit in a vise and use a hacksaw to cut the shank.

Step-by-step instructions for making the circular table are given on the following pages; it is the most tedious shape to construct because of the difficulty of cutting and sanding lengths of 4 x 4 lumber into a smooth curve. The square and rectangular variations shown on the opposite page are much easier to build.

Finishing: Pine or fir 4 x 4's can be stained almost any shade, then covered with polyurethane or lacquer and polished to a high gloss with 000 steel wool and oil. The stain should be allowed to dry at least 24 hours before the polyurethane or lacquer finish is applied; follow the instructions that come with the stain and finish that you choose. The table shown here was stained with a walnut oil stain. Because the end grain of the dowels absorbs more stain than the side grain of the 4 x 4's, the pegged construction stands out in dramatic contrast. Unstained natural pine or fir is also attractive.

Parts list

Part	Name	Quantity	Thickness	Width	Length	Material
A	Base	2	3½″	3½″	20″	4 x 4 pine or fir
B	Base	2	3½″	3½″	16″	4 x 4 pine or fir
C	Base	2	3½″	3½″	36″	4 x 4 pine or fir
D	Top	2	3½″	3½″	22″	4 x 4 pine or fir
E	Top	2	3½″	3½″	30″	4 x 4 pine or fir
F	Top	2	3½″	3½″	34″	4 x 4 pine or fir
G	Top	2	3½″	3½″	36″	4 x 4 pine or fir
H	Top	1	3½″	3½″	36″	4 x 4 pine or fir
I	Cap	18	1⅛″ dia.	—	⅝″	Hardwood dowel
J	Peg	18	¾″ dia.	—	3¾″	Hardwood dowel
K	Peg	4	¾″ dia.	—	7½″	Hardwood dowel

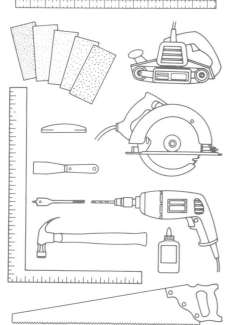

Tools and materials: Circular saw, handsaw, ⅜″ or ½″ reversible electric drill with ¾″ auger bit and 1⅛″ spade bit. Belt sander, hammer or mallet. Framing square, wooden yardstick, pencil. Putty knife. Sanding block. No. 150 sandpaper and Nos. 80 and 120 sanding belts. Carpenter's glue, 000 steel wool. Oil walnut stain, polyurethane varnish, wood filler, paintbrush, soft cloths. Three 12′ lengths of 4 x 4 pine or fir. A 1⅛″ hardwood dowel 1′ long, three ¾″ hardwood dowels 3′ long.

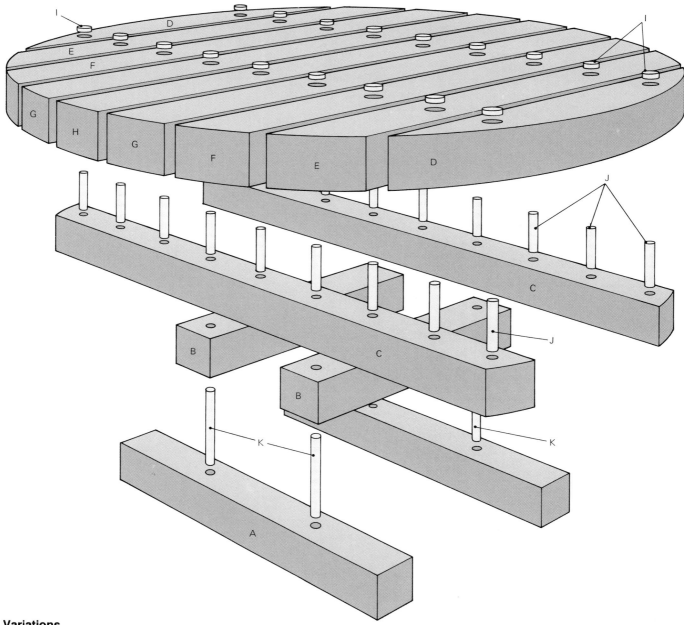

Variations

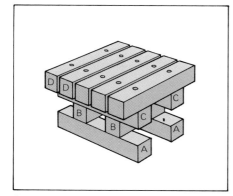

Square table can be made as large as the round table, illustrated in the exploded view (top), or it can be built as a small end table shown here. In either case, parts A, C, and D must all be the same length for a square table. There are five D's and no parts E through H.

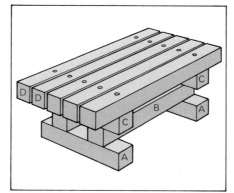

Rectangular shape can be used either as a low table or as a bench. It is built in the same way as the square table at the left, except that parts B and D are longer than parts A and C. When planning any of these variations, remember that a 4 x 4 is 3½ in. wide.

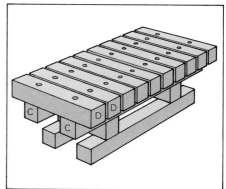

"Xylophone" variation is a square table that has been extended into a rectangle by adding more short parts D rather than extending the length of the D's. Parts C are extended to the desired table length. The xylophone requires more work than the same size rectangle.

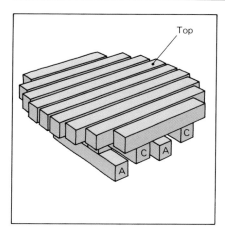

1. Cut all wood to the lengths shown in the chart on page 76. Lay out parts A through H on the floor in order to make sure that they are all the right length and will fit properly. Space the table-top parts about ½ in. apart and reject any that warp more than about ⅛ in. Parts C should be positioned under and perpendicular to parts D through H.

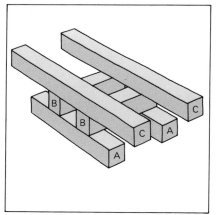

2. Remove table-top parts D through H. Position parts C so that they are flush with the ends of parts B. Assemble base (A, B, and C) using only carpenter's glue. Allow the glue to dry thoroughly so that the parts will not slide out of alignment when they are moved.

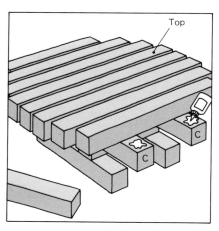

3. Reposition table-top parts perpendicular to parts C. Space the parts as evenly as possible about ½ in. from one another. Remove the table-top parts one at a time, apply a liberal coating of carpenter's glue, then attach them to the base. Reposition any parts that have shifted and allow the entire assembly to dry thoroughly.

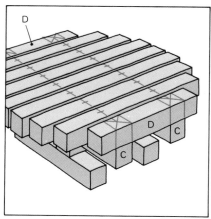

4. To mark the centers of the dowel holes, use a framing square to extend the widths of parts C up the sides and across the tops of parts D. Draw diagonals on the resulting 3½-in.-square boxes to locate the four centers on parts D. Connect two pairs of centers with lines parallel to parts C. Measure along these lines half the width of each top piece and mark each center.

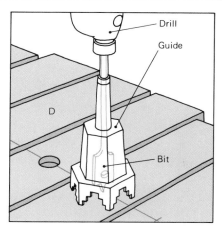

5. Use a 1⅛-in. spade bit to drill holes about ½ in. deep on each of the 18 center marks made in Step 4. Use a commercial drill guide or a framing square to make sure that the bit is absolutely perpendicular to the surface of the wood.

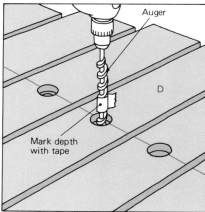

6. Use the modified ¾-in. auger bit (see text) to drill dowel holes through the table-top pieces and into parts C. Center the lead screw of the auger in the dimple left by the point of the spade bit. Keep the auger perpendicular to the surface as you drill. Reverse the drill periodically to clear wood chips from the hole. Mark the auger to make 4½-in.-deep holes.

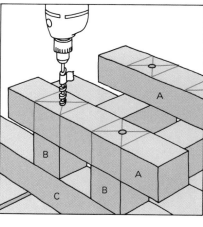

7. Turn the table upside down and drill four ¾-in. dowel holes into the base assembly. Each hole must pass through the center lines of parts A, B, and C. (To mark the centers, use a pencil and framing square as in Step 4.) Keep the bit perpendicular and drill each hole 8 in. deep so that it passes through parts A and B and penetrates 1 in. into parts C.

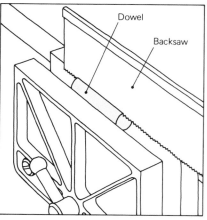

8. If you cannot obtain dowels that have spiral grooves, clamp each of the twenty-two ¾-in. smooth dowels in a vise one at a time and use a backsaw to cut a groove about ⅛ in. deep along the edge of each dowel from top to bottom. Next, put a generous amount of carpenter's glue into each of the four holes on the bottom of the base assembly.

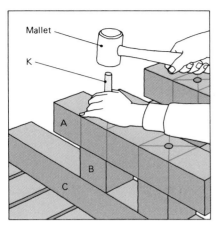

9. Use a hammer or mallet to drive one of the 7½-in.-long pegs (K) into one of the holes in the base. Use a scrap piece of dowel to drive the peg as far as it will go below the surface of the wood. Have a damp cloth handy to wipe up any glue that overflows from the hole. If no glue overflows, add more glue to the remaining holes and drive pegs into them. Clean up glue spills.

10. Turn the table right side up and squeeze a generous amount of glue into each of the 18 peg holes. Hammer a 3¾-in. peg (J) into each hole, as in Step 9, again using a scrap of dowel to drive each peg to the bottom of its hole. If glue does not overflow from the first hole, add more to the remaining ones. Then clean up the glue that overflows with damp cloths.

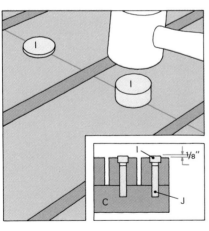

11. Blot excess glue out of each hole so that a ¼-in. air gap exists between the top of each 3¾-in. peg (J) and the wide portion of each hole. Apply a small amount of glue around the edges of each 1⅛-in. cap (I) and drive one cap into each hole. Each cap should protrude about ⅛ in. above the surface of the table. Wipe off all traces of glue from the surface so that the stain can penetrate.

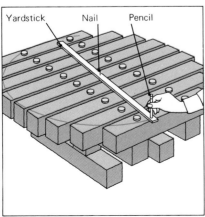

12. Mark the center of part H. Then stick a pencil through the hole at one end of a wooden yardstick. Measure in 18 in. from the pencil point and drive a 4d finishing nail through the yardstick and into the mark at the center of H. Use the yardstick and pencil as a compass to draw a circle 36 in. in diameter onto the table top.

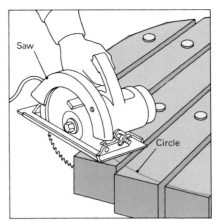

13. Use a circular saw to cut away the waste wood outside the circle drawn in Step 12. You cannot cut a curve with the circular saw; so make a series of straight cuts that are tangent to the circle in order to remove as much wood as possible and reduce the amount of sanding needed in Step 14. Use a handsaw to continue these cuts through parts C.

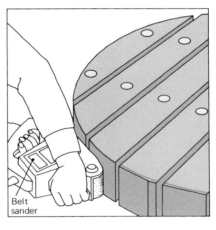

14. Use a belt sander and No. 80 sanding belt to round off the edges of the table top and edges of parts C. Sand carefully and evenly up to the circle that was drawn in Step 12. Sand the 1⅛-in. caps down flush with the surface of the table top. Resand the entire table using a No. 120 sanding belt.

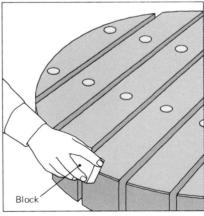

15. Use a stainable wood filler to fill in any irregularities at the joints of the 4 x 4's and any low spots on the wood surface. When the filler has dried, resand the table, first with the belt sander and No. 120 belt, then by hand using a sanding block and No. 150 sandpaper. Use the sanding block to chamfer all sharp edges on the 4 x 4's.

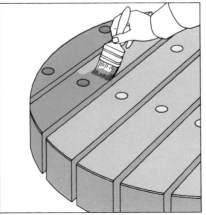

16. Apply a penetrating oil stain, if desired, following the instructions on the label. Allow the stain to dry for 24 hr., then apply a coat of polyurethane or lacquer finish. When the finish has dried, rub it to a high gloss with 000 steel wool and rubbing oil.

DINING TABLE

An exotic wood from Africa, zebrawood gives a new look to this classic extension-leaf dining table. Zebrawood is not easy to work; your tools and saw blades must be extremely sharp to handle it. But the dramatic grain of zebrawood is unsurpassed by any other. If you prefer a more subdued look, use any hardwood that is available as veneered lumber-core plywood, such as oak, teak, walnut, or cherry.

The veneered plywood top is trimmed with mitered hardwood edge strips; it measures 35½ inches x 56 inches and rests on a bearer rail and two leaves. Each leaf is 22½ inches x 35½ inches, including the edge strips. The stationary bearer rail supports the top when the two leaves are pulled out. The leaves are screwed to tapered slides, and as they are withdrawn from their storage position, the taper of the slides causes the table top to rise gradually. When the leaves are fully extended, the table top drops onto the bearer rail (see diagrams on opposite page, bottom left). It is a good idea to use your hand to support the top so that it drops gently. Dowels glued into the underside of the top are seated in the bearer rail to keep the top in position. To return the leaves to their storage position, lift the table top and slide the leaves back under it (see illustration opposite).

In order to prevent scratches, the underside of the top is covered with felt where it touches the leaves. To compensate for the thickness of the felt at the ends of the top, plastic laminate is glued to the underside of the bearer rail.

In the chart the dimensions for the legs are given as though they were a single piece of wood; actually, each leg is made from two pieces of hardwood, each 1⅜ inches thick, glued face to face. Be sure the slides are perfectly straight or the leaves will not operate smoothly. Wood of a thickness of the slides (1½ inches) is likely to change shape after being cut because of the release of fibers. Therefore, it is a good idea to cut the wood close to the required width, joint it again (see Step 7), and then cut it to the final width. When making crosscuts, follow a similar practice: cut close to the line on the first pass, then make the second pass with the

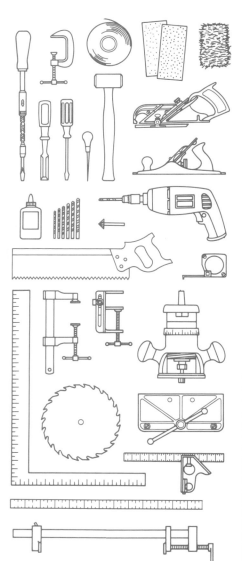

Parts list

Part	Name	Quantity	Thickness	Width	Length	Material
A	Top	1	¾"	33"	53½"	Plywood
B	Leaf	2	¾"	33"	20"	Plywood
C	Top side edge strip	2	¾" ✷	1½"	56"†	Zebrawood
D	End edge strip	6	¾" ✷	1½"	35½"†	Zebrawood
E	Leaf side edge strip	4	¾" ✷	1½"	22½"†	Zebrawood
F	Leg	4	2¾"	2¾"	28½"	Zebrawood
G	Side apron	2	1½"	2¾"	48"	Zebrawood
H	End apron	2	1½"	2¾"	27½"	Zebrawood
I	Bearer rail	1	¾"	8½"	33"	Plywood
J	Bearer end edge strip	2	¾" ✷	1½"	32½"†	Zebrawood
K	Bearer side edge strip	2	¾" ✷	1½"	11"†	Zebrawood
L	Slide	4	1½"	1⅞"	49⅜"	Hardwood
M	Center support	1	1½"	2¾"	30"†	Hardwood
N	Slide stop dowel	4	⅜" dia.	—	1½"	Dowel
O	Joining dowel	16	½" dia.	—	3¾"	Dowel
P	Positioning dowel	2	½" dia.	—	2"	Dowel

✷ Buy ¹³⁄₁₆" thick stock and plane to ¾".
†Measurement is approximate; cut to fit during construction.

Tools and materials: Table saw with fine-tooth carbide-tipped blade, carbide-tipped rip blade, miter gauge, and crosscut tray. Circular saw with plywood blade. Router with ¼" straight bit, ½" or ¾" straight bit, ¼" rounding-over bit, and ¾" core-box bit. Drill with ½" twist bit, countersink bit, and doweling jig. Tenon saw, 1½" chisel, wooden mallet, rabbet plane, smooth plane. Steel tape rule, combination square, framing square, straightedge, pencil. Standard screwdriver, spiral-ratchet screwdriver, awl. Vise, two quick-action clamps, two 6" C-clamps. Bar or pipe clamps as follows: seven 3', five 4', four 6'. Two sawhorses. White glue, contact cement, masking tape. Nos. 80, 100, 120, and 150 sandpaper. No. 220 open-coat silicon carbide paper, 0000 steel wool. High-gloss polyurethane varnish, paste wax, paraffin, cloths. A 4' x 8' panel of ¾" zebrawood lumber-core plywood. Solid zebrawood milled to ¹³⁄₁₆", 1⅜", and 1½" (see chart and Step 7). Hardwood milled to 1½" (see chart), ¼" plywood scraps. Two ½" hardwood dowels 3' long, a ⅜" hardwood dowel 6" long. Plastic laminate 8½" x 32½", ⅔ yd. felt. Four furniture glides for bottoms of legs. Flathead wood screws: eight 1½" No. 8, four 2" No. 10, two 1¾" No. 12, ten 2" No. 12, and two 2¼" No. 12.

blade on the outer edge of the cutting line. This technique will give the cut a straighter surface.

The project calls for a number of bar or pipe clamps in several sizes. If you use pipe clamps, you will need seven pairs of head and tail pieces; then you can buy black pipe, threaded on one end, cut to the required lengths (see *Tools and Materials*). Whenever you glue joints,

have someone on hand to help wipe off the excess glue, position the clamps, and move heavy assemblies.

After you complete the step-by-step instructions, remove the top and leaves; then sand and finish all parts. Sand the hardwood with Nos. 80, 100, 120, and 150 paper; sand the plywood surfaces carefully with Nos. 100 and 150 paper so that you do not break through the veneer. Glue the

felt to the underside of the top and put furniture glides on the legs.

This dining table was finished with four coats of high-gloss polyurethane, sanded between coats with No. 220 open-coat silicon carbide paper. A coat of paste wax was then applied with 0000 steel wool. (Alternative finishes might be tung oil or Danish oil.) Paraffin was used to wax the slides and their notches.

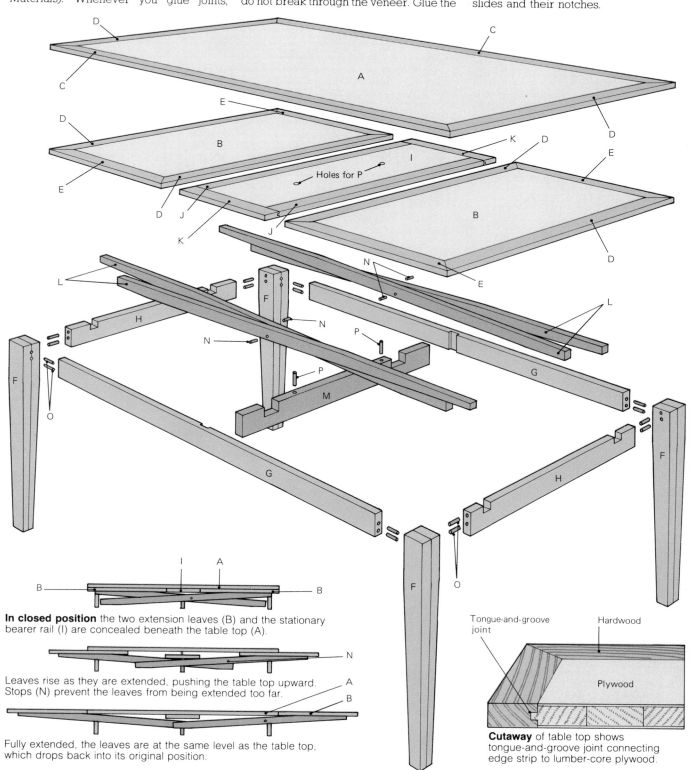

In closed position the two extension leaves (B) and the stationary bearer rail (I) are concealed beneath the table top (A).

Leaves rise as they are extended, pushing the table top upward. Stops (N) prevent the leaves from being extended too far.

Fully extended, the leaves are at the same level as the table top, which drops back into its original position.

Cutaway of table top shows tongue-and-groove joint connecting edge strip to lumber-core plywood.

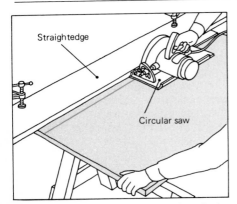

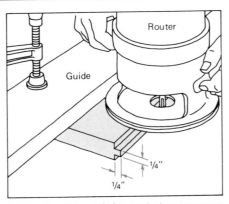

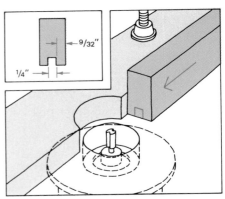

Top and leaves: 1. Rip plywood lengthwise on table saw, making first cut 33⅜ in. wide; then turn piece around and rip other edge to get a final width of 33 in. (This gives a clean cut on both edges.) Place cloths on sawhorses to protect plywood, then rest plywood on sawhorses with better side down. Using a circular saw with a straightedge as a guide, cut the top (A) and leaves (B) to length.

2. Practice this and the next step on scrap wood before cutting tongues and grooves in top, leaves, and edge strips. Using a router and any straight bit larger than ¼ in., clamp a guide and adjust depth of cut to make a cut ¼ in. x ¼ in. in plywood edges. If plywood measures less than ¾ in. thick, reduce the depth of the cut on the underside to leave a tongue exactly ¼ in. thick.

3. Rip ¹³⁄₁₆-in. zebrawood 1½ in. wide. Cross-cut pieces 2 in. longer than final lengths for edge strips (C, D, and E) for top and leaves (see *Index*, p.379) and use a ¼-in. straight bit to cut a groove in one long edge of each strip. Set the bit so that it leaves ⁹⁄₃₂ in. above and below the groove. (The extra ¹⁄₃₂ in. will be planed off later.) Mark all pieces as to their orientation.

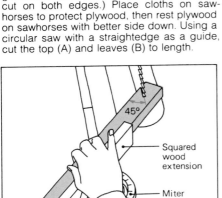

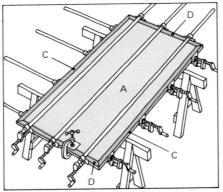

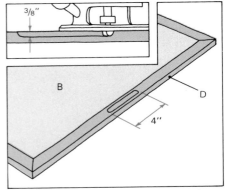

4. Extend the table saw miter gauge by screwing a squared piece of wood onto it. Mark a 45° angle on one end of an end edge strip (D); saw in two passes, the first ¹⁄₁₆ in. outside the line and the second on the line. Place edge strip on top (A) and mark 45° angle at other end; saw as before. Repeat for other end edge strip, side edge strips (C), and edge strips (D and E) on leaves (B).

5. To glue each end edge strip to top, run a thin bead of glue on both sides of tongues and on shoulders of grooves. Clamp with three 6-ft. clamps. Then immediately glue and clamp side edge strips. (If plywood is higher than edge strip at any point, press plywood down with a C-clamp and scrap wood; be careful not to break plywood.) Wipe off excess glue with damp cloths. Repeat for each leaf.

6. When glue has dried, plane upper surfaces of edge strips level with plywood; put masking tape on plywood to avoid nicking veneer. Use a router and ¾-in. core-box bit set ⅜ in. deep to make a 4-in.-long finger groove (for pulling out leaves) on underside of each leaf. Plunge router at beginning of cut; at end turn motor off, wait until bit stops, and lift out. Sand edge strips with Nos. 80 and 150 paper.

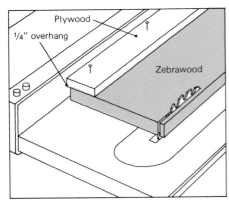

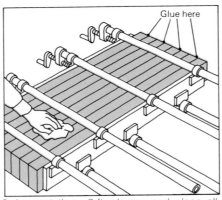

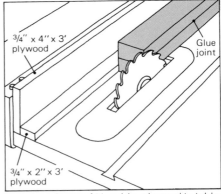

Cutting legs: 7. Joint one edge of 1⅜-in. zebrawood stock. Make a straightedge by ripping a strip of ¾-in. plywood about 3 in. wide. Nail it to one edge of stock so it overhangs ¼ in. Trim ¼–½ in. from other edge. Then with the edge you just cut riding the fence, rip enough boards to 2¹³⁄₁₆ in. wide for eight lengths of 31 in. Each leg (F) is made of two well-matched pieces glued together.

8. Lay out three 3-ft. clamps and place all eight leg pieces across clamps, inner surfaces up. Spread glue on these surfaces. Turn pieces on edge and press two glued surfaces together, making sure all ends and edges are flush. Tighten clamps, and add four more clamps across top. Wipe excess glue from all surfaces. Loosen, remove, and retighten clamps one at a time to wipe beneath them.

9. Screw a fence of ¾- x 4-in. plywood to table saw fence. Screw a second piece of plywood ¾ in. x 2 in. x 3 ft. to this fence as shown. Set saw blade 2¾ in. high, and set fence so that blade will shave ¹⁄₃₂ in. from one surface of each leg where the glue joint shows. Saw all four legs; remove small piece of plywood, set saw for a 2¾-in. cut, and saw opposite surface of each leg flush.

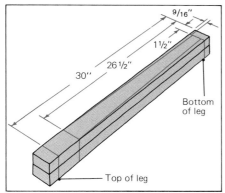

Shaping legs: 10. Use combination square to draw lines around each leg at 1½ in., 26½ in., and 30 in. from bottom. The span between 1½ in. and 30 in. is the final length of the legs—28½ in. Mark corners of each leg for taper by measuring in 9/16 in. from each edge along first line from bottom. Use a straightedge to draw lines from these points to outer edge of each leg at 26½-in. line.

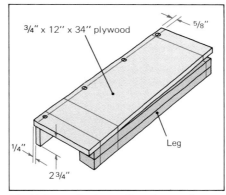

11. Make a jig for cutting tapers from a squared piece of plywood ¾ x 12 x 34 in. Transfer the lines from one of the legs to the plywood and mark them across plywood. Draw a line ⅝ in. from one edge of plywood. Cut another piece of plywood ¾ x 2¾ x 34 in. Set small piece perpendicular to large piece ¼ in. from edge and below ⅝-in. line. Insert four 1½-in. No. 8 screws along that line.

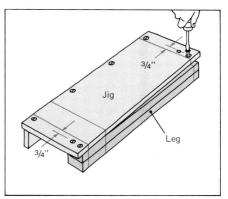

12. Drill four holes with a 3/16-in. bit in the large piece of plywood ¾ in. outside the lines indicating the top and bottom of the leg; drill two holes at each end. Align a leg's taper line, drawn in Step 10, with the edge of the jig and match the top and bottom lines of the leg with the corresponding lines on the jig. Drill into the leg through the four holes in the jig with a 3/32-in. bit; insert 1½-in. No. 8 screws.

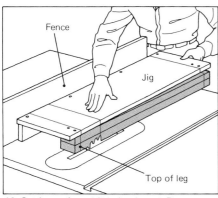

13. Set fence for a 12¹/₃₂-in. rip cut. Because of the thickness of the legs, make several passes, raising the blade about 1 in. for each pass. Reset fence for a 12-in. cut; shave off final 1/32 in. in one pass for a clean cut. Redraw lines across cut surface with combination square. Then saw opposite surface of leg by reversing it on jig; redraw lines. Save the wedges. Repeat on the other three legs.

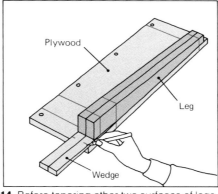

14. Before tapering other two surfaces of legs, jig must be remade to fit tapers just cut. Unscrew small plywood piece. Lay large piece of plywood on table, place a leg on it, lining up top and bottom marks. Hold down tapered portion of leg, and fit a wedge between plywood and untapered part of leg. Mark wedge where it intersects end of jig, saw at this line, and screw wedge to jig.

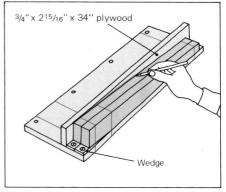

15. Mark taper on remaining surfaces. Screw a leg to large plywood piece, tapered surface up. Cut a plywood piece ¾ x 2¹⁵/₁₆ x 34 in. Hold this against leg and mark taper on it. Unscrew leg, nail large plywood piece along taper line just marked, and saw along that line with fence set at 12 in. Remove nails. Screw tapered piece to underside of large plywood piece, as before, with edge just cut down.

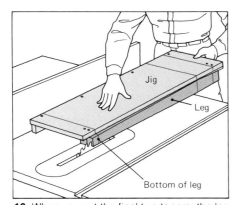

16. When you cut the final two tapers, the leg must always be oriented the same way on the jig, with the bottom of the leg being fed through the saw blade first. Saw the tapers in several passes, raising the blade for each pass, with the fence set first at 12¹/₃₂ in., then at 12 in., as you did in Step 13. Once again, be sure to redraw all the squared lines as soon as you finish cutting each surface.

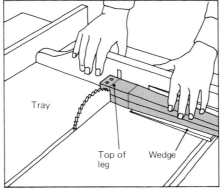

17. To saw legs to final 28½-in. lengths, you will need a crosscut tray wide enough to accommodate the length of the taper. (If you have a radial arm saw, use that instead.) Put leftover wedges beneath and behind each leg to square it with the back and base of tray. Cut off excess at tops of legs. Reverse wedges, set a stop on tray so that all four legs will be the same, and make cuts at bottoms.

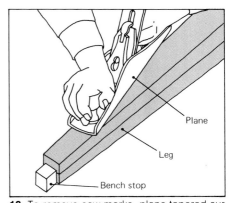

18. To remove saw marks, plane tapered surfaces very lightly with a smooth plane. Do not touch untapered parts. Decide on placement of legs (glue joints should face ends of table), and number them 1–4. Designate each joint surface as a or b; a will be joined to a side apron, b to an end apron. On a plan label aprons I–IV (see next step), and write on each joint face the part to which it will be joined.

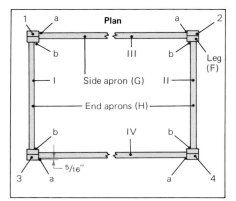

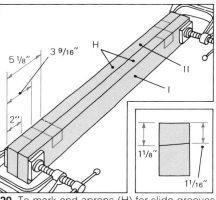

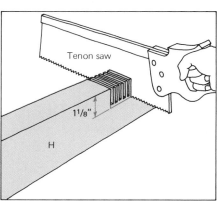

Making the aprons: 19. Joint 1½-in. stock, using method shown in Step 7. Rip and cross-cut aprons (G and H) slightly larger than their final widths and lengths. Then joint each piece; rip and crosscut to final widths and lengths. (Jointing twice helps ensure straightness, as wood changes shape when fibers are released by sawing.) Mark end aprons I and II, side aprons III and IV.

20. To mark end aprons (H) for slide grooves, clamp them inner face to inner face with ends flush. Using combination square, draw lines across top at 2 in., 3⁹⁄₁₆ in., and 5⅛ in. from each end. Unclamp. Draw lines across both faces of end apron I at 3⁹⁄₁₆ and 5⅛ in.; draw lines across faces of end apron II at 2 in. and 3⁹⁄₁₆ in. Mark depth of grooves: 1¹⁄₁₆ in. on the outer faces and 1⅛ in. on the inner faces.

21. Set crosscut blade on the table saw to height of 1¹⁄₁₆ in. and make parallel cuts in the grooves, keeping the blade inside the lines drawn (or use dado head in table saw). Use a tenon saw to angle the cuts to the 1⅛-in. depth on inner face. Use a 1½-in. chisel and a wooden mallet to chop out the remaining waste. Clean the bottom of the cut with the chisel held beveled side up.

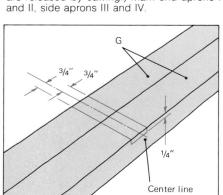

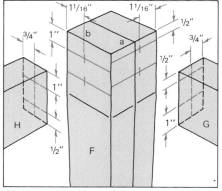

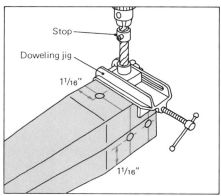

22. Clamp side aprons (G) side by side, and mark a center line across width of their inner faces (those that will face center of table). Draw lines ¾ in. to each side of center line for grooves. Unclamp pieces; mark grooves for ¼-in. depth. Cut these 1½-in.-wide grooves with a dado head in the table saw, or use a router with any straight bit. Plane outer surfaces of all aprons to remove saw marks.

23. Lay out positions of dowel joints on apron ends. For joint a on side aprons (G), measure ½ in. from top and 1 in. from bottom. Using a combination square, draw lines across ends of aprons. For joint b on end aprons (H), draw lines 1 in. from top and ½ in. from bottom. Clamp each leg in vise and hold matching apron at right angles to it. Transfer lines to leg, using sharp pencil. Draw lines across legs.

24. Set commercial doweling jig so that dowel holes will be ¾ in. from outer faces of aprons. Use a ½-in. twist bit, and set a drill stop at 2 in. plus the thickness of your doweling jig. Align the doweling jig with marks made on apron ends. Drill holes, pushing down on drill and withdrawing it several times to get rid of waste. Set jig to drill holes in legs 1¹⁄₁₆ in. from corners of legs.

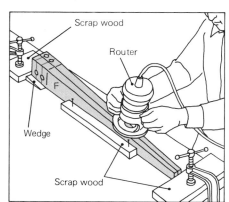

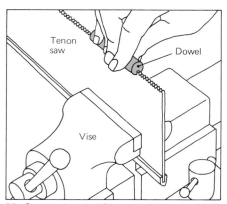

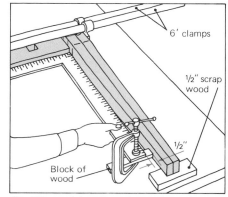

25. Round corners of legs with a router and a ¼-in. piloted rounding-over bit. To hold a leg while doing this, wedge it between bench stops or scrap wood clamped to work surface. Nail or clamp another piece of scrap behind leg to prevent its moving away from router. Start router at small end of leg and move it to the other end. Turn leg to do other three corners. Repeat on other legs.

26. Cut 16 dowels (O), each 3¾ in. long. Fit them in joints; if any dowels are too tight, sand them. Make a glue channel in each dowel by clamping a tenon saw in a vise, teeth up, and rubbing the dowels on the saw teeth. Test-fit legs and aprons. To check squareness of legs during assembly, clamp a small block of wood so it protrudes ½ in. from outer edge of long arm of framing square (see next step).

27. When gluing legs to each end apron, apply glue around edges of holes, on ends of dowels, and on joint surfaces. Rest bottoms of legs on ½-in.-thick scrap wood. Clamp across top and face of apron with 6-ft. clamps. Check squareness of legs to apron. Measure from work surface to each leg bottom; distance should be ⁹⁄₁₆ in. Wipe off glue; if it leaks into empty dowel holes, redrill them when dry.

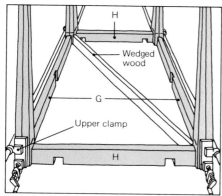

28. Glue side aprons to end assemblies, placing two 6-ft. clamps on each side. Check squareness. Adjust legs by manipulating clamps: tighten upper clamp to bring legs closer; tighten lower one to spread legs. Measure corner to corner; if measurements are unequal, cut a piece of wood the length of shorter measurement plus half the difference between the two. Wedge it diagonally.

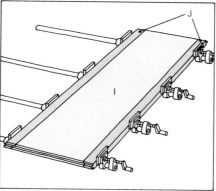

Understructure: 29. Glue plastic laminate to underside of bearer rail (I). Cut grooves in edge strips (J and K) as you did in Step 3. Cut tongues on long edges of bearer rail, and glue on end edge strips (J). Then cut tongues on short edges of bearer rail and across ends of edge strips just attached (corners are not mitered). Glue on side edge strips (K). Plane edge strips flush with plywood and laminate.

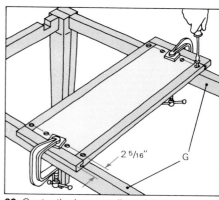

30. Center the bearer rail on side aprons; and make sure it overhangs them exactly the same distance on each side. Clamp the bearer rail in place. Draw a line 2⁵⁄₁₆ in. from each short edge of bearer rail. Drill and countersink pilot holes for four 2-in. No. 12 screws along the line on each side—two through the edge strips and two through the plywood. Insert the screws.

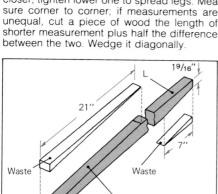

31. Mark slides (L) for taper cuts as shown. With same type of jig used for the leg tapers (Steps 11 and 12), cut the long taper on one slide; use this as a template to mark other slides. Saw those tapers, then repeat procedure for short tapers. Long tapered surfaces will be attached to undersides of leaves and will be horizontal; mark and saw adjacent ends at right angles to these surfaces.

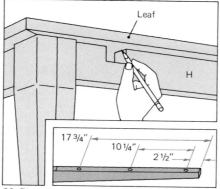

32. Place leaves in their closed position on top of aprons; mark the locations of the notches in the end aprons on undersides of leaves. Remove leaves and use a framing square to extend the lines across undersides of leaves. Mark undersides of slides at 2½, 10¼, and 17¾ in. from ends of long tapers. Drill and countersink pilot holes for No. 12 screws at these points. Screws are inserted in next step.

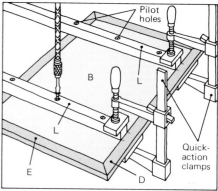

33. Center each slide between lines on undersides of leaves, aligning narrow ends with inner edges of edge strips. Clamp in place. At several points check that distance between them measures the same. Make starter holes in leaves with awl through pilot holes. Starting at narrow ends, use a spiral ratchet screwdriver to drive 1¾ in., 2 in., and 2¼ in. screws, in that order, in each slide.

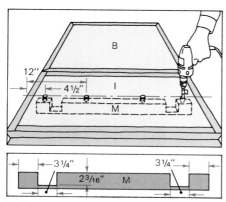

34. Cut center support (M) to fit into dadoes in side aprons. Cut notches for slides in its top 3¼ in. from ends, 3¼ in. wide, and 2³⁄₁₆ in. deep. Glue center support to side aprons. Using combination square, mark its position on top of bearer rail. When glue is dry, drill and countersink ⁷⁄₃₂-in. pilot holes in bearer rail and center support at 4½ and 12 in. from each edge of rail. Insert 2-in. No. 10 screws.

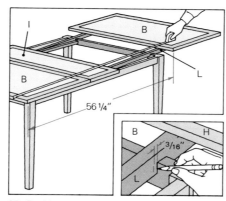

35. Position one leaf so that its inner edge is 56¼ in. from outer edge of other leaf. Mark inner faces of slides where they intersect notches in end aprons. Make a second set of marks ³⁄₁₆ in. farther in from the first set. Drill ³⁄₈-in. holes 1 in. deep in the centers of the slides at these second marks. Insert but do not glue slide-stop dowels (N). Repeat on outer faces of slides for other leaf.

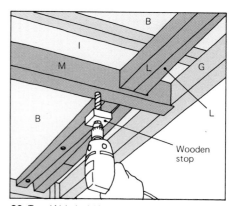

36. Top (A) is held in place by dowels (P). Drill holes for them 11 in. from one edge of bearer rail and 13 in. from other into and through center support. With leaves closed, clamp top in position, making sure all edges are flush. Put a wooden stop (see *Index*, p.379) on drill bit at 4 in. Drill up through dowel holes into underside of top. Taper dowels to fit holes, sand them, and glue into top only.

FOYER BENCH

Entrance foyers, hallways, and stair landings are generally tight spaces that need to be furnished cleverly with pieces that are attractive and useful. This bench meets both requirements. You can put it next to the hall telephone, toss mail or coats onto it, store out-of-season articles under its seat, or sit on it to change into and out of foul-weather gear.

The bench, made almost entirely of knotty pine, is finished with stain and tung oil. You can gain access to its storage chest by removing the slip-on armrests and lifting up the hinged seat. Directions for building the bench follow. To find more complete instructions for cutting dadoes, mortising hinges, and finishing furniture, see the *Index,* p.379.

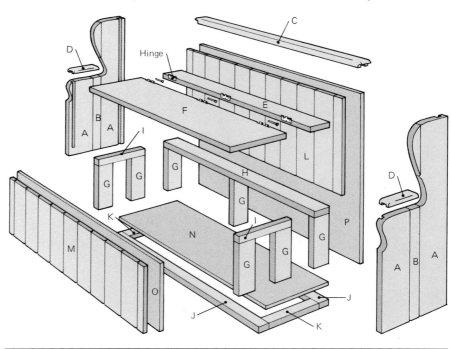

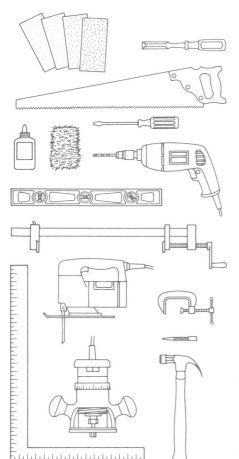

Parts list

Part	Name	Quantity	Thickness	Width	Length	Material
A	Wide end piece	4	1⅛"	7½"	36½"	5/4 x 8 pine
B	Narrow end piece	2	1⅛"	2½"	36½"	5/4 x 8 pine
C	Back rail	1	1⅛"	1¾"	50"	5/4 x 8 pine
D	Slip-on armrest	2	1⅛"	2"	10½" ✱	5/4 x 8 pine
E	Back seat section	1	1⅛"	5" ✱	47¾"	5/4 × 8 pine
F	Front seat section	1	1⅛"	11¼" ✱	47¾" ✱	5/4 x 12 pine
G	Seat-support leg	7	1½"	3½"	10⅛"	2 x 4 lumber
H	Long seat support	1	1½"	3½"	47¾" ✱	2 x 4 lumber
I	Short seat support	2	1½"	1½"	12" ✱	2 x 2 lumber
J	Long cleat	2	1½"	2½"	47¾" ✱	2 x 3 pine
K	Short cleat	2	1½"	2½"	11" ✱	2 x 3 pine
L	Backrest slat	10	¾"	5"	20¼" ✱	Tongue-and-groove pine
M	Underseat slat	10	¾"	5"	12⅜" ✱	Tongue-and-groove pine
N	Floor	1	¾"	16" ✱	47¾" ✱	Plywood
O	Underseat	1	¾"	12⅜"	49¼"	Plywood
P	Backrest	1	¾"	36½"	49¼"	Plywood

✱ Measurement is approximate; cut to fit during construction.

Tools and materials: Crosscut saw, ripsaw, saber saw. Router with ¾" straight bit, small bead bit, and 45° chamfering bit. Drill, wood chisel, screwdriver. Framing square, level, pencil. Hammer, nail set. Four 6' bar or pipe clamps or two 12' band clamps, four 4" C-clamps. Nos. 80, 100, and 150 sandpaper, 000 steel wool. Wood putty, carpenter's glue. Wood stain, tung oil, soft cloth. Wood (see above). Three 3" hinges, 6d and 8d finishing nails.

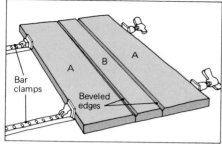

1. Cut end pieces (A and B) to size and use a router with a chamfering bit to bevel both long top edges of each narrow end piece (B) and one long edge on each wide piece (A). Glue beveled edges together for each bench end. Clamp and weight down.

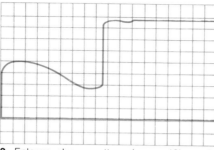

2. Enlarge above pattern (see p.48); each square on grid equals 2 in. When glue dries on bench ends, trace outline of enlarged pattern on one end and cut along outline with saber saw. Trace outline of cut bench end on other end and cut just inside traced line.

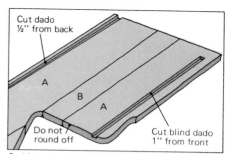

3. Use router with bead bit to round off all edges except arms and bottoms. Cut a ¾- x ¾-in. dado along inner face of each bench end from top to bottom ½ in. from its back. Cut a blind dado on each bench end from its top to 1½ in. from its bottom and 1 in. from its front.

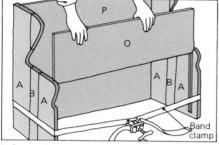

4. Cut underseat (O) and backrest (P) to size. Chisel dadoes in bench ends smooth and fill with glue. Slide underseat and backrest into dadoes. Clamp assembly together and check for squareness. Drive 6d nails through bench ends into plywood. Set nails. Let glue dry.

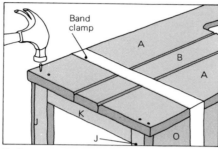

5. Check measurements, then cut cleats (J and K) and floor (N) to size. Glue cleats into place flush with bottom of assembly; reinforce with 6d nails. Set nails. When glue is dry, position floor inside assembly and fasten it to cleats with 6d nails. Set nails.

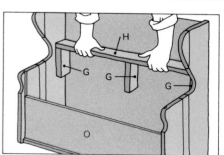

6. Cut long seat support (H) and three support legs (G) to form an E frame that will fit face down along back of inside of assembly and rise to same height as top of underseat (O). Nail E frame together with 8d nails, glue it into place, and reinforce it with 6d nails.

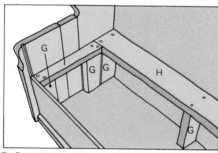

7. Cut short seat supports (I) and remaining support legs to form two inverted U frames the same height as E frame—these must fit against bench ends between E frame and underseat. Assemble U frames and glue and nail them into place. Set all nails.

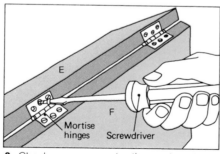

8. Check measurements, then cut seat sections (E and F) to size. Connect the two sections with hinges, mortising (sinking) the hinges into the wood. Position hinged seat over E and U frames and fasten back of seat to top of E frame with 6d nails. Set nails.

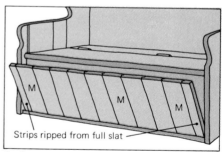

9. Cut underseat slats (M) to length and fit nine of them together. To make assembled slats fit across plywood underseat, fill in with strips ripped from 10th slat. Apply glue to backs of slats and filler strips and press assembly into place against underseat.

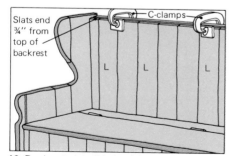

10. Backrest slats (L) should reach from top of seat to ¾ in. below the top of the plywood backrest. Cut slats to length, fit them together with filler strips, and glue them into place. Hold both slat assemblies in place with C-clamps until the glue dries.

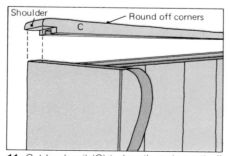

11. Cut back rail (C) to length and round off upper corners with router and bead bit. Cut dado (¾ in. x ¾ in.) along center of rail's underside and cut 1⅛-in. shoulders into its ends. Attach rail to top of backrest and backs of bench ends with glue and 6d nails.

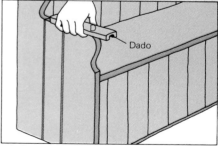

12. Set nails and fill all nail holes in bench with putty. Cut armrests (D) to length, round off edges, and cut dadoes 1⅛ in. wide and ½ in. deep into bottoms. Put armrests in position. Sand and stain entire bench, then rub it with tung oil for a rustic finish.

VINYL-COVERED COUCH

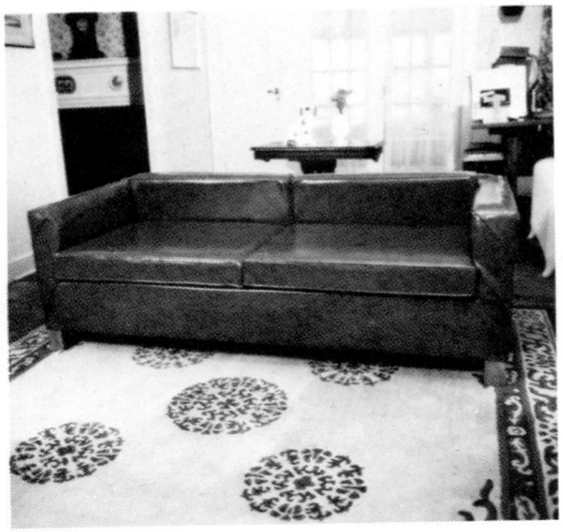

Making upholstered furniture used to be beyond the skills of home craftsmen. Today, with the availability of plywood, foam padding, and vinyl fabric, projects such as this vinyl-covered couch are within the reach of most woodworkers. Polyurethane foam, which is more durable than foam rubber, can be purchased from specialty suppliers, and the vinyl fabric (sheet vinyl reinforced with fabric) can be ordered through upholstery shops and other suppliers. Consult the Yellow Pages under "Foam and sponge rubber" and under "Plastics—fabrics" for places that sell these materials.

Variation: Our couch has two seat cushions and two bolsters. The bolsters, placed against the couch back, are optional. If you do not want them, you must reduce all front-to-back measurements by 4 inches.

Construction: Use a rasp and sander to smooth and round all edges, corners, and slots cut in the plywood panels. To secure the joints, use plenty of liquid hide glue and flathead wood screws spaced not more than 6 inches apart. Reinforce the frame with glue strips and edge strips as

Parts list

Part	Name	Quantity	Thickness	Width	Length	Material
A	Seat panel	1	¾″	33″	70½″	Plywood
B	Back panel	1	¾″	21″	72″	Plywood
C	Arm panel	2	¾″	21″	33″	Plywood
D	Fascia panel	1	¾″	4″	70½″	Plywood
E	Glue strip	9	¾″	(See Step 5).		1″ pine stock
F	Seat support	1	1½″	3½″	70½″	2 x 4 pine
G	Seat support	1	1½″	3½″	32¼″	2 x 4 pine
H	Leg	4	3½″	3½″	8″	4 x 4 ash
I	Edge strip	1	¾″	1½″	70½″	1 x 2 pine
J	Edge strip	2	¾″	1½″	32⅝″	1 x 2 pine
K	Edge strip	2	¾″	1½″	16¼″	1 x 2 pine
L	Seat pad	1	4″	34″	71½″	Polyurethane foam padding 1.25 lb./cu. ft. density
M	Back pad	2	4″	13¼″	36¼″	
N	Arm pad	2	4″	13¼″	30″	
O	Bolster pad (optional)	2	4″	13¼″*	32¼″*	
P	Seat cushion pad	2	4″	26″*	32¼″*	Polyurethane foam padding 1.8 lb./cu. ft. density
Q	Welting	1	—	—	6 yd.	Vinyl-covered cording
R	Seat cover	1	—	54″	80″	Vinyl fabric
S	Inside back cover	2	—	28″	51″	Vinyl fabric
T	Inside arm cover	2	—	27″	43″	Vinyl fabric
U	Outside back cover	1	—	25″	74″	Vinyl fabric
V	Outside arm cover	2	—	25″	36″	Vinyl fabric
W	Seat cushion cover	2	—	54″* †	72″* †	Vinyl fabric
X	Bolster cover (optional)	2	—	54″* †	72″* †	Vinyl fabric

*Measurement is approximate; cut to fit during construction (see Step 24).
† Amount of fabric needed to make two covers.

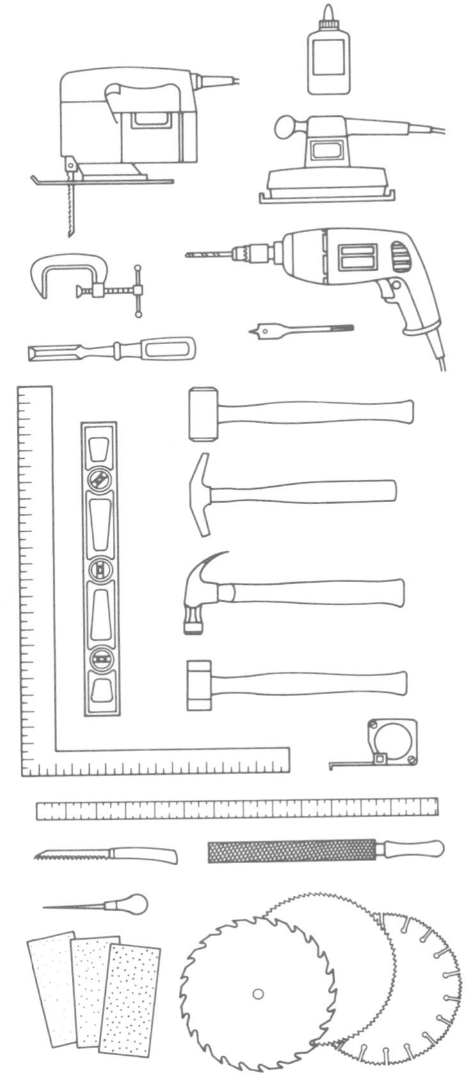

Tools and materials: Table saw or hand, circular, or radial arm saw. Dado head for power saw or handsaw, chisel, and mallet. Heavy-duty reciprocating saw or saber saw. Variable-speed electric drill with No. 8 Screwmate bit, screwdriver bit, and 1″ spade bit. Orbital sander or sanding block. Nos. 80 and 220 sandpaper. Electric carving knife or razor-sharp bread knife. Level, yardstick, steel tape rule, framing square, felt-tipped marker, pencil. Wood rasp, awl. Several 3″ and 5″ C-clamps. Claw hammer, tack hammer, plastic hammer. Liquid hide glue. Penetrating oil stain, polyurethane varnish, paste wax, beeswax. Polishing cloth, paintbrush. Curved upholstery needle, upholstery thread, tack puller, scissors. Two 4′ x 8′ sheets of ¾″ plywood, 3 running ft. of 4 x 4 ash (or maple or oak), 15 running ft. of 1 x 2 No. 2 pine, 10 running ft. of 2 × 4 No. 2 pine, 1″ pine stock for glue strips (see Step 5). Polyurethane foam padding (see above), 16 yd. of thick vinyl reinforced with fabric 54″ wide, 2 yd. cotton batting, 6 yd. vinyl welting, 2 yd. muslin. Heavy cardboard. Four 1 1/16″ furniture glides. Two boxes No. 4 carpet tacks, 50 decorative upholstery tacks. Twelve 1″ and one hundred 2″ No. 8 flathead wood screws. 6d common nails.

indicated on the following pages.

Upholstery: Have the foam pads cut to size by a dealer if possible; they can be trimmed at home if necessary. Use cotton batting along the edges of the seat, back, and arms to soften and round out these areas. Upholstery vinyl is thick and tough, so hand sewing—except the finishing stitches on page 93—is virtually impossible. However, if you have a heavy-duty sewing machine, you may want to make the seat cushions yourself (see instructions on page 99). Otherwise, have an upholsterer make the cushions, welting, and bolsters (if you want them).

A total of 16 yards of vinyl fabric 54 inches wide is needed. Add two more yards if you want the optional bolsters. You can save a yard by piecing together the outside back cover if the back of the couch will not be seen. (The sewing should be done by the upholsterer.)

Vinyl is easier to work with than leather or cloth fabrics, as it can be stretched at least 5% in any direction; this facilitates making neat folds and smooth corners. Cut each piece of the cover to its rough size first; then during the actual fitting make the smaller, more detailed cuts and trim (see p.90). When making these detailed cuts, go slowly and carefully; otherwise, you could ruin a piece of fabric with one slip of the scissors. To avoid errors, experiment with a paper pattern first. Aside from this basic approach, there is no exact rule in upholstering. Every professional has his own method.

Use carpet tacks in places where they will not be visible; it is safer to use too many tacks than too few, except where noted. Use decorative upholstery tacks along the outside edges of the arms.

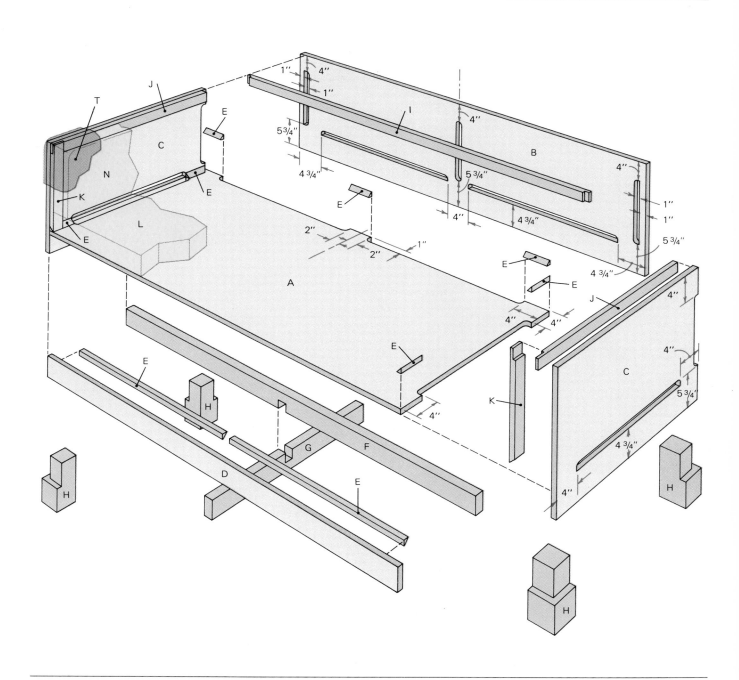

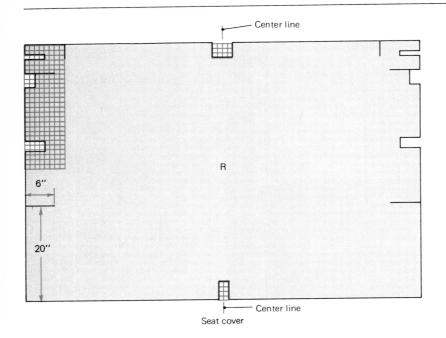

Center line

6″

20″

R

Center line

Seat cover

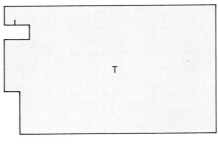

74″

U

Center line

Outside back cover

The eight patterns shown on this page represent the eight pieces of vinyl fabric needed to upholster this couch. They are keyed to the letters in the chart on page 88. The seat cover (R) is the largest and most intricate piece. Extreme caution is advised in cutting and fitting it, as a single error may ruin the entire piece. The outside back cover (U) may be one piece or three sewn together. The inside back covers (S), inside arm covers (T), and outside arm covers (V) are paired. The opposite pieces of each pair (the mirror images) share the same letter. In upholstering these parts, make sure you are using the right-hand piece for the right side and the left-hand piece for the left side. Label all parts as you cut them. All views shown here are from the fabric (back) side of the vinyl.

Because the vinyl fabric will stretch, rough-cut the fabric pieces slightly oversize wherever possible. (The excess can be trimmed later.) Most of the slits, slots, and tabs are devised so that the vinyl can be pulled through slots in the wooden frame or can be fitted to the frame's edges, corners, or hidden supports. For this reason, do not cut the slits, slots, and tabs in advance, but cut them on the spot during the actual fitting. Your final cuts may deviate somewhat from the dimensions given in these patterns.

Note: Color grids are 1″ squares.

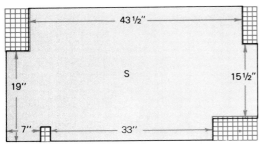

43½″

19″

S

15½″

7″   33″

Inside back cover (left)

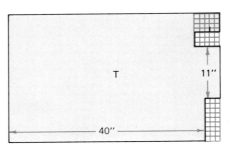

T

11″

40″

Inside arm cover (left)

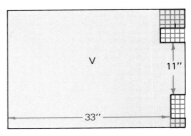

V

11″

33″

Outside arm cover (left)

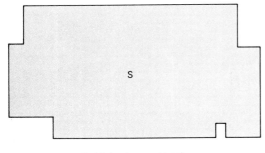

S

Inside back cover (right)

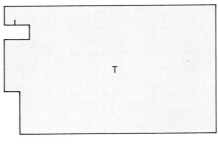

T

Inside arm cover (right)

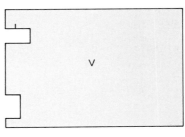

V

Outside arm cover (right)

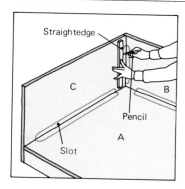

1. Set up and level a low worktable or set up and level a sheet of plywood on supports. Cut panels A, B, C, and D to the dimensions given in the chart from two sheets of ¾-in. plywood. Use a rasp and then No. 80 sandpaper to smooth all edges and to round all corners slightly. Assemble the panel pieces on the worktable and tack them together temporarily with a few 6d nails. Mark the 1-in. slots. (For their locations, see p.89.)

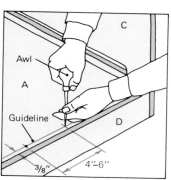

2. Take apart the panel assembly. Cut the 1-in. slots with a reciprocating saw or saber saw. Start slots that are not located on the panel edges by first drilling an entry hole with an electric drill and a 1-in. spade bit, then insert the saw blade. Rasp and sand all the slot edges so that the vinyl fabric will not get snagged when it is pulled through these slots.

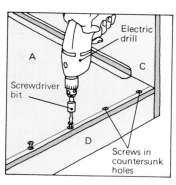

3. Tack the panels together temporarily as before. Pencil a guideline ⅜ in. from the front edge of the seat panel (A). The line should be exactly above the center line of the top edge of the fascia panel (D). Mark starting holes 4–6 in. apart with an awl along the guideline. Use an electric drill with a No. 8 Screwmate bit to drill pilot holes into the awl marks for inserting the screws in the next step.

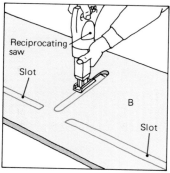

4. Untack the seat panel and lift it from the assembly. Use a brush to apply liquid hide glue under the front edge of the seat panel and on the top edge of the fascia panel. Reassemble the parts and insert 2-in. screws, lubricated with beeswax, into the pilot holes. Tighten with a screwdriver or a variable-speed drill with a screwdriver bit. Repeat the gluing and screwing process along all other joints where panels meet.

5. Let assembly cure overnight. Make glue strips (E) by cutting 1-in. pine stock with a table saw tilted at 45°. (Other types of saws may be used if they can cut at a 45° angle.) The strips will each have a triangular cross section with one 90° and two 45° corners. You will need two strips, each about 3 ft. long, plus seven strips about 4 in. long to reinforce the seat joints.

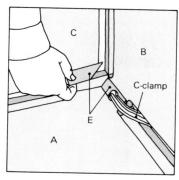

6. Install short glue strips with liquid hide glue above seat joints where parts A and B and parts A and C meet. Along the joint where parts A and D meet install the long glue strips on the underside only. Where two strips meet at a corner, miter the end of one at 45° for a close fit. Secure with C-clamps to cure overnight.

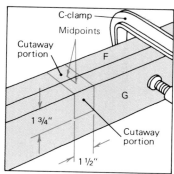

7. Cut the 2 x 4 seat supports (F and G) 70½ in. and 32¼ in. long and mark their midpoints. Clamp them together with midpoints aligned and lay out half-lap joints 1½ in. wide and 1¾ in. deep at the center of each piece. Cut both joints at once, using a dado head on a power saw or a handsaw and chisel (see *Index*, p.379).

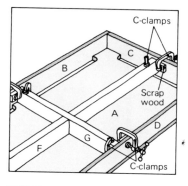

8. Turn the couch upside down. Install the long seat support (F) first with its notch facing upward. Use liquid glue and 2-in. screws to secure it to panels C. Then install the shorter support (G) by securing it to panels B and D. To prevent the supports from sliding on the wet glue, clamp scrap wood against the supports to keep them in line.

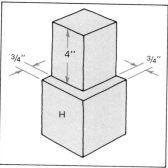

9. Rabbet adjoining faces of each leg (H) 4 in. long and ¾ in. deep as shown. Position legs at corners. If necessary, trim legs or panels so top of each leg supports the seat panel and the lips of the legs support the underside of the fascia (or back panel) and the arm panels. While legs are in position, use a straight 2 x 4 and level to make sure legs are even with each other. Trim them if they are not.

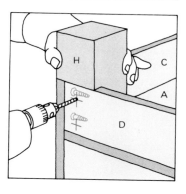

10. Using No. 220 paper, sand and stain the legs. Hold each leg in place. Drill two pilot holes through each panel into each side of a leg. Stagger the holes so the screws do not collide. Secure with 2-in. screws. Brush two coats of polyurethane varnish on legs, sanding gently between the coats. Then apply paste wax. Make a small starting hole on the center of each leg bottom and drive in a large furniture glide, using a plastic hammer.

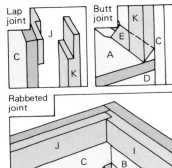

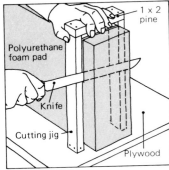

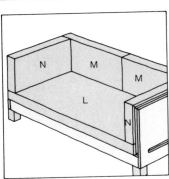

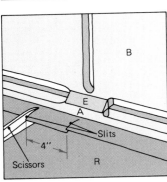

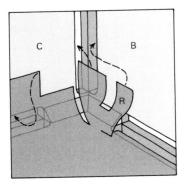

11. Install edge strips (I, J, and K) along the inner edges of back and arm panels (B and C). Use rabbeted joints at back corners, lap joints at upper front arm corners, and modified butt joints to fit the glue strips at the lower front arm corners. Apply glue and C-clamps. Drill pilot holes every 6 in. along edge strips. Insert one 1-in. screw from the inside into each corner lap joint, but insert all other screws from the outside.

12. Buy polyurethane foam padding cut to size if possible. If trimming is necessary, make a simple jig of 1 x 2 pine stock and a piece of plywood as shown. Slice the foam pad with an electric carving knife or a razor-sharp bread knife, guided by the jig to ensure a straight cut.

13. Put foam pads (L, M, and N) in place on the finished wood frame for a test fit. All dimensions for pads given in chart are 1 in. oversize in both length and width. (If the pads were cut exactly to size, the upholstery covering would wrinkle because foam pads are springy and can be easily compressed.) Label the pads and put them aside.

14. Lay the rough-cut vinyl seat cover (R) on the seat panel (A), vinyl side up, so that its rear edge is next to the back panel (B). Mark off two lines about 3 in. long and 4 in. apart as shown. Cut away the area between them. The slot should straddle the center of the back panel. Put the seat pad (L) back in place, and put the seat cover on top of it for a close fit.

15. Cut the left rear corner of seat cover (R) according to the pattern on page 90. Before cutting the right rear corner, check the fit and then proceed. Trim and correct the cuts if necessary.

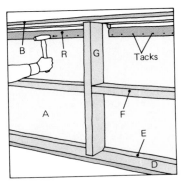

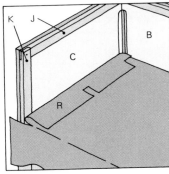

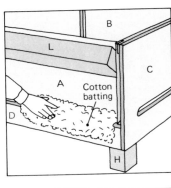

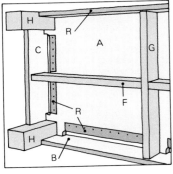

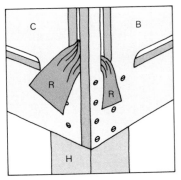

16. Take off the seat pad (L) and turn the couch onto its front edge. Insert the two segments of the rear edge of the seat cover (R) through the two horizontal slots in the back panel (B). Pull the edge of the seat cover in position and tack it permanently under the seat panel (A) with carpet tacks. Begin from the center and work toward the sides, spacing the tacks 1½–2 in. apart.

17. Put the couch back on its feet and the seat pad (L) back in place under the seat cover (R). Pull the cover taut and tack its front edge temporarily under the fascia (D) for a test fit. Cut a slot at the center of the front edge of the cover to fit seat support (G). Trim if necessary. Cut slots into the side edges similarly so that they fit around the seat support (F) when pulled through the slots of the arm panels (C).

18. Undo the temporary tacking along front edge of the seat cover (R). Lift the front part of the seat pad (L) and cover the front edge of the seat where panels A and D meet with cotton batting that is about 6 in. wide. The batting will help soften the hard edge of the couch front, creating a comfortable knee support.

19. Turn the couch on its back. Smooth and stretch the seat cover (R) from the already tacked back to the front, making the cover taut but not tight. Tack the front edge to the back of the fascia panel (D) permanently, working from the center to the sides. Pull the side edges through the slots in the arm panels (C) and tack them permanently under the seat panel (A).

20. Put the couch right side up. Insert the two tabs (see Step 15 and p.90) in the right rear corner of the seat cover (R) into the two vertical slots in the arm and back panels (C and B) as shown. Pull the tabs down, smooth the seat corner, and tack the tabs to the panels. Tack the left rear corner in the same way.

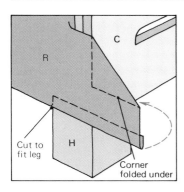

21. Turn under the loose front corners of the seat cover at the slits to make diagonal folds and at the bottom to make level folds as shown. Tack the folded corners to the outside face and under the edge of the arm panels (C) and under the edge of the fascia panel (D). This completes the upholstering of the seat panel.

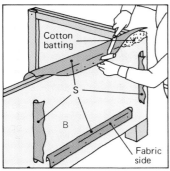

22. Position a back pad (M)—with cotton batting on its top and down its left edge—on the left side of back panel (B). Drape an inside back cover (S) in place and pull its bottom edge through slot in panel. Tack it so the fabric side is exposed as shown. Pull cover taut and tack the top edge, with the vinyl side exposed, to the back panel. Pull side edges through vertical slots and tack them. Upholster other back pad in same way.

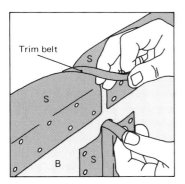

23. To cover possible exposure of wood, foam padding, or batting between the back pads, make a trim belt by folding a 3-in.-wide vinyl strip twice to make a 1-in.-wide belt. Insert one end of the belt through the center back slot and the other on top of the seat back. Pull and tighten to make the belt sink into the crack between the back pads. Tack each end of the belt to the back panel with a single tack.

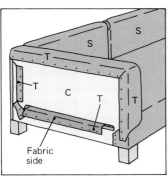

24. Position arm pads (N) and install cotton batting along their top and front edges. Drape inside arm covers (T) over pads. Pull bottom edges through horizontal slots and rear side edges through vertical slots as shown, and tack. Tack other two edges over arm edges as done with couch back. Now that inner surfaces of couch are finished, give final interior dimensions to upholsterer so he can make the seat cushions and bolsters.

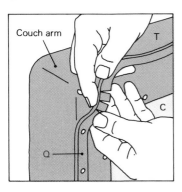

25. Tack the single length of welting (Q) all along the outside edges of the arms and back. Start from the bottom of one arm, run the welting up the arm and along its top, along the top of the back, the top of the other arm, and down the other arm. To make the welting curve easily, make three ½-in. cuts at each corner. Tack the welting only where necessary to keep it in position.

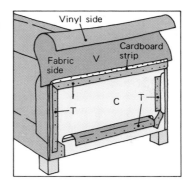

26. Begin covering the outside surfaces of the couch by tacking a 1-in.-wide strip of cardboard 36 in. long (to be used as a stiffener) through the fabric side of the top edge of an outside arm cover (V) to the outside edge of its arm panel (C). Keep the strip straight and close to the welting, using two rows of tacks. Curve the ends of the strip to round out the corners.

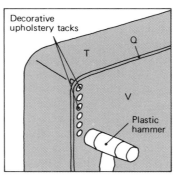

27. Drape the outside arm cover down over its cardboard strip, exposing the vinyl side. Fold the front edge under and tack it with decorative upholstery tacks, as these will be visible. Then, using carpet tacks, tack the bottom edge to the inside of the arm panel and the rear edge to the back panel. Repeat Steps 26 and 27 on other arm.

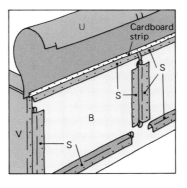

28. Tack a 1-in.-wide cardboard strip 74 in. long (which can be made from smaller pieces) through the top edge of the outside back cover (U) to the rear of the back panel (B). This should be tacked from the fabric side, as you did the outside arm covers, using two rows of carpet tacks. Make sure the top edge is straight and close to the welting.

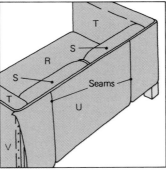

29. The outside back cover (U) may be a single piece or made of three pieces sewn together. With the latter, position the cover so that the two seams are symmetrical. Drape the cover down over the cardboard strip. Then, turning the couch on its front, gently pull the cover taut and tack its bottom edge to the inside of the back panel (B).

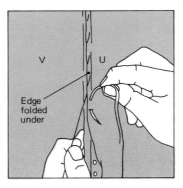

30. Put the couch right side up. Fold under the side edges of the outside back cover (U). Using a curved upholsterer's needle and heavy upholstery thread, sew the folded edges to the outside arm covers (V). Keep the stitches inside so that when the thread is pulled tight they are scarcely visible. Staple a muslin dust cover, (about 38 x 76 in.) to the entire bottom of the couch.

MODULAR COUCH

If you want living room furniture that can be adapted to a variety of arrangements, build this handsome, versatile modular couch. Actually, it is much more than a couch. It is a full living room set made up of three units—a sofa and two chairs. Each unit is faced with red oak and fitted with cushions. The units can be arranged as shown in the photograph at left or to suit your space and taste. For example, the units could be separated by an end table or two. Because of their design, the arms of the chairs can be made the backs and vice versa.

Construction: The modular units are identical except for the sofa, which differs in length only. Each unit has a plywood frame made up of a base (a box with a raised bottom), a back, and an arm. The frame is covered with oak tongue-and-groove flooring slats. The slat tops and the open edges of the arms and backs are covered with oak strips and rails.

Because the finished units are very heavy, they are put on casters. The 3-inch casters specified below are actually 3¼ inches in length. If you substitute casters of a different length, adjust the height of the base bottom accordingly by cutting the bottom dado (see p.96, Step 2) either higher or lower, depending on the size of your casters.

Complete directions for building the couch and making the cushions follow, including detailed instructions for cutting the wide dadoes in the rails with a table saw. To find directions for other ways of cutting dadoes and rabbets, see the *Index*, p.379.

Finishing: After the couch has been assembled, it must be sanded and finished. Use an orbital sander with Nos. 80, 100, and then 150 paper on all the exterior surfaces. Brush on a coat of polyurethane varnish thinned with 20% turpentine, and when it is dry, sand the pieces with No. 220 paper. Then add a final full-strength coat of polyurethane varnish. Let it dry, apply paste wax with 0000 steel wool, and buff the wax with a soft cloth.

Parts list (excluding cushions)

Part	Name	Quantity	Thickness	Width	Length	Material
A	Sofa base front	1	¾″	8½″	57¾″	Fir plywood
B	Sofa base back	1	¾″	8½″	57¾″	Fir plywood
C	Sofa base top	1	¾″	26¾″	56¾″	Fir plywood
D	Sofa base bottom	1	¾″	26¾″	56¾″	Fir plywood
E	Base side	6	¾″	8½″	26¾″	Fir plywood
F	Chair base front	2	¾″	8½″	27¾″	Fir plywood
G	Chair base back	2	¾″	8½″	27¾″	Fir plywood
H	Chair base top	2	¾″	26¾″	26¾″	Fir plywood
I	Chair base bottom	2	¾″	26¾″	26¾″	Fir plywood
J	Sofa back	1	¾″	26½″	57¾″	Fir plywood
K	Chair back	1	¾″	26½″	27¾″	Fir plywood
L	Arm	3	¾″	26½″	28½″ ✶	Fir plywood
M	Outside slat	94	¾″	2¼″	26½″	Red oak flooring
N	Inside slat	88	¾″	2¼″	18″	Red oak flooring
O	Underseat slat	88	¾″	2¼″	8½″	Red oak flooring
P	Facing strip	6	¾″	2¼″ ✶	26¼″	1 x 6 red oak board
Q	Long rail	1	¾″	2¾″	63″	1 x 6 red oak board
R	Short rail	5	¾″	2¾″	32″	1 x 6 red oak board
S	Long edging strip	1	³⁄₁₆″	1⅜″	63″	1 x 6 red oak board
T	Short edging strip	5	³⁄₁₆″	1⅜″	32″	1 x 6 red oak board

✶ Measurement is approximate; cut to fit during construction.

Tools and materials: Table saw with dado head. Electric drill with set of twist bits and countersink. Router with ⅜″ piloted rounding-over bit. Belt sander with Nos. 60 and 80 sanding belts, orbital sander. Nos. 80, 100, 150, and 220 sandpaper, 0000 steel wool. Block plane, rabbet plane, chisel. Six 3′–5′ pipe or bar clamps, two or more 6″ C-clamps. Hammer, nail set, screwdriver. Combination square, steel tape rule, pencil. White glue. Polyurethane varnish, turpentine, paste wax, soft cloth. Cushions (see p.99). Five 4′ x 8′ panels of ¾″ fir plywood, one 8′ length of 1 x 6 red oak board, six 24-sq.-ft. bundles of red oak tongue-and-groove flooring. Twelve 3″ Shepherd casters with 4 doz. ¾″ No. 2 panhead self-tapping screws. 1½″ No. 8 flathead wood screws. 3d and 4d finishing nails, 6d coated nails. 1″ brads.

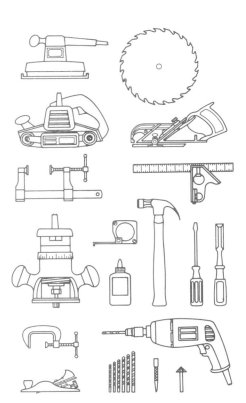

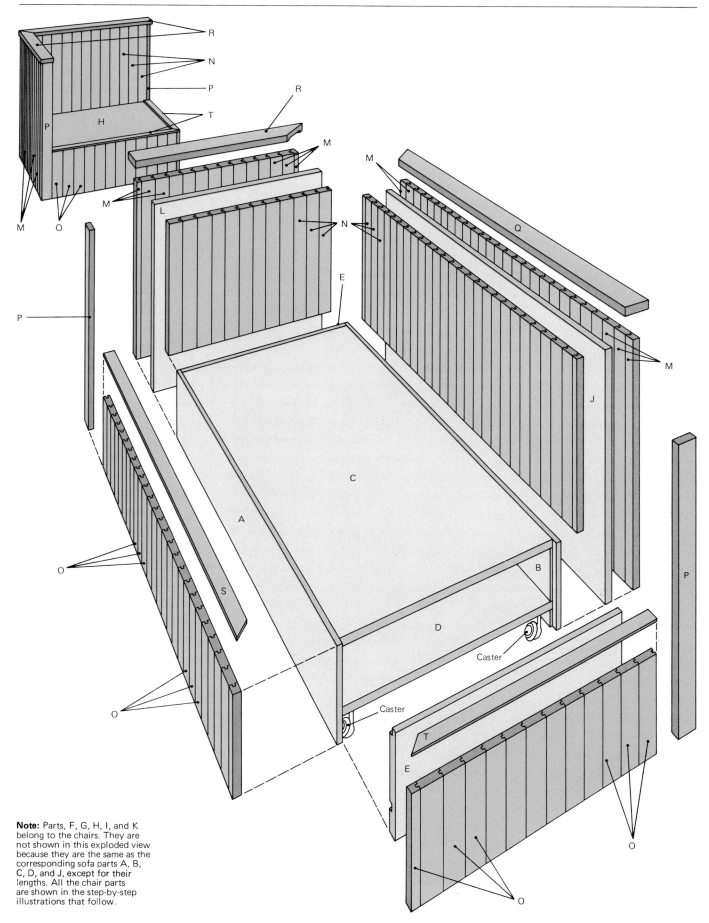

Note: Parts, F, G, H, I, and K belong to the chairs. They are not shown in this exploded view because they are the same as the corresponding sofa parts A, B, C, D, and J, except for their lengths. All the chair parts are shown in the step-by-step illustrations that follow.

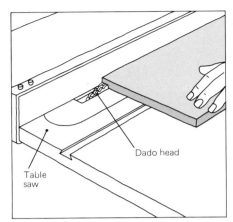

1. Cut all plywood parts of sofa and chairs except arms (L) to specifications given in chart on page 94. Cut ¼-in.-deep rabbets as wide as wood is thick along sides of sofa and chair base fronts (A and F) and backs (B and G). Cut same size rabbets into tops of sofa and chair base fronts, backs, and sides (E).

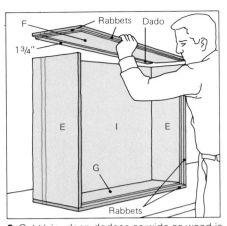

2. Cut ¼-in.-deep dadoes as wide as wood is thick 1¾ in. above bottoms of base backs, fronts, and sides. Extend lines of dadoes to outside of wood. Glue together base bottoms (D and I), fronts, backs, and sides. Drive 6d nails into corners and along lines of dadoes. Glue and nail on base tops (C and H).

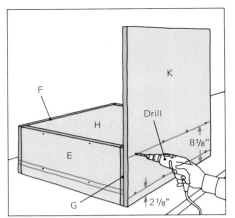

3. Apply glue to base backs (B and G) and press sofa and chair backs (J and K) into place. Secure each back with two 4d nails. Draw lines 2⅛ in. and 8⅛ in. from bottom of each back. Drill ³⁄₁₆-in. holes along each line: four holes on chair lines, six on sofa lines. Countersink holes; insert 1½-in. screws.

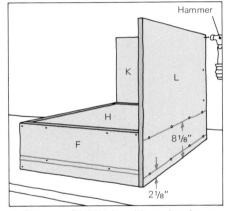

4. Cut arms (L) 26½ in. wide and as long as entire chair or sofa is deep. Draw guidelines on arms and glue and screw on arms as you did backs, using four screws along each line drawn. Nail arms and backs together where they meet above base top with 6d nails. (Do not use screws; they will not hold.)

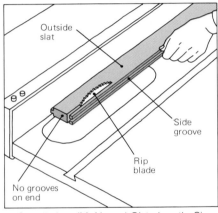

5. Cut all slats (M, N, and O) to length. Since flooring pieces vary in length, cut the long slats first to make sure you have enough of them. Pick an outside slat that has a flat end (one that has been cut at end) and use a table saw to cut the groove from its side, making a rectangle with a tongue but no groove.

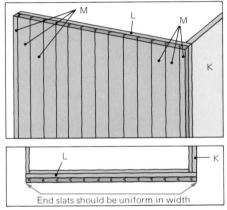

6. Test-fit outside slats (M) together on arm of one chair. If slats do not fit flush with sides of arm, you will have to cut slats at ends to uniform size. Repeat for chair back, but use slat with groove that was cut off (see Step 5) for corner back slat and allow space for it to overlap edge of corner slat on arm.

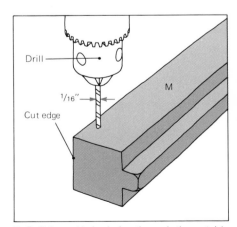

7. Drill three ¹⁄₁₆-in. holes through the outside slat that will be attached to chair arm where it meets back. (Rip slat to size first if you found it needed cutting in Step 6.) Drill the holes straight down near grooved edge of slat and through groove in slat. If groove has been cut off, drill near cut edge.

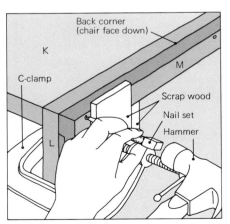

8. After drilling holes in slat, spread glue on arm where slat will go and clamp slat into place with drilled edge facing back corner. Make sure that drilled edge of slat is flush with back edge of arm and with top and bottom of arm. Nail slat into place through holes, using 3d finishing nails. Set nails.

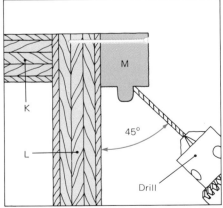

9. Drill three ¹⁄₁₆-in. holes through edge of same slat into base of tongue, as shown, holding drill at angle of about 45° to surface of slat. Drive 3d finishing nails through these holes into chair arm as far as you can with hammer. Use nail set to drive nails slightly below the surface of the wood.

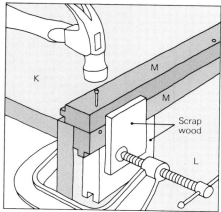

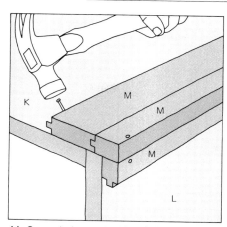

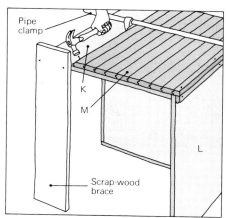

10. Drill three ¹⁄₁₆-in. holes straight down through squared-off edge of corner back slat—the one with its groove cut off (see Step 5). Glue slat into place with outer edge flush with outer edge of slat on arm. Nail back slat into place and set nails. Drill and nail slat at angle to tongue as you did in Step 9.

11. Spread glue over strip of chair back next to corner back slat and fit second slat into place over glue, slipping groove of second slat over tongue of corner one. Gently tap second slat into place with hammer. Drill three ¹⁄₁₆-in. holes through second slat at angle to tongue and nail down slat as in Step 9.

12. Add other slats to outside of chair back in same way. As you get away from corner, prop up unsupported side of chair back by nailing piece of scrap wood to it. If any slats are hard to slide in, fit a pipe or bar clamp over slats and tighten clamp against edges of slats to squeeze stubborn slats into place.

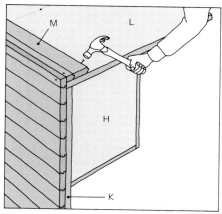

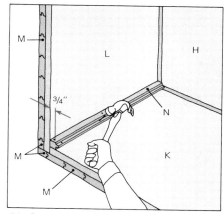

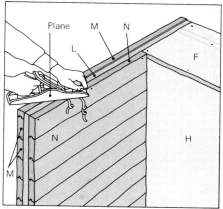

13. Use one of your straightest pieces for last outside slat on chair back and cut it to fit with a tiny bit hanging over (it will be planed flush later). Drill three ¹⁄₁₆-in. holes straight down through last slat and glue and nail it into place. Remove temporary support and clamps. Attach slats to arm as you did to back.

14. Cut a ¾-in. strip from an inside slat (N) with its tongue intact and glue it to inside of chair back where it meets arm. Glue, drill, and nail it as you did corner slat on outside of arm and add other slats as you did to outside of back (Steps 7–13). Repeat for inside of arm, but begin with a full-size slat.

15. Use block plane to smooth fronts of chair arms and open edge of chair back. Be sure to plane slightly protruding edges of outside slats even with the plywood. Cut facing strips (P) 26¼ in. long and a tiny bit wider than the thickness of the entire arm and back. (Excess will be removed when chair is sanded later.)

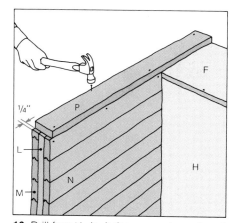

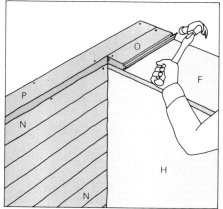

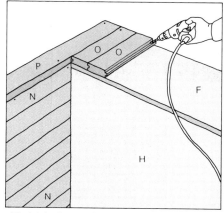

16. Drill four ¹⁄₁₆-in. holes near edges of each facing strip, spacing holes evenly but alternating sides so that there are two holes on each side of strips. Glue strips to front of arm and open edge of back, flush with bottom. Strips should fall ¼ in. short of top of chair. Drive 3d finishing nails through holes. Set nails.

17. Glue first underseat slat (O) into place with its grooved edge against facing strip on arm. Drill two ¹⁄₁₆-in. holes straight down through slat near its grooved edge. Drive in 3d finishing nails and set them. Drill two more holes through slat at an angle to its tongue, and drive in nails with hammer and nail set.

18. Add other underseat slats to front of chair as you did outside slats, but use only two nails per slat. Cut a 1⅞-in. strip from an underseat slat with its tongue intact, and glue and nail slat flush against facing strip on chair back. Add other underseat slats to chair. Add slats and facing strips to sofa and second chair.

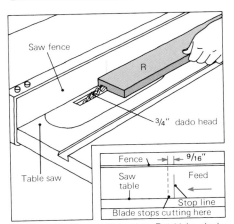

19. Cut rails (Q and R) to size. Put ¾-in. dado head on table saw and set depth of cut to ¼ in. plus 1/32 in. Set saw fence a bit less than ¼ in. from inside edge of blade. Test-cut a piece of scrap wood. Set up stop for length of cut by drawing a line on fence 9/16 in. from point nearest feeding side where blade stops cutting.

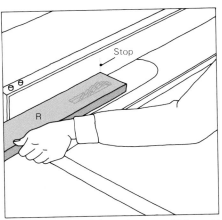

20. Push each rail through saw until its near end is even with stop. Move saw fence 1 in. from inside of blade and push rails through saw again. Finally, reset fence to 2½ in. from *outside* of blade and push rails through once again to complete dado. End of dado will be slightly rounded and must be squared off.

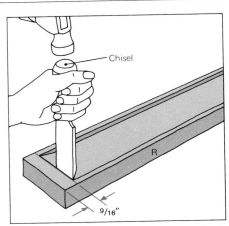

21. To square off dado, draw a line exactly 9/16 in. from solid end of each rail and clamp rail down, dado facing up. Place blade of chisel on line with beveled edge of blade facing dado, and hammer chisel down into wood. Remove chisel and cut a bit from bottom, toward line, with beveled edge of chisel up.

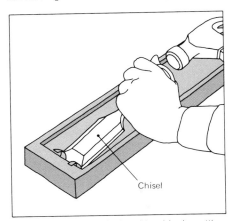

22. Go back and forth with chisel, cutting along line and from bottom, taking out a little wood at a time. Also chisel wood from sides of dado. Continue until dado is completely squared off. Test-fit rails on backs and arms of chairs and sofa. Use a rabbet plane to clean remaining ridges from dadoes.

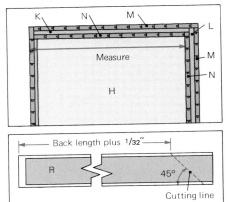

23. Use a belt sander with a No. 60 sanding belt on tops of all backs and arms. Measure chair back from inside corner to open end. Mark off this distance plus 1/32 in. on inside edge of dado in rail for chair back. Use combination square to draw 45° cutting line at this point. Cut with table saw and bevel guide.

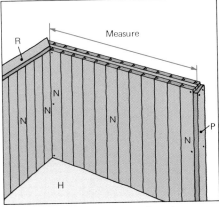

24. Slip cut rail onto chair back and measure distance from lower edge of back rail to outside edge of arm. Mark off this distance plus 1/32 in. on arm rail, then draw 45° cutting line and cut as before. Check fit. Cut rails for other chair and sofa in same way. Use a belt sander with No. 80 belt on outside of all units.

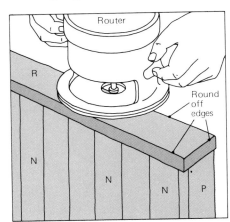

25. Glue rails into place and clamp each one down with pipe or bar clamps buffered with scrap wood. (If clamps are not available, tack rails down with 6d finishing nails, then fill nail holes later.) When glue is dry, remove clamps and use router with a ⅜-in. rounding-over bit to round off all edges of rails.

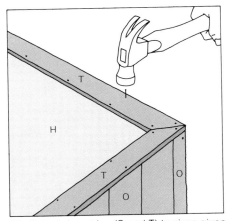

26. Cut edging strips (S and T) to sizes given in chart on page 94. Measure edges of chair and sofa seats from each facing strip (P) to open end and mark off these distances on edging strips. Use combination square to draw 45° cutting lines at marks and cut at lines. Attach strips with glue and 1-in. brads.

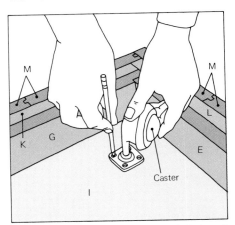

27. Position casters near corners of chair and sofa floor bottoms, allowing room for casters to swing around without hitting walls of base. Put pencil through screw holes in casters and mark positions, then drill ⅛-in. pilot hole at each mark. Attach casters with self-tapping screws. Sand and finish units (see p.94).

Making the cushions

You can either make your own cushions, as shown below, or have them made to order. You will need two seat and two back cushions for the sofa and one seat and one back cushion for each chair. If you plan to arrange the couch as shown, you will also need a cushion for the arm of the corner chair, since that arm will then function as a back.

Each cushion is made up of a cover and filler. The cover consists of a top and a bottom, a boxing strip that runs around the perimeter of the cushion, and cording, or piping, which is sewn between the boxing strip and the top and bottom. The filler is a polyurethane (rigid foam) block covered with polyester batting. Order the polyurethane in blocks cut 1 inch smaller all around than the projected sizes of the finished cushions—when you add the batting, the filler will be somewhat larger than the cover, giving resiliency to the finished cushion.

The sizes of the finished cushions are given below. The top and bottom of each seat cushion is as large as the area the cushion will cover. The length of each boxing strip is twice the length plus twice the width of the top and bottom; the width of the boxing strip is 6 inches for the seat cushions and 5 inches for the others. The height of the back and arm cushions is 6 inches less than the height of the back rests because those cushions rest on top of the 6-inch-thick seat cushions.

Cut the fabric for the tops, bottoms, and boxing strips 1½ inches longer and wider than they will be on the finished cushions to allow for a ¾-inch seam on each side. Make the cording by covering cable cord with bias strips. (A bias strip is a strip cut at a 45° angle across the fabric.) Cut the strips wide enough to go around the cord plus 1½ inches. Cut both the bias strips and the cord to the same lengths as the boxing strips.

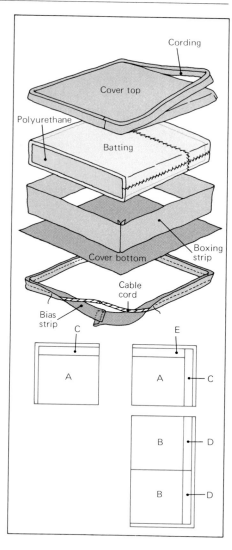

Sizes of finished cushion covers

Part	Name	Quantity	Thickness	Width	Length
A	Chair seat cushion	2	6″	27¾″	27¾″
B	Sofa seat cushion	2	6″	27¾″	29″
C	Chair back cushion	2	5″	12″	27¾″
D	Sofa back cushion	2	5″	12″	29″
E	Arm cushion	1	5″	12″	22″

Tools and materials: Sewing machine with zipper foot. Tape measure, tailor's chalk. Thread, needles, pins, scissors. Block of polyurethane for each cushion cut to size (see text). Roll of polyester batting, 12 yd. of 54″ wide upholstery fabric for cushion covers, 48 yd. of ⅛″ or ³⁄₁₆″ cable cord.

Making the cover

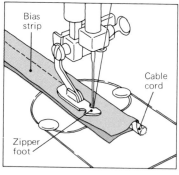

1. Cut cable cord and bias strips for cording (see text). Fold each bias strip around an equal length of cable cord with right side of fabric out and seam edges even. Pin into place. Using a zipper foot, machine-stitch fabric together close to cord, but do not crowd stitching against it. Cut fabric for tops, bottoms, and boxing strips.

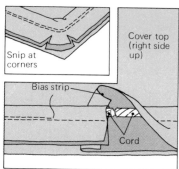

2. Pin cording to right side of a cover top with cut edges aligned. Using zipper foot, machine-stitch just inside stitching on cording, but begin 1 in. from end of cording. When stitching at a corner, snip seam allowances. Cut ends of cord flush and turn under the seam allowance at beginning of bias strip. Overlap the folded ends and stitch. Add cording to a cover bottom in same way.

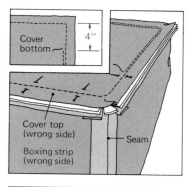

3. Stitch ends of a boxing strip together. Pin boxing strip to top with their right sides together and the seam in boxing strip at corner of top. Using zipper foot, machine-stitch top to boxing strip. As you near each corner, snip seam allowances and then stitch around corner. Add cover bottom in same way, but leave back and rear 4 in. of sides of bottom open. Make other covers in same way.

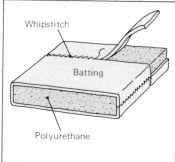

4. Wrap polyurethane blocks with batting so that batting is 1 in. thick on four sides of polyurethane. Whipstitch edges of batting together with a needle and thread. Turn cushion covers right side out and push polyurethane into covers through openings in backs. Turn under seam allowances on boxing strips and sew openings shut by whipstitching them.

TV AND STEREO CABINET

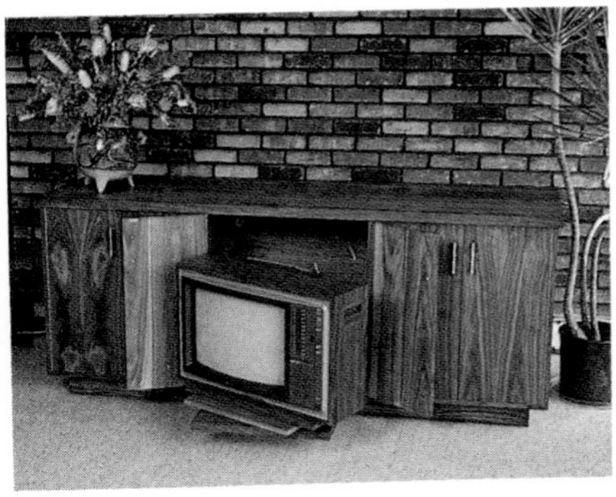

Clean, elegant lines and rich walnut veneer combine to make a handsome piece of furniture with space for a television set, stereo, and record storage. Although the design is simple, its construction demands considerable time.

Wood: Since lumber is not available in the widths required, plywood is the best choice. The cabinet shown here was built largely of A–2 interior plywood with walnut veneer on both sides. Plan your layout so the A side will be prominent, facing upward on the shelves and inward on the partitions. Pay special attention to the panel from which the top of the cabinet will be cut so that the most attractive figure will be in the center. The top's thickness of 1½ inches is achieved by layering two panels of ¾-inch plywood. All machining and nailing is done on the lower panel, or subtop.

Finishing: All exposed edges must be covered with matching veneer (see Steps 15–18). You can buy veneer in leaves (sheets of about 8 square feet) or in strips that have cloth or paper backing. In either case, the veneer—like that on the plywood panels themselves—should be no thinner than 1/32 inch. Walnut veneer requires no stain for a dark, lustrous finish. This cabinet was finished with four coats of tung oil, applied with a brush and wiped with a soft cloth. Work a small section of the cabinet at a time, but complete each large surface at one sitting. Follow the manufacturer's directions for the drying time between coats.

Because electrical cords and stereo connectors vary, the design of the cabinet does not specify the placement of holes in the back. Before finishing the back panel, determine the best places for such holes based on your own appliances. Use a drill or saber saw to make them no larger than necessary for the plugs to go through easily. Sand the edges of the holes.

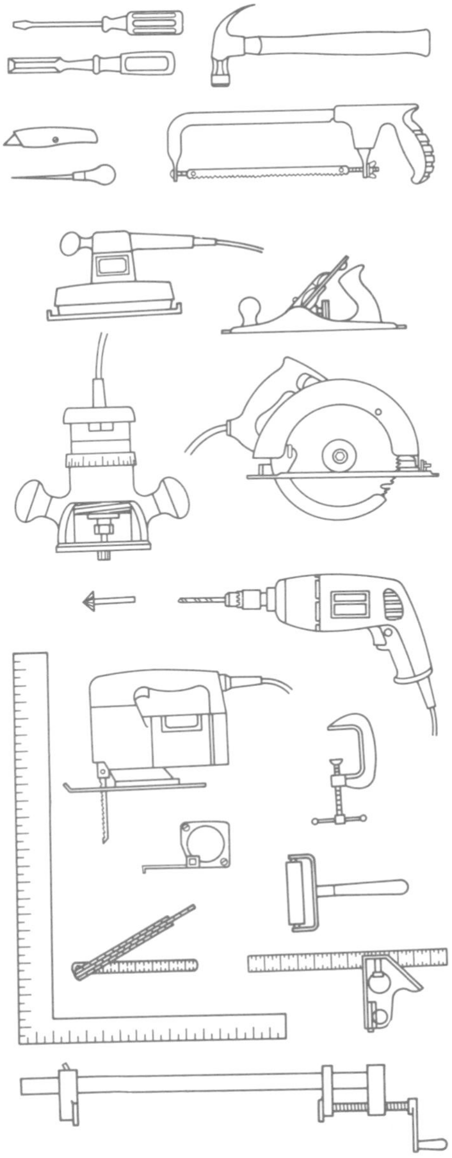

Parts list

Part	Name	Quantity	Thickness	Width	Length	Material
A	Subtop	1	¾"	21¾"	76"	4′ x 8′ panel A–D fir plywood
B	Top	1	¾"	22"	76"	
C	Bottom	1	¾"	21"	74"	4′ x 8′ panel A–2 walnut veneer plywood
D	Right shelf	1	¾"	13"	24½"	
E	Left shelf	2	¾"	20"	24½"	
F	Side	2	¾"	21¼"	27¾"	4′ x 8′ panel A–2 walnut veneer plywood
G	Partition	2	¾"	21"	27¼"	
H	Door	6	¾"	26⅝"✻	11¾"✻	
I	Front and back of base	2	¾"	3"	68"	4′ x 8′ panel A–2 walnut veneer plywood
J	End of base	2	¾"	3"	17"	
K	Record divider	6	½"	12½"✻	13¼"✻	4′ x 8′ panel A–2 walnut veneer plywood
L	Back	1	¼"	28¼"✻	49⅞"✻	4′ x 8′ panel walnut veneer plywood
M	False back	1	¼"	24½"✻	27¼"✻	
N	Front and back cleat	2	¾"	¾"	66½"	1 x 1 pine
O	End cleat	2	¾"	¾"	15"	1 x 1 pine

✻Measurements are approximate. Parts H, K, L, and M should be measured against the assembled cabinet shell before cutting.

Tools and materials: Drill with 3/16" and ⅜" bits and countersink. Table saw or circular saw with carbide-tipped panel-cutting blade. Saber saw, hacksaw. Orbital sander, softwood block. Router with carbide bits (¼", ½", and ¾" straight). Four 2" C-clamps, two 3′ and two 7′ bar or pipe clamps. Steel tape rule, steel ruler, wooden extension rule, framing square, combination square. Veneer saw or mat knife. Rubber roller, block plane, ½" and ¾" straight chisels, hammer, screwdriver, awl. Walnut wood filler, contact cement, white glue. Nos. 100 and 150 sandpaper, tung oil, paintbrush, soft cloths. Walnut veneer. A–2 walnut veneer plywood: three ¾" x 4′ x 8′ panels and a ½" x 4′ x 8′ panel. A ¼" x 4′ x 8′ panel walnut veneer plywood. A ¾" x 4′ x 8′ panel A–D fir plywood. Two 8′ lengths 1 x 1 pine. 3d and 6d common-coated nails and 6d finishing nails, 1¼" No. 8 flathead wood screws, ⅝" No. 5 chrome flathead tapping screws. Two 8′ lengths 1½" chrome piano hinges. Six magnetic door catches, six door pulls.

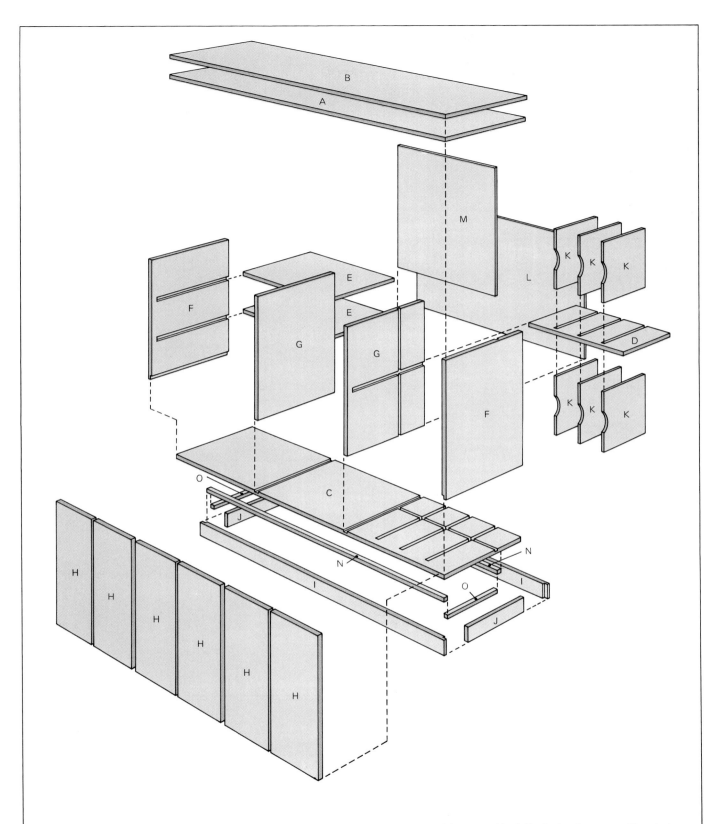

Exploded view shows exactly how and where all pieces of the cabinet fit together. The parts are keyed by letter to the chart on the previous page. Cut all pieces as specified except doors, back, false back, and record dividers; these must be measured and then cut to fit precisely within their grooves during assembly.

The basic construction technique involves cutting dadoes (internal grooves) and rabbets (grooves along the edges) in certain pieces into which other pieces will fit. Accurate measuring, mark-ing, and machining are critical. For instructions on cutting dadoes and rabbets with a router, see Steps 1–4. (It is also possible to do the job with a table saw that is equipped with special dadoing blades or with a circular saw; see *Index*, p.379.)

The finished cabinet stands 32 inches high, give or take small variances in machining the dadoes and rabbet joints. The top is 76 inches long and 22 inches wide, overhanging the cabinet by ½ inch at each end and ¾ inch in front.

Patterns for dadoes and rabbets

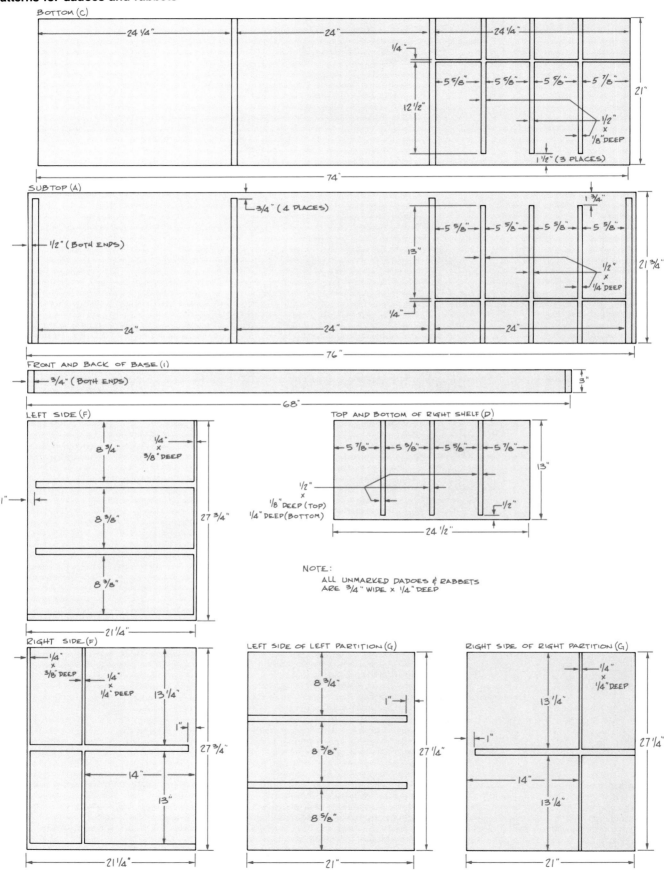

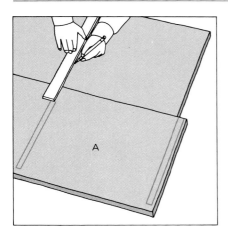

1. Use the patterns on page 102 to mark out all dadoes and rabbets. Wherever possible, lay pieces side by side while marking to ensure precision. At the same time, use a different colored pencil to mark the router guideline (the distance from the center of the dado to the guideline must equal the radius of the router's base).

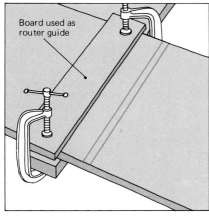

Board used as router guide

2. Use straight router bits to cut the dadoes. All the dadoes are ¼ in. deep except the three in the bottom for the record dividers (K), which are ⅛ in. deep. Test the depth on scrap wood before routing the cabinet pieces. Before routing each dado, use two C-clamps to secure a straight board or plywood strip along the router guideline.

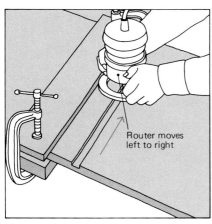

Router moves left to right

3. Always move the router from left to right along the guide strip. In cases of "blind" dadoes (those that do not run all the way across a piece) in which the blind end is at the right, stop the router at the end of the line and turn it off before lifting it from the wood. When the blind end is at the left, the router bit must be "plunged"—that is, slowly lowered into the wood while the bit is turning.

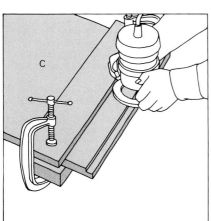

4. Rabbets can be cut just as dadoes are—or with special rabbeting bits. Note that all rabbets are ¼ in. deep except those in the side pieces, which are ⅜ in. deep. After the routing is complete, the ends of the blind dadoes must be chiseled square. Mark these out carefully; do not attempt to do the job by eye.

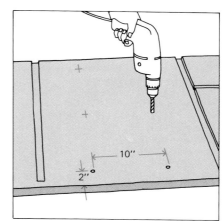

10"
2"

5. Use a ³⁄₁₆-in. bit to drill three rows of holes through the subtop (A) for screwing it onto the top. The rows should run lengthwise 2 in. from the front and back edges and along the center line. Space holes 10 in. apart, beginning 3 in. from one end. (Do not, however, drill through the dadoes; displace any such holes by 1 in.) Countersink screwheads ¼ in. deep.

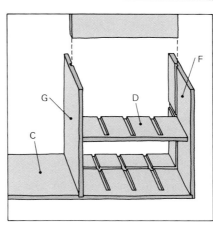

G   D   F
C

6. Veneer front edges of shelves (D and E, see Steps 15–18). Then assemble cabinet dry—without glue—to be sure everything fits. Measure and cut the false back (M) to fit within dadoes of record compartment (cut it ¹⁄₃₂ in. smaller than measurements to allow for tightening of clamps). Disassemble. Sand interior surfaces with Nos. 100 and 150 sandpaper.

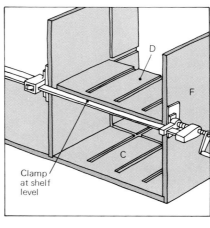

D
F
C
Clamp at shelf level

7. Begin permanent assembly with the record compartment. Preset a 3-ft. clamp to 26 in., and have a damp cloth handy to clean off excess glue (where glue dries, it will leave light spots in finish). Apply glue to all rabbets and the ¾-in. dadoes of right side, right partition, and bottom, making sure the sides of the grooves are covered. Put side and partition in place, insert shelf, and clamp firmly.

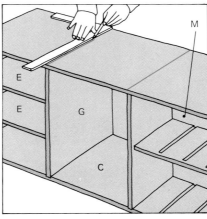

M
E
E   G
C

8. Glue and clamp the left section in the same way. Slide the false back (M) into position in the record section (no glue is needed). Then apply glue to the ¾-in. dadoes of the subtop (A) and fit it over the sides and partitions. Use a rule to draw lines on the subtop corresponding to the center of the grooves underneath, and drive 6d coated nails along these lines into upper edges of sides and partitions.

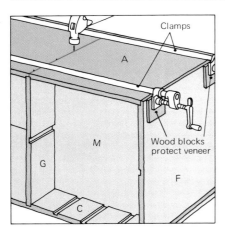

9. Turn the cabinet upside down and, after ruling the nail lines, drive 6d coated nails into partitions. Two 7-ft. bar or pipe clamps will secure the sides to the bottom (use scrap wood under the clamps to protect the veneer). If clamps are not available, drive 6d finishing nails through the sides into the bottom; set nailheads and fill with walnut wood filler.

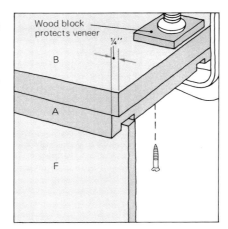

13. Turn the cabinet right side up and test alignment of the top (A) on the subtop (B); the top should be flush at front and sides and overhang rear edge by ¼ in. Adjust as needed. When top fits properly, apply a liberal coat of glue to the subtop and secure top with four C-clamps. Drive 1¼-in. No. 8 wood screws up through the holes in the subtop into the top.

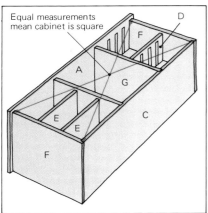

10. The cabinet must be perfectly square or the doors cannot be made to fit. To square up the cabinet, place it on its back and measure diagonally corner to corner in both directions. If the measurements differ, push or pull the corners until they match within 1/64 in. Let glue dry at least 2 hr.

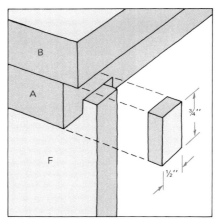

14. Cut two rectangular blocks of ¼-in. plywood measuring ½ in. × ¾ in. Glue these to the back of the subtop at both ends to fill the spaces underneath the overhanging top to complete the 1½-in. thickness. After the glue dries, use a block plane to trim front and side edges so that the two pieces of plywood are flush and square all around.

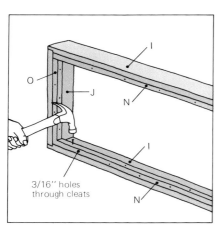

11. Assemble the base while the glue dries on the cabinet. Apply glue to the rabbets on front and back pieces (I); then clamp ends (J) in place, making sure structure is square. Glue and nail cleats (N and O) around the top inside edge, using 3d coated nails. Drill 3/16-in. holes through the cleats for screwing base to cabinet bottom (two evenly spaced holes in end cleats and seven in long cleats).

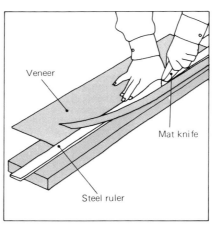

15. Veneer all exposed edges, beginning with the top. Lay the veneer leaf out on a flat softwood surface, and with a sharp pencil and steel ruler, mark each strip, as needed, slightly larger than the surface it is to cover. Cut along the penciled line with a veneer saw or mat knife, using the ruler as a guide.

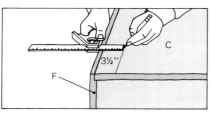

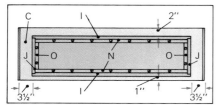

12. Apply veneer to the entire face of both ends of base to cover the exposed edges of the front and back. Remove clamps from cabinet and turn it upside down to attach base. Draw guidelines on the bottom of cabinet 3½ in. from each end, 1 in. from the back, and 2 in. from the front. Apply glue to the cleats and top of the base; place the base within ruled lines and drive 1¼-in. No. 8 wood screws.

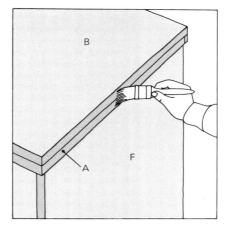

16. Veneer the sides of the top first, then the front edge. Apply a coat of contact cement to the plywood edges (do not use water-based cement). When it is dry to the touch, apply a second coat and apply one coat to the back of the veneer strip. Let both surfaces dry to the touch.

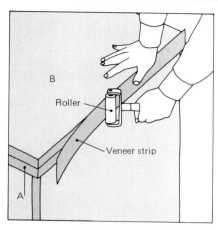

17. Align the veneer carefully before applying it; once contact is made, it cannot be repositioned! Starting at one end, press the veneer down firmly with a rubber roller. (An alternative method would be to place a flat wooden block over the veneer and tap it with a hammer, working from one end of the strip to the other.)

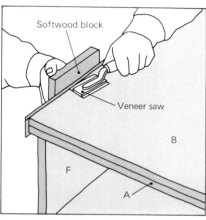

18. Trim excess veneer from each strip before proceeding to the next strip, using a veneer saw or mat knife. Hold a softwood block behind the veneer for a clean cut. Apply veneer to the exposed edges of the sides, then the bottom and partitions. At the joints, mark abutting strips carefully and cut the ends square with a mat knife or with a very sharp chisel.

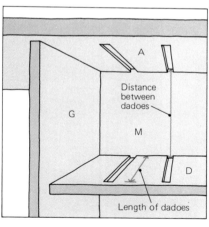

19. Measure and cut six record dividers to fit within their dadoes. They should be 9/64 in. shorter than the interior distance between the upper and lower dadoes and 1/32 in. narrower than the length of the dadoes so that they can be inserted into the upper dadoes and dropped into place. Because record dividers are removable, they should not be glued.

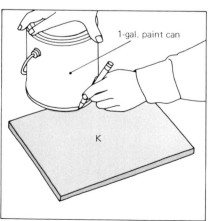

20. A 1-gal. paint can makes a good template for marking the curved "scoop" in the front of the record dividers. Mark one divider and cut it with a saber saw, then use it as a pattern for the remaining five. When the cutting is done, sand the edges all around with No. 100 sandpaper. Veneer the front edges.

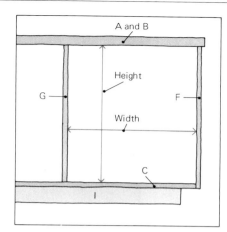

21. Measure the openings in which the doors will be hung. If they are the same size, the doors will be identical; if not, the doors must be adjusted to fit. Door height should be 7/32 in. less than the height of the opening. To calculate door width, subtract from the width of the opening two thicknesses of piano hinge, two thicknesses of veneer, and 3/32 in. clearance. Divide by two for width of door.

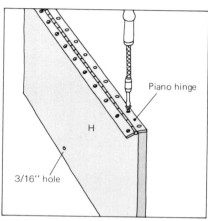

22. Cut the doors. Then veneer the tops and inner edges (unhinged sides), being careful to make three left-hand and three right-hand doors. Position and drill 3/16-in. holes for attaching door pulls. Sand all edges with Nos. 100 and 150 sandpaper. Use a hacksaw to cut piano hinges to door height. Drill 5/64-in. pilot holes, and attach hinges to doors with 5/8-in. No. 5 flathead tapping screws.

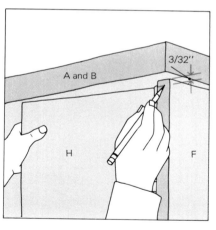

23. Position each door 3/32 in. down and mark its upper corner on the cabinet. Then hang all six doors, using only two holes in each hinge—the second from the top and the second from the bottom. Test the fit and alignment. If changes must be made, use the top and bottom holes for new positions. Mark the lower corners on the cabinet and remove the doors for finishing with the hinges still attached.

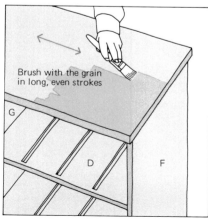

24. Cut the back (L) to fit within the rabbets and overhanging top. Sand all the remaining surfaces with Nos. 100 and 150 sandpaper. Finish with four coats of tung oil. When dry, rule guidelines and use 3d coated nails to attach the back; no glue is needed. Hang the doors permanently. Install door pulls and magnetic door catches.

WINDOW SEAT

A window seat is a good way to use the area in a bay window that might otherwise go to waste. This design has storage space beneath the seat.

Bow and bay windows come in different sizes, and the seat must be fitted accordingly. If your window differs from the one in this project, you will have to adjust the horizontal dimensions of the seat, but the vertical dimensions and the basic structure need not change.

For the stability of the seat, it is best to glue and nail all joints. Because the cushions are removed when the seat is opened, finishing nails and putty are used on the exposed top surfaces. The seat cushion is 4 inches thick to provide a normal 18-inch seating height and the bolster is 12 inches high to reach the top of the back. Add a 2 × 2 support nailed to the floor beneath the kickplate if you have children who are likely to kick it often.

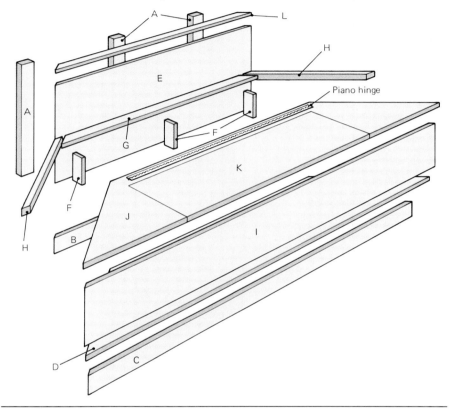

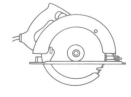

Parts list

Part	Name	Quantity	Thickness	Width	Length	Material
A	Back support	3	1½"	3½"	29¼"	2 x 4 fir
B	Base support	1	¾"	3"	58½"✶	Birch plywood
C	Kickplate	1	¾"	3"	99¼"✶	Birch plywood
D	Base	1	¾"	23⅝"	104¼"✶	Birch plywood
E	Back	1	¾"	25½"	58½"✶	Birch plywood
F	Seat brace	3	¾"	4"	9½"	Birch plywood
G	Rear seat support	1	¾"	4"	62"✶	Birch plywood
H	Side seat support	2	1½"	1½"	33"✶	2 x 2 fir
I	Front	1	¾"	10¼"	105¼"✶	Birch plywood
J	Seat	1	¾"	24¼"	107"✶	Birch plywood
K	Lid	1	¾"	21"	54"✶	Birch plywood
L	Top	1	¾"	2¼"	58½"✶	Birch plywood

✶Measurement is approximate. Cut to fit during construction.

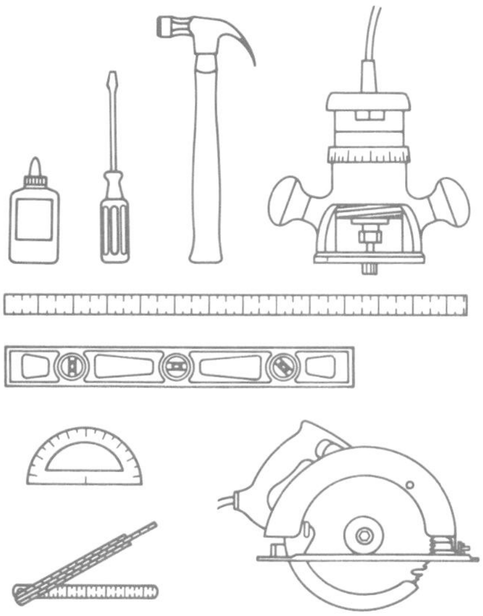

Tools and materials: Router (optional). Circular saw. Hammer, screwdriver, combination square or protractor, straightedge, wooden extension rule, level, pencil. Cardboard. Wood glue. Cushions to fit seat and back (see *Index*, p.379). Two ¾" × 4' × 10' panels of birch plywood, an 8' length of 2 × 4 fir, a 6' length of 2 × 2 fir. Brass or stainless steel piano hinge 54" long. 1¾" No. 8 flathead wood screws. 6d common and finishing nails.

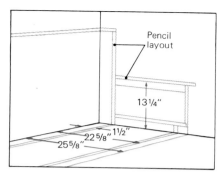

Pencil layout

13¼"

11½"

22⅝"

25⅝"

1. Measure and lay out the positions of the window-seat parts, drawing them on the floor first and then on the wall. Because walls always have irregularities, this will help you to measure, cut, and install the pieces accurately as you go along.

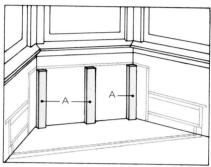

A   A

2. Cut and attach the back supports (A) to the wall, one at each corner, the third exactly in the middle. If the wall is made of wood, the supports can be nailed or screwed in. Otherwise, use anchors appropriate for plaster, plasterboard, or masonry walls.

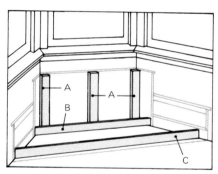

A   A

B

C

3. Bevel the ends of the base support (B) and nail it to the back supports. Bevel the ends of the kickplate (C) and fasten it to the walls. Parts B and C should be parallel and 19⅝ in. apart.

Templates

4. Lay out two pieces of cardboard, each slightly larger than half the size of the base. Position and cut them so that they fit against the side walls exactly and align at the base supports. Using the cardboard templates, mark plywood and cut base.

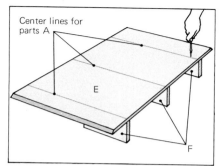

Center lines for parts A

E

F

5. Bevel the sides of the back piece (E). Be sure it fits snugly against the back supports. Cut the seat braces (F) and screw them to the front of E, flush with the bottom, so that each brace will sit directly in front of a back support when the back piece is installed.

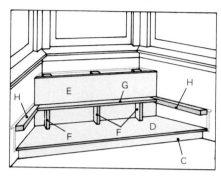

H   E   G   H

F   F   D

C

6. Nail back piece (E) to back supports (A). Cut side seat supports (H) and attach them to wall, using marks from Step 1 as guides. Be sure that front ends of H are beveled so that the front (I) will fit snugly against them. Nail the rear seat support (G) to the tops of seat braces (F).

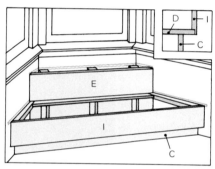

D   I

C

E

I

C

7. Bevel the sides of the front piece (I). Use a router or circular saw to cut a rabbet ¼ in. deep and ¾ in. wide along the bottom inside edge of part I. Position the rabbeted edge over the front edge of the base (D). Glue and nail front piece to base and to side seat supports.

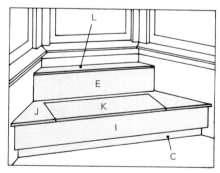

L

E

J   K

I

C

8. Make templates (see Step 4) to cut top piece (L) and nail it to back supports. Cut the seat (J), using the same procedure. Cut a rectangle from seat 21 in. x 54 in. Attach this lid (K) to seat with a piano hinge. Use a router to recess hinge. Install seat.

Plywood cutting patterns

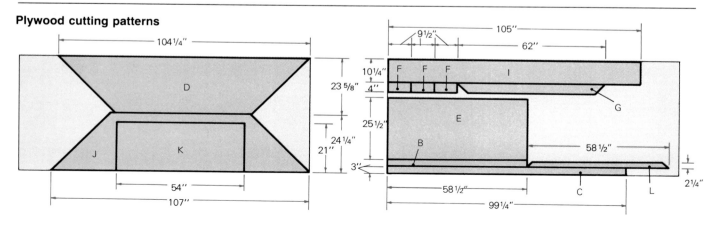

104¼"

D

J   K

54"

107"

21"

24¼"

23⅝"

9½"

105"

62"

10¼"

4"

F F F   I

G

25½"

E

B

58½"

C   L

58½"

3"

99¼"

2¼"

CHERRY END TABLE

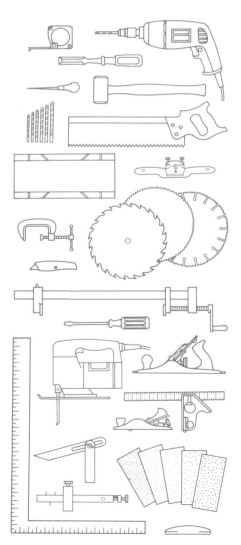

Time-honored techniques of hand joinery, executed with the help of modern tools and equipment, make this a project any craftsman can be proud of. Whether your decor is stark contemporary or cozy Early American, this end table's clean, elegant lines, highlighted by the rich tones and delicate figuring of oiled cherry, will fit right in.

Wood: For the greatest economy and the best results in matching color and figure, try to find a single piece of cherry stock that will yield all the solid parts of the table. Brush a little paint thinner on the surface to get an idea of the color and figure—it will dry harmlessly—then look for a matching piece of cherry-veneer plywood for the shelf.

With careful cutting, you can get all the solid pieces from a board that is 2 inches thick, 6½ inches wide, and 10½ feet long. First, cut a 32-inch length and rip it into two 3-inch widths for the legs (see p. 109, Step 1, for the cutting diagram). Then cut a 6-inch length and rip it into four 1¼-inch widths for the wings (B). Cut three 20-inch lengths for the top. Rip the remainder into 2½-inch widths for the aprons (C and D), then rip these pieces to a thickness of 1¼ inches. The edging (E and F) and screw blocks (H) can be made from the scrap.

Construction: The table is built in three clearly defined phases, each of which is shown on a separate page. First, the legs, wings, and aprons are cut roughly to shape and jointed to make the basic table structure (p. 109). Then these parts are more carefully shaped, the shelf is fitted into notches in the legs, and the structure is assembled with glue (p. 110). Finally, the top is formed and joined to the structure by means of slotted screw blocks (p. 111). Because of the inevitable imprecision of mortise-and-tenon joints, both the shelf and the top should be cut and shaped to fit the assembled leg-and-apron structure—not cut according to predetermined dimensions.

It may be difficult to find 2-inch-thick boards wide enough to make the legs according to the diagram on the opposite page (Step 1). If so, you can cut all four legs 1¾ inches square and 24⅞ inches long and join two wings to each, rather than one as we have done, in order to make the corner units. When rough-cutting the curved part of the tapered legs (Step 3, opposite page), guard against accidents by first making a series of parallel cuts about ¼ inch apart. If you use a band saw for the job, tape a piece of scrap wood to the lower part of the leg, as shown in Step 3, just thick enough to keep the piece level on the saw table.

Finishing: After construction is completed, use a block plane or spokeshave to gently round all sharp edges—how much you round them is a matter of personal taste and esthetic judgment. Then sand with Nos. 100, 150, and 220 sandpaper to achieve a smooth surface. To bring out the natural color and figure of the wood, apply several coats of penetrating oil, such as linseed oil, tung oil, or a commercially prepared Danish-style natural finish. If you want a protective, glossy surface, wait about a week before rubbing in a coat of wax.

Parts list

Part	Name	Quantity	Thickness	Width	Length	Material
A	Leg	4	1¾"	3" ✳	24⅞"	Cherry
B	Wing	4	1¾"	1¼"	8" ✳	Cherry
C	Side apron	2	1"	2½"	14"	Cherry
D	End apron	2	1"	2½"	12"	Cherry
E	Side edging	2	½"	⅞" ✳	16" ✳	Cherry
F	End edging	2	½"	⅞" ✳	14" ✳	Cherry
G	Top	1	1⅜"	16½"	18½"	Cherry
H	Screw block	10	⅝"	1"	1½"	Cherry
I	Shelf	1	¾"	12⅞" ✳	14⅞" ✳	A–2 cherry plywood

✳ Measurement is approximate; cut to fit during construction.

Tools and materials: Table saw with combination blade. Band saw, saber saw, or coping saw. Backsaw, miter box. Drill with ³⁄₃₂", ¹¹⁄₆₄", and ⁵⁄₁₆" twist bits. Framing and combination squares, T bevel, steel tape rule, marking gauge, mortising gauge (optional), pencil. Awl, mat knife. Screwdriver. Jack plane, block plane, shoulder plane (optional), spokeshave or drawknife. Straight chisels: ⅛", ⅜", ½", ¾", 1", and 1½". Mallet. Six 3' bar or pipe clamps, several assorted C-clamps. Orbital sander (optional), sanding block. Nos. 80, 100, 150, and 220 sandpaper. Yellow carpenter's glue, penetrating oil. Wax (optional). Wax paper, heavy paper. ³⁄₁₆" washers, 1¼" and 1½" No. 8 roundhead screws. A 2" x 6½" x 10½' board of cherry stock or the equivalent. An 18" square of ¾" A–2 cherry plywood.

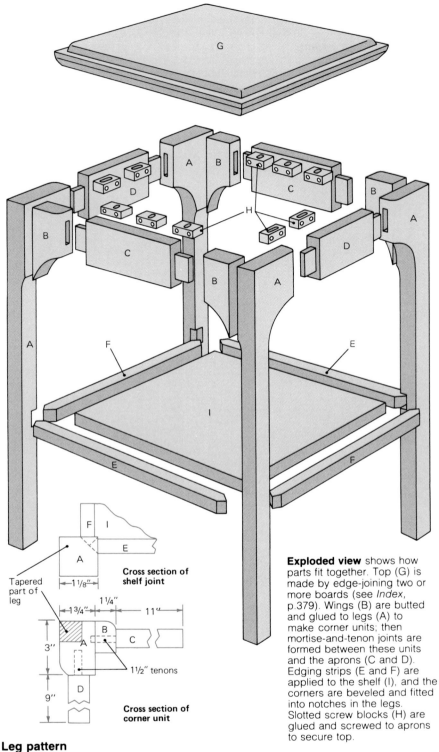

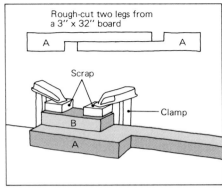

Rough-cut two legs from a 3″ x 32″ board

A   A

Scrap

Clamp

B

A

1. Plane stock to thickness for legs (A), wings (B), and aprons (C and D). Cut to length and width. Glue and clamp wings to legs to form corner units, making sure that the top edges are flush and the joints are square.

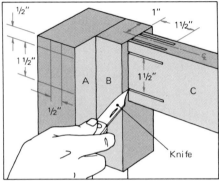

½″   1″
1½″
1½″

A   B

1½″

½″

C

Knife

2. Use a table saw to cut cheeks of tenons 1½ in. deep in ends of apron pieces (C and D). Position aprons flush with tops of corner units and mark for mortises. Cut tenon shoulders and make mortises (see *Index*, p.379).

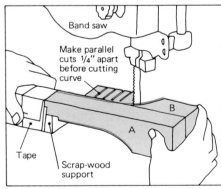

Band saw

Make parallel cuts ¼″ apart before cutting curve

B

A

Tape

Scrap-wood support

3. Use pattern below to scribe outline of tapered leg on both outer faces of corner units. Rough-cut to within ⅛ in. of scribed lines. Rip straight sections on table saw; use band, saber, or coping saw to cut curves.

Cross section of shelf joint

F   I
E
A
Tapered part of leg
⟵ 1⅛″ ⟶

1¾″   1¼″   11″

3″
A   B   C

1½″ tenons

9″
D

Cross section of corner unit

Exploded view shows how parts fit together. Top (G) is made by edge-joining two or more boards (see *Index*, p.379). Wings (B) are butted and glued to legs (A) to make corner units; then mortise-and-tenon joints are formed between these units and the aprons (C and D). Edging strips (E and F) are applied to the shelf (I), and the corners are beveled and fitted into notches in the legs. Slotted screw blocks (H) are glued and screwed to aprons to secure top.

Leg pattern

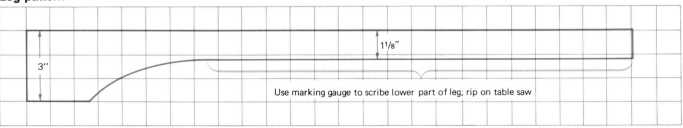

1⅛″

3″

Use marking gauge to scribe lower part of leg; rip on table saw

Use 1-in. grid to make full-size pattern of tapered leg on heavy paper. Scribe pattern on both outer faces of corner units.

Fitting the shelf

The table's sturdiness depends on custom-fitting the shelf. First, use a plane and spokeshave to reduce the rough-cut corner units to their scribed shapes. Assemble and clamp the table structure dry (no glue) with all four legs square to the ground. Cut and edge the shelf (Steps 1–3). The shelf corners are beveled so that the notches they must fit into can be cut straight across. Mark the bevel points (thickness of the edging plus 1/16 inch), then use the shelf corners themselves as patterns for the notches. After the notches are cut, doublecheck the bevel points before sawing off shelf corners.

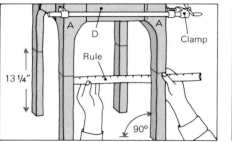

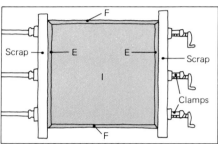

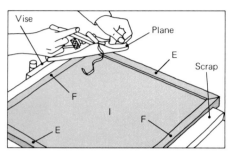

1. Rule a line around each leg 13¼ in. from the floor. Measure the distances between the legs at these marks. Add ⅛ in. to each dimension to determine the size of the shelf (I). Cut shelf from ¾-in. plywood.

2. Miter one end of each side edging (E). Clamp to sides of shelf and cut an end edging (F) to fit between miters. Mark and cut miters on opposite ends of parts E and fit other end edging. Glue and clamp edging in place.

3. Plane parts E and F and sand with No. 80 sandpaper so that they are flush with both surfaces of shelf. Label each shelf corner and the corresponding leg before disassembling the table to cut the notches.

Making the notches

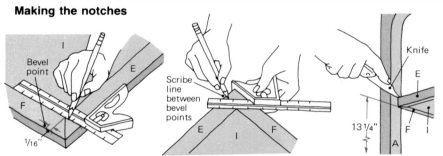

Extend outline of shelf (I) across edging (E and F); mark bevel points 1/16 in. farther from corners. Hold each shelf corner against inner faces of its matching leg, and mark shelf thickness plus distance from corner to bevel points on leg.

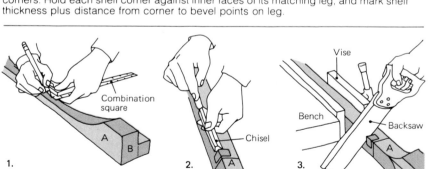

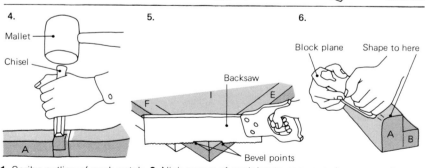

1. Scribe outline of each notch. **2.** Nick corner of each leg to ensure a clean saw cut. **3.** Cut notch to depth with backsaw. **4.** Chisel out notch, making its base flat or slightly concave. **5.** Doublecheck bevel points and saw off shelf corners. **6.** Shape upper corners of legs (A) and wings (B) to the point where they meet aprons (C and D).

Assembling the frames

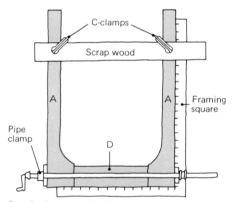

Sand all parts with Nos. 100, 150, and 220 paper. Glue tenons of end aprons (D) into their mortises and apply pipe clamps. To ensure squareness of end frames, secure scrap wood across legs with C-clamps.

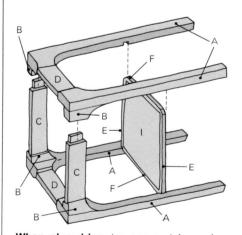

When glue dries, lay one end frame face down. Apply glue to mortises and notches and insert side aprons (C) and shelf; then glue the other end frame in place. Stand table frame upright, square it up, and apply pipe clamps across legs.

Shaping the top

The upper surface of the top is rabbeted all around to create a raised center panel. Viewed in silhouette, the edges of this panel should align with the outer surfaces of the table legs. The top's lower edge is beveled at an angle of about 40° to meet the upper edges of the corner units (A and B). Before beveling, center the table frame upside down on the underside of the top and outline the corner units; then set the angle of the table saw to cut just a hair outside these lines. Gently round all sharp corners with a plane and No. 80 sandpaper to give the top a graceful form. Attach the top as shown below.

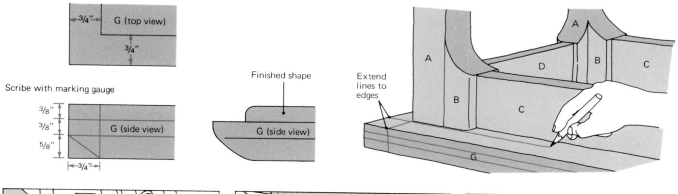

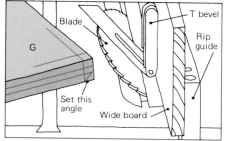

1. Use T bevel to transfer the angle from an edge of the marked-out top (G) to the table saw. The blades of most saws can be tilted only to the right, so the rip guide must be moved to the left of the blade.

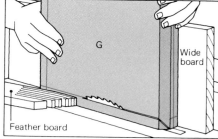

2. Make test cuts with scrap wood to find proper settings, then cut bevels along bottom edges of four sides of top. To ensure straight cuts, attach a wide board to fence and clamp feather board (see *Index*, p.379) to table.

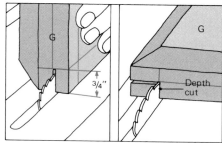

3. Move rip fence back to right side of blade and reset blade to 90°. Cut ¾-in. rabbets in all four edges of top. Lower blade to ⁵⁄₁₆ in. and adjust rip fence for depth cuts. Finish rabbets with chisel or shoulder plane.

Attaching the top

Changes in humidity will cause the top to swell and shrink. If the top is firmly secured to the table structure, such movement will eventually weaken the mortise-and-tenon joints and may cause the top to split. The problem is solved by attaching slotted screw blocks to the apron pieces, with all the slots running across the grain of the top, then driving screws through the slots and into the top. Make all the blocks from a strip of hardwood ⁵⁄₈ inch thick and 1 inch wide that is at least 20 inches long. Mark out a dozen blocks as shown below—10 are needed, the other two are spares.

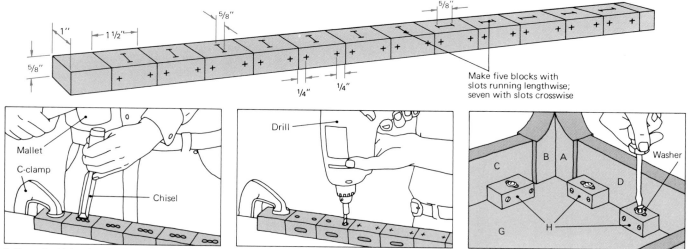

Make five blocks with slots running lengthwise; seven with slots crosswise

1. To make ⁵⁄₈-in. slots in blocks, first drill three holes, using an ¹¹⁄₆₄-in. bit. (Drill center hole first.) Then cut through waste from both sides with ½-in. chisel. Finally, clean out the slots with ⅛-in. chisel.

2. Use an ¹¹⁄₆₄-in. bit to drill two shank holes through each block for the screws that will secure the blocks to the aprons. Center the holes ¼ in. from the ends of the blocks. Then cut the blocks apart.

3. Use glue and 1½-in. No. 8 screws to mount three blocks on each side apron (C) and two on each end apron (D). Attach top (G) with 1¼-in. No. 8 roundhead screws and ³⁄₁₆-in. washers. (Use ⁵⁄₃₂-in. bit for pilot holes.)

SERVING CART

Dazzle your dinner guests by rolling out an appetizing assortment of foods on this handsome oak and glass serving cart. Although the cart is ideal for serving food on the patio or in the dining room, it is not limited to this use. It can also pinch-hit as a portable bar, as a plant stand, or as a base for a television set or microwave oven. Use the lower shelves to store magazines or utensils. The position of the center shelf is adjustable to suit your needs.

Made of sturdy oak and glass, the cart is 18½ inches wide, 30½ inches long, and 28 inches high. It is made up of four posts with casters and three frames that hold the glass shelves. Each frame consists of four interlocking inside rails that are glued and screwed to the posts and four outside rails that fit between the posts and are glued and nailed to the ends of the inside rails. Because oak is so hard, all screw and nail holes must be predrilled. The adjustable center shelf is held in place with four pin-type supports, which

you can make yourself by bending short sections of aluminum rod into L shapes.

When buying the oak board for this project, you can have the lumber dealer rip it to the widths needed. You can cut it to the lengths needed before beginning the project. After the wooden parts of the cart have all been assembled, sand the wood thoroughly with Nos. 100, 150, and 220 sandpaper; then apply several coats of tung oil, rubbing the wood down lightly with 000 steel wool between applications. (To find directions on ripping and finishing, see *Index*, p.379.)

Do not purchase the glass for the shelves until the wooden parts of the cart have all been assembled. Then check the measurements for the shelves against the actual cart and have the glass cut to the size you need by a dealer. Since the glass must fit around the tops of the four posts, you must have small squares of glass cut from the corners, a tricky process best left to an expert.

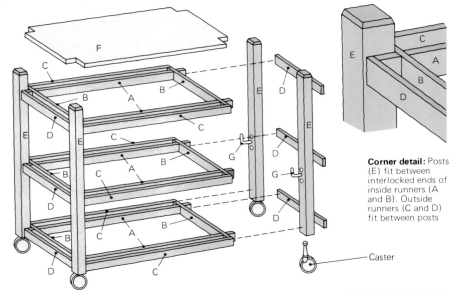

Corner detail: Posts (E) fit between interlocked ends of inside runners (A and B). Outside runners (C and D) fit between posts

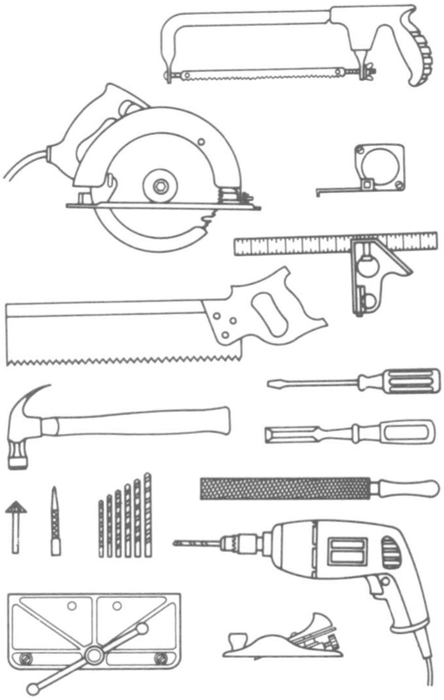

Caster

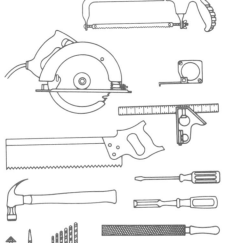

Parts list

Part	Name	Quantity	Thickness	Width	Length	Material
A	Long inside runner	6	½″	1¾″	29″	Red oak board
B	Short inside runner	6	½″	1¾″	17″	Red oak board
C	Long outside runner	6	½″	1¾″	27″	Red oak board
D	Short outside runner	6	½″	1¾″	15″	Red oak board
E	Post	4	1¾″	1¾″	27″	Red oak post
F	Glass shelf	3	¼″	18½″✶	30½″✶	Plate glass
G	Shelf support	4	¼″ dia.	—	2″	Aluminum rod

✶Measurement is approximate. Check against assembled cart before having glass cut.

Tools and materials: Circular saw, backsaw, hacksaw. Drill with set of twist bits and countersink. Block plane, coarse file or wood rasp, vise. Wood chisel, hammer, nail set, screwdriver. Steel tape rule, combination square, pencil. Nos. 100, 150, and 220 sandpaper. White glue, wood putty, 000 steel wool, tung oil, soft cloth. Six ½″ × 5½″ x 36″ oak boards, four 3′ lengths of 2 x 2 oak posts. Three sheets of ¼″ plate glass (see text). Four casters with bushings, ¼″ aluminum rod 8″ long (anodized gold finish). Two dozen 1½″ No. 8 flathead wood screws, two dozen 4d finishing nails.

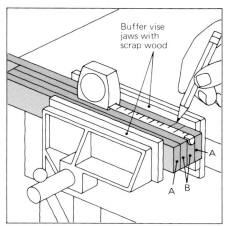

1. Cut all the wood to the specifications given in the chart on the previous page. Align the ends of two long inside runners (A) and two short inside runners (B) and clamp them together in a vise. Make pencil marks 1 in. and 1½ in. from aligned ends of the runners.

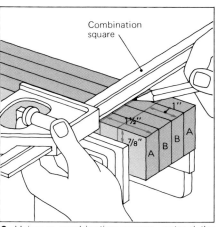

2. Using a combination square, extend the marks into rules that run across the tops of the four runners. These rules will act as cutting lines for the slots to be cut in Step 3. Extend the cutting lines ⅞ in. down each side of the aligned runners to mark depth of slots.

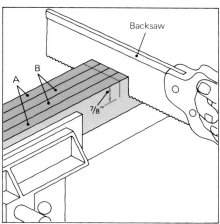

3. Use a backsaw to cut just within the outside cutting line to a depth of ⅞ in.—that is, to the point where the cutting line stops on the sides of the clamped runners. Cut along the inside cutting line in the same way, being sure to make this cut exactly even with the first cut.

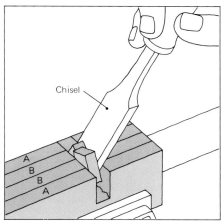

4. Use a wood chisel to remove the wood between the two cuts, then smooth the slots with a coarse file or wood rasp. Test-fit a piece of ½-in. scrap wood. File the slot, if necessary, to make scrap fit snugly. Unclamp runners, align other ends, and cut slots in same way.

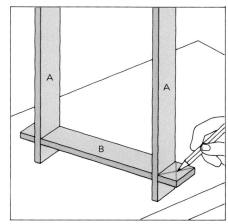

5. Temporarily assemble the shelf frame by interlocking the slots on the ends of the runners to form a rectangle. Posts will be attached to the stubs that protrude beyond rectangle. Pencil an X onto sides of stubs that will not come into direct contact with a post.

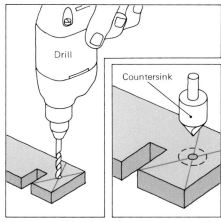

6. Disassemble the shelf frame and place the runners with the marked sides facing up. Drill a ⅛-in. screw hole through the center of each of the eight stubs. Use a countersink bit to widen the tops of the screw holes so that the screwheads will lie flush with the wood.

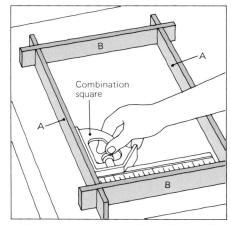

7. Run glue along the inside surfaces of the slots and reassemble the shelf frame. Wipe off excess glue with a damp cloth. Use a combination square to align and square up frame, then set frame aside to dry. Make and assemble a second shelf frame in same way.

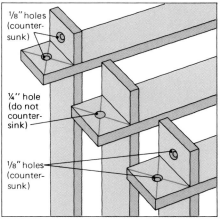

8. Make and assemble a third shelf frame (the adjustable center one) in the same way, but drill ¼-in. holes into the stubs instead of the smaller holes called for in Step 6, and do not widen the holes with the countersink. The shelf supports (G) will fit into these holes.

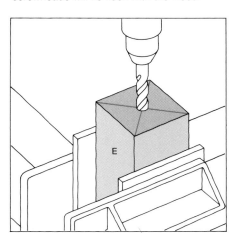

9. Mark the center of one end of each post (E) by using the combination square to draw diagonal lines across its ends from corner to corner. Drill holes for caster bushings where the lines intersect—⅜-in. holes or size recommended by caster manufacturer.

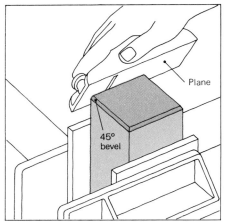

10. Turn each post right side up and use a block plane to cut a bevel around the top edges. A bevel gives the posts a more graceful look, avoids sharp edges, and reduces chance of post's splitting. Cut bevel about ⅛ in. wide and at a 45° angle.

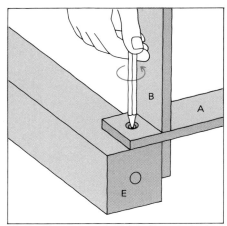

11. Position one post (E) into V made by two stubs of bottom shelf frame, aligning bottoms of post and frame. Insert pencil into holes in stubs and mark positions for holes on post. Remove post and drill ³⁄₃₂-in. pilot hole at each mark. Glue and screw frame into post.

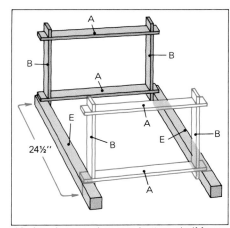

12. Attach second post to bottom shelf frame in same way, then make a mark 24½ in. from bottom of each attached post. Align top edge of top shelf frame with marks, and attach top frame as you attached bottom one. Turn assembly over and attach other two posts.

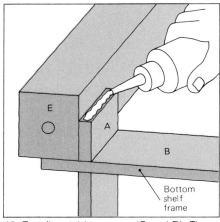

13. Test-fit outside runners (C and D). Those for unattached center shelf should not fit too snugly between posts, as shelf must be movable. Glue outside runners for center shelf to ends of inside runners. Glue other outside runners to both inside runners and posts.

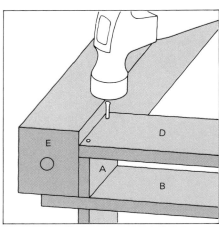

14. Drill two ¹⁄₁₆-in. clearance holes through the outside runners and into the ends of each of the inside runners. Drive 4d finishing nails into the holes and set their heads below the surface of the wood with a hammer and nail set. Fill all screw and nail holes with putty.

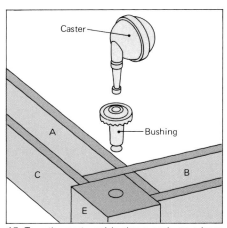

15. Turn the cart upside down and use a hammer to drive the bushings into the holes in the bottoms of the posts. Place the casters into the bushings and push them down until they are fully seated in the bushings. Turn the cart right side up again and let glue and putty dry.

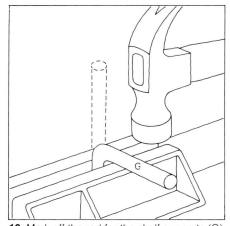

16. Mark off the rod for the shelf supports (G) into four 2-in. sections. Secure the rod in a vise and use a hacksaw to cut it at the marks. Clamp ½ in. of each piece of rod, in turn, into the vise and bend the remaining part of the rod with a hammer to form a 90° angle.

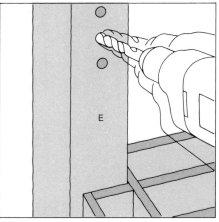

17. Place center shelf frame into position. Make pencil marks on posts through holes in frame. Lower frame, and drill ¼-in. holes into posts at marks, wriggling drill to enlarge holes. Drill series of evenly spaced holes in line with first holes for other shelf positions.

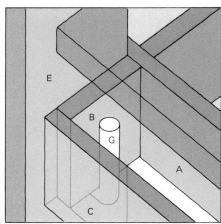

18. Finish wood and put in top and bottom glass shelves (F). Insert center shelf frame. Lower it and fit in glass, then raise shelf and push long ends of shelf supports (G) into holes in posts at desired level. Insert bent ends of shelf supports between shelf runners.

KITCHEN BASE CABINET

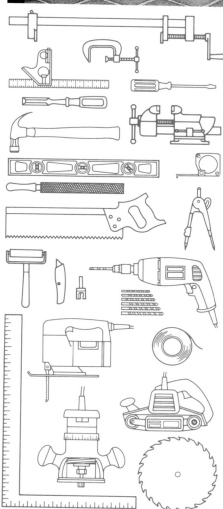

There are two sorts of kitchen cabinets: base cabinets, which sit on the floor, and wall cabinets. Base cabinets provide both storage space and work surfaces. They often house sinks, such large appliances as dishwashers, and sometimes smaller conveniences, such as slide-out shelves or cutting boards.

Construction: The basic cabinet is made of a plywood case (sides, floor, and back) and a counter top covered with plastic laminate. Hardwood trim defines

Parts list

Part	Name	Quantity	Thickness	Width	Length	Material
A	Right (wall) side	1	¾″	22½″	31″	Birch plywood
B	Left (outer) side	1	¾″	23¼″	35¼″	Cherry plywood
C	Divider	1	¾″	22¼″	31″	Birch plywood
D	Cabinet floor	1	¾″	22½″	46½″	Birch plywood
E	Shelf	1	¾″	8″	22⅞″	Birch plywood
F	Drawer side	6	½″	4½″	22″	Birch plywood
G	Drawer side	4	½″	8″	22″	Birch plywood
H	Drawer front and back	4	½″	8″	21″ ✳	Birch plywood
I	Drawer front and back	6	½″	4½″	21″ ✳	Birch plywood
J	Drawer bottom	2	¼″	20⅞″ ✳	21″ ✳	Birch plywood
K	Drawer bottom	3	¼″	20⅞″ ✳	21″ ✳	Birch plywood
L	Back	1	¼″	31¾″	46¾″	Birch plywood
M	Door panel	1	¼″	19⅝″	21⅞″	Cherry plywood
N	Drawer face	2	¹³⁄₁₆″	9⅜″	23″	4/4 cherry
O	Drawer face	3	¹³⁄₁₆″	5⅞″	23″	4/4 cherry
P	Kickplate	1	¹³⁄₁₆″	3½″	48″ ✳	4/4 cherry
Q	Trim	9	¹³⁄₁₆″	1¼″	†	4/4 cherry
R	Door stile	2	¹³⁄₁₆″	2″	25⅛″	4/4 cherry
S	Door rail	2	¹³⁄₁₆″	2″	20½″	4/4 cherry
T	Door panel clip	4	⅜″	¹³⁄₁₆″	⅞″	4/4 cherry
U	Plug	24	⅜″ dia.	—	¼″	4/4 cherry
V	Bracing strip	2	¾″	1½″	45½″	1 x 2 pine
W	Bracing strip	2	¾″	1½″	19½″	1 x 2 pine
X	Batting strip	1	½″	½″	72″ ✳	1 x 2 pine
Y	Batting strip	1	½″	½″	24½″ ✳	1 x 2 pine
Z	Platform beam	2	1½″	3½″	46¾″	2 x 4 fir
AA	Platform beam	2	1½″	3½″	16″	2 x 4 fir
BB	Counter top	1	¾″	25″ ✳	73″ ✳	Particle board
CC	Backsplash (optional)	1	¾″	18″ ✳	73″ ✳	Particle board

✳Measurement is approximate; cut to fit during construction.
†One piece 30¼″ long for divider; one 22⅞″ long for shelf; and two 22⅜″ long, two 32¼″ long, and three 45½″ long for cabinet face. Check measurements before cutting.

Tools and materials: Radial arm or table saw with dado head. Saber saw, backsaw. Router with straight veneer trimmer, bevel veneer cutter, arbor, and pilot, ⅜″ rabbeting bit, and 45° chamfer bit. Electric drill with set of twist bits, No. 10 plug cutter, and Nos. 8 and 10 combination pilot, clearance, and counterbore bits. Wide chisel, ³⁄₁₆″ chisel, fine laminate file. Hammer, screwdriver. Several 5′ pipe or bar clamps, several 6″ C-clamps, vise. Framing square, combination square, level, steel tape rule, compass, utility knife, pencil. Rubber-surfaced pressure roller or rolling pin. Belt sander with No. 120 sanding belt. Nos. 80, 100, 150, and 220 sandpaper. Masking tape, carpenter's glue, construction adhesive, contact cement. Lacquer thinner or equivalent solvent, tung oil, soft cloths. One 4′ x 8′ panel each of ¼″, ½″, and ¾″ birch-veneer lumber-core plywood and of ¾″ high-density particle board. One 2′ x 4′ panel each of ¼″ and ¾″ cherry-veneer lumber-core plywood, 48′ of 4/4 cherry, 20′ of 1 x 2 clear pine, and 11′ of 2 x 4 fir. Cedar shingles. Enough ¹⁄₁₆″ plastic laminate to cover surface and edges of counter top. Two flush-mounted pivot hinges, five pairs of 20″ metal drawer slides, one magnetic door catch, six small round drawer/door pulls. 2d, 3d, 4d, 8d, and 12d common nails, 4d and 6d finishing nails, ⅞″ No. 6 roundhead wood screws and the following flathead wood screws: ⅝″ No. 4, ½″ No. 6, 1″, 1½″, and 2″ No. 8, and 1¼″ No. 10.

the openings for the door and drawers and reinforces the case. The case is fastened to a platform that has been leveled with tapered shingles used as shims.

Do-it-yourselfers who build kitchen cabinets often order custom-made counter tops. It is a good idea to do so if you need a large or L-shaped top. Otherwise, you can make your own as shown and save a good deal of money.

Variations: The base cabinet described in this project has five drawers and a wood-paneled door that opens to reveal a shallow fixed shelf. You can easily rearrange, increase, or eliminate the elements to suit your needs. For example, you can do away with three drawers and make double doors, or you can make the shelf adjustable or change the wooden door panel to a glass one by following the directions in the next project (*Kitchen wall cabinet,* pp.120–123). You can also redesign the cabinet to house a sink.

The directions that follow are for a cabinet 3 feet high and 2 feet deep that will fit beneath the kitchen wall cabinet in the next project. The counter top is designed to cover not only the cabinet but a dishwasher or other appliance as well. You can build the base cabinet exactly as it is shown here if you wish, but you will have to adapt at least the length of the counter top to fit your own kitchen.

A base cabinet has two types of sides. One side (the right, as described in the directions that follow) reaches only to the cabinet floor, which rests on top of a platform. It should be placed against a wall or butt against another cabinet on a common platform. The other side (the left) reaches all the way to the kitchen floor, masking the platform. It should be placed against a large appliance or be left exposed. If it is exposed, use cherry-veneer plywood and fill the screw holes with cherry plugs as used on the face of the cabinet. If the left side of the cabinet will not be seen, use less-expensive birch plywood and leave out the plugs. If both sides of your cabinet will be visible, use the measurements, techniques, and materials given for the left (outer) side for both sides of your cabinet. If both sides butt against walls or other cabinets, use only the measurements, techniques, and materials shown for the right (wall) side.

You may want to install a backsplash, which will prevent liquids from running off the counter top and down the wall. Although a short backsplash is equal to the task, the 18-inch-high backsplash recommended is easier to keep clean and provides a level support for a wall cabinet. If you plan to install a wall cabinet above your base cabinet, a high backsplash will make the job easier.

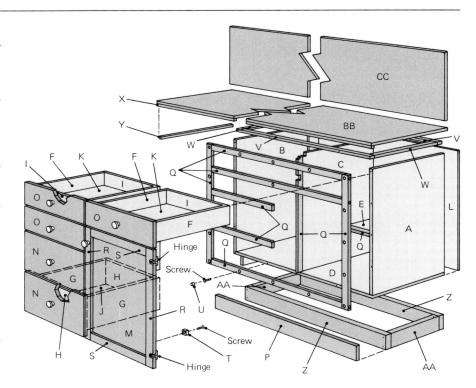

Patterns for dadoes, rabbets, and notches

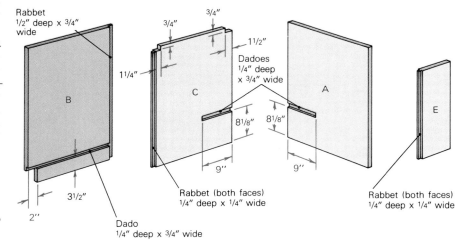

Variations

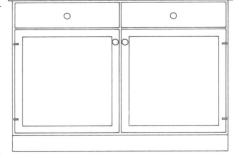

2 doors

8 drawers

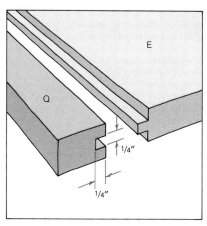

1. Cut parts A–E to sizes in chart on page 115. Then cut dadoes, rabbets, and notches shown in patterns on page 116. (To find directions, see *Index*, p.379.) Cut trim (Q) for divider (C) and shelf (E) and cut a ¼- × ¼-in. dado down center of back edge of each trim piece. Apply glue to dadoes, push trim onto tongues created by rabbets in divider and shelf. Clamp until dry. Belt-sand trim flush with divider and shelf.

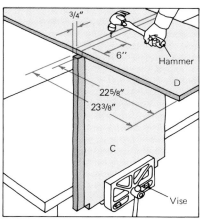

2. Draw lines across top of cabinet floor (D) 22⅝ and 23⅜ in. from left edge. Continue lines on bottom of floor. Clamp divider (C) upside down in vise and glue floor to its bottom edge so that divider meets floor between lines and divider trim extends ¾ in. beyond front of floor. Using lines on bottom of floor as guide, drive 4d common nails through floor into bottom of divider every 6 in. Keep connection squared while doing so.

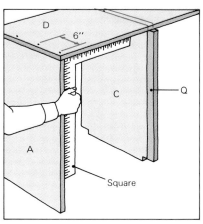

3. Apply glue to bottom edge of right cabinet side (A) and set cabinet floor (D) upside down on top of it so that all outer edges of the two pieces are flush. Drive 4d common nails through cabinet floor into bottom edge of side every 6 in., stopping to check for squareness after driving in each nail. It is of utmost importance that the cabinet be square, as the smooth operation of the drawers and door will depend upon it.

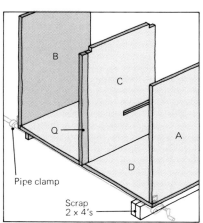

4. Turn assembly right side up. Apply glue to long horizontal dado in left cabinet side (B) and insert left edge of cabinet floor into it so that front edges of floor and side are flush. Clamp unit and prop up opposite side of cabinet floor with two scrap 2 x 4's set on edge so that cabinet will sit level until the glue dries.

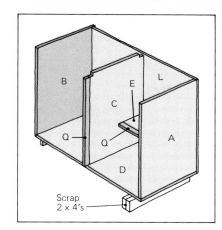

5. Slide shelf (E), with its trim facing the front, into dadoes in divider (C) and right side (A). Cut back (L) to size and glue it in place so that it sits in rabbet in left side and is flush with bottom of cabinet floor (D) and outer edge of right side. Tongue of left side will extend a bit beyond back. Secure back with 4d common nails.

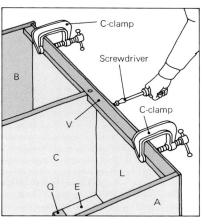

6. Check measurement and cut long bracing strips (V) to size. Clamp one strip along inside of back (L), fitting it into notch at top of divider (C) so that its ends touch insides of cabinet sides (A and B). Use No. 8 combination bit to drill five evenly spaced pilot holes through back into bracing strip. Also drill down through bracing strip into top of divider. Drive in 1½-in. No. 8 screws and remove clamps.

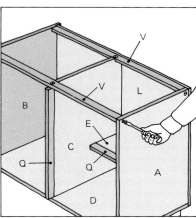

7. Fit other long bracing strip (V) into notch at front of divider so that its ends are flush with tops and fronts of cabinet sides. (Trim on divider will protrude ¾ in. at front.) Use No. 8 bit to drill through front bracing strip into divider and drive in a 1½-in. No. 8 screw. Drill one hole through each side into each end of each long bracing strip and drive 2-in. No. 8 screws into the holes.

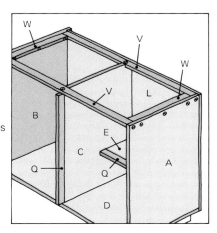

8. Check measurement and cut short bracing strips (W). Clamp one strip against inside of right cabinet side (A) with its ends butting long bracing strips (V). Use No. 8 combination bit to drill three holes through cabinet side into short bracing strip. Clamp other strip to left side. This time, drill pilot holes through strip into side. Attach strips with 2-in. No. 8 screws. Sand inside of cabinet with Nos. 80, 100, 150, and 220 paper.

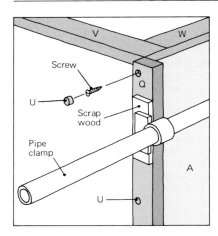

9. Cut trim (Q) for front edges of cabinet sides, and clamp trim flush with inner edges and tops of sides. Use No. 10 bit to drill pilot holes every 8 in. through trim into front edges of sides. Counterbore holes ¼ in. deep. Glue and screw trim in place. Remove clamps when glue is dry. Use No. 10 plug cutter to cut plugs (U) from cherry Glue plugs into screw holes, and chisel and sand their tops flush with trim.

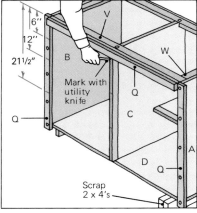

10. Mark trim on cabinet sides 6 in. from top. Mark trim on divider and left side 12 in. and 21½ in. from top. Cut a piece of trim and position it across cabinet front flush with tops of trim on sides. Use a knife to mark divider where trim crosses it. Cut and position a second piece of trim with top edge at 6-in. mark and a third piece with top edge flush with top of cabinet floor. Mark divider where these pieces cross it.

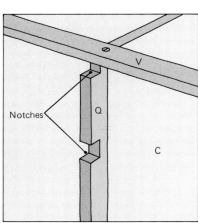

11. Use saber saw to cut ¹³⁄₁₆-in.-deep notches in divider trim where horizontal trim will hit it, using knife marks as guides. With No. 10 bit drill a deep hole through each piece of trim into divider. Glue and screw trim to divider. Drill pilot holes and glue and screw top trim to bracing and bottom trim to cabinet floor. Plug all holes. Use No. 8 bit to drill through trim on sides into ends of horizontal trim. Drive in 2-in. screws.

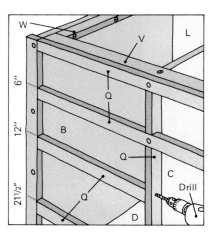

12. Cut two pieces of trim and position them between trim on divider and left cabinet side so that top of one piece is at 12-in. mark and top of other piece is at 21½-in. mark made in Step 10. Use No. 10 bit to drill holes through trim on divider and on left cabinet side into ends of short horizontal trim. Drive in No. 10 screws. Use router with chamfer bit to bevel any edges of trim that will face the door or a drawer.

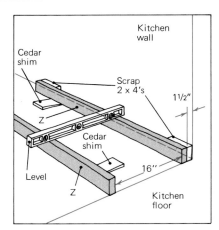

13. Cut platform beams (Z and AA) to size. Position one long beam parallel to wall and 1½ in. from it. Put two short 2 x 4 scraps into gap to maintain spacing and serve as nailing surfaces. Position other long beam parallel to first and 16 in. away. Level each beam, if necessary, by pushing a cedar shingle under it as far as needed. Level beams with each other in same way, being sure to keep each beam level along its length.

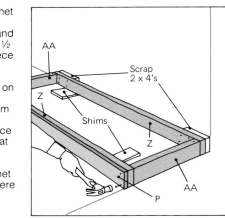

14. Position the short beams (AA) between ends of long ones. Level short beams, then level all beams with each other. Use 12d nails to toenail the 2 x 4 scraps to wall, face-nail inner long beam to scraps, toenail short beams to inner long beam, and face-nail outer long beam to short beams. Also toenail each piece to kitchen floor. Cut kickplate (P), and nail it flush with top of outside beam with 6d finishing nails every 10 in.

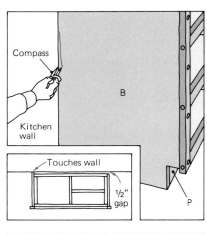

15. Position cabinet on platform with back edge of left side (B) touching wall and cabinet back (L) ½ in. from wall. Front of cabinet should be 2¾ in. from kickplate. If there are gaps between left side and wall, set a compass with its point and pencil as wide apart as widest gap. Draw point of compass down wall so that pencil will mark contours of wall on left side. Plane or sand away wood behind marks to make side fit flush with wall.

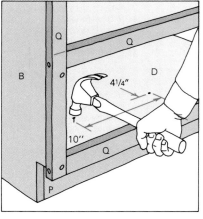

16. Drive 8d nails through cabinet floor into platform every 10 in. Using dimensions in chart on page 115 for parts F–K, make three small and two large drawers. To do so, cut drawer faces (N and O) to size, then follow the directions on page 183 for making drawers in platform bed, but skip Steps 16–18 and use 20-in. slides instead of the larger ones required for the bed. Sand and set aside drawers.

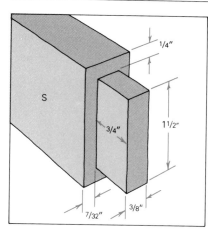

17. Cut door stiles (R) and rails (S) to size. Mark off both ends of both rails for tenons. Each tenon should be ¾ in. long, ⅜ in. thick, and 1½ in. wide, and have four shoulders. The long shoulders should be ⁷⁄₃₂ in. wide and the short shoulders should be ¼ in. wide as shown. Use table or radial arm saw with dado head to cut the tenons. To find directions for cutting the tenons (and the mortises in the next step), see *Index*, p.379.

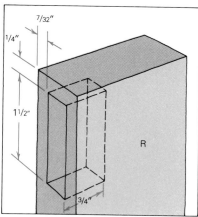

18. Draw cutting lines for mortises on door stiles (R) ¼ in. and 1¾ in. from each end of each stile and ⁷⁄₃₂ in. from each side edge. Test-fit door-rail tenons inside the lines. Cut blind mortises ¾ in. deep. Glue together, clamp, and square off door frame. When glue is dry, unclamp frame and make rabbets ⅜ in. wide and ¼ in. deep along inside perimeter of door frame to accept panel. Chisel corners of rabbets square.

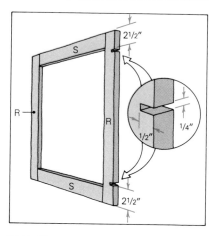

19. Sand door frame with Nos. 80, 100, 150, and 220 paper. Cut two slots on outside face of one door stile, each ¼ in. wide and ½ in. deep. Position one slot 2½ in. from top of stile and other slot 2½ in. from bottom. Set hinges into these slots and use pencil to mark positions of hinge screw holes. Drill pilot holes, and screw hinges to stile.

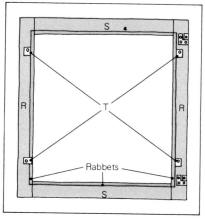

20. Cut door panel clips (T) and drill a ⅛-in. hole ³⁄₁₆ in. from one end of each. Sand clips and position them on inside of door frame so that when screwed on they can be turned one way to cover rabbets and the other to leave rabbets unobstructed. Mark clip holes on frame, drill ⁵⁄₆₄-in. pilot holes, and attach clips to frame with No. 6 roundhead screws, but leave screws loose enough that clips can be turned.

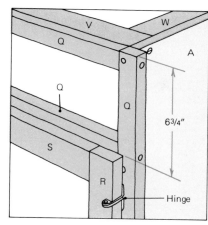

21. Cut door panel (M) to size and test its fit in frame. Trim it to fit if necessary, then sand it. Remove panel and hold frame against cabinet face with rabbets facing in and hinges at right. Top edge of frame should be 6¾ in. below top edge of cabinet. Level door frame, then mark cabinet with location of screw holes in hinges. Remove door frame and drill holes for hinge screws. Secure panel in frame, but do not install door yet.

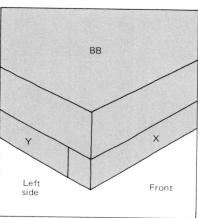

22. Cut counter top (BB) and batting strips (X and Y) to size. Attach batting strips to underside of counter top, flush with its front and side edges, with glue and 3d common nails. Cut plastic laminate for top surface and exposed edges of counter top, allowing for ¼-in. overhang on all sides. Apply laminate (see *Index*, p.379) to side edge, front edge, and then top surface of counter top. Trim each piece and bevel edges.

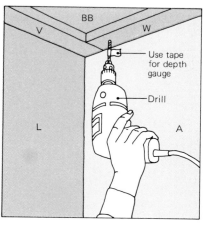

23. Position counter top on cabinet with its long batting strip overhanging cabinet front and its right side flush against wall. Use No. 8 bit to drill up through bracing (V and W) into counter top in each corner. (Do not drill deeper than 1⅛ in. or you may pierce top.) Drive in 1¼-in. screws. Sand exterior of cabinet, then rub down wood with tung oil. Attach drawer/door pulls; install door, door catch, and drawers.

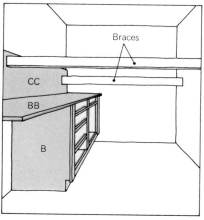

24. If you are installing a backsplash (CC), cut it to size and apply plastic laminate to edges that will show, then to front. Test-fit backsplash on wall. If there are gaps, trim as in Step 15. Glue backsplash to wall with construction adhesive. If possible, brace it with lumber wedged against opposite wall until adhesive dries. Drill pilot holes and drive 2-in. screws through bottom of the counter top into bottom of the backsplash.

KITCHEN WALL CABINET

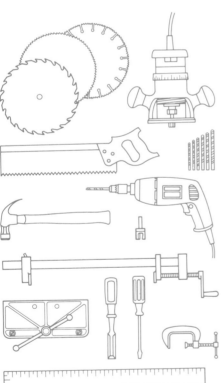

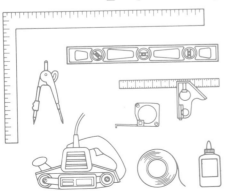

This kitchen wall cabinet was created as a companion piece to the base cabinet on pages 115–119 and shares many of its construction details. Like the base cabinet, it is made up of a plywood case with cherry door frames and trim. The wall cabinet is of standard height (30 inches) and depth (12 inches), and its 6-foot length is designed to fit over the counter top on the base cabinet.

Variations: You can build the cabinet exactly as shown or adapt its size or style to suit your needs. It may be installed over the base cabinet or over a refrigerator or stove. If it is installed over a refrigerator or other high object, its height must be reduced to make it fit. When changing dimensions, remember to take into consideration the thickness of the wood and the sizes of the dadoes and rabbets.

You can install the adjustable shelves described in this project or use permanent shelves like the one in the base cabinet. You can also make the cabinet with glass doors, as instructed, or substitute wood-paneled doors like the one in the base cabinet. If you prefer, you can build the cabinet without doors to create a hutch. The overall appearance of the kitchen can be greatly changed by choosing different woods and making doors of a different design, yet still following these basic building instructions.

Installation: Although the cabinet is relatively easy to build, installing it can be a bit tricky. First, you must locate the studs in your wall, mark the position of the cabinet on the wall, and prop up the cabinet securely in place. If your kitchen wall is slightly irregular, you will have to trim the back edges of the cabinet sides to fit the contours of the wall. Then you must attach shims made of cedar shingles between the slightly recessed cabinet back and the kitchen wall, and drive screws through the cabinet back, shims, and wall into the studs.

While building and installing the wall cabinet, be ruthless in your efforts to square and level it—even if your floor is not level. If you fail to do so, the doors may not close properly and any objects on the shelves may roll around.

If the top of the cabinet is close to the ceiling, you may want to add the optional scribes to fill the space between. If the cabinet fits snugly between two walls, use only a front scribe. If one or both sides of the cabinet are exposed, install scribes on the open sides as well.

Parts list

Part	Name	Quantity	Thickness	Width	Length	Material
A	Top	1	¾"	10½"	68¾"	Cherry plywood
B	Bottom	1	¾"	10½"	68¾"	Cherry plywood
C	Side	2	¾"	11¼"	27¾"	Cherry plywood
D	Divider	1	¾"	10½"	27¼"	Cherry plywood
E	Shelf	2	¾"	8⅝"	33⅝"	Cherry plywood
F	Back	1	¼"	27¾"	69¼"	Cherry plywood
G	Trim	7	¹³⁄₁₆"	1⅞"	✳	4/4 cherry
H	Door stile	8	¹³⁄₁₆"	2"	28"	4/4 cherry
I	Door rail	8	¹³⁄₁₆"	2"	15⁷⁄₁₆"	4/4 cherry
J	Door panel clip	16	⅜"	¹³⁄₁₆"	⅞"	4/4 cherry
K	Plug	32	⅜" dia.	—	¼"	4/4 cherry
L	Front scribe (optional)	1	¹³⁄₁₆"	To fit	72"	4/4 cherry
M	Side scribe (optional)	1–2	¹³⁄₁₆"	To fit	11¼"	4/4 cherry
N	Door panel	4	⅛"	14³⁄₁₆"†	24¾"†	Glass

✳ Two pieces 33⅝" long for shelves, two 68¼" long for top and bottom, two 30" long for sides, and one 26¼" long for divider. Check measurements before cutting.
† Measurement is approximate. Have glass cut by a glazier to fit the door frames exactly after frames are built.

Tools and materials: Radial arm or table saw with dado head. Backsaw. Router with ⅜" rabbeting bit and 45° chamfer bit. Electric drill with set of twist bits, No. 10 plug cutter, and Nos. 8 and 10 combination pilot, clearance, and counterbore bits. Wide chisel, ³⁄₁₆" chisel. Hammer, screwdriver, several 5' pipe or bar clamps, several 6" C-clamps, vise. Framing square, combination square, level, steel tape rule, compass, pencil. Belt sander with No. 120 sanding belt. Nos. 80, 100, 150, and 220 sandpaper. Magnetic stud finder (optional). Masking tape, carpenter's glue, tung oil, soft cloths. Scrap of ¾" pegboard. Glass, ¼" and ¾" cherry-veneer lumber-core plywood, and 4/4 cherry (see above). Cedar shingles. Eight flush-mounted pivot hinges, eight push-in shelf supports, four magnetic door catches, four small round door pulls. Supply of 4d common nails, 6d finishing nails, ⅞" No. 6 roundhead wood screws, 2½" No. 8 and 1¼" No. 10 flathead wood screws.

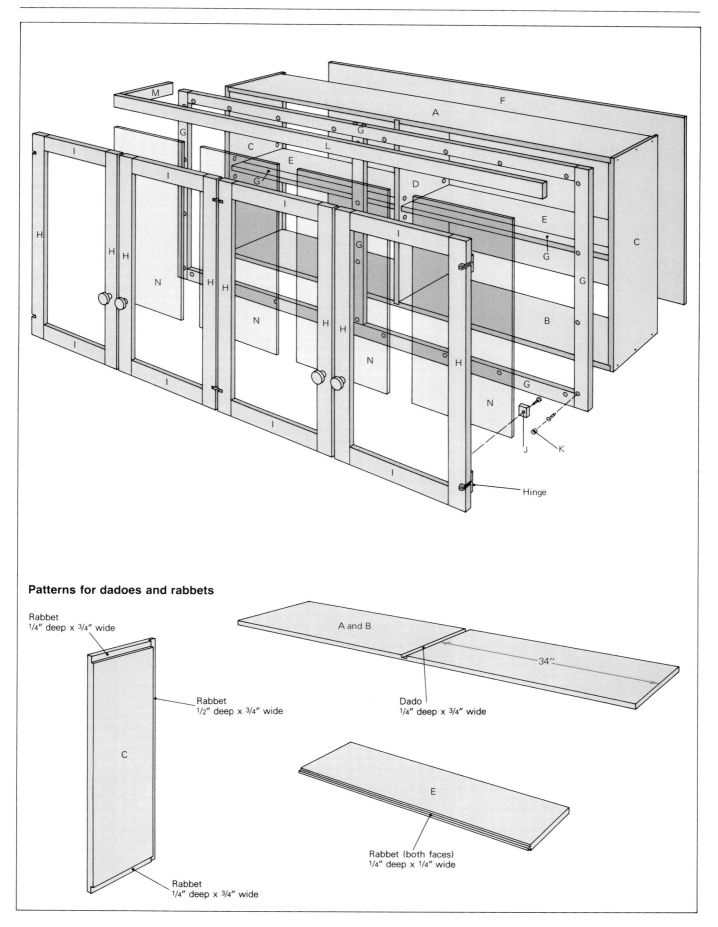

Patterns for dadoes and rabbets

Rabbet
1/4" deep x 3/4" wide

Rabbet
1/2" deep x 3/4" wide

Rabbet
1/4" deep x 3/4" wide

A and B

34"

Dado
1/4" deep x 3/4" wide

E

Rabbet (both faces)
1/4" deep x 1/4" wide

Building the cabinet

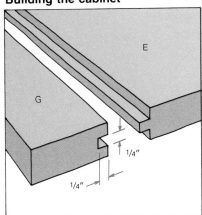

1. Cut all wooden parts except trim (G) and scribes (L and M) to sizes given in chart on page 120, then cut dadoes and rabbets shown in patterns on page 121. Next, cut trim for shelves and a ¼- x ¼-in. dado down one long edge of each piece of trim. Glue dadoes in shelf trim over tongues created by rabbets in front edges of shelves (E). Clamp until glue dries, then belt-sand trim flush with surfaces of shelves.

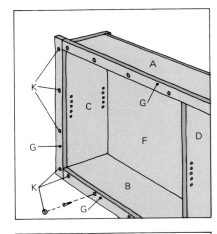

5. Add trim to top and bottom in same way, but double the number of screws. Top edge of bottom trim should be flush with top surface of bottom; bottom edge of top trim should be flush with underside of top. The trim on top, bottom, and sides will create a frame that protrudes all around front of cabinet. Use plug cutter bit to cut cherry plugs (K) for all holes. Glue plugs into holes and chisel and sand them flush.

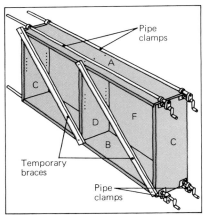

2. Cut a 3- x 27¾-in. scrap of ¼-in. pegboard with a row of holes in its center. Clamp it flush with front edge of divider (D). Put ¼-in. bit in drill and fix stop ⅝ in. from point. Drill through every other center hole in pegboard to make ⅜-in.-deep holes for shelf supports. Repeat at back edge and at both edges on other face of divider. Repeat for inner edges of sides (C), but clamp pegboard flush with rabbets at rear edges.

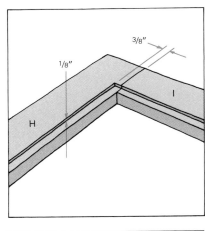

6. Center trim on front edge of divider, and use No. 10 bit to drill four pilot holes. Then glue and screw trim in place. Use No. 8 bit to drill two holes down through top trim into divider trim and two holes up through bottom trim into divider trim. Drive in No. 8 screws. Fill all holes with plugs. Use a router with a chamfer bit to bevel all inner edges of trim on front of cabinet.

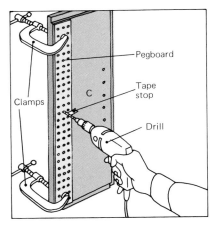

3. Glue top (A) and bottom (B) into rabbets in sides (C) and clamp unit. Slide in divider (D), then glue back (F) in place. Drive three 4d nails into each joint and nail back to top, sides, and bottom. Carefully square up cabinet and nail two scrap boards across front of unit to serve as temporary braces and hold cabinet square. When glue is dry, remove clamps and temporary braces.

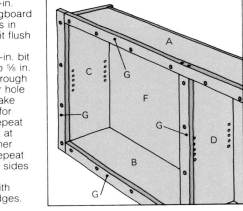

7. Cut tenons in door rails (I) and mortises in door stiles (H), then assemble to make four door frames. Rout rabbets along inside perimeters of frames, cut slots for hinges, attach hinges to frames, and attach door panel clips (J). To do all this, follow the directions for making the door for the kitchen base cabinet (p.119, Steps 17–20), but make the rabbets in the frames only ⅛ in. deep to accept the glass panels.

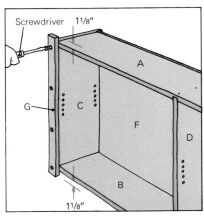

4. Check measurements and cut trim (G) for top, bottom, sides, and divider. Clamp trim pieces to sides so that they extend 1⅛ in. beyond top and bottom and their inner edges are flush with inner edges of sides. Use a No. 10 combination bit to drill four evenly spaced holes through each piece of trim into front edges of sides. Counterbore holes ¼ in. deep. Glue trim to sides and drive 1¼-in. No. 10 screws into holes.

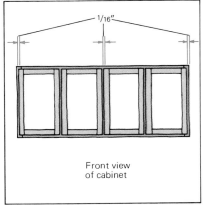

Front view of cabinet

8. Place cabinet on its back and position door frames over front of cabinet so that they are centered horizontally with the two center frames 1/16 in. apart and two outside frames 1/16 in. from side edges of cabinet. If frames are too wide, plane or sand them to fit. Trace hinge holes on cabinet, then drill pilot holes and screw on hinges. Check that door frames close flat against cabinet. Remove door frames and put them aside.

Installing the cabinet

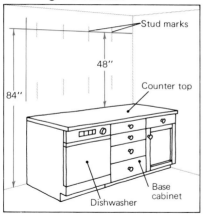

9. Use magnetic stud finder or other method (see *Index*, p.379) to locate studs in wall that will be covered by cabinet. Mark locations of studs on wall where marks will be visible when cabinet is in place. Carefully measure and draw a line across wall 84 in. above floor or 48 in. above top of base cabinet. Be sure the line is level. Also draw lines to show where cabinet sides will hit wall.

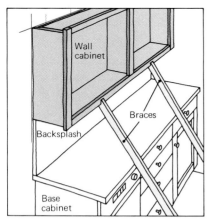

10. If you are installing your cabinet above a base cabinet that has an 18-in.-high backsplash, position wall cabinet directly on top of backsplash, then brace or prop up front of cabinet or have a helper hold cabinet in place. Check that top of cabinet meets the lines drawn in Step 9 and that it is perfectly plumb and level, then proceed to Step 12.

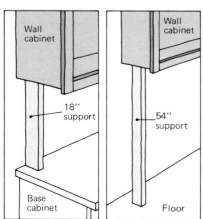

11. If you do not have an 18-in.-high backsplash to set wall cabinet on, put up a temporary support to hold cabinet in place. If you are installing cabinet over a standard (36-in.-high) base cabinet, support should be 18 in. high. If you are installing it above floor, support should be 54 in. high. Carefully level support, then position cabinet on it. Check that cabinet meets lines drawn in Step 9 and that it is level.

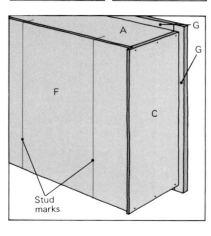

12. Check fit of back edges of cabinet sides against kitchen wall. If there are gaps, set a compass with its point and pencil as wide apart as widest gap. Draw point of compass down wall so that pencil marks contours of wall on cabinet sides. Take cabinet down and plane or sand away wood behind marks. Reposition cabinet and check fit. Mark cabinet top where studs cross it. Extend marks down cabinet back.

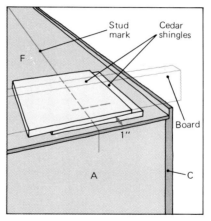

13. Center pairs of cedar shingles over all stud marks 1 in. from both top and bottom of back. Adjust shingles by pushing them together or pulling them apart until they are even with back edges of sides. Lay a straight board across back edges of sides. If shingles just touch board, tape shingles in place. Reposition cabinet on wall to be sure that shingles touch wall. Readjust shingles if necessary.

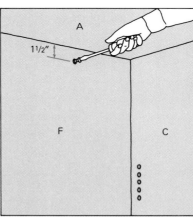

14. Sand cabinet with Nos. 80, 100, 150, and 220 paper, then rub down with tung oil. Reposition cabinet on wall and use a No. 8 combination bit to drill pilot holes through back and each pair of shingles into studs. Drill from inside of cabinet, in line with each stud mark, 1½ in. from top and 1½ in. from bottom. Drive No. 8 screws partway into holes. Check that cabinet is level and plumb, then tighten screws securely.

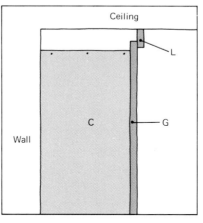

15. Remove temporary support if you used one. If you are adding scribes to cabinet, determine width of scribes by measuring distance from tops of doors to ceiling or soffit. Cut scribes and attach them with 6d finishing nails. Nail front scribe (L) to trim above doors. Nail side scribes (M), if any, to cabinet sides. Set nails, fill holes, then sand scribes and rub them down with tung oil.

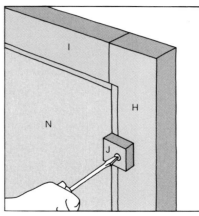

16. Press shelf supports into holes in cabinet sides and divider at desired heights and place shelves on them with trim facing forward. Have a glazier cut glass to fit door frames. Then install door frames by screwing hinges into pilot holes drilled in Step 8. Attach magnetic door catches and door pulls. Finally, put glass door panels (N) into door frames and lock them in place with door panel clips (J).

KITCHEN CUPBOARD

Few kitchen cupboards have enough shelves to hold all the groceries a family needs. This red oak cupboard does. It has 42 shelves and is 84 inches high, 30 inches wide, and 24 inches deep. There are shelves in the back, shelves in the two swing-out units, shelves in the doors, and two deep shelves at the top of the cupboard. You can reach the back shelves by opening the doors and then the swing-out units. You can reach the other shelves by simply opening the doors. The shelves vary in depth and are designed to hold cans, bottles, and packages in a wide range of sizes.

Directions for building the cupboard follow. When cutting the dadoes and rabbets, be sure to do the dadoes first in order to control any splintering that may occur. (To find detailed instructions for cutting dadoes, rabbets, mortises, and tenons, see the *Index*, p.379.)

Parts list

Part	Name	Quantity	Thickness	Width	Length	Material
A	Cupboard back	1	1/2"	29"	84"	Oak plywood
B	Cupboard side	2	3/4"	23³⁄₁₆"	84"	Oak plywood
C	Cupboard top and floor	2	3/4"	22³⁄₁₆"	29"	Oak plywood
D	Divider	1	3/4"	16"	55½"	Oak plywood
E	Upper shelf	2	3/4"	16"	28½"	Oak plywood
F	Back shelf	10	3/4"	6"	13⅞"	Oak plywood
G	Kickplate	1	3/4"	4¾"	29¾"	Oak plywood
H	Swing-out unit side	4	3/4"	6"	52¾"	Oak plywood
I	Swing-out unit top and bottom	4	3/4"	6"	10½"	Oak plywood
J	Swing-out unit back	2	3/4"	10½"	52¾"	Oak plywood
K	Swing-out shelf	10	3/4"	5¼"	10¼"	Oak plywood
L	Door	2	3/4"	13⅜"	77"	Oak plywood
M	Door unit side	4	3/4"	3⅝"	74¼"	Oak plywood
N	Door unit top and bottom	4	3/4"	3⅝"	10"	Oak plywood
O	Door shelf	20	3/4"	3⅝"	9¾"	Oak plywood
P	Face-frame stile	2	13⁄₁₆"	1¾"	80"	4/4 x 6 oak
Q	Face-frame rail	2	13⁄₁₆"	1¾"	28¼"	4/4 x 6 oak
R	Upper shelf support	4	13⁄₁₆"	3/4"	16"	4/4 x 6 oak
S	Back shelf support	20	13⁄₁₆"	3/4"	6"	4/4 x 6 oak
T	Door cleat	4	13⁄₁₆"	3/4"	75"	4/4 x 6 oak
U	Swing-out unit corner	4	7⁄₁₆"	7⁄₁₆"	7"	4/4 x 6 oak
V	Door unit corner	4	7⁄₁₆"	7⁄₁₆"	4½"	4/4 x 6 oak
W	Edging	27	1/4"	13⁄₁₆"	✳	4/4 x 6 oak
X	Upper shelf facing	2	1/4"	13⁄₁₆"	28½"	4/4 x 6 oak
Y	Back shelf facing	10	1/4"	13⁄₁₆"	13⅞"	4/4 x 6 oak
Z	Swing-out shelf facing	10	1⅛"	1¹⁄₁₆"	10¼"	5/4 x 6 oak
AA	Door shelf facing	20	1⅛"	1¹⁄₁₆"	9¾"	5/4 x 6 oak
BB	Long cupboard cleat	4	3/4"	3/4"	28½"	Pine
CC	Short cupboard cleat	4	3/4"	3/4"	21⁷⁄₁₆"	Pine

✳ Lengths vary. Measure and cut strips ¼" thick to fit all four edges of each door; the side edges of the kickplate; the front edge of the divider; the front edges of the swing-out unit sides, tops and bottoms; and the front edges of the door unit sides, tops, and bottoms.

Tools and materials: Table or radial arm saw with dado head. Backsaw. Electric drill with twist bits and countersink. Drill press with mortising attachment (optional). Block plane, wood chisel. Hammer, screwdriver. Vise, several 3' pipe or bar clamps, several cinch or band clamps. Framing square, steel tape rule, pencil. Belt sander with No. 120 sanding belt. Nos. 120, 150, and 220 sandpaper. Soft cloths, tack cloths. White glue, 1 qt. paste stain, 1 qt. paste varnish. Four 4' x 8' panels of ¾" red oak plywood, one 4' x 8' panel of ½" red oak plywood, three 10' lengths of 4/4 x 6 red oak, one 4' length of 5/4 x 6 red oak, 18' of ¾" x ¾" white pine. Two brass piano hinges 1½" x 72", 10 self-closing brass hinges. Two magnetic door catches, two brass door pulls. ⅜" No. 5 and 1½" No. 8 flathead wood screws, 3d finishing nails.

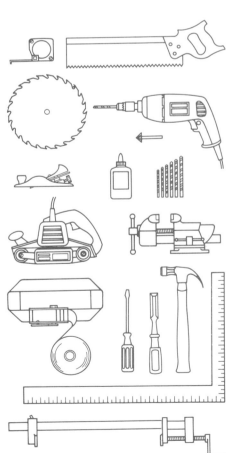

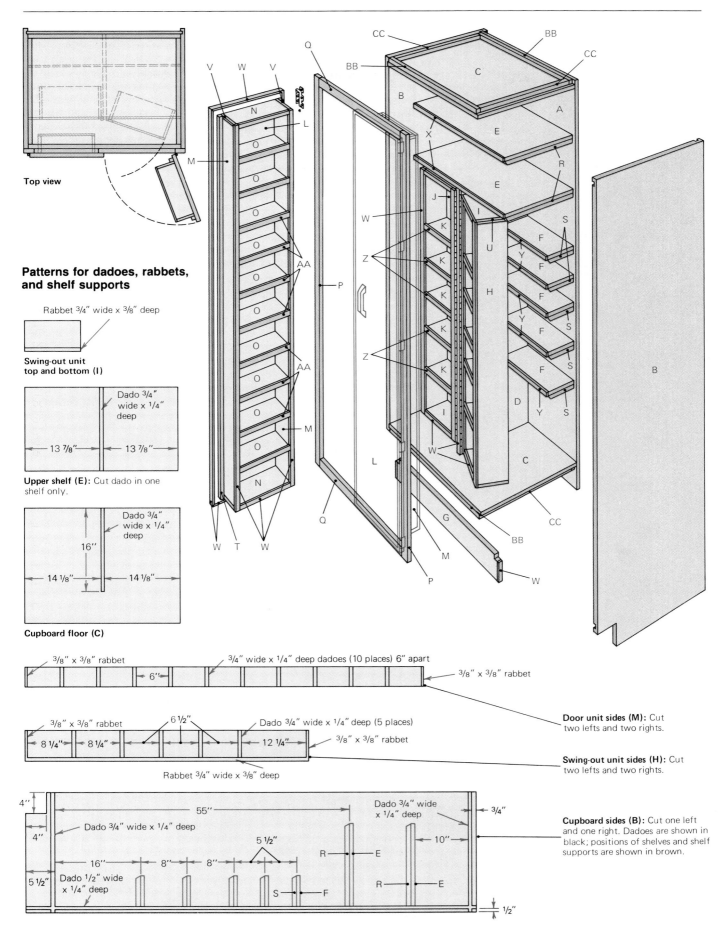

Top view

Patterns for dadoes, rabbets, and shelf supports

Rabbet ³/₄" wide × ³/₈" deep

Swing-out unit top and bottom (I)

Dado ³/₄" wide × ¹/₄" deep

13 ⁷/₈" | 13 ⁷/₈"

Upper shelf (E): Cut dado in one shelf only.

Dado ³/₄" wide × ¹/₄" deep

16"

14 ¹/₈" | 14 ¹/₈"

Cupboard floor (C)

³/₈" × ³/₈" rabbet

6"

³/₄" wide × ¹/₄" deep dadoes (10 places) 6" apart

³/₈" × ³/₈" rabbet

Door unit sides (M): Cut two lefts and two rights.

³/₈" × ³/₈" rabbet

8 ¹/₄" | 8 ¹/₄"

6 ¹/₂"

Dado ³/₄" wide × ¹/₄" deep (5 places)

12 ¹/₄"

³/₈" × ³/₈" rabbet

Rabbet ³/₄" wide × ³/₈" deep

Swing-out unit sides (H): Cut two lefts and two rights.

4"

55"

Dado ³/₄" wide × ¹/₄" deep

³/₄"

4"

Dado ³/₄" wide × ¹/₄" deep

5 ¹/₂"

R — E

16"

8"

8"

10"

5 ¹/₂"

Dado ¹/₂" wide × ¹/₄" deep

S — F

R — E

¹/₂"

Cupboard sides (B): Cut one left and one right. Dadoes are shown in black; positions of shelves and shelf supports are shown in brown.

125

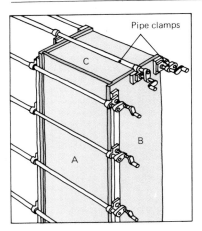

1. Cut all the parts to the sizes given in the chart on page 124. Cut one edge of each shelf support at a 30° angle. Cut the dadoes and then the rabbets according to the patterns on page 125. Glue and clamp together the cupboard back, sides, top, and floor (A, B, and C). Use a square to check the alignment of the parts as you tighten the clamps. Wipe off any excess glue.

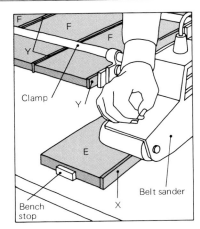

5. Glue shelf facing (X and Y) to the front edges of the upper and back shelves (E and F) with the facing overhanging slightly above and below. Glue edging (W) to the front edge of the divider in the same way. Clamp the edging to the divider. Clamp the shelves together edge to edge. When the glue is dry, use a belt sander with a No. 120 belt to sand the edging and facing flush with the sides of the divider and shelves.

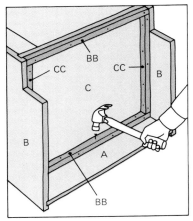

2. When the glue is dry, remove the clamps and drill 3/32-in. pilot holes through the cupboard back (A) and into the edges of the cupboard top and floor (C), using the dado patterns to help you find the places for the holes. Drive No. 8 screws into the pilot holes. Glue and nail the cupboard cleats (BB and CC) into place along the edges of the cupboard top and floor as shown. Wipe off any excess glue.

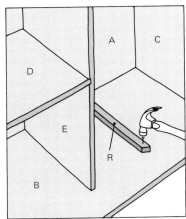

6. Position the divider and dadoed upper shelf in the cupboard. Temporarily nail each shelf support (R and S) inside the cupboard, positioning each over the mark made for it in Step 3. Drill 3/32-in. pilot holes through each support and into a cupboard side or the divider. Remove the divider, shelf, and supports. Sand the inside of the cupboard and all surfaces of the divider, shelf supports, and upper and back shelves with Nos. 120, 150, and 220 paper.

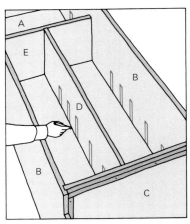

3. Dry-fit the divider (D) and the dadoed upper shelf (E) in the cupboard, fitting the bottom of the divider into the dado in the cupboard floor and fitting the dado in the shelf over the divider. Make sure that the shelf is straight, then trace the outlines of both the shelf and the divider onto the cupboard back. Following the pattern on page 125, mark locations of the shelf supports (R and S) on the cupboard sides and divider.

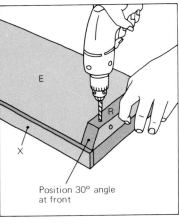

7. Position the shelf supports along the undersides of the shelves with the undrilled faces of the supports against the shelves. Drill two 3/32-in. pilot holes through each support and into its shelf. Drive No. 8 screws into the pilot holes to attach each support to its shelf. Glue the divider and upper and back shelves into place, then drive No. 8 screws into the pilot holes in the sides of the supports.

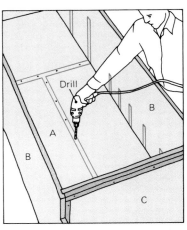

4. Remove the divider and shelf. Drill 3/32-in. pilot holes through the cupboard back between the lines marking the location of the divider and shelf. Clamp the divider and shelf back into place and drill through the pilot holes in the cupboard back into the edges of the divider and shelf. Remove the divider and shelf again.

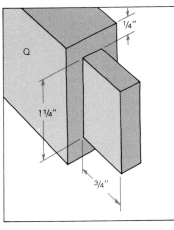

8. Mark off both ends of both face-frame rails (Q) for tenons. Each tenon should be 3/4 in. long and have four 1/4-in. shoulders. Use a table or radial arm saw with a dado head, or a backsaw and chisel, to cut the tenons. (To find directions for cutting tenons, see *Index*, p.379.)

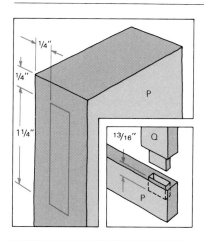

9. Draw cutting lines for mortises, as shown, on the ends of the face-frame stiles (P). Test-fit the tenons inside the lines. Adjust the lines as needed. Use a drill press with a mortising attachment or a drill and chisel to cut the mortises. Test-fit the mortises and tenons. The fit should be snug but not forced. Glue the face frame together and clamp it, making sure it is square. Let the glue dry, then glue and clamp the face frame to the front of the cupboard.

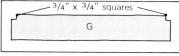

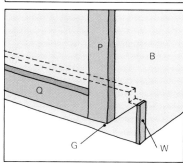

10. Cut ¾-in. squares from the top corners of the kickplate (G). Glue edging (W) to the side edges of the kickplate, and clamp the three pieces until the glue dries. Use a belt sander with a No. 120 belt to sand the edging flush with the sides of the kickplate. Glue the kickplate into place at the bottom of the cupboard. The edges of the kickplate will protrude about ⅛ in. on each side; sand them flush with the cupboard sides.

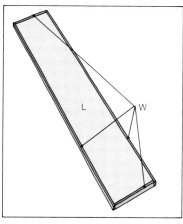

11. Add edging (W) to the four edges of each door (L). Sand the doors and the face frame, using Nos. 120, 150, and 220 paper, and remove the sawdust with a tack cloth. Following the directions on the container, use a soft cloth to apply paste stain to the face frame and to the insides of the cupboard and doors. Wipe off any excess stain. Let the stain dry. Wipe on paste varnish in the same way. There is no need to sand between staining and varnishing.

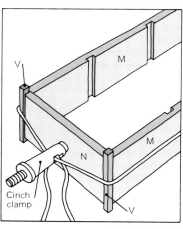

12. Glue together the sides, tops, and bottoms of each of the swing-out and door units (H and I and M and N). Clamp each unit, making sure it is square, and remove excess glue. (You can use a damp cloth placed on the blade of a screwdriver to reach excess glue in the corners.) When the glue is dry, remove the clamps and glue on the corners (U and V). Put cinch or band clamps around the units to hold all four corners at once until the glue is dry.

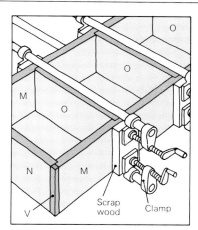

13. Saw off the protruding ends of the corners (U and V), and plane and sand their sides flush with the surfaces of the units. Glue the swing-out and door shelves (K and O) into the dadoes in the swing-out and door units. Clamp the shelves to the units until the glue dries. Glue edging (W) to the front edges of the swing-out and door units, and belt-sand the edging flush as you did in Step 5.

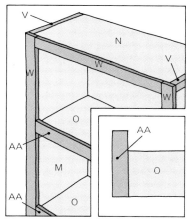

14. Glue the swing-out and door shelf facing (Z and AA) to the front edges of their shelves, with the bottom edges of the facing strips flush with the bottoms of the shelves. The lip formed on each shelf by the facing will keep goods from spilling out while the units are being swung open or closed. Glue and clamp the swing-out unit backs (J) into place. When the glue is dry, sand the swing-out and door units with Nos. 120, 150, and 220 paper.

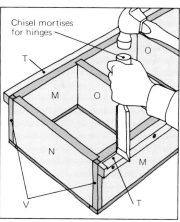

15. Position five self-closing hinges on each door (L); drill pilot holes for the hinge screws and screw on the hinges. Drill pilot holes and screw the other sides of the hinges to the face-frame stiles (P). Position door cleats (T) on the back edges of each door unit side (M); drill ³⁄₃₂-in. pilot holes, countersink the holes, and attach the cleats with No. 8 screws. Chisel shallow mortises in the cleats where the hinges will hit them.

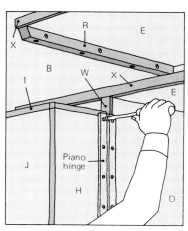

16. Position the door units, making sure that they clear the face frame. Drill ³⁄₃₂-in. pilot holes through the door cleats and into the doors; countersink the holes and drive in No. 8 screws. Attach the swing-out units to the front edges of the divider with the piano hinges; drill ⁵⁄₆₄-in. pilot holes and drive in No. 5 screws as shown. Sand, stain, and varnish the unfinished parts of the cupboard, then attach the magnetic door catches and the door pulls.

MOBILE WORK ISLAND

Few kitchens have enough storage or counter-top space, especially where it is most needed at a given time. This mobile work island, a kitchen cabinet on wheels, can help you solve such problems and will stand up to years of tough use.

First of all, it has a butcher-block top, which is an ideal chopping surface. In addition, the entire cabinet is easy to move from place to place, and its casters can be locked to freeze the cabinet in position. Moreover, the storage compartment in the back of the cabinet has adjustable shelves to accommodate kitchen utensils of various sizes.

Another handy feature is the garbage unit, which is concealed within the cabinet. It is screwed onto the inside of a self-closing door on the front of the cabinet. The garbage unit contains a roll of 30 plastic bags at the bottom and a frame that holds one bag at a time open to receive trash. You can remove a full bag by simply lifting it and tearing it away from the bag below, which will then be in place and ready for more garbage.

Construction: Directions for building the mobile work island follow, but explicit instructions for cutting dadoes and finishing the wood are not given. To find complete directions for these techniques, consult the *Index* on page 379.

Model numbers for the garbage-bag unit, casters, and pilasters (metal tracks for the shelf supports) are given below in the listing of tools and materials. The names and addresses of the manufacturers of these models can be found in the buying guide on page 377. If you prefer, you may substitute any equivalent product; but if you do, you may have to adjust some of the dimensions in the project.

Plastic laminate: The outside surfaces of the cabinet are covered with plastic laminate to make it easier to keep the cabinet clean. Directions for working with the laminate are given in the step-by-step instructions that follow, but there are a few points you should keep in mind. Always cut plastic laminate a bit larger than needed; it should overlap the wood you are covering about ⅛ inch on all sides. Do the edges of the wood first and trim the laminate flush with the wood, then proceed to the larger surfaces. When cutting laminate, clamp it down so that the teeth of the saw you are using will cut into the face of the laminate—position it face up for a handsaw, face down for a table saw. Also, make sure that as much of the surface of the laminate as possible is supported, or it may crack.

Parts list

Part	Name	Quantity	Thickness	Width	Length	Material
A	Top	1	1½"	25½"	25"	Butcher block
B	Side	2	¾"	22½"	33⅝"	Birch plywood
C	Front	1	¾"	24"	31⅛"	Birch plywood
D	Back	1	¾"	24"	33⅝"	Birch plywood
E	Bottom	1	¾"	22½"	23"	Birch plywood
F	Divider	1	¾"	23"	30⅛"	Birch plywood
G	Door	1	¾"	21"	22"	Birch plywood
H	False drawer	1	¾"	5⅛"	22"	Birch plywood
I	Shelf	2	¾"	11½"	22¼"	Birch plywood
J	Caster pad	2	¾"	5"	22½"	Birch plywood
K	Kickplate	1	¾"	3"	22½"	Birch plywood
L	Nailing strip	6	1⅛"	1⅛"	✷	¾ x ¾ pine

✷ Two 22½" long, two 10½" long, and two 9" long.

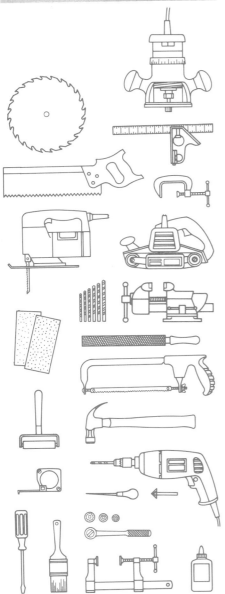

Tools and materials: Table saw or radial arm saw with dado head. Saber saw, backsaw, hacksaw. Router with straight veneer trimmer, bevel veneer cutter, arbor, and pilot (or with plastic laminate trimmer attachment and combination straight and bevel cutter bit). Electric drill with twist and countersink bits. Rubber-surfaced pressure roller or rolling pin. Three to seven 3' pipe or bar clamps, two 3" C-clamps. Hammer, awl, screwdriver, vise, fine laminate file, 7/16" socket wrench or adjustable wrench. Combination square, steel tape rule. Belt sander with No. 120 sanding belt (optional). Nos. 120, 150, and 220 sandpaper. White glue, contact cement, lacquer thinner or equivalent solvent. Wood stain, varnish, or other wood finish. Small and large paintbrushes. A 1½" x 25" x 27" butcher block, two ¾" x 4' x 8' panels of birch plywood, an 8' length of ¾ x ¾ pine, 12' of ¾" birch tape. Scrap wood, several lengths of scrap dowels. One 49" x 97" sheet of 1/32" plastic laminate. Rack-Sack garbage-bag unit. Four pilasters (Grant 120–ALB). Eight shelf supports (Grant 21B). Two locking casters (Bassick SBH13709). Two free casters (Bassick H13709). Two overlay self-closing door hinges, one door pull, one drawer pull. 1¼", 1½", and 1¾" No. 8 flathead wood screws. Sixteen ¼" lag bolts 1¼" long.

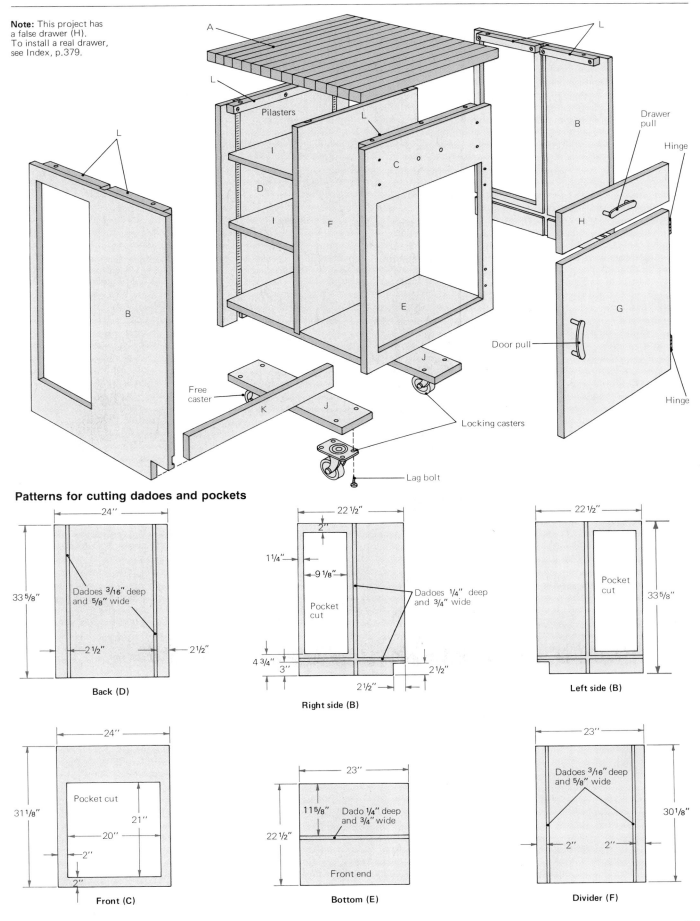

Note: This project has a false drawer (H). To install a real drawer, see Index, p.379.

A

L

L

Pilasters

L

I

D

I

F

B

C

Drawer pull

Hinge

H

Door pull

G

Hinge

B

E

J

Free caster

K

J

Locking casters

Lag bolt

Patterns for cutting dadoes and pockets

24"

33 5/8"

Dadoes 3/16" deep and 5/8" wide

2 1/2"

2 1/2"

Back (D)

22 1/2"

2"

1 1/4"

9 1/8"

Pocket cut

Dadoes 1/4" deep and 3/4" wide

4 3/4"

3"

2 1/2"

2 1/2"

Right side (B)

22 1/2"

Pocket cut

33 5/8"

Left side (B)

24"

31 1/8"

Pocket cut

21"

20"

2"

2"

Front (C)

23"

11 5/8"

Dado 1/4" deep and 3/4" wide

22 1/2"

Front end

Bottom (E)

23"

Dadoes 3/16" deep and 5/8" wide

30 1/8"

2"

2"

Divider (F)

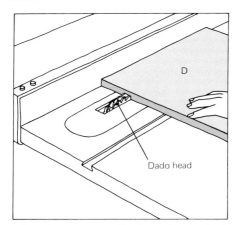

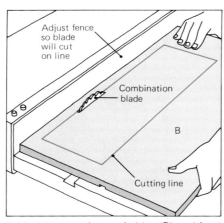

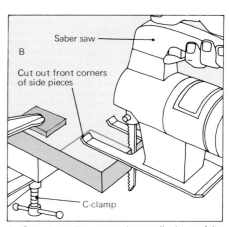

1. Cut all parts to specifications given in chart on page 128. Use a table saw with a dado head to cut dadoes into sides (B), back (D), bottom (E), and divider (F) as shown in dado patterns on page 129. Dadoes for pilasters are ³⁄₁₆ in. deep and ⁵⁄₈ in. wide. All others are ¼ in. deep and ¾ in. wide.

2. Mark inner surfaces of sides (B) and front (C) with cutting lines for the pocket cuts shown on page 129. Put combination blade in table saw and lower blade. Place front piece on saw table with cutting line facing up and just over saw blade. Turn on saw and gradually raise blade until it penetrates wood.

3. Cut along line, stopping well short of its ends. Finish cut with saber saw. Repeat for other lines of pocket. Cut pockets in sides in same way. Cut a 2½-in. square from lower front corner of each side (see patterns, p.129). Sand, stain, and varnish divider and insides of front, back, bottom, and sides.

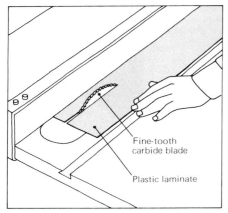

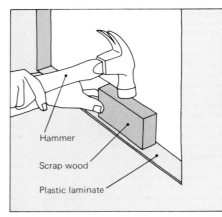

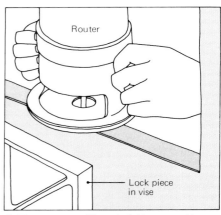

4. Cut plastic laminate to cover the edges of the openings in the sides and front. The laminate should overlap the edges of the wood by about ⅛ in. on all sides. To cut the laminate, use a table saw with a fine-tooth carbide blade, a saber saw with a metal cutting blade, a backsaw, or sheet metal snips.

5. Brush contact cement along back of laminate and on surfaces to be covered. Let cement dry until it is no longer sticky and a piece of brown paper may be moved over it without dragging. Position laminate over wood and carefully press it into place. Tap it down with hammer buffered with scrap wood.

6. Use a router with a straight veneer trimmer to cut protruding edges of laminate flush with wood. Move router in a counterclockwise direction while trimming. Use a belt sander with a No. 120 belt or No. 120 sandpaper to smooth edges of laminate. If you use a belt sander, belt should move from edge inward.

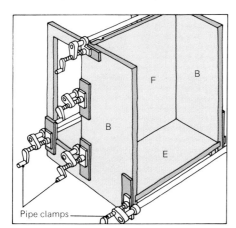

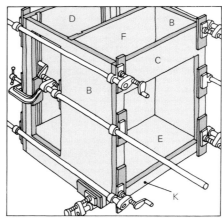

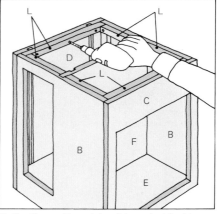

7. Test-fit the bottom (E) and divider (F) to the sides (B). If the fit is good, apply glue to the surfaces to be joined and clamp the assembly together with bar or pipe clamps. In order to protect the surfaces of the cabinet, put pieces of scrap wood between the cabinet and the jaws of the clamps. Let the glue dry.

8. Glue on the front (C), back (D), and kickplate (K), with the edges of the front and back protruding slightly (about the thickness of a paper matchbook cover) past the sides. Clamp the assembly and let the glue dry; then use a belt sander or No. 120 paper to sand the protruding edges flush with the sides.

9. Position nailing strips (L) against inside surfaces of sides (B), front (C), and back (D). They should fit snugly together around entire top perimeter of cabinet body. Drill ⁵⁄₆₄-in. pilot holes through nailing strips and into surfaces of sides, front, and back. Attach nailing strips with glue and 1½-in. No. 8 screws.

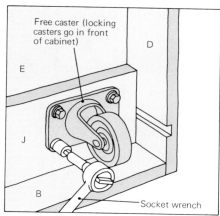

10. Glue and screw caster pads (J) to underside of bottom (E) with 1¼-in. No. 8 screws. (Drill ⁵⁄₆₄-in. pilot holes for screws.) Position casters on pads, allowing enough room for casters to swing freely. Attach the casters with lag bolts, using an awl to start the holes. Tighten lag bolts with a wrench.

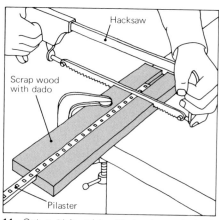

11. Cut a ⅝-in.-wide, ³⁄₁₆-in.-deep dado in piece of scrap wood. Using square and backsaw, make a ³⁄₁₆-in.-deep groove perpendicular to dado. Place each pilaster into dado and cut it to length through groove in scrap wood with a hacksaw. Nail pilasters into their dadoes in cabinet.

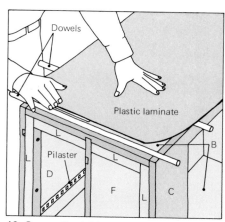

12. Cover all outside surfaces of cabinet with laminate as in Steps 4–5. When working with large surfaces, put several dowels on wood after cement is dry, and place laminate over dowels. Align laminate, then start pressing it down on one side and continue to opposite side, rolling out dowels as you go.

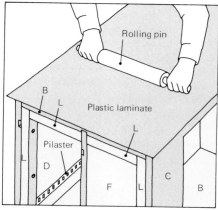

13. Use a special rubber-surfaced pressure roller (available from laminate suppliers) or a kitchen rolling pin to push large pieces of laminate firmly onto wood. (Tap edges as before with a hammer buffered with scrap wood.) Use a router with a straight veneer trimmer to cut plastic flush with wood (see Step 6).

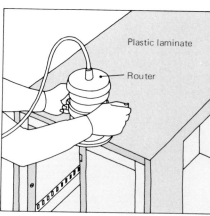

14. Use a router with a bevel veneer cutter to cut a slight bevel in the edges of the laminate. This will dress the joints and keep the edges from lifting. Smooth the beveled edges with a fine laminate file held at a slight angle. If joints are still not smooth to the touch, sand them slightly with No. 220 paper.

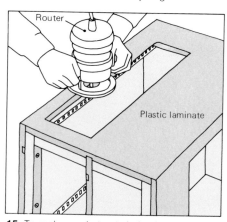

15. To make pocket cuts in laminate, first drill a hole large enough to accept blade of saber saw. Cut out laminate close to edges of wood, working in a clockwise direction. Use a router to trim laminate flush with wood and to bevel edges; then file edges smooth. Clean laminate with lacquer thinner.

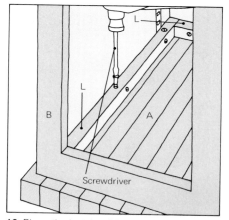

16. Place the butcher-block top (A) face down on a smooth, clean surface. Turn the cabinet body upside down and center it on the butcher block. Use a ⁵⁄₆₄-in. bit to drill pilot holes through the nailing strips (L) and ½ in. into the butcher block. Attach the butcher-block top with 1¾-in. No. 8 screws.

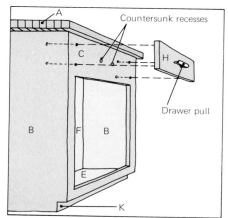

17. Cover edges and then fronts of door (G) and false drawer (H) with laminate. Trim laminate. Attach door and drawer pulls. Use drill with countersink to make small recesses in cabinet front where screwheads on drawer pull will hit; then attach drawer with 1¼-in. No. 8 screws driven in from inside of cabinet.

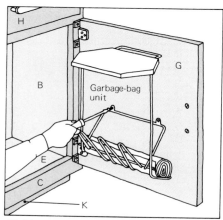

18. Mount door with overlay hinges and screw the garbage-bag unit to inside of door. Apply birch tape to edges of shelves (I) with contact cement, then sand edges smooth. Sand, stain, and varnish the shelves. Insert the shelf supports into the pilasters at desired levels and put in the shelves.

PENINSULA WORK CENTER

Homes with an open floor plan often employ a peninsula work center to divide the dining and kitchen areas. This unit features an eye-level cabinet that adds storage space without blocking light or creating a solid barrier between the two areas. The glass doors and shelf in the upper cabinet allow light to pass through.

The lower cabinets were made from inexpensive units bought at a store that sells unfinished furniture. The doors and drawers of the cabinet next to the wall open into the dining area; those of the other cabinet open into the kitchen. If you prefer, you can build custom cabinets from scratch (see *Index*, p.379), or you can modify the base of a standard kitchen cabinet. Saw away the bottom at the back to make a kickplate with the same dimensions as that on the front less ½ inch. Use lumber or plywood to frame the cutaway. Cover the back of the cabinet with ½-inch plywood and apply veneer tape to the exposed edges.

Kitchen cabinets generally come in standard lengths starting at 12 inches and increase in length by 3-inch increments. Decide how long you want the peninsula to be, divide that measurement by two, and choose the appropriate size cabinets.

The combined lengths of the two cabinets govern the length of the upper cabinet and its parts; so no lengthwise dimensions are given for them in the chart below.

The upper cabinet is 18 inches above the counter top and is positioned off-center, leaving more counter space on the kitchen side. An electric outlet box was installed by an electrician and placed between the vertical battens approximately 6 inches above the counter top. A hole to accommodate the box was cut in the outlet panel and the box cover screwed on over the hole. The outlet box should protrude 1½ inches from the wall in order to be flush with the panel.

Extra care should be taken to make sure that all parts are plumb (vertical) and level. It is important to measure precisely and recheck all measurements.

The peninsula work center is finished with white paint and contrasting brown trim. White laminate covers the counter top, the backsplash panel, and the outlet panel. Brown laminate accents the counter-top edges, and black or tan plastic track for the sliding glass doors contrasts with the white upper cabinet.

Be sure to have a helper on hand when it comes time to mount the upper cabinet.

Parts list

Part	Name	Quantity	Thickness	Width	Length	Material
A	Lower cabinet	2	✲	✲	✲	Ready-made
B	Counter top	1	¾″	✲	✲	Plywood
C	Vertical batten	2	¾″	1½″	28″	1 x 2 pine
D	Horizontal batten	4	¾″	1½″	5½″	1 x 2 pine
E	Backsplash panel	1	¾″	5″	✲	Plywood
F	Outlet panel	1	¾″	11½″	12½″	Plywood
G	Support post	1	1½″	3½″	✲	2 x 4 pine
H	Block	2	¾″	¾″	3″	Pine
I	Cabinet end	2	¾″	11½″	15½″	Plywood
J	Upper cabinet top and bottom	2	¾″	11½″	✲	Plywood
K	Cabinet divider	1	¾″	11½″	15″	Plywood
L	Center post	1	¾″	3½″	18½″	1 x 4 pine
M	Sliding glass door	8	¼″	✲	✲	Plate glass
N	Shelf	2	¼″	✲	✲	Plate glass

✲ To be determined during construction.

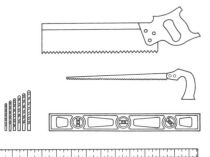

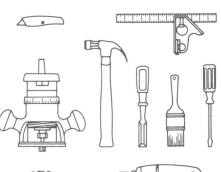

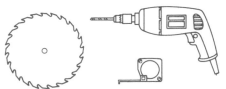

Tools and materials: Drill with twist bits. Table or circular saw with crosscut blade. Fine-tooth saw. Keyhole or saber saw. Router with flush-trim, bevel-trim, and ¾″ straight bits. Hammer, screwdriver, ½″ chisel. Combination square, straightedge, level, steel tape rule, pencil. Mat knife, single-edge razor blade, two paintbrushes. Nos. 80, 100, and 150 sandpaper. Contact cement. Duco cement, wood glue, veneer tape, wax paper. Dull-finish brown paint, glossy white paint. Wood and plate glass (see above), ½″ plywood for cabinet backs (optional, see text). Dowels (see Step 4).

Brown and white plastic laminate. Black or tan polystyrene plastic track for ¼″ bypassing doors, four plastic pin-type shelf supports. Electric outlet box. Four 1″ No. 8 flathead wood screws, thirty-two 1½″ No. 8 flathead wood screws, eight 1½″ No. 8 ovalhead wood screws and matching countersunk washers, plus other screws as needed. Toggle bolts or 3″ No. 10 flathead wood screws (or fiber anchors and self-tapping screws for masonry wall or floor). 2d and 16d nails.

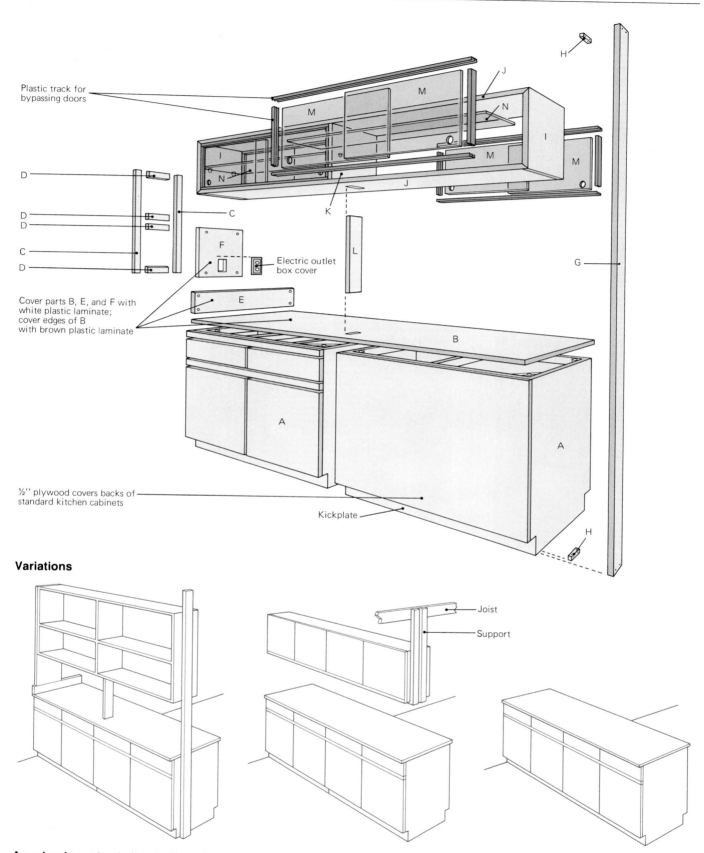

Plastic track for bypassing doors

H

J

M

N

I

D

D
D

C

D

C

F

Electric outlet box cover

Cover parts B, E, and F with white plastic laminate; cover edges of B with brown plastic laminate

E

K

L

G

B

½'' plywood covers backs of standard kitchen cabinets

A

A

Kickplate

H

Variations

Joist

Support

A peninsula can be designed with varying degrees of complexity. A simple counter with storage cabinets beneath it (right) is the easiest to build and offers a nearly unrestricted view. A unit with suspended cabinets (center) provides more storage but requires cutting through the ceiling and attaching a support to the joists. Space above the cabinets allows extra light to pass through. Overhead cabinets can also be supported by a column at the outer end, and the cabinets can be carried to ceiling height for extra storage (left). Doors can be glass or opaque.

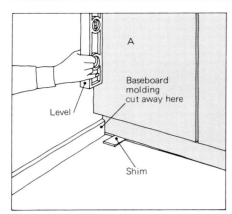

1. Use a backsaw to cut away baseboard molding, if any, where cabinet (A) will butt against the wall. With a level check that the wall surface is a true vertical. Slight high spots on the wall may be sanded flat; otherwise, use shims to fill the space. If the floor is not level, use shims to make the cabinets stand level. Locate studs by tapping the wall, by probing with a hammer and nail, or by using a stud finder.

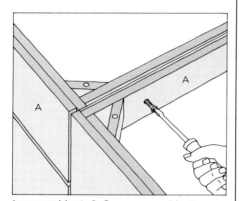

Lower cabinet: 2. Screw one cabinet through its frame into the wall and, if possible, into a stud; otherwise use wall fasteners. Bolt or screw through the frame of the second cabinet into the first; hardware for this should be ordered from the cabinet manufacturer when you buy the cabinet.

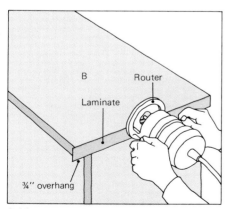

3. Measure the length and width of cabinet tops and cut a ¾-in. plywood counter top (B) the same length and 1½ in. wider. Use a fine-tooth saw to cut brown plastic laminate slightly oversize for the edges. Glue the laminate to the short edge first and trim to size with a router and flush-trim bit. Then laminate the long edges.

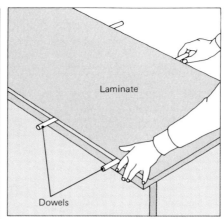

4. Cut white plastic laminate slightly oversize for the counter top. Coat the counter top and the underside of the laminate with contact cement. Allow the cement to dry to the touch. Place dowels across the counter top at 12- to 18-in. intervals. Rest the laminate on the dowels and position it accurately over the counter top. Press laminate in place at one end, then work toward the other, rolling the dowels ahead as you go. Trim the edges flush, then bevel edges with a bevel-trim bit.

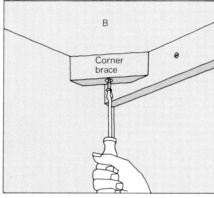

5. Glue and screw the counter top to the cabinet tops through the corner braces of the cabinets, allowing a ¾-in. overhang on each side of the cabinet.

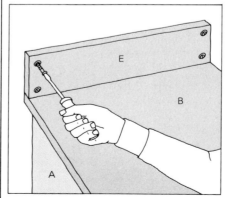

Wall panel: 6. Cover the side and top edges and front surface of the backsplash panel (E) with white laminate. Screw the panel to the wall flush with the counter top with 1½-in. No. 8 ovalhead screws and countersunk washers. Use plastic anchors to hold screws in wall.

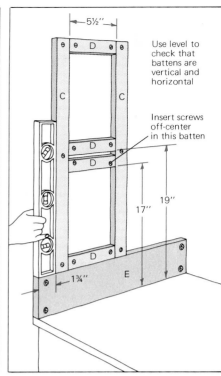

7. Sand all the battens (C and D) with Nos. 80 and 100 sandpaper. Paint the edges and the front surfaces with two coats of dull-finish brown paint.

8. Using appropriate wall fasteners, mount one vertical batten (C) 1¾ in. back from the edge of the counter top on the dining area side. The lower end of the batten should rest on top of the backsplash panel (E). Mount the other vertical batten 5½ in. from the first and parallel to it.

9. Mount the horizontal battens (D) between the vertical battens—one flush with the tops of the vertical battens, another resting on top of the backsplash panel, and the others 17 in. and 19 in. above the counter top.

10. Saw the outlet panel (F) to size. Outline the electric outlet box on back of panel and cut along outline with a keyhole or saber saw. Cover the panel's edges with white laminate. Mark the outline of the electric outlet box on the laminate for the panel's surface; cut out the opening and cement the laminate to the panel.

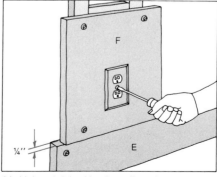

11. Using 1½-in. No. 8 ovalhead screws and countersunk washers, mount the outlet panel on the vertical battens. Place it ¼ in. above the backsplash panel and center it over the vertical battens. Screw the outlet cover to the box.

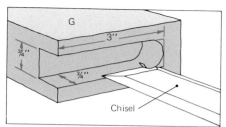

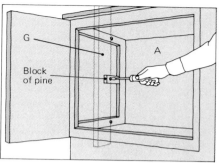

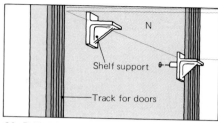

Support post: 12. Cut a 2 x 4 to length for the support post (G). Cut a slot mortise in both ends of the post, using a router and a ¾-in. straight bit set to cut ¾ in. deep. Make the mortise 3 in. long. Use a chisel to square the ends of the mortise. (The mortise will fit over wood blocks mounted on the ceiling and floor in Steps 14 and 15.)

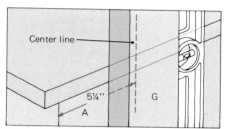

13. Mark a center line for the support post on the end of the lower cabinet (A) 5¼ in. from the edge of the cabinet that faces the dining area. Hold the post in place with its center line against this line. Use a level to make sure the support post is plumb in both directions. Have someone hold the 2 x 4 while you mark its position and the positions of the mortises on the ceiling and the floor. Remove the post, and complete the outline of the mortises.

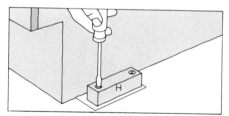

14. Cut two ¾-in. x ¾-in. x 3-in. blocks of pine (H). Mount one on the ceiling in the mortise outline with appropriate fasteners; countersink the heads of any screws used. Mount the other block on the floor with countersunk 1¾-in. No. 8 wood screws if the floor is wood. For a concrete floor drill holes with a masonry bit and insert fiber or lead anchors.

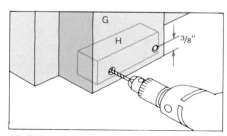

15. Drill ³⁄₁₆-in. holes into the support post (G) as shown—two holes ⅜ in. from the top and two ⅜ in. from the bottom. Countersink the holes. Slide the 2 x 4 into position. Drill pilot holes into the blocks, and drive 1-in. No. 8 screws into them.

16. Screw the end of the lower cabinet (A) to the support post in three places through the frame of the cabinet or through small blocks of pine that you mount on the inside of the cabinet wall. Use screws that will not pierce the outer surface of the support post.

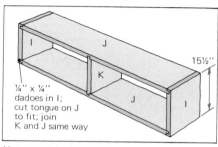

Upper cabinet: 17. Measure 18 in. above the counter top and mark that distance on vertical battens (C) and support post (G). Measure the span between them precisely; cut the cabinet top and bottom (J) 1 in. shorter. Cut the cabinet ends and divider (I and K). Make dadoes and rabbets (see *Index*, p.379) as shown above; dadoes are all ¼ in. x ¼ in. and rabbets are cut to fit. Glue and nail the cabinet and make sure it is square (see *Index*, p.379).

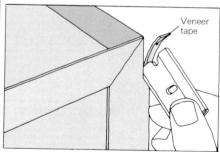

18. Apply veneer tape to all exposed plywood edges. Coat the tape and each edge with contact cement; let them dry to the touch. Give plywood edges a second application and let dry. Press the veneer tape into position and miter it at corners. On long edges cover half the length with wax paper while you lay the tape on the other half. Work from the center toward the end to press it down. Remove the wax paper and press down other half of tape. Trim any overhanging tape with a razor blade.

19. Install polystyrene plastic track for ¼-in. bypassing doors flush with outside faces of upper cabinet openings. Glue the track with Duco cement. Measure the openings for sliding glass doors, allowing for thickness of the track, and have eight doors (M) cut from ¼-in. plate glass. Have the edges polished and a ¾-in. hole cut for a fingerhold, or glue a clear plastic button to each door.

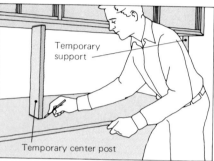

20. Drill ¼-in. holes in cabinet ends (I) and divider (K) for plastic pin-type shelf supports at midpoint of upper cabinet interiors. Have two glass shelves (N) cut from ¼-in. plate glass, allowing for the thickness of the shelf supports; have the edges polished. Do not install glass until the cabinet is in place.

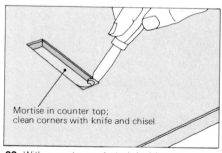

21. Cut an 18-in. length of 1 x 4 (make sure it is straight and square), and place it at the center where the center post (L) will go. (The actual center post is 18½ in. long.) Cut two more temporary supports of scrap wood, each 18 in. long. Place the upper cabinet on the supports and level cabinet. Mark outline of the 1 x 4 on the bottom of the cabinet and on the counter top.

22. With a router and straight bit cut mortises in these outlines ¼ in. deep. Square the ends of the mortises, using a chisel for the plywood and a knife for the laminate. Drill shank holes for 1½-in. No. 8 flathead screws in the ends of the upper cabinet; these holes will be used for fastening the cabinet to the battens and support post in the next step. Paint the center post brown and the cabinet white.

23. Spread glue evenly in the mortises and on the ends of the center post. Put the center post in the counter-top mortise. With someone helping, lower the cabinet into position on the center post. Use temporary supports to hold the cabinet while leveling it from front to back and from side to side. Drive screws through cabinet ends into the vertical battens (C), horizontal battens (D), and the support post (G).

24. Insert the plastic shelf supports in the predrilled holes, and place the glass shelves (N) on them. Insert the sliding glass doors (M) in the track.

BREAKFAST BAR

For many kitchens a breakfast bar is an attractive alternative to the conventional kitchen table. This tile-covered counter has no legs to trip the unwary, takes up less space than a table, and is better looking than the ubiquitous chrome and plastic-laminate table. If you mount the bar at a height of 32½ inches (midway between normal table and kitchen counter heights), you can use it as both a dining table and a work surface. It can accommodate as many as four diners.

The breakfast bar is simply a base cov-ered with ceramic tiles and framed with mahogany; it is mounted on brackets. To avoid cutting the tiles, arrange them on the base first, then cut the base to fit the tiles. A plain 4-inch tile is actually about 4⅜ inches square, and a decorative tile may be slightly smaller—about 4¼ inches square. The smaller tiles are centered between the larger ones, and the extra space filled with grout. When laying tiles, work in a well-ventilated area to avoid harmful fumes. The brackets were made to order by a welding shop.

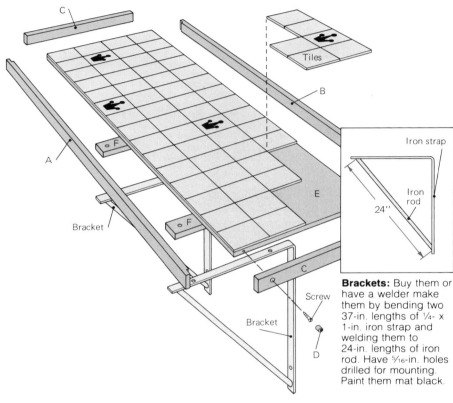

Tiles

Iron strap
Iron rod
24″

Brackets: Buy them or have a welder make them by bending two 37-in. lengths of ¼- x 1-in. iron strap and welding them to 24-in. lengths of iron rod. Have ⁵⁄₁₆-in. holes drilled for mounting. Paint them mat black.

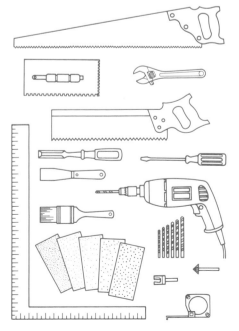

Parts list

Part	Name	Quantity	Thickness	Width	Length	Material
A	Frame front	1	¾″	1¾″	67½″ *	1 x 4 mahogany
B	Frame back	1	¾″	1¾″	67½″ *	1 x 4 mahogany
C	Frame end	2	¾″	1¾″	18″ *	1 x 4 mahogany
D	Plug	18	⅜″ dia.	—	¾″	1 x 4 mahogany
E	Base	1	¾″	17½″ *	66″ *	Construction-grade plywood
F	Support	2	¾″	3″	16″ *	Construction-grade plywood

* Measurement is approximate; cut to fit during construction.

Tools and materials: Power saw with dado head or backsaw and chisel. Handsaw. Electric drill with set of twist bits, countersink, and ⅜″ plug cutter. Wall-type saw-tooth trowel for spreading adhesive. putty knife. Framing square or combination square, level, steel tape rule, pencil Screwdriver, ⁷⁄₁₆″ wrench or adjustable wrench. Paintbrushes, stiff-bristled brush. Nos. 100, 150, and 220 sandpaper, 0000 steel wool. Commercial ceramic tile grout or mixture of 1 part lime and 5 parts portland cement. Waterproof ceramic tile adhesive, hide glue. Penetrating oil stain, polyurethane varnish, liquid floor wax. paste wax. Sponge, soft cloth. One 8′ length of 1 x 4 mahogany, one 4′ x 8′ panel of ¾″ construction-grade plywood. Sixty or so 4″ ceramic tiles with spacer lugs. Two iron brackets. Four ¼″ lag bolts 3″ long. Twenty-four 1½″ No. 8 flathead wood screws. four 1″ No. 10 roundhead wood screws.

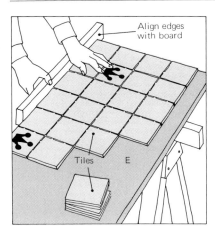

Align edges with board

Tiles

E

1. Cut the base (E) 19½ in. wide and 68 in. long (2 in. wider and longer than the finished base). Sand the bottom of the base with three grades of paper. Lay the tiles out on the oversize base to create the tile pattern desired. Push against the edges of the tiles with a straight board to make sure the tiles are aligned. Draw a line around the laid-out tiles, remove the tiles, and cut the base to size.

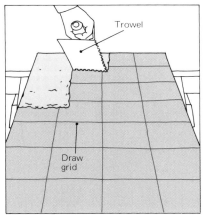

Trowel

Draw grid

2. To be safe, draw lines across the width and the length of the base to form a grid that shows where each tile should be placed. Use a putty knife to apply a gob of tile adhesive to one end on the top of the base. Use a trowel to spread out the adhesive evenly. Put down only as much adhesive as you can cover with tiles in 20 min. or less.

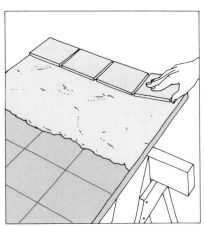

3. Put the first tile down in one corner on the adhesive, making sure that the edges of the tile are flush with the edges of the base. Press the tile down firmly. Put another tile down next to the first one. Continue putting down adhesive and tiles along the same edge. Make sure that all the tiles are flush with the edge of the base.

Putty knife

4. Put down the remaining rows of tiles in the same way, adding more adhesive to the base as needed. Keep the rows of tiles straight. The spacer lugs on the sides of the tiles will keep them the proper distance apart. Add decorative tiles after the surrounding tiles have been put down. Center the decorative tiles in the spaces left for them by pushing them in place with a putty knife. Let the adhesive cure overnight.

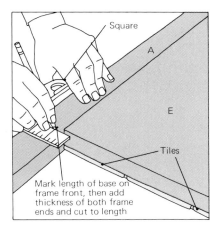

Square

A

E

Tiles

Mark length of base on frame front, then add thickness of both frame ends and cut to length

5. Rip the mahogany board down the middle to make two slats about 1¾ in. wide. Cut the frame front (A), back (B), and ends (C) to length from these slats. The frame ends should be ½ in. longer than the base (E) is wide. The frame front and the frame back should be the same length as the base plus the combined thicknesses of the frame ends.

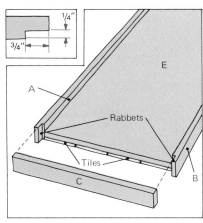

1/4"

3/4"

A

E

Rabbets

Tiles

C

B

6. Use a power saw with a dado head or a backsaw and chisel to cut rabbets in the ends of the frame front and back. These rabbets should be ¼ in. deep and as wide as the frame ends (C) are thick. (To find directions for cutting rabbets, see the *Index*, p.379.) Turn the base (E) upside down and position the frame members around the base, fitting the frame ends into the rabbets in the frame front and back.

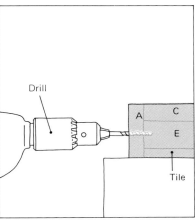

Drill

A C

E

Tile

7. Drill a ³⁄₃₂-in. pilot hole through each end of the frame front and back into each frame end. The holes should be centered on the edges of the plywood base. Drill five more pilot holes through the frame front and five through the frame back into the base. Then drill two through each frame end into the base. Use a ³⁄₈-in. bit to counterbore all these pilot holes about ³⁄₈ in. deep.

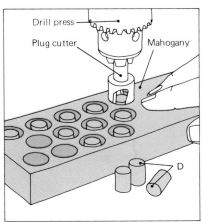

Drill press

Plug cutter

Mahogany

D

8. Apply a thin coat of hide glue to the frame members and attach them to the base. Try not to get glue on the outside of the wood; it will create stains that are hard to remove. Drive No. 8 screws as far as you can into the pilot holes. Use a plug cutter to cut mahogany plugs (D). Run the cutter to its maximum depth, then back it out. Use a screwdriver to break the plugs loose from the mahogany stock.

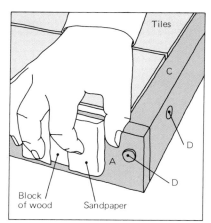

Block of wood | Sandpaper

Tiles | C | D | A | D

9. Apply a thin coat of hide glue to the lower halves of the plugs and push them into the screw holes in the frame, lining up the grain of the plugs with the grain of the frame. Let the glue dry, then wrap a piece of No. 220 sandpaper around a block of wood and sand the ends of the plugs flush with the frame. Sand the entire frame by hand with No. 220 paper, and round off the sharp edges of the frame as you sand.

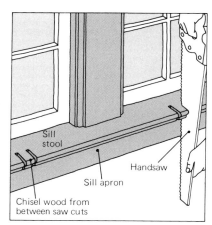

Sill stool | Handsaw | Sill apron | Chisel wood from between saw cuts

13. If you are mounting your breakfast bar on a windowsill, the mounting procedure will be a bit more complex. First, use a saw and chisel to make cutouts in the stool of the sill the width of the brackets. These cutouts will allow the legs of the brackets to pass through the stool. Drill ¹³/₆₄-in. pilot holes for the brackets into the sill apron, then proceed to the next step.

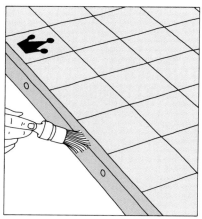

10. Brush a thin coat of stain on the frame. If you want a light stain, wipe it off in about 10 min.; if you want a dark stain, leave it on. Let the stain dry for 24 hr. or more, then brush on a coat of polyurethane varnish thinned 20%. When the varnish is dry, sand the frame with No. 220 paper and add a second coat of varnish. Let the second coat dry, then apply paste wax with 0000 steel wool. Buff with a soft cloth.

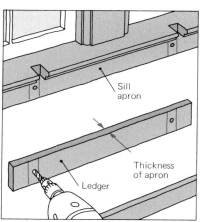

Sill apron | Thickness of apron | Ledger

14. Because of the apron, the bottoms of the brackets will not be flush with the wall. Cut a ledger as thick as the apron and a few inches longer than the distance between the brackets. Position the ledger where the bottom holes in the brackets will fall. Drill pilot holes through the ledger and into the studs. Drive lag bolts through the brackets and ledger into studs.

11. Mix the grout with water to the consistency of thick cream. Work it into the seams between the tiles with your fingers or a pencil eraser, making sure that the seams are fully filled. While the grout is still damp, wipe off the excess with a damp sponge. Let the grout dry for at least 4 hr. Add a second coat, let it dry, then smooth it down with a stiff-bristled brush. Clean the tiles and give them a coat of liquid wax.

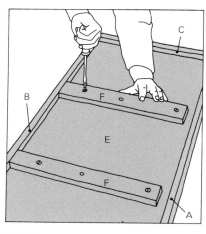

C | B | F | E | F | A

15. Cut the two supports (F) to fit under the bar. Position the bar on the brackets and mark the underside of the bar where the brackets hit it. Remove the bar and place the supports over the marks. Drill three ³/₃₂-in. pilot holes through each support and into the base, avoiding the spots where the holes in the brackets will fall. Countersink the holes. Attach the supports with hide glue and No. 8 flathead wood screws.

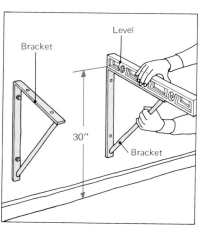

Bracket | Level | 30" | Bracket

12. To locate the wall studs to which you will fasten the brackets, tap the wall until you hear a solid rather then a hollow sound, or drill small holes in the wall and probe with a drill bit. (Use the studs closest to the center of the bar.) Position and level each bracket, then drill ¹³/₁₆-in. pilot holes through the holes in the brackets into the wall. Attach the brackets to the studs with lag bolts.

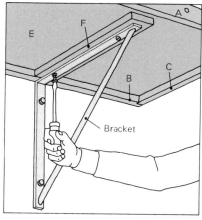

E | F | A | B | C | Bracket

16. Position the bar on the brackets so that the supports are centered on the bracket arms. Mark the locations of the holes in the bracket arms on the supports. Remove the bar and drill ³/₃₂-in. pilot holes at the marks. Reposition the bar and fasten it to the brackets with No. 10 roundhead wood screws.

CAFE TABLE AND CHAIRS

A small table and chairs can have a number of practical uses around the house. One or more sets can be used in the recreation room or on the patio. You can seat guests in pairs, or you can use the chairs for extra seating in the dining room and the table as an extra server.

The cafe table is 30 inches high and has a round top that is 29 inches across. The raw edge of the two-layered table top is finished with birch veneer tape. The chairs are 33 inches high at the back and 16¼ inches wide. Each chair has two back posts, two front legs, a number of rails, and a slat seat. The directions that follow tell you how to make one chair. If you are making two, double the quantities given in the chart below.

Construction: The basic construction is relatively simple, but some of the parts are curved or subtly beveled. Because the table top is round, you must cut it carefully with a saber saw. Cut the table braces and feet and the chair back posts, front legs, and side leg rails in two stages. First, cut them to the sizes given in the chart, then use a band saw or saber saw to cut them according to the patterns on pages 140 and 142.

Cut the table support post to the length given in the chart, then use a band saw or Surform tool to cut curves into its corners as shown in the pattern on page 140. To hold the post in place while cutting the curves, saw a deep 90° V-shaped channel in a long piece of scrap wood, and place the post in the channel with the corner to be cut facing up. To cut the rabbets in the post, use a radial arm or table saw with a dado head, a circular saw, or a backsaw and chisel.

Directions for joining the parts with screws follow; if you wish, you can join the parts with dowels instead. (To find directions for joining with dowels or more detailed instructions for cutting rabbets, see the *Index,* p.379.)

Finishing: When you are done building the table and chairs, sand them thoroughly with Nos. 100, 150, and 220 paper. Using a soft cloth, apply several coats of tung oil to the sanded pieces. Rub the wood down lightly with 000 steel wool between coats.

Parts list for table

Part	Name	Quantity	Thickness	Width	Length	Material
A	Table-top base	1	¾″	31½″ ✲	31½″ ✲	Plywood
B	Table-top slat	14	¾″	2¼″	31½″ ✲	Red oak flooring
C	Support post	1	3½″	3½″	28½″	4 x 4 poplar post
D	Brace	4	1⅛″	3″ ✲	11″ ✲	5/4 x 8 poplar
E	Foot	4	1⅛″	4″ ✲	13½″ ✲	5/4 x 8 poplar
F	Edging	1	—	2″ ✲	92″ ✲	Birch veneer tape
G	Plug	32	⅜″ dia.	—	¼″	Hardwood dowel

Parts list for each chair

Part	Name	Quantity	Thickness	Width	Length	Material
A	Back post	2	1⅛″	3¾″ ✲	33″	5/4 x 8 poplar
B	Front leg	2	1⅛″	3″ ✲	14″	5/4 x 8 poplar
C	Front and back leg rail	2	1⅛″	1⅝″	14″	5/4 x 8 poplar
D	Side leg rail	2	1⅛″	1⅝″	13″ ✲	5/4 x 8 poplar
E	Front and back seat rail	2	1⅛″	1⅜″	14″	5/4 x 8 poplar
F	Side seat rail	2	1⅛″	2½″	14″	5/4 x 8 poplar
G	Seat support	2	1⅛″	1⅛″	14″	5/4 x 8 poplar
H	Back rail	2	1⅛″	2¼″	14″	5/4 x 8 poplar
I	Inner seat slat	7	1⅛″	1¾″	16″	5/4 x 8 poplar
J	Outer seat slat	2	1⅛″	⅞″	16″	5/4 x 8 poplar
K	Plug	40	⅜″ dia.	—	¼″	Hardwood dowel

✲ Cut to this size (or larger) and then cut further according to pattern or directions.

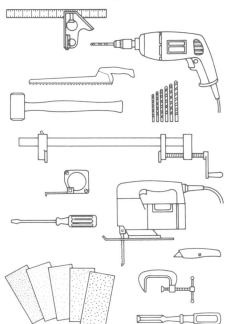

Tools and materials: Table or radial arm saw with dado head, or circular saw, or backsaw. Band saw or a Surform tool. Saber saw with edge guide. Electric drill with set of twist bits. Mallet or hammer, wood chisel, screwdriver. Framing or combination square, steel tape rule, pencil. Utility knife or single-edge razor blade, pushpins. Several 2′ pipe or bar clamps, several 6″ C-clamps, one band clamp. Nos. 80, 100, 150, and 220 sandpaper. 000 steel wool. Carpenter's glue, clear tung oil, soft cloth. Two 10-sq.-ft. bundles of oak flooring for table. Plywood, poplar, dowels, veneer tape (see above). 1″, 2″, 3″, and 3½″ No. 8 self-tapping screws.

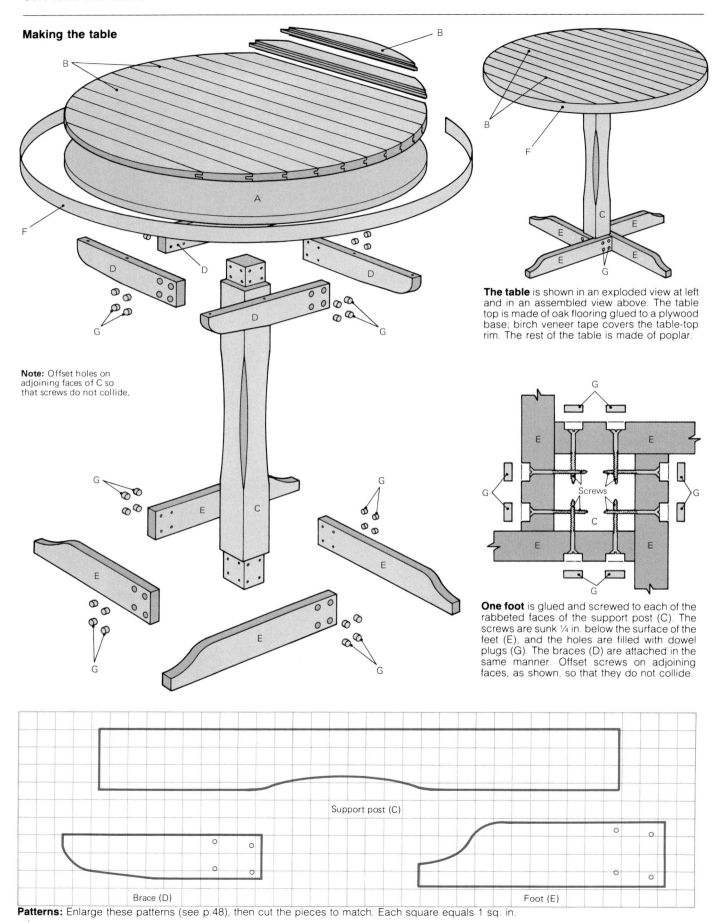

Cafe table and chairs

Making the table

Note: Offset holes on adjoining faces of C so that screws do not collide.

The table is shown in an exploded view at left and in an assembled view above. The table top is made of oak flooring glued to a plywood base; birch veneer tape covers the table-top rim. The rest of the table is made of poplar.

One foot is glued and screwed to each of the rabbeted faces of the support post (C). The screws are sunk ¼ in. below the surface of the feet (E), and the holes are filled with dowel plugs (G). The braces (D) are attached in the same manner. Offset screws on adjoining faces, as shown, so that they do not collide.

Screws

Support post (C)

Brace (D)

Foot (E)

Patterns: Enlarge these patterns (see p.48), then cut the pieces to match. Each square equals 1 sq. in.

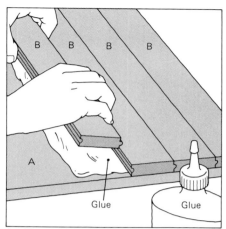

1. Glue the table-top slats (B), with their tongues and grooves together, to the table-top base (A). If any slat buckles, drill 3/32-in. pilot holes through the underside of the plywood base and into the slat; then drive in 1-in. screws. Weight the table top down for 24 hr.

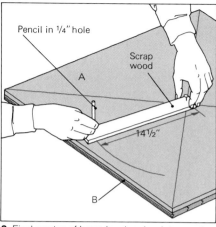

2. Find center of base by drawing intersecting diagonal lines on the 31½-in. square. Drill a ¼-in. hole through one end of a scrap of wood. Drive a nail through the scrap into center of base 14½ in. from hole. Put a pencil in hole and draw a circle.

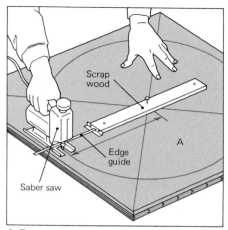

3. Remove the scrap wood and screw it to the edge guide of the saber saw. Nail the scrap wood back into place so that the saw blade is on the drawn circle. Cut out the table top along the drawn circle. Sand the table top with Nos. 100, 150, and 220 paper.

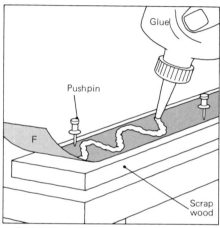

4. Test-fit the edging (F) around the rim of the table top, and mark and trim the edging to make its ends fit flush. Apply glue to the rim of the table top and the back of the edging (hold the edging down with pushpins). Allow both surfaces to get tacky.

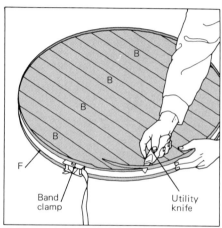

5. Press edging onto rim of table top with edging overhanging top and bottom of table top. Hold edging in place with a band clamp until glue dries, then use a utility knife to trim edging flush with top and bottom of table top. Sand the edging.

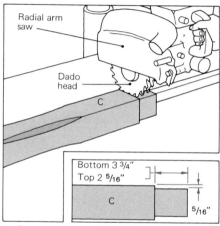

6. Cut the support post (C), braces (D), and feet (E) as described in the text on page 139. Cut a rabbet 3¾ in. wide and 5/16 in. deep into the bottom of each face of the support post, then cut a rabbet 2 5/16 in. wide and 5/16 in. deep into the top of each face of the post.

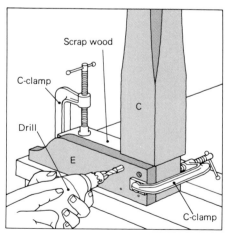

7. Clamp the feet (E) into the rabbets in the bottom of the support post and drill four 3/32-in. pilot holes through each foot into the post. Use a 3/8-in. bit to counterbore the holes ¼ in. deep. Glue the feet into place and drive 2-in. screws into the pilot holes.

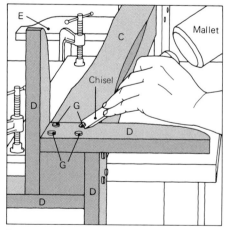

8. Attach the braces (D) to the rabbets in the top of the post as you attached the feet to the bottom. Fill all the screw holes with plugs (G). Trim the tops of the plugs with a chisel and then sand them flush with the surrounding wood, using No. 80 paper.

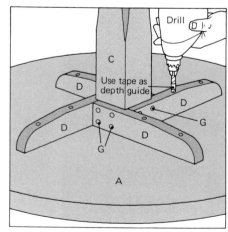

9. Center the top of the post assembly on the underside of the table top. Drill two 3/32-in. pilot holes through each brace into the table top. Counterbore the holes. Glue the post assembly down and secure it with 3-in. screws. Sand and finish the table.

Making a chair

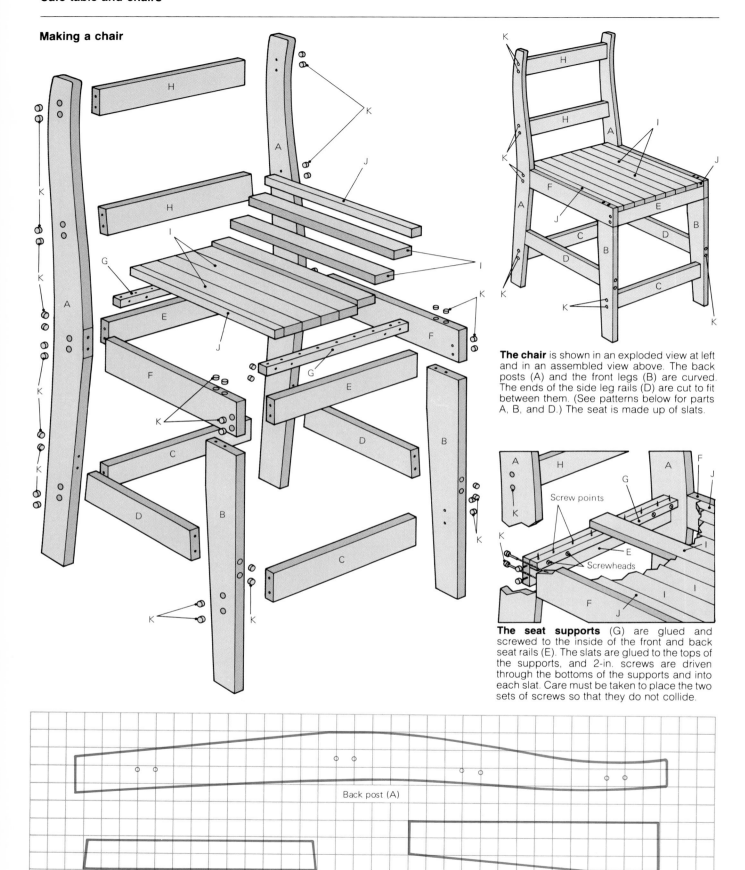

The chair is shown in an exploded view at left and in an assembled view above. The back posts (A) and the front legs (B) are curved. The ends of the side leg rails (D) are cut to fit between them. (See patterns below for parts A, B, and D.) The seat is made up of slats.

Screw points

Screwheads

The seat supports (G) are glued and screwed to the inside of the front and back seat rails (E). The slats are glued to the tops of the supports, and 2-in. screws are driven through the bottoms of the supports and into each slat. Care must be taken to place the two sets of screws so that they do not collide.

Back post (A)

Side leg rail (D)

Front leg (B)

Patterns: Enlarge these patterns (see p.48), then cut the pieces to match. Each square equals 1 sq. in.

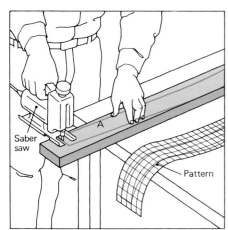

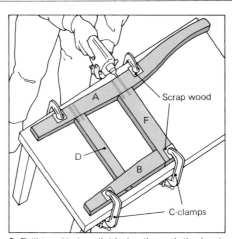

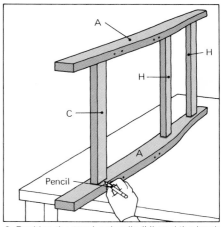

1. Cut the chair parts to the sizes and shapes given in the chart (p.139) and the patterns (p.142). Clamp one back post (A) near the edge of your workbench; then clamp a side seat rail (F), a front leg (B), and a side leg rail (D) into position next to the back post.

2. Drill two ³⁄₃₂-in. pilot holes through the back post into each rail. Drill two ³⁄₃₂-in. pilot holes through the front leg into the leg rail and two through the seat rail into the front leg. Use a ³⁄₈-in. bit to counterbore all the pilot holes to a depth of ¼ in. Disassemble.

3. Position the two back rails (H) and the back leg rail (C) on the back post 1⅛ in., 9¾ in., and 28 in., respectively, from the top of the post. Position the second back post over the free ends of the rails. Trace the outlines of the rails on both back posts.

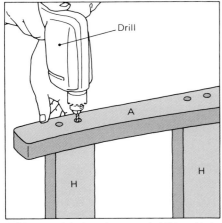

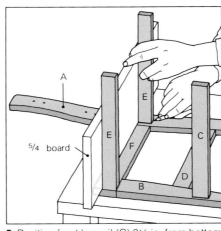

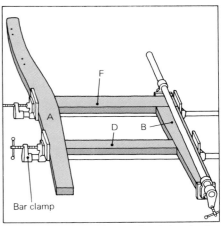

4. Disassemble the pieces and drill two ³⁄₃₂-in. pilot holes through the back posts inside the markings for each rail. Use a ³⁄₈-in. bit to counterbore the holes ¼ in. deep on the outer faces of the posts. Reassemble pieces and drill through pilot holes into rails as shown.

5. Position front leg rail (C) 3½ in. from bottom of leg. Position front and back seat rails (E) lower than the side seat rail by the thickness of a seat slat. Use a ⁵⁄₄ board to position them. Mark placement of all three rails, and drill and counterbore pilot holes for them.

6. Drill and counterbore pilot holes in the remaining front leg (B), side leg rail (D), and side seat rail (F). Glue and screw the back posts (A) to parts D and F, and glue and screw parts D and F to the front legs. Clamp the assemblies until the glue dries.

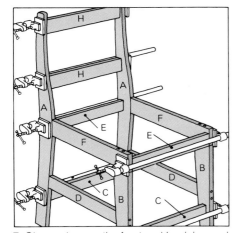

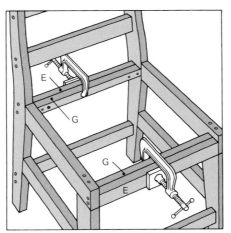

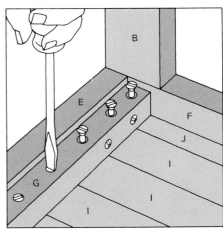

7. Glue and screw the front and back leg and seat rails (C and E) and the back rails (H) to the assembled chair sides. Clamp the chair until the glue dries. Fill all the screw holes with plugs (K) and sand the ends of the plugs flush with the chair as you did on the table.

8. Clamp the seat supports (G) to the insides of the front and back seat rails (E) with their tops flush. Drill four ³⁄₃₂-in. pilot holes through each support into its rail. Use a ³⁄₈-in. bit to counterbore the holes ¼ in. deep. Glue and screw the supports into place.

9. Clamp the seat slats (I and J) into place and drill a ³⁄₃₂-in. pilot hole through the bottom of each seat support into each slat. Glue and screw the slats down. Round off the front ends of the slats with No. 80 sandpaper. Sand and finish the chair.

143

MENU-PLANNING CENTER

If you would like to have a place in your kitchen to plan menus, keep bills, write shopping lists, and generally organize the complex affairs of running a household, this wall-mounted planning center is an ideal project. And it need not be restricted to the kitchen; it could easily serve as a secretary in another room.

There are shelves and compartments inside the unit. You can use the shelves for hiding away recipes, bills, letters, advertising circulars, and discount coupons, as well as your grocery lists; you can use the compartments for cookbooks, the telephone directory, or anything else you would like to keep handy. The fold-down door provides a writing surface at the proper height and can be closed at a moment's notice to hide any clutter.

Materials: To hold down costs, this project was built from lauan mahogany plywood and stock. If you prefer a more beautiful but costly wood, use Honduran (dark) mahogany plywood and stock.

The back is made of ¾-inch plywood, which provides a solid base for mounting the planning center to the wall studs of your home. When you install the unit, make sure that its bottom edge is 30 inches from the floor in order to provide a comfortable writing height.

When the door is closed, it is held in place by a pair of magnetic catches, which are attached to the interior dividers and to the inside of the door. When it is open, the door is held level for writing by two brass chains. A brass piano hinge serves as the fulcrum for the door, and a pair of brass door pulls completes the hardware list.

Construction: Start by laying out and cutting all parts, then cut the required dadoes and rabbets (Steps 1–5). Note that edging is glued to all exposed plywood edges. The edging strips must be cut to various sizes (see the chart below); then some of them must be trimmed to fit just before they are glued down. Do as much of the sanding as possible before assembly. Always sand with the grain; sanding across the grain will leave deep scratches, which will be difficult to remove later. Be careful when sanding the edging not to penetrate the thin mahogany veneer of the plywood. Start sanding the edging with a belt sander and a No. 120 belt, then switch to the orbital sander and progressively finer sandpaper—Nos. 120, 150, and 220. To add a final professional touch to the piece, "break the corners" at all edges—that is, sand a small radius into all exposed edges to soften their appearance. The paste stain and paste varnish recommended for this project are much easier to use than traditional liquid finishes.

For detailed instructions on cutting dadoes and rabbets, using a feather board, mounting the unit to the wall, and finishing, consult the *Index* (p.379).

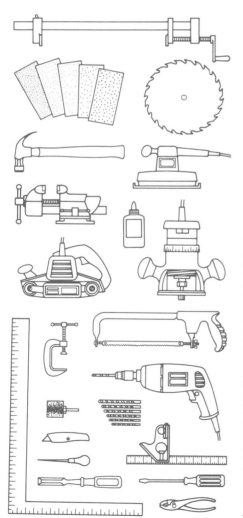

Parts list

Part	Name	Quantity	Thickness	Width	Length	Material
A	Top	1	¾″	11¾″	35″	Mahogany plywood
B	Bottom	1	¾″	11¾″	35″	Mahogany plywood
C	Side	2	¾″	11¾″	20¼″	Mahogany plywood
D	Divider	2	¾″	10½″	18½″	Mahogany plywood
E	Back	1	¾″	18¾″	35″	Mahogany plywood
F	Door	1	¾″	17″	33⅝″	Mahogany plywood
G	Side shelf	1	¾″	10½″	12½″	Mahogany plywood
H	Center shelf	4	¼″	9½″	10″	Mahogany plywood
I	Center shelf edging	4	¼″	½″	9½″	4/4 mahogany
J	Side shelf edging	1	¹³⁄₁₆″	½″	12½″	4/4 mahogany
K	Cabinet edging	14	¹³⁄₁₆″	✳	✳	4/4 mahogany

✳ All visible plywood edges are covered with edging strips cut from 4/4 stock (which is actually ¹³⁄₁₆″ thick). You will need four ⅜″ x 11¾″ strips for the tops and bottoms of the sides, two ⅜″ x 17″ strips for the sides of the door, two ⅜″ x 34⅜″ strips for the top and bottom of the door, two ½″ x 18½″ strips for the fronts of the dividers, two 1⅛″ x 21″ strips for the fronts of the sides, and two 1⅛″ x 35″ strips for the fronts of the top and bottom.

Tools and materials: Table saw with dado head, router with straight bit and arbor. Electric drill with set of twist bits and drum sander bit, hacksaw. Belt sander with No. 120 sanding belt, orbital sander. Nos. 120, 150, and 220 sandpaper. Vise, four 4' pipe or bar clamps, two 2″ (or larger) C-clamps. Combination square, framing square, sharp knife, pencil. Hammer, screwdriver, wood chisel, pliers, awl. White glue, paste stain, paste varnish, soft cloths. One 4' x 8' panel of ¾″ mahogany plywood, a 1' x 4' piece of ¼″ mahogany plywood, a 10' length of 4/4 mahogany 6″ wide. One 1½″ x 36″ brass-finish piano hinge, two brass door pulls, two 2' brass sash chains, four brass screw eyes, two magnetic latches.

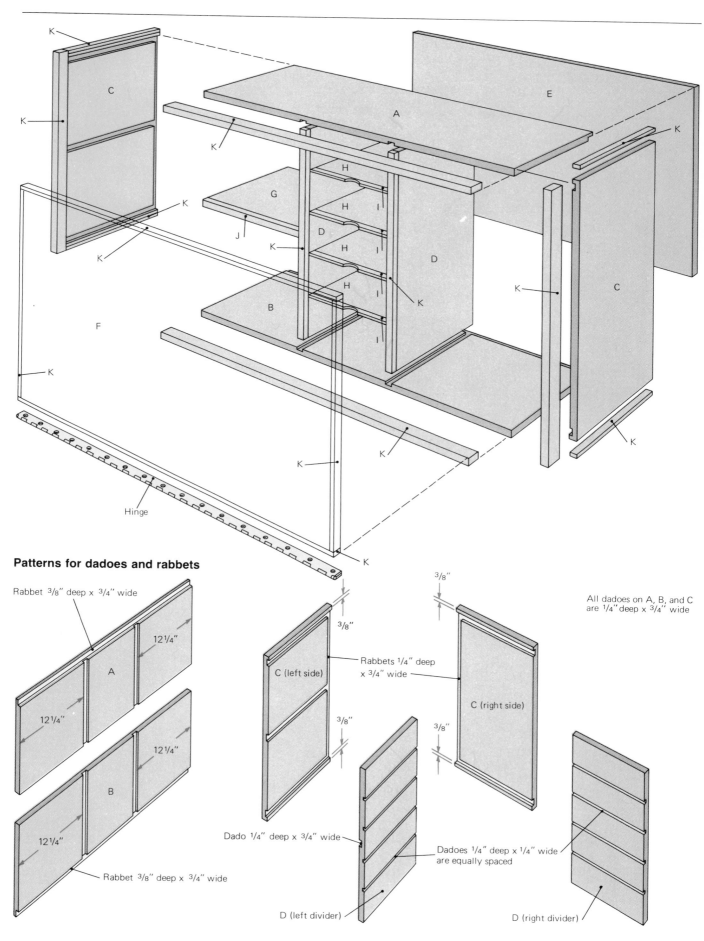

K

K

C

K

A

E

K

K

K

H

K

G

H

I

J

D

D

K

B

H

H

I

D

F

K

I

K

C

K

I

K

K

K

Hinge

K

Patterns for dadoes and rabbets

Rabbet $3/8''$ deep x $3/4''$ wide

$12^{1}/4''$

A

$12^{1}/4''$

$12^{1}/4''$

B

$12^{1}/4''$

Rabbet $3/8''$ deep x $3/4''$ wide

$3/8''$

$3/8''$

$3/8''$

C (left side)

$3/8''$

Rabbets $1/4''$ deep
x $3/4''$ wide

C (right side)

$3/8''$

$3/8''$

All dadoes on A, B, and C
are $1/4''$ deep x $3/4''$ wide

Dado $1/4''$ deep x $3/4''$ wide

Dadoes $1/4''$ deep x $1/4''$ wide
are equally spaced

D (left divider)

D (right divider)

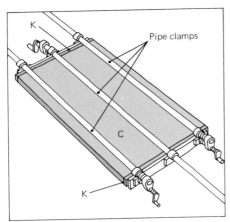

1. Cut all the parts to the dimensions given in the chart on page 144. Glue cabinet edging (K) to the tops and bottoms of the sides (C) and clamp the pieces until the glue dries. Belt-sand the edging to make it flush with the surfaces of the sides, moving the sander with the grain as much as possible.

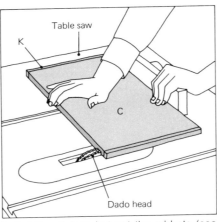

2. Cut the dadoes but not the rabbets (see patterns, p.145). The dadoes that the center shelves (H) will fit into are ¼ in. deep and ¼ in. wide. The others are ¼ in. deep and ¾ in. wide. Glue and clamp edging to the fronts of the sides. When the glue is dry, belt-sand the edging flush with the sides.

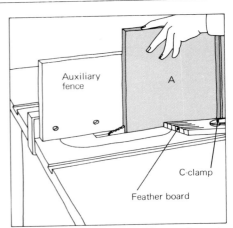

3. Attach a board to your table saw fence to make a high auxiliary fence. (Keep any mounting hardware flush with the board on the saw blade side.) Make a ¾-in.-deep cut into the back edge of the top (A) ⅜ in. from its dadoed surface, using a feather board to push the piece into the fence as you saw.

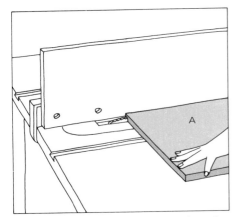

4. Remove the feather board and place the top, dadoed side down, on the saw table. Make a second cut ⁵⁄₁₆ in. deep ¾ in. from the back edge of the top. Chisel out the wood to form a rabbet ⅜ in. deep and ¼ in. wide. Repeat the procedure to cut a rabbet the same size into back edge of bottom (B).

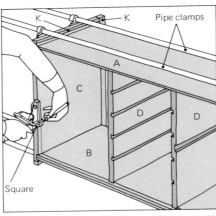

5. Dry-fit and clamp the top and bottom with the sides (C) and dividers (D). Use a pencil and a combination square to mark out the rabbets for the sides so that they are flush with the ones in the top and bottom. All the rabbets should form an even, continuous channel for the back to fit into.

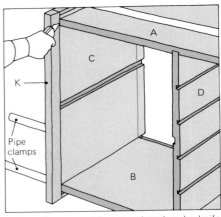

6. Turn the assembly around and make knife marks on the front edges of the top and bottom where they meet the inner surfaces of the sides. Remove the clamps and take the assembly apart. Measure the distance between the knife marks on the top and bottom and trim their edging (K) to that length.

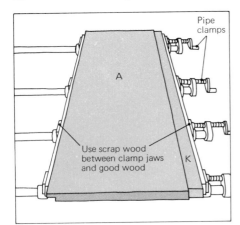

7. Glue and clamp the trimmed edging into place between the knife marks on the front edges of the top and bottom. Wipe away any excess glue; otherwise, the stain will not penetrate the wood. When the glue is dry, remove the clamps and belt-sand the edging flush with the surfaces of the top and bottom.

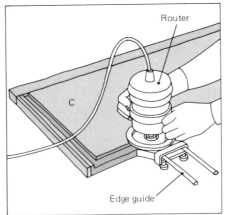

8. Following the pencil marks made in Step 5, cut ¼-in.-deep rabbets into the sides with a router and straight bit. Use the edge guide on the router to be sure you do not cut beyond the pencil marks. Sand the inner surfaces of the top, bottom, and sides with Nos. 120, 150, and then 220 paper.

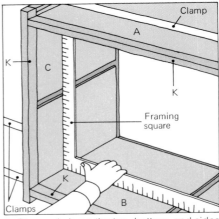

9. Glue and clamp the top, bottom, and sides together, carefully checking the unit for squareness with a framing square. (You may dry-fit the back into its rabbets to help you square the unit, but do not glue it into place yet.) Let glue dry, then remove clamps (and back). Add edging to the dividers (D).

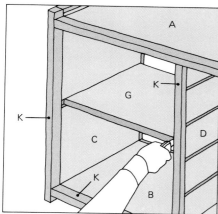

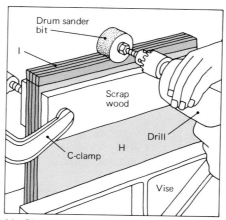

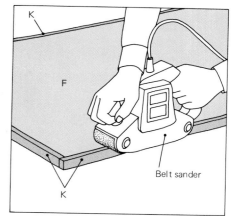

10. Slide the dividers and side shelf (G) into place and mark the shelf for its edging (J) as you marked the top and bottom in Step 6. Remove dividers and shelf, measure the distance between the marks on the shelf, then trim edging to that length. Glue and clamp the edging into place and let the glue dry.

11. Glue and clamp shelf edging (I) to the fronts of the four center shelves (H). When the glue is dry, belt-sand the edging flush with the shelves. Belt-sand the side shelf and dividers in the same way. Clamp the center shelves together in a vise, and use a drill with a drum sander bit to form curved finger notches.

12. Glue and clamp edging to the sides of the door (F). When the glue is dry, add edging to the top and bottom of the door. Belt-sand the edging flush with the door. Use Nos. 120, 150, and then 220 paper on all surfaces of the door, back, dividers, and shelves, and the outsides of the top, bottom, and sides.

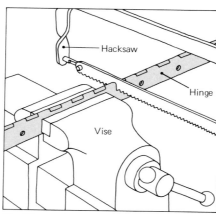

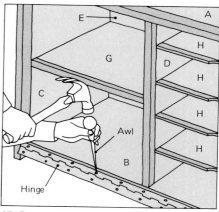

13. Glue the dividers, side shelf, and center shelves into place in that order. When the glue is dry, stain and varnish the insides of the unit, but do not get any stain or varnish in the rabbets for the back. Put masking tape over surfaces of the back (E) that will fit into the rabbets, then stain and varnish the back.

14. When the varnish is completely dry, remove the masking tape from the back and glue the back into place. Clamp it until the glue dries. Lock piano hinge in a vise in its closed position, and use a hacksaw to cut it to a length of 34⅜ in. If the cut edges are rough, smooth them with sandpaper or a file.

15. Position one leaf of the piano hinge over the edging on the bottom (B). Use a hammer and awl to punch indentations in the top of the edging through the holes in the hinge. Remove the hinge and drill pilot holes for the hinge screws at the awl marks. Then screw the hinge to the bottom.

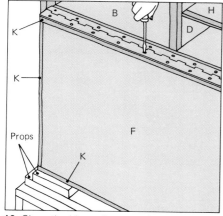

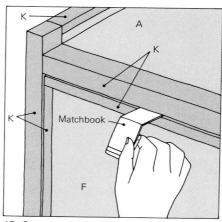

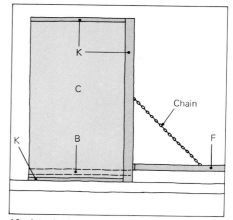

16. Close the hinge, then test-fit the door and trim and resand it if necessary—there should be 1/16-in. clearance on all sides. Align the loose leaf of the hinge over the bottom of the door. (Prop the door up to get it to the correct height.) Attach the hinge with two screws near the middle to test the fit.

17. Close the door and check the fit, using a matchbook cover or similar gauge. If the fit is okay, add remaining hinge screws; if fit is not okay, make minor corrections with the belt sander on the edges of the door. Resand door if necessary, then stain and varnish all the remaining unfinished parts of the unit.

18. Attach door pulls and magnetic latches. Place the unit on a level surface with its door open; door and bottom must be parallel. Use pliers to open screw eyes slightly. Attach screw eyes to insides of sides and to door. Stretch chain tight between screw eyes, cut off excess, then close screw eyes.

SPICE RACK

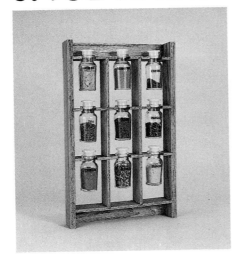

If you have trouble finding the spice you need when you need it, this handsome, easy-to-construct spice rack will help you organize and display a selection of spices. The rack is 17½ inches high and holds nine bottles, but you can add more horizontal rows to double, or even triple, its capacity. The wooden frame is made of rich oak with notched horizontal supports for the spices. Recycled vitamin bottles are scrubbed clean and labeled, then filled with your favorite spices and hung from the notches.

Construction: Cut all the lumber for the project. The chart below gives the exact measurement for each part.

Cut slots into the vertical supports (B) and into the center horizontal supports (C). This will allow you to fit the supports together like the cardboard dividers in a carton of bottles.

Next, cut dadoes into the side pieces (A), top horizontal support (D), and bottom horizontal support (E). This will allow you to fit all the pieces together and glue them. The dadoes can be made with a saw and chisel (see Steps 4 and 5) or with a circular saw or router. (To find directions for cutting dadoes with a power tool, see *Index*, p.379.)

Make U-shaped notches in the center and top horizontal supports (C and D)—but not in the bottom one (E)—by drilling holes into them and extending the holes to the edges by sawing. Sand all the wood parts, then assemble and glue them.

Finishing: Apply an oil finish to the wooden rack, or stain and varnish it. If you decide to stain it, apply the stain with a cloth (wiping with the wood grain), then wipe off the excess. Let the stain dry at least 24 hours; afterward, smooth it with 000 steel wool and brush on a coat of varnish. (To find more exact directions for finishing the wood, see *Index*, p.379.)

When the finish is completely dry, drill ¹⁄₁₆-inch pilot holes in the back of the rack where the picture-hanging hooks will be fastened. Attach the hangers with ½-inch No. 3 wood screws.

Soak the vitamin bottles in hot water so that you can peel off the old labels; then dry the bottles. (You can often buy spice labels in hardware stores, or you can make your own using blank self-adhesive labels, which are sold in stationery stores.) Apply new labels and fill the bottles with the corresponding spices. Hang the rack in your kitchen and fit the bottles into the notches.

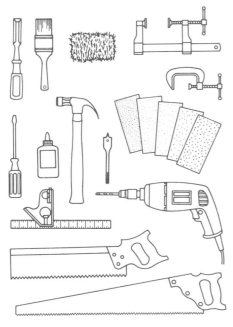

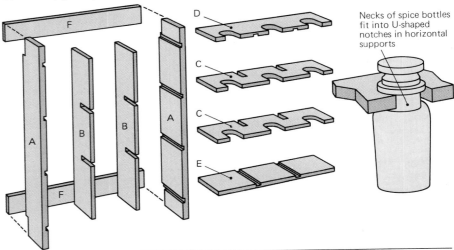

Necks of spice bottles fit into U-shaped notches in horizontal supports

Parts list

Part	Name	Quantity	Thickness	Width	Length	Material
A	Side piece	2	½"	2"	17½"	Red oak
B	Vertical support	2	¼"	2"	14¼"	Red oak
C	Center horizontal support	2	¼"	2"	9¾"	Red oak
D	Top horizontal support	1	¼"	2"	9¾"	Red oak
E	Bottom horizontal support	1	¼"	2"	9¾"	Red oak
F	Back brace	2	¼"	1½"	10½"	Red oak

Tools and materials: Drill with ¹⁄₁₆" and ⅛" bits, 1¼" spade bit. Crosscut saw and backsaw (or handsaw with at least 10 teeth per inch). Combination square. Hammer, screwdriver, ¼" chisel. Two 2" C-clamps, two bar clamps (optional). Paintbrush. White glue, No. 120 sandpaper, oil finish (or wood stain and varnish), 000 steel wool, soft cloths. Two 5½" wide red oak boards dressed on both sides, one of them ½" thick and 2' long, the other ¼" thick and 4' long. Nine bottles that generic vitamins come in, preprinted spice labels. Two ½" No. 3 wood screws. Two circular picture hangers.

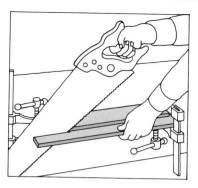

1. Cut out all wood parts for the rack according to the specifications given in the chart on the previous page. To do so, measure the boards and mark the cutting lines with a pencil. Clamp a straight piece of lumber along each line, in turn, as a guide to keep the cuts straight. Cut along the lines with a crosscut saw.

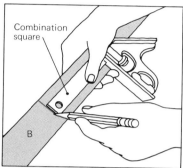

2. Mark the location of the slots in the vertical supports (B) with a combination square and pencil. Set the square to 4⅝ in. for the outsides of the slots and then to 4⅞ in. for the insides. Place the square flush against each end of each support, in turn, and draw cutting lines. Set the square to 1 in. and mark the length of the slots.

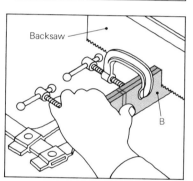

3. Clamp both vertical supports (B) together and cut along the insides of the parallel cutting lines with a backsaw. Remove the wood between the cuts with a ¼-in. chisel. Mark the slots on the center horizontal supports (C) with the square set to 3⅛ in. for the outsides, 3⅜ in. for the insides, and 1 in. for the length. Cut out the slots.

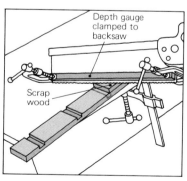

4. Mark the cutting lines for the dadoes on each top and bottom support (D and E) 3⅛ in. and 3⅜ in. from each end across the entire width. Clamp scrap wood to the blade ⅛ in. from the cutting edge to act as a depth gauge. Clamp scrap wood along each line to guide the saw. Saw along the insides of the lines.

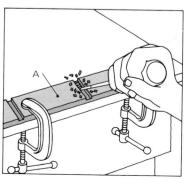

5. Mark the cutting lines for the dadoes on each side piece (A) 1½ in., 1¾ in., 6¼ in., and 6½ in. from each end. Saw ⅛ in. deep along the insides of the lines as in Step 4. Remove wood between saw cuts on all dadoes with a ¼-in. chisel. Make sure that the bottoms of the dadoes are smooth and level with the saw cuts.

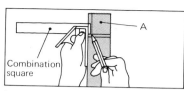

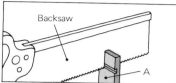

6. Mark the locations of the cutouts for the back braces (F) along the back of each side piece (A). Set the combination square to ¼ in. and draw a line from the top of the side piece to the edge of the first dado (top). Cut along inside of this line with backsaw (bottom). Finish the cut by sawing along top of dado, and remove cutout wood.

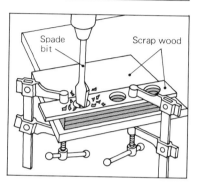

7. Clamp the top support (D) and both center supports (C) between two wood scraps to prevent supports from splitting. Drill three ⅛-in. pilot holes ¾ in. back from the front edge of the supports and positioned 1⅝ in., 4⅞ in., and 8⅛ in. from one end. Drill through the pilot holes with a 1¼-in. spade bit.

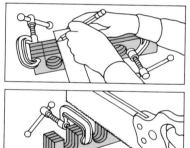

8. Use a pencil and square to extend the sides of the 1¼-in. holes to the nearest edge (top). Cut along these lines with the backsaw to create U-shaped notches that will hold the spice bottles (bottom). Sand all wooden parts with No. 120 sandpaper. Wrap sandpaper around a dowel, pencil, or scrap wood to reach the insides of the notches.

9. Test-fit all pieces and loosen any tight joints by sanding them. Assemble the vertical supports (B) and the center horizontal supports (C) without glue. Run beads of glue through the dadoes in the top and bottom horizontal supports (D and E) and through the dadoes and cutouts in the side pieces (A). Complete the assembly of the rack.

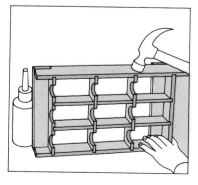

10. Place the rack on a flat surface and check to see that all pieces are fully seated. Tap lightly with a hammer if necessary. Remove excess glue with a wet cloth. If you have bar clamps, use them to hold the rack together while the glue dries. When the glue is dry, finish the rack and attach the hangers as described in the text.

BUTCHER-BLOCK TABLE

A table with a butcher-block top is both sturdy and attractive. Traditionally, a butcher block is made by laminating strips of maple to form either cubes or slabs. The top for this butcher-block table departs slightly from tradition; it is made of alternating maple and walnut strips and the surface is framed in walnut. You can make the entire top of maple if walnut is too expensive or difficult to obtain. The top is supported by a trestle base constructed entirely of maple. The completed table—63 inches long, 29 inches wide, and 30 inches high—would be a handsome and useful addition to almost any room in your house.

When ordering wood for the table, be sure it is well seasoned—preferably air dried. If you buy kiln-dried lumber, it is important that the lumber be planed down to uniform thickness; so unless you have a thickness planer, have the lumber dealer dress the lumber for you. Any minor irregularities can be removed with simpler tools: use a jack plane for the roughest areas and a smooth plane to finish the job. Sand the table to a satin finish and rub it down with antiquing oil.

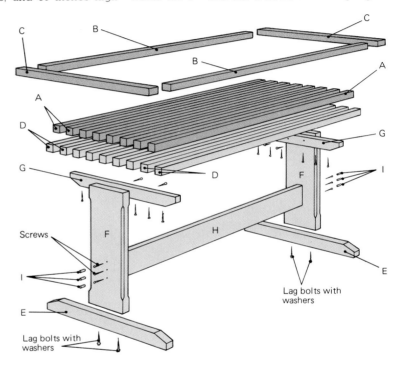

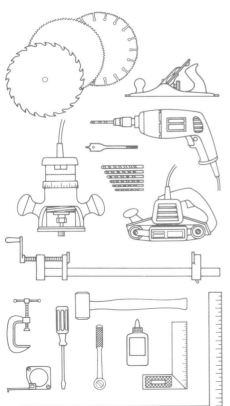

Parts list

Part	Name	Quantity	Thickness	Width	Length	Material
A	Walnut strip	8	1½"	1½"	59½"	2 x 6 walnut
B	Side strip	2	1½"	1¾"	59½"	2 x 6 walnut
C	End strip	2	1½"	1¾"	29"	2 x 6 walnut
D	Maple strip	9	1½"	1½"	59½"	2 x 6 maple
E	Foot	2	1½"	2¾"	26"	2 x 6 maple
F	Leg	2	1½"	7¼"	25½"	2 x 8 maple
G	Brace	2	1⅛"	2⅜"	24½"	5/4 maple
H	Stretcher	1	1⅛"	5"	44½"	5/4 maple
I	Plug	6	⅜" dia.	—	½"	Hardwood dowel

Tools and materials: Table saw, radial arm saw. Portable power planer or jack plane and smooth plane. Electric drill with set of twist bits and 1" spade bit. Belt sander with No. 120 sanding belt (or No. 120 sandpaper). Nos. 150, 180, and 220 sandpaper. Router with ½" cove bit and ½" corner-round bit. Four or more 6' pipe or bar clamps, four or more 6" C-clamps. Dead-blow hammer or heavy mallet. Framing square, try square, steel tape rule, pencil. Socket wrench, screwdriver. Carpenter's glue, commercially prepared antiquing oil, soft cloths. One 6' length of 2 x 8 maple and four 6' lengths each of 2 x 6 maple and 2 x 6 walnut—all dressed on two sides to uniform 1½" thickness. One 6' length of 5/4 maple 5" wide, ⅜" hardwood dowel 4" long. Four 1½" dia. glides. Four ¼" lag bolts 3" long with washers to fit. Two dozen No. 8 self-tapping screws 2" long.

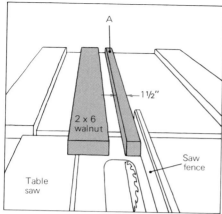

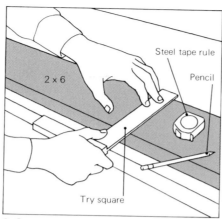

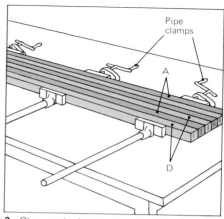

1. Check boards for walnut strips (A) for squareness and plane them, if necessary, to get at least one true edge on each board. Push true edge of one board against table saw fence, set fence for outside rip cut, and remove outside edge of board. Reset fence and rip three strips 1½ in. wide.

2. Cut other A strips from remaining squared boards. Square off boards for side, end, and maple strips (B, C, and D). Rip strips to widths shown in chart. Plane all strips to uniform thickness if necessary. Arrange strips A and D alternately for best grain effect; number ends of strips to keep them in order while gluing.

3. Glue and clamp several strips together. Use a dead-blow hammer or mallet to knock strips into alignment as you tighten clamps. Let glue dry 24 hr., then add more strips in same way. Repeat until all A and D strips have been added. Glue on side strips (B), and clamp assembly until glue is dry.

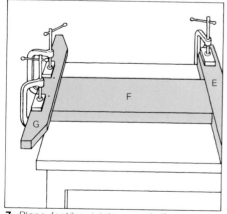

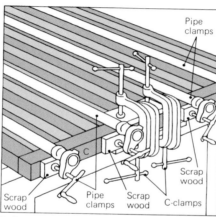

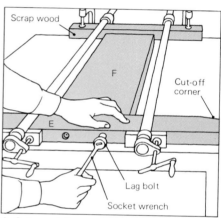

4. Belt-sand top and underside of top with No. 120 belt, moving sander across grain until joints are smooth and top is flat. Use framing square to determine cutting lines for length of top. Position top under radial arm saw and saw halfway along cutting line, then turn top around and cut along other half of line.

5. Glue and clamp end strips (C) in place. Use C-clamps to help you align ends of other strips with end strips. Let glue dry, then unclamp top and sand it with Nos. 150 and 180 paper. Use router with corner-round bit to soften sharp edges, and sand entire top with No. 220 paper until it is smooth.

6. Cut remaining parts to sizes given in chart. Cut off upper corners of feet (E) and lower corners of braces (G) at 30° angles. Position feet against legs (F) and drill two ³⁄₁₆-in. pilot holes through bottom of each foot into its leg. Use 1-in. spade bit to counterbore holes 1 in. deep. Drive in lag bolts with washers.

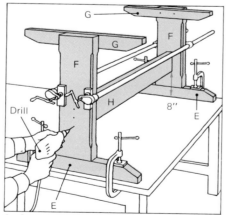

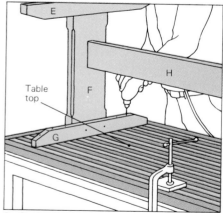

7. Plane foot/leg joints smooth if necessary. Position braces against legs with tops aligned. Drill two ³⁄₃₂-in. pilot holes through each brace into its leg. Use ³⁄₈-in. bit to counterbore holes ¼ in. deep. Glue, screw, and clamp pieces together. Rout corners of legs with cove bit for decorative relief. Sand.

8. Clamp stretcher (H) between leg assemblies with bottom of stretcher 8 in. from bottoms of feet. Drill three ³⁄₃₂-in. pilot holes through each leg into ends of stretcher, and use ³⁄₈-in. bit to counterbore holes ½ in. deep. Glue and screw stretcher to legs. Glue plugs (I) in holes; chisel and sand ends flush.

9. Center trestle base on underside of top. Drill and countersink six ³⁄₃₂-in. pilot holes through each brace into maple strips in top—you should have three holes on each side of each leg. Glue and screw trestle base to top. Hammer glides into feet. Give table final sanding, remove dust, and rub in oil.

STORAGE BINS

A precision-made, handsomely crafted set of storage bins, nestled in a cabinet shell, not only makes an appetizing display for foodstuffs but also adds a decorative accent to a well-organized kitchen.

The bins and their shell, assembled with white glue, are made of solid cherry stock and cherry-veneer plywood. Glass windows are installed in the faces of the drawerlike bins. To enhance the design of the unit, the fronts of the bins and the cabinet shell are built at an angle. If the instructions are followed, the bevel angle will be about 9½° from the vertical (or 80½° from the horizontal). To ensure that all the front parts slope at the same angle, you must make a jig so that the angle cut into each piece can be duplicated on the table saw.

All the parts, as well as their dadoes, rabbets, tenons and mortises, should be measured and cut with great precision. Before gluing, always test-fit the parts to determine if they are square and if the fit is snug. Make any necessary adjustments and then apply glue. Most clamping is done with bar or pipe clamps for joining individual pieces or web clamps for clamping all around an assembly. (See the *Index*, p.379, for techniques that are not detailed in the steps.)

Solid cherry edging is used to cover the edges of the plywood pieces and also those of the drawer face frames where the dado grooves show. The edging is made in two different ways (see Step 8) because the surfaces to which the edging is applied are beveled differently. The top edges of the drawer sides and backs, which are exposed to less wear and tear, are covered with cherry-veneer tape instead of solid cherry edging.

Parts list

Part	Name	Quantity	Thickness	Width	Length	Material
A	Top	1	¾″	11¼″	29¼″	Cherry plywood
B	Bottom	1	¾″	14¼″	29¼″	Cherry plywood
C	Back	1	¾″	17¼″	29¼″	Cherry plywood
D	Side	2	¾″	14″	17⅝″	Cherry plywood
E	Vertical divider	2	¾″	13¼″	17¼″	Cherry plywood
F	Horizontal divider	2	¾″	11¾″	14¼″	Cherry plywood
G	Upper drawer side	4	¾″	7⅜″	11⅝″	Cherry plywood
H	Drawer back	4	¾″	7⅜″	12½″	Cherry plywood
I	Lower drawer side	4	¾″	7⅜″	13⅜″	Cherry plywood
J	Upper drawer bottom	2	¼″	12¼″	11″	Mahogany plywood
K	Lower drawer bottom	2	¼″	12¼″	13″	Mahogany plywood
L	Top and bottom edging	2	¼″	13⁄16″	30¼″	4/4 cherry
M	Horizontal divider edging	2	¼″	13⁄16″	30¼″	4/4 cherry
N	Side edging	2	¼″	13⁄16″	17¼″	4/4 cherry
O	Vertical divider edging	2	¼″	13⁄16″	17¼″	4/4 cherry
P	Drawer face-frame rail	8	13⁄16″	2″	12″	4/4 cherry
Q	Drawer face-frame stile	8	13⁄16″	2″	8¾″	4/4 cherry
R	Upper drawer slide	4	⅜″	⅜″	11½″	4/4 cherry
S	Lower drawer slide	4	⅜″	⅜″	13″	4/4 cherry
T	Drawer pull	4	13⁄16″	1⅛″	10½″	4/4 cherry
U	Stile edging	8	¼″	13⁄16″	10″	4/4 cherry
V	Top rail edging	4	¼″	13⁄16″	15″	4/4 cherry
W	Corner strip	2	7⁄16″	7⁄16″	12″	4/4 cherry
X	Glass	4	1⁄16″	✳	✳	Glass

✳ Cut to fit during construction or have glass installed by a glazier.

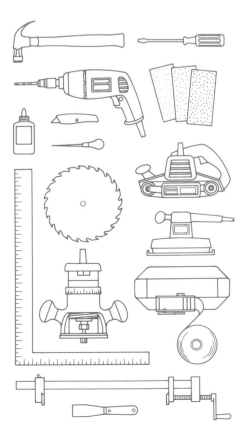

Tools and materials: Table saw with dado head and high-speed (or carbide) blade. Router with ⅜″ rabbeting bit and ⅜″ rounding-over bit (both with roller guides). Electric drill with 1⁄16″ twist bit and Screwmate bit. Hammer, screwdriver, awl, utility knife, putty knife. Framing square. Eight 3′ bar or pipe clamps, two web clamps (or ropes and tightening cylinders), vise. Belt sander, orbital sander. No. 120 sanding belt, Nos. 120, 150, and 220 sandpaper. White glue, contact cement, ½ pt. cherry paste stain, ½ pt. paste varnish, auto wax. Veneer tape. A ¾″ x 4′ x 8′ panel of cherry-veneer plywood, a ¼″ x 2′ x 4′ piece of mahogany-veneer plywood, a 10′ length of 4/4 cherry (actual thickness 13⁄16″) 6″ wide. Four pieces glass 1⁄16″ thick, metal glazier's push points. Twenty-four ¾″ No. 6 flathead wood screws, eight 1½″ No. 8 flathead wood screws, 1″ No. 17 brads.

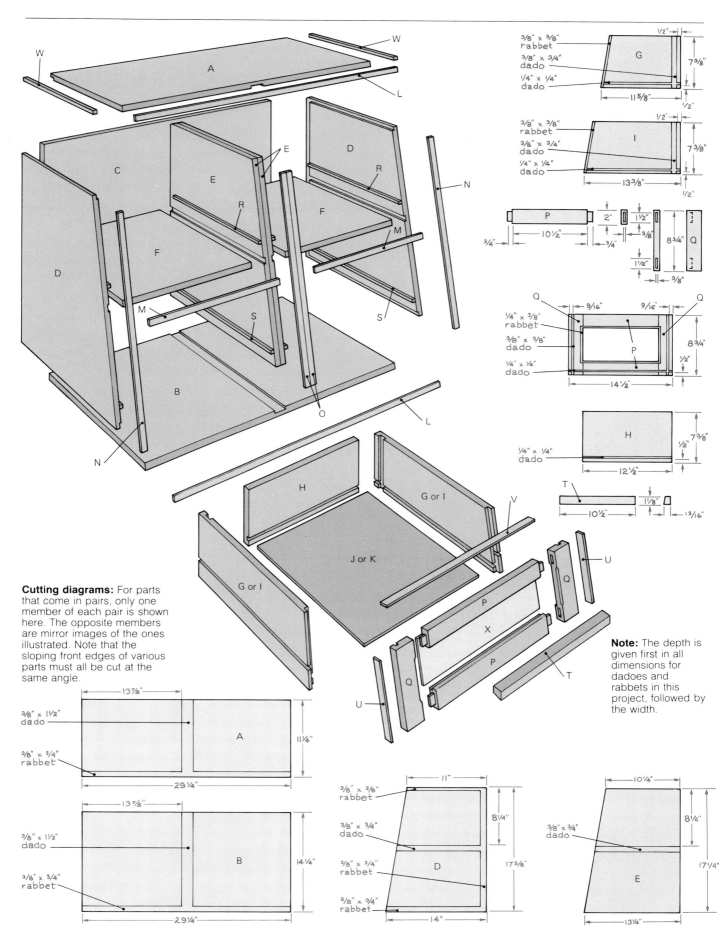

Cutting diagrams: For parts that come in pairs, only one member of each pair is shown here. The opposite members are mirror images of the ones illustrated. Note that the sloping front edges of various parts must all be cut at the same angle.

Note: The depth is given first in all dimensions for dadoes and rabbets in this project, followed by the width.

153

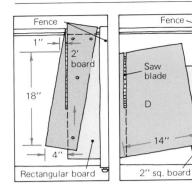

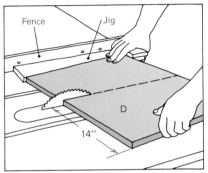

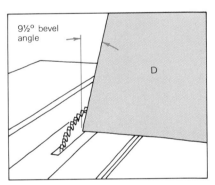

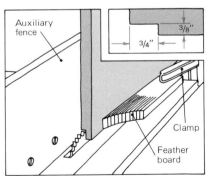

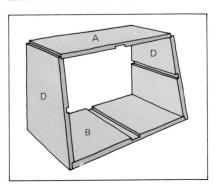

1. Make a jig by nailing a 2-ft. board to a rectangular board, skewed so that one end is 3 in. farther out than the other over an 18-in. span (left). Saw out an angled piece by moving rectangular board along rip fence. Nail a 2-in.-sq. board at a right angle to sloping side of angled piece (right). Jig now has a bevel of about 9½° from the vertical.

2. Cut two rectangles 26 x 17⅝ in. from the ¾-in. plywood panel. Position one corner of each piece in jig's right angle. Adjust fence so that saw blade will begin a cut 14 in. from opposite corner. Move jig and plywood together along rip fence to saw out angled front edges of sides (D) and vertical dividers (E). Trim parts to size.

3. Cut the top (A), bottom (B), and horizontal dividers (F) slightly wider than the dimensions given in the chart on page 152. Use one side (D) as a gauge to set the saw blade at the bevel angle. Then trim the front edges of A, B, and F to size so that, when assembled, the bevel of these horizontal edges will match the slope on the fronts of parts D and E.

4. Cut dadoes and rabbets in sides (D), vertical dividers (E), top (A), and bottom (B) according to patterns on page 153. It takes both a flat and vertical cut to make a rabbet with the table saw. A high auxiliary fence and a feather board will make the work easier and safer (see *Index*, p. 379).

5. Assemble the top (A), bottom (B), and sides (D) with white glue. Clamp with bar or pipe clamps. Let dry. Note that the bottom edges of the sides are flush with the bottom, but the top edges of the sides protrude.

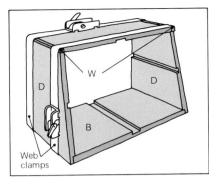

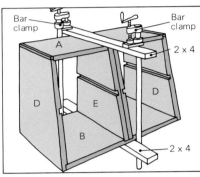

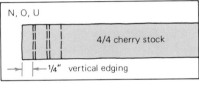

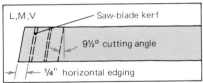

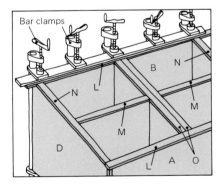

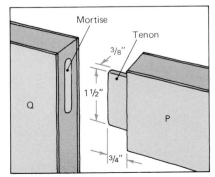

6. Glue corner strips (W) to the half-filled rabbet joints at the top edges of the sides. Clamp the cabinet shell with web clamps. When the glue dries, belt-sand the joints smooth, sanding with the grain. Take care not to sand through the thin veneer on the sides and top. Next, smooth the interior of the shell with the orbital sander.

7. Test-fit the two vertical dividers (E) back to back into the dadoes in the top and bottom. If necessary, trim their front edges to make them flush with those of the cabinet shell and their back edges flush with the rear rabbets. Glue and clamp the assembly until it is dry. Install the horizontal dividers (F) in the same way.

8. Cut ¼-in.-wide edging strips from the ⁴⁄₄ cherry stock. Saw edging for the sides, vertical dividers, and stiles (N, O, and U) straight down the board (upper diagram). Saw edging for the top, bottom, horizontal dividers, and top rail (L, M, and V) at the bevel angle (lower diagram). Cut edging to length.

9. Glue the edging around the cabinet shell first, then on the vertical dividers, and finally on the horizontal dividers. Clamp with as many bar clamps as possible. Smooth surfaces of the edging with a belt sander and No. 120 sanding belt. Then finish with the orbital sander and 220 paper. Sand sides of edging flush with adjacent surfaces.

10. Cut the drawer face-frame rails (P) and stiles (Q) to the dimensions in the chart. Cut tenons on both ends of each rail according to the pattern (p.153), and mortise the inside edge of each stile to receive the tenons. (For the technique of cutting tenons and mortises, see *Index*, p.379.)

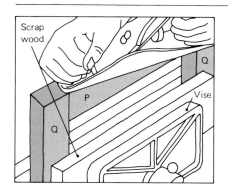

Scrap wood

Q

P

Q

Vise

11. Test-fit rails and stiles to make the four drawer face frames. Check and trim as needed. Glue and clamp. When dry, belt-sand each frame. Reduce the side and top edges slightly to make room for the edging. Apply edging (U) to sides of each frame. Glue and clamp.

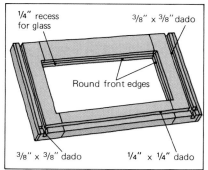

1/4" recess for glass

3/8" x 3/8" dado

Round front edges

3/8" x 3/8" dado

1/4" x 1/4" dado

12. Dado the back side of each face frame (see p.153) to receive the drawer sides (G or I) and bottom (J or K). Rout a 1/4-in. recess all around the back of each frame opening to receive the glass (X). Use a rounding-over bit all around the square edges of the front of each window to give the edges next to the glass a sculptured look.

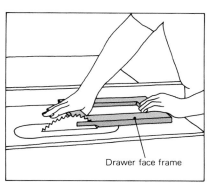

Drawer face frame

13. Set the saw blade at the bevel angle, and bevel the top and bottom edges of the drawer face frames so that their top and bottom edges can go all the way into the cabinet shell. Apply edging (V) to tops of frames only.

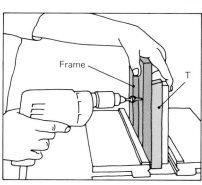

Frame

T

14. Cut the four drawer pulls (T) to size. Mark positions of drawer pulls on face frames. For each pull drill two pilot holes from the front into the marked area. Clamp the pull in place. Using a Screwmate bit, countersink the pilot holes from the back and drill into the shell. Install the pulls with 1½-in. No. 8 screws.

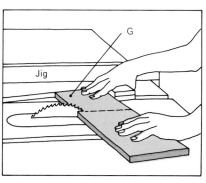

G

Jig

G

15. Cut the drawer sides (G and I) to size, using the jig for their sloping front edges as in Step 2. Note that, due to the angle, the upper drawer sides (G) are shorter than the lower ones (I). Dado the inner faces of the sides to receive the backs (H) and bottoms (J or K). Dado the outer faces for drawer slides (see p.153).

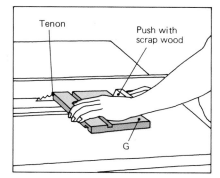

Tenon

Push with scrap wood

G

16. Cut the tenons on the front edges of the drawer sides (G and I). For instructions on cutting tenons, see *Index*, p.379. The tenons will be inserted into the backs of the drawer face frames. Cut parts H, J, and K to size (see chart, p.152). Dado parts H (see p.153).

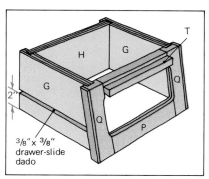

T

H

G

G

Q

P

2"

3/8" x 3/8" drawer-slide dado

17. All the major parts of the drawers are now ready for assembly: the backs (H), sides (G and I), bottoms (J and K), and the already assembled face frames. After test-fitting parts, glue and clamp each assembled drawer with bar clamps. Check for squareness and make any necessary adjustments.

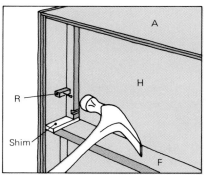

Putty knife

Tape

Drawer

18. After the assembled drawers have dried, cover the top edges of the sides and back (but not the face frame) of each drawer with cherry-veneer tape, using contact cement. The tape will hide the remaining exposed edges of the plywood.

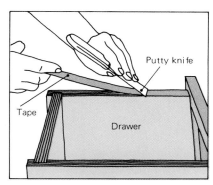

A

H

R

Shim

F

19. Insert each drawer, shimming it up to its correct position. From the still-open back of the cabinet shell, insert slides (R and S) into their dadoed outer drawer faces. Mark slide positions inside shell, and nail slides temporarily to shell through 1/16-in. predrilled holes. Slide drawers in and out to test the fit.

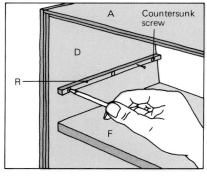

A

Countersunk screw

D

R

F

20. Drill three pilot holes through each slide into the cabinet shell with a Screwmate bit, and insert 3/4-in. No. 6 screws. Rub some auto wax on the slides. Glue and clamp the back (C) in place. Finish exterior cabinet shell and drawer faces with cherry stain and varnish. Install glass (X) in drawer recesses, using metal glazier's push points.

155

HANGING STORAGE RACK

Kitchen storage problems are handily solved with this two-shelf suspended rack of durable maple. It could serve equally well as a plant holder in any room. The design is easily modified: if space is limited, shorten the rack by one section or make only one shelf.

If you do not have a table saw or circular saw with a rip guide, purchase the maple cut to the three needed widths (see chart below). Then cut the strips to length yourself. An easy way to saw a number of pieces the same length is with a backsaw, a miter box, and a stop. Clamp the miter box to the work surface, measure from the slots for a right-angle cut, and clamp a straight piece of scrap wood to the work surface at that point. Then simply butt the strip of wood you are cutting against the stop and saw it.

The chain that holds the rack should be capable of carrying a minimum capacity of 250 pounds. Calculate the amount of chain needed by measuring the distance from your ceiling to the point where you want the lower shelf to hang, then multiply that distance by eight. As pictured, the shelves are 14 inches apart.

Before assembling the shelves, sand the wood with Nos. 80, 150, and 220 sandpaper. You can leave the wood natural or, after gluing, apply several coats of mineral oil for protection.

Hang the rack from two strips of wood fastened through the ceiling to the ceiling joists. These are usually on 16-inch centers running perpendicular to the roof ridge. Find the joists with a magnetic stud finder, or drill a hole in the ceiling and probe with a straightened coat hanger. The strips of wood should be screwed to at least four joists with lag bolts.

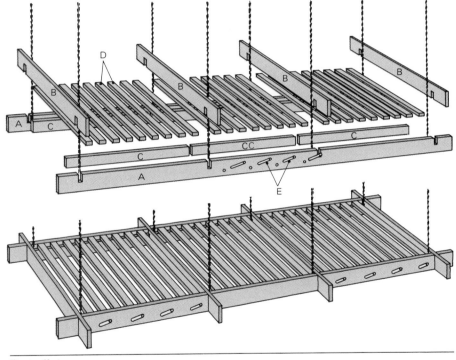

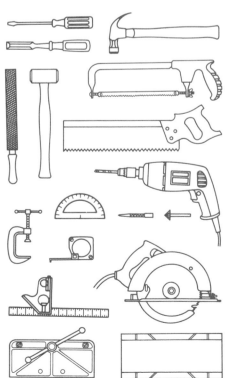

Parts list

Part	Name	Quantity	Thickness	Width	Length	Material
A	Side	4	½"	2"	61"	Maple
B	Crosspiece	8	½"	2"	20"	Maple
C	Ledge strip	8	½"	1½"	19"	Maple
CC	Ledge strip	4	½"	1½"	17"	Maple
D	Slat	52	½"	1"	15"	Maple
E	Hanging peg	12	¼" dia.	—	1½"	Hardwood dowel

Tools and materials: Drill with ⁷⁄₆₄" and ¹⁄₁₆" twist bits and countersink. Backsaw or other fine-tooth saw, miter box, hacksaw. Circular or table saw with rip guide (optional). Hammer, screwdriver, nail set. Wooden mallet, ½" wood chisel, coarse file or rasp. Two 3" C-clamps, vise. Steel tape rule, combination square, protractor, pencil.

Wood glue. Nos. 80, 150, and 220 sandpaper. Wood (see above). Eight lengths twisted-link coil brass-plated chain. Sixteen 1¼" and thirty-two ¾" No. 8 flathead wood screws. Eight ¼" lag bolts, 16 flat washers, eight screw hooks, 3d finishing nails.

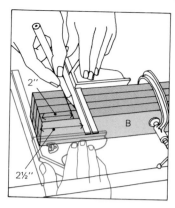

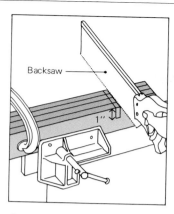

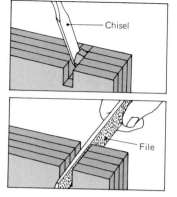

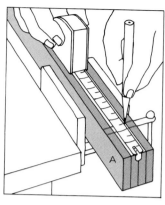

1. Align four crosspieces (B) against a combination square; clamp the crosspieces together. Mark a line across all four 2 in. from one end and another line at 2½ in. Extend the lines down surface of outer boards 1 in., and connect those two lines.

2. Leave C-clamp on, and clamp the boards in a vise. With a backsaw or other fine-tooth saw, cut inside the lines made in Step 1 to 1-in. depth. Hold the saw horizontal, and keep checking on back side to make sure it follows the line and does not go below 1 in.

3. With a ½-in. chisel and wooden mallet, chop out the waste in each board. Clean the corners of the cut with a rasp or coarse file. Test the cut with ½-in. stock and trim the notches if the fit is tight. Repeat Steps 1–3 on both ends of all eight crosspieces.

4. Clamp together all four sides (A) and lay out notches 2 in. from each end as above. Then measure in 21½ in. from each end and lay out two more ½-in. notches. Clamp the sides in the vise, and saw and chisel out the notches as shown in Steps 2 and 3.

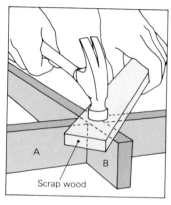

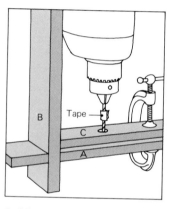

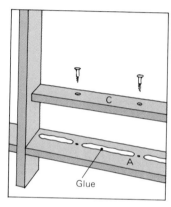

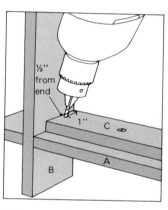

5. Spread glue in notches of one shelf. Fit pieces together; protect maple with scrap wood, and tap notches with a hammer. Check for squareness by measuring diagonally (see *Index*, p.379). Set assembly aside to dry and make frame for second shelf.

6. With a ⁷⁄₆₄-in. bit drill holes 3 in. from each end of ledge strips (C). Countersink for flathead screws. Clamp strips to sides (A) flush with bottom edges. Drill into sides ¼ in., using tape to show how deep bit should go. Number each strip and its side section.

7. Apply glue to the ledge strips one by one, and put strips in position on inner surfaces of sides. (Be sure to match the number on each strip to the numbers on the side sections.) Insert ¾-in. screws as you glue each strip. Wipe off excess glue with a damp cloth.

8. Use a ⁷⁄₆₄-in. bit to drill through ledge strips and into sides. These holes should be 1 in. from bottom of ledge strip, ½ in. over from all crosspieces, and facing center of shelf. (Holes will be used to fasten chain and will fall between the slats and crosspieces.)

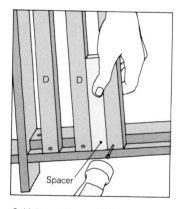

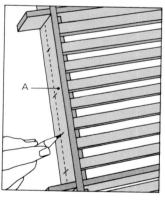

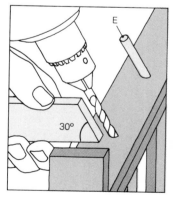

9. Using a piece of 1-in. wood as a spacer, glue the slats (D) on top of the ledge strips. Drill ¹⁄₁₆-in. holes through slats into ledge strips, and hammer in nails. Sink heads just below wood surface with a nail set. Repeat Steps 6–9 for the second shelf.

10. Decide how many hanging pegs (E) you will need; four on a side section is probably the maximum that will fit comfortably. Lay out peg positions by dividing the distance between crosspieces—19 in. here—equally. Mark positions on the sides (A).

11. Use a protractor to mark a line at a 30° angle on a piece of scrap wood about 2 in. wide. Saw along the line and use this piece of wood as a guide for drilling holes for pegs. Test-fit the pegs and then glue them. Sand their ends round after the glue has dried.

12. Screw lengths of chain to bottom rack, inserting washers between chain and screwheads. Measure the distance you want between shelves on chain; mark a link and count same number of links on all other lengths. Attach upper shelf to those links.

CORK MESSAGE BOARD

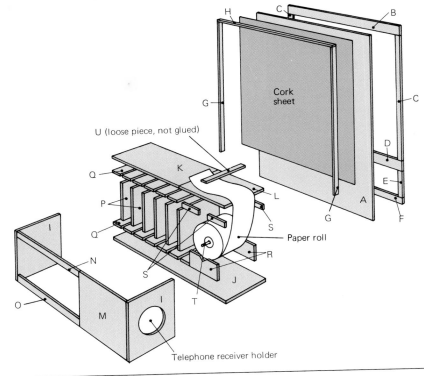

U (loose piece, not glued)

Cork sheet

Paper roll

Telephone receiver holder

Parts list

Part	Name	Quantity	Thickness	Width	Length	Material
A	Backboard	1	1/4"	15½"	20½"	Plywood
B	Top horizontal	1	1/4"	1¾"	15½"	Pine lattice
C	Long vertical	2	1/4"	3/4"	12¼"	Pine lattice
D	Center horizontal	1	1/4"	1¾"	15½"	Pine lattice
E	Short vertical	2	1/4"	3/4"	4"	Pine lattice
F	Bottom horizontal	1	1/4"	3/4"	15½"	Pine lattice
G	Side edge trim	2	1/4"	3/4"	15½"	Pine lattice
H	Top edge trim	1	1/4"	3/4"	16"	Pine lattice
I	End	2	1/4"	5¼"	5¼"	Pine lattice
J	Box base	1	1/4"	5¼"	15½"	Pine lattice
K	Fixed top	1	1/4"	4½"	8¾"	Pine lattice
L	Movable top	1	1/4"	4½"	6¾"	Pine lattice
M	Solid front	1	1/4"	5¼"	6¾"	Pine lattice
N	Top trim	1	1/4"	5/8"	8¾"	Pine lattice
O	Base trim	1	1/4"	1/2"	8¾"	Pine lattice
P	Divider	6	1/4"	4½"	4½"	Pine lattice
Q	Spacer	13	1/4"	1¼"	4½"	Pine lattice
R	Paper holder support	2	1/4"	2½"	4"	Pine lattice
S	Movable top support	4	1/4"	1/4"	2½"	Pine lattice
T	Paper holder	1	3/8" dia.	—	*	Dowel or pencil
U	Paper cutter	1	1/4"	1"	4½"	Pine lattice

✸ To be determined during construction.

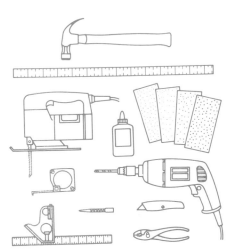

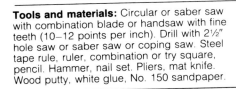

Tools and materials: Circular or saber saw with combination blade or handsaw with fine teeth (10–12 points per inch). Drill with 2½" hole saw or saber saw or coping saw. Steel tape rule, ruler, combination or try square, pencil. Hammer, nail set. Pliers, mat knife. Wood putty, white glue, No. 150 sandpaper. Danish or natural oil finish or polyurethane varnish, tack cloth. Wood (see above). Cork sheet 16" × 16", 3/8" dowel or pencil. Adding-machine paper roll 3⅞" wide. Pen with coiled cord and prepasted pad. Box of 1/2" wire brads.

Organize your household communications with this easy-to-make cork message board. Each person can have a slot for mail and messages, and there is a bulletin board for everyone. A roll of paper and a permanently attached pen ensure that messages will be recorded. A holder for the telephone receiver while it is off the hook is optional; so you can skip Step 9 if it is not needed.

Wood: The box parts are of ¼-inch-thick pine stock, known as lattice. Buy the lattice as wide as possible—at least 5½ inches—then saw it to size, starting with the widest pieces. If wide lattice is not available, use ¼-inch plywood and fill the exposed edges with putty and sand them smooth when the putty dries.

Finishing: Sand the box all over with No. 150 sandpaper, then wipe it clean with a tack cloth. Apply the finish of your choice, either penetrating resin finish (often labeled "Danish" or "natural" oil) or several coats of polyurethane varnish.

Choose a central location to hang the message board. Then attach it directly to the wall through the backboard, using toggle bolts or plastic anchors and screws. If you wish, you can simply rest the board on a counter.

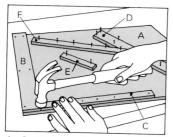

1. Sand the edges of the plywood backboard (A). Attach the stiffeners (B through F) to its back side in alphabetical order. Glue each piece, then nail with brads. Position each brad with pliers, and press it into wood so that it stands on its own; then hammer it. (You can use a staple gun and staples less than ½ in. long.)

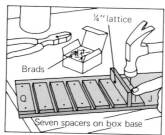

2. Glue and nail first spacer (Q) onto box base (J). Spacer should be flush with side and front edges. Glue six more spacers with their front edges flush with front edge of box base.(Use a piece of ¼-in. lattice to position these spacers.) Following the same procedure, glue six spacers to the fixed top (K).

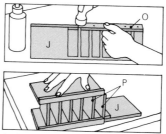

3. Glue and nail trim pieces to the front edges of the message box top and base. Top trim (N) goes on fixed top (K) flush with its lower edge; base trim (O) goes on box base (J) flush with the left and lower edges of that part. Glue the dividers (P) into the slots between spacers on the box base. Test fit of top.

4. Apply glue to tops of all dividers except the last on right end of box. (This one supports one end of the movable top.) Insert dividers in the slots of the fixed top (K), making sure they touch the top trim (N). Protect the fixed top with a piece of scrap wood and tap it lightly with a hammer to fully seat the dividers in their slots.

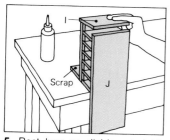

5. Rest box on divider at right end; support fixed top with a scrap of lattice. Glue and nail one end (I) onto the left side of the message box. Check the box for squareness with a try or combination square; shift it gently with your hands if it is not square. Set the box aside in order to allow the glue to dry.

6. All the dividers except the one on the far right are held in place by the spacers. The far right divider should be glued and nailed to the edge of the last spacer on the fixed top (K). To do this, rest the box on the end attached in Step 5. Squeeze some glue between divider and spacer; nail with brads.

7. Glue and nail the solid front (M) to the box base (J). Its side edge should butt against the trim pieces (N and O). Check the assembly for squareness all around with a try or combination square. Glue and nail the right end (I) to the base and the solid front. Once again make sure the box is square.

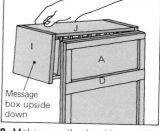

8. Make sure the backboard (A) fits the rear of the message box. If not, sand the edges of the board. Apply glue to edges across bottom and up the sides as far as the center horizontal (D). Run glue along back edge of fixed top (K). Insert backboard into message box, and nail brads through ends and base into backboard.

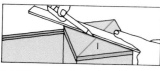
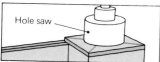

9. To mark the hole for the telephone rest, draw diagonals with a ruler placed from corner to corner on right end (I). Where the diagonals cross is the center of the hole. Cut the opening with a 2½-in. hole saw attached to your drill, or draw a circle of that diameter and use a saber saw or coping saw to cut the hole.

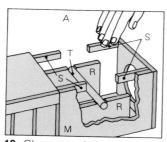

10. Glue paper holder supports (R) to front (M) and backboard (A). Cut a dowel for paper holder (T) to bridge the space between M and A. Glue movable top supports (S) to backboard and front so that their tops are level with tops of dividers (P). Place movable top (L) on supports; press paper cutter (U) into position.

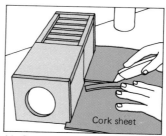

11. Cut cork sheet to fit. If it is not 16 in. wide, cut two pieces each 9 in. wide. Apply glue evenly all over backboard; press down cork sheet and work out bubbles from center toward edges. Trim edges. To eliminate overlap, slit cork down middle with a knife and a ruler as a guide. Peel away excess; press seam flat.

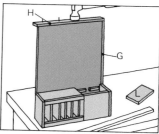

12. With cork sheet face down on flat surface, weight board with heavy objects while glue dries. Glue and nail edge trim (G and H) to sides and top. Set all brads with a nail set; fill holes with wood putty. Smooth edges of movable top (L) with sandpaper wrapped around a 1-in.-wide strip of lattice. Smooth other edges; finish.

KNIFE STORAGE BLOCK

An attractive storage block of laminated maple not only keeps an assortment of carving knives close at hand but also prevents them from jostling against one another in a kitchen drawer, which can dull their cutting edges. The block shown here is 11 inches deep to accommodate a 10½-inch knife blade and a sharpening steel. It can be made with very little waste from a single 1⅛-inch board 11½ inches wide and 38 inches long, using the cutting pattern below. You should adjust the dimensions to fit your own cutlery.

Construction: Begin by sawing a 4-inch length from the end of the maple board.

Put this piece aside; it will yield the four support laminates. Rip the remainder into two 5-inch boards. Saw these into six 11-inch pieces—the main laminates—being sure all corners are square. If you are using a radial arm saw, use a bench stop to ensure accuracy. Reset the arm to 30° and reposition the bench stop to remove one corner from each laminate. Then make the 30° angle cuts for the four support laminates (G–J). If you are not using a radial arm saw, mark and cut the angle from one main laminate and use it as a pattern for the other five. With the help of a ruler, transfer the angle to a support

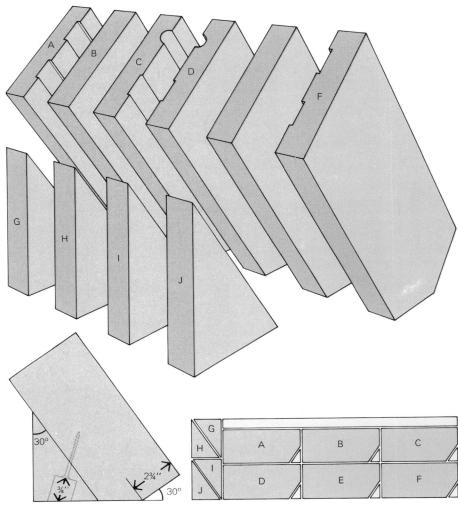

Exploded view shows how the pieces of the knife block fit together. The cutting pattern indicates how all 10 pieces can be cut from a single board 11½ in. x 38 in.

Parts list

Part	Name	Quantity	Thickness	Width	Length	Material
A–F	Main block laminate	6	1⅛"	5"	11"	Hard maple board
G–J	Support laminate	4	1⅛"	5⅝"	3⅞"	Hard maple board

Tools and materials: Drill with ⅜", 11/64", and 3/32" bits. Radial arm, hand, or circular saw. Small router with straight bit and core-box bit. Sanding disc or belt sander, sanding block. Four 7" bar clamps or hand screws. Ruler, awl, screwdriver. Nos. 80, 100, and 150 sandpaper, carpenter's glue, mineral oil, soft cloths. Two 3" No. 8 flathead wood screws.

laminate; then cut one support laminate and use it as a pattern.

Apply glue to the facing sides of the four support laminates, clamp them, and put the structure aside to dry. Label the six main laminates A–F as shown on the previous page. Knife storage slots are routed into the inner faces of laminates A and F; the groove for the sharpening steel and one more knife slot are formed by routing half the depth from laminate C and half from D. Position each knife blade on the appropriate face and trace around it, allowing a little extra room so the blades will slide easily in and out. Use a

small router with a straight bit to make each slot 1/16 inch deeper than the blade that will be stored in it; for the sharpening steel use a core-box bit. Before gluing, assemble the block with the knives and steel in place to be sure everything fits.

Apply a liberal coat of glue to the routed face of laminate A, keeping the glue 1/4 inch away from the slots. Continue building the block layer by layer, then stand it on its long edge and true up the alignment. Carefully apply two clamps and tighten lightly. Turn the block over and apply two more clamps a little more firmly. Secure the first pair of clamps, then

the second. Let the glue dry, then sand all edges to achieve even surfaces.

The support block is attached to the main block with two 3-inch No. 8 flathead wood screws, their heads countersunk 3/4 inch into the base. Drill pilot holes through the support block first, then use them as guides to drill into the main block for marking purposes. Finally, deepen the pilot holes in the main block to accommodate the full length of the screws. Finish by hand, using a sanding block and No. 150 sandpaper. Rub in several coats of mineral oil, which will penetrate the maple and bring out its distinctive figure.

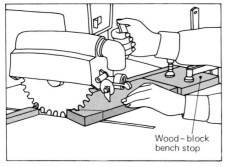

1. After cutting six 5- x 11-in. pieces for the main laminates, set radial arm saw to 30° and adjust the bench stop so that the blade will enter bottom edge of the laminate 2¾ in. from the square corner. Make angle cuts to remove a triangular piece from each main laminate.

Wood–block bench stop

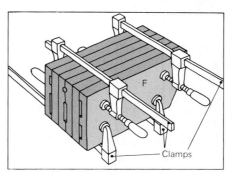

5. Before gluing, set the four clamps to the proper width. Have a damp cloth ready. Glue one laminate at a time until the block is complete; then apply clamps lightly by pairs. Alternate tightening to prevent slippage. Wipe off excess glue with the cloth.

Clamps

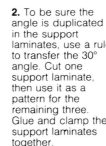

2. To be sure the angle is duplicated in the support laminates, use a ruler to transfer the 30° angle. Cut one support laminate, then use it as a pattern for the remaining three. Glue and clamp the support laminates together.

30°

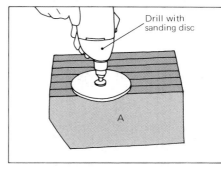

6. When the glue is dry, sand the edges of the blocks even and smooth, using a No. 80 sanding disc or belt. To prevent swirl marks with a disc sander, keep the disc moving and level. Finish the edges with No. 100 sandpaper.

Drill with sanding disc

A

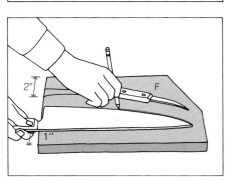

3. The knife slots are routed into the inner faces of laminates A and F and the joining faces of C and D. For even rows mark 1 in. from the long side of each laminate and 2 in. from the short side. Place the back of each knife blade on the marks and trace the outline of the blade.

2"

1"

F

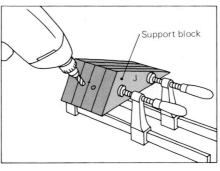

7. Use a ¹¹⁄₆₄-in. bit to drill two pilot holes through the 4-in. side of the support block at an angle that will allow No. 8 wood screws to bite at least 1 in. deep into the main block. Use a ⅜-in. bit to countersink the screwheads ¾ in.

Support block

J

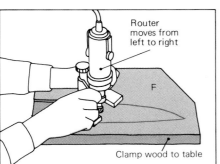

4. Rout the slots slightly larger than the blades. For laminates A and F set the router to cut ¹⁄₁₆ in. deeper than the thickest part of the blade. To cut the groove and slot between C and D, remove half the thickness from each laminate.

Router moves from left to right

F

Clamp wood to table

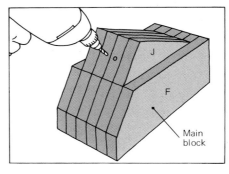

8. Position the support block and drill into the main block just deep enough to mark the angle of the pilot holes. Remove the support block and use a ³⁄₃₂-in. bit to complete the pilot holes. Attach blocks with wood screws. Sand all surfaces with No. 150 paper.

J

F

Main block

BATHROOM VANITY

Two historic models, the classic Early American dry sink and the hardwood cabinets that once graced luxury ocean liners, are combined in this handsome bathroom vanity. The materials used are a rich mixture of colors and textures—including brass, copper, marblelike Corian, and walnut—that can transform the prosaic bathroom sink into a striking addition to any home's decor.

The sink in this vanity washstand is a 12-inch copper mixing bowl with a rolled wire rim, purchased at a gourmet kitchen supply store. A hole was cut in the bottom to receive a standard 1½-inch drain. The faucets are standard brass fixtures that look like antiques.

The stiles and rails are made of 4/4 walnut stock (whose actual thickness is 13/16 inch). The panels were made from ½-inch rough-cut walnut boards, which had to be planed to a thickness of ¼ inch. It would be simpler and less expensive to use ¼-inch walnut-veneer plywood, which is much easier to find. All the cabinet parts were sanded with Nos. 100, 150, and 220 paper, then finished with tung oil.

The white marblelike top is Corian, a man-made material that is commonly used for counter tops and can be cut and sanded almost as easily as wood. Use carbide-tipped blades and bits when working with Corian, and wear a protective mask and goggles, as Corian emits fumes that can be harmful. If you wish to substitute walnut for the Corian, give it a water-repellent finish by rubbing in a base coat of linseed oil mixed with turpentine, followed by several coats of linseed oil. Do not use tung oil on any wood near the sink—it contains a toxic substance that may be released by hot water.

Variations: The dimensions given in the chart below are for a small vanity that is 37 inches high, 19 inches wide, and 17 inches deep. The sink itself is 34¼ inches above the floor. This arrangement will fit in most small bathrooms. If you have more space available, you can increase the lengths of the stiles and rails and cut the panels and other parts to fit. If you wish, you can increase the number of cabinet doors and add a second sink too (see opposite page).

Parts list

Part	Name	Quantity	Thickness	Width	Length	Material
A	Stile	6	13/16"	1⅝"	33½"	4/4 walnut
B	Side rail	4	13/16"	1⅝"	17"	4/4 walnut
C	Side bottom rail	2	13/16"	3½"	17"	4/4 walnut
D	Front top rail	1	13/16"	1⅝"	19"	4/4 walnut
E	Front bottom rail	1	13/16"	3½"	19"	4/4 walnut
F	Door stile	2	13/16"	1⅝"	28⅜"*	4/4 walnut
G	Door rail	3	13/16"	1⅝"	15¾"	4/4 walnut
H	Backsplash	1	13/16"	4"*	19"*	4/4 walnut
I	Backsplash side	2	13/16"	4"*	17"*	4/4 walnut
J	Block	6	13/16"	1¼"	2"	4/4 walnut
K	Siding strip	2	3/16"	13/16"	17"	4/4 walnut
L	Side panel	8	¼"	7"*	13⅝"*	½" walnut
M	Door panel	4	¼"	6⅜"*	12"*	½" walnut
N	Brace	3	¾"	1½"	17⅜"*	1 x 2 white pine
O	Side support	2	¾"	1¼"	15½"*	Rip from 1 x 2 white pine
P	Back support	1	¾"	1¼"	15⅞"*	
Q	Spline	2	⅛"*	½"	33½"	
R	Top	1	¾"	17"	17¼"*	Corian

*Measurement is approximate; cut to fit during construction.

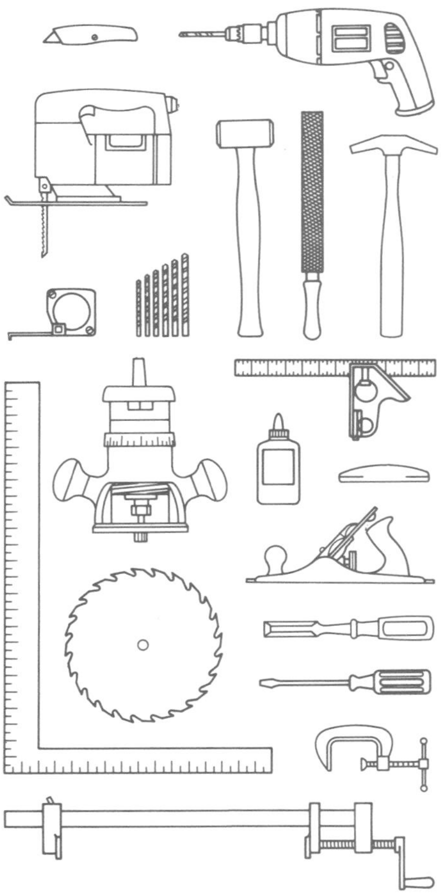

Tools and materials: Table saw and radial arm saw (optional) with carbide-tipped combination blade and dado head. Saber saw with carbide and nonferrous-metal cutting blades. Router with 3/16" rabbeting bit, 3/16" and 5/16" cove bits, and 5/16" carbide-tipped quarter-round bit. Drill with carbide twist bits and hole cutter (optional). Orbital sander or sanding block. Steel tape rule, framing square, combination square, pencil. Jack plane, mat knife, rasp, ⅝" straight chisel. Screwdriver, tack hammer, mallet. Mask, goggles. Four 3′ pipe clamps, sixteen 6" C-clamps. Nos. 80, 100, 150, and 220 sandpaper. Carpenter's glue, silicone sealant. Tung oil, soft cloths. An 18" square piece of ¾" Corian, ½" x 8" x 14′ walnut stock or a 4′ x 4′ panel of ¼" walnut-veneer plywood. A 9′ length of 1 x 2 white pine, 32′ of 4/4 walnut stock 3¾"–4" wide. A ⅛" dowel 6" long. A 12" copper mixing bowl. Plumbing fixtures. Door pull. Three 1¼" x 2½" brass butt hinges, ¾" carpet tacks, 2" No. 6 self-tapping screws, ¾" and 1¼" No. 8 flathead wood screws.

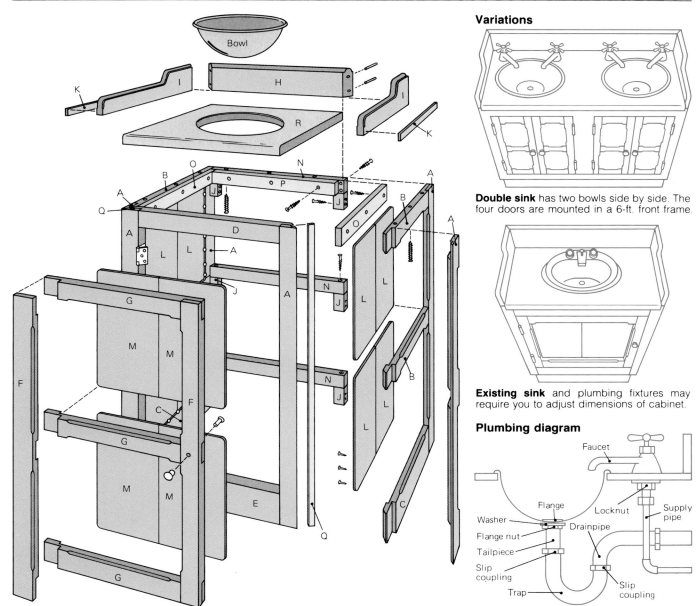

Variations

Double sink has two bowls side by side. The four doors are mounted in a 6-ft. front frame.

Existing sink and plumbing fixtures may require you to adjust dimensions of cabinet.

Plumbing diagram

Exploded view shows how parts fit together. Side and front frames are formed by lap joints, as is the door. Panels fit loosely into rabbets and are held in place by carpet tacks. Frames are joined in front by long splined miters and in back by 1 x 2 braces (N). Two bottom braces are screwed to hardwood blocks, their height determined by plumbing requirements. Top brace rests on blocks so it is flush with tops of side frames; it is screwed to 1 x 2 side supports (O) on which top (R) rests.

Top's back is supported by another 1 x 2 (P), and top's lip overhangs front frame. Top is enclosed on three sides by backsplash pieces, which are secured by 2-in. screws driven up through top side rails (B) and top brace. Joints between backsplash pieces are mitered and reinforced with ⅛-in. dowel pins. Use ½-in. grid to make pattern for backsplash sides (I). Basic vanity design can be adapted to several variations. Plumbing can be done with standard fittings.

Pattern for backsplash sides (I)

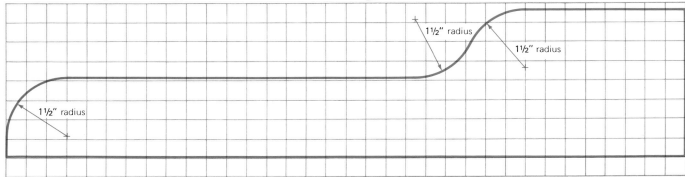

Use this grid to make a pattern (see p.48) for the backsplash sides. Make boxes ½ in. square. Cut two sides that are mirror images.

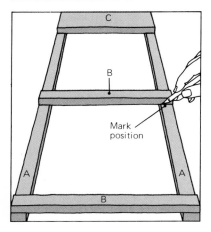

1. Rip 4/4 walnut 3½ in. wide for bottom rails and 1⅝ in. wide for all stiles and other rails. Cut stiles (A) and rails (B, C, D, and E) to length for front and side frames. Lay frames out square, placing crossmembers on top of stiles. The middle rail of each side frame should be centered in the open space between the top and bottom rails. Label all parts for reassembly later.

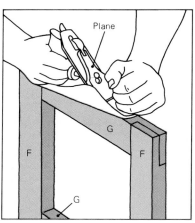

2. Use a sharp knife to mark the joints between stiles and crossmembers on underside of crossmembers; scribe width of crossmembers on stiles. Cut rabbets and dadoes for lap joints to half the thickness of the wood, using a wide dado head—determine depth of cut with scrap pieces. Lay out frames to check joints; then apply glue and C-clamps to one pair of joints at a time, making sure all joints stay square.

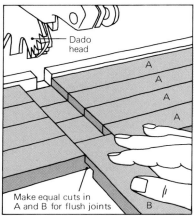

3. Cut door stiles (F) and rails (G) long enough to fit snugly within front frame. Lay out parts inside frame; then scribe, cut, and assemble lap joints as described in Step 2. After glue has dried, plane the top edge of door and the side edge that will not receive hinges for a finished appearance and to create a clearance of at least ¹⁄₁₆ in. all around.

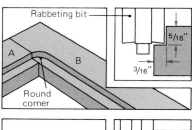

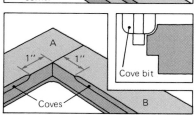

4. Use router equipped with rabbeting bit to cut rabbets for panels (L and M) ³⁄₁₆ in. wide and ⁵⁄₁₆ in. deep into the interior back edges of side frames and door. Do not attempt to square off the rabbets at the corners, but let them remain rounded. Then use a ³⁄₁₆-in. cove bit to rout decorative coves into interior front edges, stopping 1 in. from each corner of the frames.

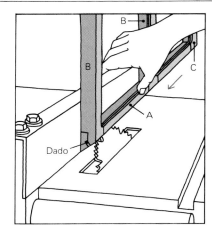

5. Set table saw blade to 45°, making test cuts in pieces of scrap wood to ensure accuracy; then miter the front stiles (A) of both side frames and both stiles of the front frame. Reset blade's depth of cut to make ¼-in.-deep dadoes for splines the width of the saw blade (about ⅛ in.) along all four mitered edges. Make splines (Q) from white pine, planed just thick enough to fit snugly into dadoes; cut each slightly less than ½ in. wide.

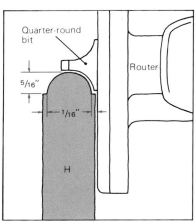

6. Cut backsplash (H) and backsplash sides (I) a little longer than needed. Miter back ends of both side pieces and one end of the back piece. Scribe pattern (p.163) onto outer faces of side pieces and rough-cut with saber or band saw; finish shaping with rasp and No. 80 sandpaper. Rout both upper edges of all three pieces with a ⁵⁄₁₆-in. quarter-round bit, set deeply enough to cut ¹⁄₁₆ in. into the wood.

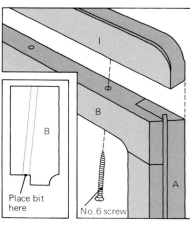

7. To attach backsplash sides (I) to side frames, first drill three ⅛-in. holes up through each top side rail (B), placing the point of the bit at the base of the rabbet in the back edge. Then hold each side piece in position and drill ⁵⁄₆₄-in. pilot holes into it. Finally, apply glue to each top side rail and secure backsplash sides with 2-in. No. 6 self-tapping screws.

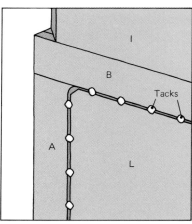

8. Cut panels (L and M) to fit within rabbets in side frames and door, allowing for ⅛ in. clearance all around. Use a rasp to round off the corners to match the way the rabbets are cut. (If you are using ¼-in. plywood instead of walnut stock, each panel may be cut to the full width of the opening, rather than half the width as indicated in the chart on page 162.) Secure panels by driving ¾-in. carpet tacks around the edges of the panels into the walnut frames.

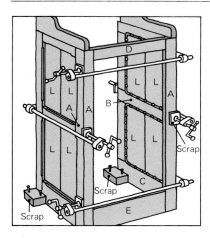

9. Glue splines (Q) into dadoes in stiles (A) of front frame. Before glue dries, apply more glue to dado in a side frame and to faces of miter, and force side frame into position, making sure that joint is square. Quickly form the other miter joint in the same way. Then apply two bar or pipe clamps across front frame and one centered across each side frame. Tighten clamps a little at a time, making sure both joints remain square and corners are flush.

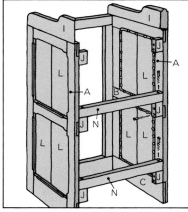

10. Glue and screw blocks (J) to back stiles (A) of side frames, using two 1¼-in. No. 8 wood screws in each; position blocks so that the braces that rest on them will be level. Cut braces (N) so their length matches the distance between the side frames. To secure the two bottom braces, drill a ⅛-in. hole through the width of the brace ⅜ in. from each end; then drill ⁵⁄₆₄-in. pilot holes into blocks and drive in 2-in. No. 6 self-tapping screws.

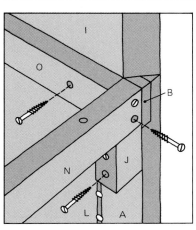

11. Before securing top brace (N), cut the side supports (O) ¾ in. shorter than the interior length of the top side rails (B). Glue and screw supports to top side rails with 1¼-in. No. 8 wood screws so that the upper edges are flush. Drill three ⅛-in. holes through the width of the top brace for attaching backsplash (H)—see Step 7. Then secure the top brace to the side supports with 1¼-in. No. 8 screws.

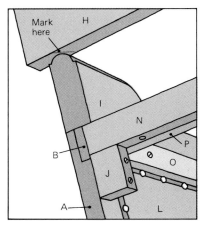

12. Cut back support (P) to length so that it fits between the two side supports (O); glue and screw it to the top brace (N) with 1¼-in. No. 8 wood screws. To fit the backsplash (H), hold its mitered end against the top edge of the miter on one of the backsplash sides (I), and mark the other end for mitering. Cut it slightly long, then trim a little at a time until the backsplash fits snugly between the miters of the two side pieces.

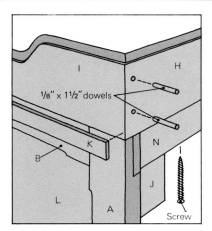

13. Hold backsplash (H) in position and drill pilot holes (see Step 7). Then apply glue to all faces of miter joints and to top edge of top brace (N) and drive 2-in. No. 6 self-tapping screws up into backsplash. Reinforce miter joints by drilling two ⅛-in. holes into each backsplash side (I) and driving glued dowels into holes. Trim with knife and sand flush. Apply glue to siding strips (K) and clamp over joints between top side rails (B) and backsplash sides.

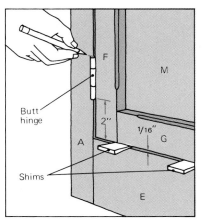

14. Position hinges and trace their outlines onto door stile (F)—center one hinge and place the others 2 in. from top and bottom. Use a mallet and ⅝-in. chisel to cut hinge mortises (see *Index*, p.379). Secure hinges to door stile with ¾-in. No. 8 wood screws. Position door in its frame, using ¹⁄₁₆-in. shims to maintain bottom space, and mark placement of hinges on stile (A). Cut mortises in stile and attach hinges with screws.

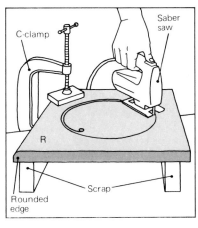

15. Cut top (R) to fit within the frame made by the three backsplash pieces (H and I) so that it overhangs the front top rail (D) by about ¾ in. Shape the top edge of the overhang with a router and ⁵⁄₁₆-in. quarter-round bit; smooth with No. 80 sandpaper. Position bowl in center of top and trace its outline. Cut ¼ in. inside traced circle with saber saw, then use rasp and No. 80 sandpaper to shape hole so that bowl rests on its rim.

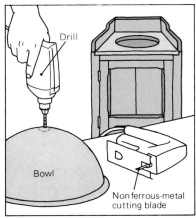

16. Position faucets and trace their outlines on top (R). Use hole cutter or appropriate bit to drill holes for pipes. Drill ³⁄₁₆ in. starter hole in bottom of bowl and use saber saw with nonferrous-metal cutting blade to enlarge hole as needed for drain. Sand top with Nos. 100 and 150 sandpaper. Then apply silicone sealant to edges of large hole in top, and seat bowl firmly. Sand all cabinet parts and apply desired finish.

EARLY AMERICAN NIGHT TABLE

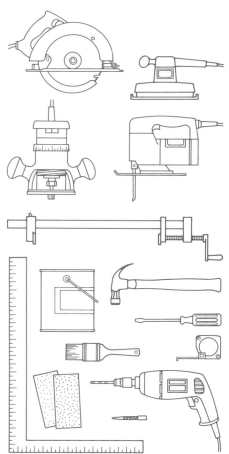

This traditional night table is made of pine, which is relatively inexpensive and easy to work with. For the top, bottom, and side pieces, edge-joined pine—random widths of pine boards already glued edge to edge—was used. It is usually available in lumberyards, but if you are unable to purchase pine that way, you can make it yourself (see *Index,* p.379). Choose pine boards that are No. 2 grade or better, and select a comparable grade for the pine plywood.

When all the pieces are cut to size and routed, do a test fit and make any necessary adjustments before final assembly. You will need a 2-foot bar clamp to glue the front rail to the sides (Step 6); but clamping is not required elsewhere, since all other parts are secured with screws or nails and glue.

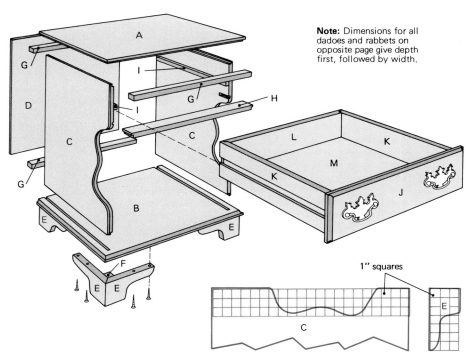

Note: Dimensions for all dadoes and rabbets on opposite page give depth first, followed by width.

1″ squares

Parts list

Part	Name	Quantity	Thickness	Width	Length	Material
A	Top	1	⅝″	16″	21″	Edge-joined pine
B	Bottom	1	⅝″	16″	21″	Edge-joined pine
C	Side	2	⅝″	15″	21″	Edge-joined pine
D	Back	1	¼″	18″	20½″	Pine plywood
E	Foot block	8	¾″	3¼″	7″	1 x 8 pine
F	Glue block	4	¾″	¾″	3″	1 x 8 pine
G	Filler block	3	¾″	1″	16¾″	1 x 8 pine
H	Front rail	1	¾″	1¾″	17¼″	1 x 8 pine
I	Drawer slide	2	½″	1¹¹/₁₆″	14¼″	Oak or other hardwood
J	Drawer face	1	¾″	5″	17¾″	1 x 8 pine
K	Drawer side	2	½″	4¼″	14¼″	Pine
L	Drawer back	1	½″	4¼″	16⅛″	Pine
M	Drawer bottom	1	¼″	14″	16⅛″	Pine plywood

Tools and materials: Circular or table saw, saber saw. Router with ¼″ rounding-over bit, ¼″ cove bit, rabbeting bit, and ¼″ and ¾″ dado bits. Electric drill with No. 8 Screwmate bit. Orbital sander with No. 180 sandpaper. Hammer, nail set. Screwdriver. Steel tape rule, framing square. A 2′ bar clamp. Stain, polyurethane varnish, silicone spray lubricant, paintbrush. An 8′ length of ¾″ No. 2 common or better grade edge-joined pine 18″ wide. A 6′ length of 1 x 8 No. 2 common pine, a 4′ length of ½″ x 5″ No. 2 common pine. A 2′ x 4′ piece of ¼″ pine plywood, ½″ x 2″ x 16″ oak or other hardwood. Two drawer pulls. Six ¾″, nine 1″, twenty 1¼″, and eight 1½″ No. 8 flathead wood screws, 1″ common nails, 1″ finishing nails, 1″ brads.

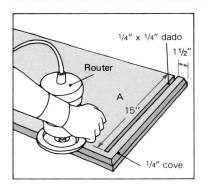

1. Cut all parts to the sizes specified in the chart. Cut two blind dadoes on the underside of the top (A) and on the top of the bottom (B) as shown. Rout the lower edges of the top along its front and sides, using a router with a ¼-in. cove bit. Do the same along the upper edges of the bottom.

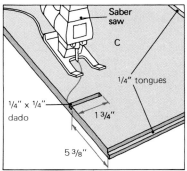

2. Rabbet top, bottom, and rear edges of sides (C) to create ¼-in. tongues. Cut a ¼- x ¼-in. dado 1¾ in. long on inner face of each side 5⅜ in. below lower edge of top rabbet, beginning from front edge. Cut decorative curves into front edges with a saber saw, and rout front edges, using a ¼-in. cove bit.

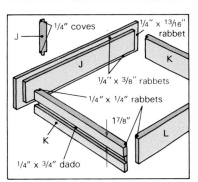

3. Rabbet the rear edges of drawer face (J) ¼ x ¹³⁄₁₆ in. along ends and ¼ x ⅜ in. along top and bottom. Rout all front edges with ¼-in. cove bit. Cut ¼- x ¼-in. rabbets on the inner faces at both ends of drawer sides (K) and drawer back (L). On outer face and along length of each drawer side cut a ¼- x ¾-in. dado 1⅞ in. from the top.

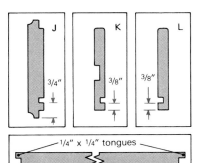

4. Cut ¼- x ¼-in. dadoes on the inner faces of parts J, K, and L: one dado should be ¾ in. from the bottom edge of part J and the others ⅜ in. from the bottoms of parts K and L. Rout the top edges of the drawer sides and back with a ¼-in. rounding-over bit. Rabbet the two ends of the front rail (H) to make ¼- x ¼-in. tongues 1¾ in. long.

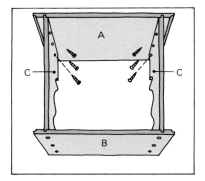

5. Before assembling the table, countersink pilot holes for all screws and apply white glue to dado and rabbet joints. Then insert three 1¼-in. No. 8 flathead wood screws through the bottom (B) into each side (C), and insert three screws at an angle through each side into the top (A).

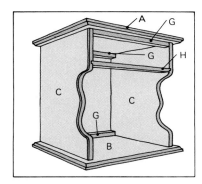

6. Use glue and three 1-in. screws to attach each filler block (G): two go on the top (A) and one on the rear of the bottom (B) as shown. Apply glue to the tongues of the front rail (H) and insert into the short dadoes on the inner faces of the sides (C). Clamp rail to sides with a bar clamp for 4 hr.

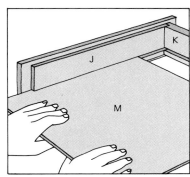

7. Using glue and 1-in. finishing nails hammered flush with a nail set, assemble the drawer. First, join one drawer side (K) to the drawer face (J), then slide the drawer bottom (M) into the dadoes cut for it in Step 4. Finally, attach other side and drawer back (L).

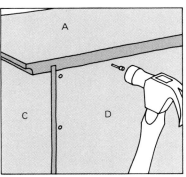

8. Test-fit the drawer slides (I) in the dadoes on the drawer sides (K). Then insert drawer and slides together and check for a smooth fit. Mark the proper positions of the slides on the inner faces of the table sides (C). Attach each slide with three ¾-in. No. 8 screws. Spray the slides and the drawer dadoes with silicone lubricant.

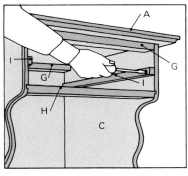

9. Using glue and 1-in. common nails spaced about 3 in. apart, attach the back (D) to the rear of the night table with its good side facing forward. Nail through the back into the rabbets in the sides (C) and into the top and bottom filler blocks (G) at the rear of the table.

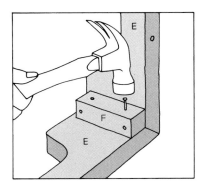

10. Shape the feet (E) with a saber saw and miter them (see *Index*, p.379) for joining. Assemble each foot and a glue block (F) with glue and four 1-in. brads as shown. Position each foot ¼ in. in from the corner edges of the bottom (B), using two 1¼-in. and two 1½-in. screws. Finish with stain and varnish. Attach drawer pulls.

GLOBE LAMP

Brighten your home with one or both of these geometric globe lamps. The simple design of a globe seated on a rectangle or cube will give any room a modern look.

The lamps are designed around pre-wired globe light fixtures, which can be purchased in many department stores and through most major mail-order catalogs. The lamp bases are made of inexpensive particle board (flake board) and covered with plastic laminate. If you prefer, you can substitute some other type of covering, such as heavy wallpaper, cork, or mirror tiles, in order to create the look of your choice. The construction techniques are the same for rectangular and square bases. The measurements given in the chart are for a rectangular base. To make a square lamp, simply change the length of the sides (A) to 5½ inches and change the length of the side laminate pieces (C) to 6⅛ inches.

Variations in size: The overall dimensions of the lamp base are governed by the diameter of the globe. The dimensions given below are for a lamp with a globe that is 7 inches in diameter. If the diameter of your globe is larger or smaller, measure its circumference (the distance around its middle) and divide by three. Subtract 1 inch from the resulting number and you will have an approximate width for the base. Round off this figure to the nearest quarter-inch for ease in measuring. This will give you the actual width of the completed lamp base. Use the same measurement for the actual height of the base if you are building a cube base. If you are constructing a rectangular base, double the width for the actual height of the completed lamp base.

To calculate the dimensions of the sides (A) of the lamp base, subtract ½ inch (the thickness of the particle board) from the actual width of the completed base and subtract ½ inch (the thickness of the bottom) from the height. The bottom (B) should have the same measurements as the actual width of the completed base. Add ⅛ inch to the actual dimensions of the completed base to get the size of the side laminate pieces (C) and top laminate (D).

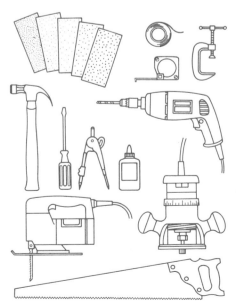

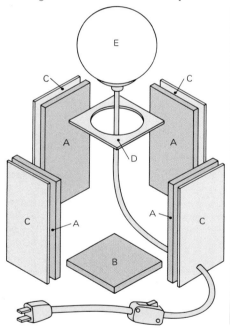

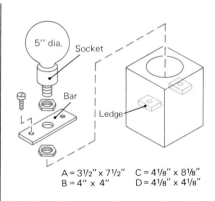

A = 3½" x 7½"   C = 4⅛" x 8⅛"
B = 4" x 4"   D = 4⅛" x 4⅛"

Variation. You can make a smaller globe lamp using a simple spherical light bulb and a porcelain socket instead of the special prewired globe light. Glue and nail a ledge to the insides of each of two opposite sides to support the light socket. The bulb should be seated about ½ in. above the top of the base to keep it from scorching the plastic. Attach lamp wire to the socket, pass the wire through a threaded nipple, and screw on a brace bar with a nut above and below it.

Parts list

Part	Name	Quantity	Thickness	Width	Length	Material
A	Side	4	½"	5½"	11½"	Particle board
B	Bottom	1	½"	6"	6"	Particle board
C	Side laminate	4	—	6⅛"	12⅛"	Plastic laminate
D	Top laminate	1	—	6⅛"	6⅛"	Plastic laminate
E	Globe light	1	7" dia.	—	—	Globe light fixture

Tools and materials: Hand or circular saw, saber or keyhole saw, fine-tooth saw. Router with laminate cutter or fine, wide file. Electric or hand drill, hammer, screwdriver. Wire cutter. Two 4" C-clamps. Steel tape rule, compass, pencil. Contact cement, white glue, electrical tape, No. 100 sandpaper. A 1' × 2½' piece of particle board (flake board) and 2' × 2½' piece of plastic laminate. Line switch, plug, 7" globe light fixture, extra lamp cord. Two dozen 4d finishing nails.

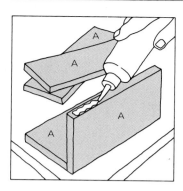

1. Use a handsaw or a circular saw to cut out the sides (A) and bottom (B). Run a generous bead of white glue down one edge of one side and fit that side together with a second side, face to edge. Nail the glued sides together with three 4d finishing nails. Add the other two sides in the same way.

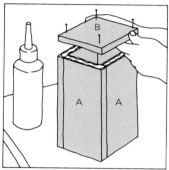

2. Carefully align the bottom (B) and then glue it into place. Drive three nails through the bottom and into the lower edge of each side (A). Check the sides for irregularities. The plastic laminate that will cover them must be applied to a perfectly smooth surface. Depressions will do no harm, but raised nailheads or high spots will cause problems.

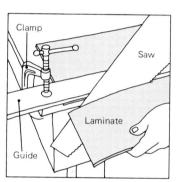

3. Clamp the sheet of laminate to your workbench or a table so that its entire length is supported. The laminate should be positioned so that the teeth of the saw you are using will cut into its face—generally clamp it face up if you are using a handsaw and face down if you are using a saber saw. Cut the four side laminate pieces (C) and the top laminate (D).

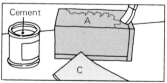

4. Coat one side (A) and the back of one side laminate (C) with contact cement. When the cement is no longer sticky, place a piece of paper over the side. Position the laminate over the paper so that it overlaps the side all around, and then remove the paper and press the laminate onto the side. Tap it down with a hammer buffered with a scrap of wood.

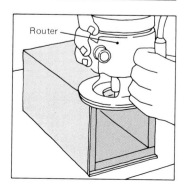

5. Use a laminate cutter in a router or use a wide file to trim the edges of the side laminate flush with the side of the lamp base. (If the overlap is extensive, cut away the excess with a fine-tooth saw before using the router.) Attach laminate to the remaining three sides in the same way, and then trim the laminate flush with the top of the lamp base.

6. Apply cement to the top edges of the lamp base and to the underside of the outer edges of the top laminate (D) and let it set. Position the laminate, trim it flush with the sides, then adjust the router cutter to make a slight bevel to dress the joints and keep the edges from lifting. If you do not have a router, use a file held at a slight angle to bevel the edges of the laminate.

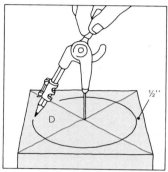

7. Mark the center of the top laminate (D) by drawing two intersecting diagonal lines across it. Drill a ⅛-in. pilot hole where the two lines cross, and then place the point of a compass into the hole and draw a circle that passes to within ½ in. of the top edges.

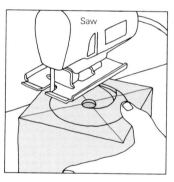

8. Using the pilot hole as a starter, drill a hole in the top that is large enough to accommodate the blade of a saber saw or keyhole saw. Use the saber saw or keyhole saw to cut out the circle drawn in Step 7. Smooth the edges of the cut with sandpaper.

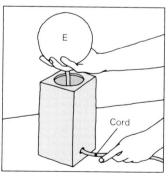

9. Drill a ½-in. hole just above the bottom of one of the sides of the lamp base. Pass the cord of the globe light (E) through the hole, set the globe light into place on top of lamp base, and pull cord tight.

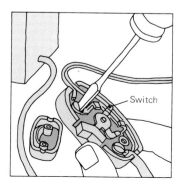

10. Cut the cord off about 1 ft. from the lamp and trim back the insulation to expose the ends of the wires. Attach one bared wire end to one of the switch terminals. Strip the end of the extra lamp cord and attach one bared wire end to the other switch terminal. Splice the free wires of the two cords together. Attach a lamp plug to the other end of the extra lamp cord.

CHEST OF DRAWERS

It is a tenet of traditional joinery that joints should be as inconspicuous as possible. Wood is selected with an eye toward blending colors and figures so that, ideally, a piece of furniture seems to be carved from a single block of wood.

Contemporary woodworkers often take the opposite tack, flaunting a well-made joint instead of trying to conceal it. The dovetail joints that secure the interchangeable sections of this chest of drawers are a case in point. The tails, which terminate the spreaders, are of dark walnut, contrasting sharply with the poplar used throughout the rest of the piece. And because the spreaders are precisely aligned one on top of the other, the blatant dovetails give the illusion of being even more blatant butterfly joints holding the sections of the chest together. (In fact, nothing holds the sections together except gravity; they are kept in alignment by pegs that fit into holes in the top and bottom spreaders.)

Materials: The wide poplar boards used for the top, sides, and drawers, on the other hand, reflect the traditional approach. Hardwood is difficult to find in the widths required, and extremely expensive when you do find it, so boards are made for the project by edge-joining narrower stock. If you select and match the boards carefully, the joints will be imperceptible to any but the most discerning eye. (For instructions on the techniques of edge-joining, see *Index,* p.379.)

The chest of drawers consists of a top unit, a base unit, and as many chest sections as you wish to make—however high you wish to make them. Ours has a 6-inch section on top of three 10-inch sections. The chart below and the instructions on the following pages are for building a single 10-inch chest section and drawer. To make a different-size section, add or subtract the appropriate number of inches from the height of the chest sides (D) and back (L) and from the drawer sides (G), back (H), and front (I). All other external measurements remain the same.

Depending on the quality and width of available hardwood stock, you will need 7–9 board feet of poplar and about 3 board feet of walnut to make the top and base units. (A board foot is equivalent to a nominal 1-inch board 12 inches square; if you order a 1 x 6 that is 2 feet long or a 1 x 4 that is 3 feet long, for example, you have bought 1 board foot. By the same token, a 2 x 12 that is 1 foot long is 2 board feet.) For each 10-inch chest section and its drawer you will need 13–15 board feet of poplar and for a 6-inch section and its drawer, 11–13 board feet; each chest section requires about 3 board feet of walnut. Four chest sections and drawers require

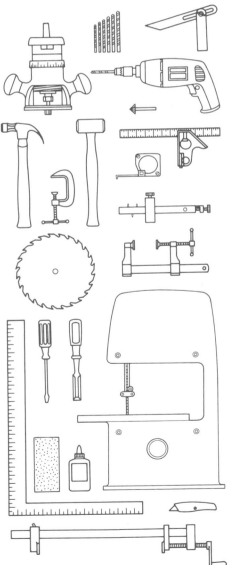

Parts list

Part	Name	Quantity	Thickness	Width	Length	Material
A	Spreader	8	¾″	2¼″	36″	Walnut
B	Top side	2	¾″	16¾″	1″	Poplar
C	Base side	2	¾″	16¾″	4″	Poplar
D	Chest side	2	¾″	16¾″	10″ ✳	Poplar
E	Top	1	¾″	17¾″	38″	Poplar
F	Base front	1	¾″	3¼″	34½″	Poplar
G	Drawer side	2	¾″	8⅜″ ✳	16¼″	Poplar
H	Drawer back	1	¾″	7⅞″ ✳	33⅝″†	Poplar
I	Drawer front	1	¾″	9¼″ ✳	35¼″†	Poplar
J	Drawer guide	2	¾″	¾″	15¼″	Poplar
K	Drawer-pull laminate	4	¾″	1½″†	5¾″†	Poplar
L	Chest back	1	¼″	9¼″ ✳	35¼″	A–D fir plywood
M	Drawer bottom	1	¼″	16⅛″	33⅜″†	A–D fir plywood
N	Peg	8	⅜″	—	1¼″	Hardwood dowel

✳ For a 6″ chest and drawer subtract 4″.
†Measurement is approximate; cut to fit during construction.

Tools and materials: Table saw with miter gauge and dado head. Band saw with adjustable table. Router with ⁹⁄₁₆″ dovetail bit, ⅝″ and ¾″ straight bits. Drill with twist bits and countersink. Steel tape rule, framing square, combination square, marking gauge, T bevel, scribe, knife, pencil. Mallet, ¾″ straight chisel. Hammer, screwdriver. Four 4′ bar or pipe clamps, at least eight 6″ C-clamps, two 12″ quick-action clamps. Carpenter's glue. Nos. 80, 100, and 150 sandpaper. Finishing material of your choice. Wood (see above). Two ³⁄₁₆″ stove bolts 2″ long with matching nuts (optional). 1″ No. 6 flathead wood screws, 1″ and 1¼″ No. 8 flathead wood screws. ¾″ brads.

a 4- x 8-foot panel of ¼-inch plywood.

Hardwood generally comes in random widths rather than standard sizes. For the greatest economy and the best-looking results, do not depend on the lumberyard workers to pick out your wood for you. Go to the lumberyard yourself and choose the boards you want. Look for boards 6–7 inches wide and at least 6 feet long. Pay attention to the color of the wood—there can be quite a difference between two boards of the same material. The boards you choose should match one another exactly after they are finished. To bring out the grain and true color of a piece of raw lumber, wet it with water.

Construction: Select straight and true walnut stock for the spreaders (A). These pieces must be identical, and they must all lie flat, face to face, if the completed sections are to form a solid, cohesive whole. To help ensure the necessary precision, work out and cut the dovetail pins on both ends of one spreader first, then use it as a master for marking all the dovetail slots in all the side pieces (see p.172). If you think that you might want to add sections to your chest of drawers at some future date, save the master spreader. If not, use it in the project.

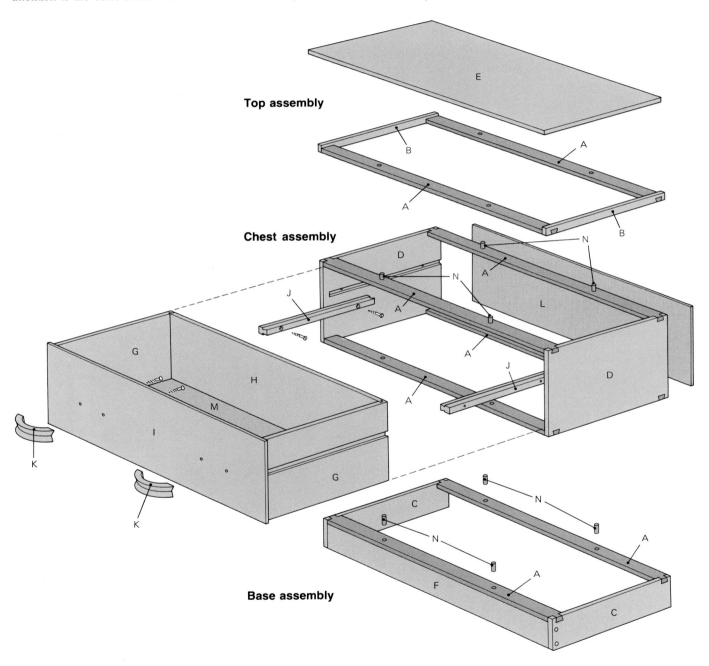

Top assembly

Chest assembly

Base assembly

Exploded view shows how units fit together. Detailed drawings of each unit appear on the following pages with step-by-step instructions for building that unit. Begin construction by ripping enough walnut to make all the spreaders (A) you will need; each additional chest section will require four more spreaders. Cut each spreader ¹⁄₁₆ in. longer than its final measurement, using a bench stop to ensure that all are the same length. Edge-join poplar stock to create boards of the widths needed for parts B–I. Note that the grain of wood runs vertically in the side parts (B, C, and D) and horizontally in all other parts. If you wish to maintain a consistent figure along the whole length of a side of the assembled chest of drawers, edge-join stock to make a single board that is long enough to yield one side of all units. Then crosscut the side parts in order, from top to base, labeling each for assembly. Take great care when cutting these and all other parts to size that all corners are perfectly square. Cuts that are even slightly askew will result in a lopsided and unsteady piece of furniture.

Cutting the dovetails

The crucial first step in making identical dovetail joints is to construct a solid and reliable hardwood jig for cutting the tails on a table saw. It is vital that the wood for the jig be straight and true. Rip a 6-ft. length to a width of 3½–4 in. Cut a 2-ft. piece for the base of the jig and screw a 1 x 2 stiffener to its back (Step 2). Secure the base to the face of the miter gauge with No. 8 wood screws or ³⁄₁₆-in. bolts. With the help of a T bevel, set the miter gauge to reflect the angle of one side of the tail. Cut marked test pieces to make precise adjustments in the angle of the cut, to set the height and angle of the blade, and to mark the position for the

arm of the jig (Step 3). Cut three pieces of hardwood to make the arm 18 in. high, and clamp them to the base (Step 4), being sure that the joint is square. To use the jig, hold a spreader (A) firmly in the corner formed by the two front pieces of the arm of the jig, then guide it over the blade. When one side of all tails is cut, reset the miter gauge to the complementary angle and repeat the process with test pieces before cutting the second side of all tails. To cut the shoulders, set the miter gauge to 90° and adjust blade height to ⁷⁄₁₆ in. Clamp a simple stop block to the jig base. Finish the shoulders with a sharp chisel.

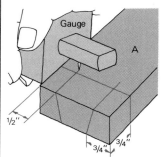

1. With marking gauge, scribe pattern of tails on both ends of all spreaders (A) and on several short test pieces.

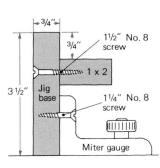

2. Cut hardwood for jig. Screw 1 x 2 stiffener to back of jig base and attach base to face of table saw's miter gauge.

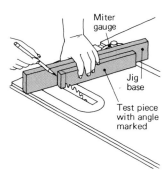

3. Set blade to 90°. Set miter gauge so jig's base matches angle of tail. Use test piece to mark position of arm.

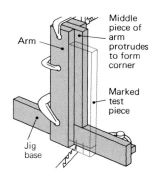

4. Clamp the three parts of jig arm in place, making sure joint is square. Cut test pieces to make final adjustments.

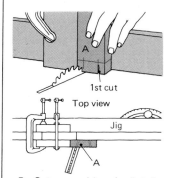

5. Cut one side of all tails. Reset miter gauge and make test cuts to reposition arm; then cut opposite angles.

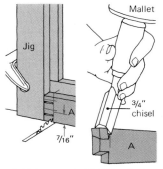

6. Set gauge to 90° (check with framing square) to cut shoulders ⁷⁄₁₆ in. deep. Finish tails with sharp ¾-in. chisel.

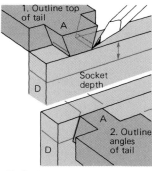

7. Scribe socket depth; mark out all sockets with master spreader. Cut test pieces to set blade angle and stop.

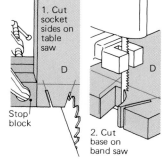

8. Cut sockets just inside the scribed lines. Rough-cut bases with band saw, then trim to final size with chisel.

Top and base units

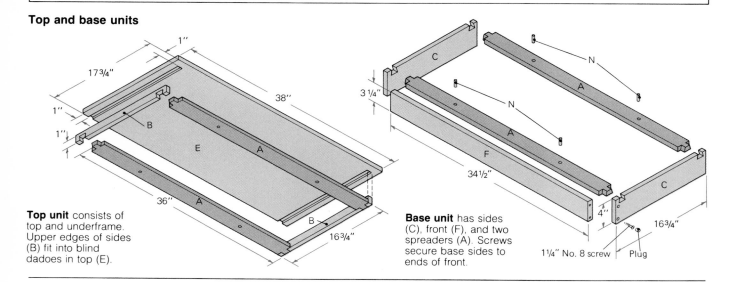

Top unit consists of top and underframe. Upper edges of sides (B) fit into blind dadoes in top (E).

Base unit has sides (C), front (F), and two spreaders (A). Screws secure base sides to ends of front.

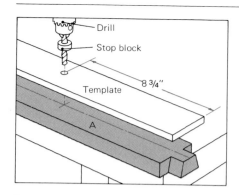

Use a template to drill ³⁄₈-in. holes along the center line of all spreaders (A), 8¾ in. from each end. Drill holes ½ in. deep in base unit spreaders and upper spreaders of chest sections; drill all the way through other spreaders.

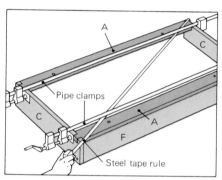

Base unit:
1. Drill two ³⁄₁₆-in. holes through each base side (C) ³⁄₈ in. from front edges to receive screws that secure sides to base front (F). Countersink for screwheads or, if you wish to use plugs, counterbore the holes ³⁄₈ in. deep (see *Index*, p.379).

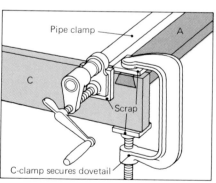

2. Assemble base unit dry and apply bar or pipe clamps from side to side to be sure that parts fit together properly. Measure unit diagonally, from corner to corner in both directions; if unit is square, measurements will be the same.

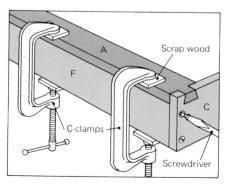

3. For final assembly apply glue to the dovetail and the shoulders of one end of each spreader (A) and insert in slots of a base side (C); then glue the other base side to its tails and apply clamps, using scrap blocks to protect the wood.

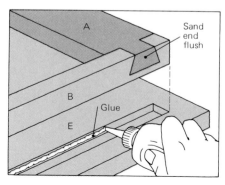

4. Apply glue to top edge and both ends of base front (F) and clamp it to front spreader, using several C-clamps to ensure a firm joint. Drill ⁷⁄₆₄-in. pilot holes in ends of base front and insert 1¼-in. No. 8 wood screws.

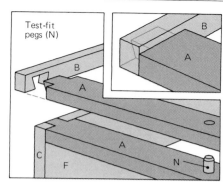

Top unit:
1. Assemble underframe dry on top of base unit to ensure that dimensions match. Then glue spreaders (A) into top sides (B) as in Step 3 for base unit—set pipe clamps before applying quick-action or C-clamps to dovetail joints.

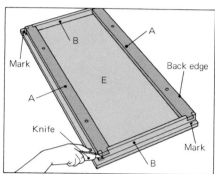

2. Place top (E) upside down and position underframe on it, centered from side to side with the back edges flush. Use a sharp knife to mark the rear corners and front edges of both sides (B) on the underside of the top.

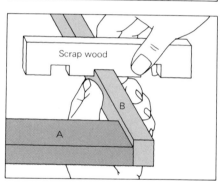

3. Use framing square to mark out blind dadoes in top (E). Before cutting dadoes, make test cuts in scrap wood to determine proper width of dado head and depth of cut, fitting the result to the protruding edge of the top side pieces (B).

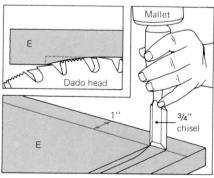

4. Cut dadoes in top (E), stopping just short of the blind end (the line, an inch from the front edge, where each dado ends). Finish cutting both dadoes by hand, using a sharp straight chisel and a hardwood mallet.

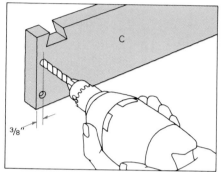

5. Use No. 80 sandpaper to sand ends of dovetails flush with top sides (B). Then sand underframe with Nos. 100 and 150 paper. Apply glue evenly to walls of blind dadoes and to faces of spreaders, and clamp the underframe to the top.

Chest unit and drawer

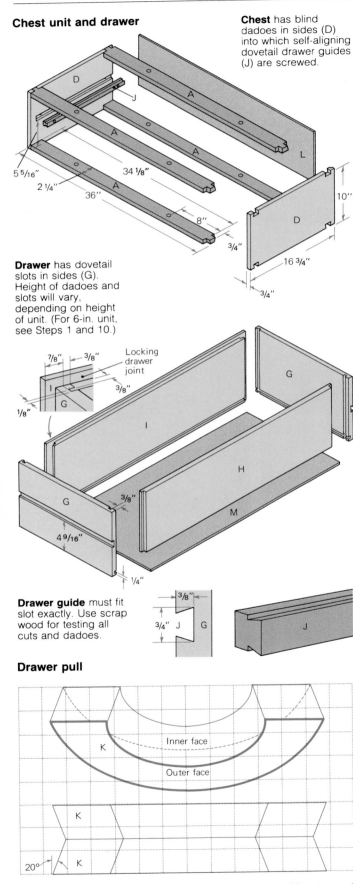

Chest has blind dadoes in sides (D) into which self-aligning dovetail drawer guides (J) are screwed.

Drawer has dovetail slots in sides (G). Height of dadoes and slots will vary, depending on height of unit. (For 6-in. unit, see Steps 1 and 10.)

Drawer guide must fit slot exactly. Use scrap wood for testing all cuts and dadoes.

Drawer pull

Use ½-in. grid to scribe pattern for drawer-pull laminates (K) on top and bottom of stock. Cut two laminates at a 20° angle for each pull.

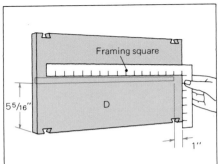

1. Mark out ¾-in. blind dadoes on inner face of all chest sides (D) to receive drawer guides (J). The 5⁵⁄₁₆ in. measurement at left is for a 10-in. chest unit; for a 6-in. unit measure up 3⁵⁄₁₆ in. from bottom edge of side. Dadoes end 1 in. from front edge.

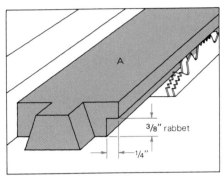

2. Cut dadoes ⅜ in. deep (see *Index*, p.379). Use ¾-in. chisel to finish blind end of each dado. Cut ¼-in. rabbets ⅜ in. deep in back edges of the chest sides (D) and in both rear spreaders (A) to receive the chest back (L).

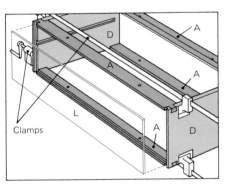

3. Assemble and clamp chest unit dry, using base unit as pattern. Cut chest back (L) to fit within its rabbets, making sure that corners are square. Measure width of front opening. Disassemble; sand interior surfaces with Nos. 100 and 150 sandpaper.

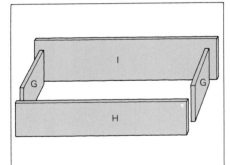

4. Cut drawer sides (G), back (H), and front (I) to size. Drawer back should be ⅞ in. shorter than the width of front opening in chest unit (measured in Step 3); the front should be ¾ in. longer.

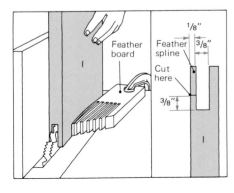

5. Cut ⅜-in. dadoes 1¼ in. deep in both ends of drawer front (I) for the locking drawer joint. Position dadoes to leave feather splines ⅛ in. wide on the rear of both ends. Cut splines to ⅜ in. long.

174

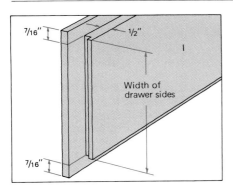

6. Cut 7/16-in. rabbets 1/2 in. deep in the top and bottom edges of the inner surface of the drawer front (I). The space between the rabbets should match the width of the drawer sides (G).

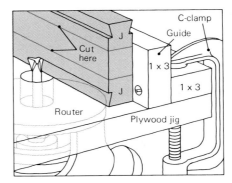

11. Cut drawer guides (J) from 3/4-in. stock about 3 in. wide. First, remove router base, then mount tool to 3/4-in. plywood jig so that 9/16-in. dovetail bit protrudes 3/8 in. (see *Index*, p.379). Position and clamp 1 x 3 guide to cut tails along both edges of stock.

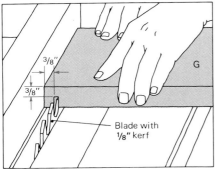

7. On the inner surface of both drawer sides (G) cut a 1/8-in. dado 3/8 in. from the front edge. Dadoes should be 3/8 in. deep to receive the feather splines on the ends of the drawer front. Test each joint as the dado is cut.

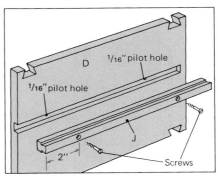

12. Rip 3/4-in.-wide drawer guides (J) from dovetailed stock. Drill a 9/64-in. hole 2 in. from each end of drawer guides for screws. Countersink. Glue guides into dadoes in chest sides (D) and secure with 1-in. No. 6 wood screws.

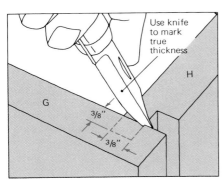

8. Cut 3/8-in. rabbets in rear corners of drawer back (H) deep enough to leave tongues 3/8 in. thick. Cut 3/8-in. dadoes 3/8 in. deep in drawer sides (G) to receive tongues. Assemble drawer frame dry and check for squareness (see "Base unit," p.173, Step 2).

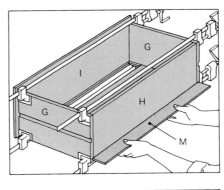

13. Sand all drawer parts with Nos. 100 and 150 sandpaper. Glue splines of front (I) and tongues of back (H) into their dadoes; square up and apply clamps. Slide bottom (M) into its dadoes without glue; secure it to bottom edge of back with 3/4-in. brads.

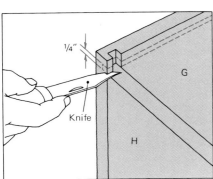

9. Mark position of bottom edge of back (H) on both drawer sides (G). Disassemble, and at that height cut 1/4-in. dadoes 1/4 in. deep in drawer sides and front (I) to receive drawer bottom (M). Reassemble frame; cut bottom to fit within dadoes.

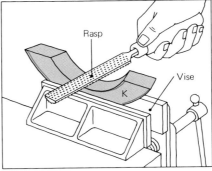

14. Rough-cut drawer-pull laminates (K) on band saw with table set at 20°. Finish with rasp and No. 80 sandpaper. Glue laminates together, then sand with Nos. 100 and 150 sandpaper. Secure to drawer front with 1 1/4-in. No. 8 wood screws, inserted from inside the drawer.

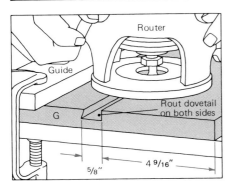

10. Scribe 5/8-in. dadoes on drawer sides (G) for dovetail slots. For 10-in. unit use measurement shown; for 6-in. unit measure 2 9/16 in. from bottom. Cut dadoes 3/8 in. deep. Finish slots with router and 9/16-in. dovetail bit.

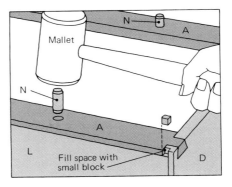

15. Glue and clamp spreaders (A) to chest sides (see "Base unit," p.173, Step 3). Glue and nail chest back (L) in place, using 3/4-in. brads. Bevel ends of pegs (N) and glue into upper spreaders (A) of all units. Sand with Nos. 100 and 150 paper; apply desired finish.

STENCILED BLANKET CHEST

The joinery in this charming chest is simple—the sides are glued and nailed into rabbets cut into the front and back, and the bottom and feet are screwed on from underneath. The fun and the challenge come in cutting the grooves that accent the front and sides of the chest (see opposite page) and in stenciling the Pennsylvania Dutch motif within the areas created by the grooves (p.178).

The materials are basic too. Edge-joined pine comes in varying widths and lengths and is generally available at lumberyards. Each width is made of several boards already glued edge to edge. If you cannot find this material, you can do your own edge-joining (see *Index*, p.379). The no-mortise hinges are easy to install.

After you have assembled the chest (p.179), paint the unstenciled parts, including the interior, with a semigloss oil-base paint. The barn-red paint used here was custom mixed. While painting, keep the stenciled areas covered with several layers of newspaper or heavy brown paper cut to the shape of these areas and taped in place. Be careful not to get any paint in the grooves.

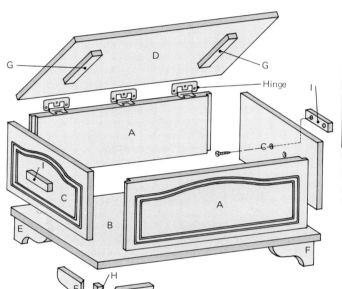

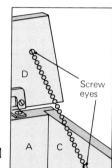

Chains to hold back while it is open are mounted with screw eyes.

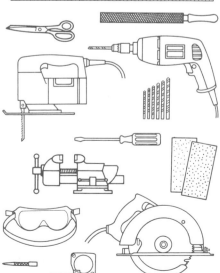

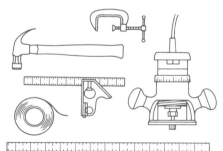

Parts list

Part	Name	Quantity	Thickness	Width	Length	Material
A	Front and back	2	⅝"	12½"	34"	Edge-joined pine
B	Bottom	1	⅝"	17"	36"	Edge-joined pine
C	Side	2	⅝"	12½"	15"	Edge-joined pine
D	Lid	1	⅝"	17"	36"	Edge-joined pine
E	Right foot	4	¾"	4"	8"	1 x 6 common pine
F	Left foot	4	¾"	4"	8"	1 x 6 common pine
G	Cleat	2	¾"	2½"	13½"	1 x 6 common pine
H	Glue block	4	¾"	¾"	3½"	1 x 6 common pine
I	Handle	2	¾"	1"	4¼"	1 x 6 common pine

Tools and materials: Table saw or circular saw. Saber saw with medium-tooth blade. Router with ⁵⁄₁₆" rounding-over bit without pilot and ¼" rounding-over bit with pilot. Drill with ⅜" and ³⁄₁₆" bits. Vise, C-clamps. Steel tape rule, combination square, straightedge. Hammer, rasp, screwdriver, nail set. Safety goggles. Nos. 80 and 150 sandpaper. Scissors, paper plates, masking tape. Wood putty. Acrylic paint in tubes: medium green, medium blue, light blue, and white. Semigloss oil-base paint, small can 5-lb.

white shellac, polyurethane varnish, three paintbrushes, tack cloth. Accent Art stenciling kit (for address, see p.377). Two ½" plywood pieces 21¼" x 24" and 21¼" x 41" for templates. Large plywood scrap about 32" x 50". Edge-joined pine (see above). An 8' length of 1 x 6 common pine. Three 2½" no-mortise butt hinges with ½" screws. Two 18" chains, four ¼" screw eyes. Box of 1¼" No. 8 flathead wood screws, sixteen 1½" No. 8 flathead wood screws, 6d finishing nails.

Routing grooves in front and sides

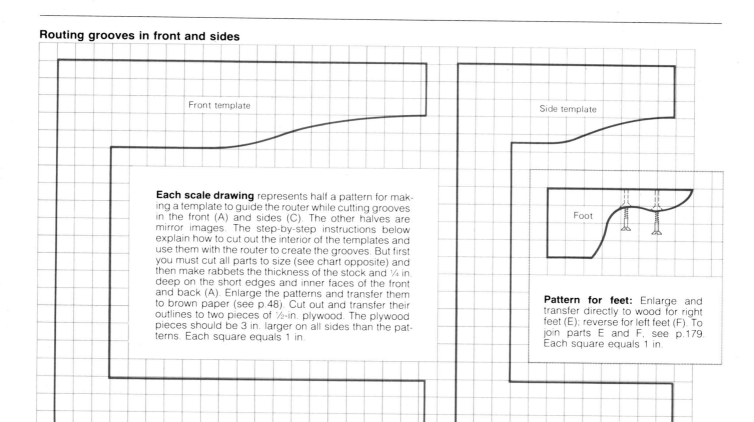

Front template

Side template

Foot

Each scale drawing represents half a pattern for making a template to guide the router while cutting grooves in the front (A) and sides (C). The other halves are mirror images. The step-by-step instructions below explain how to cut out the interior of the templates and use them with the router to create the grooves. But first you must cut all parts to size (see chart opposite) and then make rabbets the thickness of the stock and ¼ in. deep on the short edges and inner faces of the front and back (A). Enlarge the patterns and transfer them to brown paper (see p.48). Cut out and transfer their outlines to two pieces of ½-in. plywood. The plywood pieces should be 3 in. larger on all sides than the patterns. Each square equals 1 in.

Pattern for feet: Enlarge and transfer directly to wood for right feet (E); reverse for left feet (F). To join parts E and F, see p.179. Each square equals 1 in.

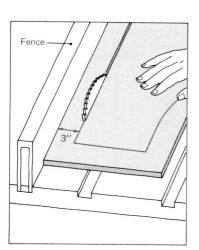

Fence

3″

1. To saw out the interior of template for front, set the saw fence 3 in. from the blade. Lower saw blade below table surface, and position template against fence. Start saw and very slowly raise the blade until it penetrates template. Finish the cut to each corner. Repeat on each of template's straight sides. If you do not have a table saw, cut out the template with a saber saw and a straightedge.

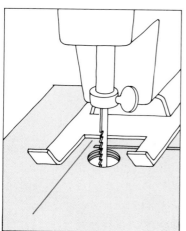

2. To cut the curved line on template, use a saber saw with a medium-tooth blade. Clamp template to work surface with line to be cut overhanging edge. Make an entry hole with a drill and ⅜-in. twist bit close to a corner and inside the line. Insert saw blade and cut along line. Clamp template in a vise, and use a rasp to smooth edges of cuts. Repeat Steps 1 and 2 to cut out template for sides.

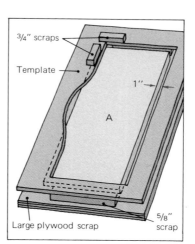

¾″ scraps

Template

1″

A

Large plywood scrap

⅝″ scrap

3. Nail two scraps of ¾-in. wood at a corner of each template with their inner edges aligned with the cutout in the template. Raise templates above surfaces being grooved by setting each on ⅝-in. scraps of wood; nail through each template and scraps into large plywood scrap. Center the front (A) and sides (C) inside templates from side to side and place bottom edges 1 in. above template edges. Secure front by screwing through large plywood scrap from below. (Fill holes afterward.)

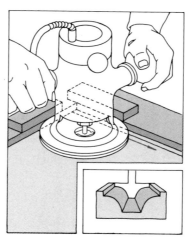

4. Use router and pilotless ⁵⁄₁₆-in. bit set to cut slightly less than ⅝ in. deep. Test depth on scrap; bit should cut a narrow, flat area above the round (inset). Use the scraps at the corner to guide the router as you lower the bit gradually, with the power on, into the wood. Move router clockwise slowly around each template. To secure each side (C) to scrap under its template, drill two screw holes 4½ in. from the top edge and 1½ in. to each side of center. (Use these same holes later to attach the handles.)

Applying the stencil design

Stenciling is an ancient technique for painting repetitive designs on furniture or on floor, wall, or ceiling surfaces. It was widely used on Early American furniture, especially Pennsylvania Dutch designs, which inspired the tulip, heart, and love-bird motif for this blanket chest. To obtain this motif, order the Accent Art stenciling kit from the Hunt Manufacturing Company (see p.377 for the address). The kit contains two other designs as well.

Prior to stenciling, sand all surfaces of the chest that will be exposed with Nos. 80 and 150 sandpaper, and sand the edges of the routed grooves to remove any roughness. Wipe all surfaces with a tack cloth to remove dust, and apply a sealer coat of 5-pound white shellac. Do not shellac surfaces that will form joints.

Modern stencilers recommend acrylic paint because it is easy to use and dries quickly. Use the paint directly from the tube, squeezing only a small amount onto a paper plate. If you want to use colors other than those on our chest and find that you must mix paints to get a desired color, mix enough for all of that color at one time. (A baby-food jar about half full will be ample for one color.) To prevent paint from drying out, keep it capped tightly.

When the painted designs are dry, brush a coat of polyurethane varnish over all stenciled areas to protect them.

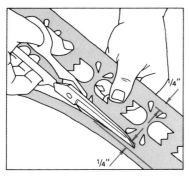

1. Remove the Pennsylvania Dutch design from the kit. Carefully push out the pieces of paper for the tulip borders. Draw lines ¼ in. from the edges of the tips of the leaves at the top and bottom of the stenciling strip. Cut along these lines.

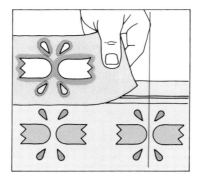

5. Stencil two more pairs of tulips to each side of center three pairs, spacing them by placing the end cutout on the stencil paper over an already painted pair. After finishing the line of tulips and leaves across the bottom, paint one pair of tulips and its leaves at the center of the top, placing stencil edge ¼ in. from the edge of the groove.

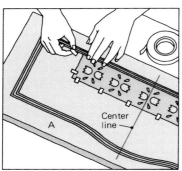

2. Draw a light center line from top to bottom on the front (A). Place the stencil with one pair of tulips on the center line and the bottom edge of the stencil paper flush with the edge of the bottom groove. Tape the stencil in place with masking tape. Cover the leaves with masking tape, leaving the tulips uncovered.

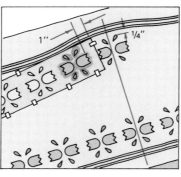

6. When center tulips have dried, remove stencil. Cut ends of stencil 1 in. from the tips of tulips. Angle stencil to follow curve of groove, and place it ¼ in. from edge of groove with tips of tulips exactly 1 in. apart. Paint one pair of tulips and leaves, let dry, then move stencil so next pair will be 1 in. from pair just finished. Continue until there are three pairs to each side of center pair.

3. Cut the sponge supplied with kit into ½-in. strips. Squeeze a small amount of medium blue paint onto a paper plate. Dip the end of a sponge strip into paint, then remove excess by blotting it on plate. Apply paint with a straight up-and-down dabbing motion. You will get a smooth surface if paint is not too thick and if you apply it with a firm touch.

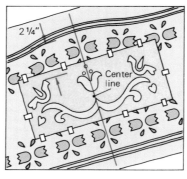

7. On each side of the front, stencil two pairs of tulips equidistant from top and bottom grooves and ½ in. from side grooves. Position stencil for center design by aligning stencil with center line drawn in Step 2. Tops of birds' heads should be about 2¼ in. below edge of groove. Paint the birds and three small dots white, the flower and hearts light blue, and the curlicue green.

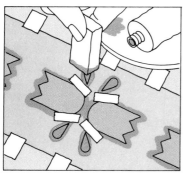

4. Allow paint to dry (it dries quickly). Remove tape from leaves, and place bits of tape along edges of tulips—not on freshly painted surfaces. Use another paper plate and follow the same procedure to paint the leaves green. Let paint dry, then remove the stencil paper. If paint dries on the sponge strip, cut off ⅛ in. to get a clean surface.

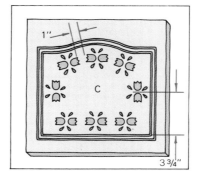

8. Stencil each of the two sides (C) with three pairs of tulips across the bottom, one pair centered at the top with one pair to each side of it—spaced 1 in. apart as in Step 6—and a pair on each side placed with the center line of the tulip design 3¾ in. from the edge of the bottom groove. Position stencils ¼ in. from the nearest groove.

Assembling the chest

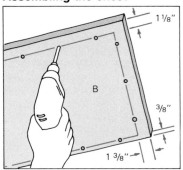

1. Draw lines on underside of bottom (B) 1⅜ in. from short edges, ⅜ in. from rear edge, and 1⅛ in. from front edge. Drill ³⁄₁₆-in. holes along these lines, three on short edges and five on front and back edges. Countersink the holes for No. 8 screwheads.

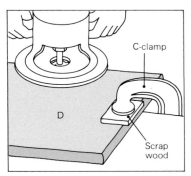

2. Use a router and ¼-in. rounding-over bit with pilot to round the front and side edges of the bottom and the lid (D). Do this on both the top and bottom surfaces.

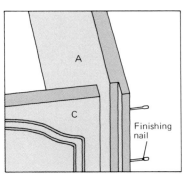

3. Spread glue in rabbets of front and back (A) and on the ends of the sides (C). Join sides to front and back, nailing each joint with several 6d finishing nails. Measure diagonally to check that the chest is square (see *Index*, p.379). Set nails below surface with nail set. Fill holes with wood putty.

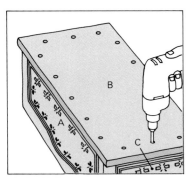

4. When glue has dried, rest the chest on its top edges. Position the bottom (B) with its rear edge flush with the back (A) and its short edges overhanging each side (C) by an equal amount. Drill pilot holes into front, back, and sides through clearance holes drilled in Step 1. Insert 1¼-in. No. 8 screws.

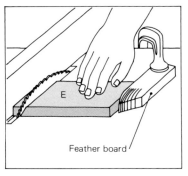

5. Tilt blade of saw to 45°. Make a practice cut on scrap wood and check with a combination square that the angle is correct. Using a feather board (see *Index*, p.379), miter the 4-in. left edges of the right feet (E) and the right edges of the left feet (F). Pair off right and left feet and mark them so that they can be reassembled the same way.

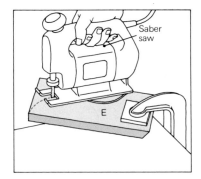

6. Enlarge the pattern on page 177 for shaping the feet. Lay pattern on each right foot (E) and trace the outline. Reverse the pattern for each left foot (F). Saw along the lines with a saber saw. Soften the edges with No. 80 sandpaper.

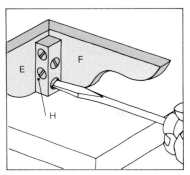

7. Drill pilot holes for 1¼-in. screws through two adjoining sides of each glue block (H); offset holes and make two in each side. Match a left and right foot, put block in corner, and mark through block for pilot holes in feet; drill holes. Glue feet, then glue and screw block in place. Check for squareness. Repeat for other feet.

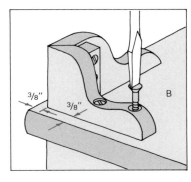

8. Drill clearance holes in the undersides of the feet, positioned as shown in the foot pattern. Counterbore the holes so that screwheads will be hidden. Position each foot ⅜ in. from the edge of the bottom (B). Drill pilot holes in the bottom through the clearance holes in the feet, and insert 1½-in. screws.

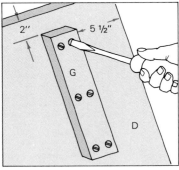

9. Drill two rows of three ³⁄₁₆-in. pilot holes ½ in. from long edges of each cleat (G). Make sure screws do not enter any joints in lid (D). Using 1¼-in. screws, mount cleats on underside of lid 2 in. from front edge and 5½ in. from side edges.

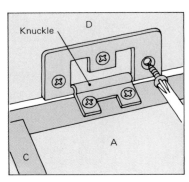

10. Center one hinge along underside of lid and place other two 3 in. from short edges with knuckles (round part) against back edge of lid. Screw large flaps to lid with ½-in. screws and small flaps to top edge of back (A). Soften outer edges of handles (I) with a rasp and sandpaper. Screw handles to sides (C) through holes made when routing the sides; use 1¼-in. screws. Mount chains.

PLATFORM BED

Queen-size comfort, striking design, and extra storage space are combined in this platform bed of oak and walnut. Three kinds of joints are used. The walnut side frames have butt joints reinforced with dowels. The walnut facings around the top are mitered and glued without reinforcement. All other joints, including those of the drawers, are tongue and groove. You can complete the design with the sunburst headboard of matching veneers (Steps 21–29) or with the cabinet headboard unit described in the next project (pp. 185–187).

Buying material: Walnut is expensive and usually comes rough sawed in random widths. You must joint one edge before ripping. A jointer is the ideal tool for the job, but it is possible to use a table saw (Step 1). Select walnut carefully to minimize waste; choose boards about 5 inches wide. The top rails do not show in the finished bed; you can save money by making them of a less expensive hardwood, such as poplar.

The drawers are of birch plywood with oak plywood faces. If Finnish birch plywood is available, use it; its many thin layers make it stronger and more warp resistant than American plywood. It need not be veneered; simply round the edges.

Finishing: Begin by brushing on a mixture of four parts satin polyurethane to one part turpentine. Wipe it off with a soft cloth and sand with No. 220 paper. Then brush on two coats of full-strength satin polyurethane, sanding each when dry. Apply a third, and when it dries, use 0000 steel wool to work in a coat of wax. Buff with a soft cloth.

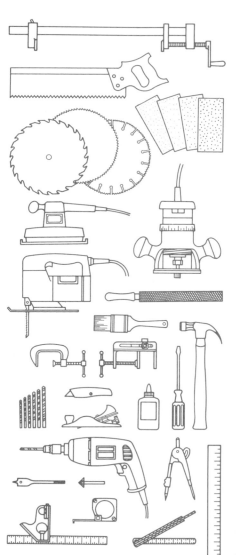

Parts list

Part	Name	Quantity	Thickness	Width	Length	Material
A	Top rail	2	¾″	2½″	76″	Walnut or poplar stock
B	Bottom rail	2	¾″	2¼″	76″	Walnut stock
C	End stile	4	¾″	2¼″	14¼″	Walnut stock
D	Center stile	2	¾″	2¼″	9½″	Walnut stock
E	Drawer support	4	¾″	14¼″	56½″	A–D fir plywood
F	Spacer	2	¾″	14¼″	37⅜″ ✻	A–D fir plywood
G	Filler	1	⅜″	2½″	56″	Softwood
H	Foot	1	¾″	14¼″	56½″	A–2 oak plywood
I	Side overhang	2	1½″	2½″	80½″	2 x 3 fir
J	Foot overhang	1	1½″	2½″	60½″ ✻	2 x 3 fir
K	Side facing	2	¾″	4¼″	84″ ✻	Walnut stock
L	Foot facing	1	¾″	4¼″	64″ ✻	Walnut stock
M	Drawer side	8	½″	8¹⁵⁄₁₆″	26″	2–2 birch plywood
N	Drawer front	4	½″	8¹⁵⁄₁₆″	35¹³⁄₁₆″ ✻	2–2 birch plywood
O	Drawer back	4	½″	8⁵⁄₁₆″	35¹³⁄₁₆″ ✻	2–2 birch plywood
P	Drawer bottom	4	¼″	26¼″ ✻	35⁵⁄₁₆″ ✻	A–4 birch plywood
Q	Drawer face	4	¾″	9½″	37⅜″	A–2 oak plywood
R	Lid panel	2	¾″	30¼″ ✻	80½″ ✻	A–D fir plywood
S	Headboard	2	¾″	46³⁄₁₆″ ✻	60⅜″	Particle board

✻ Measurement is approximate; cut to fit during construction.

Tools and materials: Drill with twist bits, 1″ spade bit, and countersink. Router with bits (¼″ straight, ¼″ and ⅜″ quarter-round, and 1″ ball-bearing flush trim) and template guide. Table saw, radial arm saw, saber saw. Orbital sander. Doweling jig. Steel tape rule, wooden extension rule, framing square, combination square, compass, pencil. Hammer, screwdriver. Backsaw, mat knife. Block plane, rasp. Two 2″ paintbrushes. At least twelve 6″ C-clamps, several 3′ and 8′ bar or pipe clamps. Nos. 80, 100, 150, and 220 sandpaper. White glue, contact cement, wood putty, 0000 steel wool. Satin polyurethane finish, turpentine, wax, soft cloths. Safety goggles. Six ¾″ x 5″ x 8′ boards walnut stock or equivalent. A ⅜″ x

2½″ x 56″ softwood strip. Three ¾″ x 4′ x 8′ panels A–D fir plywood. A ¾″ x 4′ x 8′ panel A–2 oak plywood. Two ¼″ x 4′ x 8′ panels A–4 birch plywood, a ½″ x 4′ x 8′ panel 2–2 birch plywood. Two ¾″ x 4′ x 8′ panels particle board. Three 8′ lengths 2 x 3 fir. Walnut and oak veneers. Twenty-four ⅜″ hardwood dowels 2″ long. 4d and 6d finishing nails, 6d coated nails, 2d common nails. ⅝″ No. 4 flathead wood screws, ½″ No. 6 flathead wood screws. 1″, 1¼″, and 2½″ No. 8 flathead wood screws. 2½″ and 3″ No. 10 flathead wood screws. Eight ¼″ flathead stove bolts 2″ long with matching T nuts. Four pairs 26″ drawer slides (Grant No. 329). Eight 2⅛″ round walnut drawer pulls.

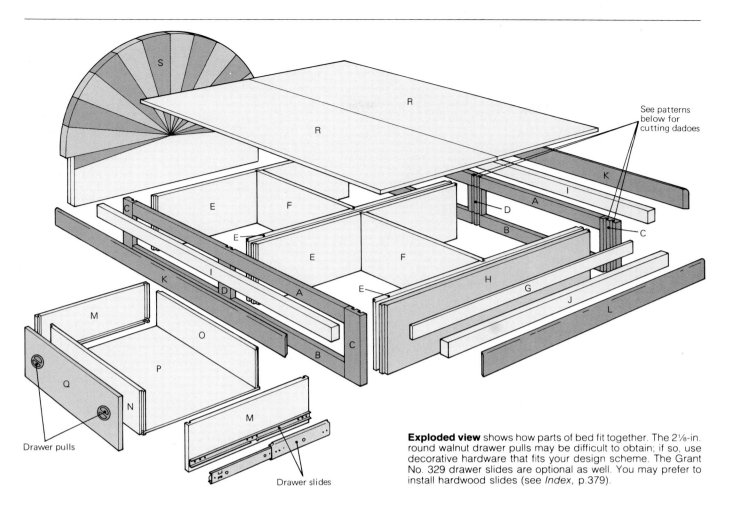

See patterns below for cutting dadoes

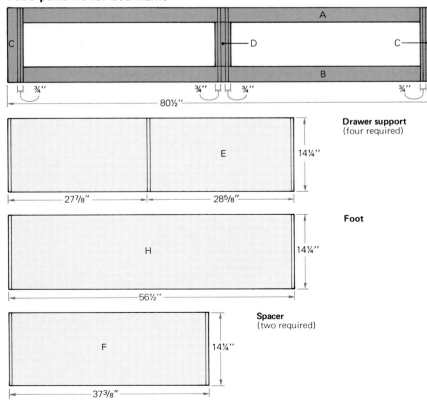

Drawer pulls

Drawer slides

Exploded view shows how parts of bed fit together. The 2⅛-in. round walnut drawer pulls may be difficult to obtain; if so, use decorative hardware that fits your design scheme. The Grant No. 329 drawer slides are optional as well. You may prefer to install hardwood slides (see *Index*, p.379).

Dado patterns for bed frame

Drawer frame
(make 2nd frame a mirror image)

14¼"

¾"   ¾" ¾"   ¾" ¾"

80½"

Drawer support
(four required)

E

14¼"

27⅞"   28⅝"

Foot

H

14¼"

56½"

Spacer
(two required)

F

14¼"

37⅜"

Use patterns to lay out dadoes and rabbets for tongue-and-groove joints in side frames, drawer supports, spacers, and foot. To ensure precise alignment, it is best to lay the pieces side by side, marking across several at once. At the same time, use a different-colored pencil to rule lines against which to clamp guide strips when you rout out the dadoes and rabbets (the distance from the center of the dado to the guideline must equal the radius of the router's base). Although a router equipped with a ¼-in. straight bit is the best tool for this job, dadoes and rabbets can also be cut with a table saw, circular saw, or radial arm saw. (For instructions on cutting dadoes and rabbets with all these tools, see *Index*, p.379.) All dadoes are ¼ in. wide and 9/32 in. deep. When cutting the ¼-in.-wide rabbets for the tongues, it is important to allow for any variance in the thickness of the wood; the idea is not to cut to a specific depth but to be left with a tongue that is exactly ¼ in. thick. Measure each piece and adjust the depth of the cut accordingly.

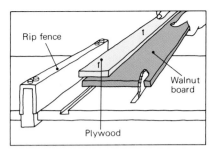

1. Rip walnut stock for rails, stiles, and facings. To joint stock with table saw, rip a strip of ¾-in. plywood 3 in. wide and nail it to one edge of board. Set saw to cut ¼ in. from other edge. Put this straight cut against fence and rip stock to widths needed.

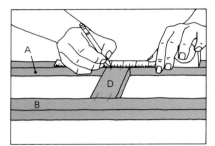

2. Cut rails (A and B), and stiles (C and D) to length. Use framing square to lay side frames out on table. To mark joints for doweling, mark both pieces of each joint 9/16 in. from both edges of the butting piece. Label all joints for accurate reassembly.

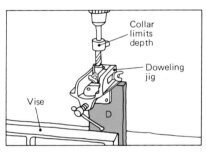

3. Use a doweling jig to drill ⅜-in. holes 1 1/16 in. deep, centered on thickness of wood, at points marked in Step 2. To avoid discrepancies, orient jig with front face of each piece. If dowels are not grooved, cut small grooves with backsaw. Assemble frames dry to ensure fit.

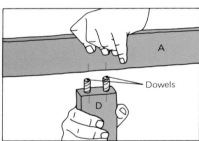

4. Begin final assembly by joining center stiles to rails. Apply glue to faces of joints and lips of holes. Insert dowels in stiles, then force rails over them. Join end stiles in the same way. Align bar or pipe clamps with rails and center stiles; square up and tighten.

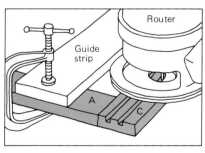

5. Wipe off excess glue and let dry; then remove clamps and plane joints even. Cut drawer supports (E), spacers (F), and foot (H). Use patterns on page 181 to mark out dadoes and rabbets for tongue-and-groove joints. Cut with router and ¼-in. straight bit.

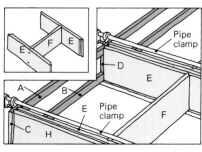

6. Glue tongues of spacers into grooves of drawer supports; secure with 6d coated nails. Then glue tongues of drawer supports and foot into grooves of walnut frames. Square by measuring corner to corner; apply bar or pipe clamps across bed frame.

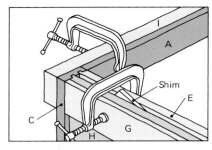

7. Cut filler (G) to fit across the top edge of the foot. Glue and clamp filler in place. Cut 2 x 3 for the overhang pieces (I and J). Glue and clamp the side overhangs (I) flush with the top edge of the side frames, securing with several C-clamps.

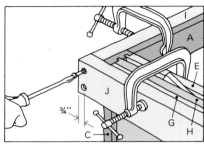

8. Drill and countersink two 3/16-in. holes ¾ in. from both ends of foot overhang (J). Glue and clamp foot overhang in place. Drill 5/64-in. pilot holes through holes in foot overhang into ends of side overhangs and drive 2½-in. No. 8 wood screws.

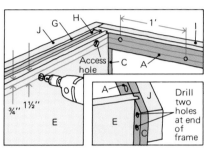

9. Plane upper surface flush. Rule lines ¾ in. and 1½ in. down along sides and foot. Drill 3/16-in. holes at 1-ft. intervals, alternating between lines. Counterbore ⅜ in. deep. (Use 1-in. spade bit to make access holes in end drawer support.)

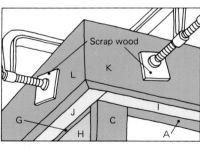

10. Cut miters on one end of each side facing (K) and foot facing (L), leaving extra wood on uncut ends. (Check carefully for accuracy.) Clamp one side facing and the foot facing in place, the miters tightly joined, the bottom edges flush with bottom of overhang.

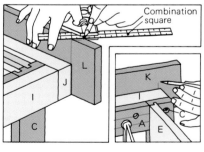

11. Mark the point for the second miter of the foot facing; then cut it a little long. Clamp the other side facing in place and trim foot facing to fit snugly. Then saw head ends of the two side facings off square. Apply glue to miters and facing pieces and clamp them in place.

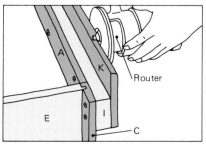

12. Drill 7/64-in. pilot holes into facings through holes drilled in Step 9, and drive No. 10 wood screws. Use 2½-in. screws for sides and 3-in. screws for foot. Plane upper surface of facings. Then use router and ¼-in. quarter-round bit to round the outer edges.

Dado patterns for drawers

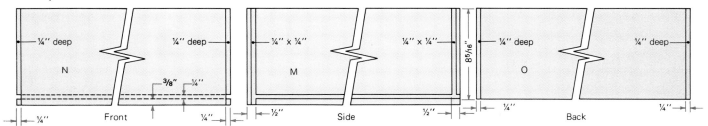

13. Cut drawer sides (M), fronts (N), and backs (O). (For lengths of fronts and backs subtract 1⁹⁄₁₆ in. from width of opening in side frames; if widths differ, make each drawer to fit its own opening.) Cut dadoes and rabbets as shown above. (If you are using Finnish birch plywood, round the top edges of the drawer sides using a router and ¼-in. quarter-round bit.)

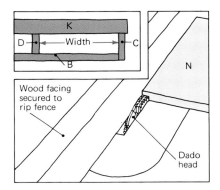

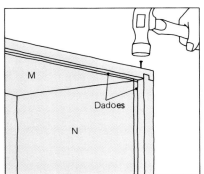

14. Sand inside surfaces of drawer parts with No. 100 sandpaper. Glue tongues of front and back into grooves of sides, aligning the upper edge of the dado for the bottom all around, level with the bottom edge of drawer back. Secure joints by driving 4d finishing nails through sides into front and back.

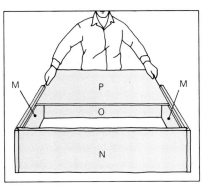

15. Square up drawers by measuring corner to corner in both directions, adjusting until measurements match. Then cut drawer bottoms (P) to fit within dadoes (allow ¹⁄₃₂-in. clearance), the rear edges flush with backs of drawers. Slip bottoms in place and secure them to drawer backs with a few 2d common nails.

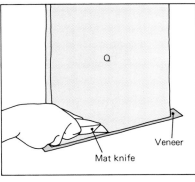

16. Cut drawer faces (Q) so the figure of the oak plywood will be continuous on each pair of drawers. Apply oak veneer, first to both ends, then to top of each face and—if drawers are made of plain birch plywood—to top edges of drawer sides. (For veneering instructions, see *Index*, p.379.) Trim veneer and hand-sand edges lightly with No. 100 paper.

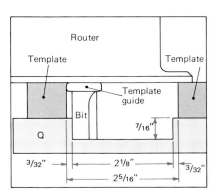

17. Drawer pulls are set into mortises made with a router equipped with a template guide and straight bit. To make the template, first rule two perpendicular lines on ½-in. plywood. Use a compass to draw a circle from intersection point large enough to allow for the difference between bit and template guide. Cut out circle with saber saw; sand edges as needed.

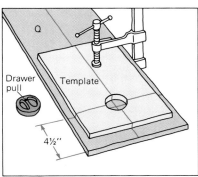

18. To position template, rule a line across center of drawer face, and rule perpendicular lines 4½ in. from both ends. Match lines on template with those on face, clamp template in place, and rout out mortises. Sand drawer faces with Nos. 100 and 150 paper. Drill ¹⁄₁₆-in. pilot holes and attach pulls from rear with two ⁵⁄₈-in. No. 4 wood screws.

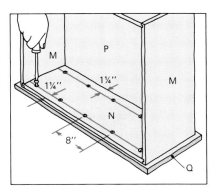

19. Rule lines 1¼ in. from top and bottom of inside drawer fronts (N). Then, starting 1½ in. from one side, drill ³⁄₁₆-in. holes 8 in. apart along both lines. Countersink. Position faces on drawer fronts so that they are centered side to side and overhang bottom by ⁵⁄₁₆ in. Secure with 1-in. No. 8 wood screws.

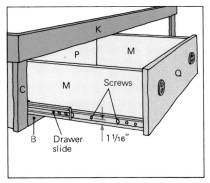

20. Hang drawers with 26-in. drawer slides. Use two ½-in. No. 6 wood screws in slotted holes to attach runners to sides so that screws align 1¹⁄₁₆ in. from bottom. With two more screws attach slides to drawer supports (E), square with frame and resting on bottom rails (B). Insert drawers to test for fit. Adjust as needed, then drive remaining screws.

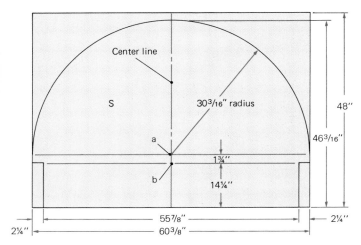

Center line

S

30³/₁₆″ radius

48″

46³/₁₆″

a

1¾″

b

14¼″

55⅞″

2¼″

60⅜″

2¼″

Sunburst headboard is made by laminating two pieces of ¾-in. particle board (S). First, cut two rectangles 48 in. x 60⅜ in. On one mark out pattern above; use trammel points or a compass made from a pencil, a nail, and a piece of 1 x 2 to draw a semicircle from point a with a radius of 30³/₁₆ in.

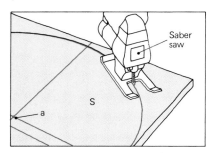

Saber saw

S

a

21. With a saber saw rough-cut the semicircle, sawing just outside the line. Use a rasp and No. 80 sandpaper for final shaping. When the arc is as close to perfect as you can get it, trace the pattern onto the second piece of particle board and rough-cut with the saber saw.

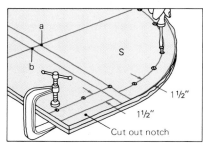

a

b

S

1½″

1½″

Cut out notch

22. Glue and screw the two pieces of particle board together with bottoms flush, using 1¼-in. No. 8 wood screws. (Pilot holes are unnecessary with particle board; drill ³/₁₆-in. shank holes only through piece that will be back of headboard, and countersink.)

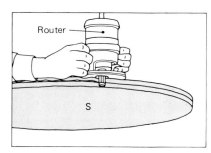

Router

S

23. Use saber saw to cut 2¼- x 14¼-in. notches in both bottom corners. Then, with router and 1-in. ball-bearing flush trim bit, trim the rough-cut arc flush with the finished piece. Hand-sand all edges with No. 80 sandpaper.

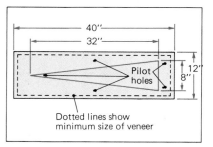

40″

32″

Pilot holes

12″

8″

Dotted lines show minimum size of veneer

24. Select seven good pieces of walnut veneer and seven of oak at least 9 in. x 36 in. Stack them between two pieces of ½-in. plywood. Mark out the top piece as shown; then drill ¹/₁₆-in. pilot holes and drive 6d finishing nails through the veneer sandwich.

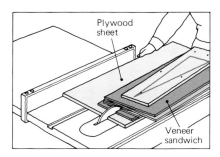

Plywood sheet

Veneer sandwich

25. Nail the sandwich to a larger sheet of plywood so that one leg of the triangle is parallel with the long edge of the plywood. Set the table saw to cut through the sheet and the sandwich together along this leg. Reposition on plywood sheet to cut the other leg of the triangle.

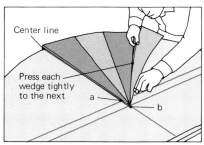

Center line

Press each wedge tightly to the next

a

b

26. Apply two even coats of contact cement to face of headboard and backs of veneer wedges, allowing each to dry to the touch. Align first wedge with center line, its tip on point b. Alternate oak and walnut until half of headboard is covered; then start again at center line.

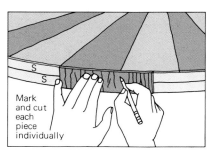

S

S

Mark and cut each piece individually

27. Rub veneer down firmly with wood block. Then rout edges flush (see Step 23). Cut 2-in. veneer strips across grain for edges; cut each piece to fit, and label. Apply contact cement, press veneer down one strip at a time, starting at center and abutting tightly.

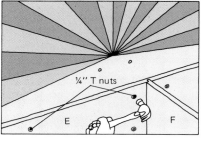

¼″ T nuts

E

F

28. Position headboard on bed frame and drill eight ¼-in. holes through headboard and drawer support; countersink for bolt heads. Remove headboard and enlarge holes in drawer support with ⁵/₁₆-in. bit. Hammer T nuts in place from inside bed frame.

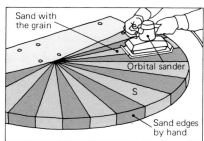

Sand with the grain

Orbital sander

S

Sand edges by hand

29. Sand veneered surfaces of headboard with No. 80 paper. Fill where necessary with wood putty. Sand again—and sand all unsanded surfaces of bed with No. 100 and then No. 150 paper. Apply satin polyurethane finish.

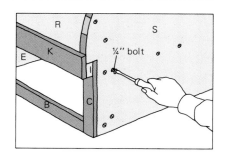

R

S

E

K

¼″ bolt

I

B

C

30. Cut two pieces of ¾-in. plywood for lid panels (R), joining along edge of spacers (F). Apply walnut stain. Secure to overhangs (I and J), the edge of the drawer supports (E), foot (H), and spacers with 6d coated nails. Secure headboard with flathead stove bolts.

CABINET HEADBOARD UNIT

Designed to go with the platform bed shown on pages 180–184, this walnut and oak headboard is made largely of plywood. Its solid oak top is almost 9 feet long and stands just under 5 feet from the floor, so it is a practical alternative to the sunburst headboard if you have a spacious bedroom. If you are making both projects, consolidate the lists of materials. Each project, for example, calls for a 4- x 8-foot panel of ¾-inch oak plywood, but with careful planning you can make one panel serve both projects.

Construction: Each of the three cabinets is assembled individually with the same tongue-and-groove joints that were used for the platform bed. The completed units are joined by driving wood screws into the top through holes in the top shelves. The oak reveals between the cabinets are screwed into the sides of the center cabinet and fit loosely into dadoes in the end cabinets. The drawers in the end cabinets, though smaller than those of the platform bed, are made in the same way, with this exception: the oak plywood faces do not sit flush against the frames, but fit inside, so each must be cut ³⁄₁₆ inch shorter than the distance between the sides of the end cabinet in which it belongs to allow for two thicknesses of veneer and ⅛-inch clearance. The 10-inch drawer slides are installed ¾ inch back to allow for the faces. The walnut drawer pulls in these drawers and in the sliding doors of the center cabinet match those used in the drawers of the platform bed. Finish the headboard with satin polyurethane (see text, p. 180).

The cabinet headboard design can easily be adapted for use with any queen-sized bed. Instead of building the headboard and center filler units, simply cut a dado all around the inside of the opening in the center cabinet ⅜ inch from the front, and fit in a piece of walnut plywood.

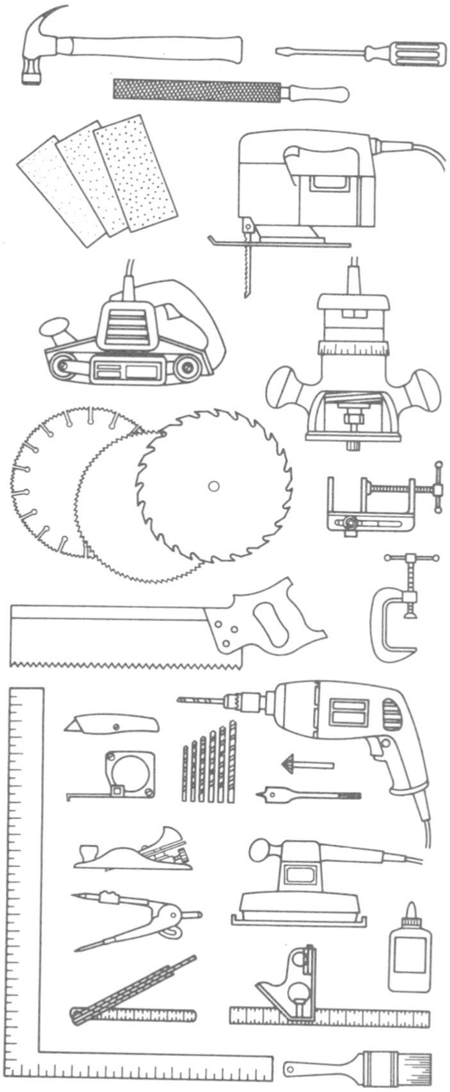

Parts list

Part	Name	Quantity	Thickness	Width	Length	Material
A	Outer side	2	¾″	11½″	55¼″	A–2 walnut plywood
B	Inner side	4	¾″	11¼″	55¼″	A–2 walnut plywood
C	End-cabinet shelf	6	¾″	11¼″	19″	A–2 walnut plywood
D	Adjustable shelf	4	¾″	11″	18⅜″	A–2 walnut plywood
E	End-cabinet filler	2	¾″	1½″	18½″	A–2 walnut plywood
F	Center-cabinet shelf	3	¾″	11¼″	60¹⁵⁄₁₆″	A–2 walnut plywood
G	Top partition	1	¾″	11¼″	14½″	A–2 walnut plywood
H	Bottom partition	1	¾″	8¾″	14½″	A–2 walnut plywood
I	Headboard face	1	¾″	9¾″	58¹⁵⁄₁₆″ ✳	A–2 walnut plywood
J	Headboard side	2	¾″	3″	10½″ ✳	Walnut stock
K	Headboard top	1	¾″	3″	60⁷⁄₁₆″ ✳	Walnut stock
L	End-cabinet back	2	¼″	19⅝″ ✳	53¾″ ✳	A–2 walnut plywood
M	Center-cabinet back	2	¼″	30¹⁵⁄₁₆″ ✳	30¼″ ✳	A–2 walnut plywood
N	Center filler	1	¾″	16″	60⁷⁄₈″	Particle board
O	Filler spacer	1	¾″	1⅜″	58¹⁵⁄₁₆″	Particle board
P	Filler block	2	¾″	¾″	14⅝″	1 x 1 pine
Q	Drawer side	4	½″	5½″	10″	2–2 birch plywood
R	Drawer front	2	½″	5½″	16¹⁵⁄₁₆″ ✳	2–2 birch plywood
S	Drawer back	2	½″	4⅞″	16¹⁵⁄₁₆″ ✳	2–2 birch plywood
T	Drawer bottom	2	¼″	9¾″ ✳	16¹⁵⁄₁₆″ ✳	A–4 birch plywood
U	Drawer face	2	¾″	6″	18⅜″ ✳	A–2 oak plywood
V	Sliding door	2	¾″	14″ ✳	30¹⁵⁄₁₆″	A–2 oak plywood
W	Reveal	2	¾″	1¼″	55¼″	Oak stock
X	Top	2	1½″	6⅛″ †	105⅜″ †	Oak stock

✳ Measurement is approximate; cut to fit during construction.
† Final measurement; cut slightly oversize and trim to measure.

Tools and materials: (See *Platform Bed*, p. 180, for tools, joining materials, and finishing materials, with these additions: ⁵⁄₁₆″ and ⅜″ straight router bits, jack plane or belt sander, 1½″ and 2″ No. 8 flathead wood screws.) A ¾″ x 3″ x 8′ board walnut stock. Two 1½″ x 6½″ x 9′ boards oak stock, a ¾″ x 3½″ x 5′ board oak stock. Three ¾″ x 4′ x 8′ panels A–2 walnut plywood, two ¼″ x 4′ x 8′ panels A–2 walnut plywood. A ¾″ x 4′ x 8′ panel A–2 oak plywood. A ¼″ x 1′ x 3′ piece A–4 birch plywood, a ½″ x 2′ x 4′ piece 2–2 birch plywood. A ¾″ x 4′ x 8′ panel particle board. A 3′ length 1 x 1 pine. Walnut and oak veneers. Two 6′ lengths ⅛″ Fibertrack door runners with four sheaves. Two pairs 10″ drawer slides (Grant No. 328). Four 2⅛″ round walnut drawer pulls.

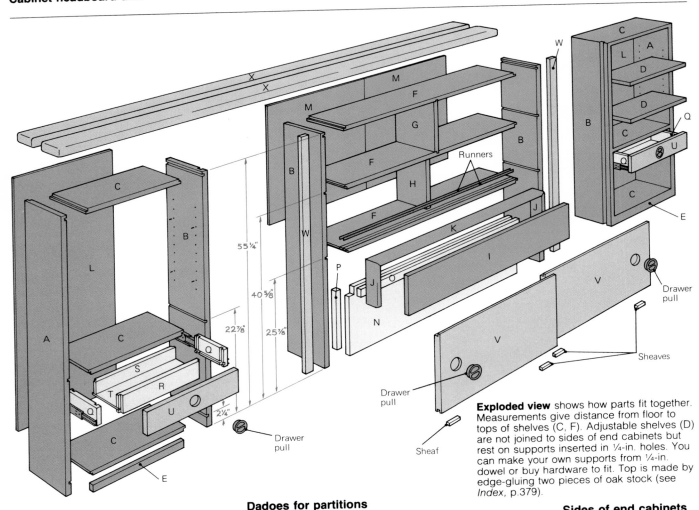

Exploded view shows how parts fit together. Measurements give distance from floor to tops of shelves (C, F). Adjustable shelves (D) are not joined to sides of end cabinets but rest on supports inserted in ¼-in. holes. You can make your own supports from ¼-in. dowel or buy hardware to fit. Top is made by edge-gluing two pieces of oak stock (see Index, p.379).

Use diagrams to lay out dadoes and rabbets for center-cabinet shelves (F) and sides of end cabinets (A, B). Note that the dadoes that receive the tongues of the bottom partition (H) are blind—they stop 8½ in. from back of shelf—and must be finished with a chisel. The rabbets on the end-cabinet shelves (C), top partition (G), and bottom partition (H), like those of the center-cabinet shelves, are ¼ in. wide and are cut deeply enough to leave tongues ¼ in. thick. Not shown are dadoes across side pieces (A, B) to receive tongues of shelves (C, F); these are ¼ in. wide by 9/32 in. deep and are positioned according to measurements given in the exploded view; take measurements for width of dadoes from thickness of shelves. (See caption that accompanies patterns on page 181.) After you have cut the dadoes, drill two rows of ¼-in. holes for shelf supports 1¼ in. from front and back edges of end-cabinet sides; use a template to guide your drill bit (see Index, p.379). Space holes on 2-in. centers, starting 6 in. above the middle dado, and drill them ⅜ in. deep. To protect the plywood veneer at the edges of the holes, use bits specifically ground for wood or plastic. In addition, 3/16-in. holes must be drilled through the top shelves for attaching the oak top (X). Drill one hole in each corner 1½ in. from the edges and two more near the middle groove of the top center-cabinet shelf (F); countersink. After all machining is finished, sand interior surfaces with No. 120 sandpaper, followed by No. 150.

Dadoes for partitions

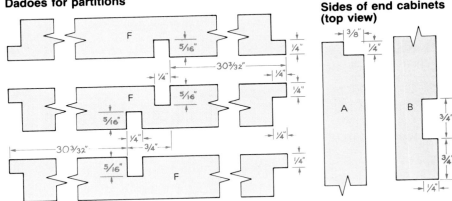

Sides of end cabinets (top view)

Dadoes for sliding doors

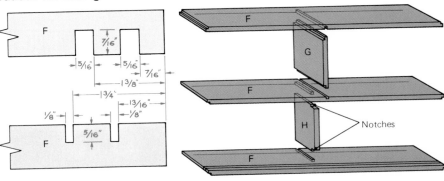

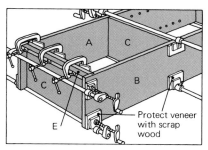

1. To assemble each end cabinet, first glue tongues of shelves (C) into grooves of outer side (A); then glue inner side (B) onto its tongues. Apply clamps loosely across shelves. Square cabinet up and tighten clamps. Glue and clamp filler (E) to bottom shelf.

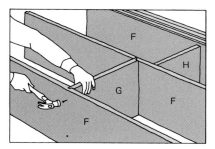

2. Cut ¼-in. notches ⅜ in. deep in front corners of bottom partition (H); veneer edge. Glue tongues into grooves of two lower center-cabinet shelves (F); secure with 6d finishing nails. Glue top partition (G) and top shelf (F) in place, nailing through top shelf only.

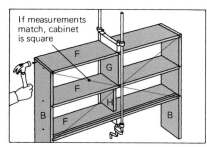

3. Glue and nail inner sides (B) onto center-cabinet shelves (F), using one 6d coated nail per joint. Align bar or pipe clamps with the partitions. Square cabinet by measuring corner to corner, then tighten clamps. Drive two more 6d coated nails to secure each joint.

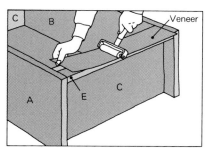

4. Veneer front edges of all three cabinets and adjustable shelves (D). Use a single 3¾-in. veneer strip to cover filler (E) and edge of bottom shelf of each end cabinet. On center-cabinet sides (B), veneer only to a line 12½ in. up from floor. (See *Index*, p.379, for veneering instructions.)

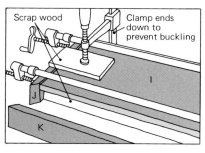

5. Cut headboard face (I) to size (width of opening in center cabinet minus two thicknesses walnut stock). Cut and fit mitered corners of headboard sides (J) and top (K); see p.182, Steps 10–11. Glue and clamp sides (J) to face (I), allowing about ¹⁄₁₆-in. protrusion.

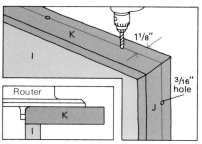

6. Glue and clamp headboard top (K) in place. Plane and sand protruding edges flush. Round off edges with router and ⅜-in. quarter-round bit. Along a line 1⅛ in. from back edge of sides and top, drill and countersink several ³⁄₁₆-in. holes for screwing headboard to cabinet.

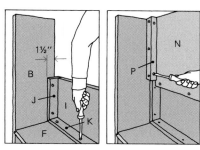

7. Cut ¾-in. notches 1⅜ in. deep in top corners of center filler (N). Glue and clamp filler spacer (O) to front between notches. Use 1¼-in. No. 8 wood screws to attach filler blocks (P) to back. Drill and countersink several ³⁄₁₆-in. holes through filler and spacer and along center line of filler blocks.

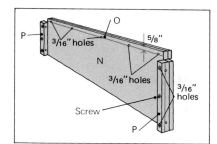

8. With 1¼-in. No. 8 screws, secure headboard unit and center filler unit to center cabinet. Drive 2-in. No. 8 screws through filler and filler spacer into headboard face. Veneer bottom part of sides with 3¼-in.-wide strips, covering the part of the filler that will show.

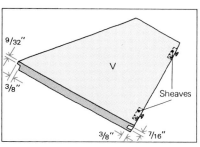

9. Cut sliding doors (V) to fit between center-cabinet shelves. Rabbet front of each door's top edge, leaving ⅜-in. tongue ⁹⁄₃₂ in. thick. On table saw cut slot along bottom edge ⅜ in. deep to accommodate sheaves. Screw two sheaves into slot in each door. Install Fibertrack runners.

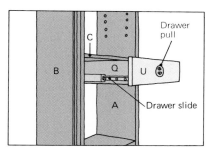

10. Make drawers (Q, R, S, T) 1¹⁄₁₆ in. narrower than opening in end cabinets (see p.183, Steps 13–20). Cut drawer faces (U) ³⁄₁₆ in. shorter than width of opening. Install walnut drawer pulls. Hang drawers with 10-in. slides so that upper edge of face is ⅛ in. below middle shelf.

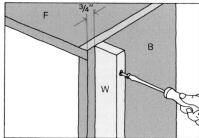

11. Cut end-cabinet backs (L) to fit in rabbets on outer sides (A) flush with all other edges. Cut center-cabinet back (M) in two panels. Sand and finish panels, then nail in place. Screw reveals (W) to center-cabinet sides ¾ in. from front, using 1½-in. No. 8 wood screws.

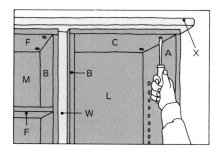

12. Edge-glue oak stock for top (X). Cut to length and use plane or belt sander to smooth all surfaces. Round edges and corners with router and ⅜-in. quarter-round bit. Sand and finish top, then secure to cabinets by driving 1½-in. No. 10 wood screws.

MISSION-STYLE HEADBOARD

Reflecting the simple mission style, this headboard consists of only eight pieces plus an optional ninth. Five pine boards, glued edge to edge, form the backboard; pine also crowns the headboard. The posts are made of 4 x 4 cedar. For decoration you can glue a relief carving (found at gift shops and flea markets) to the center of the headboard. You can avoid gluing together individual boards for the backboard by using ¾-inch plywood instead, but the finished project will not be as attractive.

The top of the backboard is cut in a scoop design, following the pattern below (see p. 48 for instructions on enlarging and using patterns).

Each 4-foot-long cedar post is beveled on all four sides at the top to produce a pineapple crown. Bevel crosscuts also create the pad feet at the bottoms. The posts are rounded on all edges, and the inner side of each post has a ¾-inch-wide dado cut to a depth of 1 inch. The ends of the backboard are glued into these dadoes to join the backboard and posts.

The crown piece has a blind dado on its underside so that it can fit onto the top of the backboard. The facing edge and ends of the crown are rounded.

Glue is the only fastener used in this project. If the glue is carefully applied and the parts are clamped overnight, or until the glue dries, the joints will be stronger than the wood itself.

Our headboard is designed for use with a double-size angle-iron bed frame that is 53 inches wide. The headboard is 56½ inches wide, edge to edge, which allows the screw holes for attaching the frame to the headboard to be centered on the flats of the posts. You must plan your headboard so that it is 3½ inches wider than your bed frame.

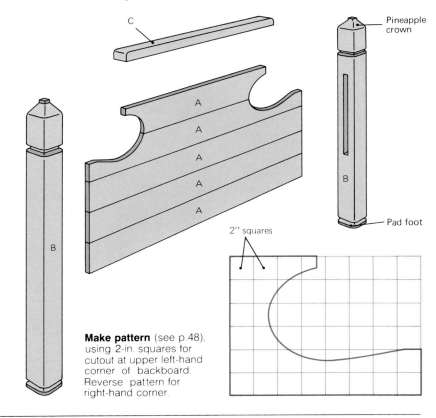

Pineapple crown

Pad foot

Make pattern (see p. 48), using 2-in. squares for cutout at upper left-hand corner of backboard. Reverse pattern for right-hand corner.

2″ squares

Parts list

Part	Name	Quantity	Thickness	Width	Length	Material
A	Backboard	5	¾″	5½″	51½″	1 x 6 pine board
B	Post	2	3½″	3½″	48″	4 x 4 cedar
C	Crown	1	1⅛″	1½″	35″	⁵⁄₄ x 4 pine board

Tools and materials: Radial arm saw with 72-point carbide-tipped blade and dado head. Saber saw. Surform scraper or router with ½″ rounding-over bit. Belt sander with Nos. 100 and 150 belts. Orbital sander and sanding block with No. 180 paper. Four 4′ pipe or bar clamps. Rubber mallet, wooden mallet, ¾″ and 2″ chisels, medium file. Steel tape rule. Wood glue, clear varnish, paintbrush. Several weights (bricks, barbells, or sandbags). Five 8′ lengths of 1 x 6 clear pine, one 8′ length of 4 x 4 cedar, one 4′ length of ⁵⁄₄ x 4 pine board.

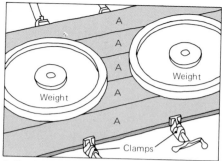

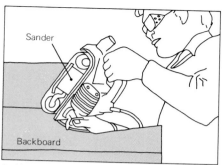

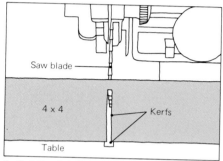

1. Cut backboards (A) 51½ in. long, selecting best portions of each board. Edge-join boards and clamp them together. Place clamps below boards and put weights on top to prevent the boards from buckling.

2. Transfer scoop patterns to rear of backboard and cut them out with a saber saw. Saber saw blades cut on the upstroke, producing frayed edges, so sand the cutouts with Nos. 100 and 150 sanding belts.

3. Use belt sander with Nos. 100 and 150 belts on all surfaces of backboard, giving special attention to glued joints. Finish with orbital sander, using No. 180 paper. Board-to-board joints should be almost undetectable.

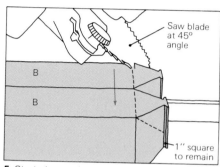

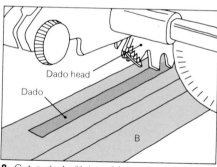

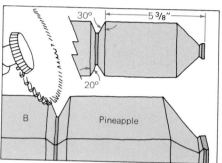

4. Cut the 8-ft.-long 4 x 4 in half. Since the radial arm saw will only make a cut 3 in. deep, you will have to turn the post over and align the first-cut kerf with the kerf on the saw table before making the second cut.

5. Start pineapples on posts (B) by making 45° bevel cuts with a crosscut blade on all four sides of both posts. Use scrap 4 x 4 to determine depth of cut and distance from the ends needed to produce 1-in.-sq. caps.

6. Shape bottoms of pineapples with two more sets of bevel cuts to form an asymmetrical V 5⅜ in. from post caps. Upper cuts are 30° bevels, base cuts are 20° bevels. Cut the pad feet at bottoms of posts the same way.

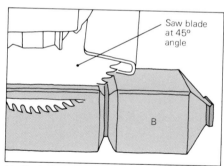

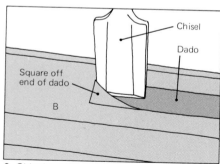

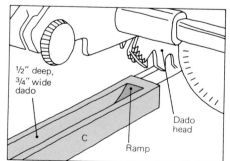

7. To help round the edges of the posts lengthwise, make 45° bevel rip cuts from end to end. Later (Step 10) complete the rounding of the posts, using a Surform scraper or a router with a rounding-over bit.

8. Cut a dado ¾ in. wide and 1 in. deep in each post, beginning 18 in. from the bottom. Lower spinning dado head into post, raise it, stop saw, and measure depth until you reach 1 in. Then cut each dado 19½ in. long.

9. Chisel out the curved ramps at the ends of the dadoes. First, tap the 2-in. chisel along the side walls. Next, use the ¾-in. chisel to make vertical cuts at the ends of each dado; then chisel out the waste.

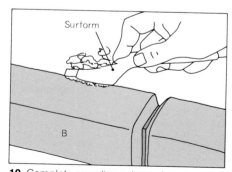

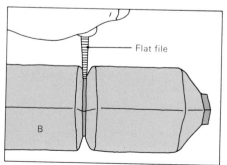

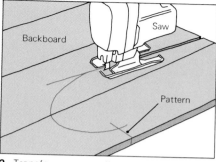

10. Complete rounding edges of posts, using a Surform scraper (shown) or a router with a rounding-over bit, depending on the look you wish to achieve. The Surform works best with the grain; across the grain use a file.

11. Clean the kerfs at the base of each pineapple with the edge of a file. Finish off squares on post tops with the flat of the file. Apply glue to the dadoes and force posts onto the backboard with a rubber mallet.

12. Cut ⁵⁄₄ board to size for crown (C). Cut a ½-in.-deep blind dado as long as top of backboard and chisel out ramps. Round off facing edge and ends of crown; glue it on. Stain headboard if you wish, then varnish it.

READING LAMP

When reading in bed, you should be able to direct the pattern of light so that it will not disturb your sleeping spouse. This lamp pivots and telescopes to let you do so. Begin construction by cutting all the parts according to the chart and patterns below. Use a saber saw to cut out the brackets, and snips to cut the metal. Once all the parts are cut, follow the step-by-step directions. (For details on cutting dadoes, finishing wood, and soldering, see the *Index,* p.379.)

Enlarge patterns below to serve as cutting guides (see p.48). Each square equals ½ in.

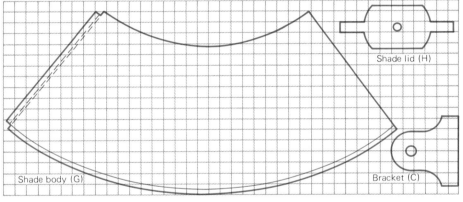

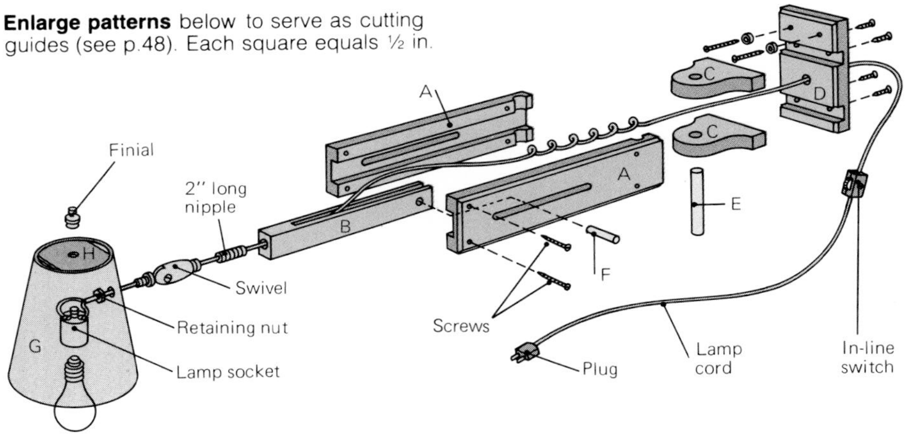

Finial

2″ long nipple

Swivel

Retaining nut

Lamp socket

Screws

Plug

Lamp cord

In-line switch

Shade lid (H)

Shade body (G)

Bracket (C)

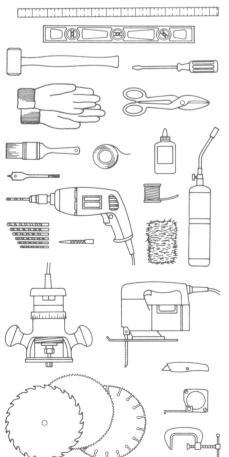

Parts list

Part	Name	Quantity	Thickness	Width	Length	Material
A	Housing side	2	¾″	2½″	12″	1 x 4 maple
B	Extension arm	1	¾″	1″	10″	1 x 4 maple
C	Bracket	2	¾″	3″	3¼″	1 x 4 maple
D	Base	1	¾″	3¼″	6″	1 x 4 maple
E	Support post	1	½″ dia.	—	4¼″	Hardwood dowel
F	Stop	1	¼″ dia.	—	1½″	Copper or brass rod
G	Shade body	1	—	9″	20″	Copper flashing
H	Shade lid	1	—	2½″	5½″	Copper flashing

Tools and materials: Power saw. Dado head for saw, router with straight bit, or backsaw and chisel (for cutting dadoes). Saber saw. Drill press or router with bead and quarter-round bit. Drill with ½″ spade bit and set of twist bits. Propane torch. Two 4″ C-clamps. Wooden mallet, screwdriver. Wire stripper or sharp knife, metal snips, punch. Metal straightedge, steel tape rule, level, pencil. Nos. 100, 150, and 220 sandpaper, 0000 steel wool. Paintbrush, work gloves. Thin cardboard, two wood blocks, plastic friction tape, white glue. Acid-core solder, flux, detergent, penetrating oil stain, polyurethane varnish, paste wax. Short length of ½″ dowel, 4′ length of 1 x 4 maple or other hardwood, 1′ length of 20″ copper flashing, 1½″ length of ¼″ copper or brass rod (slightly thinner rod used in toilet tanks will do). A 10′ length of lamp cord with matching plug and in-line switch, porcelain lamp socket with threaded nipple 1″ long, ⅜″ threaded nipple 2″ long, brass retaining nut, brass finial, lamp swivel, 75-watt light bulb. Eight 1″ No. 8 brass roundhead wood screws, four 1½″ No. 8 brass flathead wood screws. Two 3″ No. 14 brass flathead wood screws with collar washers.

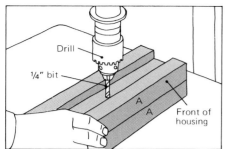

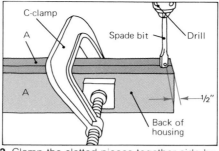

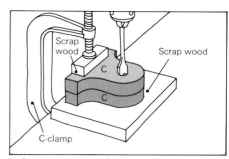

1. Draw lines along inner face of each housing side (A) ¾ in. from each long edge. Cut ⅜-in.-deep dadoes between lines. Drill ¼-in. holes through dadoes 1⅞ in. from front and 4⅛ in. from back. Cut slots between holes large enough to accept stop (F) easily.

2. Clamp the slotted pieces together side by side and cut shallow notches across both ½ in. from back ends. Reclamp pieces together with notches facing each other; use a ½-in. spade bit to drill one hole at point of notches, making half hole in each housing side.

3. Clamp brackets (C) together and use a ½-in. spade bit to drill through both. Push support post (E) into holes. If it will not fit, reduce its diameter by sanding. Further reduce its diameter at center to allow lamp housing to swivel freely on completed lamp.

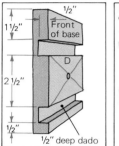

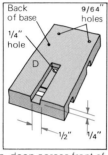

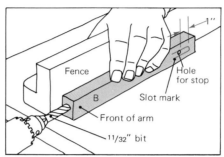

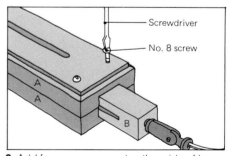

4. Cut ¾-in. dadoes ½ in. deep across front of base (D), 1½ in. from top and ½ in. from bottom. Cut ½-in. dado on back of base ¼ in. deep, from center of bottom going up 2¾ in. Drill ¼-in. hole through top of dado and two 9/64-in. holes through top of base.

5. Sand down extension arm (B) until it slides easily into clamped-together housing. Mark outline of slot in housing on arm. Drill a hole the diameter of stop (F) on arm 1 in. from back of slot outline. Drill an 11/32-in. hole 2¼ in. deep into front end of arm as shown.

6. Cut a ½-in.-deep slot for lamp cord along top of extension arm from back end to 1 in. from front. Trim top and bottom edges of housing sides (A) with bead and quarter-round bit. Sand, stain, varnish, and wax all wooden parts. Wax arm to make it slide easily.

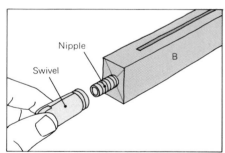

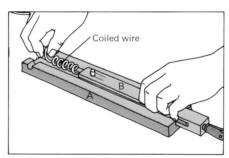

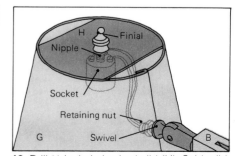

7. Twist ⅜" nipple halfway into hole in end of extension arm. As it has a slightly larger diameter than hole, nipple will form threads in wood. Thread swivel onto nipple and push lamp cord into slot in extension arm and through nipple hole, nipple, and swivel.

8. Coil remaining lamp cord around a dowel. Push extension arm and coiled wire into dado in one housing side. Remove dowel. Glue housing sides together. Drill 3/32-in. pilot holes and drive a No. 8 roundhead screw into each corner of housing.

9. Add four more screws to other side of housing, but off-set these screws so that they do not collide with first four. Push support post (E) through brackets (C) for alignment. Attach brackets to base (D) with glue and No. 8 flathead screws. Countersink screws.

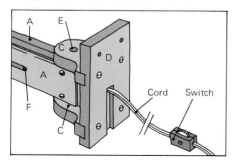

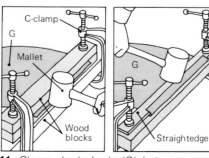

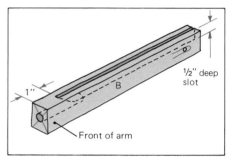

10. Remove support post. Slide housing into place between brackets. Apply glue to support post and tap it into place. Glue stop (F) into hole near back of extension arm. Attach in-line switch to lamp cord at point where it will be most easily reached. Attach plug.

11. Clamp shade body (G) between wood blocks and bend down one end with a mallet. Turn shade over and bend end even more over a metal straightedge. Bend other end of shade in opposite direction. Pull shade into a circle, hook edges together, and solder.

12. Drill ⅜-in. hole in shade lid (H). Solder lid to shade. Drill hole for swivel in seam of shade. Push swivel through hole; screw on retaining nut. Wire on socket and wrap its posts with tape. Add nipple, then finial, to top. Mount lamp with No. 14 screws.

JEWELRY BOX

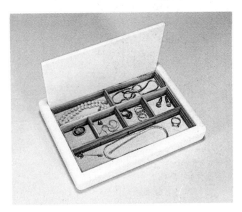

Sleek and clean lined, this jewelry box looks as if it were made of alabaster, but its translucence comes from a durable, man-made material called Corian. The project, of course, could also be made of solid hardwood if you prefer.

To open the box, press on the rear of the top, place a finger under the front edge, and lift up. The top fits into a slot behind the back liner and stays upright. To close the box, lift the top slightly and lower the front edge.

Corian is dense but easy to work. It was developed for use in bathrooms and kitchens and is sold at lumberyards or through custom kitchen and bathroom contractors. You may be able to buy scraps left over from a job.

A special glue bonds Corian so that no seams show. Follow the manufacturer's instructions in mixing the glue. It has a very short pot life before it sets—about 5 minutes—so have all the Corian parts test-fitted and cleaned with denatured alcohol before mixing the glue. Do not touch the joint surfaces thereafter.

A carbide-tipped blade is recommended because the resins in Corian will quickly dull an ordinary blade. If your blade cuts a 1/8-inch kerf (as most carbide-tipped blades do), you can notch the teak dividers and liners with one pass (Steps 8–10). Make a test cut in scrap wood and measure it; if it is not 1/8 inch wide, you will have to make two passes.

The appearance of the box depends on the care you give to finishing it. Sand all surfaces except the top and bottom with No. 80 paper. Follow with No. 150 paper on all surfaces, sanding the length of the pieces just as with wood. The final sanding with No. 320 (or finer) sandpaper results in a satin-smooth surface with no visible sanding marks.

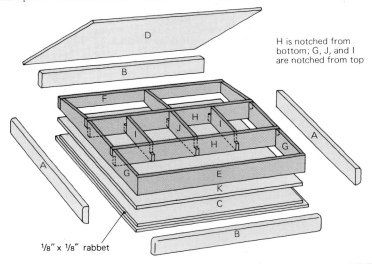

H is notched from bottom; G, J, and I are notched from top

1/8" x 1/8" rabbet

Parts list

Part	Name	Quantity	Thickness	Width	Length	Material
A	Side	2	3/4"	2"	7 1/2"	Corian backsplash
B	Front and back	2	3/4"	2"	12"	Corian backsplash
C	Bottom	1	1/4"	7 3/4"	10 3/4"	Corian sheeting
D	Top	1	1/4"	7 1/2"	10 1/2"	Corian sheeting
E	Front liner	1	1/8"	1 1/4"	10 1/2"	Teak
F	Back liner	1	1/8"	1"	10 1/2"	Teak
G	Side liner	2	1/8"	1 1/4"	7"	Teak
H	Long divider	2	1/8"	1 1/4"	10 1/4"	Teak
I	Short divider	2	1/8"	1 1/4"	2 5/8" ✱	Teak
J	Center divider	1	1/8"	1 1/4"	4 13/16" ✱	Teak
K	Bottom liner	1	1/4"	7 1/2"	10 1/2"	Hardboard or plywood

✱ Cut slightly oversize and sand to fit.

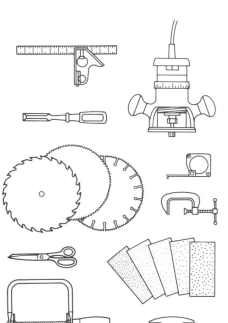

Tools and materials: Table or radial arm saw with carbide-tipped combination blade. Coping saw. Router with 1/2" rounding-over bit with pilot. Combination square, steel tape rule, pencil. Three 4" C-clamps. Scissors, 1/2" wood chisel. Sanding block, Nos. 80, 150, and 320 sandpaper. Denatured alcohol, a kit of joint adhesive for Corian, wood glue, aluminum foil, wax paper, rubber gloves, soft cloth. Corian backsplash 3/4" x 3" x 42", Corian sheeting 1/4" x 12" x 16". Teak 1/8" x 5 1/2" x 18", hardboard or plywood 1/4" x 7 1/2" x 10 1/2".

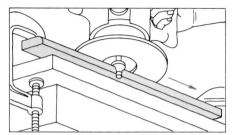

1. Rip the backsplash piece to a 2-in. width, but do not saw parts to length yet. Clamp piece to work surface with one edge slightly overhanging. Shape edge with router and ½-in. rounding-over bit with pilot. Do not force the bit, but make several light passes, repositioning clamp as needed. Smooth edge with No. 80 sandpaper.

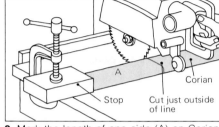

2. Mark the length of one side (A) on Corian. Align with saw blade so that blade will cut on outside of line. Place a bench stop (squared piece of wood) against end of Corian and clamp stop to table. Make the cut; move strip to stop and cut a second piece the same length. Reposition stop and cut front and back (B), each 12 in. long, in same way.

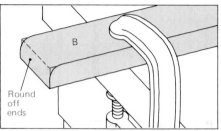

3. Clamp the front (B) to the work surface with one end overhanging slightly. Shape that end with the rounding-over bit. Reverse the part and repeat at the other end. Shape the back piece in the same way. Sand with No. 80 sandpaper. Do not round the ends of the sides (A); these are left straight so that they can be glued to the front and back.

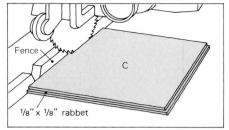

4. With the saw set for a rip cut, saw the top (D) and bottom (C) to size. Then set the blade flush to the fence and at a level to make a cut ⅛ in. deep. Test-cut the edge of a scrap to make sure you are cutting a rabbet ⅛ in. x ⅛ in. If not, move the blade away from fence enough to make the cut ⅛ in. wide. Then cut rabbets on all four edges of the bottom.

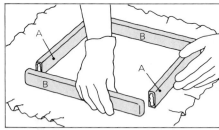

5. Test-fit parts A, B, C, and D. Wearing rubber gloves and working on a piece of aluminum foil, mix glue following manufacturer's instructions. Spread an even coat of glue on both faces of joints of sides, front, and back. Place parts A and B, rounded edge up, on aluminum foil and join them. Check for squareness with a combination square.

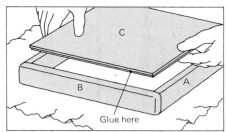

6. Coat the rabbets on the bottom (C) with an even bead of glue and place the bottom in position on the rounded edges. After about 10 min. remove excess glue on the bottom with a wood chisel. Allow the glue to dry overnight. Then use No. 80 sandpaper wrapped around a sanding block to smooth the joints until they are almost invisible.

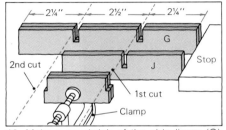

7. Saw a squared scrap of wood 1⅞ in. thick to the length of the box interior. Place in box, up against front, to support router. Clamp another scrap to hold box as shown. Round outer edge of box with rounding-over bit. Repeat on back edge. Then saw support to width of box interior; repeat procedure to round the edges of the sides of the box.

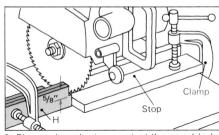

8. Place a bench stop against the saw blade and clamp stop to saw table. Adjust height of blade to cut ⅝ in. deep into the 1¼-in.-wide teak parts. Clamp the two long dividers (H), touching the stop, to fence. With a single pass of the saw blade, cut a notch ⅝ in. deep and ⅛ in. wide at one end of the dividers; repeat the cut at other end.

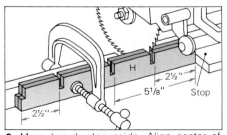

9. Move bench stop aside. Align center of long dividers (5⅛ in. from ends) with center of saw blade; clamp dividers to fence. With blade at same height as in Step 8, make a notch. Cut two more notches, each 2½ in. from ends of dividers. Mark for first of these notches only, then position bench stop, make cut, reverse dividers, and cut other notch.

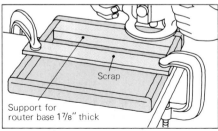

10. Make a sandwich of the side liners (G), center divider (J), and short dividers (I) as shown. Clamp sandwich to fence so that blade will notch dividers 2¼ in. from one end of G and J. Place stop at end of sandwich and make cut. Turn sandwich end to end, placing a scrap in notch to keep parts aligned. Clamp to fence and make second cut.

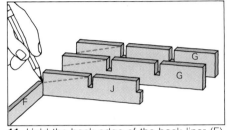

11. Hold the back edge of the back liner (F) even with the lower edge of the center divider (J), and mark where the top of the liner hits J. Draw a line from this mark to the top of the nearest notch. Align back edges of the side liners (G) with center divider, clamp them in a vise together, and saw the taper with a coping saw following the line on J.

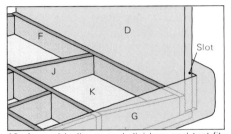

12. Assemble liners and dividers and test-fit; trim if necessary. Glue grid of liners and dividers with wood glue. Line box with wax paper. Place grid in box and stand top (D) in slot at back of box; in this position top will hold grid while glue dries. Finish box (see text). Cover bottom liner (K) with velvet. Place bottom liner in box with the grid on top of it.

OLD-WORLD WORKBENCH

Woodworking benches have been developed over the centuries to suit the needs of the craftsmen who use them. Our hardwood bench is a close copy of a Scandinavian one. It has two vises. The bench dogs and end vise allow the bench to act as a giant clamp. It can hold boards for planing or blocks of wood for carving.

The bench top is constructed of hard maple. It is made by reinforcing the edges of two center boards and several thicker rails with dowels, then gluing the edges together. While working on the bench top, use a sturdy pair of sawhorses or a strong table to hold it. As the top takes shape, it will become very heavy. When you join the boards and rails, align their tops carefully; do not worry about the bottoms. This aligning will save you considerable time in sanding the hard maple when the top is completed.

The vises are attached to the underside of the bench top. You can buy the vise hardware (the base and the vise-screw and guide-rod assembly), as well as the vise dogs, from any dealer in fine tools. If you choose the Garrett Wade vise models listed below, use the instructions given on the following pages for attaching them. If you use any other models, follow the manufacturer's instructions instead (even the screw sizes may change). Make your own vise heads from maple.

The bench legs are made from construction-grade pine. The tops and bottoms of the legs are fitted into supports with mortise-and-tenon joints, and the legs are connected with stretchers; then the entire assembly is screwed to the prepared bench top.

The finished bench should be sanded down and given several coats of tung oil sealer to keep the wood from drying out. As the bench wears, the top can be resanded and given another coat of sealer. If properly cared for, this workbench could be passed down from one generation of woodworkers to the next.

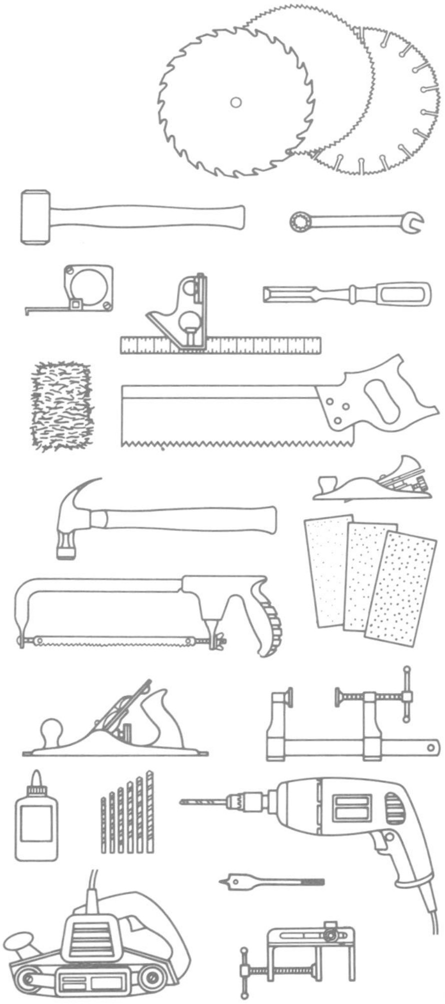

Parts list

Part	Name	Quantity	Thickness	Width	Length	Material
A	Outer side rail	2	2½"	2½"	60"	Hard maple
B	Inner side rail	2	2½"	2½"	60"	Hard maple
C	End rail	1	2½"	2½"	22"✲	Hard maple
D	Center board	2	1¾"	6"	60"	Hard maple
E	End-vise face	1	1¾"	5½"	22"✲	Hard maple
F	End-vise head	2	1¾"	5½"	22"✲	Hard maple
G	Side-vise head	1	1¾"	5½"	17"	Hard maple
H	Side-vise head	1	1"	5½"	17"	Hard maple
I	Leg	4	3½"	3½"	32½"	4 x 4 pine
J	Support	4	3½"	3½"	21"	4 x 4 pine
K	Stretcher	2	1½"	5½"	45"	2 x 6 pine
L	End-vise handle	1	1" dia.	—	18"	Hardwood dowel
M	Side-vise handle	1	⅞" dia.	—	14"	Hardwood dowel
N	Long dowel	52	½" dia.	—	4"	Hardwood dowel
O	Short dowel	14	½" dia.	—	3"	Hardwood dowel
P	End-vise cap	2	1" dia.	—	—	Furniture leg cap
Q	Side-vise cap	2	⅞" dia.	—	—	Furniture leg cap
R	End-vise hardware	1	—	—	—	Model B shoulder vise
S	Side-vise hardware	1	—	—	—	Model A shoulder vise
T	Bench dog	4	¾"	¾"	6"	Steel bench dog

✲Measurement is approximate; cut to fit during construction.

Tools and materials: Table or radial arm saw, hacksaw, backsaw. Heavy-duty drill with extra-long twist bits and ⅞" and 1¼" spade bits. Bench plane, block plane. Jointer plane (optional). Mallet, ½" and 1¼" wood chisels. Hammer, ½" wrench, commercial doweling jig. Four 2' bar clamps. Combination square, steel tape rule, pencil. Belt sander with Nos. 16 (open coat), 80, and 120 sanding belts. Nos. 80 and 120 sandpaper, carpenter's glue. Tung oil sealer, 000 steel wool, soft cloth. Wood and dowels (see above). Garrett Wade Model A shoulder vise 70G03.01 and Model B shoulder vise 70G04.01 (or equivalent). Two ⅞" and two 1" furniture leg caps, four steel bench dogs. Four 5⁄16" bolts 6" long with nuts and double washers, four 5⁄16" lag screws 5" long with washers. Seven 1" and eight 1½" No. 12 flathead wood screws, eight 1½" No. 14 flathead wood screws. Four small brads.

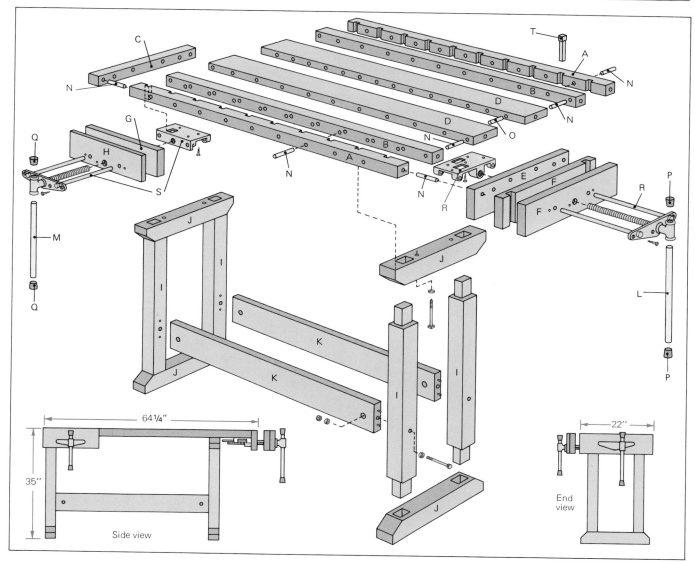

1. Cut the center boards (D) to length (see chart). Prepare their edges for joining by planing them smooth with a bench plane, then with a jointer plane if you have one.
2. Lay the two center boards side by side and look for gaps between the edges to be joined. Plane away any gaps. The two edges must fit snugly together, for the strength of the edge joint depends on the full contact of the adjoining edges.

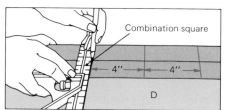

3. Clamp the center boards together with the edges that will be joined facing up. Mark the locations of the dowel holes every 4 in. along the edge of one of the boards. Use a combination square to draw a straight line through each of the dowel marks and across both boards. Make sure that the lines are drawn perfectly straight, as dowel alignment must be accurate.

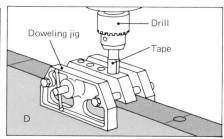

4. Separate the boards and place the doweling jig on the marked edge of one of them. Align the jig with the first dowel mark. Put a ½-in. bit into a drill and wrap tape around the bit to act as a depth gauge. The distance of tape from the point of drill bit should be 1½ in. plus the thickness of the jig. Drill through the jig and into the wood until the tape hits the jig. Drill the other dowel holes in this board and then into the other center board in the same way.
5. Cut the short dowels (O) to length. Clamp each dowel in a vise and cut a shallow groove along its length with a backsaw to let excess glue escape. Sand the ends of the dowels so that they will fit into the holes easily. Test-fit the dowels and boards before you start gluing.

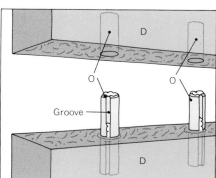

6. Put a liberal amount of glue on one end of each dowel and insert the glued ends into the holes in one of the center boards. Put more glue on the protruding ends of the dowels and on the edge of the board. Spread an even coat of glue along the drilled edge of the other center board and fit that board over the first one so that the dowels go into the dowel holes.
7. If necessary, use a hammer buffered with scrap wood to tap the boards together. Then clamp them together, wipe off any excess glue with a damp cloth, and let the joint dry thoroughly.

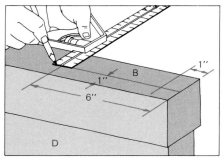

8. Cut side rails (A and B) to length. Position an inner side rail (B) against an edge of the assembled center boards (D) and plane the pieces until they fit together snugly. Draw straight lines across the long outside edge of the side rail every 6 in. and also 1 in. from each end. Use a combination square and pencil to draw a second line through the first lines on the edge, making crosses 1 in. from what will be the top of the bench. These crosses mark the dowel hole locations. Note that the dowel holes must be 1 in. from the top of the rail and not centered on its edge because the rail is thicker than the center boards.

9. Clamp the inner side rail into place against the center boards and drill ½-in. dowel holes wherever the lines on the edge intersect. The holes should be 4 in. deep, going through the inner side rail and into the center board. No jig is needed, as both pieces are drilled at once.

10. Glue the inner side rail into place as you glued the center boards together, but use the long dowels (N). Clamp the assembly and let it dry; then add the other inner side rail in the same way.

11. Position the outer side rails (A) against the inner ones and plane them for a snug fit. Clamp the two outer rails together and draw a line across the thickness of both rails 4 in. from one end and every 6 in. beyond to mark the locations for the bench dog slots.

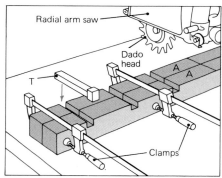

12. Test-cut a slot in a piece of scrap wood. Use a radial arm or table saw with a dado head and cut the slot as wide and as deep as the base of a bench dog (T). Check the fit of the bench dog. It should fit snugly into the slot without being tight. With the outer side rails still clamped together, cut slots at all the lines drawn in Step 11. Check the depth of the cut frequently, and test-fit with a bench dog after each cut.

13. Clamp the outer side rails (A) into place with the slots positioned against the inner side rails (B); be sure the facing slots are aligned across the bench top. Check the fit of the joints and plane the pieces if necessary; then lay out dowel hole locations between the bench dog slots.

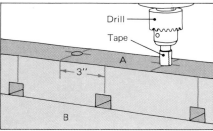

14. Drill ½-in. dowel holes 3¾ in. deep between the slots. The dowel holes should go through the centers of the edges of the outer side rails (A) and into the edges of the inner side rails (B). Attach the outer side rails with glue and long dowels (N).

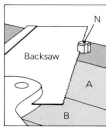 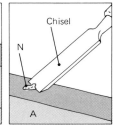

15. Use a backsaw to cut the dowels off flush with the edges of the bench. Trim the dowel ends with a ½-in. chisel, then plane the edges of the bench top smooth.

16. Measure the width of the bench top and cut the end rail (C) to that length. Clamp the end rail into place at the end of the bench top where the slots are closer.

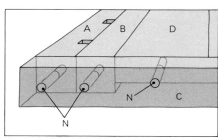

17. Drill ½-in. dowel holes 3¾ in. deep through the end rail and into each of the six bench top sections. The holes that go into the side rails (A and B) should be centered on the edge; those that go into the two center boards (D) should be 1 in. from the top of the bench.

18. Attach the end rail with long dowels (N) and glue. Cut and trim the dowel ends and plane the edges smooth (see Step 15).

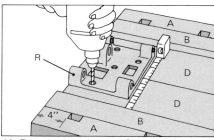

19. Turn the bench over. Center the base of the end-vise hardware (R) on the underside of the bench top where the bench dog slots are 4 in. from the end. Drill ¹³/₆₄-in. pilot holes 1¼ in. deep for the No. 14 screws. Screw the base down.

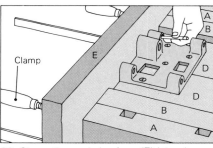

20. Clamp the end-vise face (E) into place. Put a pencil through the holes in the vise base to mark the locations of the vise-screw and guide-rod holes on the vise face. Unclamp the face.

21. Drill a 1¼-in. hole for the vise screw through the vise face at the appropriate mark. Drill a ⅞-in. hole for each of the two guide rods. (The sizes of all these holes may be different for your vise; check the manufacturer's instructions.)

22. Reclamp the vise face into place. Check its alignment and mark the width of the bench on the face. Remove the face and use it as a pattern to mark the vise-screw and guide-rod holes on the end-vise heads.

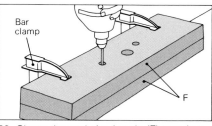

23. Clamp the end-vise heads (F) together and drill the marked holes completely through the first and partially into the second. Unclamp the heads and finish the holes in the second.

24. Reclamp the vise face (E) into place and align all the holes by pushing the vise screw and guide rods through them. Drill dowel holes as you did in Step 17.

25. Remove the vise face (E) and cut it to length, using the bench-width marks made in Step 22. Attach the vise face with glue and long dowels (N). Trim the dowels and plane the face (see Step 15).

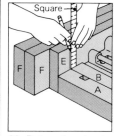 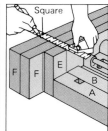

26. Return the vise heads (F) to their place, with the vise-screw and guide-rod assembly inserted, and tighten the vise screw. Use a combination square and pencil to transfer the location of the bench dog slots on the bench to the top of the inner vise head. Mark the length of the vise face (E) on the vise heads. Remove vise heads, and cut bench dog slots where marked on inner vise head. Cut both heads to length.

27. Test-fit the bench dogs, then glue the two end-vise heads together with the bench dog slots inside. Clamp, and let them dry.

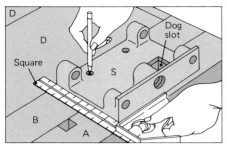

28. Place the base of the side-vise hardware (S) into position on the underside of the bench top. Align the square hole in the base so that it is over the nearest bench dog slot. Use a square to make sure that the side of the vise base is parallel to the side of the bench top. Drill 5/32-in. pilot holes 1½ in. deep for the No. 14 screws. Screw the base down.

29. Cut the side-vise heads (G and H) to size and glue them together. When the glue is dry, hold the heads in place against the side of the bench—the top edge of the combined heads should be flush with the top of the bench. Put a pencil through the holes in the vise base to mark locations of vise screw and guide rods on heads.

30. Drill a 1-in. hole through the vise heads for the vise screw and 7/8-in. holes for the guide rods (or whatever size holes your vise calls for). Reposition the vise heads and slip the vise-screw and guide-rod assembly into place. Tighten the vise screw.

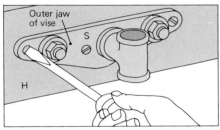

31. Drill 5/32-in. pilot holes 1 in. deep through the holes in the faces of the vise-screw and guide-rod assemblies and into their vise heads. Fasten the assemblies to their heads with 1-in. No. 12 screws.

32. Smooth the top surface of the bench with a belt sander. If the top has ridges formed by a slight misalignment, start with a very coarse open-coat belt (No. 16). Finish with a No. 80 sanding belt.

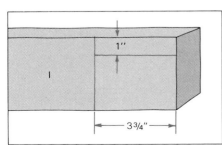

33. Cut the legs (I) to length. Make a mark 3¾ in. from one end of one leg. Use a combination square to extend this mark across the width of the leg. Set the blade of the square to protrude 1 in. and use it to draw a line 1 in. from one side of the leg, running from the end of the leg to the 3¾-in. line. These lines will be used to cut a tenon into the end of the leg.

34. Set up the saw for the widest possible dado cut. Place the leg on the saw table and adjust the blade to cut up to the 1-in. line. Make a cut, then push the leg over and continue the cut. Repeat until you reach the 3¾-in. line; then clamp a piece of scrap wood to the table to act as a stop. Using the stop as a guide, make the same cuts in the facing side of the same end. Cut the other end of the leg in the same way. Cut the other three legs as you cut the first.

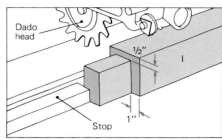

35. Place a leg on the saw table so that one of the uncut sides of a tenon is facing the blade and the end is tight against the stop. Adjust the blade for a ½-in.-deep cut; make the cut along the length of the tenon. Repeat on the facing side. The completed tenon will have two 1-in. shoulders and two ½-in. shoulders. Repeat the cuts at the other end of the leg and on both ends of the remaining three legs.

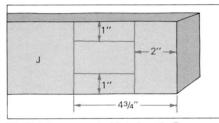

36. Cut the supports (J) to length. Draw lines across facing sides of each support 2 in. and 4¾ in. from each end. Draw lines perpendicular to these lines 1 in. from the sides of the supports to form rectangles. The wood inside each of these rectangles must be removed to create the through mortises. Check the fit of the tenons inside the rectangles. Adjust the cutting lines, if necessary, to fit the tenons.

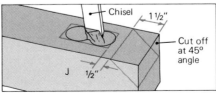

37. Drill two 1¼-in. holes into the center of each rectangle. Use a 1¼-in. chisel to remove the rest of the wood from the mortise. Hold the flat side of the chisel against the cutting lines and make the cut straight down. When you have cut halfway through the piece, turn it over and finish the chiseling from the other side. Test-fit the mortises and tenons. Cut off the tops of the supports at a 45° angle ½ in. from mortises.

38. Drill a 3/8-in. hole for the stretcher bolt through each leg 11 in. from its bottom. Apply glue to the mortises and tenons and clamp the legs and supports together until the glue dries.

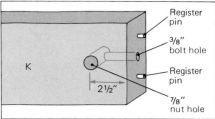

39. Cut the stretchers (K) to length. Drill a 3/8-in. bolt hole 3 in. deep into the center of each end of each stretcher. Use a doweling jig to help align the hole. Drill a 1/8-in. hole above and below each bolt hole halfway between the bolt hole and the edge of the wood. Screw 1½-in. No. 12 screws into the 1/8-in. holes, leaving the portion without threads exposed. Use a hacksaw to cut off the heads of these screws, leaving about ½ in. of the headless screws exposed to serve as register pins. Drill a 7/8-in. hole through the side of each end of each stretcher in line with the bolt hole and 2½ in. from each end of the stretcher. These holes will house the nuts and washers.

40. Unclamp the legs and supports. Use a backsaw to trim off any excess tenon from the tops and bottoms to make the tenons flush with the mortises.

41. Temporarily assemble the legs and stretchers with the bolts, washers, and nuts. Align the stretchers and tighten the bolts to make impressions where the register pins in the stretchers hit the legs. Take the legs and stretchers apart again and drill ¼-in. holes ½ in. deep where the pins left impressions. Reassemble the legs and stretchers, align them carefully, then tighten the bolts securely.

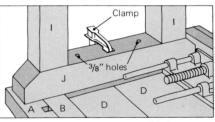

42. Clamp the entire leg assembly into place on the underside of the bench top. Drill a 3/8-in. hole about 1 in. from each of the legs through the top support and slightly into the bench top. Remove the leg assembly and deepen the holes in the bench top. Use tape on the drill bit as a depth gauge to make certain you do not drill through to the other side. Replace the leg assembly and fasten it to the bench top with lag screws and washers. Tighten the lag screws with a ½-in. wrench.

43. Cut the vise handles (L and M) to length. Sand them with Nos. 80 and 120 paper, then set them aside.

44. Give the bench top several sandings, using a belt sander with a No. 80 belt and then a No. 120 belt. Smooth the edges of the workbench with a block plane, cutting into the edges to prevent splitting. Apply a penetrating sealer to all exposed wood and to the vise handles. Apply several coats of sealer to the bench top and give it a final rubdown with 000 steel wool.

45. Slip the vise handles into place and push the caps (P and Q) over the ends of the handles. Fasten the caps into place by driving a small brad through each cap.

ROOM DIVIDER

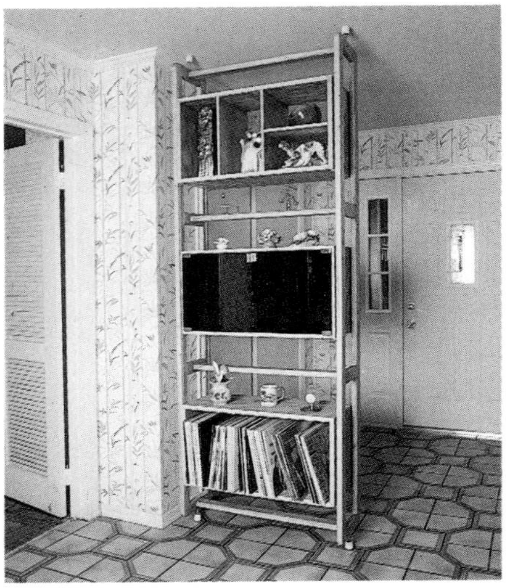

A room divider creates two living areas where only one existed, providing semiprivacy for different activities. Our divider contains storage space as well and has the look of a permanent installation; however, should the occasion arise, it can be disassembled and set up elsewhere quickly and easily. This divider was built to fit a room with an 8-foot ceiling.

The project combines hardwood, plywood, and acrylic plastic. The basic ladderlike framework is a pair of side frames joined by stretchers. Three cabinets rest between the stretchers on adjustable shelf supports that are clipped into metal pilasters. Two cabinets have backs; of these, one has bronze smoked acrylic plastic doors that are nearly opaque and the other has metal dividers for storing records. The third cabinet is open on both sides and contains dividers and a shelf.

Materials: The framing members—stiles, rails, and stretchers—were ripped from so-called 5/4 oak stock, which is actually 1 1/16–1 1/8 inches thick, not a full 1 1/4 inches. To make the 3/8-inch-square corner fillers (K), joint a board (see *Index*, p.379); then saw a 3/8-inch slice from the jointed edge. Lay this piece flat on the saw table, and cut enough 3/8-inch strips for the 12 corner fillers, making them slightly longer than the finished size given in the chart. Follow the same procedure for the edge strips (L, M, N, and O).

You can get all the 3/4-inch plywood parts from one panel if you piece the cabinet backs (p.201, Step 3). For the 1/2-inch plywood parts try to buy a piece 16 x 48 inches with its grain running lengthwise.

When working with the acrylic plastic, leave the protective paper in place until you have installed the doors. Cut the acrylic to size on the table saw, using a fine-tooth carbide-tipped blade. If a door's fit is tight, you can sand its edges, starting with No. 120 paper. Do the final sanding with No. 400 wet-or-dry paper used wet on a sanding block.

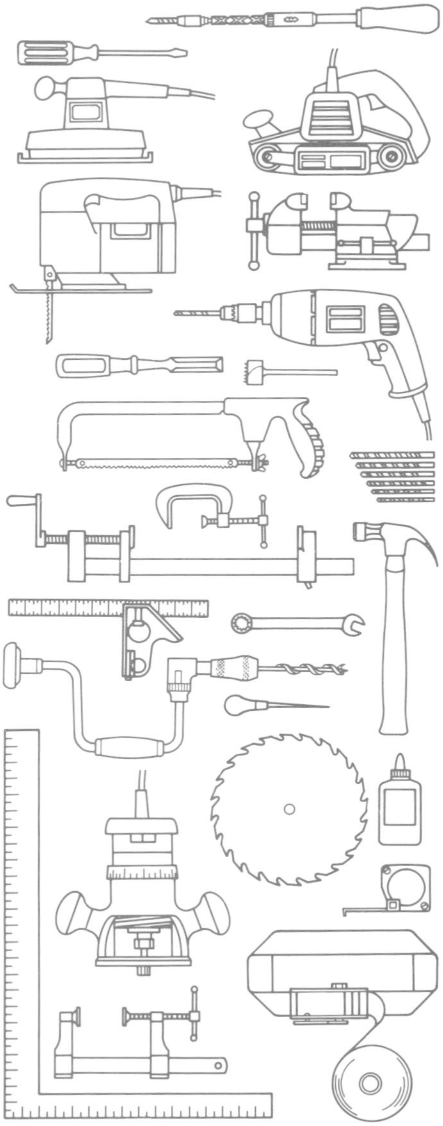

Parts list

Part	Name	Quantity	Thickness	Width	Length	Material
A	Stile	4	1 1/8″	2 1/2″	90″	5/4 red oak
B	Rail	8	1 1/8″	2 1/2″	10″	5/4 red oak
C	Stretcher	4	1 1/8″	2 1/2″	31 1/2″	5/4 red oak
D	Top and bottom	4	3/4″	12″	29″	Red oak plywood
E	Side	4	3/4″	12″	15 1/4″	Red oak plywood
F	Back	2	3/4″	15 1/4″	29″	Red oak plywood
G	Top and bottom	2	3/4″	12″	29″	Red oak plywood
H	Side	2	3/4″	12″	15 1/4″	Red oak plywood
I	Divider	2	1/2″	12″	15″	Red oak plywood
J	Shelf	1	1/2″	12″	12″	Red oak plywood
K	Corner filler	12	3/8″	3/8″	16″	5/4 red oak
L	Horizontal edge strip	12	1/4″	3/4″	30″	5/4 red oak
M	Vertical edge strip	12	1/4″	3/4″	16″	5/4 red oak
N	Divider edge strip	4	1/4″	1/2″	15″	5/4 red oak
O	Shelf edge strip	2	1/4″	1/2″	12″	5/4 red oak
P	Door	2	1/4″	14 1/4″	14 3/4″	Acrylic plastic

Tools and materials: Table saw with combination blade, fine-tooth carbide-tipped blade, and dado head (optional). Router with 3/8″ rounding-over bit with pilot and 1/2″ and 5/8″ straight bits. Drill with 3/16″, 3/8″, and 7/16″ twist bits, 1″ Forstner or multispur bit, guide, and stop. Saber saw, hacksaw. Vise, six 4′ and eight 3′ bar or pipe clamps, two cinch or band clamps, two 6″ C-clamps, two quick-action clamps. Screwdriver, hammer, awl, push drill, two 9/16″ open-end wrenches. Steel tape rule, combination square, framing square. Brace and 3/8″ auger bit, 3/8″ mortise chisel, 1″ firmer chisel. Belt sander, orbital sander, sanding block. Nos. 120, 150, and 220 open-coat sandpaper. No. 120 sanding belt. No. 400 wet-or-dry sandpaper. Wax paper. Soft cloths, 1 pt. golden oak paste stain, 1 pt. clear paste varnish. White glue. One 3/4″ x 4′ x 8′ panel of A–2 red oak plywood, a 1/2″ x 16″ x 48″ piece of A–2 red oak plywood with grain running lengthwise, three 10′ lengths of 5/4 x 6 red oak boards. One 16″ x 30″ sheet of 1/4″ smoked acrylic plastic. Four 84″ pilasters (Grant No. 120 ALB). Twelve shelf supports (Grant No. 21B). Four 3/8″–16 T nuts, eight 3/8″–16 hex nuts, 3/8″–16 threaded rod 16″ long, four 1″ aluminum or steel dowels 1″ long with 3/8″–16 threaded holes. Four 1″ crutch tips. Two pairs no-bore clip-on hinges for exterior doors (Selby No. HT960P). Two combination pull and strike plates (Selby No. TK–150P). One double magnetic push latch (Selby No. M–559). Five record dividers (Selby No. 50B). Sixteen 5/8″ No. 6 roundhead wood screws.

Finishing: Sand the hardwood parts with a belt sander and No. 120 belt. (Make sure the belt sander does not come in contact with the plywood parts—it will rapidly remove the oak veneer.) Then finish sanding the hardwood parts with an orbital sander and No. 150 paper, followed by No. 220. Sand all the plywood parts with Nos. 120, 150, and 220 sandpaper, using the orbital sander. The finish is a polyurethane-based paste stain, which you wipe on with a soft cloth and then buff lightly to remove any excess. Follow with a clear paste varnish.

When you have finished the framework, install it by adjusting the hex nuts. After you mount the cabinets and load them, readjust the hex nuts.

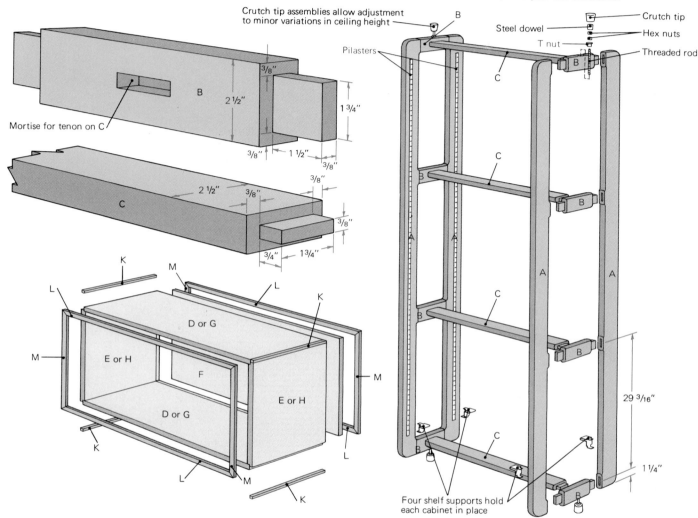

Crutch tip assemblies allow adjustment to minor variations in ceiling height

Mortise for tenon on C

B

2½"
1¾"
3/8"
3/8"
1½"
3/8"

C
2½"
3/8"
3/8"
3/8"
3/4"
1¾"

Pilasters
Crutch tip
Steel dowel
Hex nuts
T nut
Threaded rod
B
C
B
A
A
A
A
C
B
C
B
B
C
29 3/16"
1¼"

K
M
L
L
K
D or G
E or H
F
E or H
M
M
D or G
K
L
M
K

Four shelf supports hold each cabinet in place

Making the side frames

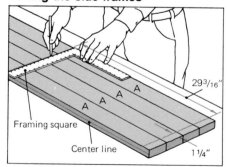

Framing square
Center line
29³/₁₆"
A
A
A
A
1¼"

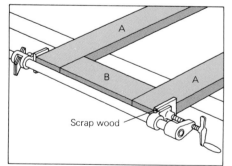

A
B
A
Scrap wood

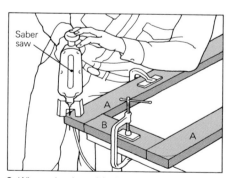

Saber saw
A
B
A

1. Mark tenons on both ends of each rail (B), using the measurements shown at top of page. Mark and cut tenons and mortises; see *Index,* p.379. For positions of mortises in stiles (A), draw a center line on a long edge of each stile; then with a framing square draw crosslines 1¼ in. from each end and 29³/₁₆ in. from each 1¼-in. line.

2. Test-fit the rails and stiles. Number the rails and corresponding positions on the stiles. Take the assembly apart. Spread glue on all tenon surfaces except the ends. Join rails and stiles again, and place a clamp across each rail; protect the oak from the clamp jaws with scrap wood. Check for squareness (see *Index,* p.379). Wipe off glue with wet cloths.

3. When glue has dried, sand surfaces with a belt sander and No. 120 belt. Mark a quarter circle with a 1¼-in. radius on each corner. Saw just outside the lines with a saber saw, using a blade with 10 teeth per inch. If the saw overheats, stop and allow it to cool before you resume cutting. Use the belt sander to sand the wood to the lines.

Making the side frames (continued)

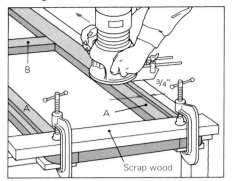

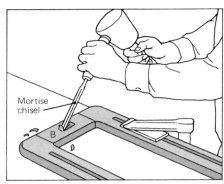

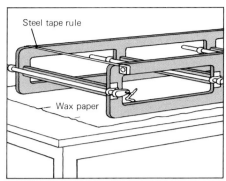

Steel tape rule

Wax paper

4. Place frames side by side, ends aligned; center pilasters on inner faces of stiles; mark tops and bottoms. (Dadoes for pilasters should be ¾ in. from outer edges.) Clamp scrap wood at top and bottom of each stile to stop router; allow for rounded ends of cuts. Make two passes with a ½-in. straight bit to cut dadoes ³⁄₁₆ in. deep and ¹⁹⁄₃₂ in. wide.

5. Round edges of rails and stiles with ⅜-in. rounding-over bit. Mark and cut tenons on ends of stretchers (C) and mortises in inner faces of rails (B). (See illustration on page 199 for the dimensions.) Round edges of stretchers. Test-fit the stretchers in the side frames; number stretchers and corresponding positions on rails. Take the assembly apart.

6. Glue and clamp the assembly as shown, using four 4-ft. bar or pipe clamps. Rest it on a level surface, protected with wax paper, or on two sawhorses. Check for squareness by measuring diagonally; also measure the distance between the stiles at several points to make sure the distance is the same over the entire length of the assembly.

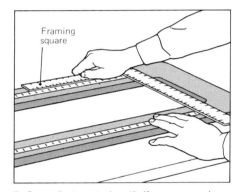

Framing square

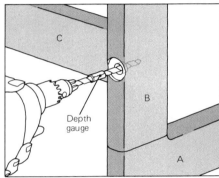

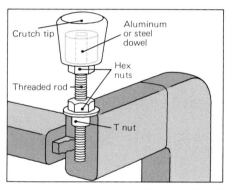

Crutch tip — Aluminum or steel dowel

Hex nuts

Threaded rod

T nut

7. Saw pilasters to length if necessary (see *Index,* p.379). Lay one pilaster in a dado. Starting at the bottom, make starter holes with push drill through single round holes; hammer in nails. Place next pilaster in its dado and use framing square to align holes and numbers on pilasters; nail in place. Install other two pilasters in same way.

8. Mark centers of the four top and bottom rails on their outer edges. Use a 1-in. Forstner or multispur bit to drill shallow holes the depth of the T-nut flanges. Then use a ⅜-in. straight bit to drill holes 2 in. deep, centered in the first holes. Finally, drill ½-in.-deep holes with a ⁷⁄₁₆-in. bit, centered in the ⅜-in. holes. Sand and finish all surfaces (see text).

9. Tap the T nuts into holes. Clamp the threaded rod in a vise (protect wooden vise jaws with scrap wood). Cut four 4-in. lengths of rod with a hacksaw. Screw hex nuts onto rods at one end and screw those ends into metal dowels; screw hex nuts onto other ends of rods and screw these ends into T nuts. Put crutch tips over dowels. Install assembly in room.

Rabbets and dadoes for cabinets

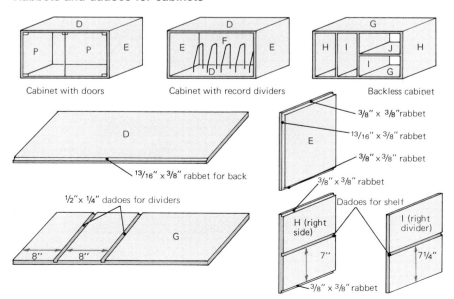

Cabinet with doors

Cabinet with record dividers

Backless cabinet

¹³⁄₁₆″ x ⅜″ rabbet for back

½″ x ¼″ dadoes for dividers

8″   8″

⅜″ x ⅜″ rabbet

¹³⁄₁₆″ x ⅜″ rabbet

⅜″ x ⅜″ rabbet

⅜″ x ⅜″ rabbet

Dadoes for shelf

H (right side)

I (right divider)

7″

7¼″

⅜″ x ⅜″ rabbet

Use diagrams at left to cut rabbets and dadoes in cabinet parts. All rabbets are ⅜ in. deep; those on top and bottom edges of cabinet sides (E and H) are ⅜ in. wide, and those for cabinet backs are ¹³⁄₁₆ in. wide. Cut rabbets on a table saw in two passes with an extra-high fence of plywood screwed to the table saw fence to keep the piece you are working on perpendicular during the vertical passes. Use a feather board (see *Index,* p.379) clamped to the table to hold work against fence. Make vertical cuts first, then remove extra fence and make horizontal cuts to complete rabbets. The top and bottom (G) of the backless cabinet require dadoes to seat the dividers. One side (H) and one divider (I) are dadoed to hold the shelf (J). These dadoes are ½ in. wide (less if plywood is thinner) and ¼ in. deep. They can be cut with a router or on the table saw with a dado head.

Making the cabinets

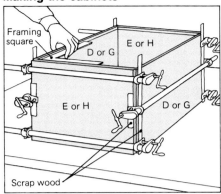

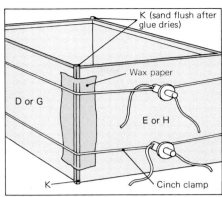

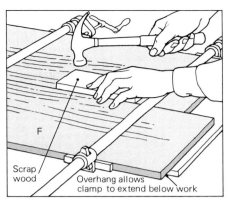

1. Sand inner surfaces of cabinet tops and bottoms (D and G) and sides (E and H). Glue and clamp one cabinet at a time, using six 4-ft. clamps on cabinet and thin strips of scrap wood to protect the plywood from the jaws of the clamps. Check each cabinet for squareness with the framing square or by measuring diagonally. Adjust if necessary.

2. Clean corners of rabbets with a chisel. Glue corner fillers (K)—see text for how to make these—into the four outer corners of each cabinet. Hold them in place while the glue dries with two cinch or band clamps; put wax paper between the wood and the clamps. When glue has dried, remove clamps and belt-sand corner fillers flush with plywood.

3. To make backs (F), cut plywood pieces overly long. Position them side by side so that their grains match. Lay pieces to be joined on top of scrap ¾-in. plywood almost the size of a back. Glue edges. Tighten pipe clamps one at a time. Press surfaces flush; if necessary, hammer to get them flush, protecting back with scrap wood. Repeat for other back.

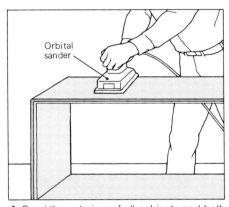

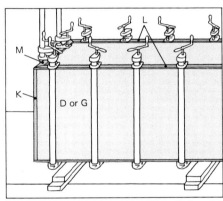

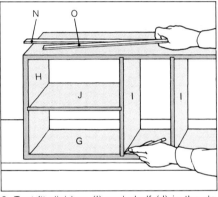

4. Sand the exteriors of all cabinets and both surfaces of the cabinet backs with orbital sander and No. 120 paper. Put glue in the rabbets of one cabinet and on the edges of one back. Clamp the back in place, using two clamps across the top, two across the bottom, and one across each side. Repeat the procedure for the other cabinet with a back.

5. Saw corners of edge strips (L and M) to 45°, using miter gauge on table saw. Cut miter at one end of each strip; then measure edge to which it will be glued and saw other end to fit. Glue and clamp edge strips on the two cabinets that have backs as shown. On the backless cabinet glue front edge strips only. Sand edge strips with No. 120 paper.

6. Test-fit dividers (I) and shelf (J) in the dadoes of the backless cabinet; trim them for fit if necessary. Remove dividers and shelf, and glue and clamp edge strips (N and O) to the front and back edges of parts I and J. When glue has dried, belt-sand edge strips flush. Then sand all parts and cabinet interior with Nos. 150 and 220 paper.

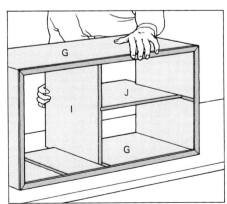

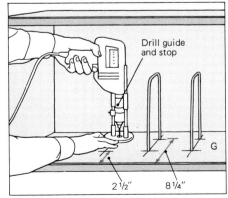

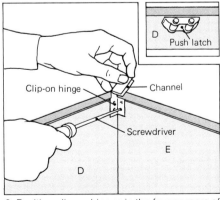

7. Put glue in dadoes and on edges of dividers and shelf. Insert dividers and shelf into dadoes from rear as follows: join the shelf and its divider and slide them in, then slide second divider into place. Glue and clamp edge strips (L and M) to back edges of cabinet. Sand all cabinet exteriors with Nos. 150 and 220 paper, then apply finish (see text).

8. Choose one cabinet with a back and mark five equally spaced front-to-back lines on its bottom. Lay framing square along the bottom, and make crossmarks 2½ in. and 8¼ in. from the front edge of the cabinet. Use a drill guide and stop (see *Index*, p.379) to make ³⁄₁₆-in. holes ⅜ in. deep at these marks. Insert legs of record dividers into holes.

9. Position clip-on hinges in the four corners of the third cabinet; use push drill to start holes for ⅝-in. screws. Be sure hinges are square to edges of cabinet. Insert screws. Center and attach magnetic push latch under cabinet top. Slide doors (P) into hinge channels; mount pull and strike plates on inner top edges of doors. Install supports and cabinets in frame.

201

SEWING CENTER

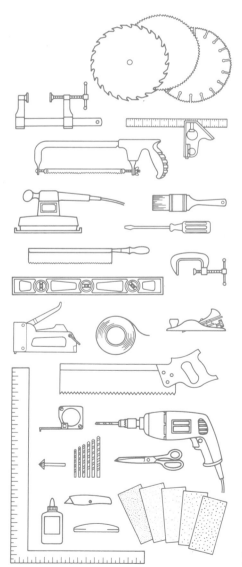

There is plenty of room behind the fold-down door of this wall-mounted sewing center to store a portable sewing machine and its accessories, along with all manner of tools, notions, sundries, patterns, and materials. When the door is open, it becomes a worktable, supported in front by a broad leg that is itself a shallow, open-faced cabinet.

The main cabinet has three shelves and a divided storage compartment. The dimensions of this compartment are governed by the size of the sewing machine. Measure your machine and adjust the dimensions if necessary.

This sewing center was made from a combination of solid teak and lumber-core teak plywood (plus one small piece of veneer-core fir plywood), chosen to match other teak furniture in the room. You can use less expensive hardwood, such as birch or cherry, with no loss of strength. However, if you attempt to make the sewing center from the usual veneer-core plywood, you must modify the design. Screws will not seat well in the edge of veneer-core plywood, so hinges cannot be attached the way ours are. Nor can the corners of the two cabinets be securely joined by the method shown; tongue-and-groove joints are recommended if you must use veneer-core plywood (see *Index*, p.379).

Wood: When ordering solid stock planed to size, ask for 4/4 (four-quarter) thickness—a nominal measurement of greater precision than the usual 1 inch. The actual thickness should be 13/16 inch.

If you use teak, be aware that the color of the wood may vary from tawny yellow to dark brown. Match the tones of the plywood, hardwood, and veneer; and be sure to specify FEQ (first European quality) for the solid stock.

Finishing: Veneer for covering exposed plywood edges is available in two forms: as cloth-backed rolls of tape or in leaves of about 8 square feet each. Teak requires no stain; sand lightly with 220 paper and apply a clear penetrating oil.

Parts list

Part	Name	Quantity	Thickness	Width	Length	Material
A	Cabinet side	2	¾"	10¼"	47¼"	Cut from a 4' x 8' panel A–2 lumber-core teak plywood
B	Cabinet end	2	¾"	10¼"	35¼"	
C	Cabinet shelf	3	¾"	9½"	35"	
D	Divider	1	¾"	9½"	15½"	
E	Leg end	2	¾"	2¾"	23¼"	
F	Leg shelf	3	¾"	2⅛"	23"	
G	Leg side	2	¾"	2¾"	27¼"	Cut from a 4' x 8' panel A–2 lumber-core teak plywood
H	Cabinet back	1	¾"	35¼" ✻	47¼" ✻	
I	Door	1	¾"	35½"	47¾"	
J	Leg back	1	½"	23⅛" ✻	27⅛" ✻	A–D fir plywood
K	Foot	1	13/16"	1½"	22"	4/4 teak FEQ
L	Top edging	1	¼"	13/16"	36" ✻	4/4 teak FEQ
M	Side edging	2	¼"	13/16"	48" ✻	4/4 teak FEQ
N	Cabinet corner	4	⅜" ✻	⅜" ✻	11" ✻	4/4 teak FEQ
O	Leg corner	4	⅜" ✻	⅜" ✻	3" ✻	4/4 teak FEQ
P	Molding end	2	¼"	1"	24" ✻	4/4 teak FEQ
Q	Molding side	2	¼"	1"	28" ✻	4/4 teak FEQ
R	Ledge	1	13/16"	3"	36"	4/4 teak FEQ
S	Spool peg	12	¼" dia.	—	2"	Hardwood dowel

✻ Measurement is approximate; cut to fit during construction.

Tools and materials: Table saw with dado head and combination blade. Drill with twist bits and countersink. Orbital sander. Steel tape rule, combination square, framing square, level, pencil. Hacksaw, backsaw, dovetail saw, veneer saw. Block plane, mat knife, scissors. Screwdriver. Ten 5' bar or pipe clamps, two band clamps, several 2"–6" C-clamps. Staple gun and staples. Sanding block. Nos. 80, 100, 150, and 220 sandpaper. Masking tape. Carpenter's glue, contact cement. Penetrating oil, 2" paintbrush, soft cloth. A 3' x 3' piece of burlap. Two ¾" x 4' x 8' panels of A–2 lumber-core teak plywood, a ½" x 2' x 2½' piece of A–D fir plywood, a 6' length of 4/4 FEQ teak 6" wide. Teak veneer. A ¼" hardwood dowel 2' long. Two brass cabinetry hooks and matching staples, 12 small brass cup hooks. A 1½" brass piano hinge 5' long. 4d and 6d finishing nails, 1" brads. Flathead wood screws: ¾" and 1" No. 6, 1" and 1¼" No. 8, 1¼" No. 10.

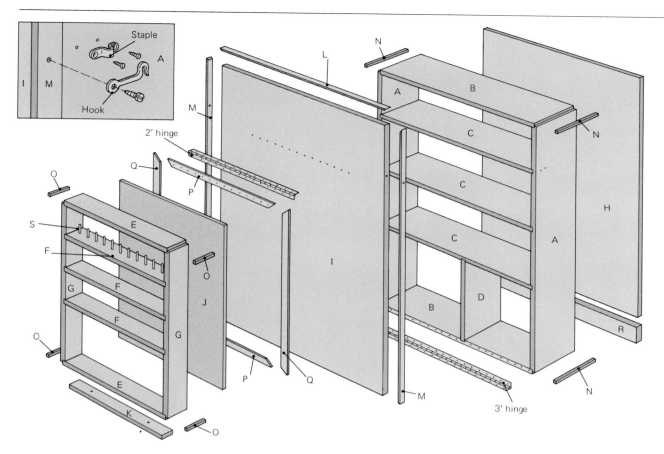

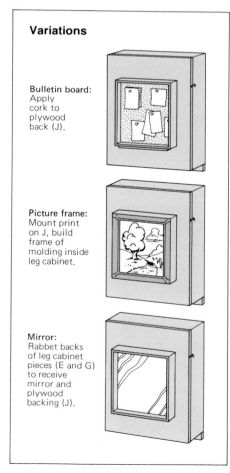

Exploded view shows how the parts of the sewing center are assembled. With careful planning you can cut all the teak plywood parts from two 4- x 8-ft. panels and all the solid teak parts from a 6-ft. board of 4/4 stock that is 6 in. wide (for instructions on laying out and cutting plywood, see top of page 50). Two flat brass cabinetry hooks hold the door closed, and the shallow leg cabinet simply rests against the door. When the hooks are released, the door swings open from the top, pivoting on a 3-ft.-long piano hinge at the bottom, and the leg cabinet swings out on its own 2-ft. piano hinge to support the worktable. The ¼-in. pegs in the top shelf of the leg cabinet hold spools of thread. Small brass cup hooks

screwed into the burlap-covered back are for packaged sewing supplies, such as buttons, zippers, and needles. A pincushion and other loose items can rest on the two middle shelves; for more security, you can stretch elastic cord across these shelves.

The sewing center was built for a clothing designer's home workroom, where the open-faced leg cabinet is not at all out of place. You may prefer to use one of the decorative variations shown at the right, or another variation of your own design, for the leg cabinet. Just be sure that the main weight is on the back of the cabinet, in line with the hinge. If the leg's center of gravity is too far forward, it will not swing all the way out when the door is opened.

Closed position

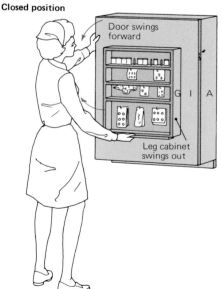

Open position

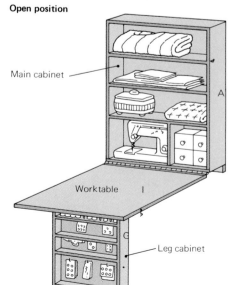

Variations

Bulletin board: Apply cork to plywood back (J).

Picture frame: Mount print on J, build frame of molding inside leg cabinet.

Mirror: Rabbet backs of leg cabinet pieces (E and G) to receive mirror and plywood backing (J).

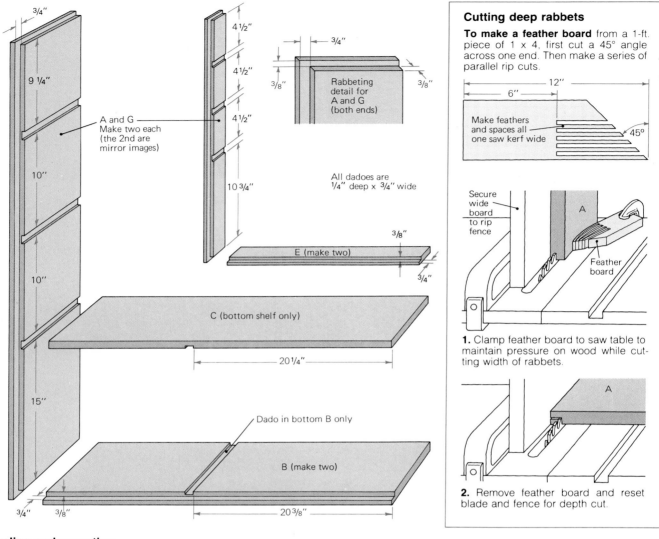

3/4"

9 1/4"

10"

10"

15"

3/4"   3/8"

A and G —
Make two each
(the 2nd are
mirror images)

4 1/2"

4 1/2"

4 1/2"

10 3/4"

3/8"

3/4"

3/8"   3/8"

Rabbeting
detail for
A and G
(both ends)

All dadoes are
1/4" deep x 3/4" wide

E (make two)

3/8"

3/4"

C (bottom shelf only)

20 1/4"

Dado in bottom B only

B (make two)

20 3/8"

Cutting deep rabbets

To make a feather board from a 1-ft. piece of 1 x 4, first cut a 45° angle across one end. Then make a series of parallel rip cuts.

12"

6"

Make feathers
and spaces all
one saw kerf wide

45°

A

Secure
wide
board
to rip
fence

Feather
board

1. Clamp feather board to saw table to maintain pressure on wood while cutting width of rabbets.

A

2. Remove feather board and reset blade and fence for depth cut.

Leveling and mounting

You will need two helpers to mount the sewing center. Have them hold the main cabinet against the wall with the door open. Place a level on the worktable (open door) and have helpers adjust the cabinet's position until the worktable is level in all directions (below, left). Draw a line on the wall across the bottom of the cabinet, marking both corners (center). Secure the ledge (R) along this line, screwing directly into the wall studs if possible, or use plugs or toggle bolts to fasten it. Then support the cabinet on the ledge while you secure its back to the wall in at least six places (right).

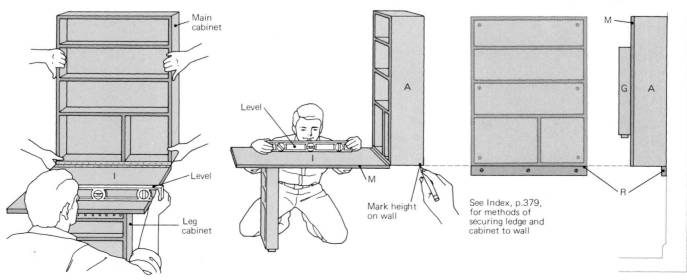

Main
cabinet

I

Level

Leg
cabinet

Level

Mark height
on wall

M

See Index, p.379,
for methods of
securing ledge and
cabinet to wall

M

G   A

R

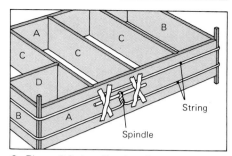

1. Cut dadoes and rabbets as shown on facing page. Rule a center line along the upper face of top leg shelf (F). Beginning 1⅞ in. from one end, drill twelve ¼-in. holes ½ in. deep along this line, spaced on 1¾-in. centers, to receive spool pegs (S).

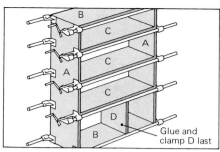

2. Sand inner faces of cabinet and leg parts with Nos. 100, 150, and 220 sandpaper. Assemble cabinet sides (A), ends (B), shelves (C), and divider (D) dry to ensure squareness; then glue and clamp. Assemble leg sides (G), ends (E), and shelves (F) in the same way.

3. Rip a 6-ft. length of teak stock to ½ in. square; cut cabinet corners (N) and leg corners (O) from it. Glue these pieces into the ⅜-in. rabbets formed by the joints of the cabinet and leg sides and ends; secure with band clamps, or use string and spindles.

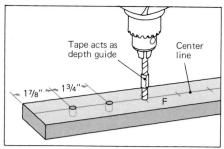

4. Trim ends of corner pieces (N and O) with a dovetail saw, then plane their sides and ends until almost flush with adjoining surfaces. Hand-sand with No. 80 paper to make surfaces flush, taking care not to sand away the thin veneer covering the teak plywood.

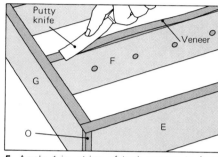

5. Apply 1-in. strips of teak veneer to front edges of cabinet and leg units, then trim to size and sand with No. 220 paper. (See *Index*, p.379, for instructions on veneering.) Be sure to veneer top and bottom pieces first, then sides, shelves, and finally cabinet divider.

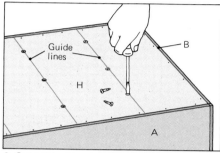

6. Cut cabinet back (H) to fit within its rabbets. Sand with Nos. 100, 150, and 220 paper. Rule lines across its rear face to coincide with center lines of cabinet shelves (C). Secure to cabinet sides and ends with 6d nails; fasten to shelves with 1¼-in. No. 8 screws.

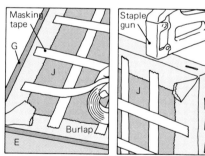

7. Cut leg back (J) to fit within its rabbets with ¹⁄₁₆-in. clearance all around. Cover its face with burlap and put it back in place; stretch burlap and secure it with masking tape on rear face of J. Remove back, staple edges, and trim excess burlap.

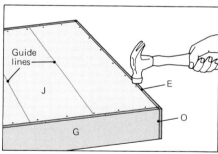

8. Sand spool pegs (S) and glue them into their holes. Finish inner surfaces of leg unit with penetrating oil before securing leg back (J). Rule lines on rear face of J (see Step 6), then drive 4d nails into sides and ends and 1-in. No. 8 screws into shelves.

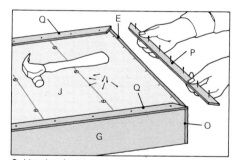

9. Use backsaw and miter box to cut molding strips (P and Q), covering joints between leg back (J) and sides and ends (G and E). Glue and secure molding with 1-in. brads; set heads slightly. Sand carefully with Nos. 100, 150, and 220 sandpaper.

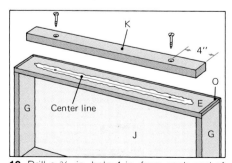

10. Drill a ³⁄₁₆-in. hole 4 in. from each end of foot (K), centered front to back; countersink. Center foot on bottom of leg unit and drill ³⁄₃₂-in. pilot holes into bottom of E. Apply glue and secure foot to bottom of unit with 1¼-in. No. 10 wood screws.

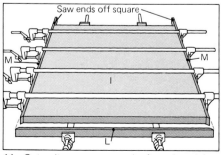

11. Cut miter on one end of each edging piece. Clamp side edging (M) to door (I) and cut second miter in top edging (L) to fit. Glue and clamp edging in place; cut ends off square with bottom of door. When glue dries, carefully plane and sand edging flush.

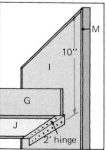

12. Use 1-in. No. 6 wood screws to attach 2-ft. piano hinge to back of leg unit; use ¾-in. screws to attach the other half to door face, centered on a line 10 in. from door top (left). Attach 3-ft. piano hinge to back of door, then to edge of cabinet bottom (right).

ENTERTAINMENT CENTER

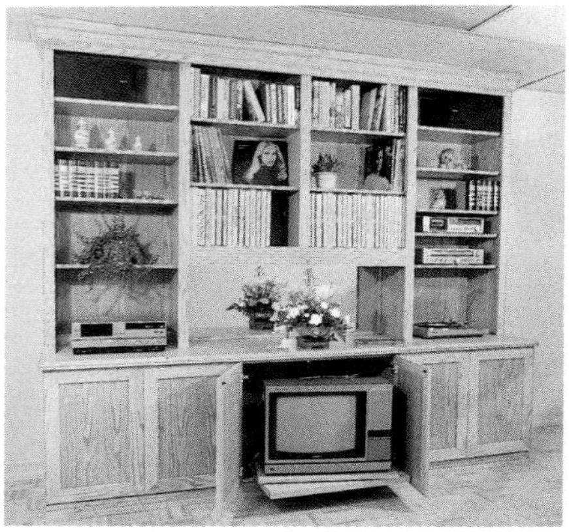

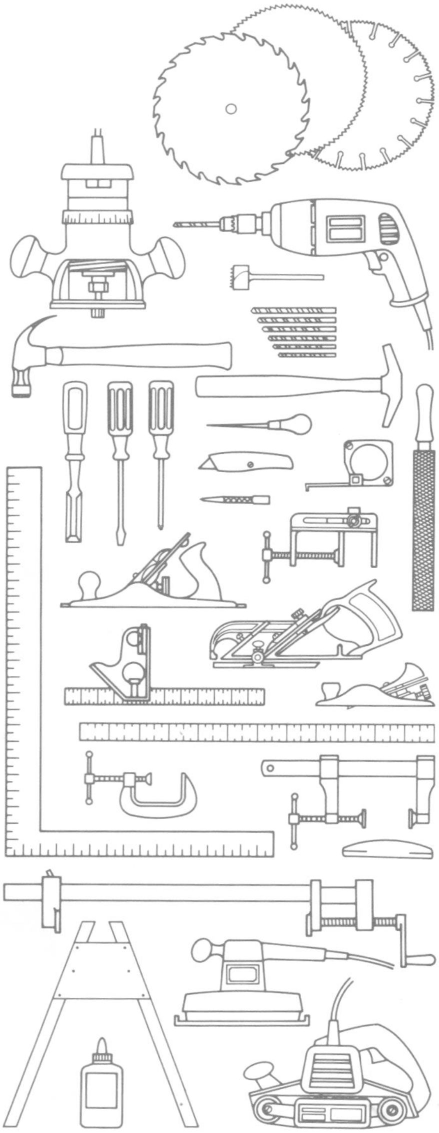

Parts list

Part	Name	Quantity	Thickness	Width	Length	Material
A	Upper end-cabinet side	4	3/4″	13 1/4″	62 3/4″ ✲	Oak plywood
B	Upper center-cabinet side	2	3/4″	13 1/4″	62 3/4″ ✲	Oak plywood
C	Upper end-cabinet facing	2	3/4″	13 1/4″	62 1/2″ ✲	Oak plywood
D	Center partition	1	3/4″	13 1/4″	39 3/4″ ✲	Oak plywood
E	Fixed shelf	1	3/4″	13 1/2″	51 7/8″	Oak plywood
F	Upper end-cabinet top	2	3/4″	13″	25 3/4″	Oak plywood
G	Upper center-cabinet top	1	3/4″	13″	51 7/8″	Oak plywood
H	Counter top	1	1 1/2″	25 1/2″	109 1/2″	Oak
I	Lower cabinet side	2	3/4″	23 7/8″	26″	Oak plywood
J	Lower cabinet inner wall	2	3/4″	22 7/8″	26″	Birch plywood
K	Lower cabinet partition	3	3/4″	22 7/8″	25″	Birch plywood
L	Lower small-cabinet top and bottom	2	3/4″	22 7/8″	35″	Birch plywood
M	Lower large-cabinet top and bottom	2	3/4″	22 7/8″	71″	Birch plywood
N	Base side	2	1 1/2″	3 1/2″	23 7/8″	2 × 4 pine
O	Base center	1	1 1/2″	3 1/2″	20 3/8″†	2 × 4 pine
P	Base front and back	2	1 1/2″	3 1/2″	104 1/2″	2 × 4 pine
Q	Upper cabinet shelf	16	3/4″	11 7/8″	25 3/16″	Oak plywood
R	Large shelf	4	3/4″	22 9/16″	20 7/8″	Birch plywood
S	Lower right-cabinet shelf	2	3/4″	22 9/16″	13″	Birch plywood
T	Lower left-cabinet shelf	2	3/4″	22 9/16″	12 5/8″	Birch plywood
U	Glue block	2	1 1/8″	1 1/8″	3 1/4″	Pine
V	Door frame top and bottom	12	3/4″	2 3/4″	17 15/16″	Oak
W	Door frame side	12	3/4″	2 3/4″	25 29/32″	Oak
X	Door panel	12	1/4″	13 1/4″	21 1/4″	Oak plywood
Y	Dowel	48	3/8″	—	2″	Dowel
Z	Mirror	1	1/4″	21 1/2″	51 1/4″	Plate glass
AA	Upper center-cabinet back	2	1/4″	26 1/8″†	40 1/2″†	Oak plywood
BB	Upper end-cabinet back	2	1/4″	26 7/8″†	62 1/2″†	Oak plywood
CC	Lower large-cabinet back	1	1/4″	26″†	71 1/2″†	Oak plywood
DD	Lower small-cabinet back	1	1/4″	26″†	35 1/2″†	Oak plywood
EE	Front crown molding	1	1 1/2″	4 1/8″	9′3″†	Oak
FF	Side crown molding	2	1 1/2″	4 1/8″	15 1/2″†	Oak
GG	Fascia molding	1	3/4″	4 1/4″	50 5/8″†	Oak
HH	End pilaster molding	2	3/4″	2 1/4″	59 3/4″†	Oak
II	Inside pilaster molding	2	3/4″	2 1/4″	59 3/4″†	Oak
JJ	Center pilaster molding	1	3/4″	2 1/4″	37 1/8″†	Oak
KK	Front base molding	1	1″	3 1/2″	108 1/4″†	Oak
LL	Side base molding	2	1″	3 1/2″	24 7/8″†	Oak
MM	Cabinet interior molding	2	3/4″	2 1/2″	25 5/16″†	Oak
NN	Shelf edge strip molding	16	3/4″	3/4″	25 3/16″	Oak
OO	Crown molding support	1	3/4″	2 3/4″	9′†	Oak
PP	Mirror frame top and bottom	2	3/4″	3/4″	51 1/2″†	Oak
QQ	Mirror frame side	2	3/4″	3/4″	21 3/4″†	Oak
RR	Mirror backing top and bottom	2	3/4″	3/4″	51 1/2″†	Pine
SS	Mirror backing side	2	3/4″	3/4″	20 1/4″†	Pine
TT	TV tray	1	3/4″	22 3/4″	29″	Birch plywood
UU	Swivel top	1	3/4″	20″	27 1/2″	Birch plywood
VV	Small tray	††	3/4″	19 1/2″	18 3/4″	Birch plywood
WW	Tray lipping	††	5/8″	3/4″	††	Pine

✲ Unit is designed to fit against an 8′ ceiling. Alter dimension to suit your ceiling height; allow 2 1/2″ for crown molding.
† Measurement is approximate; cut to fit during construction.
†† To be determined during construction.

You can entertain your friends and family handsomely with this home entertainment center designed to store all your audiovisual equipment. The lower cabinet holds the TV on a pullout tray. In the cabinets to either side of the TV there is space for a stereo receiver, cassette deck, turntable, and videocassette player. All shelves rest on adjustable supports, except the bottom shelf in the center of the upper cabinet.

Because of the entertainment center's size—9 feet 1½ inches long, 8 feet high, and 25½ inches deep—this is an ambitious project. Accuracy and careful planning are important. Make sure you have enough space to store and handle the plywood panels and to rip the long oak boards required for the solid oak parts.

If you make the unit of oak, as shown, the wood will cost over $1,000, but you will have a custom piece of furniture that is worth several times that amount. Using birch would cut the cost substantially. However, birch does not stain well, so finish it with a clear finish, such as tung oil.

Before you start, make cutting diagrams of all plywood pieces to be sure you can cut them from the panels. As you cut, letter each part and mark its orientation.

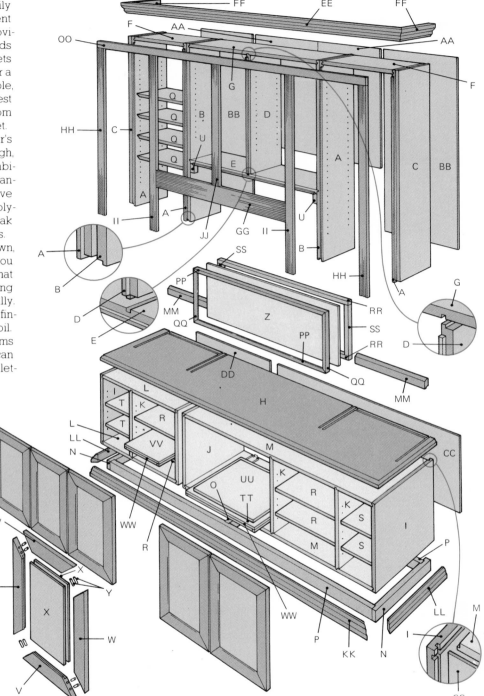

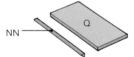

The plywood upper cabinet shelves (Q) are edged with ¾- x ¾-in. oak strips (NN). Glue strips to shelves before shaping with Roman ogee bit. Clamp with three bar clamps per shelf; do not nail. When glue has dried, lightly plane edge strips, but do not touch the plywood. (Designate "top" and "bottom" for each shelf.) Rout edge strips with Roman ogee bit in same way parts of mirror frame will be routed (see p.212), placing top surface of each shelf up so that its lower edge is routed. For shelves that are to be installed above eye level, have the better plywood surface facing down.

Tools and materials: Table saw with rip and fine-tooth carbide-tipped blades, dado head, crosscut tray, and miter gauge or miter tray. Circular saw, radial arm saw. Router with guide, ¼" and ¾" straight bits, ¼" and ⅜" rounding-over bits, ⅜" core-box bit, and Roman ogee bit with ¼" radius. Drill with depth stop, 1⅜" multispur or Forstner bit, ¼" bit for cutting acrylic plastic. Twist bits as follows: 1/16", 7/64", 3/16", ¼", ⅜". Brad awl, 1/32" nail set. Hammer, tack hammer, regular screwdriver, Phillips screwdriver, 1" chisel. Mat knife or veneer saw, rasp or file. Bullnose plane, block plane, jack or smooth plane. Doweling jig. Steel tape rule, framing square, combination square, straightedge. Two quick-action clamps, four 3" C-clamps, ten 3' bar or pipe clamps, four 6' bar or pipe clamps, two sawhorses. Orbital sander, belt sander, sanding block. Finishing materials (see p.213). Goggles. Carpenter's glue (for counter top only), white glue. Wood putty, contact cement. Oak veneer or 13/16" veneer tape, ¾" × 3' × 3' chipboard. Five ¾" × 4' × 8' panels A–2 oak plywood, four ¼" × 4' × 8' panels A–4 oak plywood, three ¾" × 4' × 8' panels 2–2 birch plywood. Seven 8' lengths ¾" × 2¾" oak for door frames. Oak for counter top (see p.211). Remaining oak and pine (see chart). Forty-eight ⅜" spiral-cut dowels 2" long. Mirror (see chart). One pair 22" drawer slides (Grant No. 3320). One pair 18" drawer slides (Grant No. 3320) for each additional pullout shelf (optional). Four pairs concealed hinges (Grass No. 1210/12), two pairs concealed hinges (Grass No. 1211/02). Metal shelf rests. Six minilatches. Sixty-two ⅝" No. 6 Phillips-head wood screws, twenty 1¼" and twelve 1½" No. 8 flathead wood screws, four 1¼" and twelve 2" No. 10 flathead wood screws, ten 1¼" No. 10 brass flathead wood screws. 3d, 4d, 6d finishing nails. ⅝", ¾", 1¼" brads.

Tongue-and-groove joints: The cabinet parts are joined by tongues and grooves. Except for tongues on the back edges of parts B, tongues and grooves are on surfaces facing the cabinets' interiors. For example, part A is shown as it appears on the right-hand side of a cabinet, part B as it appears on the left. For their opposites, make mirror images of the parts.

The tongues are all ¼ inch × ¼ inch,

and the grooves are ¼ inch wide and ⁹⁄₃₂ inch deep, except for the ³⁄₈-inch-deep grooves at the back edges of parts I. As a rule, the tongues—or the rabbets that make the tongues—are best cut on a table saw with a dado head. They may also be cut with a router, but do not use a circular saw. Cut the grooves with a ¼-inch router bit set to cut ⁹⁄₃₂ inch deep. Test blade and bit settings on scrap wood.

If your plywood measures less than ¾

inch thick, even by ¹⁄₃₂ inch, compensate for this difference by adding twice that amount to the length of the cabinet tops and bottoms—¹⁄₁₆ inch in the case of a ¹⁄₃₂-inch deviation. Also lengthen partitions by twice the plywood deviation. When marking the grooves near the top and bottom edges of the cabinets' sides and inner walls, remember to allow for deviations in plywood thickness by cutting the grooves that much closer to the edges.

Upper cabinets

1. Mark and cut grooves ½ in. below the top edges of upper cabinet sides (A and B).

2. Make tongues on the bottom edges of parts A and B. These will enter grooves in counter top (H).

3. Measure up 20½ in. from bottom edges of the upper center-cabinet sides (B), and cut a groove to hold fixed shelf (E).

4. Cut tongues on front edges of the upper end-cabinet sides (A) and the back edges of the upper center-cabinet sides (B). The tongues of parts A will fit into grooves in the backs of pilaster moldings (HH and II). Saw off the parts of the tongues above the grooves made in Step 1.

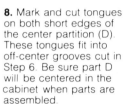

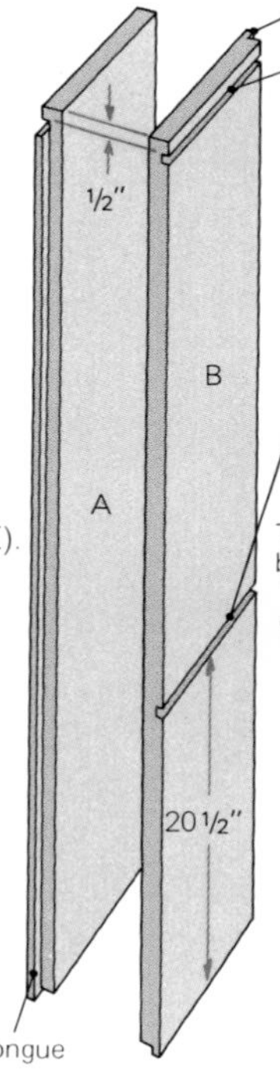

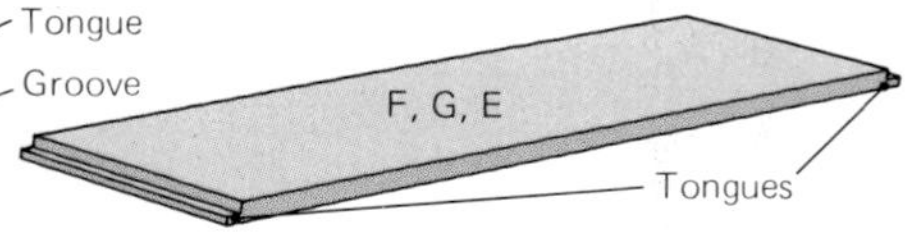

5. Mark and cut tongues on each short edge of the upper cabinet tops (F and G) and the fixed shelf (E).

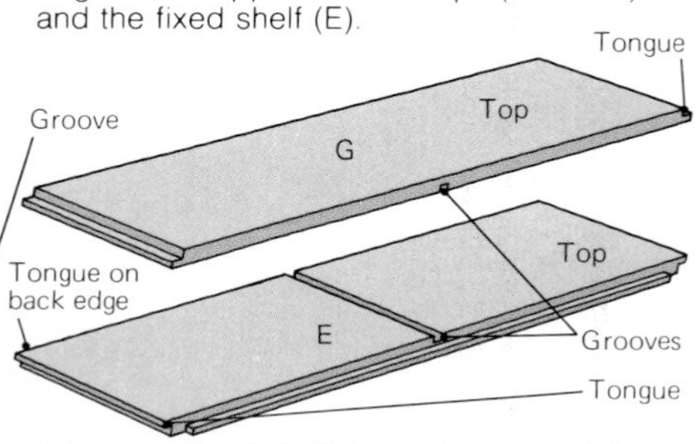

6. Lay the fixed shelf, top side up, and the upper center-cabinet top (G), bottom side up, next to each other; mark and cut ¼-in. grooves across both so that the centers of the grooves are ¼ in. from the centers of the boards.

7. Cut tongues on bottom of front and back edges of fixed shelf (E). Saw off ½ in. from each end of tongue on front edge.

8. Mark and cut tongues on both short edges of the center partition (D). These tongues fit into off-center grooves cut in Step 6. Be sure part D will be centered in the cabinet when parts are assembled.

9. Mark and cut a tongue on the front edge of the center partition; saw off ¼ in. from the bottom of this tongue.

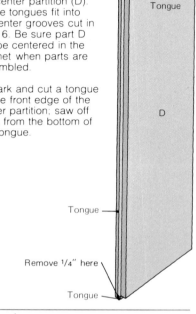

Lower cabinets

10. Mark grooves that will hold partitions by laying paired tops and bottoms (parts L and M) side by side with ends aligned. On the lower small-cabinet top and bottom (L), mark and cut grooves 13½ in. in from the outer edges.
11. On lower large-cabinet top and bottom (M), mark and cut grooves 13⅞ in. and 36¾ in. in from the outer edges.
12. Mark tongues on short edges of L and M. Cut these tongues with a router, as the parts are too large for a table saw.
13. Mark and cut tongues on the top and bottom edges of the partitions (K).
14. Mark and cut grooves on the top and bottom edges of the lower cabinet sides (I) and inner walls (J) so that tops and bottoms (L and M) will be flush.

15. To mark lines about 1 in. from back edges of lower cabinet sides (I), lay an inner wall (J) on each with the front edges flush, and use rear edge of J to draw lines. Draw a second set of lines ¼ in. outside the first lines, toward the back edges. Use these lines to make grooves ³⁄₈ in. deep on parts I.

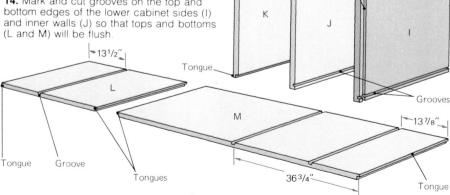

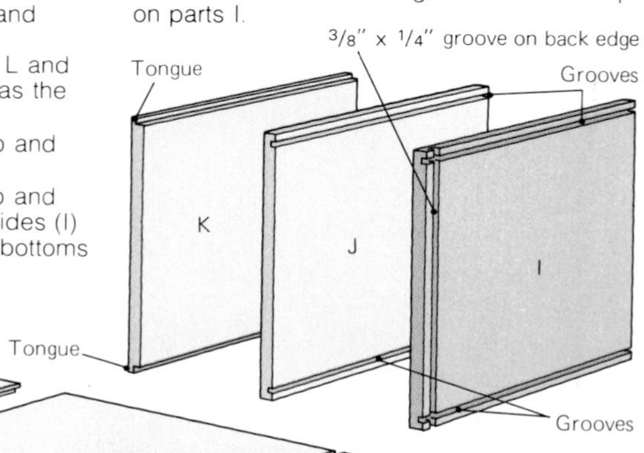

Shelf support holes

Make a template of ¼-in. pegboard 3 in. x 62 in. (see *Index*, p.379). Tape over all holes above 6½-in. mark and every other row of holes below it. Align top of template with tops of parts requiring shelf support holes. Align template's long edge as follows: on the edge of a rabbet if there is one, on a line ¼ in. from the edge of a face with a tongue, or just flush with a back edge. Where a part will have holes in both faces, offset template ⁹⁄₁₆ in. on one face so that holes will not go through. Drill through center row of holes in template with a ¼-in. bit used for cutting acrylic plastic (it will not splinter). Set a stop on the bit so that it penetrates ³⁄₈ in. In the upper center-cabinet sides (B) drill top and bottom holes through so that you can screw cabinets together. Do not make holes in TV compartment.

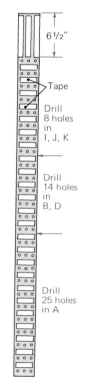

Assembling the cabinets: Test-fit the cabinets before gluing them. If the fit is tight, trim the tongues with a bullnose plane. Take the cabinets apart and sand all interiors with Nos. 100 and 150 paper. Ask someone to help with the gluing because these are big pieces that are difficult to handle alone. Have the interior moldings (MM) ready (see p.212).

The lower small cabinet is glued and nailed in the same way as the large one. However, since it only has one partition, you will have to turn the cabinet on edge to glue on the top. When the glue has dried on the lower cabinets, cover the exposed plywood edges on the front of the unit with either veneer or veneer tape (see *Index*, p.379).

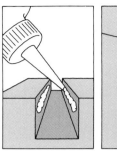 

Upper center cabinet: 1. If you do not have a large worktable, do the gluing on a level floor. Apply a thin, continuous bead of glue along each edge of a groove, but not in its bottom. Apply another bead along the part of a rabbet that will touch the surface of the matching grooved piece.

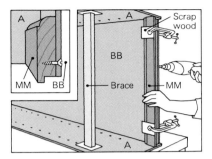

5. Cut brace to fit inside end cabinets. Prop up each cabinet. Use a $7/64$-in. bit to drill seven holes through each back (BB) near bottom edges; countersink holes. Clamp interior moldings (MM) to backs. Use a $3/32$-in. bit to drill $3/8$ in. into moldings through holes in backs. Insert No. 6 wood screws.

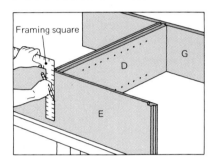

2. Glue partition (D) to upper center-cabinet top (G) and to the fixed shelf (E) with back edges flush. Use framing square to rule lines on outer surfaces of top and fixed shelf to indicate center of partition. Drive one 3d finishing nail through each line into partition.

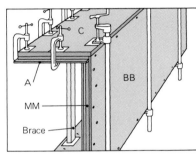

6. Lay end cabinets on their inner sides. Coat the outer cabinet sides (A) and upper end-cabinet facings (C) with glue. Align front edges of parts C with edges of rabbets on parts A. Clamp as shown. Use the brace to prop up the interior of cabinet.

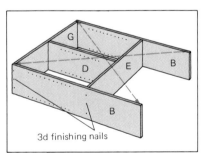

3. Glue on the upper center-cabinet sides (B). Rule lines on outer surfaces indicating the centers of parts E and G; drive three 3d finishing nails into each joint. Check assembly for squareness by measuring diagonally. If diagonals are unequal, push against corners of the longer diagonal.

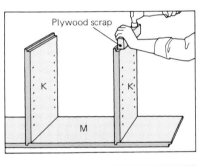

Lower cabinets: 7. Place large-cabinet bottom (M) on work surface with grooves up; glue two partitions (K) into grooves with front edges flush. To help seat tongues of partitions, hold a plywood scrap in the rabbets and tap with a hammer.

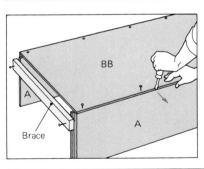

Upper end cabinets: 4. Glue and nail upper end-cabinet tops (F) and sides (A) as in Step 3. Make a brace $26 7/8$ in. long and nail it to bottom edges. Measure for and cut backs (BB). Drive 3d finishing nails into backs and sides. If sides are not flush with backs, pry sides outward with screwdriver.

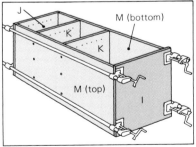

8. Glue on large-cabinet top (M); hammer to seat joints. Rule lines at joints and drive in 6d nails. With front edges of large cabinet assembly down, glue and nail inner wall (J) to left end. Glue on lower cabinet side (I); clamp, but do not nail. Check for squareness. Assemble lower small cabinet in same way.

Base: The base is $23 7/8$ in. wide and $106 1/2$ in. long. Use the end of a 2 x 4 to mark notches at front and rear of base sides (N). Cut them with a dado head or make multiple saw cuts and chisel out waste. Lay base front and back (P) side by side, mark center line, and mark notches for base center (O). Join base front, back, and sides; square them and cut base center to fit. Glue and screw parts together with 2-in. screws. Drill and countersink from inside $3/16$-in. holes staggered $3/4$ in. from top and 1 in. from bottom of sides and front.

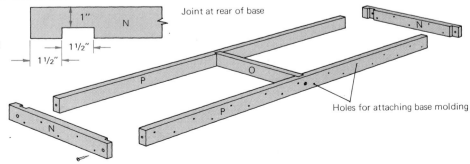

Doors and hinges: The door frame pieces (V and W) are mitered and doweled at the corners and have rabbets in their backs into which panels are set. You need one 8-foot length of ¾- x 2¾-inch oak for each door frame plus an extra length in case of error. Each panel inset (X) is made from two pieces of ¼-inch plywood with their good sides facing out. (You could also make the doors entirely of ¾-inch oak plywood, using veneer tape on the exposed edges.) Dimensions for

the door parts in the chart on page 206 and the measurements given in the step-by-step instructions below assume that the overall length of the lower cabinets is 108 inches, their height (not including the base) is 26 inches, and the ends of the unit will not butt against walls. If your cabinets differ, calculate dimensions for the door parts as described in Step 1.

The router setup (Steps 3 and 4) is for shaping the door frame stock. The same setup is used to make the moldings.

The instructions for mounting the hinges (Steps 9–14) are for the specific hinges listed on page 207. If you use different hinges, follow the manufacturer's instructions for installing them. Two of the doors on the large cabinet are mounted on a single ¾-inch partition. These doors require hinges with a different model number, but these hinges are mounted in the same way as the other door hinges. After making the door frames, indicate which edges will receive hinges.

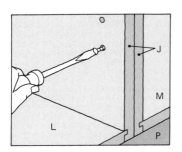

1. Set lower cabinets on base and screw together through top and bottom shelf holes with four 1¼-in. No. 10 screws. Measure length and height. Subtract ½ in. from length for spaces between all doors. Subtract an additional ¹⁄₁₆ in. if an end butts against a wall. Divide this sum by six to get the doors' width. For the doors' height, subtract ³⁄₃₂ in. from the cabinet height.

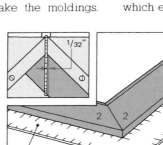

6. Make each miter cut in two passes, the first ¹⁄₃₂ in. over the line, the second on the line. Miter one end of each long piece. Then set a stop on jig and saw other ends ¹⁄₃₂ in. long. Reset stop and shave off final ¹⁄₃₂ in. Repeat procedure for short pieces. Test-fit joints; mark adjoining surfaces 1–1, 2–2, and so on. Use a block plane to smooth joints.

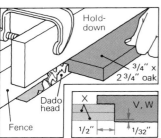

2. Joint the oak stock for the door frame pieces (V and W) on a table saw (see *Index*, p.379). Then measure the thickness of two plywood door panels (X), add ¹⁄₃₂ in., and set ½-in.-wide dado head to that height. Move saw fence close to dado head, and clamp on two pieces of scrap wood, one to act as a fence, one as a hold-down. Cut the rabbets in stock.

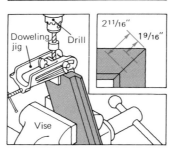

7. Lay parts of each door frame on work surface. Draw lines for dowels (Y) across miter joints at right angles, 1⁹⁄₁₆ in. and 2¹¹⁄₁₆ in. from each corner. Use a doweling jig and a drill with a ⅜-in. twist bit. Center jig on thickness of wood. Set depth guide so that full width of bit penetrates 1 in. into wood. As you drill, raise bit to pull sawdust from hole.

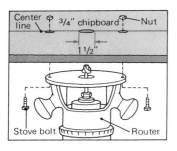

3. Mount router to a piece of ¾-in. chipboard as follows: unscrew baseplate of router and locate or drill two holes in router base. Draw a line down center of board. Align center of router with line and mark board for bolt holes in line with holes in base. Drill a 1½-in. hole for router bit. Mount router with stove bolts and countersunk nuts.

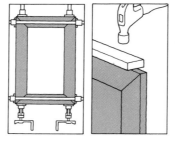

8. Test-fit each frame with dowels in place. Pull joints together with four 3-ft. bar clamps (left). Take frames apart. Spread glue evenly on joint surfaces and inside holes. Drive joints together with hammer (right) and clamp as before. When glue has dried, plane rough surfaces with a jack plane. Trim corners of rabbets with bullnose plane and chisel.

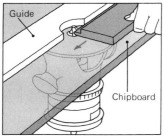

4. Clamp chipboard to work surface. Make a guide of ¾-in. plywood with a semicircle cut from one edge. Position guide so that its edge is in line with pilot on router bit; clamp to board. Use a ¼-in. rounding-over bit to shape edges of oak stock above rabbets. Pass wood from right to left. Have a helper steady pieces as they go through.

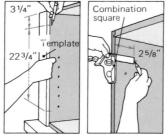

9. Make a template of ¾-in. plywood 26 in. long. Label "top." Mark lines on one edge ³⁄₃₂ in., 3¼ in., and 22¾ in. from top. Hold template against each cabinet wall flush with top of cabinet. Mark cabinet at 3¼ in. and 22¾ in. Extend lines. Set blade of combination square at 2⅝ in. and make crossmarks on those lines. Make holes with an awl where lines intersect.

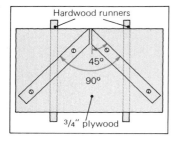

5. Cut each piece of stock into two 27-in. and two 19-in. lengths. Make a mitering jig by screwing two pieces of wood to ¾-in. plywood, leaving just enough space for the saw blade to pass between their ends. Clamp jig to the table of a radial arm saw; to use this jig on table saw, you must equip it with two hardwood runners to ride in the table's grooves.

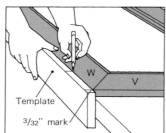

10. Hold the template along the hinge edge of each door frame with the ³⁄₃₂-in. mark at the top of the frame. Mark inner faces of frames at 3¼ in. and 22¾ in. Extend lines. Set blade of combination square at ⅞ in. and make crossmarks on the lines just drawn.

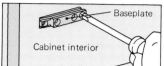

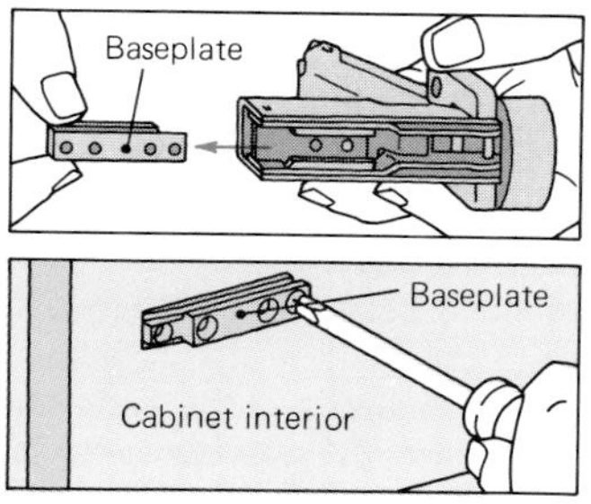

Baseplate

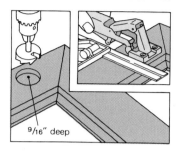

Baseplate

Cabinet interior

11. Remove the metal baseplate from the back of a hinge. Position plate so smaller tab extends into cabinet with the rearmost of its four holes over an awl hole; insert a ⅝-in. No. 6 Phillips-head screw in that hole. Make an awl hole through the front hole, and insert another screw. Repeat for all hinges.

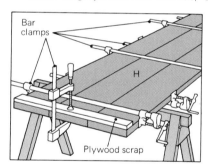

9/16" deep

12. If possible, use a drill press and set depth gauge for 9/16 in. Using a 1⅜-in. multispur or Forstner bit, drill holes centered where lines made in Step 10 intersect. If you use a hand drill, stop frequently to check depth of hole. Set cups of hinges in holes, using combination square to ensure that hinges are set square. Insert Phillips-head screws in hinge holes.

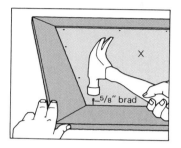

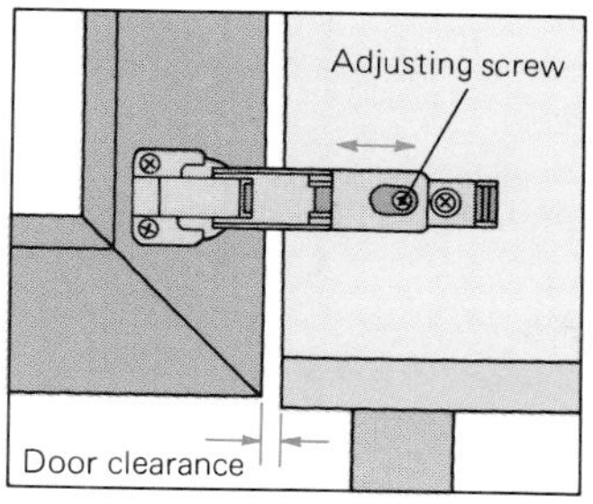

Adjusting screw

Door clearance

13. Slide the parts of the hinges attached to the frames over the baseplates. Tighten rear screws, which fix hinges to baseplates. Adjust hinges so that the frames stand slightly in front of cabinet edges; otherwise, the doors will not have room to open and close. When you have the doors properly positioned, tighten other screws in hinges. Remove frames.

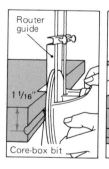

X

⌐5/8" brad

14. Measure insides of rabbets, and cut door panels (X) to fit. Sand frames with Nos. 80, 100, and 150 paper and the door panels with Nos. 100 and 150 paper. Apply polyurethane finish (see text, p.213). Glue and nail panels in place, using ⅝-in. brads at 4-in. intervals. Set brads below surface with a 1/32-in. nail set, and fill holes with wood putty. Reinstall frames.

Counter top: The upper cabinets rest in grooves that are cut into the counter top (H). This unusual feature gives the unit an elegant appearance. Normally, the upper cabinets would be made with floors and simply rest on top of the lower cabinets.

Three edge-joined oak boards, each 1½ x 8½ x 109½ inches, form the counter top. Start with boards 5–6 inches longer than you need and cut them to 109½ inches after gluing. Joint the boards (see *Index,* p.379) and rip them to 8½ inches wide. Make sure you have enough space on each side of your table saw to pass the boards through, and have someone on hand to help guide them. After jointing the boards, clamp them together. Inspect with a framing square and flashlight for high spots, and plane any high spots level. (Lay the boards across a pair of sawhorses to do the gluing.)

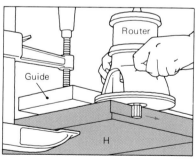

Bar clamps

H

Plywood scrap

1. Spread carpenter's glue on all edges, and apply five 3-ft. bar clamps across the top, five across bottom. Press boards into alignment, or hammer them with scrap wood. Clamp plywood scrap across ends. Wipe off excess glue with wet cloths. If glue dries, remove it with a cabinet scraper.

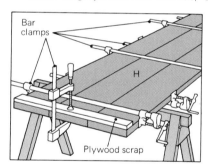

Router

Guide

H

2. Remove clamps; check surface again for evenness (light will shine through low spots). Plane high spots. Sand with a belt sander, then an orbital sander, using No. 80 paper. Set a guide, and saw across one end with a circular saw. Smooth that end with a straight router bit that has a 1-in. cutting surface.

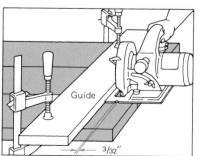

Guide

3/32"

3. Measure 109½ in. from cut end, and draw a line across counter top. Mark a second line 3/32 in. outside that line, and saw on the second line. Trim back to first line with router bit; make two passes and lower the bit for the second pass. Stop router short of the corner and reverse its direction of travel to avoid splitting wood at corner.

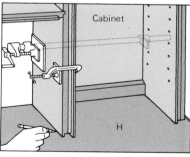

Router guide

1 1/16

Core-box bit

Guide

Roman ogee bit

4. Practice this step on scrap removed from end. Using a ⅜-in. core-box bit, set router guide 1 1/16 in. from center of bit. Make cut as shown near counter top's bottom edge. Cut upper edge with Roman ogee bit in several passes, using a straightedge as a guide. Stop short of right-hand corners and reverse direction.

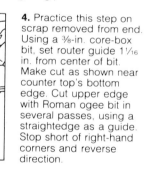

Cabinet

H

5. Assemble lower cabinets, counter top, and upper cabinets with back edges flush. Clamp three upper cabinets together; make sure they are centered. With a sharp pencil, mark back corners and front edges of tongues to be grooved into counter top. Remove upper cabinets and use a framing square to connect these lines.

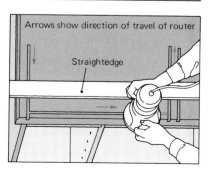

Arrows show direction of travel of router

Straightedge

6. Draw a parallel line ¼ in. from each line drawn in Step 5. Check that lines coincide with tongues on cabinets. Use a straightedge for each groove. Use ¼-in. straight bit set 9/32 in. deep and move router left to right (counterclockwise). On far left groove, make a plunge cut with router. Do not cut any grooves to side edges.

Moldings: The various decorative moldings created especially for this entertainment center give it a distinctive elegance. The moldings are made with a router set on the underside of a piece of chipboard, as described in Steps 3 and 4 on page 210. Use bits with carbide-cutting edges, and always wear goggles when routing. Test each setting of the bit and guide on scrap wood. If a molding has a groove in the back for attachment to a tongue, rout that groove last. Make sure the wood used is straight and square. If you joint and rip the wood on a table saw (see *Index*, p.379),

check the wood for squareness afterward because sawing sometimes releases fibers, resulting in bowing or warping. Rout the moldings in pieces longer than their final lengths.

Ordinarily you would do a dry run of the glue-up after all parts are cut to size. But during this dry run you must saw the moldings to their final lengths and cut cabinet backs (AA, CC, and DD). Then take everything apart for sanding and finishing (see text, p.213). Use an orbital sander on the flats of the moldings, but do the flutes by hand. Fold the sandpaper so

it fits into the flutes, and sand with Nos. 80, 100, and 150 paper.

The base and crown moldings and the mirror frame pieces require mitered corners. The base and crown moldings are best done on a radial arm saw with its blade tilted at 45° and each molding lying on its back surface. Make a cut on scrap wood and check the angle of the cut with a combination square. When sawing each molding, make one pass slightly outside the miter line and a second pass on the line. Saw the mirror frame pieces as you did the door frame parts.

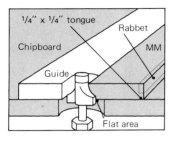

Cabinet interior moldings: To make these moldings (MM), use a rounding-over bit with a ⅜-in. radius. Position the bit high enough so that it cuts a small flat area. Then use the table saw to cut the rabbet that forms the ¼- x ¼-in. tongue.

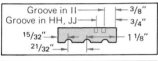

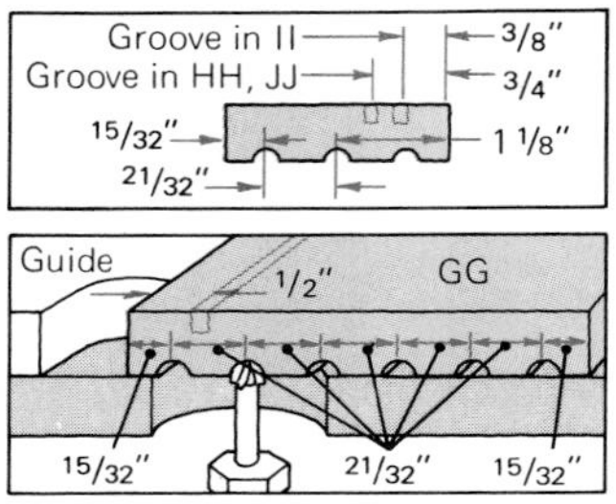

Fascia and pilaster moldings: Set a ⅜-in. core-box bit to cut a flute ⅛ in. deep. Set fence ¹⁵⁄₃₂ in. from center of bit. Cut two outer flutes on pilasters (HH, II, and JJ) and on fascia molding (GG) first; reset fence and cut center flutes on pilasters and the next two flutes on fascia molding. Finally, cut the two inner flutes on fascia. Make grooves on backs.

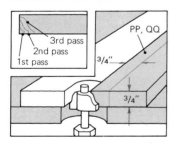

Mirror frame: Rout edges of ¾-in. boards with Roman ogee bit. Set fence so that pilot bears on wood. Draw a line at edge of fence. Move fence forward of line so that bit removes half of wood on frame pieces (PP and QQ). Move fence halfway to line; make second pass. Set fence on line for third pass. A fourth pass at same position will smooth the cut. Saw pieces to width.

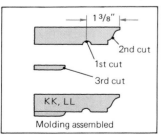

Front and side base moldings: Set core-box bit as for pilasters; cut flute in ¾- x 3½-in. stock. Cut edge with Roman ogee bit as for mirror frame. Rout one edge of ¼-in.-thick stock with ¼-in. rounding-over bit. Saw stock to 1¼-in. width, and attach to ¾-in. stock with glue and ¾-in. brads for moldings KK and LL. Do not nail where miters will be cut. Set brads.

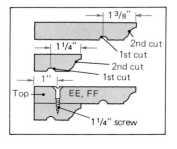

Crown moldings: To make parts EE and FF, set core-box bit as for pilasters; cut flutes. Rout edges of both as for mirror frame pieces. On backs of 4⅛-in.-wide stock draw lines 1 in. from tops. Drill ³⁄₁₆-in. holes and countersink holes at 8-in. intervals on lines, avoiding ends where miters will be cut. Glue and screw stock together with 1¼-in. No. 8 screws.

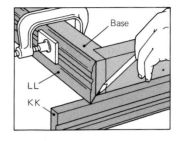

Fitting base moldings: Miter front ends of side moldings (LL); clamp to base. Miter one end of front molding (KK). Mark other end for length. Saw longer than mark, test-fit; saw off a bit at a time until fit is perfect. Use a ⁷⁄₆₄-in. bit to drill holes ½ in. deep into moldings; drill through existing holes in base. Saw side moldings flush with base sides (N). Screw moldings to base.

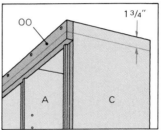

Crown molding support: Clamp support (OO) across cabinets with tops flush. Mark length, and mark where tongues on cabinets intersect. Saw to length and cut grooves for tongues. Screw to cabinets ⅜ in. from top of support at 12-in. intervals, using countersunk 1½-in. No. 8 screws. Rule a line 1¾ in. from cabinet tops on support and on cabinet facings (C).

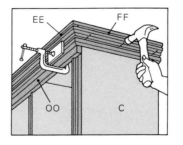

Fitting crown moldings: Miter front ends of side crown moldings (FF). Drill three ¹⁄₁₆-in. holes, evenly spaced, in each lower groove and one hole in each top groove ½ in. from miters. Mount at 1¾-in. line with 4d nails driven partway into lower holes. Mark front molding (EE) for miters; fit as you did base moldings. Drill ¹⁄₁₆-in. holes in lower groove of EE.

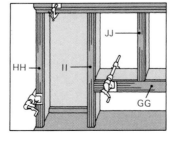

Fitting pilasters and fascia: Measure from bottom of crown molding support to counter top for lengths of pilaster moldings (HH and II). Saw them to length and clamp in place. Measure and cut the fascia molding (GG) to length and clamp it in place. Measure and cut the center pilaster molding (JJ) to length.

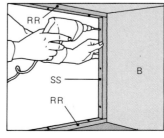

Mirror backing and frame: Drill ³⁄₁₆-in. holes in backing pieces (RR and SS) at 12-in. intervals; countersink holes. Drill matching holes in counter top. With rear edges flush, screw parts RR and SS to counter top, fixed shelf, and center-cabinet sides with 1¼-in. No. 8 screws. Drill three ¹⁄₁₆-in. holes at an angle through thinnest part of each mirror frame piece (PP and QQ).

Trays and lower cabinet shelves: A pullout tray (TT) for the TV is mounted on 22-inch slides attached to the cabinet floor. If you want pullout trays for your videocassette recorder, turntable, and other components, use 18-inch slides mounted on small trays (VV) attached to the shelves. To prevent the trays from tipping, such shelves must be screwed to shelf rests through holes drilled in the rests. If you want the TV to swivel, as well as slide in and out, cut a swivel top (UU) 1 inch longer and wider than the TV, put veneer tape on its edges, and install it on lazy-Susan hardware. Cover the edges of the shelves with veneer tape.

The TV tray is made by gluing and nailing a tray lipping (WW) to the underside of the tray's front and side edges. (Use 1¼-inch brads.) When the glue has dried, plane the lipping and plywood flush, and cover the edges with veneer. The instructions that follow are for the Grant slides listed on page 207.

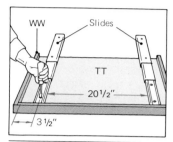

1. Turn the TV tray (TT) upside down. Position the slides, fully extended, so that the centers of the screw holes are 3½ in. from the lipping. Use roundhead screws in oval holes to screw the slides to the tray. Check that the slides are parallel; they should be 20½ in. apart. Adjust them if they are not parallel, and tighten the screws.

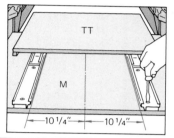

2. Turn tray right side up. Draw a center line on cabinet floor, then draw a parallel line 10¼ in. to each side. Extend slides, place case members over lines, and have someone hold the tray while you drive flathead screws into holes in case members. (If you mount slides on shelves, position them less than 3½ in. from lipping because shelves are narrower.)

Finishing and assembly: Sand oak plywood surfaces with Nos. 100 and 150 paper and solid oak with Nos. 80, 100, and 150 paper. Apply one coat of golden oak stain, leave it on for 15 minutes, and wipe it off. Make a mixture of 5 parts high-gloss polyurethane to 1 part turpentine. Brush this on, then immediately wipe off the excess with cheesecloth. Make three applications of this mixture on oak surfaces and two on birch surfaces. You need not sand between coats. Finally, apply a coat of brown Minwax to all surfaces with 0000 steel wool.

Assemble the parts in the room the entertainment center will occupy. Using holes already drilled, install the parts in this order: base, lower cabinets, counter top, upper center cabinet, light, upper side cabinets, end and inside pilasters, fascia molding, center pilaster, lower cabinet backs, upper cabinet backs, mirror and frame, crown molding, metal shelf rests, and shelves. Screw the upper cabinets together through the top and bottom shelf holes; countersink the screwheads and use 1¼-inch No. 10 brass screws. Insert two more screws 1½ inches below the fixed shelf, one on each side; the fascia molding will cover them.

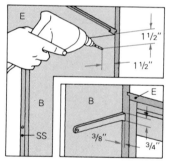

Light: Before installing the upper side cabinets, attach a light fixture to bottom of the fixed shelf (E), making sure it will be hidden by fascia molding. To allow a cord to pass from behind unit to fixture, drill a 5/16-in. hole in upper center-cabinet side (B) 1½ in. below fixed shelf and 1½ in. from front edge. From this hole rout a groove on the outer face of center-cabinet side to its back edge with a ¾-in. bit set to cut ⅜ in. deep.

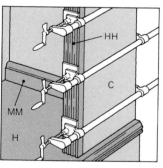

Gluing the pilasters: Put glue in grooves of pilasters HH and on leading edges of upper end-cabinet sides (A); clamp each with five bar clamps. Glue pilasters II, being careful not to get glue on edges of center-cabinet sides (B) in case you ever need to take the unit apart. Glue the center pilaster (JJ) in place after fascia molding is in place (next step).

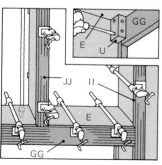

Gluing the fascia molding: Place a 2 x 4 across top of upper center cabinet at its back edge, and extend a bar clamp from the 2 x 4 to underside of fixed shelf (E); this holds shelf level while you attach fascia molding (GG). Glue and screw glue blocks (U) under fixed shelf flush with its front edge. Glue and clamp fascia molding to fixed shelf; screw through back of each glue block into molding with two 1½-in. No. 8 screws.

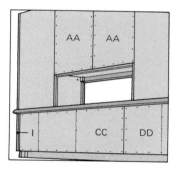

Cabinet backs: Backs AA, CC, and DD were cut to fit during preassembly (p.212); be sure you added ⅜ in. to each lower cabinet back for the grooves in lower cabinet sides (I). Rule lines on outer surfaces where backs will cover partitions; nail backs with 3d nails on these lines and to rear edges of cabinets. Use glue only on the lower cabinet backs, since they are inserted in grooves.

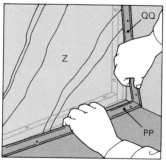

Installing the mirror: Place the mirror (Z) against mirror backing pieces (RR and SS), and have someone hold it while you fit mirror frame pieces (PP and QQ) in place. If fit of last frame piece is too tight, pull the frame bottom slightly away from the mirror, and push the bottom and a side piece in position simultaneously. Use a tack hammer to drive ¾-in. brads through predrilled holes into surrounding wood surfaces.

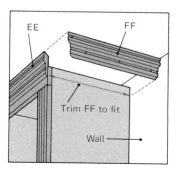

Attaching crown moldings: This step is left to last so that you can adjust the molding to meet the wall behind the unit and the ceiling. Nail the front molding (EE) in place with 4d finishing nails through predrilled holes. Measure distance to wall from its lower edges at both corners; transfer these measurements to the bottom edges of the side moldings (FF) and cut them to length. Nail the side moldings in place.

BUILT-IN BOOKCASE

Designed to fit between two walls, this built-in bookcase provides maximum storage at a minimum depth. Knotty pine tongue-and-groove boards that have beveled edges (a feature called V-jointing) are used for the wall coverings and cabinet doors. You can add shelves to the cabinets for more storage space.

No dimensions are given for the overall length of the unit or the length of the horizontal parts because these dimensions depend upon the space available. The unit in the photograph has cabinet sections 3 feet 4 inches wide, and the top shelf is 7½ feet above the floor.

Planning: Measure the available space, and make a scale drawing on graph paper. From this calculate the quantities of lumber needed. Tongue-and-groove boards come in nominal sizes: 4-inch boards are 3½ inches wide, and because of the tongue that fits into the groove of the adjoining board, the exposed face is 3¼ inches.

Check whether the floor is level, the walls are vertical, and the corners square. If not, compensate by shimming or cutting pieces to fit.

Finishing: Sand all parts with No. 80 sandpaper, then No. 100, and finally No. 150. Paint the bookshelves and the wall behind them, the shelf brackets, and the interior of the cabinet and lower shelf. Apply three coats of mat-finish polyurethane to the unpainted parts. Test the finish on a scrap piece of wood; if a darker color is desired, stain the wood before applying polyurethane.

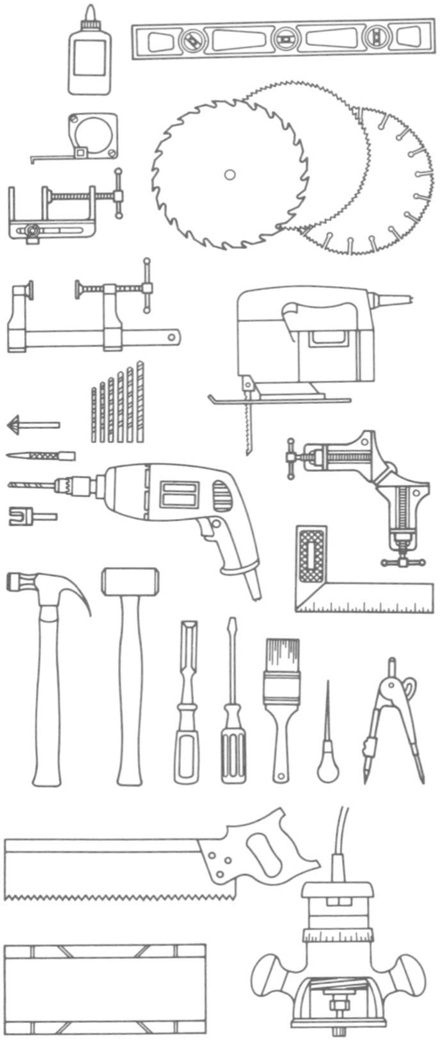

Parts list

Part	Name	Quantity	Thickness	Width	Length	Material
A	Base support	2	1½"	3½"	✳	2 x 4 fir
B	Cabinet floor	1	⅝"	14⅜"	✳	Birch plywood
C	Kickplate	1	¾"	3½"	✳	1 x 4 knotty pine
D	Edge strip	2	¼"	⅝"	✳	Knotty pine
E	Furring strip	7	¾"	1½"	49⅜"	1 x 2 common pine
F	Horizontal batten	1	¾"	1½"	✳	1 x 2 common pine
G	Cabinet wall	4	⅝"	13¾"	24⅜"	Birch plywood
H	Door frame	4	¾"	2½"	25"	1 x 3 clear pine
I	Wide shelf	1	¾"	15¼"	✳	4" tongue-and-groove pine floorboards
J	Front rail	1	¾"	3½"	✳	1 x 4 knotty pine
K	Bookshelf	4	¾"	7¼"	✳	1 x 8 common pine
L	Bookcase end	2	¾"	7¼"	34½"	1 x 8 common pine
M	Bookcase divider	5	¾"	7¼"	10"	1 x 8 common pine
N	Furring strip	7	¾"	1½"	✳	1 x 2 common pine
O	Wall covering	3	½"	✳	✳	4" tongued, grooved, and V-jointed knotty pine boards
P	Shelf	1	⅝"	13⅛"	✳	Birch plywood
Q	Cabinet door	4	½"	✳	✳	4" tongued, grooved, and V-jointed knotty pine boards
R	Door brace	20	¾"	2½"	✳	1 x 3 common pine
S	Cleat	4	¾"	¾"	14"	Rip from 1 x 2 common pine
T	Door backing	4	⅛"	✳	✳	Hardboard
U	Door edging	16	¼"	1⅜"	✳	Knotty pine

✳ To be determined during construction.

Tools and materials: Drill with twist, countersink, and counterbore bits and plug cutter. Table or radial arm saw with crosscut and rip blades. Backsaw, miter box. Router, saber saw, doweling jig. Hammer, nail set, screwdriver, chisel, wooden mallet. Awl, level, try square, compass, steel tape rule. Four bar clamps, four corner clamps. Nos. 80, 100, and 150 sandpaper. Carpenter's glue, wood putty, paint, mat-finish polyurethane, brushes. Veneer tape, ¼" x 1⅜" pine or hardwood edging, 12' of ⅜" dowel. Wood (see above). Three-in. No. 10 flathead wood screws (or fiber anchors and self-tapping screws for masonry wall), 1¾" No. 10 flathead wood screws, 1¼", 1½", and 2" No. 8 flathead wood screws. 4d and 6d finishing nails, ¾" brads. Eight 2" butt hinges with 1½" leaves. Four magnetic catches, four knobs, 26 steel shelf brackets 6" x 8". Toggle bolts (for hollow walls).

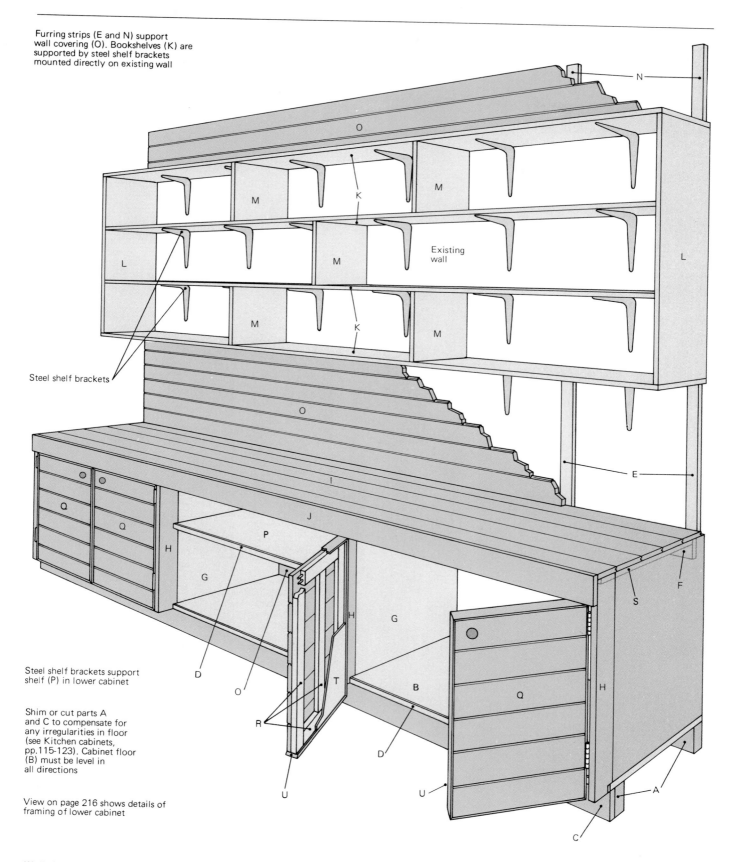

Furring strips (E and N) support wall covering (O). Bookshelves (K) are supported by steel shelf brackets mounted directly on existing wall

N

O

M

K

M

Existing wall

L

M

L

M

M

Steel shelf brackets

O

I

E

J

Q

Q

P

H

G

D

O

H

G

R

T

B

Steel shelf brackets support shelf (P) in lower cabinet

Shim or cut parts A and C to compensate for any irregularities in floor (see Kitchen cabinets, pp.115-123). Cabinet floor (B) must be level in all directions

View on page 216 shows details of framing of lower cabinet

S

F

H

Q

A

U

D

U

C

Wall fasteners: When filled with books, games, stereo set, and records, the bookcase unit will be very heavy; therefore, it must be securely anchored to the wall. The most secure anchoring is provided by screwing the framework into the studs; this is done with the rear base support (Step 1). If possible, one or more of the furring strips should be located over a stud and fastened in the same way. Otherwise, use toggle bolts in hollow walls; they have "wings" that open out on the hollow part of the wall. Use fiber anchors and self-tapping screws in masonry walls; the anchors are inserted in predrilled holes and the screws driven into them.

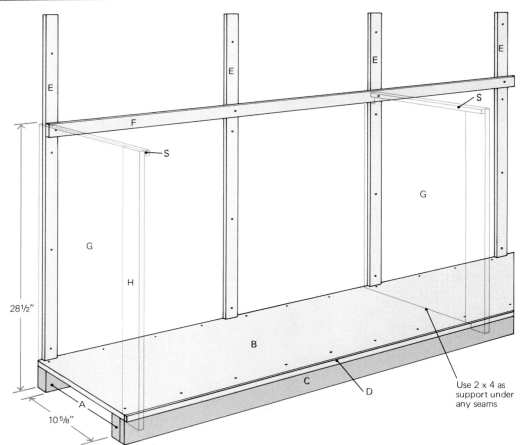

1. Locate the studs, usually on 16-in. centers, by tapping the wall or probing with a ⅛-in. twist bit. If there is a baseboard molding, cut it away so that the unit will be flush with the wall. Attach the rear base support (A) through the wall to the studs with 3-in. flathead screws (or use fiber anchors and self-tapping screws in a masonry wall).

2. Position the front base support (A) so that it is 10⅝ in. from the rear base support. Align its ends with those of the rear base support. Cut scraps of wood to serve as spacers for holding the front base support in position while you screw it into the floor with 3-in. screws through counterbored holes.

3. Place the cabinet floor (B) on top of the base supports. Nail it with 6d finishing nails to the base supports. If floor is over 8 ft. long, two pieces of plywood will be needed. Support their butting edges with a 2 x 4.

Use 2 x 4 as support under any seams

28½″

10⅝″

4. Nail the kickplate (C) to the surface of the base support with 4d finishing nails. Drive the nails ⅛ in. below the surface with a nail set and fill the depressions with wood putty. The edge of the cabinet floor will overlap the surface of the kickplate by 1 in.

5. Glue and nail the edge strip (D) to the edge of the cabinet floor with ¾-in. brads. Set them below the surface, as you did with the nails in Step 4, and fill the holes with wood putty.

6. Fasten furring strips (E) to the wall ⅝ in. from each end of the rear base support with their ends on cabinet floor. Space the five others equidistant from each other and from the end strips. Predrill holes in strips and mark wall through holes. Drill holes in wall. If a strip coincides with a stud, you can attach it with 1½-in. flathead screws; otherwise, use toggle bolts or plastic screw anchors. Countersink the screwheads.

7. Screw the horizontal batten (F) to the furring strips with 1½-in. flathead screws. Countersink the screwheads. The batten's upper edge should be 28½ in. above the floor.

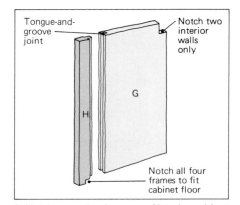

8. Notch upper back corner of interior cabinet walls (G) only to fit horizontal batten (F). To attach door frames (H) to cabinet walls, cut a lengthwise tongue on each frame ¼ in. x ¼ in with a router or power saw. In front edge of each cabinet wall cut a groove ⁵⁄₁₆ in. deep and ¼ in. wide. Glue and clamp walls and frames. Cut a notch at back edge of each door frame to fit cabinet floor (B).

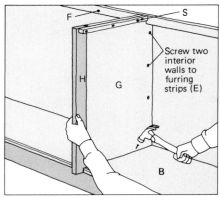

9. Glue and screw a cleat (S) to top edge of each cabinet wall (G). Predrill holes near back edge of interior walls for screwing to furring strips (E). Attach with 1½-in. screws. Screw end cabinet walls to walls of room. Make sure no screwheads will interfere with shelf (P) to be installed in Step 15. Check that walls are square with adjoining parts; toenail them to cabinet floor.

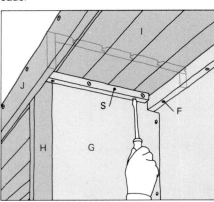

10. Fit together tongue-and-groove floorboards for 15¼-in.-wide shelf (I). Rip board at front edge of shelf. Glue and clamp boards. Drive screws up through horizontal batten (F) and cleats (S) into shelf, using 2-in. and 1¼-in. screws respectively. Glue and screw front rail (J) to shelf and door frames. Counterbore the screwheads and then fill the holes with wooden plugs.

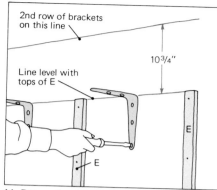

11. Draw a line level with the top of the furring strips (E), and install six steel shelf brackets spaced evenly along line. (Use fasteners appropriate to the type of wall as in Step 6.) Measure 10¾ in. up from the line (less if you are adjusting the height of the unit for a low ceiling); draw a level line for the second row of shelf brackets; install the brackets. Repeat for third and fourth shelves.

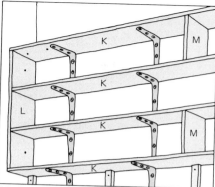

12. Saw the top and bottom shelves (K) to extend the full length of the unit; saw the middle two shelves shorter by the thickness of the ends (L). Place the shelves on the brackets. Screw the brackets to the top shelf, then to the other shelves, working downward. Nail the dividers (M) in place. Screw the bookcase ends to the walls of the room. Counterbore all screws and fill the holes.

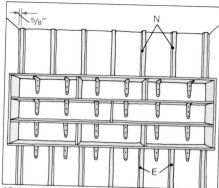

13. Measure from the top shelf to the ceiling all along the length of the unit (the ceiling may vary in distance from the top shelf). Cut seven furring strips (N) to match the space available. Using the same fasteners as in Step 6, mount two strips to the wall with their outside edges ⅝ in. from each end of the top shelf. Align the five other strips with the lower furring strips (E), and mount them.

14. Fit boards (O), tongued edge up, for wall covering. Mark top board to fit ceiling line by holding it level and using a compass to scribe a line parallel to ceiling; rip along that line. Mark the board to go below lowest bookshelf in the same way. Use a saber saw to shape its upper edge to fit brackets. Nail the boards to furring strips by blind-nailing brads at an angle as shown.

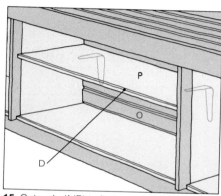

15. Cut a shelf (P) to fit the space in the center between the cabinet walls. (You may also want to equip the cabinets with additional shelves. If so, measure for them and cut.) Trim the outer edge of the shelf with edge strip (D). Mount two shelf brackets to the wall covering (O) with screws. (Decide where to place the brackets according to the tallest item you plan to store under the shelf.)

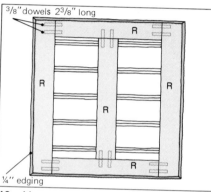

16. Measure the two cabinet openings. Divide the long dimension of each opening in half for the width of one cabinet door. Then subtract ½ in. from each dimension (to allow for ¼-in. edging all around) minus another 3/16 in. horizontally and 1/16 in. vertically to allow for clearance. The illustration shows a sample door. Use your own measurements to cut door braces (R) for the next step.

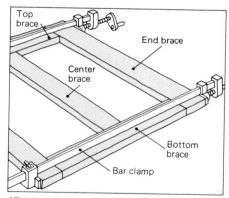

17. Use a doweling jig (see *Index*, p.379) to drill ⅜-in. holes 1¼ in. apart in door braces. Saw pieces of ⅜-in. dowel into 2⅜-in. lengths. Saw a lengthwise groove in each dowel, and bevel ends. Glue center brace to top and bottom joints first, then glue end braces. Clamp until glue has dried. Meanwhile, fit boards for doors (Q), tongued edge up; saw to correct length and rip top board for correct height.

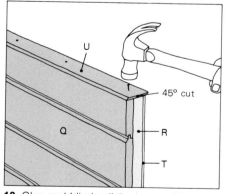

18. Glue and blind-nail the boards (Q) to braces (R). Nail ⅛-in. hardboard (T) to the back of the braces. Use a miter box and backsaw to cut ¼-in. x 1⅜-in. edging (U) to fit around outside of cabinet doors. Nail edging to doors with brads; recess brads with a nail set, and fill holes with wood putty. Sand edging, if necessary, to make it flush with front and back of cabinet door.

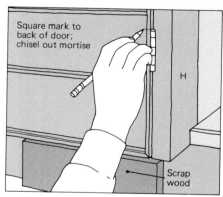

19. Each hinge leaf should be 1½ in. wide so that all screws can enter the brace. You may have to drill additional holes in the leaf. Chisel out a mortise (see *Index*, p.379) the thickness of the leaf in the door frame (H). Insert one screw completely and the others partially. Support the door with scrap wood while marking for mortise on door. Chisel out mortise, check fit, and finish inserting screws.

KITCHEN OR BAR STOOL

Our contemporary oak stool is 26 inches high and perfect for sliding under a kitchen counter. If you need a bar stool, adjust the height to that of your bar. The stool's wide, sturdy base will provide steady support at any reasonable height. The comfortable sling seat is made from durable corduroy, but any heavy material will do. The stool is relatively easy to build. A doweling jig is the only specialized tool needed; all other necessary tools are indicated below in the listing of tools and materials. The legs and crossmembers are all the same width, which makes cutting the stock go quickly. Dowels are used to strengthen all joints.

Construction: Rip the legs and crossmembers to their 2¼-inch widths first, then cut them to their proper lengths.

Lay out the dowel holes on the sides of the legs first. Since careful measuring is

required to transfer the locations of these holes to the ends of the front and rear crossmembers, transfer the locations of only the top holes to each crossmember and drill them (see Step 3). Later, after the stool is assembled, drill the bottom holes in the crossmembers by using the bottom holes in the legs as drilling guides (see Step 9 on the opposite page).

The doweling of the legs and side crossmembers is easier, since all the holes can be drilled in the edges of the pieces with the help of the doweling jig. Mark and drill them all at the same time (see Step 4). After assembling the stool, use a plane to round off the sharp edges of the hardwood parts.

Finishing: Sand all parts with Nos. 100 and 150 sandpaper. Apply several coats of an aerosol tung oil, rubbing lightly between coats with 000 steel wool.

Installing the seat

Pass the loops through both end slots. Insert the dowels into the loops in the seat fabric and pull the excess fabric out through the slots. Pull the seat tight to hold the dowels in place, and smooth the fabric. Ease your weight down on the seat gradually the first time to set the seams and tighten the fabric around the dowels.

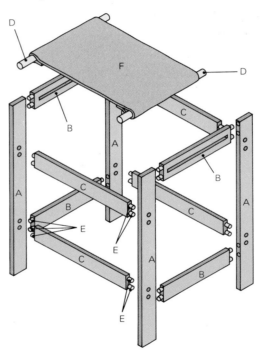

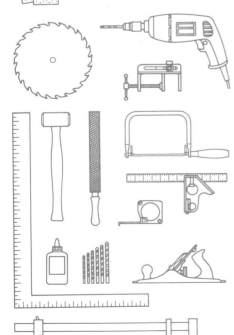

Parts list

Part	Name	Quantity	Thickness	Width	Length	Material
A	Leg	4	¾"	2¼"	26"	Oak
B	Side crossmember	4	¾"	2¼"	11½"	Oak
C	Front and rear crossmember	4	¾"	2¼"	15½"	Oak
D	Seat dowel	2	½" dia.	—	11"	Hardwood dowel
E	Frame dowel	32	⅜" dia.	—	1½"	Hardwood dowel
F	Seat	1	—	21"	30"	Corduroy

Tools and materials: Electric drill with ⅜" twist bit. Coping saw or saber saw. Table, radial arm, or circular saw. Fine-tooth handsaw or backsaw. Steel tape rule, combination square, framing square, pencil. Doweling jig. Wooden mallet, coarse file or rasp, plane. Four 2' bar or pipe clamps. Nos. 100 and 150 sandpaper and a sanding block or orbital sander. Spray-on tung oil, 000 steel wool, wood glue. One yd. of at least 24" wide corduroy or other heavy fabric. One ½" hardwood dowel 3' long and two ⅜" hardwood dowels 3' long. Eighteen running ft. of 1 x 3 oak dressed to ¾" x 2¼" or wider.

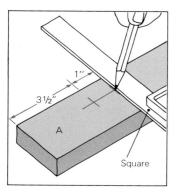

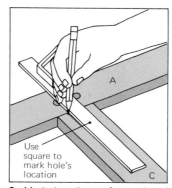

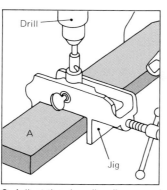

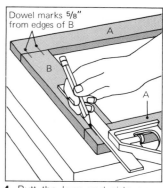

1. Mark the locations of the dowels for the front and rear crossmembers (C). They should be centered on the sides of the legs (A) 3½ in. and 4½ in. from the top of each leg and 7 in. and 8 in. from the bottom of each leg. Use the combination square to make straight lines through these marks so they are aligned vertically.

2. Adjust the doweling jig according to the manufacturer's directions so that it will guide the bit to drill ⅜-in. holes in the centers of the 2¼-in.-wide legs. Center the jig over the lines you drew in Step 1 and drill the dowel holes completely through one leg. Repeat this procedure on each of the remaining three legs.

3. Mark locations of top dowel holes on ends of front and rear crossmembers (C) by placing each crossmember against its leg in alignment with the holes; then use the square to transfer locations of top dowel holes to ends of each crossmember. Use doweling jig to center ⅜-in. holes in the ends of their crossmembers.

4. Butt the legs and side crossmembers (B). The upper members must be flush with the tops of the legs. The bottom edges of the lower members must be 4 in. from the bottoms of the legs. Mark locations of dowel holes ⅝ in. from each edge of B. Use doweling jig to drill ⅜-in. holes ¾ in. deep centered in parts A and B.

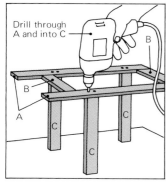

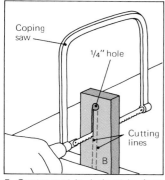

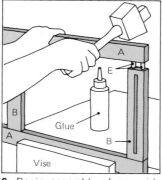

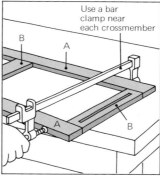

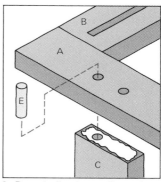

5. Center a ¼-in. hole ½ in. from each end of the upper side crossmembers (B) to start the seat fabric slots. Draw straight lines to connect the outside edges of the holes, then cut along the lines with a coping saw or saber saw. Use a rasp or coarse file to smooth the inside of the cut and to round the edges slightly.

6. Begin assembly of one side frame by placing a little glue on the ends of four ⅜-in. dowels (E) and inserting them into the holes on the edges of one leg (A). Put glue on the end of an upper side crossmember (B) and tap it into place. Do the same for a lower side crossmember (B). Remove excess glue with a damp cloth.

7. Place the other leg in position after applying glue and tap it tightly against the crossmembers. Wipe away any excess glue immediately. Clamp the frame together. Set it on a flat surface and check that it is not bowed or skewed. Reposition clamps to straighten frame. Assemble the other side frame the same way.

8. Round all edges with a plane, then sand with Nos. 100 and 150 sandpaper. Attach front and rear crossmembers (C) to one side frame. Position a crossmember, apply glue to its end, align its dowel hole with top hole in leg, and drive a dowel through leg and into crossmember. Repeat on other three crossmembers.

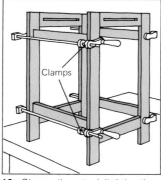

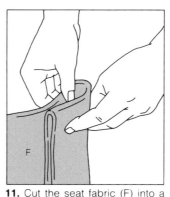

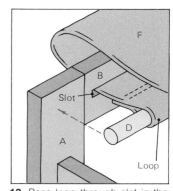

9. Carefully align the crossmembers, and drill a hole for the second dowel in one crossmember by using the hole in the leg as a guide. Repeat on the other three crossmembers. Then cover dowels with glue and tap them into place, leaving a little of each dowel protruding. Repeat Steps 8 and 9 on the other side frame.

10. Clamp the stool lightly, then check to be sure that the legs are in alignment and that the stool sits squarely on a flat surface. True it up if necessary. Tighten the clamps and allow the glue to dry. Cut the dowels flush with the leg surface and sand frame smooth. Round all edges with Nos. 100 and 150 sandpaper.

11. Cut the seat fabric (F) into a strip at least 21 in. wide and 30 in. long. Fold the fabric lengthwise with the finished side inward. Seam the fabric along the long edges to form a tube, then turn the tube right side out and smooth it, keeping the seam near one edge. Fold one of the ends over to make a 2-in. loop and sew it in place.

12. Pass loop through slot in the stool frame and insert a ½-in. dowel (D). Stretch the fabric across the frame and pass it through the other slot. Wrap it around a dowel and mark location for second seam. Remove dowels and fabric, then sew up the loop. Be sure loops are square with edges of seat.

PREP AND SERVE CENTER

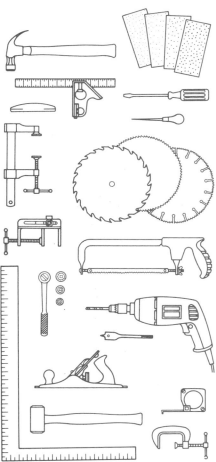

Versatility best describes this handsome prep and serve center. It can be used as a rolling work center in the kitchen or as a portable bar in the rec room to host a party. The unit is 5½ feet tall and has a work surface of over 3½ square feet. The drop leaf will nearly double the work surface when it is raised and will provide concealed storage space on the lower shelf when it is down.

The main frame is made of oak and the shelf panels are birch-veneer plywood. Dowels are used to strengthen all joints. The upper half of the center is detachable, and it has display and storage racks for stemware.

Construction: Begin by ripping the wood to the proper width for the side rails and crossrails. Then cut the pieces for the sides and ends of the shelves. Consult the chart for the exact dimensions. Lay out the sides, mark and drill the dowel holes, then glue the frame parts together.

The shelves are made from ¼-inch plywood that is reinforced on all four sides by hardwood framing ½ inch thick and 1½ inches wide. The table top itself is made of heavier ¾-inch plywood. All exposed plywood edges are covered by the hardwood framing or by solid oak trim.

The shelf units are joined to the sides with lag bolts, which are concealed beneath the plywood shelving. This type of construction will enable you to easily dismantle the structure for storage.

The stemware holders can be adjusted to fit your special requirements, and inexpensive brass hooks can be positioned wherever they are needed.

The drop leaf is supported in its raised position by a drawerlike pullout frame hidden under the table. This support frame is exactly like the shelf framing and is cut at the same time.

The entire piece rolls about on spherical casters. If mobility is not important, furniture glides can be substituted.

The frame and shelf sides were given a natural finish with tung oil, which is easy to apply and is rubbed in by hand. To protect the surfaces of the shelves and table, apply several coats of a quality varnish, sanding lightly between coats, and follow with a coat of furniture wax.

Parts list

Part	Name	Quantity	Thickness	Width	Length	Material
A	Base side rail	4	¾"	2½"	28"	Oak
B	Base side crossrail	6	¾"	2½"	15"	Oak
C	Top side rail	4	¾"	2½"	37"	Oak
D	Top side crossrail	6	¾"	2½"	15"	Oak
E	Top rail	2	¾"	2½"	28½"	Oak
F	Top crossrail	2	¾"	2½"	12½"	Oak
G	Shelf side	6	½"	1½"	28½"	Oak
H	Shelf end	6	½"	1½"	17¼"	Oak
I	Table end	2	¾"	2½"	17½"	Oak
J	Table side support	2	½"	1½"	27"	Oak
K	Table end support	2	½"	1½"	17¼"	Oak
L	Table support slide	2	¼"	1½"	17½"	Oak
M	Stemware holder support	4	¾"	¾"	16"	Oak
N	Stemware holder shelf	4	¼"	1¾"	16"	Oak
O	Fixed table top	1	¾"	17½"	28"	Birch plywood
P	Drop leaf	1	¾"	14½"	27½"	Birch plywood
Q	Drop-leaf front trim	1	¼"	¾"	28"	Oak
R	Drop-leaf side trim	2	¼"	¾"	14½"	Oak
S	Shelf panel	3	¼"	17"	28"	Birch plywood
T	Edge trim	3	1/16"	¾"	28"	Oak edging

Tools and materials: Table or radial arm saw with dado head. Hacksaw. Drill with ¾" bit and 1" spade bit. Doweling jig. Four 4' bar clamps, two 4" C-clamps. Hammer, mallet, screwdriver, awl. Steel tape rule, combination square, framing square. Socket wrench, plane, sanding block. Nos. 80, 100, and 120 sandpaper. Small brush, contact cement. Three strips 1/16" x ¾" x 36" oak edging. Two ¼" x 5½" x 30" oak boards, five ½" x 5½" x 30" oak boards, eight ¾" x 5½" x 38" oak boards. Two pieces birch plywood: ¼" x 3' x 4', ¾" x 2½" x 3'. Three ⅜" hardwood dowels 3' long. One 36" piano hinge. Four casters with ⅜" shafts. Four brass hooks. Twenty ¼" lag screws 1" long with washers, four ¼" lag screws 3" long. Ten 1¼" No. 8 flathead wood screws.

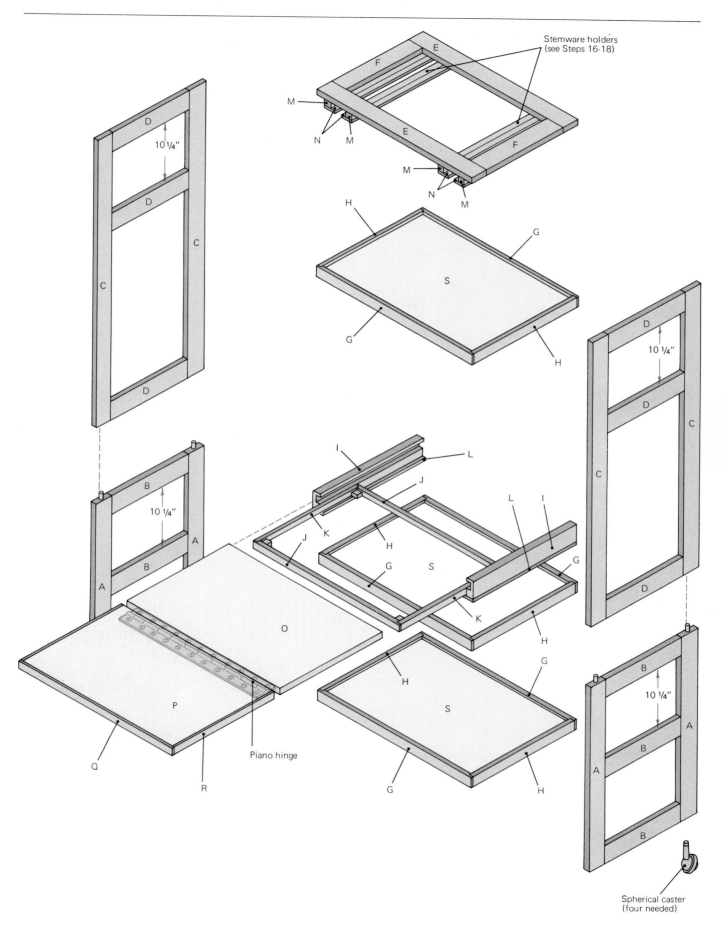

Stemware holders
(see Steps 16-18)

E

F

M

N

M

E

F

M

N

M

D

10 1/4"

D

C

C

D

H

G

S

G

G

H

D

10 1/4"

D

C

C

D

I

L

J

B

10 1/4"

B

A

A

J

K

K

H

G

S

G

K

L

I

G

H

A

H

O

H

G

S

G

P

Q

R

Piano hinge

S

G

H

B

10 1/4"

B

A

A

Spherical caster
(four needed)

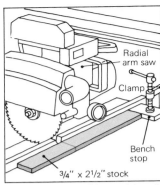

1. Rip the top and base side rails (C and A) and top and base side crossrails (D and B) to 2½-in. widths. Cut the top and base side crossrails to 15-in. lengths. Use a bench stop to make repeated cuts accurately and quickly. Then cut parts A to 28 in., parts C to 37 in., parts E to 28½ in., parts F to 12½ in., and parts I to 17½ in.

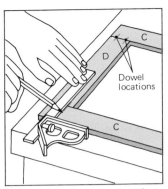

2. Plane the edges smooth to remove saw marks. Lay out two top side rails (C) and a top side crossrail (D) on a flat surface and in position, forming a U. Square up the assembly with a framing square. Use the combination square to mark locations of dowel holes, centered ⅝ in. from each edge of part D.

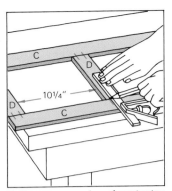

3. Place upper edge of center top side crossrail 10¼ in. below the bottom edge of the top crossrail. Mark the location for four dowel holes as shown in Step 2. Be careful to keep the center crosspiece aligned. Draw marks for the dowel holes on the lower crossrail in the same way. Cut 56 dowels 1½ in. long and four 1 in. long.

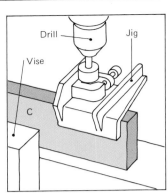

4. Align doweling jig with each of the pencil marks made in Steps 2 and 3, and adjust it to center a ⅜-in. hole. With a ⅜-in. drill bit in the guide hole of the jig, drill a hole ¾ in. deep. Test-fit long dowels in the holes; they should be snug. Assemble frame parts C and D without glue to test the alignment of the dowel holes.

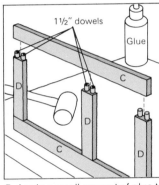

5. Apply a small amount of glue to the end of each dowel; insert each in its hole and tap in place. Run a bead of glue over the dowel ends and along the joints. Assemble the parts and wipe any excess glue away with a damp cloth. Clamp the assembly with bar clamps. Repeat Steps 2–5 for all remaining parts A–F.

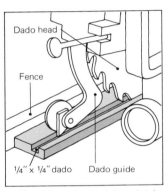

6. Rip ½-in. oak stock into 1½-in.-wide strips for the shelf sides and ends (G and H) and table supports (J and K). Then set the dado head for a ¼-in.-wide cut. Position the blade to make a dado ¼ in. from the edge of each part and ¼ in. deep. Cut strips 28½ in. long for shelf sides (G) and 27 in. for table side supports (J).

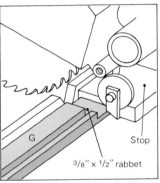

7. Cut pieces of the same stock 17¼ in. long for the shelf ends (H) and table end supports (K). Use a bench stop for the repetitive cuts. Cut rabbets ⅜ in. deep and ½ in. wide from the ends of parts G and J (see *Index*, p.379). Cut the shelf panels (S) to 17 in. x 28 in. Test-fit each shelf panel and its sides (G) and ends (H).

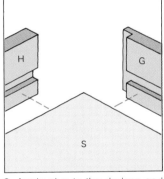

8. Apply glue to the dadoes and end joints of a shelf side (G) and two ends (H). Place a plywood panel (S) into the dadoes, fit the ends, and squeeze the parts together. Apply glue to the remaining side and place it in position. Check the fit of the joints and then clamp shelf unit until dry. Repeat for other two shelves.

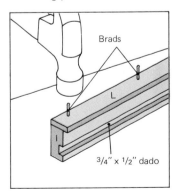

9. Set up the dado head for a ¾-in.-wide cut. Cut a dado ¼ in. from the top of the table ends (I) and ½ in. deep. Cut the pair of table support slides (L) from ¼-in.-thick stock to a width of 1½ in. and to a length of 17½ in. each. Attach the table support slides to the bottoms of the table ends with glue and brads.

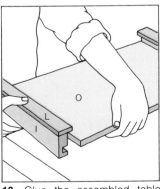

10. Glue the assembled table ends from Step 9 to the short edges of the fixed table top (O). Run a bead of glue into the ¾-in. dadoes in the table ends, and place the pieces together with their edges in alignment. Clamp the ends against the top and allow the glue to dry thoroughly before proceeding.

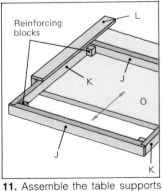

11. Assemble the table supports (J and K) in the same way as the shelf frames (Steps 6–8). Reinforce their corners with small blocks cut from scrap. The support assembly should slide easily in the slots under the fixed table top. If necessary, sand the slots for more clearance. Cut the piano hinge to a length of 24 in.

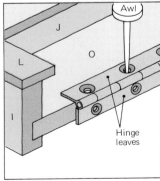

12. Center the hinge on the bottom of the table top. Hold it carefully so that one hinge leaf rests on the bottom of the fixed table top and the other on its front edge. Use an awl to make starting holes for the hinge screws under the table. For clearance, cut a recess along the top edge of support J the length of the hinge.

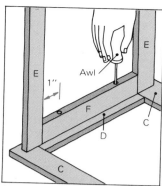

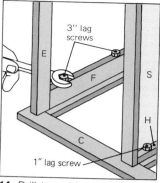

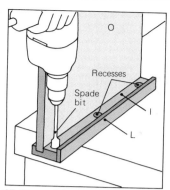

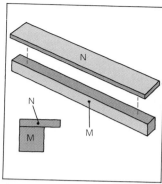

13. Place the assembled parts E and F on end and drill two ¼-in. clearance holes through the crossrails (F) 1 in. from the top rails (E). Center this assembly on the top side crossrails (D) and push an awl through the holes to mark their locations on parts D. Drill ¹³⁄₆₄-in. pilot holes ½ in. deep for lag screws at each mark.

14. Drill two ¼-in. holes in each shelf end (H) 1 in. from each side and below the plywood shelves. Center each shelf on its crossrail and mark the positions of the holes with an awl as in Step 13. Drill ¹³⁄₆₄-in. pilot holes. Attach the shelves to the sides with 1-in. lag screws and the top with 3-in. lag screws.

15. Use a 1-in. spade bit to make recesses for three washers and lag-screw heads in inner face of each table end (I). The lag-screw heads must be flush to permit the support assembly to be inserted. Drill the recesses first and then center ¼-in. clearance holes in the spade bit dimples to allow screws to go through.

16. Rip four pieces ¾ in. wide for the stemware holder supports (M) from ¾-in. stock; they should be square. Cut them to a length of 16 in. Cut four stemware holder shelves (N) from ¼-in. stock 1¾ in. wide and 16 in. long. Glue these shelves and supports together so that each shelf is flush with one side of the support.

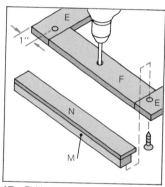

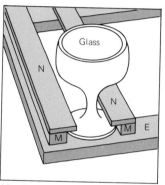

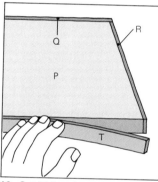

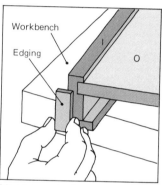

17. Drill three ⅛-in. clearance holes along the center lines of top rails (E and F). Center one hole and position the other two holes 1 in. from each end. Countersink the holes. Clamp one stemware holder assembly in place on the underside of a crossrail, centering it between the front and back edges of the top.

18. Drill through the clearance holes into the stemware holder with a ³⁄₃₂-in. bit ½ in. into the stemware holder. Insert wood screws and tighten. Place a glass in position and set down the other half of the stemware holder. Fasten it with two screws and repeat the operation for the other stemware holder assembly.

19. Cut ¾-in.-wide strips from ¼-in. stock. Trim two to a length of 14½ in. for the side trim (R) of the drop leaf (P). Apply glue and place flush against the side edges of the leaf. Cut the front trim (Q) 28 in. long and glue it along the front edge of the leaf. Attach ¹⁄₁₆-in. oak edging (T) to the rear edge with contact cement.

20. Use contact cement to apply oak edging (T) to the exposed edges of the fixed table top (O). Cover the table ends (I) with small pieces of edging. Sand the edging until it is flush with the top and bottom of the table, then round the edges to keep them from lifting. Be careful not to sand through the thin veneer.

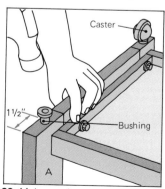

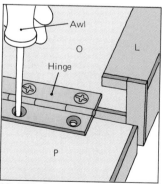

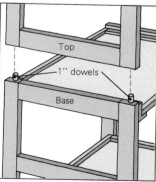

21. Sand all solid parts with No. 80 paper to round the edges, then follow with Nos. 100 and 120. Disassemble where necessary. Sand the plywood veneer very carefully with No. 120 paper if needed. Turn the base unit upside down and locate the positions of the casters on the bottom of the base.

22. Make marks on the bottom of each base side rail (A) 1½ in. from the outer edges. Place the doweling jig in alignment with each mark, and drill a ⅜-in. hole 1¼ in. deep on the center line of each rail. Remove the metal bushings from the casters, insert them in the holes, and drive them home with a hammer. Then insert the casters.

23. With the base unit still upside down, place the drop leaf (P) in position. Carefully align it with the hinge and use the awl to mark the locations of the screws on the leaf. Tap the awl with a mallet to form the pilot holes for the small hinge screws. Insert the screws to attach the drop leaf to the fixed table top.

24. Place the top unit on base unit and align the sides. Mark positions for four aligning dowels on the side rails (A and C). Use the doweling jig to drill ⅜-in. holes ½ in. deep in these rails. Glue the 1-in. dowels into the holes in the base unit only. Insert the dowels into the holes in the top unit to keep the two units aligned.

MOBILE DRY BAR

A bar fits into the entertainment plans of many homes. It can be used not only for serving drinks but for serving food as well. This mobile dry bar (dry because it has no plumbing) can be folded up and tucked out of the way when not in use. When guests arrive, it can be rolled to where it is needed and the bar top can be opened out to nearly double its size. The entire bar, which is made of solid cherry stock and cherry plywood, is about 42 inches high and 21 inches deep. When open, it is almost 7 feet wide; when closed, only 3½ feet wide.

The bar has a storage cabinet for bottles and glasses—or anything else you may want to put there. It can be reached through self-closing glass doors at the back of the bar. The four shelves inside the cabinet are adjustable for greater convenience. They are mounted with movable shelf supports and pilasters

Parts list

Part	Name	Quantity	Thickness	Width	Length	Material
A	Front	1	¾″	36″	37½″	Cherry plywood
B	Side	2	¾″	17″	37½″	Cherry plywood
C	Bottom	1	¾″	16½″	36½″	Cherry plywood
D	Divider	1	¾″	16¼″	36″	Cherry plywood
E	Top	1	¾″	20″	39″	Cherry plywood
F	Extension	2	¾″	20″	20″	Cherry plywood
G	Swing-out panel	2	¾″	18″	36¾″	Cherry plywood
H	Shelf	4	¾″	10½″	17½″	Cherry plywood
I	Doubler	2	¾″	3″	33″	Cherry plywood
J	Doubler	6	¾″	3″	20″	Cherry plywood
K	Doubler	6	¾″	3″	14″	Cherry plywood
L	Cleat	6	¾″	¾″	✳	Cherry plywood
M	Face-frame rail	2	¹³⁄₁₆″	2″	35″	4/4 cherry
N	Face-frame stile	2	¹³⁄₁₆″	2″	37½″	4/4 cherry
O	Center stile	1	¹³⁄₁₆″	2″	35″	4/4 cherry
P	Door rail	4	¹³⁄₁₆″	2″	14½″	4/4 cherry
Q	Door stile	4	¹³⁄₁₆″	2″	34½″	4/4 cherry
R	Front trim	2	¹³⁄₁₆″	2″	38″	4/4 cherry
S	Front trim	1	¹³⁄₁₆″	2″	34″	4/4 cherry
T	Top trim	1	¹³⁄₁₆″	2″	40″	4/4 cherry
U	Extension trim	4	¹³⁄₁₆″	2″	22½″	4/4 cherry
V	Swing-out panel edging	4	¹³⁄₁₆″	¼″	38″	4/4 cherry
W	Swing-out panel edging	2	¹³⁄₁₆″	¼″	19″	4/4 cherry
X	Shelf edging	4	¹³⁄₁₆″	¼″	18″	4/4 cherry
Y	Extension latch	2	¹³⁄₁₆″	1½″	6″	4/4 cherry
Z	Latch pin	2	¼″ dia.	—	1¼″	Birch dowel

✳ Cut to fit during construction.

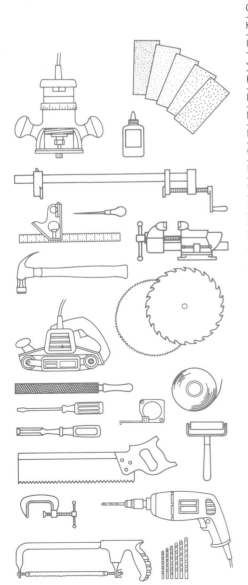

Tools and materials: Table or radial arm saw with dado head. Backsaw, hacksaw. Electric drill with twist bits and combination bit for drilling and countersinking pilot holes. Drill press with mortising attachment (optional). Router with straight veneer trimmer, bevel veneer cutter, arbor, and pilot (or with plastic laminate trimmer attachment and combination straight and bevel cutter bit), ⅜″ piloted rounding-over bit, ⅜″ rabbet bit. Fine laminate file, ¾″ chisel, ⅜″ mortising chisel. Belt sander with No. 120 sanding belt. Nos. 120, 150, 180, and 220 sandpaper. Several 4′ pipe or bar clamps, several 6″ C-clamps, vise. Rubber-surfaced pressure roller or rolling pin. Hammer, Phillips and standard screwdrivers, awl. Combination or framing square, steel tape rule, pencil. Masking tape. White glue, contact cement, paste stain, paste varnish, soft cloths. Two ¾″ x 4′ x 8′ panels and one ¾″ x 4′ x 4′ piece of A–2 cherry lumber-core plywood, 20 running ft. of 4/4 cherry 8″ wide, a ¼″ dowel 3″ long. A 2′ x 8′ sheet of ¹⁄₁₆″ plastic laminate, ⅛″ glass to fit bar doors (have glazier cut and install it). Two fixed and two swivel casters with 100-lb. capacity and sixteen ¼″ dia. x ¾″ screws for attaching casters. Two 1½″ x 20″ and two 1½″ x 37″ brass piano hinges. Two pairs of brass self-closing hinges, two brass door pulls. Eight 36″ lengths of brass pilasters (Grant No. 120–ALB), 16 brass shelf supports. 1½″ No. 6 flathead wood screws.

(metal tracks that hold the supports), which fit flush with the inner faces of the bar sides and with both faces of the divider that splits the cabinet in half.

The bar top is expanded by raising the two extensions that hang along the sides when not in use. These extensions are supported by two hinged panels that swing out from the sides. The bar top is screwed to the bar through cleats at the top of the storage cabinet, and the exten-

sions are hinged to the top. Both the top and the extensions are covered with plastic laminate to protect them from moisture. Lengths of plywood, called doublers, are attached to the perimeters of the top and extensions. The doublers provide a thick edge for the plastic laminate at the back of the bar, a gluing surface for the trim around the front and sides, and a proper anchor for the hinges that join the extensions to the top.

Begin construction of the bar by cutting all the parts (except the cleats) to the specifications given in the chart on the preceding page. Next, cut all the dadoes shown in the patterns at the bottom of this page, using a router or saw. Then follow the step-by-step directions on the following two pages. (To find detailed directions for cutting dadoes, rabbets, mortises and tenons, and for applying plastic laminate, see the *Index*, p.379.)

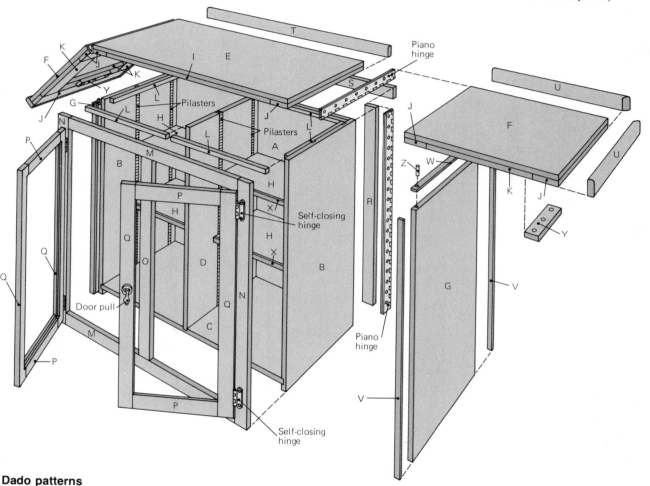

Dado patterns

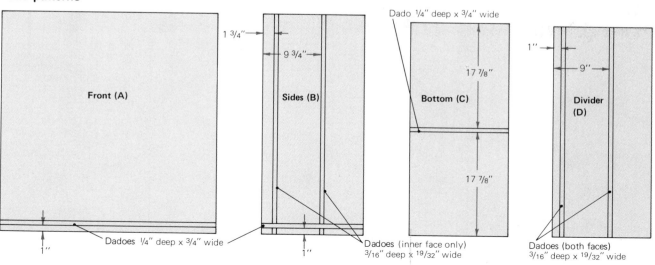

Front (A)

1" Dadoes 1/4" deep x 3/4" wide

Sides (B)

1 3/4"
9 3/4"
1"
Dadoes (inner face only) 3/16" deep x 19/32" wide

Dado 1/4" deep x 3/4" wide

Bottom (C)

17 7/8"
17 7/8"

Divider (D)

1"
9"
Dadoes (both faces) 3/16" deep x 19/32" wide

225

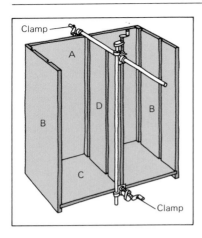

1. Cut dadoes in front (A), sides (B), and bottom (C), making sure to make one left side and one right. Cut dadoes in both faces of divider (D); when positioning dadoes, measure from front on both faces so that dadoes will be back to back. Glue and clamp front and bottom to sides so that bottom fits into dadoes in sides and front, and sides butt against front. Square up assembly. Glue and clamp divider in place.

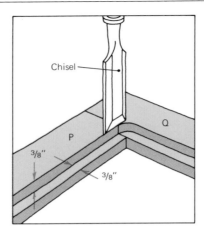

5. Glue and clamp door rails and stiles together to make two doors. When glue is dry, remove clamps and sand door frames. Then rout out rabbets 3/8 in. deep and 3/8 in. wide along inside perimeter of each door frame to accept glass. Square off corners of rabbets with a chisel. Screw self-closing hinges to doors with screws provided, then fit doors in place and screw hinges to face frame. Remove doors and hinges and sand any rough areas.

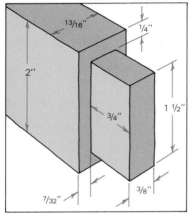

2. Mark both ends of both face-frame rails (M), all four door rails (P), and the center stile (O) for tenons. Each tenon should be 3/4 in. long, 3/8 in. thick, 1 1/2 in. wide, and have four shoulders. The long shoulders should be 7/32 in. wide and the short shoulders should be 1/4 in. wide as shown. Use a table or radial arm saw with a dado head, or a backsaw and chisel, to cut the tenons.

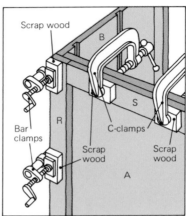

6. Position the long pieces of front trim (R) along the side edges of bar front (A), covering the glue joint. Cut the edges of the trim flush with the top and bottom edges of the bar front. Mark and cut the short piece of front trim (S) to fit between the long ones along the top edge of the bar front. Sand the inner edges of the pieces of trim (it will be too awkward to do later), and glue and clamp the trim in place. Remove the clamps when the glue dries.

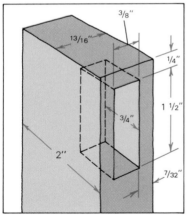

3. Draw cutting lines for mortises on face-frame stiles (N) and door stiles (Q) 1/4 and 1 3/4 in. from each end of each stile and 7/32 in. from each edge. Test-fit tenons inside the lines on stiles N and Q. Adjust lines if necessary. Use a drill press with a mortising attachment or a drill and chisel to cut blind mortises 3/4 in. deep. (Put tape on drill bit and chisel blade to act as depth gauges.) Test-fit tenons in mortises. They should be snug but not forced.

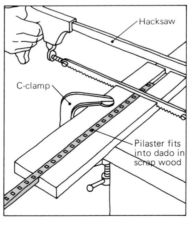

7. Cut pilasters to size; be sure that their holes line up when the pilasters are placed side by side, or shelves will be uneven when installed. To cut a pilaster, first cut a 3/16-in.-deep, 5/8-in.-wide dado in a piece of scrap wood, then cut a groove perpendicular to dado and of same depth. Place a pilaster into dado and use a hacksaw to cut it through groove in scrap wood. Push cut pilasters into dadoes in bar sides and divider, and secure them with nails provided.

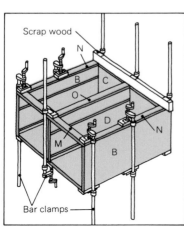

4. Mark off and cut mortises in exact centers of face-frame rails (M) for tenons on center stile. Mortises should be same size as those on face-frame stiles. Test-fit tenons in mortises and adjust, if necessary, by chiseling or adding shims. Glue together, clamp, and square off face frame. When glue is dry, unclamp face frame and glue and clamp it on back of bar. When glue is dry, remove clamps. Sand frame and joints where front and sides meet.

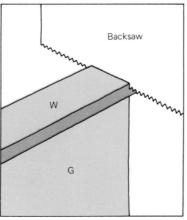

8. Center short pieces of swing-out panel edging (W) on tops of swing-out panels (G); glue and clamp in place. When glue is dry, remove clamps and trim ends of edging. Glue and clamp long pieces of swing-out panel edging (V) to sides of panels and trim ends. Add shelf edging (X) to fronts of shelves (H); trim ends. Use belt sander with No. 120 belt to trim sides of edging flush with adjoining surfaces of shelves and panels. Test-fit shelves.

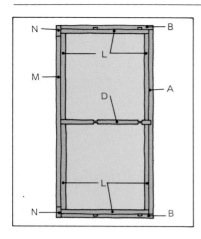

9. Measure and cut a cleat (L) to fit along inside top edge of each side (B). Use combination bit to drill pilot holes through cleats into sides, then glue and screw cleats in place. Measure and cut cleats to fit along the inside top edges of the front (A) and face-frame rail (M), reaching from the divider (D) to cleats on sides. Drill pilot holes, then glue and screw these cleats in place.

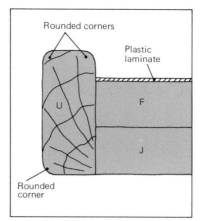

13. Cut ends of extension trim (U) that will meet in front corners at 45° angles to form miter joints. Use router and rounding-over bit to shape the two top edges and outer bottom edge of each piece of extension trim and top trim (T). Check and adjust lengths of trim, then sand. Glue and clamp trim pieces in place, with the remaining square edges flush with the bottom edges of doublers, using scrap-wood buffers to protect laminate.

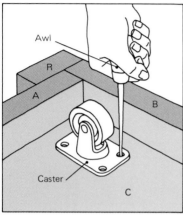

10. Turn bar upside down and position swivel casters in corners on one side of bar bottom (C), allowing enough space for the casters to swing around freely without hitting the side, front, or face frame. Using an awl and hammer, punch starter holes in the bar bottom through the screw holes in the casters, then drive in ¼-in. screws to secure the casters to the bottom. Install fixed casters with ¼-in. screws in corners on opposite side of bar bottom.

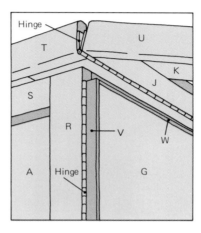

14. Center top (E) on bar, leaving enough clearance room for extensions and swing-out panels on each side. Use combination bit to drill pilot holes through cleats up into doublers on underside of top. Screw down top. Use piano hinges to mount swing-out panels (G) to edges of front trim (R), drilling pilot holes and screwing hinges in place. Mount the two extensions (F) with piano hinges, screwing hinges into adjacent bottom edges of doublers.

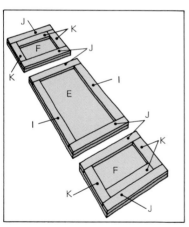

11. Position doublers (J) under side edges of top (E) and extensions (F). Align edges carefully, then drill pilot holes through doublers and glue and screw them in place. Add doublers (I and K) under back and front edges of top and extensions in same way. Attach remaining doublers to extensions' outer sides. If edges are uneven, pass doubled pieces through saw to shave edges smooth, or you will have trouble installing laminate.

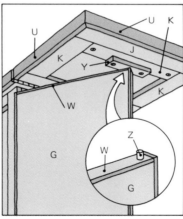

15. Drill a ¼-in. hole ¾ in. deep into center of each extension latch (Y) and into top edge of each swing-out panel (G) near free side of panel. Glue latch pins (Z) into holes in swing-out panels. Position latches on inner edges of inner doublers (K) under extensions. Align latches so that latch pins slip into holes in latches when extensions are in use. If extensions are not level when locked in, trim down thickness of latches. Drill pilot holes and screw latches in place.

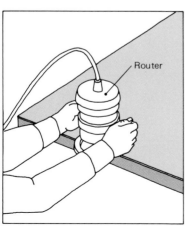

12. Apply laminate (with ¼-in. overlap on all sides) to back edges of top (E) and extensions (F). Use belt sander with No. 120 belt to trim ends of laminate. Add laminate to both side edges of top and to inner side edge of each extension. Belt-sand tops and bottoms of laminate edges flush with adjacent surfaces. Apply laminate to bar top and extensions and trim it. Use router with bevel veneer cutter on edges of laminate. File smooth.

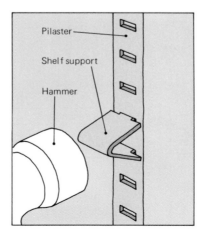

16. Sand all parts of bar that have not already been sanded. Use masking tape to protect plastic laminate, and apply paste stain, then varnish, to the bar according to directions on containers. When varnish is dry, take doors to a glazier and have the glass installed. Then reinstall doors and attach door pulls. Tap shelf supports into the pilasters and place the shelves (H) over the supports.

BUILT-IN FIREPLACE

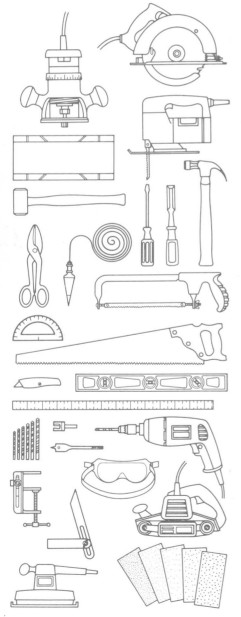

Parts list

Part	Name	Quantity	Thickness	Width	Length	Material
A	Baseplate	1	1½″	3½″	43″	2 x 4 pine
B	Baseplate	1	1½″	3½″	61″	2 x 4 pine
C	Baseplate	1	1½″	3½″	21″ ✳	2 x 4 pine
D	Baseplate	1	1½″	3½″	47″ ✳	2 x 4 pine
E	Baseplate	1	1½″	3½″	29½″ ✳	2 x 4 pine
F	Baseplate	1	1½″	3½″	23″ ✳	2 x 4 pine
G	Baseplate	1	1½″	3½″	18¾″ ✳	2 x 4 pine
H	Baseplate	1	1½″	3½″	12″	2 x 4 pine
I	Baseplate	1	1½″	3½″	40″ ✳	2 x 4 pine
J	Baseplate	1	1½″	3½″	20″	2 x 4 pine
K	Baseplate	1	1½″	3½″	15″ ✳	2 x 4 pine
L	Baseplate	1	1½″	3½″	32″	2 x 4 pine
M	Hearth support	2	1½″	2⁹⁄₁₆″	13″	2 x 4 pine
N	Hearth support	3	1½″	3½″	13″	2 x 4 pine
O	Long stud	1	1½″	3½″	93″ ✳	2 x 4 pine
P	Long stud	1	1½″	4″ ✳	93″ ✳	2 x 4 pine
Q	Long stud	1	1½″	3½″ ✳	93″ ✳	2 x 4 pine
R	Top plate	1	1½″	3½″	51″ ✳	2 x 4 pine
S	Top plate	1	1½″	3½″	16″ ✳	2 x 4 pine
T	Header	1	1½″	5½″	48″ ✳	2 x 6 pine
U	Vent support	4	1½″	2½″	45″ ✳	2 x 3 pine
V	Short stud	1	1½″	2½″	42¼″ ✳	2 x 3 pine
W	Back bin support	2	1½″	5½″	40¼″ ✳	2 x 6 pine
X	Front bin support	2	1½″	5½″	43¾″ ✳	2 x 6 pine
Y	Mantel support	4	1½″	2½″	16″	2 x 3 pine
Z	Mantel support	2	1½″	2½″	18″	2 x 3 pine
AA	Base frame	1	1½″	3½″	45⅛″ ✳	2 x 4 pine
BB	Base frame	1	1½″	3½″	68¼″ ✳	2 x 4 pine
CC	Base frame	1	1½″	3½″ ✳	19⅜″ ✳	2 x 4 pine
DD	Base frame	1	1½″	3½″ ✳	49″ ✳	2 x 4 pine
EE	Base frame	1	1½″	3½″	28½″ ✳	2 x 4 pine
FF	Base frame	1	1½″	3½″	25″ ✳	2 x 4 pine
GG	Base frame	1	1½″	3½″	20″ ✳	2 x 4 pine
HH	Base frame	1	1½″	3½″	14″ ✳	2 x 4 pine
II	Base frame	1	1½″	3½″ ✳	34″ ✳	2 x 4 pine
JJ	Base frame	1	1½″	3½″	22″ ✳	2 x 4 pine
KK	Base frame	1	1½″	3½″	20″ ✳	2 x 4 pine
LL	Base frame	1	1½″	3½″	28¾″ ✳	2 x 4 pine
MM	Fireplace platform	1	⅜″	40¼″ ✳	25½″ ✳	Plywood
NN	Plywood hearth	1	⅜″	9½″ ✳	9½″ ✳	Plywood
OO	Plywood hearth	1	⅜″	27″ ✳	32″ ✳	Plywood
PP	Nailer	5	1½″	2½″	†	2 x 3 pine
QQ	Mantel	1	1½″	5¾″ ✳	60½″ ✳	Oak board
RR	Mantel	3	1½″	6″ ✳	24¾″ ✳	Oak board
SS	Log bin side	2	⅜″	16″	36¾″ ✳	Plywood
TT	Log bin top	1	⅜″	16″	17″	Plywood
UU	Hearth facing	1	¾″	5¾″	33″ ✳	Oak board
VV	Hearth facing	1	¾″	5¾″	19½″ ✳	Oak board
WW	Hearth facing	1	¾″	5¾″	33″ ✳	Oak board
XX	Hearth facing	1	¾″	5¾″	21″ ✳	Oak board
YY	Molding	11	¾″	⅞″	†	Oak base ogee molding
ZZ	Molding	6	¾″	2¼″	†	Oak casing molding

✳Measurement is approximate. Cut slightly oversize and trim, miter, or notch to fit during installation (see step-by-step instructions).
†Cut to fit during construction.

The crackle of an open fire often contributes more romance than heat to a room, but modern fireplaces with heat-circulating ducts, combustion air intakes, and glass doors are much more efficient than old-fashioned designs. This Heatilator Advantage model amounts to several kits that can be installed by a contractor or by an ambitious do-it-yourselfer. The installation may require a building permit and inspection. Even if inspection is not required by your municipality, it may be demanded by your home's insurer.

In planning and building your fireplace, you must follow the manufacturer's safety precautions and your local building code scrupulously. If there is a conflict between them, call or write to the manufacturer for help. If the conflict cannot be resolved, you should be allowed to return the fireplace for a full refund.

Installation: This fireplace was positioned in a tight corner that measured only 3 feet 10 inches on its short side. The small Heatilator model FP28 was chosen for this reason and was canted at a 63° angle instead of the usual 45°.

It is a good idea to burn several hot fires before the wallboard is installed to check for excess heat on the outside of the firebox and chimney. Any part of the fireplace that comes in contact with the studs should remain cool enough to touch.

Tools and materials: Table saw (optional), circular saw with abrasive cutoff wheel. Saber saw, reciprocating saw, handsaw, hacksaw. Miter box. Router with ½" x 2" straight bit, ⅜" rounding-over bit, and template guide. Doweling jig. Hammer, mallet, chisel, 5/32" Allen wrench. Screwdriver, offset Phillips screwdriver. Tin snips. T bevel, torpedo level, plumb line, straightedge, protractor. Mat knife. Drill with twist bits, 1" and ⅜" spade bits, No. 10 combination bit, and No. 10 plug cutter. Safety goggles. Belt sander with No. 80 belt. Orbital sander and Nos. 100, 150, and 220 sandpaper. Tile cutter. Corner trowel, ¼" x ¼" notched trowel, and 4", 6", and 10" taping trowels. Cardboard. Golden oak stain, polyurethane varnish, 1 gal. flat latex wall paint, mat black aerosol stove paint. Paintbrushes. White glue, panel adhesive. Masking tape, one roll paper joint tape. One gal. wallboard joint compound, 2 qt. ceramic tile adhesive, 10-lb. pkg. brown floor tile grout, 4" x 4" ceramic tiles (22 sq. ft.). Lumber in 8' lengths: six 2 x 3's, fifteen 2 x 4's, two 2 x 6's, and two 2 x 6's or 2 x 8's to match joists and rafters. Oak boards: ¾" x 5¾" x 10', 1½" x 7" x 6', and 1½" x 7" x 7'. Three 8' lengths of ¾" x ⅞" base ogee molding, three 8' lengths of ¾" x 2¼" casing molding. A 4' x 8' panel of ⅜" plywood. Two 4' x 8' panels of ½" gypsum wallboard. Four ½" dowels 2" long. Heatilator Advantage model FP28 fireplace with AK20 outside air kit, GD28 glass doors, HX28 metal hearth, CD10 heat circulation kit, GR28 grate, three IC848 chimney pipes 4' long, RB48 red brick chimney termination kit, and FS838 firestop. Four ¼" x 4" and two ¼" x 6" lag screws with washers. Two ¼" x 4" toggle bolts. A 4' length of 1¼" x 1¼" aluminum angle 1/16" thick. Wood screws: three ½" No. 4 self-tapping, eight 1¼" No. 4 Phillips-head, eighteen 1½" and six 3" No. 10 flathead, twelve 2" No. 10 roundhead with washers. 6d, 10d, and 16d common nails, 4d finishing nails, and 1⅜" grooved dry-wall nails.

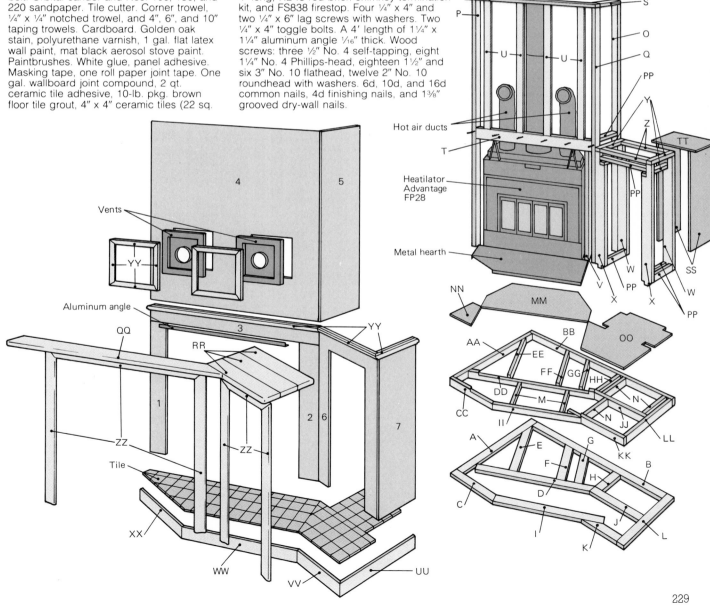

Chimney termination

Chimney

Firestop

Hot air ducts

Heatilator Advantage FP28

Metal hearth

Vents

Aluminum angle

Tile

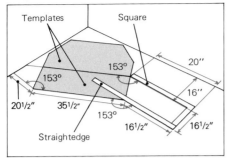

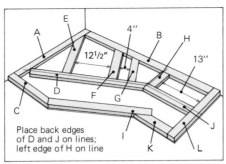

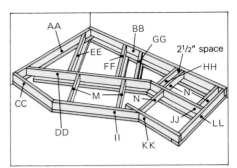

1. Make cardboard templates of fireplace and metal hearth. Lay templates in corner 1 in. from walls if possible. Use a framing square and straightedge to mark outlines for baseplates on floor.

2. Cut and lay out baseplates (A–L) along the marks made in Step 1. Miter ends as necessary to fit. Drill 5/32-in. pilot holes to prevent splitting 2 x 4's, then nail them through the floor and into the subfloor with 16d nails.

3. Cut the base frames (AA–LL) and hearth supports (M and N). Position them on edge as shown. Drill pilot holes and toenail through them and into the baseplates, using 16d nails. Do not nail parts CC, DD, II, or M yet.

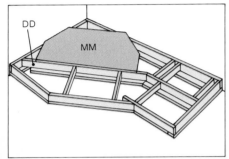

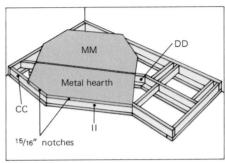

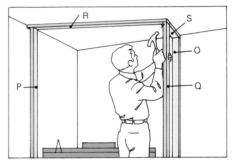

4. Cut the fireplace platform (MM) from 3/8-in. plywood, making it 1 in. larger all around than the fireplace template. Nail it to the frame (but not to part DD) with 6d nails. Platform should be flush with part DD and not overlap it.

5. Center metal hearth and trace its outline onto parts CC, DD, II, and M. Cut a notch 15/16 in. deep along outline and test-fit hearth; it must be 3/8 in. higher than frame. Cut off overhanging hearth corner with abrasive wheel.

6. Nail parts CC, DD, II, and M to frame. Drill pilot holes in metal hearth and nail it to frame. Center kit's fiberglass insulation and fireplace on platform (MM). Cover gap between platform and hearth with metal strip in kit.

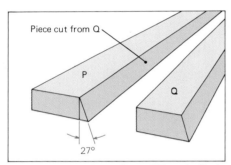

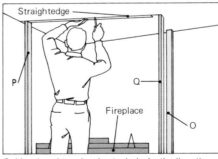

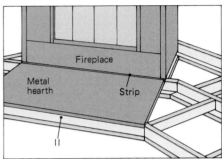

7. Rip front face of stud Q at a 27° angle. Tack the piece you cut off stud Q to the front of stud P to form a flush nailing surface. Cut studs O, P, and Q so that they fit snugly between the ceiling and the baseplates.

8. Use level to plumb studs in both directions. Move studs by tapping with a hammer. When studs are plumb, trace their outlines onto ceiling and connect the lines with a straightedge to form outlines for top plates (R and S).

9. Remove studs and cut top plates to fit inside lines drawn in Step 8. Nail plates into ceiling joists with 16d nails. Trim studs to fit between base and top plates. Plumb studs and toenail them in place with 10d nails.

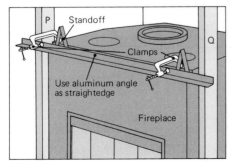

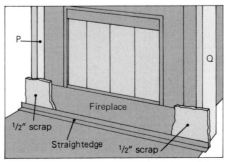

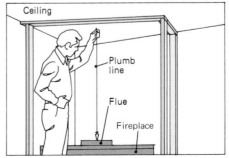

10. To position fireplace so that wallboard will fit flush in Steps 41–42, clamp a straightedge to the metal standoffs on top of fireplace. Move fireplace until straightedge is flush with beveled faces of studs P and Q.

11. Place straightedge across base of fireplace. There must be room for pieces of 1/2-in. wallboard between straightedge and studs. When fireplace is correctly positioned, drive 16d nails next to fireplace so it cannot shift.

12. Use plumb line to mark center of flue on ceiling. Center firestop on mark and trace its outline. Check attic for interfering wires or pipes, then use a saber saw to cut out ceiling along outline. Wear safety goggles.

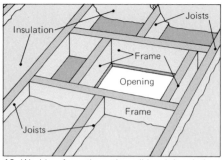

13. Working from the attic, roll back insulation around opening. Cut through any interfering joists 1½ in. beyond each side of opening. Frame opening with lumber that matches joists (2 x 6's or 2 x 8's). Extend frame to joists.

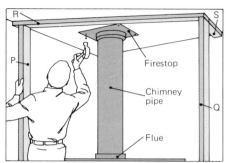

14. Tack firestop in place temporarily. Stack chimney pipes from flue to firestop. Center firestop, then nail bottom half through ceiling into frame. Nail top half to frame from attic. Then install kit's hot and cold air ducts.

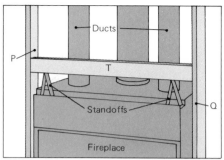

15. Use T bevel to set saw blade to angle of studs P and Q. Cut header (T) to fit snugly between studs. Rest header on metal standoffs and drill 3/32-in. pilot holes through header into studs. Attach header with 3-in. screws.

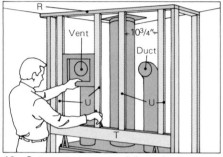

16. Cut vent supports (U) to fit between header and top plate R. Position supports at each side of ducts and 10¾ in. apart. Test-fit vents between supports. Plumb supports; mark their positions; drill 7/64-in. pilot holes.

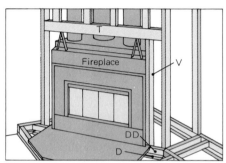

17. Use 10d nails to nail supports to header and plate without moving supports off their marks. Cut short stud (V) to fit and nail between header and baseplate D to provide a nailing surface for wallboard.

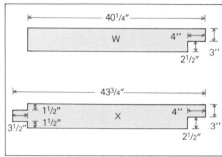

18. Cut back and front bin supports (W and X) from 2 x 6 lumber as shown. Distance from tops of W and X to ceiling should be 50 in. or less so that 48-in. wallboard will fit between mantel and ceiling.

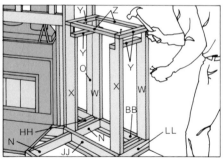

19. Attach back supports (W) to wall with ¼-in. toggle bolts and toenail to base frame BB and stud O with 10d nails. Nail front supports (X) to parts HH, JJ, LL, and N. Nail mantel supports (Y and Z) between W and X.

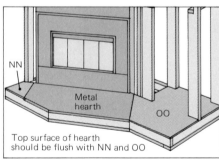

20. Piece together cardboard to make patterns for plywood hearth (NN and OO). Trace patterns onto 3/8-in. plywood and cut out parts. Draw center lines of parts N onto OO. Nail OO and NN to base with 6d nails 4 in. apart.

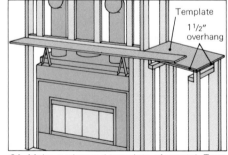

21. Make a plywood template of mantel. Template's front edges should be straight and square. Use a plane to shape back edges to fit snugly along framework. Template should overhang log bin 1½ in. at front and right side.

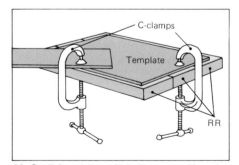

22. Cut 7-ft. oak board into three equal lengths for mantel parts RR and edge-join them (see *Index*, p.379) to make a rectangle. Smooth top of rectangle with belt sander and No. 80 belt. Clamp template to rectangle.

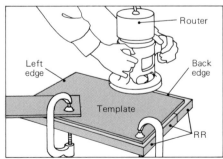

23. Cut out back and left edges of rectangle, using a router equipped with a ½-in. bit 2 in. long and a template guide. Cut rectangle in several passes, starting with a ⅛-in. cut and lowering the bit ⅛ in. for each pass.

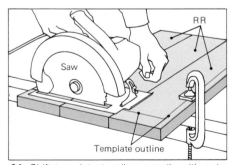

24. Shift template to align exactly with cuts made in Step 23. Trace outline of template onto remaining two edges of rectangle, and cut them. Rout a ½- x ½-in. rabbet into upper left edge of rectangle.

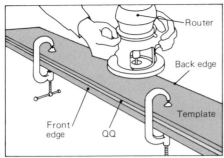

25. Clamp 6-ft. oak board (QQ) to long arm of template and cut its back edge with a router as in Step 23. Shift template; mark and cut other edges as in Step 24. Cut a ½- × ½-in. rabbet into back edge for wallboard.

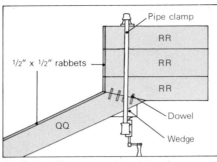

26. Rule a line across template where parts QQ and RR will join. Transfer this line to QQ and RR and cut them exactly on line. Use doweling jig (see *Index*, p.379), ½-in. dowels, and glue to join mantel parts as shown.

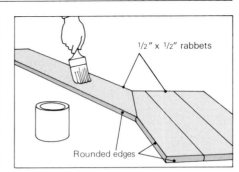

27. When glue has set, unclamp mantel and use a ⅜-in. rounding-over bit (see *Index*, p.379) to round top and bottom of mantel's front and right edges. Sand and stain with golden oak stain, then varnish.

28. Position mantel on framework, prop it up to make it level, and trace its outline onto header and studs. Remove mantel and use a ⅜-in. spade bit to drill oversize clearance holes for lag screws through header and studs.

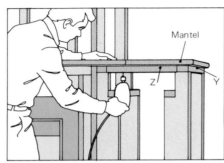

29. Reposition mantel. Push a pencil through clearance holes to mark their positions on mantel. Drill twelve ⅛-in. pilot holes through supports Y and Z into mantel. Remove mantel and enlarge holes in Y and Z to ⁵⁄₁₆ in.

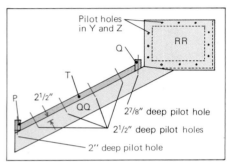

30. Drill ³⁄₁₆-in. pilot holes into mantel to depths shown. Reposition mantel. Insert 4-in. lag screws with washers through header, 6-in. lag screws with washers through studs, and 2-in. screws with washers through supports.

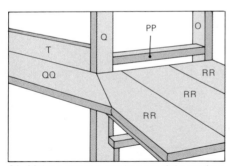

31. Make screws snug but not tight against washers to allow mantel to expand and contract. Cut and install two nailers (PP): one to fit between studs O and Q just above the mantel; another to fit between W and X above LL.

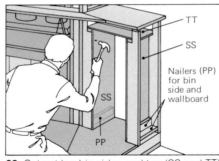

32. Cut out log bin sides and top (SS and TT). Cut two nailers (PP) about 13 in. long and attach them between log bin supports with 10d nails. Then nail bin sides to supports and nailers with 6d nails spaced 6 in. apart.

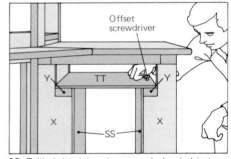

33. Drill eight ⅛-in. clearance holes in bin top. Drive Phillips-head screws through top and into lower supports (Y), using an offset screwdriver. Toenail a fifth nailer about 17 in. long to the front edge of bin top (TT).

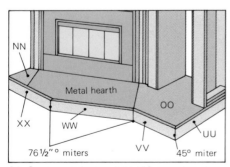

34. Cut hearth facing (UU-XX) oversize, then set saw to 45° and miter ends of parts UU and VV. Set saw to 76½° to cut ends of VV, WW, and XX. Starting at junction of VV and WW, position facing and trim parts to fit.

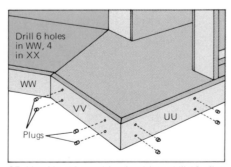

35. Use No. 10 combination bit to drill 18 pilot holes through facing and into base. Attach facing with glue and 1½-in. screws. Cut oak plugs to fill screw holes (see *Index*, p.379). Mask floor and finish facing (see Step 27).

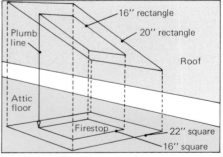

36. Working from the attic, draw two squares concentric with the firestop frame, one 16 x 16 in. and the other 22 x 22 in. Use plumb line to project corners of squares onto roof and connect them to form two rectangles.

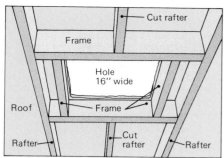

37. Drill a 1-in. starting hole. Rent a reciprocating saw to cut through roof, shingles, and rafters along inner rectangle; you need not square the corners. Cut rafters back to outer rectangle and build a frame as in Step 13.

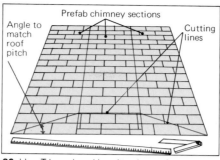

38. Use T bevel and level to determine pitch of roof. Lay three sections of prefab chimney termination side by side and transfer pitch line to outer panels. Draw horizontal line on center section and draw a 4-in. flap.

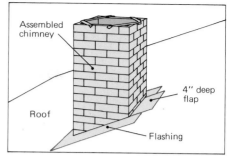

39. Use tin snips to cut sections as shown, then assemble chimney. Use hacksaw blade to cut roofing nails, and slip flashing under shingles. Nail through flashing and flap into frame made in Step 37.

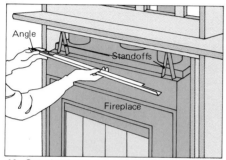

40. Cut aluminum angle to width of fireplace, notch it to fit around standoffs, and drill three pilot holes for self-tapping screws. Paint angle black and screw to top of fireplace; wallboard will fit between angle and standoffs.

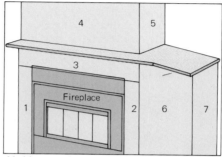

41. Measure framework and cut wallboard in order shown. Maintain ½-in. clearance between third piece and fireplace top. Cut wallboard with handsaw or by scoring paper face, snapping board, then cutting opposite face.

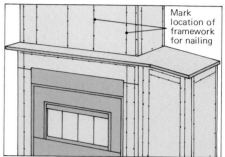

42. Mark outline of framework onto ceiling and hearth, then use a plumb line to transfer outline to wallboard. Drive dry-wall nails into framework every 4–6 in. Dimple nailheads so they can be covered with compound.

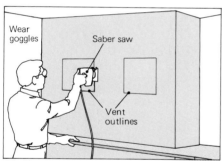

43. Trace outlines of vents onto wallboard. Openings must measure 10¾ in. wide and 12 in. high. Plunge saber saw through wallboard, cut along horizontal lines until you hit vent supports (U), then cut vertical lines.

44. Cut log bin opening in the same way as the vent openings. Fill all nail holes and seams in wallboard with joint compound. Press joint tape on seams and cover with more compound. Fold tape at corners.

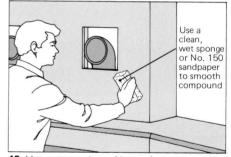

45. Use a corner trowel to apply compound to 90° corners. Use 4- to 10-in. trowels to apply progressively wider and thinner coats of compound to seams. Let compound dry between coats and smooth with a wet sponge.

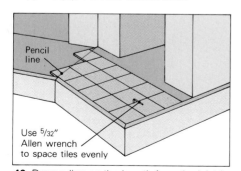

46. Draw a line on the hearth from the joint in the hearth facing to the joint in the wallboard. Lay out tiles, starting at front corner of the hearth and covering the line. Use ⁵⁄₃₂-in. Allen wrench to space tiles evenly.

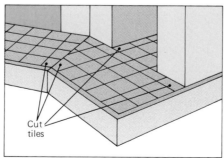

47. Sighting between tiles, transfer line on hearth to tops of tiles. Rent a tile cutter to cut tiles along lines. Mark and cut other tiles to fit log bin and left side of hearth. Cement tiles and apply grout (see *Index*, p.379).

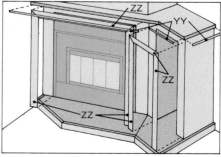

48. Mask mantel and hearth; paint wallboard. Install vents. Cut molding ZZ to fit around fireplace and log bin; molding YY under mantel and around vents. Sand, stain, and varnish molding; install with panel adhesive.

FREE-STANDING FIREPLACE

If you want to heat your home more efficiently than you can with a conventional fireplace, you should install a wood stove or freestanding fireplace, which radiates heat in all directions. Either unit must rest on a fireproof platform that will not transmit heat to the floor. If it is to be placed closer to the walls than the distances specified by the manufacturer and your local building code, those walls must be protected by a shield.

The platform shown here is made up of a sheet of asbestos sandwiched between a plywood base and a tile top. The wall behind the shield is covered with asbestos. The shield itself, made of copper-covered sheet metal, is attached to the wall with channel-iron spacers, which hold the shield 1½ inches from the wall. Air circulating between the wall and shield keeps the shield from transmitting heat and creating a fire hazard. Although the copper can be bent, as in Step 5, the job is tedious; you may prefer to have the work done by a sheet-metal shop.

The firestop and chimney termination are installed in a similar manner to those in the *Built-in fireplace* (pp.228–233). The fireplace and chimney termination are connected with stovepipe. Keep the pipe as short and straight as possible. Try to avoid 90° bends, but if you must use them, do not use more than two. Horizontal sections of pipe should rise at least ¼ inch per running foot.

Placement: The unit shown here is a Shenandoah FP–S freestanding fireplace. It must not be closer than 38 inches from any unprotected wall and the stovepipe should not be closer than 18 inches, but both can be as close as 12 inches from a shield. The front of the fireplace door opening should be no closer than 48 inches from any combustible material.

Safety notes: Because asbestos can be hazardous to your health, order it cut to fit. If you must cut it yourself, work outdoors and wear a face mask.

After installation, clean the chimney at least twice a year and replace the stovepipe every 2 years. For further safety advice, send for the pamphlet *Heating with Wood* from the U.S. Department of Energy, Washington, D.C. 20508.

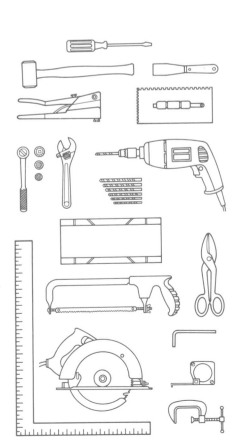

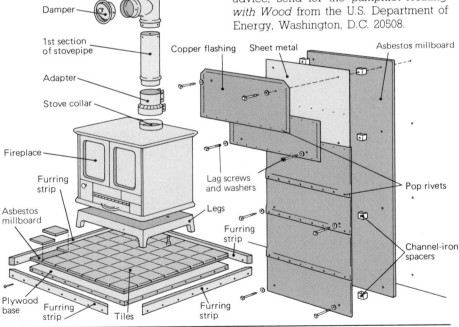

Firestop
Slip connector
Top section of stovepipe
Damper tee
Damper
1st section of stovepipe
Adapter
Stove collar
Fireplace
Furring strip
Asbestos millboard
Plywood base
Furring strip
Tiles
Furring strip
Copper flashing
Sheet metal
Asbestos millboard
Lag screws and washers
Legs
Furring strip
Pop rivets
Channel-iron spacers

Tools and materials: Circular saw, hacksaw. Miter box. Electric drill with set of twist bits. Sheet-metal shears, pop riveter. Socket wrench, adjustable wrench, ¼" Allen wrench. Mallet, screwdriver. Two 6" C-clamps. Framing square, steel tape rule, pencil. Wall-type saw-tooth trowel for spreading tile adhesive, putty knife. Black ceramic tile grout, ceramic tile adhesive, stove cement. Five dozen 6" x 6" quarry tiles. A piece of ¾" plywood about 4' x 6', ½" asbestos millboard cut to exact size of platform and wall shield. About 16' of 1 x 2 common furring. Scrap wood. A 4' x 8' panel of 24-gauge sheet metal and copper flashing to cover it. Shenandoah FP–S freestanding fireplace. Universal stove-top adapter. Air-Jet all-fuel chimney termination. Air-Jet heavy-gauge 8" dia. stovepipe as needed, including ceiling firestop and damper tee with damper and slip connector. Channel iron 1½" sq. Copper pop rivets, ¼" lag screws 3" long with washers to fit, 2" self-tapping screws, No. 8 sheet-metal screws, 1½" ring-type nails.

1. Lay out tiles to cover an area at least 43 x 49 in. Use ¼-in. Allen wrench to space tiles evenly. Then cut plywood base the same size. Buy asbestos millboard cut to same size and glue it to plywood with tile adhesive. Cement tiles to asbestos surface. (For directions on laying tiles, see *Index*, p.379.)

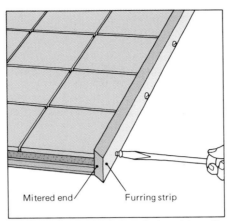

2. When adhesive is dry, cut furring strips with mitered ends (see *Index*, p.379) to form frame around platform. Drill eight ³⁄₃₂-in. pilot holes through each strip into edge of plywood base. Drive in 2-in. screws. Grout tiles and rub down frame with grout. Fire unit outdoors to burn off odors; let it cool, then bolt on legs.

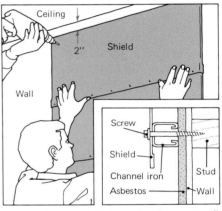

3. Nail asbestos millboard to parts of wall that will be covered by shield. Cut sheet metal 43 in. wide with a 2-in. gap at the ceiling and floor for air circulation. Cut enough panels of copper to cover sheet metal, with 1-in. overlap and overhang on all sides. Snip off four corners as shown.

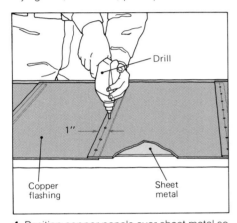

4. Position copper panels over sheet metal so that they overlap each other by 1 in. Center panels so that they overhang sheet metal by 1 in. at top and bottom and along sides. Carefully square up shield. Drill lines of ⅛-in. holes through shield where copper panels overlap, and install pop rivets through these holes.

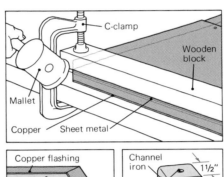

5. Clamp shield between wooden blocks and use a mallet to bend down one overhanging edge of copper. Turn shield over and bend same edge down over sheet metal. Repeat with remaining copper edges. Slice channel iron into eight 1½-in. spacers for mounting shield. Drill a ⅜-in. hole through each spacer.

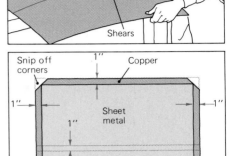

6. Have helper hold shield in place on wall, then drill holes through shield into studs. Pull top of shield away from wall a bit and slip lag screws and washers into top holes. Slip channel-iron spacers over ends of screws and drive screws into studs with socket wrench. Do same with lower rows of holes.

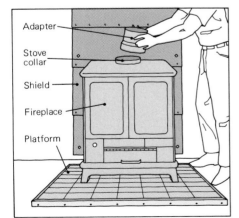

7. Move platform in place. Position fireplace on platform with its back 8 in. from back of platform, front of door opening 16 in. from front of platform, and sides of door opening 8 in. from sides of platform. Install firestop (see p.231). Attach adapter to stove collar, following manufacturer's directions.

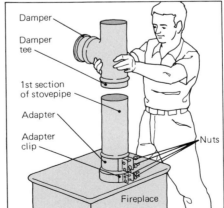

8. Tighten all nuts on adapter (except top one) against adapter clip. Push bottom of first section of pipe into top of adapter until pipe bead contacts top of adapter, then tighten top nut on adapter. Install damper in damper tee and damper tee in top of first section of stovepipe, as instructed by manufacturer.

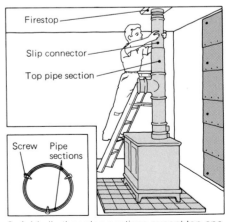

9. Add all other pipe sections except top one, securing each with three sheet-metal screws and sealing joints with stove cement. Install slip connector in top section. Install top section. Slide slip connector up and attach it to firestop, following manufacturer's directions. Install chimney termination (see p.233).

FOLDING SCREEN

This delicate-looking but sturdy folding screen of wood and fabric is perfect for dividing a room or closing off a corner. Each panel is 14 inches wide and 69 inches long. You can adjust the dimensions, but do not make the panels any wider than 18 inches. The red-oak frame could be made of another hardwood or clear pine. Slot mortise-and-tenon joints are used at the corners.

The dowels run all the way through the rails so that the fabric is easy to remove. Use a guide when drilling the dowel holes so that they will be properly aligned. The rails are stained a teak color and are finished with tung oil.

A nice touch is to match the panels to another fabric in the room. The panels are made of two thicknesses of fabric, each cut 2 inches longer and wider than the final dimensions. Stitch three sides together with right sides facing in, as you would a pillowcase, then turn the panel right side out. Leave space for the dowels at each end of the side seams, and finish the fourth side by hand.

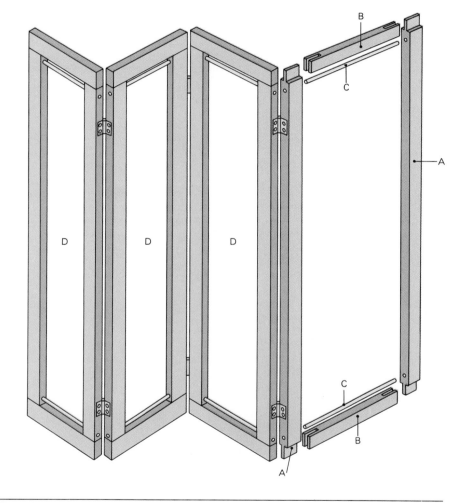

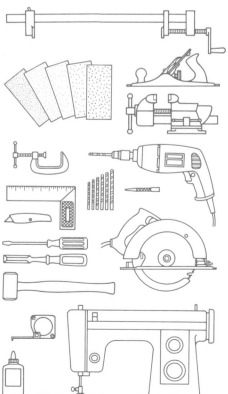

Parts list

Part	Name	Quantity	Thickness	Width	Length	Material
A	Side rail	8	¾"	1"	69"	Red oak or pine
B	Top and bottom rail	8	¾"	1½"	14"	Red oak or pine
C	Fabric rod	8	¼" dia.	—	14"	Hardwood dowel
D	Fabric panel	4	—	12"	66"	Fabric of choice

Tools and materials: Table saw or radial arm saw or circular saw with rip or combination blade and dado blade. Drill with ¹⁷⁄₆₄" and ³⁄₃₂" twist bits and guide. Sewing machine. Try square, steel tape rule, pencil. Block plane, bench plane, ½" chisel, wooden mallet. Screwdriver, nail set. Four 4" C-clamps, bar clamp, vise, mat knife. Carpenter's glue, Nos. 100 and 150 sandpaper, stain, tung oil, soft cloths. Six yd. of 48" wide fabric (more for matching repeat in pattern). Wood (see above). Six 1½" brass butt hinges with attaching screws.

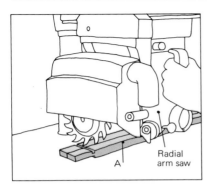

1. Cut all side rails (A) to identical 69-in. lengths. Mark a line 1½ in. from each end on all faces to indicate the tenon. Set dado blade on saw to make a cut ¼ in. deep. Make the first cut along the marked line. Move the rail and continue with enough passes to remove wood to end of rail. Turn rail over and repeat on other face.

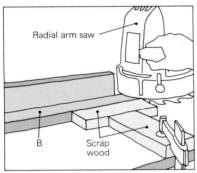

2. Make sure all top and bottom rails (B) are identical in length. Set dado blade so that it will cut a slot mortise ¼ in. wide and 1 in. deep, leaving ¼ in. of wood on either side of the slot. Protect the work from splitting by clamping an extra piece of wood against edge where blade will emerge. Cut mortises on each end of remaining top and bottom rails.

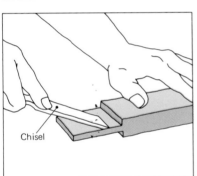

3. Smooth the tenons with a wood chisel. Use a bench plane to smooth all faces of the rails; sand them with No. 100, then No. 150 sandpaper. Pair off two side rails with a top and bottom rail; check the fit of the joints. For a tight joint chisel the tenon smooth; if a joint is loose, add a wedge of wood. Number the joints.

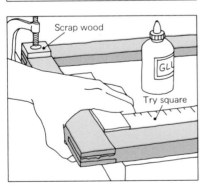

4. Clamp the four corners of a panel with C-clamps, protecting the work with scrap wood. Use a try square to check the four corners for squareness. Unclamp the top or bottom rail; apply glue on joint surfaces; reclamp and recheck for squareness. Wipe off excess glue with a damp cloth. Repeat on other end of panel.

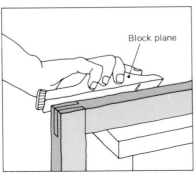

5. When the glue is dry, use a block plane to trim and smooth the joints. Plane toward the center of the work to prevent the edges from splitting. Round the edges of panels with the plane; then sand them smooth with No. 150 sandpaper. Repeat Steps 4–5 for remaining three panels.

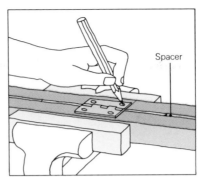

6. The hinges are mortised (sunken) into the rail by the thickness of the hinge leaf. Clamp two panels in a vise using a ¼-in.-thick scrap of wood as a spacer between them. Mark the hinge position 12 in. from end of rail. Lay hinge on line and mark the screw holes. Make starter holes with a nail set, then drill a pilot hole with a ³/₃₂-in. bit.

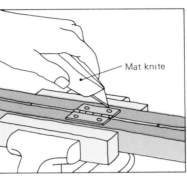

7. Temporarily attach the hinge with one screw in each leaf to hold the hinge firm. Use a sharp knife to mark and cut around the ends of the hinge. Remove the hinge and deepen the cut with a chisel, its bevel side facing the hinge area.

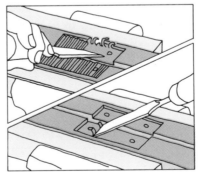

8. Holding the chisel at an angle, make a series of shallow parallel cuts close together inside the outline of the hinge. Use a wooden mallet to strike the chisel handle.

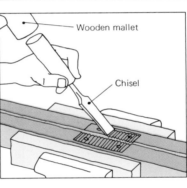

9. With the chisel's bevel facing down, remove the loosened wood. When the area is the correct depth, smooth the surface. Replace the hinge and insert all the screws. Repeat for the other five hinges. Mark dowel holes 2 in. from top and bottom of each side rail.

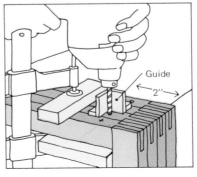

10. Use a ¹⁷/₆₄-in. twist bit to drill dowel holes in the center of each rail. Use a commercial drill guide to ensure perpendicular holes, or make a guide from four pieces of wood squared and glued as shown. To prevent wood from splitting when bit exits, clamp scrap wood to underside of rails. Make fabric panel (see text), and insert dowels through panel and holes.

237

INLAID CHECKER OR CHESS BOARD

Wood absorbs more liquid on its end grain than it does on its side grain—that is the secret of this stained oak checker or chess board, which is made of oak floor tiles. The tiles are glued together in groups of 12, with all the grain in each group running in the same direction. Each group forms one square on the inlaid board, and 64 squares are needed for a total of 768 tiles.

Oak flooring tiles are sold by commercial flooring firms for use in factories and restaurant kitchens. Four hundred tiles ⅞ x ⅞ x 5⁄16 inch are glued to a single sheet of backing paper in order to speed installation. To remove the backing paper, use a sponge to soak it with water. You will need at least two sheets of tiles in order to select 768 good ones. Discard any tiles that are chipped or cracked.

Finishing: After the board is assembled, apply the stain with a cloth or large brush. The squares with their end grain exposed will soak up more stain—and will turn darker—than those with their side grain exposed. Wipe off the. stain when the light squares have reached the shade you desire. If the contrast between light and dark squares is not great enough, you can apply more stain to the dark squares (see Step 8). Be sure to test the stain on extra tiles or on the back of the board first.

Over the years some tiles may swell and shift, but you can resand and refinish the board (Steps 5–9) if this happens.

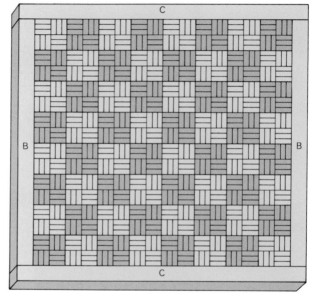

How to make the squares

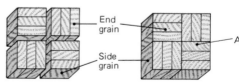

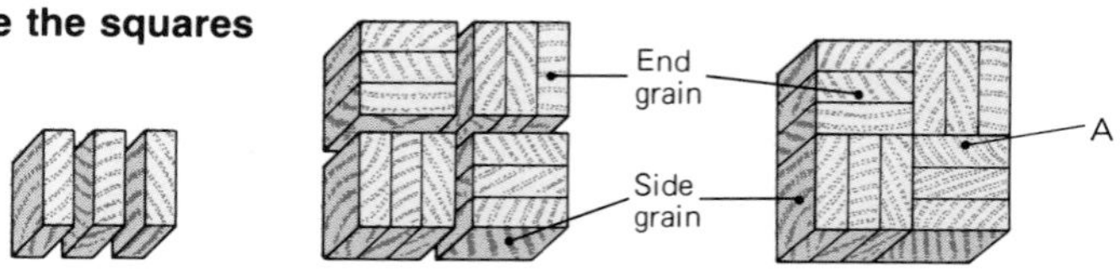

Glue floor tiles together in groups of three (left) with all the grain running in the same direction. Glue four groups of three together to form each square (center). Again, make sure that all exposed grain is the same—either all end grain (right) or all side grain.

Parts list

Part	Name	Quantity	Thickness	Width	Length	Material
A	Square	768	5⁄16″	⅞″	⅞″	Oak floor tile
B	Short frame	2	¾″	1½″	14½″ ✳	1 x 2 oak
C	Long frame	2	¾″	1½″	16″ ✳	1 x 2 oak
D	Base	1	⅜″	18″	18″	Plywood

✳ Lengths of parts B and C are approximate. Cut parts B to match the length of two opposite sides of the assembled squares. Cut parts C to match the length of each remaining side plus two thicknesses of parts B.

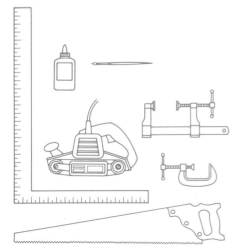

Tools and materials: Crosscut saw. Belt sander with Nos. 80 and 120 sanding belts. Two 4″ C-clamps, four 18″ pipe or bar clamps. Framing square. No. 4 artist's brush. White glue, oil stain, finishing oil, soft cloths. Two sheets of 400 oak flooring tiles, a 6′ length of 1 × 2 oak framing, a piece of ⅜″ plywood at least 18″ square.

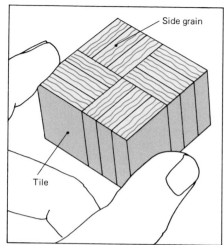

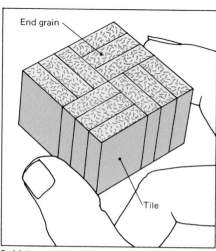

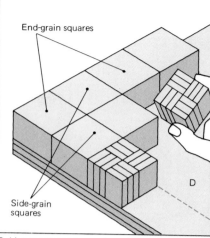

1. Make 32 squares of 12 tiles each (A), as shown on the previous page. Be sure that the side grain of each tile is exposed when the square is lying flat. Set squares aside to dry.

2. Make another 32 squares of 12 tiles each, this time with the end grain of each tile uppermost. Keep squares level and set them aside to dry. Clamping is not necessary.

3. Use a square to mark and trim one corner of plywood base (D). Starting at that corner, glue squares to base and to one another, alternating end- and side-grain squares.

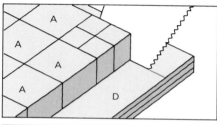

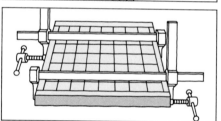

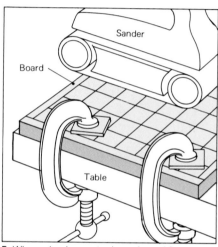

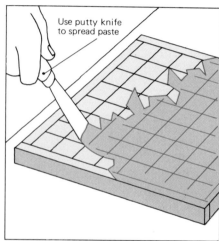

4. Press squares tightly together and let glue set. Saw off excess plywood. Cut framing (B and C) to fit board (see previous page). Glue and clamp frame flush with top of board.

5. When glue has set, clamp board face up to worktable and sand all irregularities, using No. 80, then 120 sanding belts. Sand half of board; reposition clamps, sand other half.

6. Make your own matching filler by mixing some of the sanding sawdust with white glue to form a paste. Force paste into any gaps between tiles, let it dry, and resand board.

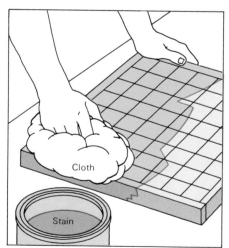

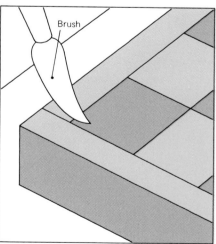

7. Apply walnut penetrating oil stain (not a thick, pasty, or opaque stain) to entire board using a paintbrush or cloth. Wipe off excess when light squares reach desired shade.

8. If dark squares are not dark enough, carefully apply more stain only to the dark squares using a No. 4 artist's brush. Wipe off excess stain when squares reach desired shade.

9. When the stain has dried, apply furniture finishing oil recommended for oak or other hardwoods. Periodically rub more oil into the surface as you would with any fine furniture.

ACRYLIC CHESS SET

These modern chessmen, made entirely of clear acrylic rod, are shaped with only small cuts, using several types of files. The cuts exploit the way acrylic transmits light, and the abstract renditions of the chess pieces are easily recognizable.

The kings, queens, bishops, knights, and rooks are all made from 1-inch clear acrylic rod cut to different lengths and filed as described on the following page. The pawns are cut from ¾-in. clear acrylic rod and are left unfiled. Their tops and the tops of the other pieces are smoothed with emery cloth and then buffed with a paste-type metal polish.

These pieces can be used with a conventional wooden chessboard or with a matching acrylic board, such as the one in this project. The light-colored squares on the black acrylic board are created by rubbing alternate squares with steel wool. It is important that you buy acrylic sheet that comes with protective paper covering. If it does not come that way, you can order it with the paper, which will only cost a bit more.

Acrylic rod is not generally available in different colors (as acrylic sheets are), so one set of chessmen must be dyed. This is done after the pieces have been carved. Because the dye will highlight the filed areas, take care when working with the acrylic that you do not make any nicks or scratches—or these will be highlighted by the dye as well. Use polish to remove any scratches.

Look in the Yellow Pages under "Plastics" for stores that sell acrylics.

   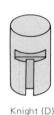  

King (A)   Queen (B)   Bishop (C)   Knight (D)   Rook (E)   Pawn (F)

Top and side views of pieces

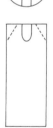 

Parts list

Part	Name	Quantity	Thickness	Width	Length	Material
A	King	2	1" dia.	—	2⅞"	Acrylic rod
B	Queen	2	1" dia.	—	2½"	Acrylic rod
C	Bishop	2✶	1" dia.	—	2¼"	Acrylic rod
D	Knight	4	1" dia.	—	2"	Acrylic rod
E	Rook	4	1" dia.	—	2"	Acrylic rod
F	Pawn	16	¾" dia.	—	1"	Acrylic rod
G	Board	1	3⁄16"	12"	12"	Acrylic sheet

✶Each piece is made into two bishops.

Tools and materials: Hacksaw, ¼" round file, 3⁄16" square file, small triangular file, flat file. Steel ruler, paper with straight edge, pencil. Mat knife or craft knife. Fine emery cloth, 000 steel wool. Saucepan. Cellophane tape. Paste-type metal polish, black dye, soft cloth. A 31" length of 1" clear acrylic rod, a 16" length of ¾" clear acrylic rod. A piece of black acrylic sheet 3⁄16" x 12" x 12" with paper covering.

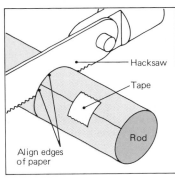

1. Using a hacksaw, cut 16 pieces 1 in. long from the ¾-in. acrylic rod. Cut two 2⅞-in. pieces, two 2½-in. pieces, two 2¼-in. pieces, and eight 2-in. pieces from the 1-in. rod. Tape a piece of paper around the rod to guide each cut; when the straight (machine-cut) edges of the paper align, they provide a guide to ensure that the cuts you make in the rod will be straight.

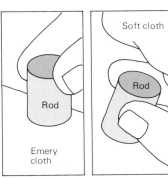

2. Rub both ends of each piece on a sheet of fine emery cloth until they are even and smooth. Place a few drops of metal polish on a soft cloth and rub one end of each piece—except the bishops (C) and the knights (D)—until you attain a high polish. The polished edges are the tops of the pieces. The pawns (F) are now finished, except for dyeing (Step 8).

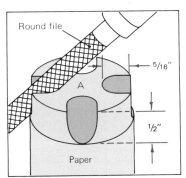

3. Tape a piece of paper ½ in. from the top of each of the two kings (A). Use a ¼-in. round file to make four equally spaced diagonal grooves ½ in. deep, starting ⁵⁄₁₆ in. from the edge of the top of each king and meeting the paper guide at the sides.

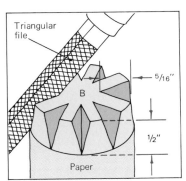

4. Tape a paper guide ½ in. from the top of each of the queens (B). Use a triangular file to cut eight diagonal notches ½ in. deep, beginning ⁵⁄₁₆ in. from the edge of the top of each queen and meeting the paper at the sides. Cut the notches in pairs, one opposite the other, to help get the spacing even.

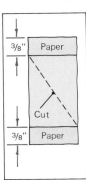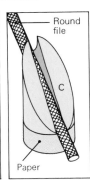

5. Tape two ⅜-in. paper guides at each end of the bishops (C). Use a hacksaw to cut diagonally between these guides, creating two identical pieces with long slanting tops. Finish the cut surfaces with emery cloth and polish (see Step 2). Then use a ¼-in. round file to cut a groove down the center of each diagonal face, tapering the depth of the cut from ⁵⁄₁₆ in. at the top to zero at the bottom.

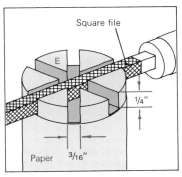

6. Tape a paper guide ⅛ in. from one end of each of the knights (D). Use a flat file to make a dome that curves down to meet the paper. Smooth and polish the dome. Attach guide ⁹⁄₁₆ in. wide below the dome. File a slit ¾ in. long along the paper guide with a ³⁄₁₆-in. square file. File a vertical slit to meet the horizontal one at its center. Do not nick the top of the horizontal slit.

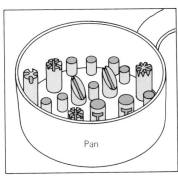

7. Tape a strip of paper to each of the four rooks (E) ¼ in. from the top. Use a ³⁄₁₆-in. square file to cut three grooves straight across the top of each rook, 60° apart, to a depth of ¼ in.

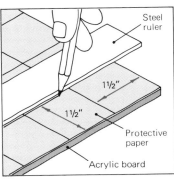

8. Place one set (16 chessmen) upright in a saucepan and mix enough black dye so that it will cover them entirely. (Smooth and polish any nicks on unfiled surfaces of the men first; otherwise, dye will highlight them, as it will surfaces you have filed.) Pour the dye into the pan without knocking over any of the pieces, and simmer for about 10 min. Wash and polish the pieces once they have cooled.

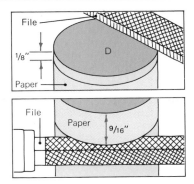

9. With a steel ruler and pencil mark the protective paper on the chessboard (G) every 1½ in. along all four edges. Lay the ruler across the board to connect opposite marks, and cut the paper along the ruler with a mat knife or a craft knife. When you have cut all the rows, you will have a grid made up of 64 squares.

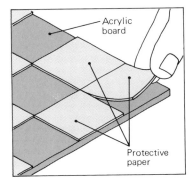

10. Peel the paper off every other square. Rub the exposed squares with steel wool until you attain a mat finish that you can easily distinguish from the shiny black squares. Remove remaining paper and wash board with soap and water.

PICTURE FRAME

The practical purpose for framing a picture is to protect it; esthetically, the frame serves to set the picture apart and to enhance its unique qualities. A work on paper—such as a watercolor or the print for which the frame in this project was made—needs a different kind of protection than does a painting on canvas.

A canvas painting, whether oil or acrylic, must breathe, so it should not be covered by glass; and because stretched canvas is subject to distortion over the years, the frame should be substantial. On the other hand, a work on paper should be protected by glass or a lightweight substitute. The glass must not touch the paper, however, so a mat is used as a spacer; the mat also serves as a frame within the frame.

Molding: Frame molding must be rabbeted on the back, making a channel just deep enough to accommodate the picture, backing board, mat, and glass. You can purchase molding with a precut rabbet from framing shops and some lumberyards. You can also buy standard molding from almost any lumberyard and rabbet it yourself, either by cutting into the back or by gluing an extra thickness of wood onto the back. In any case, be sure the rabbet is the proper depth for your needs. The best way to decide which molding looks best with your picture is to take the picture with you when you shop.

There is a standard formula for determining how much molding you need: double the length and width of the picture or mat, add eight times the width of the molding, and throw in an extra foot or two for waste. If you are less than expert with a miter box, buy twice this amount.

The frame in this project was made for a print mounted behind an 11- x 14-inch mat and covered with glass of the same dimensions. After the picture was attached to the backing board (Step 9), the board and picture, together with the mat and glass, were secured into the rabbet with glazier's push points gently hammered into the frame. The back was sealed against moisture and dust with a sheet of brown paper taped to the back of the frame. Mat, backing board, masking tape, and most other materials can be found in artists' supply shops. Buy the glass, cut to the exact size you need, from a glass shop; be sure to specify picture glass, which is lighter than window glass. Nonreflective glass, though expensive, eliminates annoying glare.

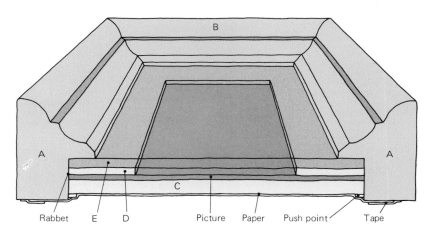

Rabbet E D Picture Paper Push point Tape

Parts list

Part	Name	Quantity	Thickness	Width	Length	Material
A	Side	2	1¼″	1¾″	16¾″ ✻	Basswood frame molding
B	End	2	1¼″	1¾″	13⅝″ ✻	Basswood frame molding
C	Backing board	1	1/16″	11″	14″	4-ply museum mount board
D	Mat	1	1/16″	11″	14″	Mat board
E	Glass	1	1/16″	11″	14″	Picture glass

✻ Measurement is approximate; cut to fit during construction.

Tools and materials: Backsaw, miter box. Combination square, framing square, nail set. Hammer. Two corner clamps. Scissors, mat knife, putty knife, bevel cutter. Sanding block, 1″ paintbrush. White glue, wood filler. Nos. 100 and 150 sandpaper. Glazier's push points. Brown paper, 1″ masking tape, 1″ linen framing tape. White antiquing base, red antiquing base, brown antiquing glaze. A 7′ length basswood frame molding. A 1/16″ x 11″ x 14″ piece 4-ply museum mount board. A 1/16″ x 11″ x 14″ piece mat board. A 1/16″ x 11″ x 14″ piece 16-oz. picture glass. One-inch No. 18 brads.

Making the frame

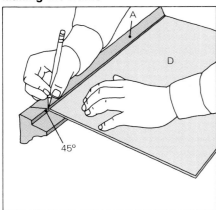

1. To cut a side piece (A), first saw 45° angle on one end of rabbeted molding strip. Place side of mat in rabbet, its corner flush with sawed end. Mark opposite corner at base of rabbet. Scribe complementary 45° angle across molding at that point.

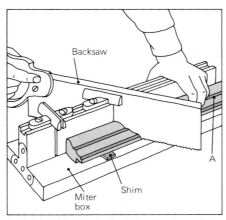

2. Hold molding strip firmly in miter box with a shim below lip to maintain square position, and cut 45° angle making side piece ¹⁄₁₆ in. longer than marked. Repeat Step 1, measuring against end of mat, and cut an end piece (B) in same way. Check joint with square.

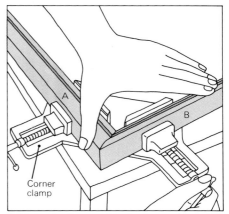

3. Make duplicates of both pieces. Assemble one L-shaped half of frame by applying glue to both faces of miter joint and positioning pieces face up in corner clamp. Adjust both pieces carefully to achieve perfect alignment, and tighten clamps.

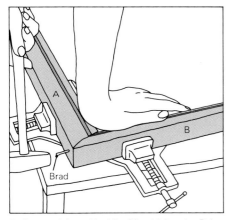

4. Secure joint with 1-in. No. 18 brads. Drive one or two brads from each side, depending on the size of the molding. Be sure nails do not interfere with each other. Set heads. Use another corner clamp to assemble the opposite L-shaped half of frame in the same way.

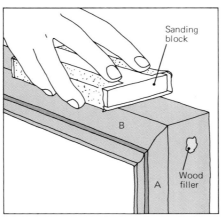

5. When glue dries, remove clamps and use them to join the two L-shaped halves, gluing and nailing each corner as in Steps 3 and 4. Fill holes left by nailheads. After glue is dry, remove clamps and sand frame by hand, using No. 100 and then No. 150 sandpaper.

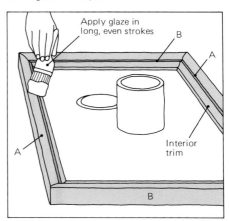

6. Apply desired finish. This frame was antiqued with a base coat of white on the entire frame, followed when dry by a coat of red antiquing base on the interior trim. After base coats dried, a warm brown antiquing glaze was brushed over the surface.

Making the mat

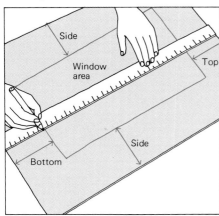

7. With framing square and mat knife, cut mat (D) and backing board (C) the same size as glass (E). On back of mat, rule outline of window through which picture will show; it should be centered from side to side, but the bottom border should be ½ in. wider than the top.

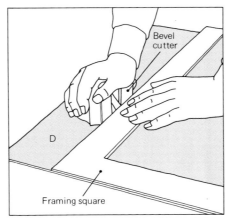

8. Using framing square as guide, cut along outline with a bevel cutter so that the bevel slopes inward from the front, showing thickness of mat when framing is complete. Finish cutting corners with mat knife. Trace outline of window on backing board.

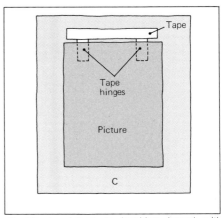

9. Attach picture to backing board with "hinges" of framing tape. First, moisten two strips of tape and apply them to back of picture so that they project an inch above the top; then position picture on backing board and secure both flaps with a single strip of tape.

CHINESE BOXES WALL UNIT

Boxes within boxes make a striking wall unit that can be equally useful and attractive as a room divider. However you use it, it should be secured to the wall or ceiling in at least two places. The unit in this project is held in place by two keyhole plates located near the top of the second largest box. To install the unit as a room divider, attach one side directly to the wall and secure the opposite corner to a ceiling joist or to an upright tension pole.

The unit shown here is 7 feet 11½ inches square and rests on a 1½-inch base, placing the top shelf less than 1 inch from the ceiling of this room. Make adjustments, either in the height of the base or in the measurements of the unit itself, to fit your room. This unit was built from 1 x 12 clear white pine, a relatively inexpensive wood, and painted to match the black-

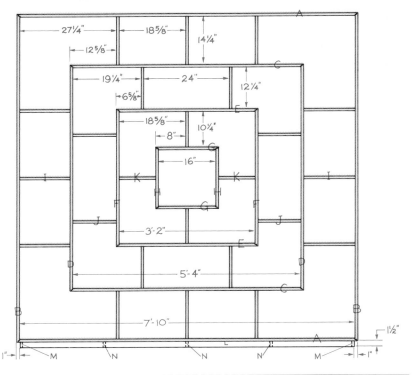

Parts list

Part	Name	Quantity	Thickness	Width	Length	Material
A	Box 1 shelf	2	¾"	11¼"	7' 10¾"	1 x 12 clear pine
B	Box 1 side	2	¾"	11¼"	7' 11½"	1 x 12 clear pine
C	Box 2 shelf	2	¾"	11¼"	5' 4¾"	1 x 12 clear pine
D	Box 2 side	2	¾"	11¼"	5' 5½"	1 x 12 clear pine
E	Box 3 shelf	2	¾"	11¼"	3' 2¾"	1 x 12 clear pine
F	Box 3 side	2	¾"	11¼"	3' 3½"	1 x 12 clear pine
G	Box 4 shelf	2	¾"	11¼"	1' 4¾"	1 x 12 clear pine
H	Box 4 side	2	¾"	11¼"	1' 5½"	1 x 12 clear pine
I	Outer spacer	12	¾"	11¼"	1' 2¾" ✳	1 x 12 clear pine
J	Middle spacer	8	¾"	11¼"	1' ¾" ✳	1 x 12 clear pine
K	Inner spacer	4	¾"	11¼"	10¾" ✳	1 x 12 clear pine
L	Front and back of base	2	¾"	1½"	7' 9½"	1 x 2 clear pine
M	End of base	2	¾"	1½"	10"	1 x 2 clear pine
N	Base spacer	3	¾"	1½"	9¼" ✳	1 x 2 clear pine

✳ Measurements are approximate. Parts I, J, K, and N should be cut to fit within the dadoes.

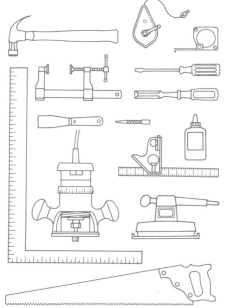

Tools and materials: Router with ¾" single flute straight bit and ⅜" rabbeting bit. Orbital sander. Circular saw or handsaw, backsaw. Two or more 8' bar or pipe clamps. Chalk line, framing square, combination square, steel tape rule, ruler. Hammer, nail set, screwdriver, ¾" straight chisel, putty knife. Wood filler, white glue. Nos. 100 and 150 sandpaper. Paint, stain, or other finishing material. Fifteen 8' lengths of 1 x 12 pine, three 8' lenghts of 1 x 2 pine. Keyhole plates or other hardware for attaching bookcase to wall or ceiling, 4d finishing nails.

and-white room decor. It could just as easily—though more expensively—be made from hardwood and finished to match the floor, the woodwork, or a furniture piece in the room. The baseboard was cut away from the wall and the base of the unit set flush with the back of the bottom shelf so that the unit sits against the wall. You might prefer to match the height of the base to the height of the baseboard and allow the shelf to overhang the base in back as it does in front in order to clear the baseboard. It would then be possible to extend the baseboard around the unit with matching pieces.

Construction: The corners of all four boxes are made with double rabbet joints, reinforced with 4d finishing nails. The spacers between the boxes are fitted into blind dadoes; each dado stops ¾ inch from the front of the board, and each spacer is notched so that the front edges will be flush. The unit is assembled face down on the floor, one box at a time, beginning with the center box. The boxes are joined with spacers, then swung upright and lifted onto the base. In order to clear the ceiling while being raised, the unit (minus its base) must be at least 2 inches shorter than the room height.

Dado patterns

Cut all lumber to length except the spacers; these will be cut to fit as the unit is assembled. Before marking the dadoes, choose the front edge for each board and rule a line ¾ in. back along both faces; all dadoes will end at these lines. Use the patterns above to measure the dadoes and rabbets; mark with a combination square. (Note that the boards for Boxes 2 and 3 are dadoed on both sides.) All dadoes are ¼ in. deep and ¾ in. wide; rabbets are ⅜ in. x ⅜ in. (For instructions on cutting dadoes and rabbets with a router, see *Index*, p.379.)

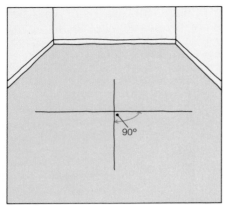

1. Begin by making a pattern on the floor to guide assembly of boxes: use a chalk line to make two perpendicular lines, each 11½ ft. long, intersecting in the center to form a large X. After the lumber for the boxes is cut, dadoed, and rabbeted, assemble the boxes dry (without glue) so that their corners are on these lines. Be sure all corners are square.

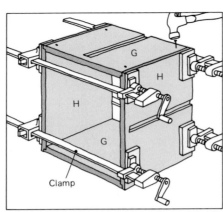

2. Begin final assembly with the inner box (4). Apply glue to the rabbets on both ends of top shelf (G) and place them into the rabbets on sides (H). Apply a clamp across the shelf, securing both sides. Then do the same with the bottom shelf. Secure by driving 4d finishing nails through the sides; set heads. (To avoid splitting wood, blunt tips of nails.)

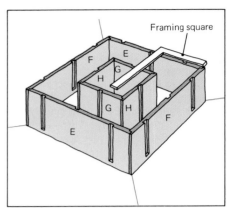

3. Place Box 4 face down on the floor, forcing the corners into alignment with the chalked X if necessary. Glue, assemble, and nail Box 3 together in the same way and align its corners with the X. Use a framing square to be sure the dadoes on Boxes 3 and 4 are exactly aligned. Then measure and cut all the inner spacers (K) to the same size.

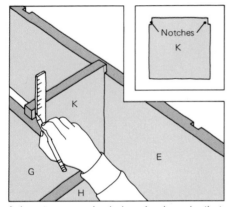

4. Insert spacers in dadoes backward—that is, with the front edge up—and use a ruler to mark notches on the protruding corners. Remove spacers one at a time to cut the notches with a backsaw.(For safety's sake, cut just inside the lines, then trim with a straight chisel for exact fit.) Replace each spacer frontward before going to the next.

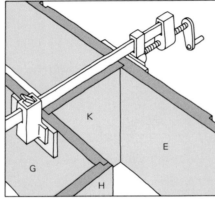

5. When all the spacers have been notched and reversed, begin gluing. Once again, remove the spacers one at a time; apply glue to both dadoes (the edges as well as the bottoms) and replace each spacer. Apply a clamp, making sure that as you tighten it the square is maintained. Then go on to the next inner spacer.

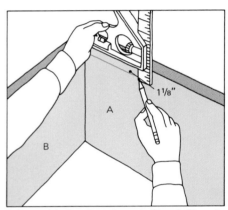

6. Assemble Box 2 as shown in Step 2. Place it face down, its corners aligned with the X; then cut, fit, and glue the middle spacers (J) as indicated in Steps 3–5. Before repeating the process with Box 1 and the outer spacers (I), rule a line on the upper face of the bottom shelf 1⅛ in. from its front edge to serve as a guide for nailing into the base.

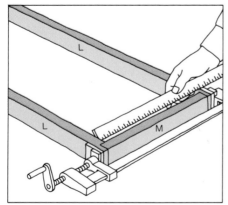

7. Glue the ends of the base (M) into the rabbets of the front and back pieces (L) and apply a clamp across each end. Drive 4d finishing nails through the ends into the front and back pieces. Measure the interior distance across the ends and cut spacers (N) to match. Glue and nail them at equidistant intervals; set all nailheads.

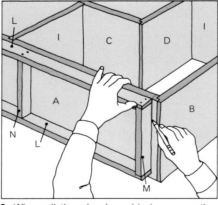

8. When all the glue has dried, remove the clamps. Trace the outline of the base on the underside of the bottom shelf flush with the back edge. At both ends of base, extend markings onto back edge. Attach hardware to wall unit at appropriate places for securing it to wall or ceiling. Then, with the aid of a helper, stand unit upright.

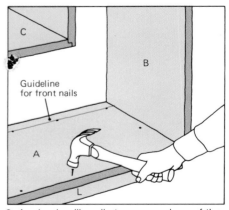

9. Apply glue liberally to upper edges of the base and lift the shelf unit onto it, making sure the ends of the base align with the marks on the back of the bottom shelf. Drive 4d finishing nails through bottom shelf into base; set heads. Fill all nail holes and sand all surfaces with No. 100, then No. 150 sandpaper. Paint or finish the unit.

PICNIC OR PATIO TABLE

Nothing could be better for those family get-togethers on warm, sunny days than this octagonal table with its four matching benches. Not only does the set have a distinctive design, but it is also solidly constructed, durable, and convenient. It seats up to eight people and has plenty of extra room in the center to accommodate serving dishes and decorations.

The four benches, each of which seats two adults comfortably, are angled to reflect the table's octagonal design. They are extremely sturdy and have none of the disadvantages of the traditional long benches made to seat three or four. These benches are easy to move, and when they are pulled back slightly from the table, there is enough space between them for diners to maneuver without disturbing one another.

Although the table is unusually large, it can be knocked down for ease of handling—if you move or if you want to store it for the winter—by simply taking out the bolts that anchor the legs and braces to the table supports.

Lumber and hardware: The table and benches should be built of either construction-grade cedar, as indicated below, or redwood. Both woods, while relatively expensive, are highly resistant to pests, rot, and foul weather. If you use any other softwood, make sure it is treated to prevent rot and pest damage.

In order to have enough wood to build the table and benches, you will need nine 10-foot 2 x 6's, one 14-foot 2 x 4, eleven 8-foot 2 x 3's, and one 14-foot 2 x 3. Be sure to cut the two outside table supports (E in the chart below) from the 14-foot 2 x 3, and cut the bench supports (H) and the bench-leg braces (I) from four of the 8-foot 2 x 3's—that is, cut four supports and

four braces from each length. To prevent rust, use solid brass, stainless steel, or coated or galvanized hardware.

Construction: The table and benches are designed with a rough look for the outdoors. A rough look, however, does not imply rough or careless construction. Accuracy in measuring and cutting is extremely important. Once you have laid out the boards for the table top and secured them, you must carefully square the top and scribe out the octagonal shape in order to make the eight sides equal in length. You must also be careful to get the correct angles in the benches and in the legs, leg braces, and lap joints. Directions are given for making the lap joints—the cutout portions of the legs that enable you to fit them together into X shapes—with a backsaw and chisel. (For making lap joints by other methods, see *Index,* p.379.)

Be careful when drilling pilot and clearance holes for screws and bolts. Remember that you are working with wood that is very soft. Avoid drilling beyond the depths indicated. To facilitate drilling into the table-leg and bench-leg braces in Steps 19 and 27, start drilling at an angle of 90° to the brace and then, once the drill has penetrated the wood, change the angle and drill straight down.

The table and benches need not be stained, merely sanded and brushed with a clear weatherproofing finish. If you prefer to stain the set, use a clear oil stain. Do not use a paintlike opaque "redwood" stain on expensive cedar or redwood—it will hide the wood's lovely grain. Opaque stains can be applied to hide the greenish tint of chemically treated lumber. Test any stain on a piece of scrap wood before you apply it to the table and benches.

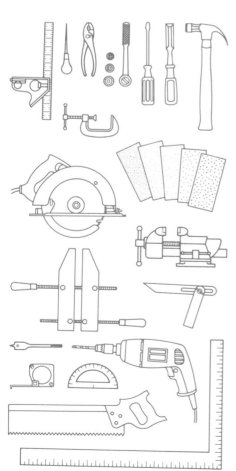

Parts list

Part	Name	Quantity	Thickness	Width	Length	Material
A	Table-top slat	10	1½"	5½"	60"	2 x 6 cedar
B	Bench slat	16	1½"	5½"	30"	2 x 6 cedar
C	Table leg	4	1½"	3½"	40"	2 x 4 cedar
D	Center table support	2	1½"	2½"	56"	2 x 3 cedar
E	Outside table support	2	1½"	2½"	24"	2 x 3 cedar
F	Table-leg brace	2	1½"	2½"	24"	2 x 3 cedar
G	Bench leg	24	1½"	2½"	21"	2 x 3 cedar
H	Bench support	16	1½"	2½"	12"	2 x 3 cedar
I	Bench-leg brace	16	1½"	2½"	13"	2 x 3 cedar

Tools and materials: Drill with extra-long twist bits and ⅞" spade bit. Circular saw, backsaw. Framing square, combination square, T bevel, protractor, steel tape rule. Hammer, screwdriver, awl. Pliers, socket wrench, broad chisel. Vise, two 4" C-clamps, a 12" adjustable hand screw. No. 80 sandpaper, weatherproofing wood finish (available at most lumberyards).

Construction-grade cedar or redwood (see above), three 2 x 3 scrap pieces 60" long, ¼" plywood scraps. Solid brass, stainless steel, or coated or galvanized hardware, including one hundred and twenty-four 2½" No. 10 flathead wood screws, forty 3" stove bolts ¼"-20 with 40 nuts and 80 washers, sixteen 5" stove bolts ¼"-20 with 16 nuts and 32 washers. Nails.

Table construction

Letters refer to parts
in chart on page 247

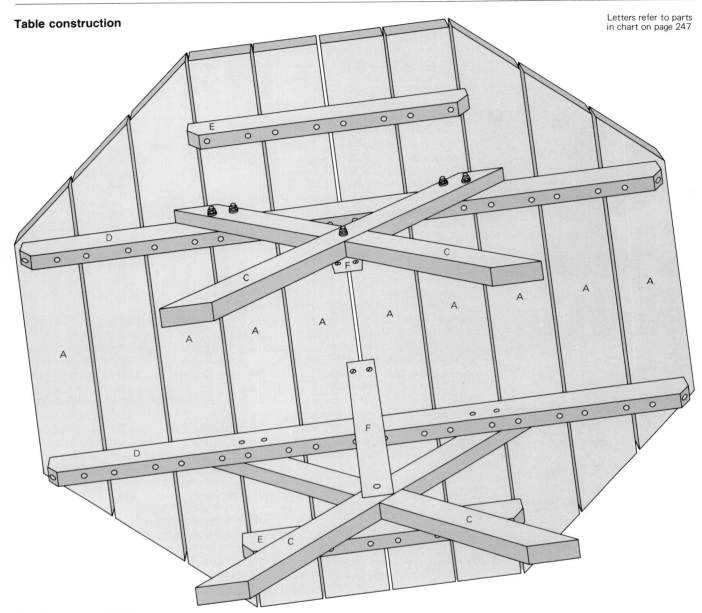

Bench-support details

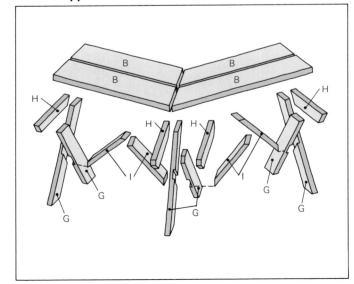

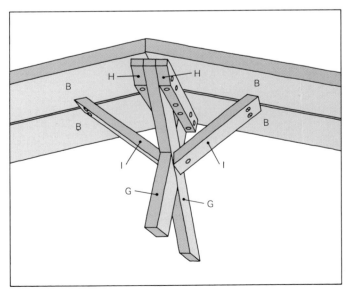

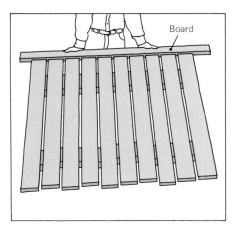

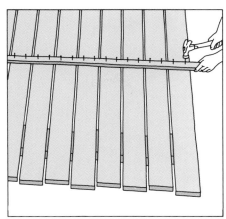

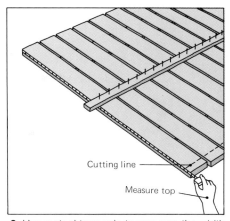

1. Cut all lumber to specifications given in the chart on page 247. Put table-top slats (A) in position on a flat surface, inserting spacers of ¼-in. plywood scraps between slats. Use two spacers per slat about 1 ft. from each end. Align the slats by pushing against one side of the table top with a board.

2. Place a piece of scrap wood for a temporary support across the center of the table top and nail it to each slat, in turn, drawing the slats tightly against the spacers before nailing. Nail securely, but do not drive the nails all the way into or through the table top, since you will have to remove them later.

3. Use a steel tape rule to measure the width of the table top parallel to the scrap support. Measure the table top in the opposite direction to determine how much to cut from each end to make the table top perfectly square. Draw cutting lines to form a square. Then lay out an octagon within this square (Step 4).

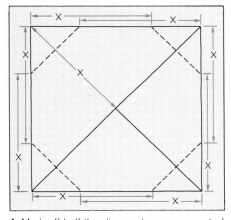

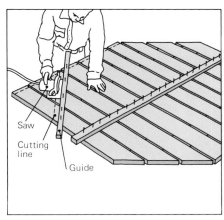

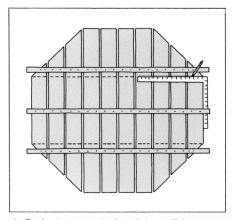

4. Mark off half the diagonal measurement of the square (shown as X) in both directions from each corner. You will have eight marks in all. Connect these marks by drawing straight lines (indicated by dotted lines) across the corners of the square to mark the eight sides of the octagonal table top.

5. Use a circular saw to cut off the corners and then the edges of the table top that protrude outside the cutting lines to form an octagon. Nail down a strip of wood to act as a cutting guide, but be sure to allow for the distance between the saw's baseplate and blade when positioning the cutting guide.

6. To further steady the slats, nail two more temporary supports across the table top just outside the angles of the octagon. Using a framing square, mark positions for permanent center table supports (D) by drawing a line parallel to each new temporary support and connecting outer angles of octagon.

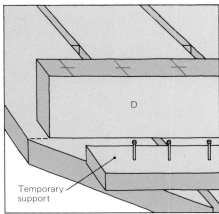

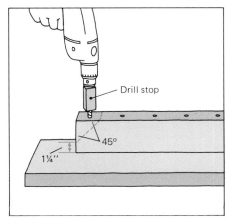

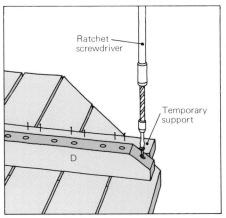

7. Position the permanent supports along the insides of the lines. Mark each support for screw holes—two for each table-top slat (A) 1 in. in from the edges of each slat. Remove the supports from the table top. Start the holes with an awl, then drill completely through the supports with a 7/32-in. drill bit.

8. Counterdrill (drill into holes made in Step 7) 1-in.-deep recesses for screws using a ⅜-in. bit. Make a drill stop with scrap wood to keep the drilling depth uniform. With a protractor and pencil, measure and mark off 45° angles 1¼ in. from the bottoms of the supports, and cut the bevels as shown.

9. Attach supports with 2½-in. screws using a hand or spiral ratchet screwdriver. If you use a variable-speed drill with a screwdriver attachment, proceed slowly or wood may split. Remove all temporary supports and spacers. Mark, drill, and bevel, but do not attach outside table supports (E).

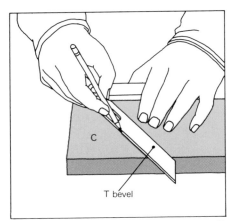

10. Set the T bevel to a 50° angle. Place the T bevel against one end of each table leg (C), in turn, and mark off the angle for a 50° bevel. Cut bevels with a circular saw. Cross two legs 19¹³/₁₆ in. below their tops, with their bevels facing in opposite directions, and join them with a single nail.

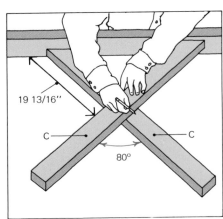

11. Butt the bevel-cut ends of the legs against a flat surface to get the correct (80°) angle for the lap joint. Mark one leg, then turn the assembly over and mark the other leg. Separate the legs and extend the marks around the legs using a combination square. Mark each lap for a ¾-in. depth.

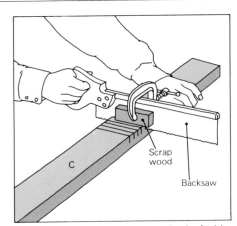

12. Repeat Step 11 on the second pair of table legs. Clamp a length of scrap wood to the backsaw blade exactly ¾ in. from its cutting edge to act as a depth gauge. Make a series of ¾-in.-deep parallel saw cuts on each table leg between the lines marked in Step 11. The cuts should be made about ¾ in. apart.

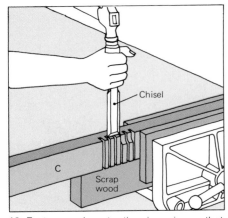

13. Fasten one leg at a time in a vise so that the lap cuts rest on a thick piece of scrap wood. Chisel out waste wood from the lap joint using the widest possible chisel and cutting away only a little wood at a time. Keep the beveled edge of the chisel facing the waste to be cut away.

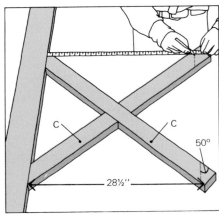

14. Fit the lap joints of one pair of legs together and place the bevel-cut ends of the legs against a flat surface. Measure and mark off points 28½ in. from the tops of the legs. Mark off and cut 50° bevels at these marks as in Step 10. Measure other two legs against first pair and cut bevels in them.

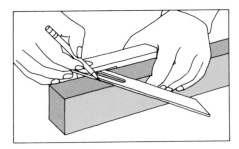

15. Using a protractor and T bevel, mark off a 55° angle on one end of one table-leg brace (F) for a bevel cut. Mark off a 35° angle on the other end so that when cut the longest side of the brace will be 18⅞ in. Cut both bevels. Mark off the second brace on the first and cut bevels into it.

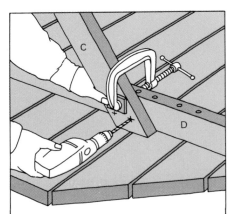

16. Clamp the legs (C) into place on the outside of the center table supports (D), making sure they are centered. With a ¹³/₆₄-in. drill bit, bore two holes in each leg 1½ in. from the table top, being careful to avoid screws already in the supports. Drill through the entire thickness of the legs and supports.

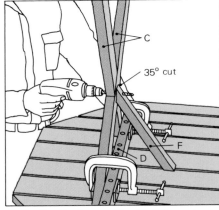

17. Position the braces (F) with 35° bevel cuts against the legs. Drill single holes through the braces and lap joints with a ¹³/₆₄-in. drill bit. Counterbore ½ in. into all holes on the inner sides of the supports and in the braces with a spade bit slightly larger than the washers. Complete the holes with a ¼-in. drill bit.

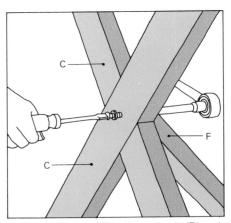

18. Fasten the legs (C) to the supports (D) and braces (F) with bolts, nuts, and a washer on each side of the wood to keep the bolts from working into the wood. Tighten nuts as firmly as possible with wrench while holding the bolts with a screwdriver. If bolts are not tight, they may work loose when table is used.

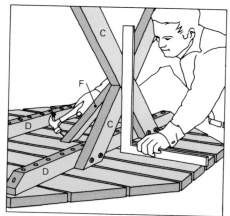

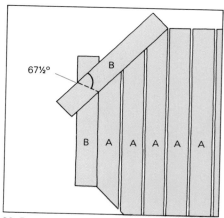

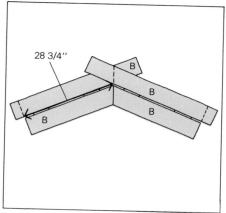

19. Make sure that the table legs are perpendicular to table top, then temporarily nail braces to top. Drill two pilot holes through each brace and ½ in. into top with ³⁄₁₆-in. bit. Counterbore holes ½ in. deep with a ½-in. bit. Screw down the braces and remove the nails. Attach outside supports (E).

20. Begin the benches by placing two bench slats (B) flush against the table top with the end of one slat overlapping the end of the other slat. The opposite ends of the slats must be even with the corners of the top. Mark the points where the slats overlap, draw a line connecting the marks, and cut the bevels.

21. Line up two more slats behind the beveled slats, mark them, and cut new slats to exactly the same angle. Position the four slats with ¼-in. plywood spacers between the front and back slats. Cut off the outer edges of the slats straight and square. Use these slats as patterns for the other 12.

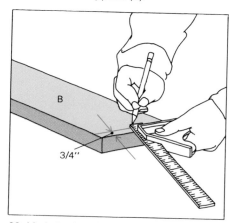

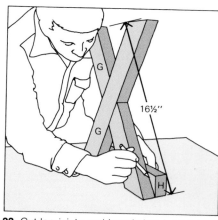

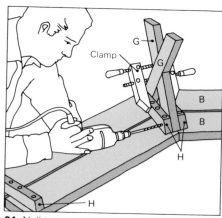

22. Mark the location for the bench supports (H) by drawing rules exactly ¾ in. in from each end of each bench slat (B). Measure carefully, since the center legs must fit snugly between the center supports. Mark and drill screw holes in the bench supports as you did in the table supports (Steps 7–8).

23. Cut lap joints and bevels into bench legs (G), as you did for table legs (Steps 10–14), but nail legs together at midpoint, and mark off and cut bevels at bottoms of legs only 16½ in. from their tops. Line up bench legs against supports. Mark parts of supports that protrude beyond legs and cut them off.

24. Nail temporary scrap-wood supports into the bench slats, screw the permanent supports into place, then remove the temporary supports. Clamp the bench sections together. Insert the legs between the inner supports, and drill through the legs and supports with a ¼-in. drill bit. You need not counterbore.

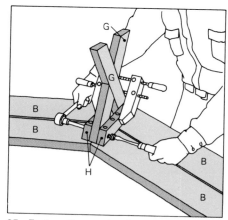

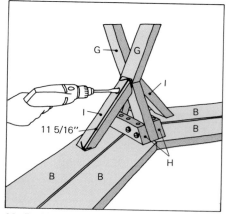

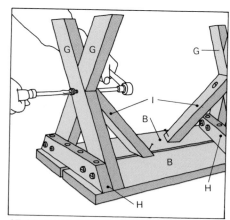

25. Fasten the center legs and supports together with 5-in.-long ¼-in. bolts, nuts, and washers (one washer on each side of the wood). Cut bevels on all bench-leg braces (I), as you did for the table-leg braces (Step 15), but cut them so that the longest sides of the finished braces are only 11⁵⁄₁₆ in.

26. Position one brace on each side of the center leg and mark for a bolt hole at the thickest part of the assembly. Bore through assembly with a ¼-in. drill bit. Counterbore either side with a spade bit to a ½-in. depth. Insert a bolt with a washer through the counterbored side. Fasten with a second washer and nut.

27. Mark and drill holes into the side legs and braces and fasten the side legs to the braces, as was done in Steps 17–18, but fasten the legs to the insides of the braces. Fasten all bench-leg braces to the bench slats as in Step 19. Sand the table and benches with No. 80 sandpaper and apply the finish.

OUTDOOR TABLE AND BENCH

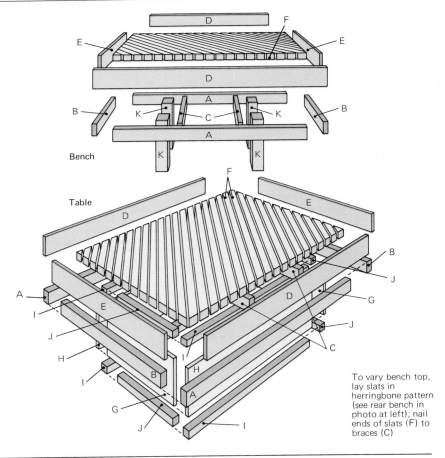

To vary bench top, lay slats in herringbone pattern (see rear bench in photo at left); nail ends of slats (F) to braces (C)

Parts list for table

Part	Name	Quantity	Thickness	Width	Length	Material
A	Side	2	1½"	3½"	48"	2 × 4 pine
B	End	2	1½"	3½"	30"	2 × 4 pine
C	Brace	2	1½"	3½"	30"	2 × 4 pine
D	Side trim	2	¾"	5½"	49½"	1 × 6 pine
E	End trim	2	¾"	5½"	33"	1 × 6 pine
F	Top slat	✷	1½"	1½"	✷	2 × 2 pine
G	Base end	2	¾"	11¼"	20"	1 × 12 pine
H	Base side	2	¾"	11¼"	35"	1 × 12 pine
I	Side base support	4	1½"	1½"	33½"	2 × 2 pine
J	End base support	4	1½"	1½"	18½"	2 × 2 pine

Parts list for bench

Part	Name	Quantity	Thickness	Width	Length	Material
A	Side	2	1½"	3½"	48"	2 × 4 pine
B	End	2	1½"	3½"	17½"	2 × 4 pine
C	Brace	2	1½"	3½"	17½"	2 × 4 pine
D	Side trim	2	¾"	5½"	49½"	1 × 6 pine
E	End trim	2	¾"	5½"	20½"	1 × 6 pine
F	Top slat	✷	1½"	1½"	✷	2 × 2 pine
K	Leg	4	3½"	3½"	15"	4 × 4 pine

✷To be determined during construction.

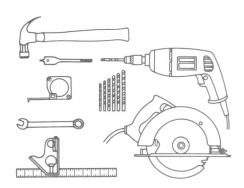

Tools and materials: Circular saw with combination blade. Drill with 1" spade bit, ⅜" and 3/16" twist bits. Hammer, ½" wrench. Combination square, steel tape rule, pencil. Wood stain. *For table,* pine in following amounts: thirteen 10' 2 × 2's, two 10' 2 × 4's, one 10' 1 × 12, two 8' 1 × 6's.

16d galvanized common nails, 8d and 16d galvanized finishing nails. *For bench,* pine in following amounts: seven 10' 2 × 2's, two 8' 2 × 4's, one 12' 1 × 6, one 6' 4 × 4. 16d galvanized common nails, 8d galvanized finishing nails, eight ⅜" lag screws 3" long, eight washers.

Easily made by the novice woodworker, this outdoor table and bench are ideal for the patio or deck. The table is 49½ inches long by 34½ inches wide and stands 16½ inches high. The bench is the same length and height but only 22 inches wide.

The frames and tops of the bench and table are similar, but the bases differ. Lag screws are used to hold the 4 × 4 bench legs in place; the outside lag screws are covered by the side trim and must therefore be recessed to lie flush with the sides. The table, however, rests on a base of 1 × 12 boards supported by two rectangles of 2 × 2's. One rectangle is nailed to the base; the other is mounted on the table framework, allowing easy removal of the base for winter storage.

The lumber should preferably be pressure treated with a preservative to withstand exposure, then protected with a top-quality latex or oil stain.

Construction: Cut the lumber to the lengths in the chart. Assemble the bench and table framework in the same way (Step 1). Then attach the bench legs (Steps 2–4). Next, cut the top slats slightly oversize as you install them at a 45° angle, and trim them all at once (Steps 5–9). Finally, add the table base (Steps 10–12).

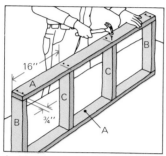

1. Mark center lines for ends (B) and braces (C) onto the sides (A) ¾ in. and 16 in. from each edge. Drive two 16d common nails nearly through the sides on each line. Position the ends, then drive the nails home. Do the same with the braces.

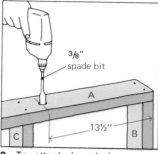

2. To attach bench legs, use spade bit to make two recesses in each side just deep enough for the lag screw heads and the washers. Center each recess 13½ in. from each end of the sides. Drill through the center of each recess with a ⅜-in. bit.

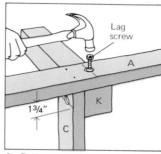

3. Drill ⅜-in holes in each brace (C) 1¾ in. from each end and below center (so that lag screws will not collide). Put screws in side holes, position legs (K), and tap screws with hammer to mark legs. Drill ³⁄₁₆-in. pilot holes in the legs where marked.

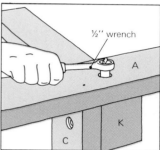

4. Temporarily attach legs by tightening screws through sides just a few turns. Drill through holes in braces with ⅜-in. bit to mark legs. Remove legs and drill ³⁄₁₆-in. pilot holes. Reattach legs with lag screws and washers. Tighten screws fully.

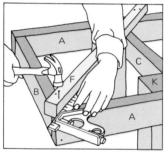

5. Cut 9 slats 48 in. long for table and 13 slats 32 in. long for bench. Use combination square to draw a 45° angle at corner of frame. Align one slat (F) with line. Check that the other end crosses frame at 45°. Nail each end of slat with two 8d finishing nails.

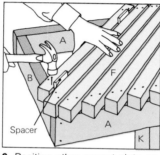

6. Position other precut slats on frame, using a spacer of ¼-in. plywood. Check to be sure that slats all cross the frame at 45°. After nailing all precut slats, cut the remaining 2 × 2's slightly oversize and nail them to the frame in the same manner.

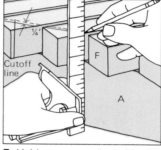

7. Hold square against side (A) with its ruler between slats. Mark each slat where the ruler touches it. Repeat this procedure across both ends (B) and the other side. Connect the marks with a straight line. Draw cutoff lines ¼ in. inside the first lines.

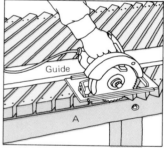

8. Measure the distance from the circular saw blade to edge of saw's base. Draw a third line that distance from one of the cutoff lines. Temporarily nail a straight board along this line. Use this board as a guide and cut off ends of slats in a single pass.

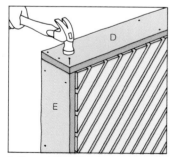

9. Repeat Step 8 on each edge of table and bench. Remove cutting guide and attach side trim (D) and end trim (E) with 8d finishing nails. The top edge of all trim boards must be flush with the upper surface of the 2 x 2 slats on the table and the bench.

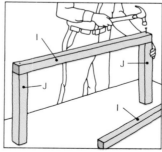

10. Join the side and end base supports (I and J) to form two rectangles. Nail them together with 16d common nails, butting end base supports against side base supports. Check rectangles for squareness (see *Index*, p.379); adjust with hands.

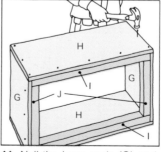

11. Nail the base ends (G) and the base sides (H) onto one rectangle with 8d finishing nails. Make sure that the edges of the ends and the sides fit flush with the rectangle. Drive the finishing nails along the edges of the sides into the ends.

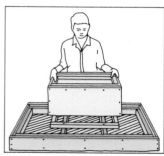

12. Center the other rectangle over the frame on the underside of the table. Nail through the rectangle and into the braces with 16d finishing nails. The base fits over this rectangle but is not nailed to it; so it comes apart easily for moving.

OUTDOOR LIGHTING FIXTURE

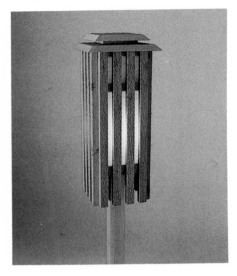

An outdoor lighting fixture must be weather resistant if it is to last. The simple and attractive lantern shown here meets this test. It is built from durable cedar, and its light chamber is enclosed by plastic diffusion panels that are firmly set, top and bottom, into ⅛-inch rabbets. Waterproof glue is used on all joints except those between the center supports and the slats (so a center support can be removed if necessary to replace a panel), and the heads of the 3d finishing nails that secure all joints are set and covered with waterproof wood filler. The porcelain light socket is designed for safe outdoor use.

Construction: With careful planning all wood parts can be cut from a single 1 x 12 board 6 feet long. First, saw two 6¼-inch pieces from one end; from these make the two base pieces (A), the insert (I), and three of the four center supports (E). Then rip two ¾-inch strips from one side of the remainder of the board; from these make the corner posts (C), the upper supports (D), and the top spacers (H). Saw a 9¾-inch piece from the remaining board for the large top (G) and a 7¼-inch piece for the small top (F) and the fourth center support (E). (Note that the two top pieces, F and G, are sawed slightly oversized, then cut to exact size in the process of beveling the edges.) Finally, rip the rest of the board into 1-inch strips for the 16 slats. The diffusion panels are cut from a plastic sheet intended for a fluorescent light. Use a saber saw with a fine-tooth blade to cut the plastic, making sure the edge is well supported.

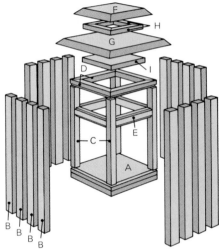

Exploded view shows how the pieces of the light fixture fit together. Parts are keyed by letter to the chart below. Note that the plastic diffusion panels (J and K) will be inset into ⅛-in. rabbets, top and bottom.

Variations. The light fixture can be mounted in several ways: on a tall pole it will serve as a patio or driveway light (1), on a short post it will brighten a garden path (2), or on a wall it will illuminate a doorway (3).

Parts list

Part	Name	Quantity	Thickness	Width	Length	Material
A	Base	2	¾"	6¼"	6¼"	1 x 12 cedar
B	Slat	16	¾"	1"	20½"	1 x 12 cedar
C	Corner post	4	¾"	¾"	14¼"	1 x 12 cedar
D	Upper support	4	¾"	¾"	6¼"	1 x 12 cedar
E	Center support	4	¾"	1¼"	4¾"	1 x 12 cedar
F	Small top	1	¾"	7"	7"	1 x 12 cedar
G	Large top	1	¾"	9½"	9½"	1 x 12 cedar
H	Top spacer	4	¾"	¾"	4½"	1 x 12 cedar
I	Insert	1	¾"	4¾"	4¾"	1 x 12 cedar
J	Upper panel	4	⅛"	4¾"	3¼"	Diffusion panel
K	Lower panel	4	⅛"	4¾"	10¼"	Diffusion panel

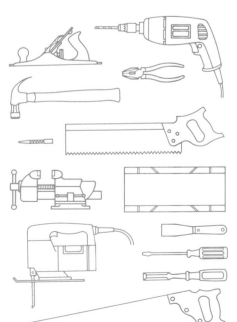

Tools and materials: Drill with ½" bit. Hand or power saw. Saber saw with fine-tooth blade. Backsaw, miter box. Hammer, ¼" straight chisel, nail set, screwdriver. Block plane, vise. Electrician's pliers, putty knife. Waterproof glue, waterproof wood filler. A 6' length of 1 x 12 cedar. Outdoor porcelain light socket, ⅛" plastic diffusion panel (10¼" x 26" min.). Two 1" No. 8 wood screws (for mounting socket), 3d finishing nails.

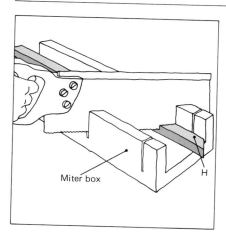

1. Use a backsaw and miter box to make square, even cuts on the ends of the slats (B), corner posts (C), and center supports (E) and to make 45° angles on the ends of the upper supports (D) and top spacers (H). Cut all other pieces to size with a power saw or handsaw; cut the two top pieces (F and G) a little larger than specified, then bevel the edges and plane to size.

Miter box

H

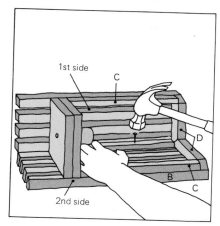

1st side

C

2nd side

5. Support the joined ends of the slats while you glue and nail the loose ends to the base. The base should butt firmly against the ends of the corner posts. Assemble four more slats as in Step 4, but attach only one corner post; join the two sides by nailing through a corner post of the first side. Then glue and nail the slats of the second side to the base.

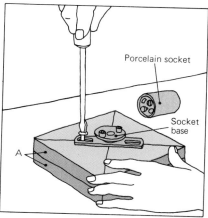

Porcelain socket

Socket base

A

2. Glue the two base pieces (A) together to form a 1½-in. laminate; use several 3d finishing nails to secure it. After the glue dries, find the center by ruling two diagonal lines corner to corner. Drill a ½-in. hole in the center of the base. Install the porcelain socket, centered over the hole, and wire the socket.

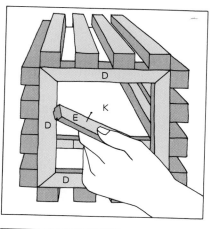

D

D

E

K

6. Continue until all four sides are assembled and joined. Set all nailheads. Then, working on one side at a time, insert the upper and lower diffusion panels (J and K) into their respective rabbets. (Use chisel to enlarge the rabbets if necessary.) Put each center support (E) in place between the panels, and nail the support to two slats. No glue is needed.

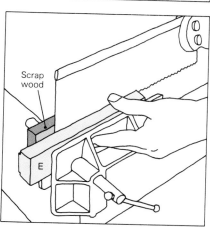

Scrap wood

E

3. Use a backsaw to cut ⅛-in.-deep rabbets around the upper edges of the base (A), both edges of the center supports (E), and the bottom edges of the upper supports (D). First, nail a piece of scrap wood to the edge being rabbeted; then use the scrap wood as a guide for the ⅛-in.-deep cut. Remove the guide and finish the rabbet with a ¼-in. straight chisel.

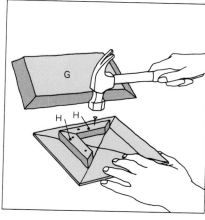

G

H   H

7. Rule diagonal lines corner to corner on the underside of the small top piece (F), and use them to guide placement of the four top spacer pieces (H) so that they form a square. Glue and nail through the spacers into the small top piece. Apply glue to top of spacers, center the large top piece (G) on them, and nail through it into the spacers.

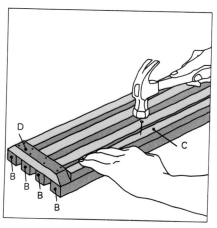

D

C

B
B
B
B

4. Lay out four slats (B) side by side, spaced ¾ in. apart; use scrap wood to ensure even spacing. Glue and nail an upper support (D) across the slats. Glue and nail a corner post (C) flush with the edges of the outer slats.

F

G

I

8. Before attaching the insert (I), make sure it fits inside the body of the light unit. Then center it on the underside of the large top piece and glue and nail it in place. Set all exposed nailheads and fill with waterproof wood filler. Neither sanding nor finishing is needed—the texture of rough-sawed cedar is ideal for the lamp.

DECK OR PATIO PLANTER

As simple in concept as a Lincoln log set, these easily constructed planters visually unify a display of plants and conceal their pots. Made of pine, they can be painted or stained to complement your outdoor decor, but be sure to use a weatherproof finish. If the pots containing your plants are too short and need to be raised, place scap boards between the long members in order to elevate the pots to whatever height is suitable.

Instructions are given on the following page for making the corner planter. It measures 36 inches on the two sides that form the corner and is 16¾ inches high.

The two variations, the rectangle and the square shown in the exploded views, are each 11¾ inches high; the square measures 18 inches and the rectangle 18 inches x 36 inches.

All members are 1 x 4's except the half-width members that form the base of the planters. Unless you have a table saw, ask the lumberyard to rip enough stock to provide the half-width pieces.

Before cutting the notches, measure the thickness of the lumber. One-inch stock is usually ¾ inch thick, but this can vary. If so, be sure the width of the notches corresponds to the lumber's thickness.

Basic units

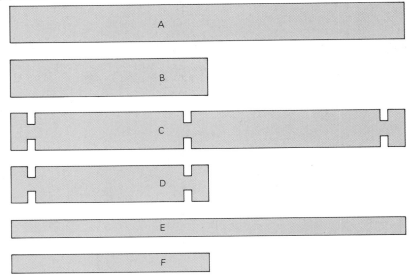

Parts list for corner planter

Part	Name	Quantity	Thickness	Width	Length	Material
A	Long member	4	¾"	3½"	36"	1 x 4 pine
B	Short member	4	¾"	3½"	18"	1 x 4 pine
C	Long notched member	4	¾"	3½"	36"	1 x 4 pine
D	Short notched member	4	¾"	3½"	18"	1 x 4 pine
E	Half-width long member	2	¾"	1¾"	36"	1 x 4 pine
F	Half-width short member	1	¾"	1¾"	18"	1 x 4 pine

Parts list for square planter

Part	Name	Quantity	Thickness	Width	Length	Material
B	Short member	4	¾"	3½"	18"	1 x 4 pine
D	Short notched member	4	¾"	3½"	18"	1 x 4 pine
F	Half-width short member	2	¾"	1¾"	18"	1 x 4 pine

Parts list for rectangular planter

Part	Name	Quantity	Thickness	Width	Length	Material
A	Long member	4	¾"	3½"	36"	1 x 4 pine
D	Short notched member	4	¾"	3½"	18"	1 x 4 pine
E	Half-width long member	2	¾"	1¾"	36"	1 x 4 pine

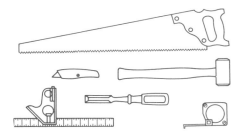

Tools and materials: Crosscut saw. Wooden mallet, ½" chisel. Scissors or mat knife. Steel tape rule, combination square, pencil. Paint or outdoor stain, cardboard.

No. 2 grade 1 x 4 pine: for corner planter 40½', for square planter 15', for rectangular planter 21', plus allowances for saw cuts and waste.

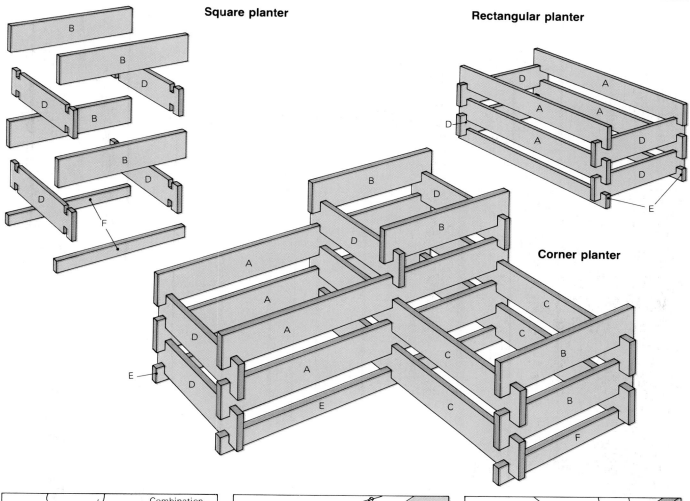

Square planter

Rectangular planter

Corner planter

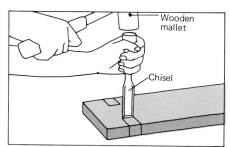

1. Make a template of cardboard for notches 1 in. deep, ¾ in. wide (or the thickness of the lumber), and 1½ in. from the ends of the boards. Cut out notches with a scissors or a sharp knife.

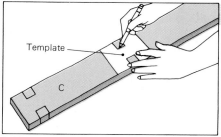

2. Use template to mark notches on both sides of boards C and D. Place a short member (B) on a long notched member (C), and draw a line across C at end of short member. Place template on line for center notch on C.

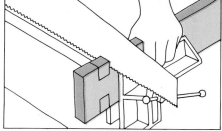

3. Cut the sides of all notches with a crosscut saw. (The saw should be just inside of the marked lines.) Keep the saw level and watch on both sides to make sure the cuts are of uniform depth.

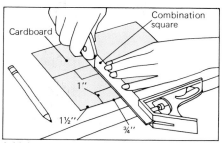

4. With a ½" chisel vertical and its beveled side facing a notch, chop out all waste wood by striking the chisel with a wooden mallet. Clean out the corners of the cut with the chisel. Repeat for remaining notches.

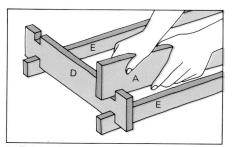

5. Finish all members with paint or outdoor stain before assembling the planter. With half-width members (E and F) on the bottom, add short notched members (D), alternating with unnotched members (A and B).

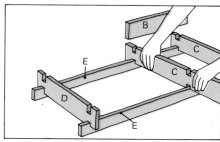

6. To make the L shape, place a long notched member (C) part of the way along the half-width long members (E). The exact position can be determined by using a short member (B) as a spacer.

257

GREENHOUSE

If you have a sunny patio or deck on the southern wall of your house and a door leading out to it, you can build this greenhouse and extend your gardening season year round. The greenhouse is framed with redwood and glazed with panels of Lucite. The lower walls, beneath the glazed sections, are insulated and covered with gypsum wallboard on the inside and plywood sheathing, felt, and double-course siding on the outside. The yellow shake siding was chosen to match that on the house. If your home has a different siding, you should choose a matching siding for the greenhouse.

To provide proper ventilation, the greenhouse contains an exhaust fan in the upper wall on one side and a double vent in the lower wall on the opposite side. There are electrical outlets on each wall.

The directions that follow assume that you are building on a deck 6 feet deep by 12 feet wide and that there is a door leading from the deck into the house. If your deck is a different size, change the measurements of the parts to fit it. If you do not have an appropriate deck, you can build one by adapting the plans for the wooden deck on pages 301–305.

Construction: Begin by laying down the soleplates along the perimeter of the deck. Next, cut away the siding on the house wall and install the ledger and king studs. Build and erect the front wall and add the rafters and side-wall studs. Install the other structural pieces, followed by the plywood sheathing, felt, and siding. Glaze the greenhouse, then add the electrical work, insulation, and inner walls. Finally, install the vents, the tile floor, and the molding.

Cut the parts to size as you work. Use the chart below for the measurements of the redwood parts, checking the sizes against the structure as you proceed. Determine the correct measurements for the Lucite, insulation, siding, and other materials by measuring the areas they must fill on the greenhouse structure.

Glazing: Each panel of Lucite glazing spans the redwood structural members and is framed by redwood parting strips. The Lucite panels are held in place by caulking and by redwood battens that are screwed down over the parting strips, forming lips to cover the edges of the Lucite. Before beginning the glazing, rip all the parting strips and battens to their required thicknesses and widths on a table saw in one session. Also cut the Lucite, using a table saw with a carbide-tipped blade. Leave the protective paper on the Lucite panels while cutting them and feed them slowly into the saw to prevent heat from building up.

You will need a helper to install the glazing, as the panels are fairly large and flexible. Start on the roof. The roof panels overhang the front of the greenhouse to form a drip edge; so there is no parting strip along the front edge. Finish by glazing the front and side walls.

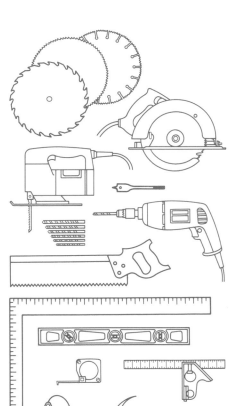

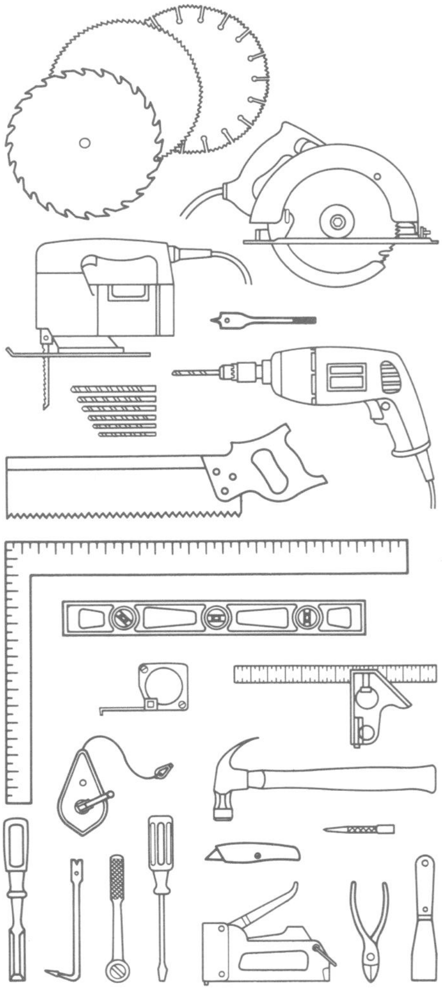

Parts list (wooden parts only)

Part	Name	Quantity	Thickness	Width	Length	Material
A	Ledger	1	1½"	5½"	144"	2 x 6 redwood
B	Rafter	7	1½"	5½"	76"	2 x 6 redwood
C	Outer front sill	1	1½"	5½"	149"	2 x 6 redwood
D	Inner front sill	1	1½"	5½"	138"	2 x 6 redwood
E	Outer side sill	2	1½"	5½"	75"	2 x 6 redwood
F	Inner side sill	2	1½"	5½"	68"	2 x 6 redwood
G	Inner blocking	4	1½"	5½"	22½"	2 x 6 redwood
H	Outer blocking	2	1½"	5½"	21¾"	2 x 6 redwood
I	Front soleplate	1	1½"	3½"	144"	2 x 4 redwood
J	Side soleplate	2	1½"	3½"	68½"	2 x 4 redwood
K	Top plate	2	1½"	3½"	144"	2 x 4 redwood
L	King stud	2	1½"	3½"	108"	2 x 4 redwood
M	Rear side-wall stud	2	1½"	3½"	108¾"	2 x 4 redwood
N	Center side-wall stud	2	1½"	3½"	105"	2 x 4 redwood
O	Front side-wall stud	2	1½"	3½"	98"	2 x 4 redwood
P	Front-wall stud	9	1½"	3½"	84"	2 x 4 redwood
Q	Fan-box side	2	1½"	3½"	✱	2 x 4 redwood
R	Front-wall center bridging	4	1½"	3½"	22½"	2 x 4 redwood
S	Front-wall side bridging	2	1½"	3½"	20¼"	2 x 4 redwood
T	Side-wall front bridging	2	1½"	3½"	19¾"	2 x 4 redwood

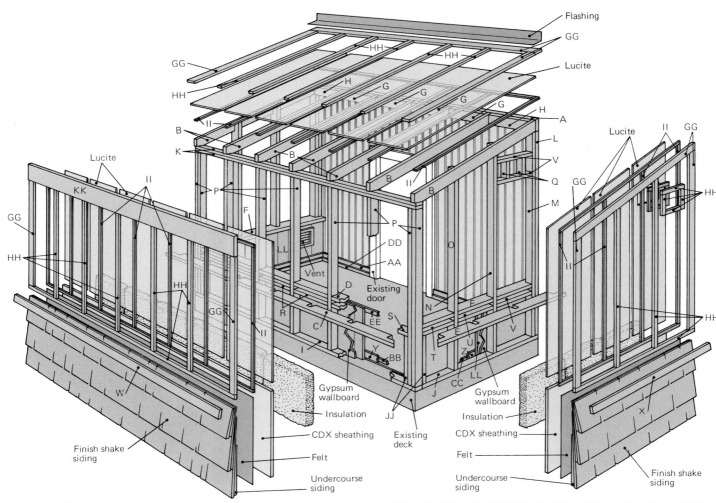

Flashing
GG
Lucite
HH — HH
GG
HH
H — G
B G G G H A
K L
II B V
Lucite — II GG
B Q
B GG HH
P II M
F
P O
LL DD
Vent AA II
D HH
R N E
S E
C U
I Y V
BB Z
T LL
EE CC LL
J
Existing door
Gypsum wallboard
Insulation
Existing deck
CDX sheathing
Felt
Undercourse siding
Finish shake siding
KK
GG
HH
HH
GG
II
W
Lucite
Finish shake siding
Gypsum wallboard
Insulation
CDX sheathing
Felt
Undercourse siding
JJ

Parts list (wooden parts only)

Part	Name	Quantity	Thickness	Width	Length	Material
U	Side-wall center bridging	2	1½″	3½″	22½″	2 x 4 redwood
V	Side-wall back bridging	4	1½″	3½″	20¼″	2 x 4 redwood
W	Front trim	1	¾″	3½″	149″	2 x 4 redwood
X	Side trim	2	¾″	3½″	63″	2 x 4 redwood
Y	Front-wall base molding	1	½″	3½″	138″	2 x 4 redwood
Z	Side-wall base molding	2	½″	3½″	68″	2 x 4 redwood
AA	House-wall base molding	2	½″	3½″	✳	2 x 4 redwood
BB	Front-wall shoe molding	1	½″	1½″	137″	2 x 4 redwood
CC	Side-wall shoe molding	2	½″	1½″	67½″	2 x 4 redwood
DD	House-wall shoe molding	2	½″	1½″	✳	2 x 4 redwood
EE	Front-wall apron molding	1	½″	1½″	138″	2 x 4 redwood
FF	Side-wall apron molding	2	½″	1½″	68″	2 x 4 redwood
GG	Wide batten	11	½″	3″	✳	2 x 4 redwood
HH	Narrow batten	21	½″	1½″	✳	2 x 4 redwood
II	Parting strip	33	³⁄₁₆″	½″	✳	2 x 4 redwood
JJ	Nailer	4	1½″	3½″	30″	2 x 4 redwood
KK	Header	1	¾″	7¼″	144″	1 x 8 redwood
LL	Wall paneling	52	¾″	5½″	31½″	1 x 6 redwood†

✳ Cut to fit during construction.
† For an attractive finish, use tongue-and-groove V-jointed redwood.

Tools and materials: Table, circular, back, and saber saws. Electric drill with twist and spade bits. Framing square, combination square, level, chalk line, steel tape rule. Hammer, mallet, nail set, chisel. Wrecking bar, socket wrench. Phillips and standard screwdrivers. Stapler. Wire cutters, tile cutter. Caulking gun. Wall-type saw-tooth trowel. Utility knife, putty knife. Stiff-bristled brush, sponge. Two units epoxy mortar, 50 lb. grout, eight cartridges clear silicone rubber caulk, one cartridge caulk the color of house wall. Lumber (see chart at left). Seven .125″ x 4′ x 8′ and one .125″ x 4′ x 10′ sheets of SAR (super-abrasion-resistant) Lucite. Three ½″ x 4′ x 8′ sheets of CDX plywood sheathing, three ⅝″ x 4′ x 8′ sheets of T-111 siding, four squares (100 sq. ft. each) of undercourse siding, three squares of 18″ striated finish shake siding. Three ½″ x 4′ x 8′ sheets of gypsum wallboard, 80 sq. ft. of 3½″ R-11 insulation, 80 sq. ft. of building paper or 15-oz. felt, 90 sq. ft. of 4″ x 8″ flat quarry tiles. Two 8″ x 16″ screened vents, 4″ x 146″ aluminum flashing. Kitchen exhaust fan, three electrical boxes 2″ x 3″ deep with duplex receptacles and cover plates, electrical wire. Six ⁵⁄₁₆″ lag bolts 4″ long. Three hundred 1½″ No. 8 trusshead stainless steel wood screws. 8d, 10d, and 12d common hot-dipped galvanized nails, 6d and 8d finishing nails, 6d rosin-coated nails, annular ring nails, shake nails.

Greenhouse

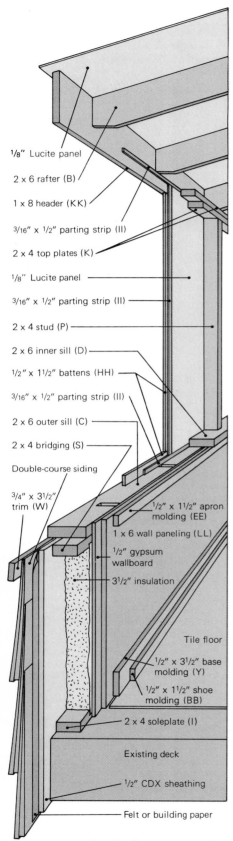

1/8" Lucite panel

2 x 6 rafter (B)

1 x 8 header (KK)

3/16" x 1/2" parting strip (II)

2 x 4 top plates (K)

1/8" Lucite panel

3/16" x 1/2" parting strip (II)

2 x 4 stud (P)

2 x 6 inner sill (D)

1/2" x 1 1/2" battens (HH)

3/16" x 1/2" parting strip (II)

2 x 6 outer sill (C)

2 x 4 bridging (S)

Double-course siding

3/4" x 3 1/2" trim (W)

1/2" x 1 1/2" apron molding (EE)

1 x 6 wall paneling (LL)

1/2" gypsum wallboard

3 1/2" insulation

Tile floor

1/2" x 3 1/2" base molding (Y)

1/2" x 1 1/2" shoe molding (BB)

2 x 4 soleplate (I)

Existing deck

1/2" CDX sheathing

Felt or building paper

Some construction details are shown in this cutaway side view of the greenhouse. The Lucite panels fit into grooves created by nailing thin parting strips between battens and parts of the greenhouse.

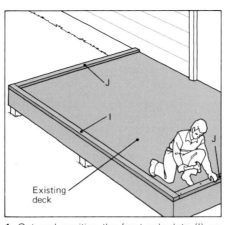

1. Cut and position the front soleplate (I) on top of the deck flush with the front edge of the deck. Cut and position the side soleplates (J) along the side edges of the deck with the ends of the side plates butted against the inner edge of the front plate. Fasten all three soleplates to the deck with 12d nails.

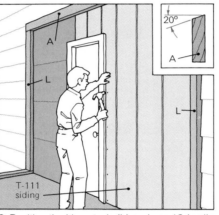

3. Position the king studs (L) and use 12d nails to fasten them to house studs or headers. Cut the top of the ledger (A) at a 20° angle and use lag bolts to fasten it over the king studs. Fill the area enclosed by the studs and ledger with T-111 siding, fitting it around the door and securing it with 8d finishing nails.

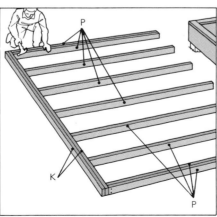

5. Center one end of a front-wall stud (P) on each mark on the top-plate assembly, and toenail each stud to the top plates with four 8d nails. Toenail double studs to each end of the top-plate assembly so that the outer edges of the outer studs are flush with the ends of the top plates. Square off the assembly.

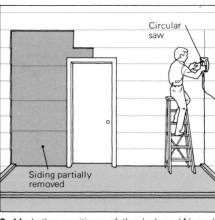

2. Mark the positions of the ledger (A) and king studs (L) on the house wall, cut through the house siding along these lines, and remove the siding inside these lines up to the door. Use a wrecking bar to pry the siding along the ledger line a bit away from wall to make it easier to insert flashing strips later.

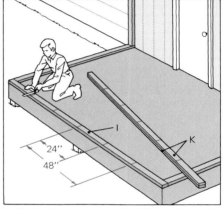

4. Fasten the two top plates (K) together with 8d nails. Mark the top and underside of the top-plate assembly at its exact center. Also mark it 24 and 48 in. from each side of the center marks. These marks will help you position the studs and rafters. Mark the top of the front soleplate (I) in the same way.

6. Attach a temporary brace across the assembly near the bottom. With a helper, erect the assembly over the front soleplate to form the front wall. Toenail the doubled studs to the soleplate flush with the ends of the plate. Toenail the other studs to the soleplate, centering them on the marks. Remove brace.

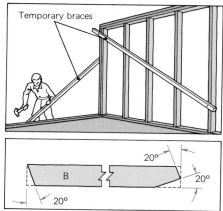

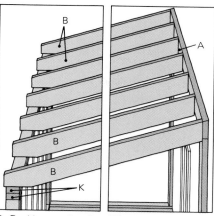

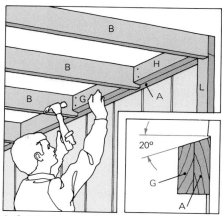

7. Use a level to plumb and square the front wall, then nail temporary braces between it and the deck and one diagonally across wall to lock it in place. Cut 20° angles in both ends of one rafter (B) as shown. Test-fit the cut rafter in all rafter positions, then use it as a pattern for cutting the others.

8. Position each rafter (B) with its lower end flush with the outside of the top plates (K). Center the lower ends of the inner rafters on the marks on the upper top plate and fasten them with 8d nails. Nail the outer rafters flush with the ends of the top plates, then nail the tops of all the rafters to the ledger (A).

9. Cut the inner and outer blocking (G and H) to fit against the ledger (A) between the rafters (B). Bevel the tops of the blocking to the same angle as the ledger, then use 8d nails to fasten the blocking to the ledger. The blocking doubles the thickness of the ledger, providing a good base for the Lucite.

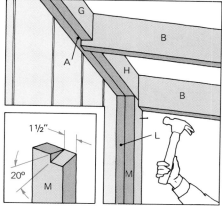

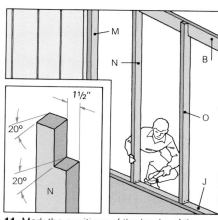

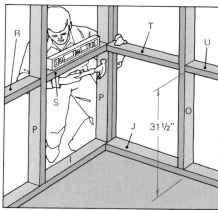

10. Remove the temporary braces from the front wall. Bevel and notch the tops of the rear side-wall studs (M) to fit around the outer rafters (B) and under the outer blocking (H). Do each stud separately; because of the angle, cuts will be different. Fasten notched studs to king studs (L) with 10d nails.

11. Mark the positions of the backs of the center side-wall studs (N) 20¼ in. from the fronts of the rear studs (M). Mark each front-wall stud (O) 44¼ in. from its rear stud. Bevel and notch studs N and O to fit around the outer rafters so their tops and outer edges are flush. Nail them to the rafters and side soleplates.

12. Cut the bridging (R–V). Two of the side-wall back bridging pieces (V) are used to box in the exhaust fan; put these aside and nail the others in place between the studs with 10d nails. The undersides of the bridging pieces should be 31½ in. from the top of the deck. Make sure the pieces are level.

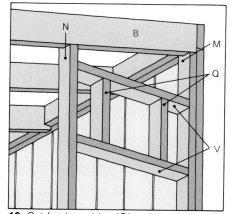

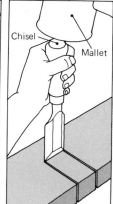

13. Cut fan-box sides (Q) to the same length as the sides of the exhaust fan. Nail them between the two remaining pieces of side-wall back bridging (V), spacing them so that the fan will fit into the resulting box. Nail the fan box between the rear and center studs of one of the side walls just under the rafter.

14. Measure the greenhouse walls from the bottom of the deck to the tops of the bridging, and cut panels of CDX sheathing to fit. Position each panel of sheathing in turn on its wall, and nail it in place with 6d rosin-coated nails. Be sure panels are aligned and flush with the edges of the bridging and studs.

15. Cut both ends of the outer and inner front sills (C and D) and the front ends of the outer and inner side sills (E and F) at 45° angles to form miter joints. Cut notches in the sills to fit around the studs, making the crosscuts with a saber saw and cutting out the waste wood with a chisel and mallet.

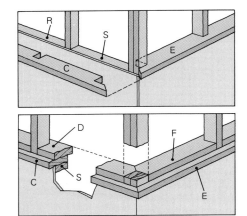

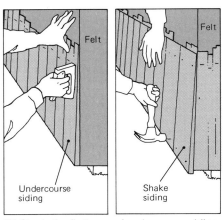

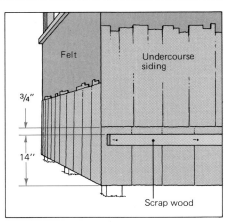

16. Push the outer sills in place from the outside with the notches hugging the studs, and nail the sills to the bridging with 10d nails. Push the inner sills in place from the inside and nail them to the outer sills. Cut felt (or building paper) to fit over the front of the sheathing and staple it in place.

17. Staple the first rows of undercourse siding over the felt to the greenhouse walls with the bottom edges flush with the bottom of the deck. Position the first rows of shake siding over the undercourse with the bottom edges a bit below the bottom of the deck. Use shake nails to attach the shake siding to the walls.

18. Nail and level a length of scrap wood horizontal to and 14 in. above the bottom of the deck on each wall in turn. Staple on a second row of undercourse siding so that its bottom edge is about ¾ in. above the scrap wood. Then rest the bottom of the second row of shake siding on the scrap wood and attach it.

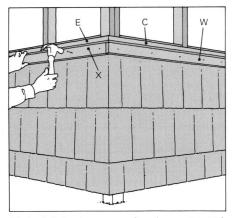

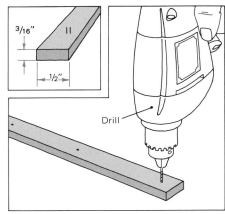

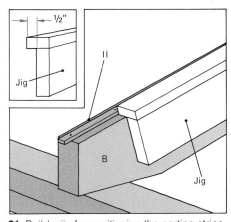

19. Install the top rows of undercourse and shake siding, butting the tops of the siding against the undersides of the outer sills (C and E). Cut the front trim (W), position it under the front outer sill, and attach it to the wall with 8d finishing nails. Nail the side trim (X) under the outer side sills.

20. Make the parting strips (II) by ripping 2 x 4's to a thickness of ³⁄₁₆ in. and a width of ½ in. Determine their lengths from the greenhouse and cut them accordingly. To prevent splitting the thin strips when nailing, drill holes slightly smaller than the diameter of a 4d finishing nail down their centers.

21. Build a jig for positioning the parting strips by nailing a strip of scrap 1 x 2 over the edge of a scrap of 1 x 4 so that the 1 x 2 overhangs the 1 x 4 by ½ in. Place the jig over the corner of an inside rafter and position its parting strip next to it. Nail the parting strip down with 4d finishing nails.

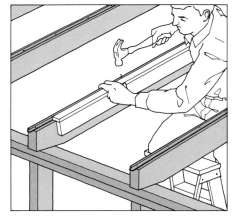

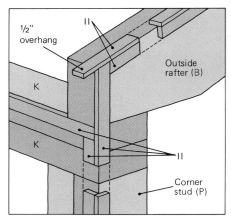

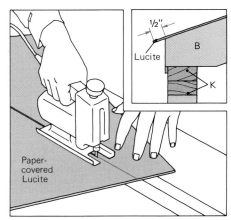

22. Nail parting strips to the remaining inside rafters in the same way; to the top, bottom, and sides of the fan box; and to all the studs except those at the corners and against the house. Then nail parting strips to the outer edges of the ledger (A), inner sills (D and F), upper top plate (K), and king studs (L).

23. Nail two overlapping parting strips along the outside corner of each outside rafter and corner stud as shown. Cut battens (GG and HH) ½ in. thick and 3 and 1½ in. wide to cover all the strips except the one on the top plate. Temporarily position each batten and drill ⁵⁄₆₄-in. pilot holes through it.

24. Measure the frames created by the parting strips and cut a Lucite panel ¹⁄₁₆ in. smaller all around for each, but cut the roof panels ½ in. longer to form an overhang. With the protective paper still on, cut the Lucite on a table saw with a carbide-tipped blade or with a saber saw and metal cutting blade.

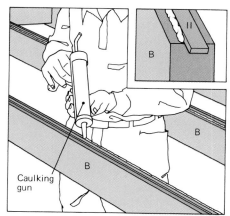

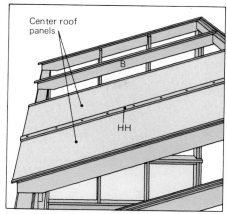

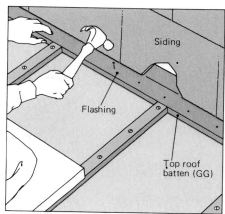

25. Place all glazing tools and materials close by and have a helper peel the protective paper from one of the two center Lucite roof panels while you use a caulking gun to lay a bed of caulking around the perimeter of the frame the panel will fit into. With your helper, position the panel over the caulking.

26. Lay the other center roof panel and screw a batten to the parting strip between the two panels. Shoot more caulking between the batten and the Lucite panels. Install the other roof panels and battens, positioning the battens on the outside rafters so that they will overlap the battens that will go on the sides.

27. Screw down the top roof batten and shoot caulking under it. Cut a piece of folded aluminum flashing as long as the roof is wide and slip one side of it under the house siding that you pried out in Step 2. Position the other side of the flashing over the top roof batten. Secure the flashing with 8d nails. Nail down siding.

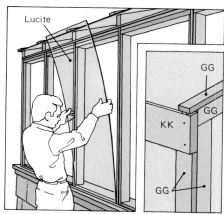

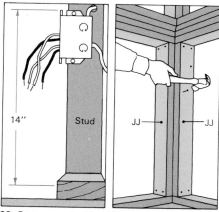

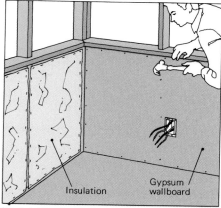

28. Install the Lucite panels on the walls in the same way with one person working on the inside of the greenhouse and another on the outside. Remember to cut a square hole for the fan box and screw battens to the parting strips on the box. Bevel the header (KK) to the angle of the roof and install it with 8d nails.

29. Screw an electrical box to a stud on each wall 14 in. above the deck floor and far enough forward to make it flush with the finished walls. Have an electrician wire the boxes and fan. Attach nailers (JJ) to front studs to form ledges on the front inside corners for nailing on wallboard and paneling.

30. Add the insulation to the walls below the inside sills by stapling it, foil facing in, to the studs. Cut the wallboard to cover the lower inside walls of the greenhouse, making cutouts in the board to fit around the electrical boxes. Secure the wallboard to the studs with annular ring nails.

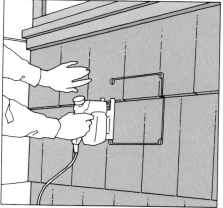

31. Fit the wall paneling (LL) together on the inside walls and use 6d finishing nails to attach it to the inner edges of the soleplates, outer sills, studs, and nailers (JJ). Attach the front-wall and side-wall apron moldings (EE and FF) to the wall paneling just under the inner sills with 6d finishing nails.

32. Drill starter holes, then use a saber saw to make a cutout for the vents in the lower part of the wall opposite the fan. (Cut through the entire wall.) Screw one vent to the siding and the other to the wall paneling. Install the duplex receptacles in the electrical boxes and attach the cover plates.

33. Lay out the tiles on the greenhouse floor. Use the herringbone pattern shown or a pattern of your choice. Cut the tiles as needed. Lay the tiles and grout them. (To find instructions for tiling, see *Index*, p.379.) Let the grout cure, then use 6d finishing nails to attach the base and shoe moldings (Y–DD).

TIE GARDEN

Ties have many applications in landscaping; they can be used to form stairs, checkerboard gardens, and retaining walls, to name just a few examples. Here they are arranged on a slope, visually uniting upper and lower areas of an uneven lawn and preventing erosion. Stepping stones provide access between the areas. The flat beds created by excavating for the ties hold shrubs, bulbs, flowering plants, and pachysandra.

Ties made especially for landscaping are widely available. Thinner and lighter than railroad ties, they usually measure 6 inches x 6 inches x 96 inches and weigh approximately 75 pounds. The stepping stones are less expensive than flagstones.

Planning: Begin by stretching a string from the slope's brow to a tall stake at the bottom of the slope. Level the string with a string level, and measure from the ground to where the string is tied to the stake for the vertical height, and measure the string for the horizontal distance. The height (in inches) divided by six tells how many ties are required as risers. The number of risers, minus one, can be divided into the horizontal distance to get the width of each terrace—that is, assuming you step up the level by just one riser at a time. However, your tie garden will look better and be more useful for planting if the beds range from 20–30 inches wide. Unless the slope is very gradual, this will necessitate doubling and even tripling ties for some of the steps. Doubled and tripled ties look best at the top and middle of the slope (see drawing below). You can break the linear pattern of risers by sawing some short in order to allow stepping stones on a different level from the bed. Crossties, cut from the ties, separate the stepping stones from the beds. Slight "pinwheeling" of the risers—spreading them wider at one end—adds to the visual interest.

Materials: No two yards are alike; therefore, the amounts of materials are not specified for this project. Once you have a plan made, you can calculate the number of ties and stepping stones that you need. Figure on using 2 feet of steel rod for each tie resting on the ground and 1½ feet for each doubled or tripled tie. You will need two 20d nails for each crosstie that is not held in place by soil on both sides.

The wood used for landscaping ties is usually green and, therefore, difficult to saw or drill. Clean the blade or bit often as you work. After sawing a tie, coat the raw end with creosote, matching the same treatment applied by the mill. Use an inexpensive, disposable brush.

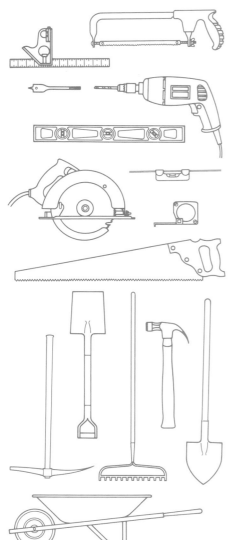

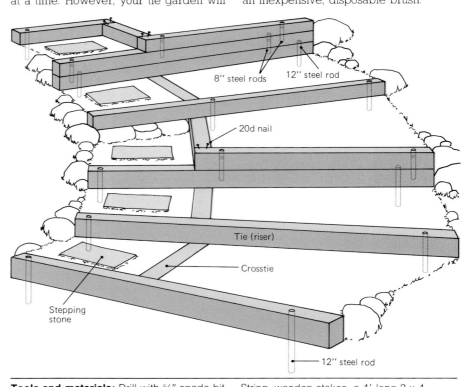

8" steel rods

12" steel rod

20d nail

Tie (riser)

Crosstie

Stepping stone

12" steel rod

Tools and materials: Drill with ⅝" spade bit and extender or brace with auger bit. Circular saw and handsaw or chain saw. Hacksaw, hammer. Square-ended spade, long-handled shovel, pick, iron rake, wheelbarrow, hand trowel. Carpenter's level, string level, combination square, steel tape rule, pencil. String, wooden stakes, a 4' long 2 x 4. Creosote, paintbrush. Landscaping ties, stepping stones, marble chips or tan pea gravel. Unthreaded ½" mild-steel rod, 20d galvanized common nails. Flowering plants, bulbs, shrubs, and ground cover as desired.

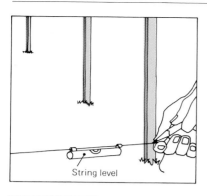

1. After planning the number and width of levels (see text), set stakes marking the back corner of each riser. For each pair of stakes, tie a string at base of stake where ground is higher. Run string to other stake, and level it with a string level; mark stake. The strings become the lines of excavation for the risers.

String level

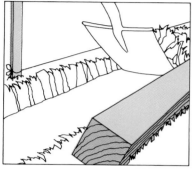

2. Start at the bottom so that excavated dirt falls in place behind each riser. Place the bottom riser on ground and mark around it with a spade. Roll the riser away; dig up grass or other plants and only enough soil to provide a level bed for the riser. Lay the riser; check across its length and width for levelness. Do this each time you lay a riser.

3. Using the next string as a guide, cut away slope for placement of the next riser. Make sharp vertical cuts with the spade, and let the soil fall into place behind the lower riser. Rake the soil level with an iron rake. Cart away any excess soil.

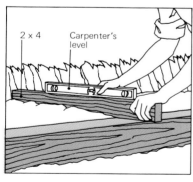

2 x 4   Carpenter's level

4. Lay a 2 x 4 across the lower riser and the soil bed made in Step 3; check with a level on top of the 2 x 4 that the bed is level. Move the 2 x 4 across the soil, making the soil level and even with the top of the lower riser. Repeat this with each bed that you make.

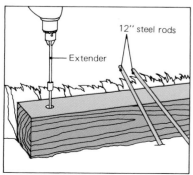

12" steel rods

Extender

5. Single risers are held to the ground with two 12-in. lengths of mild-steel rod. (Cut rod with a hacksaw.) Drill holes near each end of ties with a ⅝-in. spade bit and extender, or use a brace and auger bit. Drive rods into holes and sink 1 in. below surface; hole will quickly fill with soil and not be seen.

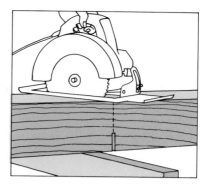

6. To make a crosstie, place a landscaping tie in position and mark where it crosses the lower riser. Roll crosstie over and connect marks. Square lines to opposite surface. Saw with chain saw or circular saw. If using latter, make two or three passes on each side, cutting as deep as saw permits, and finish cut with handsaw. Apply creosote to cut surfaces.

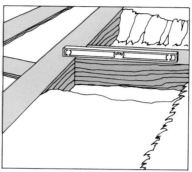

7. Outline crosstie on soil bed; remove crosstie and dig a trench deep enough so that the top of crosstie sits level with the soil bed and lower riser. Crosstie should extend under the next higher riser at least 3 in. Check that the crosstie is level. Lay next riser over it and insert steel rods into riser before excavating to next string.

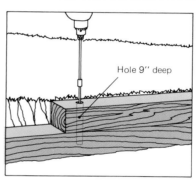

Hole 9" deep

8. When the vertical surface of a cut is too high for one riser, double or triple the ties. Secure bottom tie to earth as in Step 5. Then bind top tie to bottom tie with steel rods cut 8 in. long. Drill through the top tie and 3 in. into the lower tie. Drive rod 1 in. below surface. (The top tie in this case is cut 30 in. shorter than the bottom one.)

9. Where the end of a crosstie butts against a riser and is not supported on both sides by soil, it should be toenailed to the riser. This is done by driving a 20d nail at an angle through the riser into the crosstie (or vice versa). Counterbore for the nailhead and sink it below the surface.

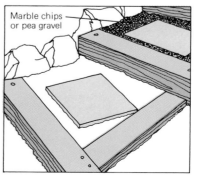

Marble chips or pea gravel

10. Place carefully chosen stones (they may come from the excavated material) at both ends of the risers to hold the soil. Lay stepping stones on the soft soil and stand on them to set them firmly. They should not teeter. Scoop out earth around them to a depth of 1 in.; fill with marble chips or pea gravel. Plant flowers, bulbs, shrubs, and ground cover as desired.

BASKET-WEAVE GARDEN FENCE

The basket-weave design of this garden fence ensures privacy and protection from bad weather yet allows air to pass through so that the fence is less likely to be damaged by strong winds.

The secret of building a fence that will last is to set the posts firmly—so that they are plumb and properly aligned—and to guard in every possible way against moisture and decay. Use lumber that has been pressure treated. Seal joints by applying a thick coat of paint to all wood parts and by securing the parts with galvanized nails while the paint is wet.

As a rule of thumb, one-third of any fence post should be below the ground; but 2 feet is the minimum. For example, a fence 6 feet high requires posts 9 feet long set 3 feet deep. The holes must be dug 42–44 inches deep with 6–8 inches of gravel at the bottom to allow for drainage. Let the quality of the soil dictate your choice of digging tools. Screw-type soil augers work best in firm soil. Blade-type augers will shore up the sides of a hole in loose, sandy soil, and clamshell diggers will chew through rocky soil.

Tamp the gravel down firmly, then position a post and add another 2 or 3 inches of gravel. Hold the post plumb, its face aligned with the line of the fence, while you fill the hole with concrete or heavy clay soil, banking the top so that water will run off to the sides.

After laying out the fence lines (see p.290) and digging all post holes, set the corner posts. Stretch level lines between them on their front faces, one along the top and another near the bottom. Mark off measurements for the intermediate posts along the top line, drop a plumb line at each point, and dig post holes. Set posts so that their tops are level with the top line and their centers are parallel to the plumb line.

After all posts are set, do not touch

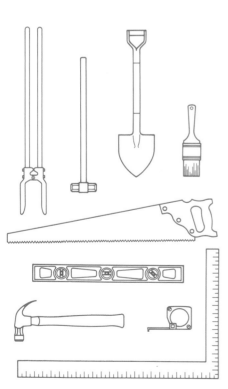

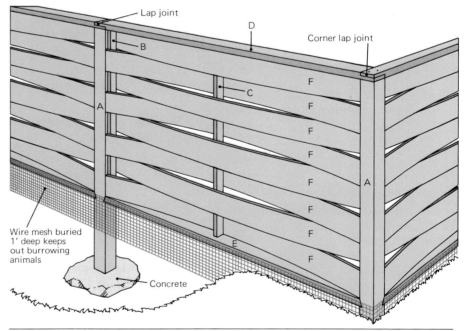

Lap joint
B
D
Corner lap joint
F
C
A
F
F
F
F
A
Wire mesh buried 1' deep keeps out burrowing animals
E
F
Concrete
F

Parts list (for 7' section of fence 62" high)

Part	Name	Quantity	Thickness	Width	Length	Material
A	Post	2	3½"	3½"	91"	4 x 4 pressure-treated lumber
B	Nailing strip	2	¾"	1½"	58" ✶	1 x 2 pressure-treated lumber
C	Divider	1	¾"	1½"	58" ✶	1 x 2 pressure-treated lumber
D	Top rail	1	1½"	3½"	87½" ✶	2 x 4 pressure-treated lumber
E	Bottom rail	1	1½"	3½"	82" ✶	2 x 4 pressure-treated lumber
F	Crossboard	8	¾"	7¼"	80⅝" ✶	1 x 8 pressure-treated lumber

✶ Measurement is approximate; cut to fit during construction.

Tools and materials: Post-hole digger, shovel. Saw, hammer, sledgehammer. Framing square, level, steel tape rule, mason's line, plumb line. String, wooden stakes. Batter boards (see p.291).

Paintbrush, waterproof paint. Pressure-treated lumber (see above). Gravel, concrete, 1" galvanized wire mesh. 6d, 8d, and 10d galvanized common nails.

them for about 2 days. Then nail the top rails in place. Lay out the crossboards side by side and cut the nailing strips and dividers to match the accumulated widths. Then use a nailing strip to determine the placement of the bottom rails. Before securing a bottom rail, paint its underside and attach a divider by nailing up through the center of the rail. When the bottom rail is in place, secure the top of the divider by nailing down through the top rail. Paint the divider.

Saw the crossboards about ⅛ inch longer than the distance between the posts. Use 6d galvanized nails to attach the nailing strips to the posts and then to attach the bottom two boards to alternate sides of one nailing strip, arranged so that they cross over each other and around the divider. Force the other ends of the boards around their nailing strip and secure them. Continue in this way to the top, nailing two boards at a time.

Joints for rails

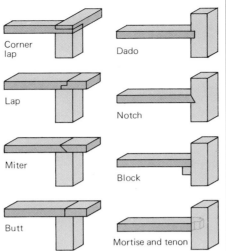

Corner lap

Lap

Miter

Butt

Dado

Notch

Block

Mortise and tenon

Several joints can be used for top rails (D). Secure with 8d galvanized common nails. Seal all joints with wet paint. Joints for bottom rails (E) should be reinforced by toenailing.

Variations

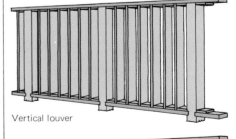

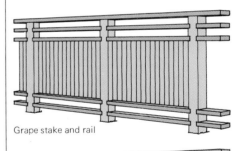

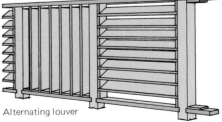

Solid board

Board on board

Grape stake

Grape stake and rail

Vertical louver

Alternating louver

Post-and-rail construction can be used for fences of many kinds, including those shown above. All fences must be kept painted to protect against moisture and decay.

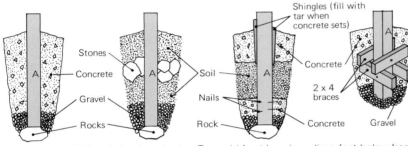

Stones
Concrete
Gravel
Rocks

Set posts in concrete (left) or in hard-packed clay soil reinforced with large stones near top of hole (right). Rock supports base of post; gravel keeps moisture from accumulating.

Shingles (fill with tar when concrete sets)
Soil
Nails
Rock
Concrete
Concrete
2 x 4 braces
Gravel

To avoid frost heaving, dig a foot below frost line and drive 10d galvanized nails near base of post (left). If water table is high, set posts above water level; reinforce with 2 x 4's (right).

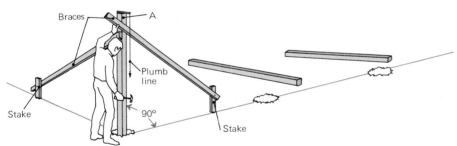

Braces
A
Plumb line
Stake
90°
Stake

To align and plumb posts, nail braces to stakes driven along fence lines and at 90° angles to posts. Use level on two sides of post to achieve vertical plumb. Hang plumb line from top of post to ensure that post remains true while hole is being filled.

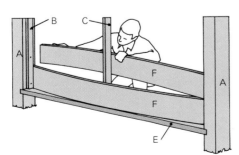

1. Secure nailing strips (B) to posts (A) with 6d galvanized common nails. Attach two bottom crossboards (F) to alternate sides of one nailing strip, crossing around divider (C).

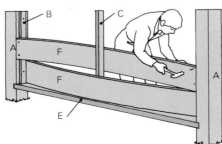

2. Force ends of crossboards around nailing strip on other post and secure with 6d galvanized nails so that each board is attached to the same side of both nailing strips.

CONCRETE DRIVEWAY, PATIO, OR WALK

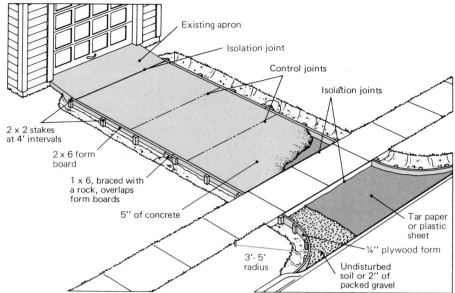

Existing apron

Isolation joint

Control joints

Isolation joints

2 x 2 stakes at 4' intervals

2 x 6 form board

1 x 6, braced with a rock, overlaps form boards

5" of concrete

3'- 5' radius

Tar paper or plastic sheet

¼" plywood form

Undisturbed soil or 2" of packed gravel

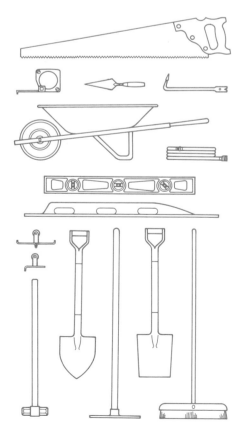

Long lasting and carefree, a concrete driveway repays the time and effort required for its construction. Plan this project carefully, for when the concrete arrives (assuming you buy transit-mixed concrete), you must work fast.

Early in the planning consult your municipal building or public works department to find out what local regulations apply. For example, wire reinforcing mesh may be necessary in areas of severe freezing conditions.

Timing: Concrete cures best in moderately cool weather. In hot, dry weather it dries so fast it becomes difficult to work with. If you must lay a driveway in summer, have the concrete delivered in the cool morning hours.

The driveway shown here is 10 feet wide and 30 feet long. Its thickness of 5 inches is adequate to support the weight of heavy trucks. For passenger cars and light delivery trucks, 4 inches will suffice. The techniques shown here can be used for laying patios and sidewalks, where a 3½-inch slab is normally adequate.

Ideally, to carry off water, your driveway should slope toward the street a minimum of ⅛ inch per running foot. More than a 1¾-inch slope per running foot, or too abrupt a change in grade, may cause the car to hit the pavement. If, on the other hand, the site slopes from the street toward the garage, you will need a drain at the low point. Where snow and ice are not a problem, dig a 2-inch-deep ditch to

lead water away from the garage, and seed the ditch with grass. On a level site drainage is best provided by raising one side of the driveway as shown in Step 7.

Concrete—a mixture of portland cement, sand, aggregate (crushed stone or washed gravel), and water—comes in cubic yards. (A cubic yard is 27 cubic feet.) When you order transit-mixed concrete, give the supplier the dimensions of your form (including thickness). Ask for coarse aggregate (maximum size ¾–1 inch), a "slump" of 4 inches (slump is a measure of consistency), and 6% air entrainment. Have two or more able helpers on hand when the truck arrives. Also have a place set aside for the driver to dump excess concrete; he cannot take it back—it will harden in the truck.

Form boards: These should be of green (wet) 2 x 6's. They can be coated with engine oil to ensure easy removal.

Joints: Control joints placed every 5–10 feet allow the slab to contract and expand without cracking. They are crosswise grooves cut into the damp concrete with a special tool called a groover. Isolation joints separate the fresh concrete from an existing structure, such as a garage floor, sidewalk, or street pavement. You can purchase ½-inch semirigid material for this purpose.

Caution: Concrete is caustic to the skin. Be sure to wear gloves, rubber boots, and protective clothing, and quickly wash any concrete off the skin.

Tools and materials: Spade, wheelbarrow, tamp, square-ended shovel. Margin trowel, 5' darby, edger, groover, stiff-bristled broom, garden hose. Prybar or crowbar. Crosscut saw, sledgehammer. Steel tape rule, 4' level, 100' of string. Screed of 2 x 6 lumber 12' long, 2 x 2 stakes 18" long,

2 × 6 lumber as needed for form boards. Isolation joint material if needed (see text), transit-mixed concrete, gravel for fill if needed (see Steps 1 and 2). Opaque plastic sheeting for curing, tar paper or plastic sheeting for covering base. Engine oil. 10d duplex-head nails, 6d common nails.

1. Drive temporary stakes at four corners of driveway, allowing 4 in. on each side (a total of 8 in.) beyond planned width. Add stakes along length of driveway at 10-ft. intervals and run string between them to outline shape of driveway. Excavate to depth of 5 in. (You can hire someone with a backhoe or tractor equipped with a scoop to do this part.) Retain turf. If water table is high, dig 2 in. deeper and spread 2 in. of gravel.

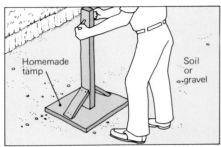

Homemade tamp

Soil or gravel

2. Remove stakes. Tamp soil or gravel so that it is firm and level. Dig out any small areas of dampness and fill with gravel.
3. Firmly drive corner stakes next to garage or apron. These should be 10 ft. 3 in. apart. Where driveway enters road, drive stakes the same distance apart. Run string between them and use as a guide for driving form stakes at 4-ft. intervals. Where form boards will butt (see Step 6), set a stake back an additional ¾ in. Plot curve of driveway where it enters street (see diagram, opposite page), and set stakes on curve at 1- to 2-ft. intervals.

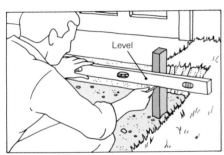

Level

4. Place level on ground next to a corner stake, and draw a line where bottom of level crosses stake. Top of form board will be positioned at this line. Continue marking other stakes in this manner for a driveway on level or gently sloping ground. See text for limits on amount of slope per foot.

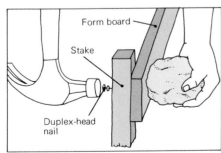

Form board

Stake

Duplex-head nail

5. Nail the form boards to the inner faces of the stakes by driving duplex-head nails through the stakes into the boards. If the ground impedes the hammer, scoop out some earth behind the stakes. To steady the stakes, hold a sledgehammer or a rock against the boards.

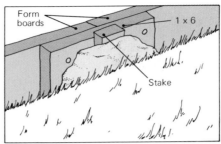

Form boards

1 × 6

Stake

6. Where form boards butt, lap the joint with a 1 × 6 board nailed with common nails, and drive a stake for support. Brace the stake with a rock.
7. If site is level, check that driveway is level by placing a straight 2 × 6 across the form boards and laying a level on the 2 × 6. Allow for drainage by raising one side of the form higher than the other (⅛ in. higher for each foot of width—1¼ in. in this case). Use a prybar or crowbar to raise form.

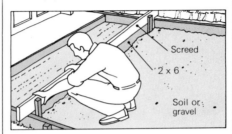

Screed

2 × 6

Soil or gravel

8. Saw off tops of stakes level with form boards. Temporarily fasten a 2 × 6 to the board that will be your screed. Move it the length of the driveway to check that the base is level. Wet down the base; cover with tar paper or a plastic sheet.
9. Pour concrete in sections of 8–10 ft. blocked off with a 2 × 6. Spread concrete with shovel. Do Steps 10 and 11 quickly, remove the 2 × 6, and pour next section.

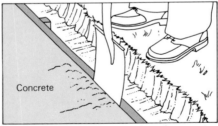

Concrete

10. Move shovel between edge of concrete and form with spading motion. This pushes large pieces of aggregate away from the form. Tap side of the form with a hammer to eliminate air pockets.

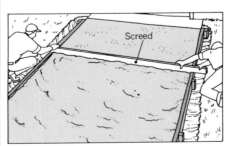

Screed

11. Place a screed (a 12-ft.-long 2 × 6) across concrete. Move it back and forth to level high spots. After one pass, fill in any low spots and level again if necessary.

Darby

12. Work a darby across concrete in a sweeping motion with trailing edge pressed down lightly. This forces large stones below surface. Make no more passes than necessary to smooth surface.

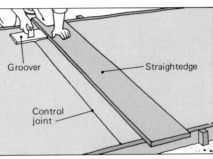

Groover

Control joint

Straightedge

13. Lay a straight-edged board across the form to serve as a guide for cutting control joints. Board should be wide and thick enough for you to crawl on. Use groover to cut control joints 1¼ in. deep (one-quarter thickness of slab) at 5- to 10-ft. intervals.

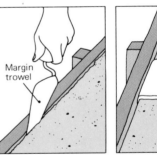

Margin trowel

Edger

14. Cut the concrete away from the form to a depth of 1 in. with a margin trowel. When the surface is no longer shiny with water, run edger between form and concrete.

15. For a skid-resistant finish, draw a damp, stiff-bristled broom across the driveway perpendicular to traffic.
16. When concrete is hard, wet it and cover it with opaque plastic sheeting weighted down at the edges. Remove form next day. Cure 5–8 days (the longer time for cooler weather) before allowing cars on it—twice that time for heavy vehicles. Fill the trench and replace the turf.

TRELLIS

A trellis is an open structure used to train vines and other climbing plants. It will also serve as a more attractive screen than a fence. The trellis in this project is 5 feet high and 6 feet wide. The dimensions can easily be changed to suit the area you need to screen or the number of plants you want to train.

The trellis is supported by two 4 x 4 posts made of pressure-treated pine. The posts are sunk below the frost line so that the trellis will be unaffected by frost heaving. (Consult your local building department to find out the location of the frost line in your area.) The rails of the trellis are also made of pressure-treated wood; but you could treat the wood yourself with a preservative before or after construction, which is a cheaper alternative.

Temporary braces are attached to the posts to prevent them from shifting during hammering. The braces are made of long pieces of scrap wood.

Horizontal rails are nailed to the posts to span the front of the trellis. Pilot holes are drilled through the horizontal rails and part of the way into the vertical rails. The holes will enable you to nail these rails together without splitting them. You will need a helper to stand behind the trellis to hold the vertical rails and absorb the hammer blows. If you have an expanse of level ground or floor and sufficient help to lift the trellis, assemble it on the ground or floor and then raise it.

If the trellis is placed next to a patio or paved surface, leave 12–15 inches of uncovered dirt for a planting area.

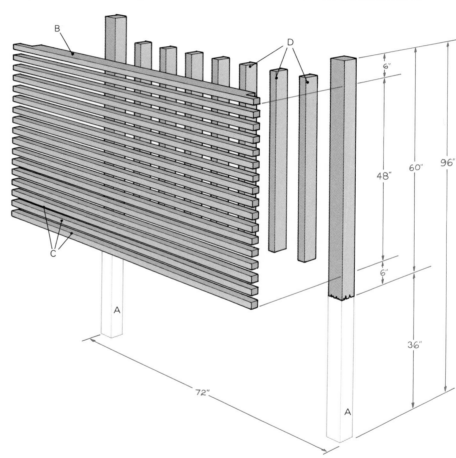

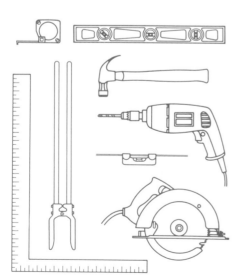

Parts list

Part	Name	Quantity	Thickness	Width	Length	Material
A	Post	2	3½"	3½"	96"	4 x 4 pressure-treated pine
B	Cap rail	1	1½"	5½"	72"	2 x 6 pressure-treated fir
C	Horizontal rail	16	1½"	1½"	72"	2 x 2 pressure-treated fir
D	Vertical rail	7	1½"	3½"	48"	2 x 4 pressure-treated fir

Tools and materials: Circular saw or handsaw. Electric drill with ³⁄₃₂" bit. Post-hole digger or shovel. Line level, carpenter's level, framing square, steel tape rule, pencil. Hammer. One qt. wood preservative. Wood (see above) and scrap wood for braces. One lb. galvanized 12d nails.

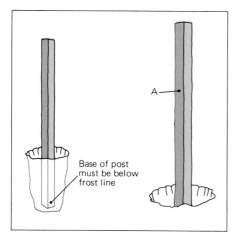

1. Dig two holes for the posts (A) 6 ft. apart and to a depth below the frost line (3 ft. for this trellis); be sure that the trellis will be properly oriented toward the sun. Insert the posts into the holes (see p.267).

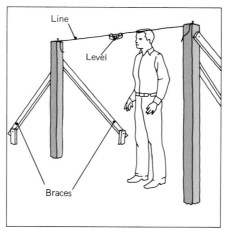

2. Use a line level to even the height of the posts. Check each post for plumbness with a carpenter's level and backfill the holes. Nail temporary braces to the posts to support them during construction.

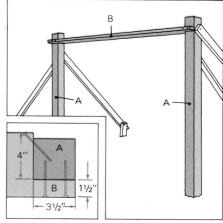

3. Saw a 3½- x 4-in. piece from each end of the cap rail (B). Nail rail 4½ in. below the top of the posts so that it projects toward the back of the trellis and is also flush with the front of the horizontal rails (C).

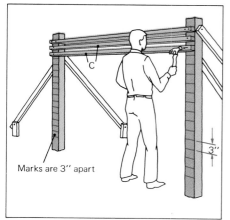

4. Make a mark on each post 1½ in. below the cap rail, then every 3 in. below the first mark until there are 16 marks on each post. Align the top of each horizontal rail (C) with these marks and nail each to the posts.

5. Mark back of each horizontal rail 6³/₁₆ in. from left post. Make a second mark 8⁵/₁₆ in. to the right of the first and every 8⁵/₁₆ in. thereafter until there are seven marks. Drill ³/₃₂-in. pilot holes ¾ in. to the right of each mark.

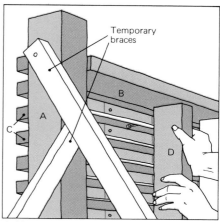

6. Line up vertical rails (D) on marks made in Step 5. Drill through holes in horizontal rails partway into vertical rails. Drive nails into holes; remove braces. Coat wood with preservative if necessary.

Variations

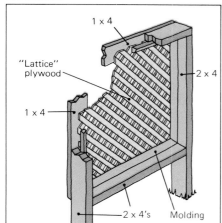

In some areas plywood can be bought precut to resemble a lattice, which is a simple way to build a trellis. The plywood can be attached to 2 x 4 stakes (sunk below the frost line) with a frame made of 1 x 4's and 1¼-in. quarter-round molding.

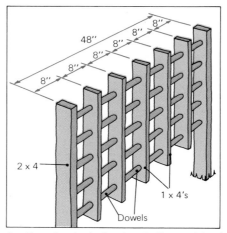

Another simple design for a trellis consists of dowels running between 2 x 4 posts (sunk below the frost line) and through vertical 1 x 4's in which holes are drilled to accommodate the dowels. The dimensions given can be varied to suit the site.

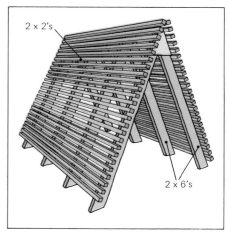

This A-frame is both a trellis and a light, airy shelter in which you can lie and enjoy the fragrance of your plants. The A-frame should be at least 8 ft. high. The horizontal rails are made of 2 x 2's, spaced 2 in. apart, and span the legs, which are 2 x 6's.

ROCK GARDEN

A rock garden can lend a pleasing touch to a manicured lawn or can convert a slope that may erode into a miniature alpine landscape. It typically consists of rock outcrops, already existing in nature or created by man, and low-growing plants. It may be located anywhere, except in heavily shaded areas or swampy ground, and its size may vary from a few square feet to several acres.

Planning: Locate your rock garden, if possible, on a slope with existing rock outcrops and away from rigid shapes, such as a garage or a straight brick wall. Sketch a map of your site with its topographical features; then include the areas where you want to add rocks, shrubs, flowers, and ground cover. If desired, you can design a garden on a natural or man-made hillside with miniature valleys, cliffs, plains, and even a stream or pool.

Arrange plants individually or in clumps to harmonize with the rocks but not in straight lines or geometric patterns. Put dwarf shrubs in crevices as accents for flowers that bloom seasonally.

Construction: Light and gravelly soil is ideal for a rock garden. Heavy soil tends to become waterlogged; and rich soil encourages lush growth, which is subject to winterkill. Dig down at least a foot and cultivate. Good drainage is essential for rock gardens. If necessary, you can improve the drainage of heavy clay soil by placing a layer of fist-size stones or gravel at the bottom of the area cultivated. Any additional soil should consist of equal parts of topsoil, coarse sand, and leaf mold or peat moss.

Rocks should not be strewn on the ground but should be firmly secured by burying them halfway into the soil. On level ground the effect of a slope can be achieved by using rocks and plants of varying heights. Design the rock garden so that it has a natural appearance and is easy to maintain.

Plants: Thousands of plants can be used for rock gardens, including rock and alpine shrubs (prostrate barberry, rock spray cotoneaster, sargent juniper, dwarf Alberta spruce, dwarf Japanese yew), ground cover (ground-hugging sedum, pachysandra, creeping thyme, English ivy), and low-growing flowers (bulbs, perennials, annuals). The plan below is for the 14- x 20-foot rock garden in the photo at the left.

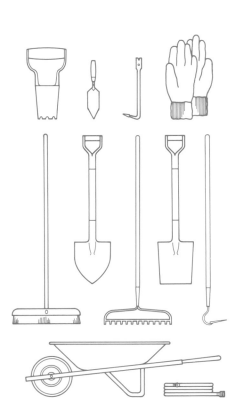

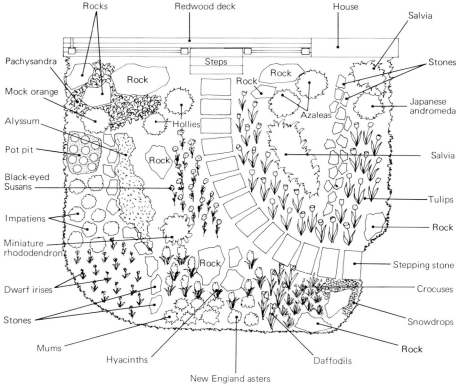

Tools and materials: Digging fork or spade. Shovel, hoe, garden trowel. Bulb planter. Lawn rake, broom. Crowbar. Wheelbarrow. Garden hose with spray head. Work gloves. Marking stakes, string. A 1" x 18" x 5' plank, four to six round logs 2' long. Clay pots. Rocks, stepping stones, gravel, marble chips. Garden soil, leaf mold, fertilizer, sand. Dwarf shrubs, tulips and other bulbs, annual and perennial flowers. Pachysandra or other ground cover.

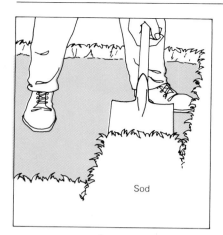

1. After carefully planning the rock garden, clear the site by removing sod with a spade and pulling out all unwanted plants and shrubs. Rake the bare ground and remove loose stones and debris. Mark out areas according to your sketch with stakes and string. If desired, you can reshape the contour of the ground to create hills and valleys. But be sure the reworked areas are covered with topsoil.

Sod

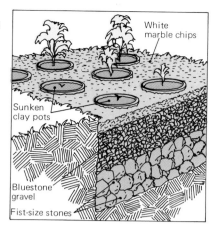

White marble chips

Sunken clay pots

Bluestone gravel

Fist-size stones

5. To build a well-drained pot pit for seasonal flowers, dig a pit about 2 ft. deep. Fill the bottom with fist-size stones, the middle with bluestone gravel, and the top with white marble chips. Sink several clay pots into the gravel and chips so that the rims of the pots are flush. Potted flowers that are in season can then be placed in the empty pots.

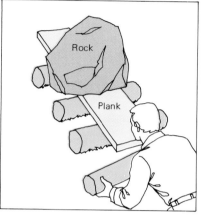

Rock

Plank

2. To move a large rock, place a sturdy plank on at least four round logs and turn the rock onto the plank with a crowbar. Move the plank by pushing the rock slowly until the rear log can be released; insert this log under the front end of the plank and continue. (Avoid placing your feet or hands under the plank and wear work gloves.) This method works well on relatively level ground. Use a wheelbarrow for removing smaller rocks.

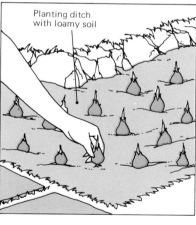

Stepping stones

Sand

6. To create a curved path of stepping stones, dig holes half an inch deeper and larger than the stones. Fill the holes with about half an inch of loose soil or sand. Put the stones in the holes, leveling them by adding or scooping out the loose soil or sand with a garden trowel. Fill the spaces around the stones with topsoil, and plant grass or ground cover in the surrounding areas.

Imbedded rock

Stub wall

3. Each rock should be partially embedded in the ground on its broadest surface. This positioning secures the rock and minimizes erosion. Dig a hole and wriggle a sizable rock into it (rear). Any terrace is an ideal spot for a stub wall (foreground); assemble the wall with smaller rocks. Add soil between rocks and pack it down. Use a broom to sweep off loose soil.

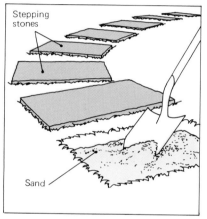

Planting ditch with loamy soil

7. Using a bulb planter, dig holes for planting daffodils, crocuses, tulips, or other flowers, or plant them in a ditch lined with loamy soil laced with bone meal. Cover holes or ditch with soil, firm down soil, and water. Arrange flowers in irregular patterns. Dwarf shrubs can be planted individually to accent rocks or flower beds.

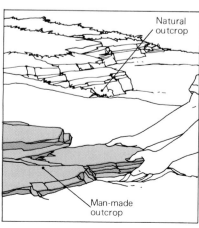

Natural outcrop

Man-made outcrop

4. If the garden has an existing rock outcrop (rear), add rocks of your choosing to harmonize with it (foreground). Select lichen-covered, weathered, or irregularly shaped rocks. Pitted limestone and porous volcanic tufa are also good. Rocks with strata lines should be arranged so that their grain runs in the same general direction.

8. Plant pachysandra or other evergreen ground cover in selected areas where there is partial shade. Dig holes several inches apart with a broom handle or garden trowel. Insert plants or cuttings and fill holes with additional soil. Press down soil around the plants with your fingers before spraying with a garden hose.

PVC AND CANVAS CHAIR

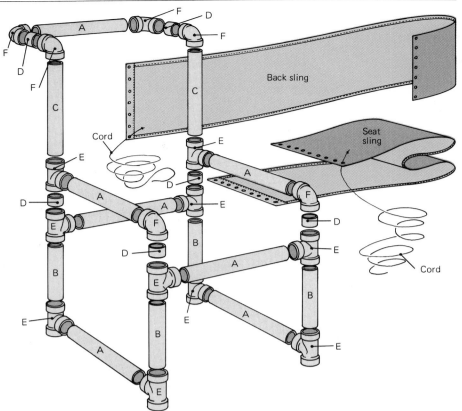

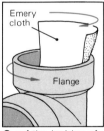
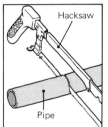
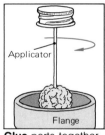
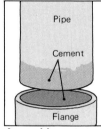

Working with PVC pipe

Cut PVC pipe to the lengths given in the chart below by placing the pipe in a vise and making vertical cuts with a hacksaw. You can judge the cuts by eye; you need not use a miter box.

Sand the insides of the elbows and T's and the ends of the pipes with emery cloth in order to roughen the surfaces and provide a better bond with the cement. Wipe off all joints.

Glue parts together carefully and accurately, one joint at a time. Use cement applicator to apply PVC cement to adjoining parts. Work in a well-ventilated area.

Assemble parts quickly. PVC cement sets in 10–15 sec.; so you must join parts accurately on the first try. Push pipes all the way into elbows and T's until pipes hit seats in joints.

Parts list

Part	Name	Quantity	Diameter	Length	Material
A	Rung	7	1½" OD	18"	PVC pipe
B	Leg	4	1½" OD	8"	PVC pipe
C	Upright	2	1½" OD	14"	PVC pipe
D	Connector	6	1½" OD	1¼"	PVC pipe
E	T	10	1½" ID	—	PVC T-fitting
F	Elbow	6	1½" ID	—	90° PVC elbow

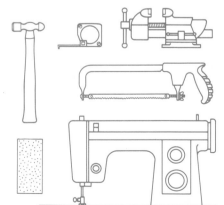

Tools and materials: Hacksaw, vise. Steel tape rule, pencil. Ball peen hammer. Sewing machine or a needle and thread. PVC cement. Lacquer thinner, cloths. Medium emery cloth. Two 10' lengths of 1½" (OD) PVC plastic plumbing pipe. Elbows and T's (see above), 1½ yd. of 34" wide canvas chair duck, 15' of ⅛" cord. Grommet kit, 32 No. 0 or No. 1 grommets and washers.

Polyvinyl chloride (PVC) plastic plumbing pipe is a popular material for building sturdy, weatherproof outdoor furniture. This design, with its pipe frame and comfortable canvas sling seat and back, can be used on a patio, deck, or lawn, but it is also attractive enough to bring indoors for use in a playroom or solarium. You can build your own chair for about one-third the cost of a ready-made one.

PVC pipe is easily cut with a hacksaw. The joints fit snugly and accurately, so there is little need to check for squareness as you go along. Just push each length of pipe into its elbow or T until it seats firmly. Cut all the pipe to the lengths shown in the chart, and assemble the chair without cement to be certain that everything fits properly. Then disassemble the chair and reassemble it with

cement. Work in a well-ventilated and flame-free area, preferably outdoors; the cement vapors are highly toxic and flammable. Do not smoke while working!

Buy weather-resistant canvas chair duck for the seat and back slings. The slings are laced with cord to the frame with a gap of about 2 inches. The canvas will stretch with use, but the slings can be tied more tightly later on.

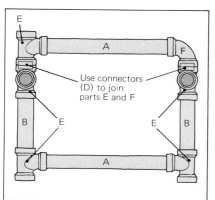

1. Using the techniques shown on the opposite page, join two T's (E) and a rung (A) to form the bottom of the chair's base. Lay assembly on a bench to make sure T's are parallel. Next, join two legs (B), three T's, a rung, and an elbow (F) as shown. Use connectors (D) to join T's and elbows to one another. Then insert the legs into the parallel T's.

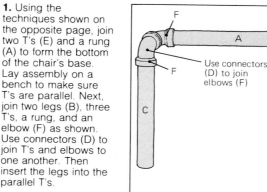

3. Assemble the back by joining two uprights (C), four elbows (F), and a rung (A) as indicated. Use connectors (D) to join the elbows to one another. The rung is set back from the plane of the uprights so that it does not touch your back when you lean against the sling. Use lacquer thinner and cloths to remove the writing stenciled on the pipe.

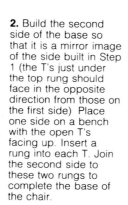

2. Build the second side of the base so that it is a mirror image of the side built in Step 1 (the T's just under the top rung should face in the opposite direction from those on the first side) Place one side on a bench with the open T's facing up. Insert a rung into each T. Join the second side to these two rungs to complete the base of the chair.

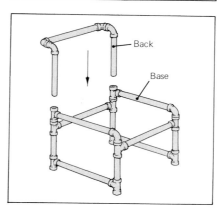

4. Join the back and base to complete the chair's frame. PVC pipe is flexible enough that the back can be bent slightly to compensate for minor misalignment between the back and base. Make slings as shown below and lace them to the frame with ⅛-in. cord so that the lacing is on the bottom and back of the chair.

Making the slings

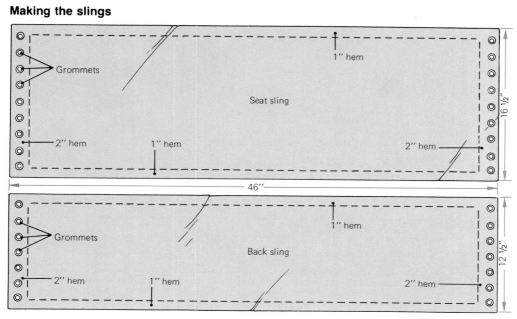

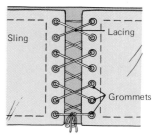

Cut the canvas for the seat sling 18½ in. x 50 in. and the back sling 14½ in. x 50 in. Sew a 2-in. hem along each short edge and a 1-in. hem along each long edge so that the finished dimensions are 16½ in. x 46 in. and 12½ in. x 46 in. Insert nine grommets at each end of the seat sling and seven at each end of the back, equally spaced about 1¾ in. apart. Pull slings tightly around frame and lace them.

PVC BICYCLE RACK

Children tend to leave their bicycles strewn around the lawn, driveway, or garage, where they are not only unsightly but also prone to damage. This bicycle rack, made of PVC plastic pipe, will keep your family's and visitors' bicycles in a neat row and hold them securely so that they cannot be easily knocked over.

Planning: The secret in designing a bicycle rack lies in planning it so that the handlebars of adjoining bikes will not interfere with one another. Commercial metal racks usually have the wheel slots spaced too close to one another, leaving it up to the good sense of the users not to bang their handlebars together or skin their knuckles. This design takes no chances, since children may be the principal users, and spaces adjoining bicycles over 14 inches apart.

The wheel slots are over 5½ inches wide in order to make room for the thick tires and wide forks of the popular BMX bicycles. If you expect to keep only 10-speed touring or racing bikes in your rack, you can make the wheel slots narrower in order to hold the bikes more upright by reducing the length of the bottom parts (A). If you own BMX bicycles with exceptionally wide forks, you will have to make the bottom parts wider than 3½ inches. Before you glue up the U-shaped wheel slots (Step 1), see how your bicycles fit and adjust the slot sizes if necessary. You may want to use several different widths in a single rack. You can also make the rack shorter or longer in order to accommodate more or less than the four bikes this rack will hold.

Construction: Instructions for working with PVC pipe are given in the previous project (*PVC and canvas chair,* pp.274–275). It bears repeating, however, that the PVC cement dries within a few seconds and that it is virtually impossible to reposition parts once they are joined. Therefore, test-fit all the parts after they have been cut (and labeled to avoid confusion), then assemble them carefully. Be sure to work in a well-ventilated area, away from fire or flame, and avoid inhaling the cement fumes.

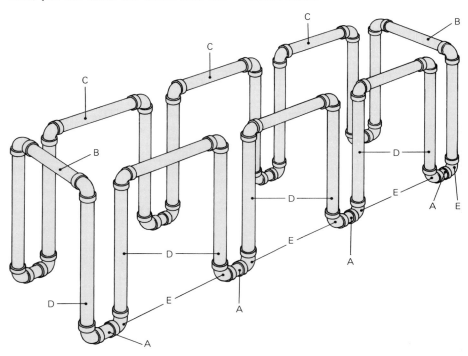

Parts list

Part	Name	Quantity	Diameter	Length	Material
A	Bottom	8	1½" OD	3½"	PVC pipe
B	End	2	1½" OD	10"	PVC pipe
C	Crosspiece	6	1½" OD	14"	PVC pipe
D	Upright	16	1½" OD	16"	PVC pipe
E	Elbow	32	1½" ID	—	90° PVC elbow

Tools and materials: Hacksaw, vise. Steel tape rule, pencil. Hammer. Plastic enamel spray paint or lacquer thinner, soft cloths, medium emery cloth. Safety goggles (optional). Thirty-two 1½" (ID) 90° PVC elbows. At least 35 running ft. of 1½" (OD) PVC plastic plumbing pipe.

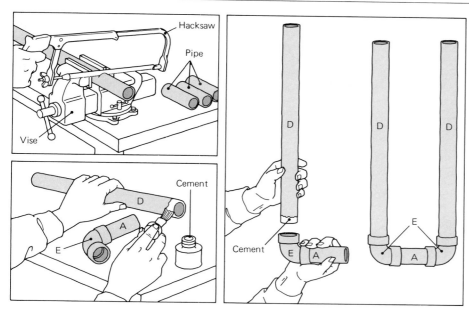

1. Cut PVC pipe to the lengths given in the chart on the opposite page by placing the pipe in a vise and making vertical cuts with a hacksaw. You can judge the cuts by eye; you need not use a miter box. Label each pipe (A, B, C, and D) with a pencil as it is cut to avoid confusion. Sand and clean all parts (see p.274). Dry-fit them to check for proper fit and alignment, then apply cement and join eight bottoms (A) and 16 uprights (D) with 16 elbows (E) to make eight U-shaped wheel slots. Be sure to push each pipe into its elbow as far as it will go.

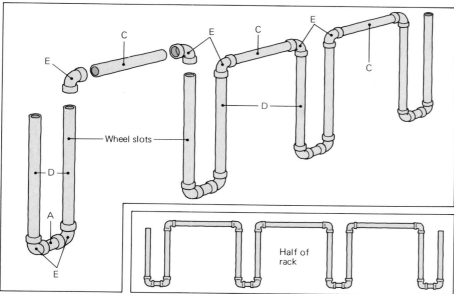

2. Add elbows to the tops of four of the wheel slots as shown. Connect the four wheel slots with three crosspieces (C) to make half the rack. Join the remaining four wheel slots with elbows and crosspieces in the same way to complete the second half of the rack. If any parts are joined improperly, you may be able to knock them apart with a hammer before the cement cures. If not, a hard blow from the hammer may shatter the faulty part without harming its neighbors—wear safety goggles!

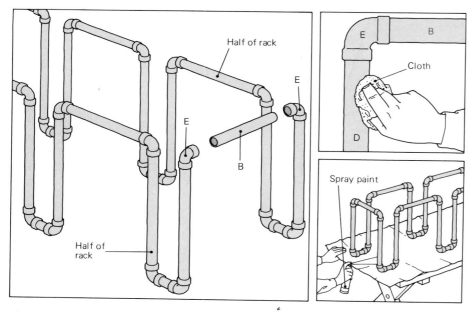

3. Glue the remaining four elbows to the ends of the two halves as shown. Then connect the two halves of the rack with the end pieces (B). The PVC pipe is flexible enough that it can be bent slightly to compensate for minor misalignment of the parts. Use lacquer thinner and cloths to remove the writing that is stenciled on the pipe if you want the rack to be white. If you want to paint the rack, choose a spray-on enamel that is compatible with plastic. (This type of enamel is often sold in hobby shops.)

STORAGE SHED

A full complement of backyard tools and appliances, as well as a workbench, can fit into a backyard storage shed the size of this one. Check to make certain that whatever you wish to store will fit through the 35½-inch x 71-inch door opening shown here. If you want to enlarge the shed or doorway, be sure to space the studs and rafters to accommodate the sheathing. Also be sure that the 4 x 4's flanking the door are installed square and plumb to simplify the task of installing the door.

The shed is built with standard wood-frame construction. The studs are spaced so that a 48-inch-wide piece of plywood may be used on each side at each corner; the overall dimensions are calculated to use a 96-inch length of plywood on the roof and at the center of the back wall.

The shed is supported by four pressure-treated posts sunk into the ground a foot below the frost line. This positioning ensures that the posts supporting the shed will not shift during the winter. If your frost line is deeper than 8 inches, which is common, you will have to buy 10-foot-long posts and saw them off. A shallower frost line allows you to buy 8-

Parts list

Part	Name	Quantity	Thickness	Width	Length	Material
A	Corner post	4	3½"	3½"	96" ✳	4 × 4 pine†
B	Front and back sill	2	3½"	3½"	128"	4 × 4 pine†
C	Side sill	2	3½"	3½"	89½"	4 × 4 pine†
D	Top-plate support	4	1½"	3½"	12"	2 × 4 fir
E	Lower side top plate	2	1½"	3½"	95"	2 × 4 fir
F	Lower front and back top plate	2	1½"	3½"	126½"	2 × 4 fir
G	Upper side top plate	2	1½"	3½"	88"	2 × 4 fir
H	Upper front and back top plate	2	1½"	3½"	133½"	2 × 4 fir
I	Door-frame stud	2	3½"	3½"	72"	4 × 4 fir
J	Wall stud	13	1½"	3½"	72"	2 × 4 fir
K	Low ridge support	4	1½"	3½"	15¼"	2 × 4 fir
L	Center ridge support	2	1½"	3½"	19"	2 × 4 fir
M	Ridgeboard	3	1½"	5½"	90"	2 × 6 fir
N	Lower rafter	10	1½"	3½"	40⅛"	2 × 4 fir
O	Upper rafter	10	1½"	3½"	31⅛"	2 × 4 fir
P	Short stud	4	1½"	3½"	16⅞"	2 × 4 fir
Q	Door-casing top	1	¾"	4"	37½"	1 × 6 pine
R	Door-casing side	2	¾"	4"	73"	1 × 6 pine
S	Doorstop	2	⁷⁄₁₆"	1⅜"	71¼"	Pine molding
T	Sheathing	14	½"	††	††	C–D plywood
U	Corner trim	4	1½"	1½"	76½"	2 × 2 cedar
V	Eave trim	2	¾"	1½"	96"	1 × 2 cedar
W	Lower gable trim	4	¾"	3½"	41⅛"	1 × 4 cedar
X	Upper gable trim	4	¾"	3½"	33⅛"	1 × 4 cedar
Y	Gable corner trim	4	¾"	2¼"	6"	1 × 4 cedar
Z	Door side trim	2	1½"	1½"	73¼"	2 × 2 cedar
AA	Drip cap	1	1¹⁄₁₆"	1⅝"	40"	Pine molding
BB	Door-frame side	2	¾"	3½"	73"	1 × 4 cedar
CC	Door-frame top and bottom	2	¾"	3½"	36"	1 × 4 cedar
DD	Door-frame center	1	¾"	3½"	29"	1 × 4 cedar
EE	Door board	5	¾"	7¼"	73"	1 × 8 cedar
FF	Long crossbrace	2	¾"	3½"	42⅝"	1 × 4 cedar
GG	Short crossbrace	4	¾"	3½"	19¾"	1 × 4 cedar

✳Length depends on the depth of the frost line (see text).
†Use pressure-treated lumber.
††These must be cut into six different shapes (see illustration on page 281).

Tools and materials: Circular or radial arm saw. Handsaw. Hammer, chisel, mallet. Shovel. Protractor, steel tape rule, level, string. Building paper (300 sq. ft.). Asphalt shingles (100 sq. ft.). Cedar shingles (200 sq. ft.). Paving stone (80 sq. ft.). Polyethylene sheet (80 sq. ft.). Sand. Lumber (see above). Metal flashing (37½" length). Door latch, handle, three T hinges. 1¼" No. 10 flathead wood screws. 6d, 8d, and 12d common nails. Roofing and galvanized siding nails.

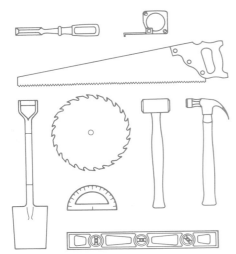

foot lengths, the next smaller size.

The shallow gambrel roof is covered with asphalt shingles. A more weatherproof, if less attractive, roofing is asphalt roll roofing, which is especially appropriate if the shed will be exposed to heavy precipitation or high wind. If you alter the dimensions of the roof, the new angles of the rafter ends can be determined with a careful scale drawing.

The walls are covered with cedar shingles, installed so that the levels of their bottom edges alternate. Cedar shingles change color with age—to a deeper brown if they are red cedar and to silver if they are white cedar. These effects can be duplicated with stains. Preservatives will retard changes in color.

The wood trim at the corners, gables, eaves, and door, as well as the door itself, offers you many possibilities for finishing with stains, paints, and preservatives.

The floor is made of paving stone, laid loose over a layer of sand and a polyethylene sheet. Other types of stone can be used if you adjust the dimensions of the screed board (Step 5) as necessary. The floor can also be made of pressure-treated lumber, a poured concrete slab, or simply left as dirt.

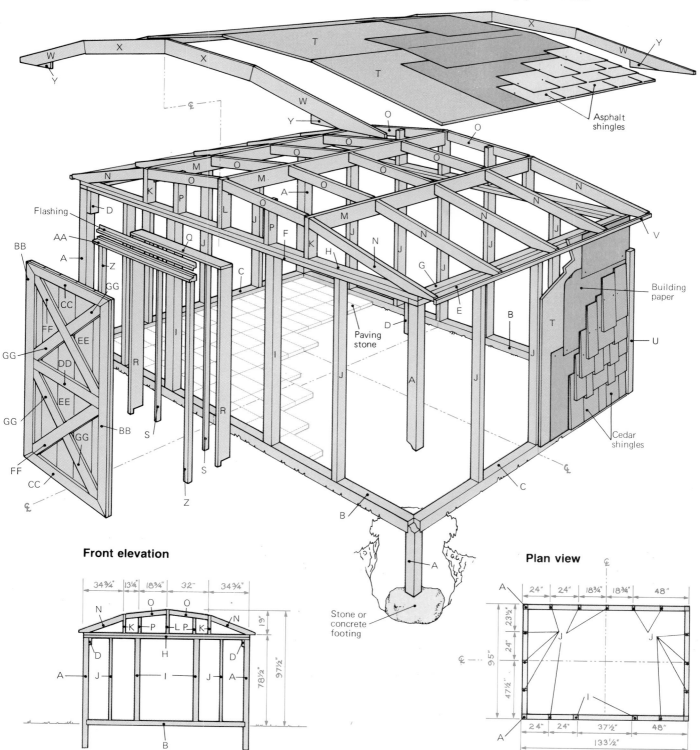

Front elevation

Plan view

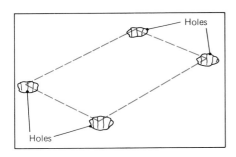

1. Measure out and mark the corners of the shed. Be sure the rectangular area inside the corners is fairly level. Dig a hole at each corner to 1 ft. below the frost line (consult your local building department).

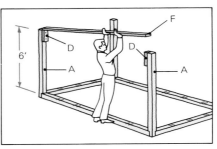

6. Lay one lower side top plate (E) beside one side sill (C). Measure and mark location of wall studs (J) on both the top plate and sill (see p.279). Repeat with the other lower top plates (E and F) and the remaining sills (B and C).

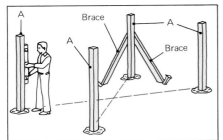

2. Lift the pressure-treated posts (A) into the corner holes. Measure the diagonals of the rectangle; if they are equal, the corners will be square. Brace posts and check for plumbness.

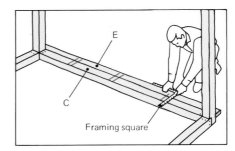

7. Measure 6 ft. up each post from the top of the sills and saw off the excess. Nail supports (D) to sides of posts to support the lower top plates. Raise the lower top plates and attach them to the posts with 12d nails.

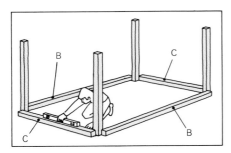

3. Backfill holes with rocks, gravel, and dirt. Using a level on top of each of the sills (B and C) as a guide, dig below each one, if necessary, until all four sills are exactly level and meet at the corners at the same height.

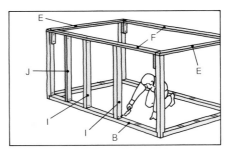

8. Using the guide marks made on the sills and top plates (Step 6), put the studs (I and J) in place. Check them for plumbness, then toenail them to the sills with 8d nails and end-nail them to the lower top plates with 12d nails.

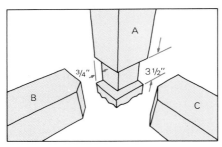

4. Using a saw, mallet, and chisel, cut a notch ¾ in. deep and 3½ in. high on both inside faces of each post to accept sills. Miter the insides of the sills, as shown, and toenail them to the posts with 8d nails.

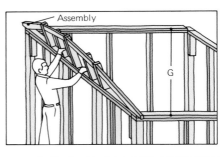

9. Install the upper side top plates (G). Cut pieces H, K, L, N, O, and P and assemble them as shown on page 279. Raise the assembly and nail the upper front top plate (H) to the lower front top plate (F) already in place.

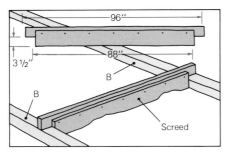

5. Make a screed board to the dimensions at left. Rest the ends of the board on the sills and draw it across the ground. This will indicate where the ground must be dug or filled so that the floor of the shed will be level.

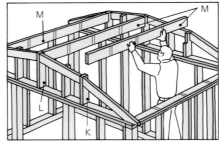

10. Repeat Step 9 for the back of shed and install it. Cut the ridgeboards (M). Mark the location of the rafters (N and O), which have the same spacing as the studs (J), on each ridgeboard. Toenail the ridgeboards to pieces K and L.

Roof framing and trim: Notch ridge supports (K and L) as indicated. Cut the 20 rafters (N and O) at precise angles shown so that the roof is secure. Gable trim (W, X, and Y) is decorative.

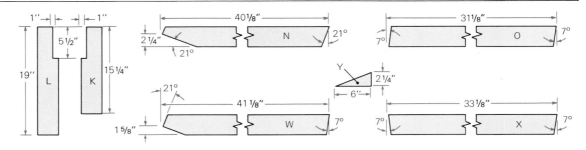

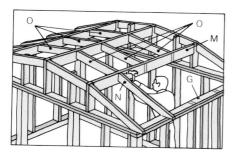

11. Nail the inner rafters (N and O) to the ridgeboards (M) at the marks made in Step 10. The lower rafters (N) should meet the upper side top plates (G) directly over the wall studs (J). Toenail the rafters to top plates.

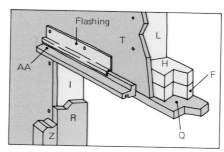

16. Attach the door casing (Q and R) to neighboring door studs (I), notching pieces R to fit over the front sill. Attach the door side trim and drip cap (Z and AA). Cut metal flashing and nail to sheathing as shown.

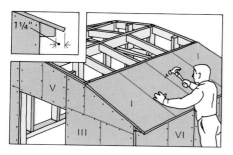

12. Measure diagonally to check walls for squareness. Position sheathing (T) so that all seams are centered over a stud. Mark locations of hidden studs on outside of sheathing. Attach sheathing to framing with 6d nails 8 in. apart.

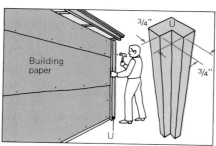

17. Cover the walls with building paper so that higher pieces overlap those below. Cut a rabbet ¾ in. × ¾ in. into the corner trim pieces (U), then nail the pieces to the corners of the shed.

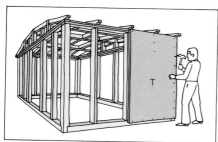

13. Cut sheathing (T) for roof (see the illustration at bottom of page). Position sheathing so that its factory-cut edge overhangs the rafter ends by 1¼ in. Mark positions of hidden framing on outside of sheathing and attach with 6d nails.

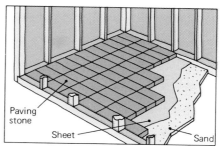

18. Install the cedar shingles from the base up, using two galvanized nails per shingle. Leave an 8-in. exposure and a ¼-in. gap between shingles. Stagger the gaps between courses. Use a string as a guide to keep the courses straight.

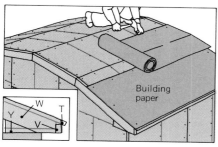

14. Attach the eave and gable trim (V, W, X, and Y) as shown on page 279. Working from the eaves up, tack or staple building paper over the roof with higher pieces overlapping those below by several inches.

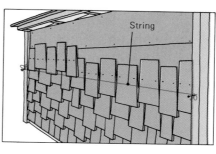

19. Assemble door frame (BB, CC, and DD). Attach door boards (EE), using two screws where boards and frame meet. Screw crossbraces (FF and GG) to door boards. Attach hinges, handle, and latch. Hang door and install doorstops (S).

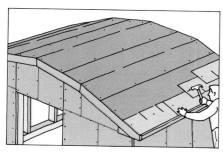

15. Install the asphalt shingles, working from the eaves toward the ridge, leaving 5 in. of each course of shingles exposed when the next course is installed. (Adequate instructions are usually supplied by the manufacturer.)

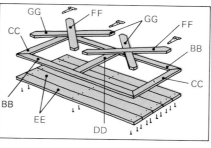

20. Place and level 1½ in. of sand over the floor of the shed, and cover it with a polyethylene sheet (a moisture and vapor barrier). Lay the paving stone in a tight pattern over the polyethylene.

Sheathing: Cut plywood as shown at right. The front of the shed is covered with two III's and a V, the back with two III's and a IV, the roof with two I's and two II's, and each side with two VI's.

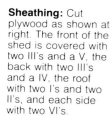

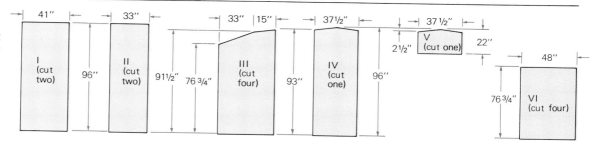

BIRD FEEDER

Birds will flock to this attractive feeder, which dispenses seeds on one side and holds suet on the other. The hopper floor is tilted so that the seeds slide downward, keeping the trough full. To replenish the feeder, withdraw the two long nails from their holes in the roof gables and separate the roof and body of the feeder.

The step-by-step instructions are for making the feeder with a table saw, but all the cuts can be made with a circular saw if you mark them carefully and use a straightedge as a guide. Before cutting the grooves and dadoes, make test cuts in scrap wood to ensure accuracy. If you use a combination blade instead of a dado head, make parallel cuts and then use a chisel to remove the waste and smooth

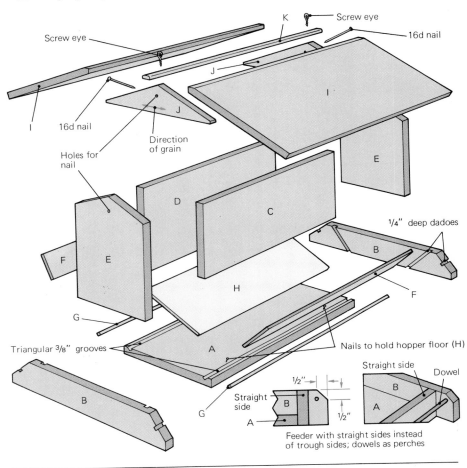

Feeder with straight sides instead of trough sides; dowels as perches

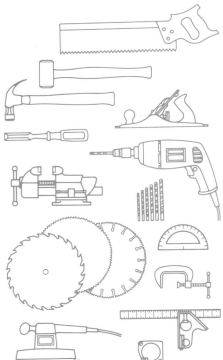

Parts list

Part	Name	Quantity	Thickness	Width	Length	Material
A	Base	1	3/4"	6 3/4"	11 3/4"	Redwood
B	Base end	2	3/4"	2"	12"	Redwood
C	Seed side	1	3/4"	4 3/4"	10 1/4"	Redwood
D	Suet side	1	3/4"	6 1/4"	10 1/4"	Redwood
E	End	2	3/4"	5 1/4"	8"	Redwood
F	Trough side	2	1/4"	2 1/8"	12 1/4"	Redwood
G	Perch	2	1/4"	1/4"	13 1/4"	Redwood
H	Hopper floor	1	1/4"	4 1/4"	10 1/4"	Exterior plywood
I	Roof	2	3/4"	6 3/4"	15"	Redwood
J	Gable	2	3/4"	2 1/8"	7"	Redwood
K	Roof ridge	1	3/8"	5/8"	15"	Redwood

Tools and materials: Drill with 1/16", 5/64", and 3/16" twist bits. Table saw (with miter gauge and combination blade or dado head) or circular saw. Backsaw or dovetail saw. Orbital sander with No. 120 paper. Steel tape rule, combination square, protractor. Hammer, wooden mallet, 1/4" chisel. Jack or smooth plane. Vise, 6" C-clamp. A 10' length of 1 x 8 redwood tongue-and-groove siding (with tongue and groove sawn off), a 1/4" x 4 1/4" x 10 1/4" scrap of plywood. Two 1/2" screw eyes and wire for hanging feeder. Box of 1 3/4" aluminum cedar shake nails, eleven 1" galvanized nails, two 16d nails.

the grooves and dadoes (these can also be cut with a router, using a V-grooving bit and a ¼-inch straight bit).

Redwood splits easily; therefore, you should drill pilot holes for the 1¾-inch nails that are used to join the main parts of the feeder. Use a ¹⁄₁₆-inch bit to drill pilot holes through the pieces being joined, and drill the holes the full length of the

nails. Then enlarge the clearance holes in each outer piece with a ⁵⁄₆₄-inch bit.

You can make the ¼-inch stock by slicing a ¾-inch board on the table saw, using a tenoning jig (see *Index,* p.379), or by making a number of overlapping, parallel cuts in the surface of the board and then planing it smooth. You can also use ¼-inch exterior plywood, but you may prefer the

variation on the opposite page (see inset). For this alternative, make the base 8 inches wide, and in place of the trough sides (F) nail ¾- x 2- x 11¾-inch sides to the base (A) and the base ends (B). Make perches of ¼-inch dowels, insert them in holes drilled in the base ends, and cut ½-inch triangles from the corners of the base ends (see Step 2).

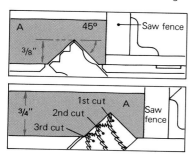

1. Sand one side of board smooth. Cut all parts but E and J to sizes shown in chart, with grain parallel to their longest dimensions. Use a ¼-in. dado head, tilt the saw 45°, and cut a triangular groove (top) ⅜ in. deep and ⅛ in. from each long edge of base (A). Or make several cuts with a combination blade, lowering the blade for each cut (bottom).

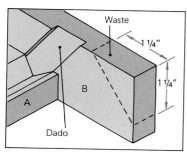

2. Mark center lines on top of base (A) and inner faces of base ends (B). Align them, and transfer positions of grooves to base ends. With dado head or saw blade upright, and using the miter gauge, cut dadoes ⁵⁄₁₆ in. wide and ¼ in. deep at 45° in base ends. Cut off 1¼-in. triangles from upper corners of each base end.

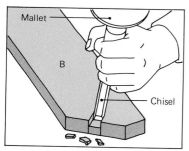

3. Lay out ¼-in. x ¼-in. dadoes centered on the angled edges of the base ends cut in Step 2. Saw the sides of the dadoes with a backsaw or dovetail saw. Chop out the remaining waste with a ¼-in. chisel and a wooden mallet.

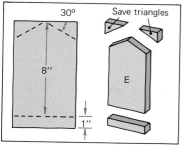

4. Cut the board for the ends (E) 9 in. long. Mark center lines. Set the miter gauge at 60°, and saw off the corners of the top edges at 30°, making a peak at each center line. Save the triangles. Saw across bottoms so that each end measures 8 in. from peak to bottom edge. In the following steps assemble all parts with their sanded sides facing outward.

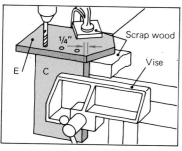

5. Clamp each side (C and D), in turn, in a vise. Position each end (E) so its upper corners are ¼ in. higher than the top edges of the sides. Drill pilot holes (see text) at 1½-in. to 2-in. intervals through each end and into the sides; make three holes for each joint. Nail sides and ends together with 1¾-in. nails. Make sure box is square.

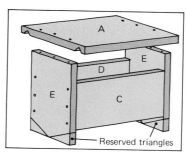

6. Stand the box upside down, drill pilot holes as shown, and nail on base (A). Position base ends (B) so that trough sides (F) fit into their dadoes and grooves. Nail base ends to sides; file off ends of nails inside feeder. Nail perches (G) into dadoes in base ends with 1-in. nails.

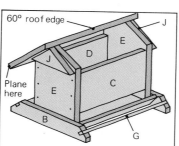

7. Grain in gables (J) should run the length of wood. Cut gables as you did the ends, then saw each gable to 2⅛ in. from peak to bottom edge. Make an extra gable of scrap wood to use as a jig in Step 10. Tilt saw blade 30°, and trim one edge of each roof piece (I). Round the corners of outer roof edges with a jack or smooth plane.

8. Measure between outer surfaces of ends (E); join gables to roof ⅛ in. farther apart. Nail gables to one roof piece as shown (left), making sure gables are parallel to each other. Turn assembly over, and rest gables on a 2 x 4 while you drill pilot holes (right). Position second roof piece tightly against first, drill pilot holes in it, and nail both roof pieces in place.

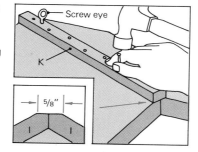

9. Use a jack or smooth plane to make a flat area ⅝ in. wide at the peak of the roof (inset). Attach the roof ridge (K) with a staggered row of 1-in. galvanized nails so that nails enter each roof piece. Drill holes for inserting two ½-in. screw eyes directly over gable peaks.

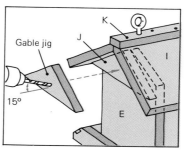

10. Use a ³⁄₁₆-in. bit to make a hole in the gable jig at a 15° angle as shown. Place roof on feeder, hold jig against gable, and drill through jig, gable, and end. Put a 16d nail in hole. Repeat for other gable. Drive two 1-in. nails partway into base (A) ¼ in. from groove on seed side; these will hold hopper floor (H) in place.

BIRDHOUSE

One of the easiest projects in this book, this birdhouse—or nesting box—meets the requirements for dryness, ventilation, and safety from larger birds.

Construction: The front corners of the floor are cut at an angle for ventilation. Four holes in each side and an opening beneath the roof at the back give cross ventilation. The entrance is high enough so that predators cannot reach the baby birds. Access through the removable front makes it easy to clean out an old nest in preparation for another tenant. The front is held in position by cleats and is secured with just one screw.

The cedar lumber used is weather resistant, so it does not need finishing. Redwood can be substituted. Paint the roof with off-white latex; it will reflect heat and make the box cooler inside.

Placement: Most songbirds prefer a relatively open, sunny area. The edges of woods, a field, or a clump of trees are good spots. Woodland birds, such as chickadees, nuthatches, and titmice, prefer shaded areas. Bluebirds, for which this house was built, nest in open country

fields (not suburban lawns), and they prefer a box mounted on a post 5–10 feet above the ground. Locate the box where the morning sun's rays can reach it. Other species will occupy a box on a tree or building. Where cats are numerous, ring the tree or post with a metal baffle.

Mount the box by driving screws or nails through the large holes in the mounting strip. For added security, run wire through the small holes in the strip and wrap it around the tree or post.

Put the box out by March when birds start looking for nesting sites—earlier in some areas. Birds are particular about not having another family of the same species nearby, but you can lure several species to your yard by setting out boxes built to different specifications (see chart opposite). Place the boxes at least 25 feet apart. Bluebirds are a special case: they do not like to be closer than 300 feet to any other birds.

If you clean the box as soon as the fledglings have left, you may get a second brood in one season. Your box may even serve as a winter storm shelter.

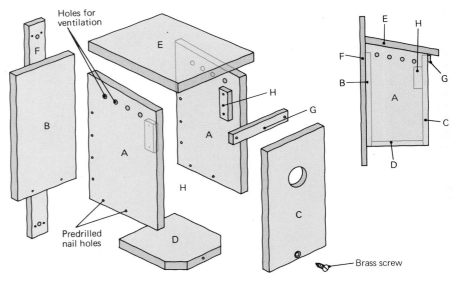

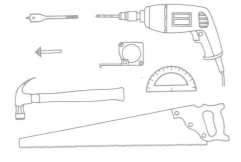

Parts list

Part	Name	Quantity	Thickness	Width	Length	Material
A	Side	2	¾″	6½″	10″	Cedar
B	Back	1	¾″	5″	9⅝″	Cedar
C	Front	1	¾″	5″	8½″	Cedar
D	Floor	1	¾″	5″	5″	Cedar
E	Roof	1	¾″	7½″	9″	Pine
F	Mounting strip	1	¾″	2¼″	19″	Cedar
G	Exterior cleat	1	⅜″	1″	6½″	Cedar
H	Interior cleat	2	⅜″	¾″	2¾″	Cedar

Tools and materials: Drill with ¹⁄₁₆″ twist bit, 1½″ spade bit, and countersink. Crosscut saw, hammer. Steel tape rule, protractor, pencil. Pine ¾″ x 7½″ x 9″, rough, unplaned cedar ¾″ x 7⅜″ x 48″. Three 1¼″ No. 8 brass flathead wood screws. Twenty-five 5d galvanized steel common nails, four 2d galvanized steel common nails.

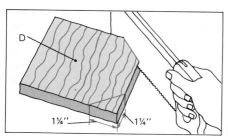

1. Cut all pieces to size. (For the cleats, split a 1-in.-wide piece of cedar.) Holding the floor (D) so that the grain will run from side to side in the finished box, measure 1¼ in. from each front corner. Draw diagonal lines, and saw off the triangles.

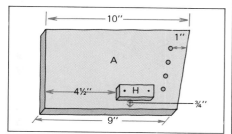

2. Drill four ¼-in. holes 1 in. below the top of each side (A). Nail the interior cleats (H) on the inside ¾ in. from the front edges and 4½ in. above bottom edges; use 2d nails.

3. Drill entrance in front (C) with 1½-in. spade bit. Center the bit 6¾ in. above the bottom edge of the front.

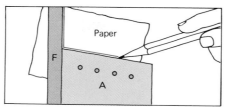

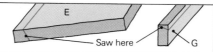

4. Trace angle of side (A) to mounting strip (F) on paper as shown; transfer that angle to the back edge of roof (E) and top edge of exterior cleat (G). Saw angle. Paint the roof with two coats of off-white latex on all sides, allowing paint to dry between coats.

5. Predrill holes with a ¹⁄₁₆-in. twist bit in the sides (A) and the back (B) where nails will enter. Glue and nail with 5d nails from the sides into the back and then from the back and sides into the floor (D).

6. Predrill holes for nails in roof (E). Glue and nail with four nails driven into each side (A). Paint the top of the roof. Nail the exterior cleat (G) across the front, driving nails into the leading edges of sides.

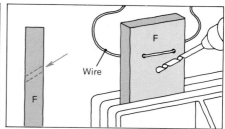

7. Drill a ⅛-in. hole in mounting strip (F) 2 in. from each end. Slant top hole downward. Drill ¹⁄₁₆-in. holes on either side of those holes ¼ in. from edge of strip for wire (see text). Glue, nail, and screw strip to back so that it extends 4⅜ in. beyond bottom of box.

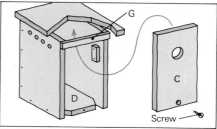

8. Drill and countersink a hole for screw in front (C) centered ⅜ in. from bottom edge. Position front under exterior cleat; drill through hole for pilot hole in floor (D).

Variations

A nesting box made to the specifications in the *Parts list* is suitable for bluebirds; tree swallows may occupy it too. Other species have different requirements as shown in the box at right. Modify the basic box according to these dimensions and the variations shown below to attract other species to your yard. The list includes the more common birds native to North America that are cavity nesters and therefore will use a man-made box. The depth of the cavity is measured from the box floor to the roof at the front of the box; entrance height is from the floor to the center of the hole.

Species	Floor of cavity	Depth of cavity	Entrance height	Entrance diameter	Above ground
Chickadee ✻	4″ x 4″	8″–10″	6″–8″	1⅛″	6′–15′
Titmouse ✻	4″ x 4″	8″–10″	6″–8″	1¼″	6′–15′
Nuthatch ✻	4″ x 4″	8″–10″	6″–8″	1¼″	12′–20′
House wren	4″ x 4″	6″–8″	1″–6″	⅞″	6′–10′
Violet-green swallow	5″ x 5″	6″	1″–5″	1½″	10′–15′
Tree swallow	5″ x 5″	6″	1″–5″	1½″	10′–15′
House finch	6″ x 6″	6″	4″	2″	8′–12′
Flicker	7″ x 7″	16″–18″	14″–16″	2½″	6′–20′
Downy woodpecker ✻	4″ x 4″	8″–10″	6″–8″	1¼″	6′–20′
Hairy woodpecker ✻	6″ x 6″	12″–15″	9″–12″	1½″	12′–20′
Screech owl ✻	8″ x 8″	12″–15″	9″–12″	3″	10′–30′
Saw-whet owl ✻	6″ x 6″	10″–12″	8″–10″	2½″	12′–20′
Wood duck	10″ x 18″	10″–24″	12″–16″	4″	10′–20′

✻ Requires log-type nesting box.

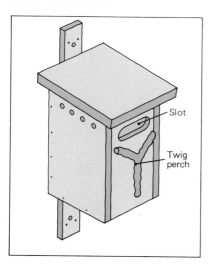

Wren house. Wrens build nests with long sticks; a slot entrance makes it easier to get the sticks into the box. Cut the slot with a saber saw or keyhole saw. Make the slot 2–2½ in. long and ⅞ in. high for a house wren, 1 in. high for a Bewick's wren, and 1½ in. high for a Carolina wren. The box dimensions and height above the ground are the same for all three (see chart above for house wren). Wrens like a perch, but do not use one for most other species; it will invite predators.

Log nesting box. Some species (see chart above) will use a box only if it resembles a hollow in a tree. Choose a log 2 in. larger in diameter than the floor dimensions. Saw a slab off one side for the roof. Saw the top of the log so that it is 1 in. lower in front than in back. Drill the entrance hole with an expansion bit. Hollow the interior with a chisel. Nail and glue the log to the back and floorboards. Put at least 1 in. of sawdust or wood chips inside. Nail box directly to main trunk of a tree.

A-FRAME DOGHOUSE

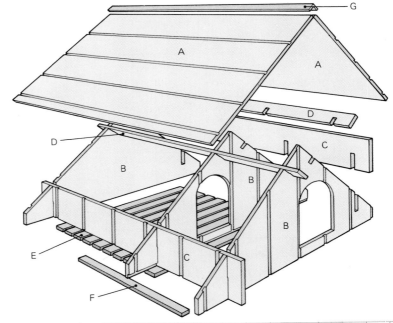

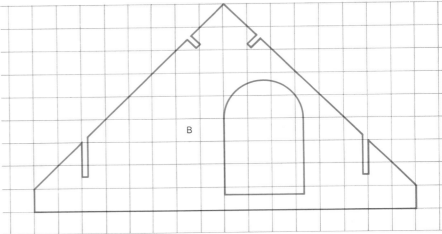

Make a pattern (see p.48) using 3-in. squares to build a house for a medium-size dog, 2-in. squares for a small dog, and 4-in. squares for a large dog (see text).

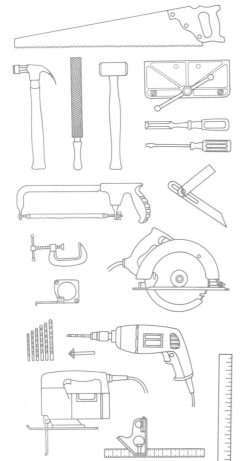

Parts list

Part	Name	Quantity	Thickness	Width	Length	Material
A	Roof	2	19/32″	34¼″ ✻	54″	T–111 siding
B	End	3	19/32″	48″	27″	T–111 siding
C	Side	2	19/32″	9″	48″	T–111 siding
D	Brace	2	19/32″	3″	48″	T–111 siding
E	Floor slat	13	¾″	1½″	34″ ✻	1 x 2 fir or pine
F	Floor support	2	¾″	1½″	25″ ✻	1 x 2 fir or pine
G	Peak	1	⅛″	2″	54″	2″ x 2″ aluminum angle

✻Measurement is approximate. Cut to fit during construction.

Tools and materials: Electric drill with set of twist bits and countersink. Circular saw and saber saw with plywood blades. Crosscut saw, hacksaw. Hammer, mallet, ½″ chisel, rasp. Two 2″ C-clamps, two 4″ C-clamps, woodworker's vise. Combination square, framing square, T bevel, steel tape rule, pencil. Two or three sawhorses. Stapler with ¼″ long staples. Waterproof glue, a qt. of cedar penetrating oil stain, 3″ paintbrush. Piece of tar paper 3″ x 54″. Two 4′ x 9′ sheets of 19/32″ T–111 grooved siding, eight 1 x 2's of fir or pine 8′ long. Nine 1¼″ No. 8 brass wood screws, twenty-four ½″ No. 8 zinc-coated wood screws. Four 3″ zinc-coated strap hinges. A 6′ length of 2″ x 2″ aluminum angle ⅛″ thick. Sixty 4d finishing nails.

An animal's own body heat is all that keeps it warm inside a doghouse. In order for this "heating system" to be effective, the doghouse should be as small as possible, have little or no ventilation, and have some sort of windbreak at the entrance. A slatted floor keeps the animal off the damp ground and prevents it from digging inside the doghouse. A hinged roof provides access to the back room so that you can clean the room or reach your animal if it is sick or in hiding.

Variations: The doghouse should be sized to fit its occupant. Measure your dog's width and height at the shoulders. The doorway should be 2 inches wider than the dog and about the same height. The house shown here is fine for medium-size dogs 12–18 inches tall. For smaller dogs use 2-inch squares in the pattern on the opposite page and reduce all other dimensions by one-third. For larger dogs use 4-inch squares and increase the other dimensions by one-third. You will also need a third sheet of siding.

Materials: The doghouse shown here is made from two 4- x 9-foot sheets of grooved T–111 outdoor siding. It can also be made of the less-expensive exterior-grade plywood, although three sheets of plywood will be needed because of its slightly smaller 4- x 8-foot size.

Construction: Support the siding with sawhorses so that it does not droop. Mark cutting lines on the siding so that the ends and sides (B and C) will be on one sheet with their grooves running from top to bottom. Lay out the roof (A) on the second sheet so that the grooves run from front to back. Position the braces (D) between the grooves. Use the edge of one uncut sheet as a cutting guide for the roof.

After the final assembly (Step 12), cut a scrap of tar paper 3 inches wide by 54 inches long and staple it along the peak of the roof. Cut the aluminum angle 54 inches long and place it over the tar paper. Its weight will hold it in place.

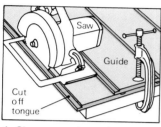

1. Clamp one piece of siding to the second piece to serve as a cutting guide. Remove the tongue along one edge of each sheet so that you are left with two sheets exactly 48 in. wide. Lay out all pieces as described in text. Measure diagonal edge of ends (34¼" in this case) and cut roof width to match this dimension.

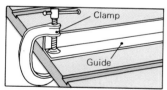

2. Use aluminum angle and small C-clamps as a cutting guide and cut out parts A, B, C, and D. Be careful to position the sawhorses so that you do not cut into them! Have a helper support one end of the sheet so that it does not twist and splinter as the cut is completed.
3. Align matching parts to make sure that they are exactly the same size. If they do not match exactly, clamp them together and cut the parts back to the size of the smallest part.

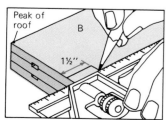

4. Align the three ends (B), two face down and one face up, and clamp them together so that the

ungrooved back sides are exposed. Mark cutting lines for the four slots 6 in. from each edge and 6 in. from the peak. Slots should match the width of the siding (use a scrap as a guide) and be half as deep as sides and braces (C and D)— 4½ and 1½ in. respectively.

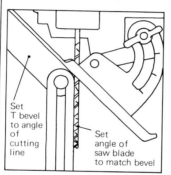

5. Use combination square to extend cutting lines for slots across the edges of all three clamped parts. Set T bevel to match the angle between the deep slots and the diagonal edge of B. Set circular saw's blade to maximum cutting depth, then set the cutting angle to match the bevel. Cut just inside lines with circular saw. Extend the cuts to the bottoms of the slots with a crosscut saw.

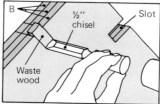

6. Reset cutting depth of circular saw to match depth of short slots (1½ in.). Cut just inside of lines with circular saw. Use ½" chisel to clean out bottoms of all slots. Hold chisel so that its beveled side faces the waste wood (part to be removed). Chisel from both sides of stacked ends (B) toward center to avoid splitting the wood.

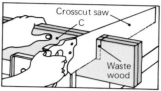

7. Clamp braces (D) face to face and mark cutting lines for slots 3 in. from each end and another 18 in. from one end. Cut out slots with circular saw still set to depth from Step 6. Clean out slots with a chisel. Clamp sides (C) face to face and trace these slots from D onto C. Cut slots in sides (C) 4½ in. deep using the circular saw and then the crosscut saw as in Step 5.
8. Assemble parts B, C, and D to make sure they fit snugly. If necessary, enlarge slots slightly with a rasp. The tighter the fit, the stronger the doghouse. (Tap tight-fitting parts into position with a mallet.) Hold straightedge along diagonal edges of ends to make sure sides and braces will not interfere with roof.

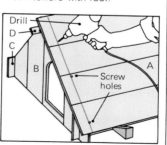

9. Prop one side of roof (A) in position so that upper edge is flush with peaks of ends and overhang is equal at front and rear. Drill pilot and countersink holes for nine 1¼" No. 8 screws on one side only. Use combination square to mark position of the three top screws first; insert them partway. Insert the three bottom screws partway, then lay straightedge between top and bottom screws to locate the three center screws. Position all screws so that they will not penetrate sides, braces, or grooves in ends.

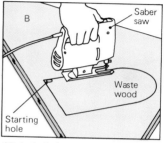

10. Label, then disassemble all parts. Align front and center ends (B) face to face. Mark cutting lines for doorway to suit your dog (see text). Drill a large starting hole, then cut out doorway with a saber saw.
11. Stain all exposed surfaces of siding with cedar oil stain; let siding dry overnight. Lay roof parts (A) face down so that their top edges butt tightly together, and attach them with four 3-in. strap hinges. Use ½-in. screws, not the longer screws supplied with the hinges. Position hinges so that they do not interfere with ends (B) when roof is in place.

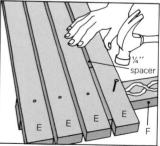

12. Reassemble parts B, C, and D. Measure inside dimensions of large room and make a platform of 1 x 2's approximately 1 in. smaller than the room. Cut two pieces 25 in. long (F) and 13 pieces 34 in. long (E). Set the short pieces 2 ft. apart and coat their upper surfaces with waterproof glue. Nail long pieces across short ones, spacing them ¼ in. apart with a scrap of ¼-in. plywood. Place floor inside doghouse and attach roof with the nine 1¼-in. screws.

POTTING CART

If you are a home gardener who maintains plants either indoors or outdoors on your deck or patio, this is the ideal project for you—a potting cart that can be wheeled to where you want it. The trough at the top of the cart will prevent loose soil from spilling out, and the sturdy slatted shelf can be used to store peat and potting soil. If this project appears too fancy for a potting cart, that is because it was designed so that you can cover it to create a TV stand or serving cart.

The cart is made of oak throughout, except for the plywood base and removable cover. The oak stock must be ripped to the proper widths before it is cut to length. The oak legs and the sides and ends of the cart are relieved with decorative grooves cut with a router. The parts are glued and screwed together in butt joints, and all visible screw holes are filled with plugs cut from dowels.

To finish the cart, sand it thoroughly with Nos. 100, 150, and 220 paper, paying particular attention to the decorative grooves. Remove any sawdust, then apply stain to the oak. When the stain is dry, apply two coats of penetrating oil.

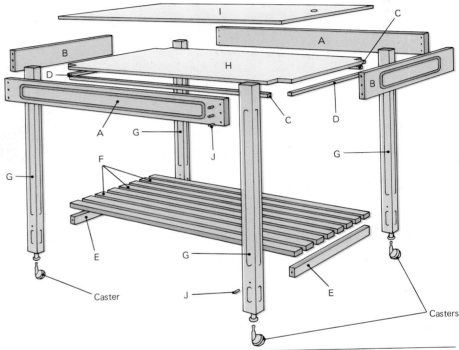

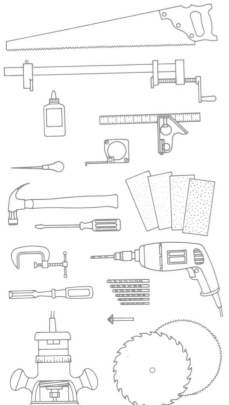

Parts list

Part	Name	Quantity	Thickness	Width	Length	Material
A	Side	2	3/4"	3⅞"	30"	1" oak
B	End	2	3/4"	3⅞"	16½"	1" oak
C	Cleat	2	3/4"	3/4"	25"	1" oak
D	Cleat	2	3/4"	3/4"	14"	1" oak
E	Leg brace	2	3/4"	1¼"	14 1/16" ✱	1" oak
F	Shelf slat	8	3/4"	1¼"	27 9/16"	1" oak
G	Leg	4	1¼"	1¾"	30 13/16"	2" oak
H	Base	1	½"	16½" ✱	28½" ✱	Plywood
I	Cover	1	½"	16½" ✱	28½" ✱	Oak plywood
J	Plug	16	3/8" dia.	—	¼"	Hardwood dowel

✱ Measurement is approximate; cut to fit during construction.

Tools and materials: Table, radial arm, or circular saw. Handsaw. Router with ¾" classic bit. Electric drill with set of twist bits and countersink. Two 3' pipe or bar clamps, four 6" C-clamps. Hammer, screwdriver, chisel, awl. Combination square, steel tape rule, pencil. Nos. 80, 100, 150, and 220 sandpaper. Carpenter's glue. Cherry or other wood stain, penetrating oil, soft cloths.

Twenty running ft. of 1" oak board at least 4" wide, a 3' length of 2" oak board at least 7" wide, ¼ panel of ½" A–C plywood and ½" oak-veneer plywood. A 3/8" hardwood dowel. Four ball casters (1⅝" dia.) with bushings. Flathead wood screws as follows: sixteen 1¼" No. 8, thirty-two 1½" No. 8, eight 2" No. 10, and four 3" No. 12.

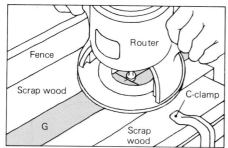

1. Cut parts A, B, C, D, F, and G to size (see chart). Measure distance from edge of router base to center of bit. Center one leg (G) that distance from saw fence or wall and fill space between with scrap wood. Clamp more scrap against other side of leg.

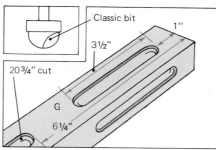

2. With router base pressed against saw fence, make a 3½-in.-long cut with classic bit, beginning 1 in. from bottom of a leg (G). Make a 20¾-in.-long cut beginning 6¼ in. from bottom. Repeat cuts on other three faces of leg. Cut other legs in same way.

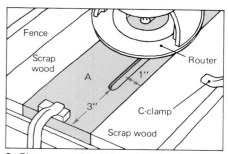

3. Clamp one side (A) against fence so that center of router bit is 1 in. from one edge of side. Make cut beginning 3 in. from one end of side and ending 3 in. from other end. Turn side and make parallel cut 1 in. from opposite edge. Repeat on other side and ends (B).

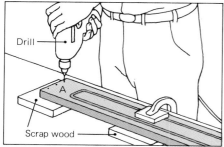

4. Join cuts on each side (A) and end (B) with connecting cuts. To do this, clamp each piece with its end against saw fence and cut with router. Drill three 3/32-in. pilot holes 3/8 in. from each end of each side. Use a 3/8-in. bit to counterbore holes ¼ in. deep.

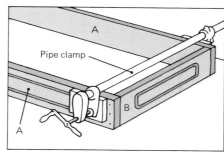

5. Glue and clamp sides to ends, checking for squareness. Use a 3/32-in. bit to drill pilot holes into ends, then drive in 1½-in. screws. Cut plugs (J) and glue 12 of them into screw holes. Trim tops of plugs with chisel and sand them flush with No. 80 paper.

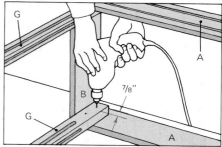

6. Glue and clamp tops of legs (G) 7/8 in. below tops of sides with thickness of each leg butting against inner face of end. Drill two 3/32-in. holes through each leg into side and two at different levels through leg into end. Countersink. Drive in 1½-in. and 2-in. screws.

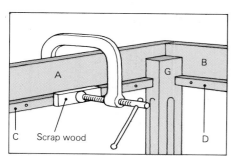

7. Glue and clamp cleats (C and D) at bottom edges of sides and ends—they should fit snugly between the legs. Drill five 3/32-in. pilot holes through each long cleat into side and three through each short cleat into end. Countersink holes. Drive in 1¼-in. screws.

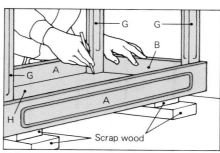

8. Check measurements for base (H), then cut it to size and position it over legs. Holding base in place, turn cart upside down and mark four corners of base for cutouts around legs. Remove base, make cutouts with handsaw, then glue base to tops of cleats.

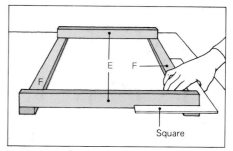

9. Measure distance between insides of legs on end of cart and cut two leg braces (E) to that length and to width of 1¼ in. Glue and clamp the two outside shelf slats (F) to tops of leg braces flush with ends of braces, checking assembly for squareness.

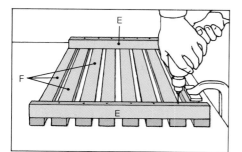

10. Position six remaining slats with equal spacing between them. Glue on slats; clamp assembly upside down to work surface. Drill a 3/32-in. pilot hole through each brace into bottom of each inside slat. Countersink pilot holes and drive in 1½-in. screws.

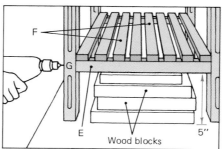

11. Position shelf so it sits between decorative grooves on legs and prop it up on wood blocks. Drill a 1/8-in. hole through each leg into leg brace. Use 3/8-in. bit to counterbore holes ¼ in. deep. Drive in 3-in. screws; fill screw holes with plugs and trim plugs.

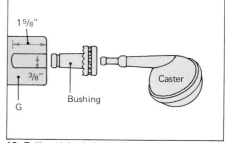

12. Drill a 3/8-in. hole 1 5/8 in. deep into bottom of each leg. Hammer caster bushings into holes and push casters into bushings. Cut cover (I) and drill hole through it near one end to serve as a finger grip. Position cover over tops of legs. Sand and finish cart.

PICKET FENCE AND GATE

There is nothing like an old-fashioned picket fence for enclosing an area in an attractive and friendly way. Use 4 x 4's for the corner and gate posts of this 3-foot fence. Be sure that they are firmly set at least 2 feet deep in concrete or hard-packed clay (see pp.266–267 for instructions in setting fence posts). In most cases the intermediate posts for a low, lightweight fence, such as this one, need be no more than 2 x 4's driven 30 inches into the ground; however, if the soil is unstable or subject to frost heave, these posts should be set more firmly. Chamfer the tops of all posts so that rain water will run off.

Laying out the fence: Drive a preliminary short stake to mark each corner of the area to be fenced in. Then, along each line of the fence, stretch a string between two batter boards, extending at least 3 feet past the preliminary corner stake. By adjusting the positions of these strings, square corners can be achieved.

Decide where the gate is to be—choose a level area with good drainage—and drive stakes to mark the positions of the gate posts. A gate for admitting foot traffic only does not have to be wider than 30–36 inches, but a gate through which wheelbarrows and garden equipment

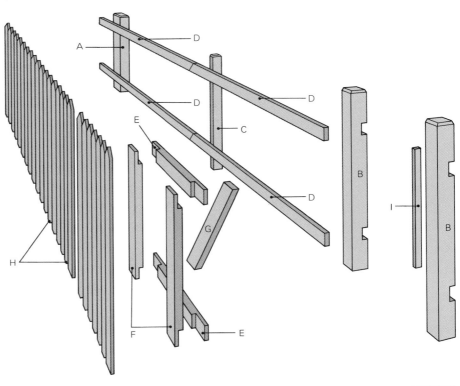

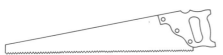

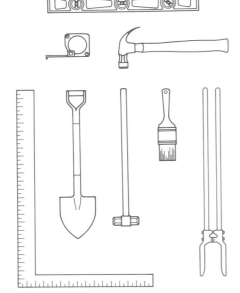

Parts list (for two sections of fence and gate)

Part	Name	Quantity	Thickness	Width	Length	Material
A	Corner post	1	3½"	3½"	57"	4 x 4 pressure-treated lumber
B	Gate post	2	3½"	3½"	63"	4 x 4 pressure-treated lumber
C	Intermediate post	1	1½"	3½"	63"	2 x 4 pressure-treated lumber
D	Fence rail	4	1½"	3½"	✳	2 x 4 pressure-treated lumber
E	Gate rail	2	1½"	3½"	✳	2 x 4 pressure-treated lumber
F	Stile	2	1½"	3½"	25½"	2 x 4 pressure-treated lumber
G	Crossbrace	1	1½"	3½"	✳	2 x 4 pressure-treated lumber
H	Picket	✳	¾"	2½"	36"	1 x 3 pressure-treated lumber
I	Gate stop	1	¾"	1½"	36"	1 x 2 pressure-treated lumber

✳ To be determined during construction.

Tools and materials: Post-hole digger, shovel. Saw, hammer, sledgehammer. Framing square, level, steel tape rule, mason's line, plumb line. String, wooden stakes, batter boards. Paintbrush, waterproof paint. Pressure-treated lumber (see above). Gravel, concrete. Two 6" T hinges, two steel mending plates. Gate latch. 1¼" and 2" No. 10 flathead wood screws. 4d, 6d, 8d, and 10d galvanized common nails.

must pass should be 40–48 inches wide.

Set the corner posts (A) first, being sure that they are plumb and squarely aligned. Then set the gate posts (B) so that their rear faces line up with the string. Position and set intermediate posts (C) at equal intervals of 6–8 feet, their front faces along the string. The tops of the corner and intermediate posts should be level, the gate posts 6 inches higher.

After about 2 days cut dadoes across the rear faces of the gate posts to receive the fence rails (D). The upper edge of the top rail should be about an inch below the tops of the other posts; that of the bottom rail should be 10 inches above the ground. Cut and secure the rails so that they are level, working from the gate posts outward. To seal joints as you assemble them, paint all surfaces and nail the parts together while the paint is still wet. Nail the pickets (H) to the rails with 6d galvanized nails, spacing them evenly no more than 2½ inches apart. Ideally, the spacing will work out so that a picket falls directly in front of each 2 x 4 post.

Making the gate: Cut the gate rails (E) an inch shorter than the distance between the gate posts (B); cut the stiles (F) long enough to overlap both fence rails. Use corner lap joints to assemble the frame (see p.267), testing it before nailing to be sure that it fits properly between the gate posts. Cut the crossbrace (G) to run from the bottom hinge corner to the upper corner of the opposite side, and secure it with steel mending plates. Nail the outer two pickets (H) flush with the edges of the gate frame and space the remaining pickets evenly between them. Hang the gate with two T hinges on the back of one gate post, and nail the gate stop (I) to the opposite gate post. A wide variety of gate latches are available, or the gate can be secured with a single hook and eye.

Building the fence

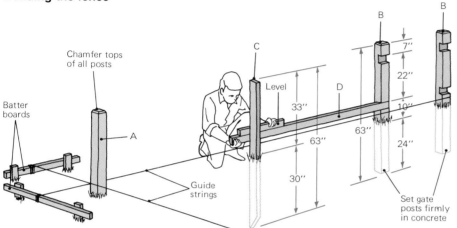

Nail a 2-ft. strip of 1 x 3 across two stakes to make a batter board. Move strings along boards to square corners. Align front faces of corner and intermediate posts (A and C) and rear faces of gate posts (B) along string.

Cut dadoes in rear faces of gate posts to receive rails (D). Tack end of bottom rail into its dado; level rail to mark its position on front edge of intermediate post (C). Do the same with the top rail.

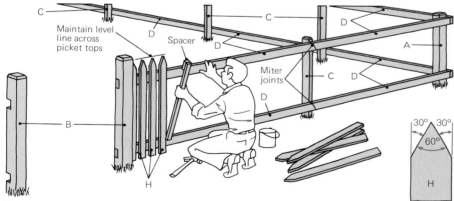

Mark and cut top and bottom rails for miter joints. Then nail them in place with 8d or 10d galvanized common nails. Cut matching miters on ends of next rails; then tack, level, cut, and secure them in the same way.

For uniform spacing of pickets, cut a slat to the width desired and attach a small cleat to one end. Hang it from the top rail. To make standard Gothic pickets, cut tops of 1 x 3's at 60° angles; sand away sharp edges.

Making the gate

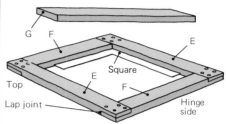

1. Assemble gate frame face down, driving four 4d galvanized nails into each corner lap joint. Cut crossbrace (G) to butt against rails (E), running from bottom hinge corner to upper corner of opposite side.

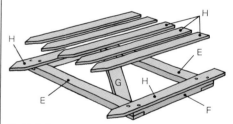

2. Nail the two outer pickets (H) flush with edges of stiles (F), being sure they will be level with pickets of fence. Space the remaining pickets evenly between them, maintaining a level line across the top.

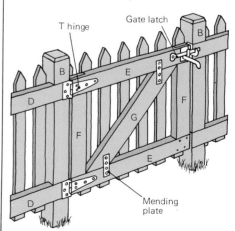

3. Attach strap sides of T hinges to gate rails (E) with one 1¼-in. screw in each end hole. Secure base end of hinge to rear of gate post (B) with a 2-in. screw, then drive remaining screws into gate rails.

Variations

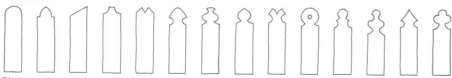

Pickets are available from many lumberyards in a variety of decorative styles.

COMPOST BIN

Successful compost bins, which convert leaves, grass clippings, and other vegetable matter into rich soil, can be made from scrap lumber or even poultry netting. But on a city lot, where nearly everything in the backyard is in plain sight, a well-designed bin of good lumber is preferable. The compost bin shown here has a capacity of 54 cubic feet. It is made of redwood, the most rot resistant of all woods and a material that ages beautifully without the need of paint or stain. The bin can also be made of cedar.

To build the bin, put together the frames for the four sides, then nail on the slats with gaps between them to let in air, which is needed for the decaying process. Add cover strips over the tops of the slats to mask them.

Since redwood is soft and does not hold nails well in areas that receive stress, use annular (ring) nails and attach strips of spruce or other sturdy wood to the corners to help hold the nails. Although the spruce strips will rot before the redwood, they make the bin sturdier and can easily be replaced when necessary.

Either nail on both end sections or nail on one and attach the other with hooks and eyes so that you can open that end for easier access. If you use the hooks and eyes, the structure will be weaker, however, and you will have to add on braces to keep the sides from spreading apart when the bin is open.

You can place the compost bin flat on the ground or prop it up on bricks. The bricks will help you level the bin if the ground is uneven, and they will permit air to flow under the bottom of the bin.

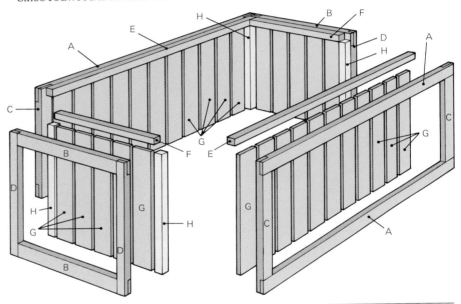

Parts list

Part	Name	Quantity	Thickness	Width	Length	Material
A	Front and back rail	4	1½"	3½"	72"	2 x 4 redwood
B	End rail	4	1½"	3½"	36"	2 x 4 redwood
C	Front and back stile	4	1½"	3½"	36"	2 x 4 redwood
D	End stile	4	1½"	1½"	36"	2 x 2 redwood
E	Front and back cover strip	2	1½"	1½"	69"	2 x 2 redwood
F	End cover strip	2	1½"	1½"	33"	2 x 2 redwood
G	Slat	32	¾"	5½"	34½"✳	1 x 6 redwood
H	Nailing strip	4	1½"	1½"	34½"	2 x 2 spruce
I	Brace (optional)	2	1½"	1½"	39"	2 x 2 redwood

✳Measurement is approximate; cut to fit during construction.

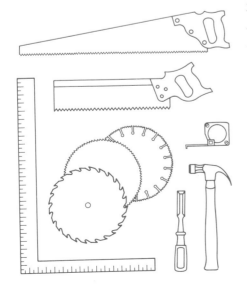

Tools and materials: Crosscut saw, backsaw. Power saw (preferably with dado blade) or router. Wood chisel, hammer. Framing square, steel tape rule, pencil. Twelve 6′ lengths of 2 x 4 construction-grade redwood, five 6′ lengths of 2 x 2 construction-grade redwood (two additional 6′ lengths of 2 x 2 construction-grade redwood if braces needed), sixteen 6′ lengths of 1 x 6 clear-heart redwood, two 6′ lengths of 2 x 2 spruce. Two 6″ gate hooks with matching screw eyes if open-end design with braces used. 3d, 6d, and 8d galvanized annular (ring) nails.

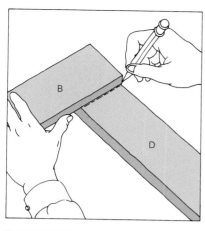

1. Cut all the wood except the wood for the slats to the sizes given in the chart. Overlap the ends of the rails (A and B) and stiles (C and D) at right angles to create two rectangular and two square frames. (Do one frame at a time.) Mark the part of each piece that is overlapped by another in preparation for cutting laps for joining the pieces.

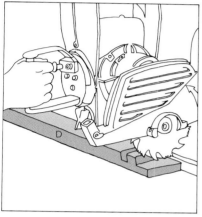

2. Cut away half the thickness of the marked area on each rail and stile with several passes of a power saw with a dado blade (or with a router or backsaw). Smooth the cut areas with a chisel. (To find detailed instructions for cutting a lap joint, see the *Index*, p.379.) Fit the lapped pieces together on a flat surface and use a framing square to get the corners perfectly square. Secure each lap joint with 3d annular nails.

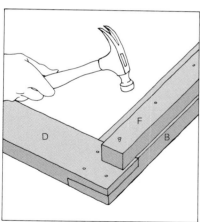

3. Center an end cover strip (F) on top of the inside edge of each of the two end frames in turn. Nail each strip to its frame with 8d annular nails. Nail the front and back cover strips (E) to their respective frames in the same way.

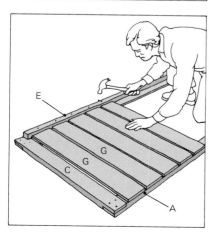

4. Measure the distance from the bottom of one of the cover strips to the bottom of its frame and cut the slats (G) to that length. Nail the slats to the backs of the frames, using two 6d annular nails at each end of each slat. Use a framing square to make sure that the slats are parallel with the stiles. Leave ½-in. spaces between the slats on the front and back of the bin and 1-in. spaces between the slats on the ends.

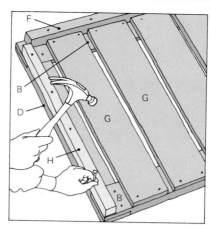

5. Position a spruce nailing strip (H) on the inside of each end stile (D) so that it is flush with both the outer edge of the stile and the bottom of the frame. Fasten the strips to the frame with several 6d annular nails.

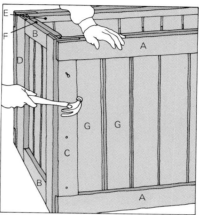

6. Hold the four sections of the bin in position. (The end sections should fit between the ends of the front and back sections.) Check for squareness. Fasten the first end section in place by driving 8d annular nails through the front and back sections and into the nailing strips on the end section. Nail the other end section in place in the same way or use the hook-and-eye system described in Steps 7–8.

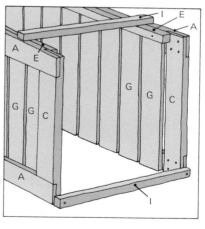

7. If you make one of the end sections of the bin removable, position one brace (I) across the bottom of the open end with the ends of the brace flush with the outsides of the front and back sections. Fasten the brace into place with 6d annular nails. Position the second brace across the top of the bin about 1 ft. from the open end. Fasten brace to the tops of front and back sections with 6d annular nails.

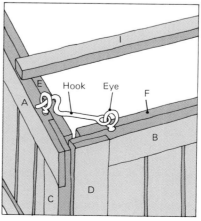

8. Screw gate hooks into the top of the upper rail (B) of the removable end section about 2 in. from both the front and back sections. Fit the bottom of the end section behind the bottom brace (I), and align the top of the end section with the ends of the front and back sections. Put screw eyes into the tops of the upper rails (A) of the front and back sections, positioning them so that they can be engaged by the hooks. Fasten hooks.

WINDOW GREENHOUSE

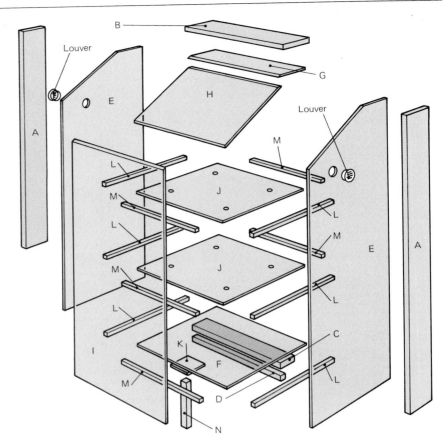

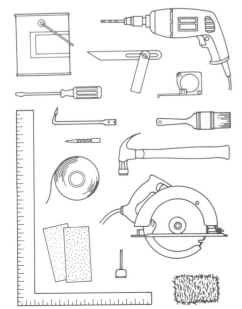

Parts list (for a 27" x 52" window with 8" jambs)

Part	Name	Quantity	Thickness	Width	Length	Material
A	False side jamb	2	½"	8"	51½"	Pine
B	False head jamb	1	½"	8"	27"	Pine
C	False sill	1	¾"	4"	27"	1 x 8 pine
D	False sill support	1	¾" ✳	2"	27"	1 x 8 pine
E	Side	2	¼"	24"	51"	Acrylic sheet
F	Bottom	1	¼"	24"	25⅞"	Acrylic sheet
G	Flat top	1	¼"	10"†	25⅞"	Acrylic sheet
H	Sloping top	1	¼"	21"†	25⅞"	Acrylic sheet
I	Front	1	¼"	25⅞"	41"†	Acrylic sheet
J	Shelf	2	¼"	24"	25⅜"	Acrylic sheet
K	Support plate	1	¼"	6"	6"	Acrylic sheet
L	Shelf support rod	6	⅜"	⅜"	24"	Acrylic rod
M	Shelf support rod	5	⅜"	⅜"	24⅝"	Acrylic rod
N	Bottom support rod	1	1"	1"	Cut to fit	Acrylic rod

✳ Will be tapered (see Step 2).
†An extra 1" is included for beveling of edges (see Step 3).

Tools and materials: Circular or table saw with guide and carbide-tipped blade (40 teeth or more). Electric drill with ⁵⁄₃₂" Screwmate bit, ³⁄₁₆" bit, cloth wheel, and 1" and 2" hole saws. Hammer, nail set, screwdriver, wrecking bar. Framing square, spirit level, protractor, steel tape rule, T bevel. Paint or stain, paintbrush, soft cloth. Acrylic solvent (cement), 1" masking tape, 0000 steel wool, Nos. 180 and 220 sandpaper. Jeweler's rouge, silicone rubber sealant.

Fine-tipped eyedropper, syringe, or hypodermic needle. Polyethylene sheet. Two 4' x 8' sheets of ¼" clear acrylic. One 1" x 1" x 6' square acrylic rod, five ⅜" x ⅜" x 6' square acrylic rods. A 3' length of 1 x 8 select pine, a 12' length of ½" x 10" select pine. Two 2" dia. aluminum louvers with screens. Two 2" dia. cork stoppers. Eight 1¼" No. 8 roundhead brass screws and eight No. 8 flat brass washers, 6d galvanized finishing nails.

A clear acrylic greenhouse projecting from a sunny window will extend the growing season for flowers, herbs, seedlings, and vegetables. The dimensions of the greenhouse depend on the size of your window opening (27 x 52 inches in this project); so do not have the acrylic cut to size until you have measured the converted window opening (after completing Step 2). While the opening is exposed, tape a polyethylene sheet over it to keep out rain and dust. The clearance between the greenhouse and the window must not be more than 1/8 inch.

Clear acrylic may be precut by the dealer, but you must bevel the edges at home. Add an extra inch to any part that will have a beveled edge to allow recutting if the first bevel is not cut properly; then trim the part to its final size along the opposite edge once the bevel has been cut correctly (see Step 3). Be sure to use sharp blades and feed the acrylic slowly into your saw.

Use a fine-tipped eyedropper or syringe to apply the solvent to the seams. The clear liquid will cement the acrylic rapidly and any overflow will fog up the shiny surface; so practice first on scraps.

To prevent scratches, do not remove the protective paper that comes on both sides of the acrylic sheets until after the greenhouse has been installed. However, during construction you will have to peel off narrow strips along the edges that must be cemented.

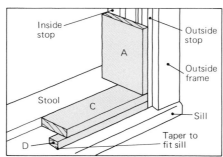
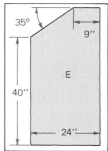

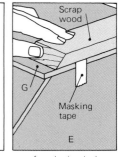

1. On old-type double-hung windows (shown), remove inside stops, parting strips, and sashes. Then put inside stops back in place. For newer type double-hung windows, remove sashes and metal channel balances. For casement windows, remove sashes at hinges. Store removed parts.

2. Measure window dimensions. Cut false side jambs (A), false head jamb (B), false sill (C), and false sill support (D) to fit. These will cover remaining woodwork so no unsightly part will be visible through transparent greenhouse. Paint or stain new wood to match existing woodwork of window.

3. Using T bevel, measure for desired slope of part H (in this case 35° from the horizontal), then use a protractor to set the angle of the saw blade. Cut the beveled edges for the flat top (G), sloping top (H), and front (I) after test-cutting on scrap wood. Trim the straight edges to size.

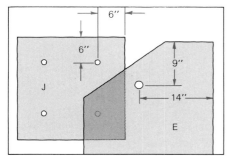

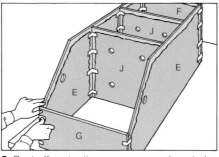

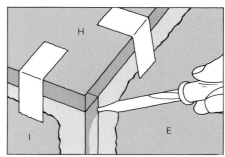

4. Drill four 1-in. vent holes in each shelf (J) and one 2-in. louver hole in each side (E) with hole saws. Polish all exposed edges of acrylic that will not be cemented with No. 220 sandpaper and 0000 steel wool. Then, using a cloth wheel sprinkled with jeweler's rouge, buff the edges.

5. Peel off protective paper near edges to be cemented. Assemble acrylic parts E–M with masking tape. Check for squareness. Cement flat top (G) and bottom (F) to the sides (E) first. Then cement shelves (J) and shelf support rods (L and M) in place. Finally, add sloping top (H), front (I), and support plate (K).

6. Apply solvent slowly along each seam with an eyedropper or syringe. It will be quickly drawn into the seams by capillary action. Firm bonding will take place in 10 min. Immediately wipe off any overflow. If a "scar" results, polish it with 0000 steel wool and a cloth dipped in jeweler's rouge.

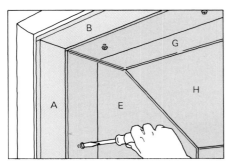

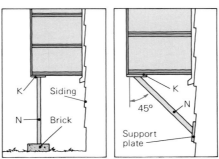

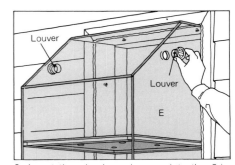

7. Fit the assembled greenhouse into the window opening. Drill eight 3/16-in. holes (two along each edge of the greenhouse) into the acrylic where it meets the window frame, and drill eight corresponding 5/32-in. pilot holes into the frame. Secure the greenhouse to the window with No. 8 brass screws and washers.

8. Cut the bottom support rod (N) to fit between the support plate (K) and a brick, rock, or pavement directly underneath (left). Cement rod to plate. If window is high, rod may be installed at a 45° angle (right), resting on a second support plate secured with screws through the building's siding.

9. Insert the aluminum louvers into the 2-in. holes in the sides (E). Use silicone rubber sealant to glue them to the acrylic and to caulk between greenhouse and window frame. If required, aim a small fan at the greenhouse in summer; mount louver covers and install an electric heating cable in winter.

GARDEN
FOUNTAIN

If nature dealt you a cruel blow by scattering rocks across your backyard or by putting small boulders where you want to plant a vegetable garden, this project can turn the tables in your favor—beautifully. A garden fountain arranges those annoying rocks in sculptural elegance and, with the help of a small recirculating pump, gives you the cool, refreshing babble of falling water.

In building the fountain, you will be using wet-wall construction techniques but applying several dry-wall techniques as well. The difference between a wet and a dry wall is that a wet wall employs mortar and a dry wall does not, relying instead on gravity and rock-against-rock friction. The rocks are mortared together as in a wet wall. However, the rocks in the base course (layer) are much larger than the rocks in the higher courses, thus forming the pyramidal structure used in dry-wall construction.

Access to the pump is provided by incorporating two U-shaped chimney blocks into the back wall. The blocks also provide a strong base for the back wall that rises above the basin in the back and holds the spout for the fountain.

Use an old agateware bowl or a galvanized tub for the basin. You can probably

find one at a flea market. If it has any rust on it, sand it thoroughly before using it. If you prefer, you can get a fancier basin from a restaurant supply house.

You will also need a pump to keep the water circulating. Use a dual-purpose pump—one that can be operated fully submerged in water or in open air if the water is fed by gravity. Have an electrician install a grounded outlet to accept the pump's three-pronged plug.

Since the fountain must be made to fit the space you have for it, the dimensions may vary. Before you begin the project, develop a ground plan based on the space available for the fountain and on the size and shape of the basin you are using. Plot the fountain to scale on graph paper. Start your design with the rear access opening (formed by the two chimney blocks). To provide easy access to the pump and electrical cord, allow at least 3 feet of clearance between the opening and the nearest immovable object.

Instructions for building the fountain follow, but directions for mixing mortar and soldering are omitted. (To find directions for these techniques, see the *Index*, p.379.) **Caution:** When working with mortar, wear work gloves over rubber gloves. Mortar can irritate the skin.

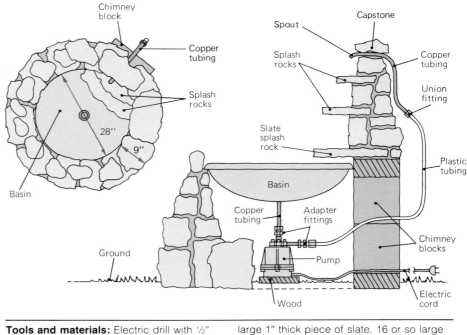

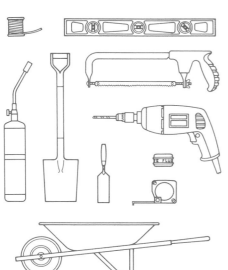

Tools and materials: Electric drill with ½" high-speed bit, pipe cutter or hacksaw. Mapp gas canister torch. Shovel, trowel, cement-mixing pan or wheelbarrow, water bucket or watering can. Steel tape rule, level, graph paper, pencil. Solid-core solder, flux, 1 qt. rust-preventive primer, one or two spray cans of rust-preventive paint in colors of your choice. Work gloves, rubber gloves, small brush. No. 100 sandpaper, emery cloth. Two concrete chimney blocks. One large 1" thick piece of slate, 16 or so large rocks, 2–4 bu. of medium and small rocks. Two to four 80-lb. bags of premixed homogenized standard cement (mortar). Large metal bowl or tub for basin (see text). Dual-purpose pump rated 140–170 gal. per hr. at 6' elevation. Two ½" (OD) x ¼" (ID) male adapter compression fittings, one ½" (OD) compression union fitting. Two ft. of ⅜" soft copper tubing, 6' of ⅜" flexible plastic tubing.

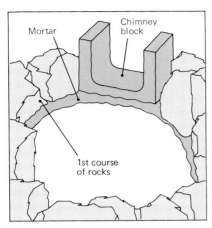

1. Level the ground of your building site, then dig a circular trench 4–6 in. deep and 9 in. wide. Mix a batch of mortar and trowel some into the back half of the trench. Set first chimney block into position about 2 in. into mortar, then set first large rocks into mortar, working out from both sides of chimney block. For a good bond dampen rocks before positioning them. Fill rest of trench with mortar and complete first course of rocks.

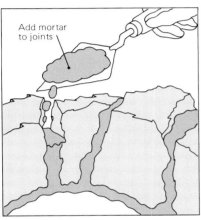

2. Fill in gaps in first course with more rocks. Fit each rock so that it stays in place without mortar. Then remove rock and lay down a full bed of mortar where rock will go. Squeeze rock back into place. Add more mortar to fill all joints. Use trowel to tamp mortar smooth. Let mortar and rocks set overnight, then sprinkle mortar with water for even curing. If soil around rocks is dry, water it too.

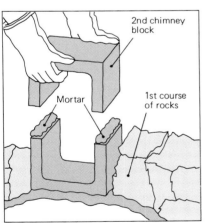

3. Apply mortar to ends of first chimney block and set second block onto it, as shown, to form an opening. Using progressively smaller rocks, continue to build up circular wall until it is about 4 in. below height of top chimney block. Check fit of basin, then continue to build up wall until basin can be fully supported and is level.

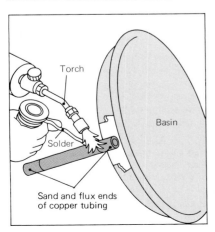

4. Use a ½-in. high-speed drill bit to bore hole in center of basin. Test-fit copper tubing in hole. Measure and cut tubing so that it is long enough to connect basin and pump in fountain well. Sand end of tubing smooth and rub it with emery cloth until shiny. Brush flux onto end of tubing and onto metal around hole in basin. Insert tubing into hole flush with inside of basin. Solder on inside and outside of basin.

5. Temporarily plug hole in basin with a stick and paint all surfaces of basin with primer, then two coats of spray paint. When dry, remove plug and put basin in position. Place a straight board across basin and put a level on board. Adjust basin until it is perfectly level, then remove board and level. Camouflage front lip of basin with one more course of rocks. Some rocks should rest against basin to wedge it into place.

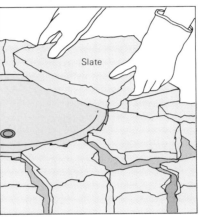

6. Mortar a large, flat 1-in.-thick piece of slate to top of upper chimney block in such a way that it extends over the back lip of basin to form the lowest splash rock. Build up back wall of fountain to a height of 18 in. or more above basin, using at least one large rock to serve as a focal point and adding a few more splash rocks.

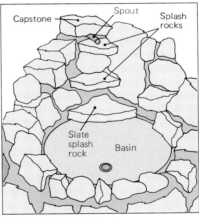

7. Bend remaining length of copper tubing to form fountain spout. Hook spout over back wall with short end pointing down toward center of basin. (If spout is pointed correctly, it will send a main jet of water out in a graceful arc with the rest of the water running down over splash rocks.) Mortar spout into place, then mortar a capstone into place over it.

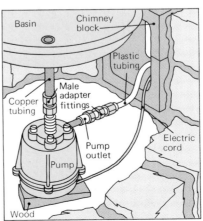

8. Screw male adapter fittings onto pump. Attach plastic tubing to the compression end of fitting on pump outlet (horizontal fitting). Reach through opening in chimney blocks and position pump under basin. Attach pump inlet to copper tubing from basin. Wedge a piece of wood under pump to adjust its height. Use union fitting to join plastic tubing to back of spout. Fill basin with water and plug in pump.

REFUSE LOCKER

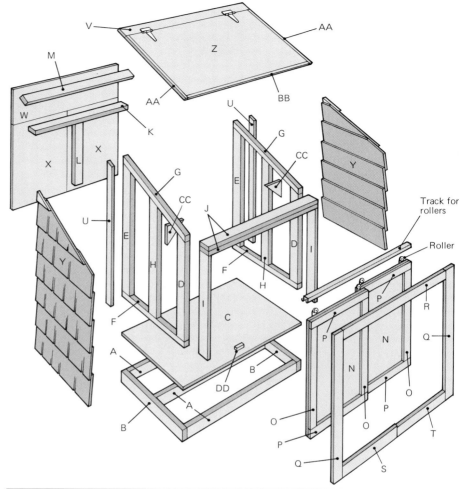

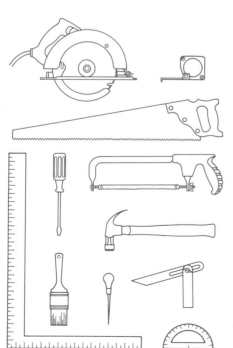

Parts list

Part	Name	Quantity	Thickness	Width	Length	Material
A	Long base	3	1½"	3½"	47"	2 x 4 pressure-treated pine
B	End base	2	1½"	3½"	30"	2 x 4 pressure-treated pine
C	Base top	1	¾"	30"	50"	Plywood
D	Front side stud	2	1½"	3½"	33"	2 x 4 pine
E	Rear side stud	2	1½"	3½"	48"	2 x 4 pine
F	Bottom plate	2	1½"	1½"	30"	2 x 2 pine
G	Top plate	2	1½"	1½"	38"✳	2 x 2 pine
H	Center side stud	2	1½"	3½"	42"✳	2 x 4 pine
I	Side cripple	2	¾"	3½"	31½"	1 x 4 pine
J	Header	2	1½"	3½"	47"	2 x 4 pine
K	Rear horizontal stud	1	1½"	3½"	47"✳	2 x 4 pine
L	Center rear stud	1	1½"	3½"	33¼"	2 x 4 pine
M	Rear plate	1	1½"	3½"	47"	2 x 4 pine
N	Door panel	2	¾"	23¼"	30¼"	Plywood
O	Vertical door trim	4	¾"	1¾"	30¼"	Rip from 1 x 4 pine

Tools and materials: Circular saw with rip blade and guide. Handsaw, hacksaw. Hammer, awl, screwdriver. Steel tape rule, framing square, straightedge, protractor, T bevel. Caulking compound, water-resistant glue, 1 qt. exterior paint, 1 qt. primer, paintbrush. Three 8' lengths of pressure-treated 2 x 4 pine. Construction-grade lumber as follows: eight 8' lengths 1 x 4 pine, two 8' lengths 2 x 2 pine, seven 8'

Thrown about carelessly by refuse collectors, garbage cans will quickly become unsightly. Left unprotected, they are often raided by varmints who will strew trash across your lawn. The solution is to store the cans out of sight in this attractive refuse locker that holds two large (32-gallon) cans. The hinged lid of the locker lifts for waste disposal. On collection day the front doors, hung from rollers, are pushed aside to remove the cans.

The tools required for this project are those most homeowners already have in their workshops. The level of skill required is that of elementary carpentry.

You can cover the sides of the locker with siding to match your house or use aluminum siding. As shown here, the locker is covered with a prefinished siding that resembles split cedar; the siding is easy to install and maintenance free.

The refuse locker can be placed against your house or left freestanding. If it is to go against the house, cover the back with ¼-inch hardboard; if freestanding, purchase an extra sheet of siding and use it for the back panels.

The base is made of pressure-treated 2 x 4's to withstand the dampness of constant contact with the ground. The rest of the framework is made of construction-grade common pine. The plywood for the base top, door panels, and lid should be A–C exterior grade.

Trim applied to the front and side

edges of the lid prevents water from soaking into the plywood. Attach this trim with nails and liberal amounts of water-resistant glue. The edges of the plywood door panels and the end grain of all lumber that has not been pressure treated should be primed and painted with several coats of paint for weather protection.

Rollers fastened to the top edges of the door panels glide in a track mounted with screws. The bottom trim, wider on the left side, prevents the door at the front of the track from swinging out. A small piece of wood nailed to the floor and butting against the door on the right side prevents it from swinging inward.

Finishing: When you have completed the construction of the locker, fill the joints between the siding and the trim with caulking compound. Put caulking compound into any other cracks where water might seep in. Inspect the joint along the front bottom trim and caulk it. Raise the lid and press some adhesive-backed foam weather stripping along the lower edge of the top trim where it will seal the crack between the trim and lid.

All exposed wood should get a coating of top-quality primer, then three coats of exterior paint. Give the lid an extra coat, and make sure that the joints between the lid trim and the plywood are completely filled with paint. Choose simple, functional door handles, and screw them to the outer edges of the door panels.

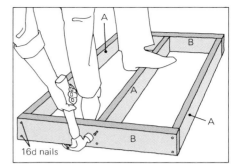

1. Nail together the 2 x 4's for the base (A and B) as shown. Use two 16d galvanized nails in each butt joint. Nail the base top (C) in place over the base framework with 10d nails at approximately 8-in. intervals.

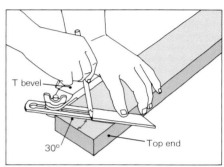

2. Using a protractor, set the T bevel for a 30° angle. Transfer angle to tops of front and rear side studs (D and E). Saw tops on these lines; saw bottoms so D and E measure 33 in. and 48 in. peak to bottom respectively.

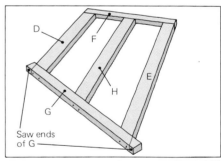

3. Nail bottom plates (F) to studs (D and E) with 10d nails. Cut top plates (G) oversize, nail to studs, and saw ends at an angle even with studs. Lay center side studs (H) in position, mark angle, saw, and nail to parts F and G.

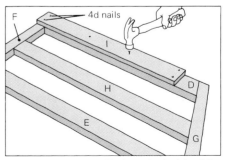

4. Nail side cripples (I) along the inside of the front side studs (D) flush with their bottoms. (A cripple is a framing member that is shorter than usual—in this case, shorter than its corresponding stud.)

Part	Name	Quantity	Thickness	Width	Length	Material
P	Horizontal door trim	4	¾"	1¾"	19¾"	Rip from 1 x 4 pine
Q	Front vertical trim	2	¾"	3½"	37½"	1 x 4 pine
R	Top front trim	1	¾"	3½"	45¾" ✲	1 x 4 pine
S	Wide bottom trim	1	¾"	3½"	23¼"	1 x 4 pine
T	Narrow bottom trim	1	¾"	3"	22¼" ✲	Rip from 1 x 4 pine
U	Back vertical trim	2	¾"	2"	57"	Rip from 1 x 4 pine
V	Top trim	1	¾"	3½"	53¾" ✲	1 x 4 pine
W	Top back panel	1	†	18" ✲	50" ✲	Siding (or ¼" hardboard)
X	Bottom back panel	2	†	38" ✲	25" ✲	Siding (or ¼" hardboard)
Y	Side panel	2	†	†	†	Siding
Z	Lid	1	¾"	33¾"	52¼"	Plywood
AA	Lid side trim	2	¾"	¾"	34½"	Rip from 1 x 4 pine
BB	Lid front trim	1	¾"	¾"	52¼"	Rip from 1 x 4 pine
CC	Corner stiffener	2	¾"	6"	6"	Plywood
DD	Doorstop	1	¾"	2"	4"	Rip from 1 x 4 pine

✲ Measurement is approximate; cut to fit during construction.
† To be determined during construction.

lengths 2 x 4 pine. Two 4' x 8' panels ¾" exterior-grade plywood. For freestanding locker, two sheets prefinished siding. For locker that stands against house, one sheet prefinished siding and one sheet ¼"

hardboard. Roll of adhesive-backed foam weather stripping. Two large hinges with screws. Double-track 48" hanging door hardware. Two door handles. Box each of 4d, 10d, and 16d galvanized common nails.

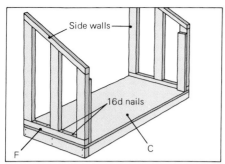

5. Stand the side walls on the base platform. Carefully align each side wall with the end of the base so that they are flush. Drive 16d galvanized common nails through the bottom plates and into the base.

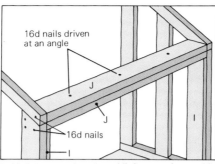

6. Nail the two headers (J) face to face with 16d galvanized nails driven at a slight angle so that the two become one piece. Rest this piece on the cripples, and drive 16d nails through the sides and into the header ends.

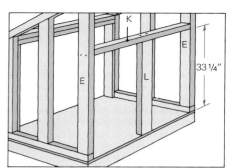

7. Measure between rear side studs (E), and cut the rear horizontal stud (K) to fit. Nail it 33¼ in. up from the base. Center the center rear stud (L) between the rear side studs, and nail it with 16d galvanized nails.

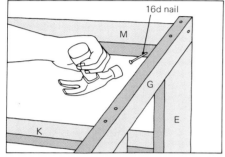

8. Nail rear plate (M) with its wider face flush with top plates (G) and its back edge flush with rear side studs (E). Nail through top plates, and toenail from inside as shown. Cut the door panels (N) to size.

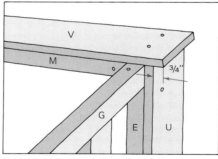

9. Using 4d nails, nail door trim (O and P) to front of door panels, flush with edges. Attach rollers to the doors, following manufacturer's directions. Cut track with hacksaw, and attach to underside of header (J).

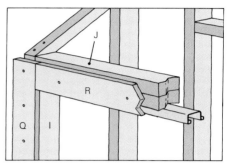

10. Nail the front vertical trim (Q) flush with inside edge of the side cripples (I). Measure between vertical trim pieces, and cut top front trim (R) to fit. Nail it ⅝ in. below top of header so that it hides the track.

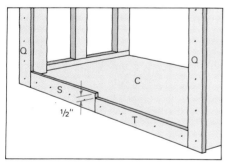

11. Nail wide bottom trim (S) to front bottom of locker so that it extends ½ in. above base top (C). Measure from end of S to edge of front vertical trim (Q); cut narrow bottom trim (T) to fit, and nail flush with base top.

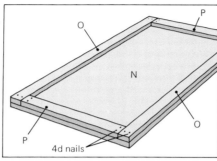

12. Nail back trim (U) to studs (E), extending trim ¼ in. beyond rear edges of studs or far enough to cover edges of rear siding (if any). Cut top trim (V) to overhang U by ¾ in. at each end; nail with back edge flush with U.

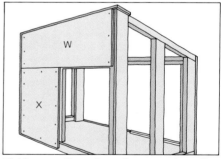

13. Measure dimensions of rear openings. Cut top back panel (W) and bottom back panels (X) to fit. Nail them in place. If locker will be freestanding, cover the rear with prefinished siding instead of hardboard.

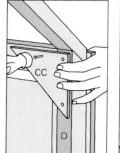 

14. Saw a 6-in. square of plywood diagonally for corner stiffeners (CC). Nail inside to front side studs (D) and header (J). Install door panels—left one in forward track. Nail stop (DD) at center of locker against right door.

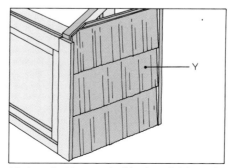

15. Install side panels (Y) of prefinished siding, following manufacturer's directions. Mark slope on back of siding and saw it. Glue and nail lid front trim (BB) and side trim (AA) to edges of lid with 4d nails.

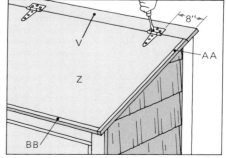

16. Install hinges on lid, positioning them approximately 8 in. from side edges. Make starter holes with an awl, and insert the screws. Place lid (Z) on locker and screw the hinges to the top trim (V).

WOODEN DECK

Adding a deck to your house is an ambitious undertaking: it requires time, patience, money, and help from friends. But you will gain an outdoor living space and a valuable addition to your home.

This deck, with its series of descending steps, is suitable for a level or gently sloping site. The outer edge of the main level is 28 inches off the ground, and the main level itself measures 21 feet wide at the house, extends 12 feet out, and measures 15 feet wide at its outer edge (see illustration on next page). The steps extend another 4 feet 3 inches into the yard. Although precise dimensions for the deck parts are given (pp.302–303), the dimensions must be checked on site, as they may differ depending on such conditions as the slope of your land.

The floor of the deck is made of 3-foot-square modules nailed together ahead of time. You can assemble them indoors in winter or on rainy days and have them ready in advance. Two edges of each module are set back, leaving protruding crosspieces through which the modules are nailed to the joists; the top boards of the adjoining modules overlap the crosspieces, covering the exposed nails.

The joists extend 17 inches beyond the sides of the modules to hold 6-foot-long redwood planters, available at garden centers. The beams, running perpendicular to the house, are supported by posts anchored to concrete footings.

The first step in planning a deck is to call or visit your local building department to find out what regulations apply and to obtain a permit. For example, the depth and size of footings are dictated by local building codes, and zoning laws determine how close to the property line a structure can be. Next, determine whether there are any underground electric, gas, septic, sewer, telephone, or water lines where you will be digging. Consult your site plan (if you have one) or your utility companies for this information. Stake out these lines; if necessary, shift the deck to avoid them.

If your house was built recently, the soil around it may be fill that has not yet settled. If so, you will have to dig down to undisturbed soil for the footings or else

rent a compactor from a tool rental agency and compact the soil.

Materials: This deck is built of redwood with posts of pressure-treated pine, which is rot-, insect-, and water-resistant. Redwood on or within 6 inches of the ground must be of "construction heart" grade. (Local codes may specify construction heart for up to 18 inches above the ground.) Above that level you can use less expensive "construction common" redwood, which contains streaks of light sapwood. A less costly alternative is to use pressure-treated lumber throughout; this treated lumber is gray-green in color and can be left natural or stained.

To retain the reddish tone of new redwood, this deck was stained with an opaque redwood stain, which must be reapplied every couple of years. As an alternative, you can coat the deck with a clear mildewcide that contains a water repellent. Redwood will weather gradually from a buckskin tan to a soft gray with this finish; reapplying the treatment every 2 years retains the tan color longer and retards checking and splintering. Freshly cut ends of lumber should be coated with the mildewcide before being nailed.

Concrete for the footings can be bought ready mixed, or you can mix your own. The amount of concrete required will vary with the depth and size of the footings. In areas where deep footings are called for, it is not necessary to pour concrete to the tops of post holes. Instead, you can pour 10 inches or so into the bottoms of the holes and make the posts long enough to extend down to the concrete, since the pressure-treated lumber will not be harmed by contact with soil.

Nails, bolts, and other hardware should be of stainless steel, aluminum alloy, or hot-dip galvanized iron so that they will not corrode and stain the wood. Because redwood splits easily, it is best to predrill all nail holes with a bit three-quarters the size of the diameter of the nail. (For bolts, drill holes the full diameter.) Since long pieces of lumber are seldom straight, you should secure a warped piece of lumber at one end and have a helper push the other end into alignment as you nail the rest of the piece in place.

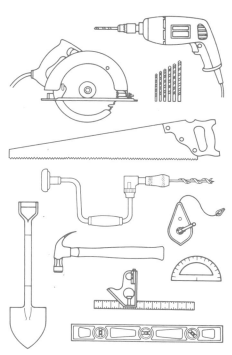

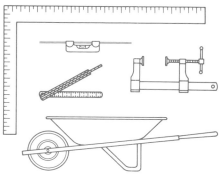

Tools and materials: Circular saw, handsaw. Drill with twist bits. Brace and ⅜" auger bit or ⅜" brad-point bit. Hammer, shovel, wheelbarrow. Protractor, framing square, combination square, carpenter's level, line level, mason's cord, plumb bob, wooden extension rule. Quick-action clamp. Redwood stain (optional), clear mildewcide with water repellent. Piece of cardboard 21" x 64". Black plastic sheeting. Portland cement, sand, and gravel or bags of ready-mixed concrete. Pressure-treated 4 x 4 pine as dictated by local building code.

Redwood as follows: 1,754' of 2 x 4's, 327' of 2 x 6's, 152' of 2 x 8's, 7' of 2 x 12's. Wooden stakes and 1 x 3's for batter boards. Four joist hangers, seven post caps. Metal flashing (21' length). Bolts or sixteen ½" lag screws 6" long and expansion anchors, 4" and 5½" carriage bolts with hex nuts and large washers, 10d and 16d grooved nails, 12d annular grooved or spirally grooved nails, 1¼" galvanized roofing nails, twelve 8" spikes. (All hardware must be noncorrosive.)

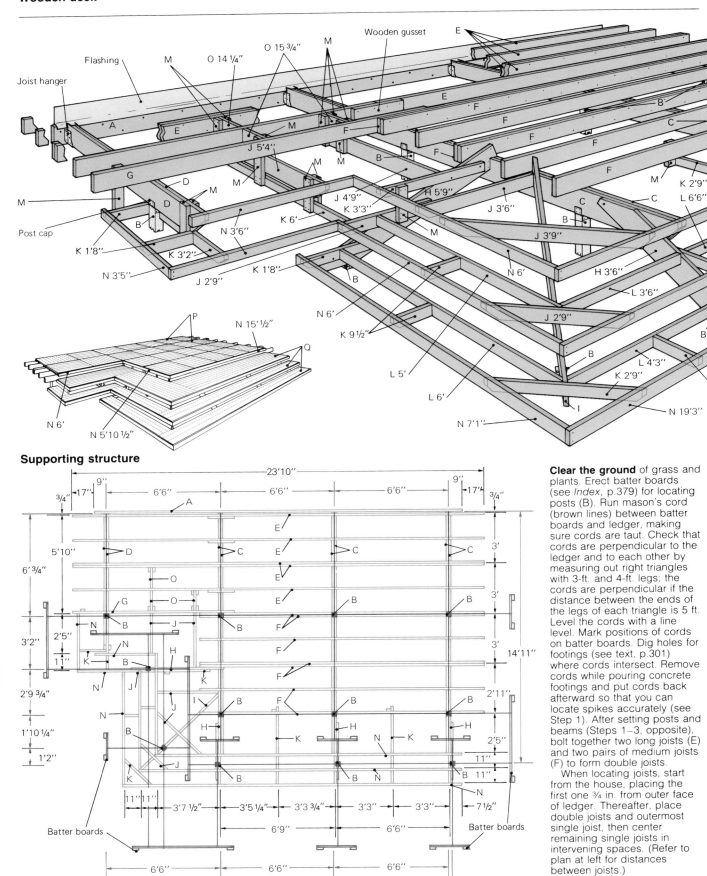

Flashing

Joist hanger

Wooden gusset

O 14 1/4"

O 15 3/4"

M

M

M

E

E

A

E

M

F

F

B

F

C

J 5'4"

F

F

F

C

B

M

M

M

F

G

B

M

K 2'9"

D

M

M

J 4'9"

L 6'6"

M

D

K 3'3"

H 5'9"

C

B

B

K 1'8"

N 3'6"

K 6'

M

C

C

Post cap

K 3'2"

K 1'8"

J 3'6"

N 3'5"

B

J 3'9"

B

J 2'9"

N 6'

H 3'6"

L 3'6"

P

N 15'1/2"

Q

N 6'

J 2'9"

B

N 6'

K 9 1/2"

L 4'3"

N 6'

N 5'10 1/2"

L 5'

K 2'9"

K 19 3/4"

B

K 9 1/2"

L 6'

I

N 19'3"

N 7'1"

Supporting structure

23'10"

9"

17"

6'6"

6'6"

6'6"

17"

9"

3/4"

3/4"

A

5'10"

D

C

E

C

E

C

3'

6' 3/4"

E

O

E

3'

O

B

G

B

J

B

B

B

3'

2'5"

N

B

F

N

11"

K

H

F

3'2"

K

B

H

F

14'11"

N

N

J

F

2'9 3/4"

N

I

B

F

B

B

2'11"

J

H

H

H

1'10 1/4"

N

B

F

N

K

N

K

2'5"

1'2"

B

K

11"

J

N

B

B

N

B

11"

K

N

11" 11"

3'7 1/2"

3'5 1/4"

3'3 3/4"

3'3"

3'3"

7 1/2"

Batter boards

6'9"

6'6"

Batter boards

6'6"

6'6"

6'6"

2 1/4"

2 1/4"

2 1/4"

2'4 1/4"

1'

2'11 1/2"

6'10

6'6"

Clear the ground of grass and plants. Erect batter boards (see *Index*, p.379) for locating posts (B). Run mason's cord (brown lines) between batter boards and ledger, making sure cords are taut. Check that cords are perpendicular to the ledger and to each other by measuring out right triangles with 3-ft. and 4-ft. legs; the cords are perpendicular if the distance between the ends of the legs of each triangle is 5 ft. Level the cords with a line level. Mark positions of cords on batter boards. Dig holes for footings (see text, p.301) where cords intersect. Remove cords while pouring concrete footings and put cords back afterward so that you can locate spikes accurately (see Step 1). After setting posts and beams (Steps 1–3, opposite), bolt together two long joists (E) and two pairs of medium joists (F) to form double joists.

When locating joists, start from the house, placing the first one 3/4 in. from outer face of ledger. Thereafter, place double joists and outermost single joist, then center remaining single joists in intervening spaces. (Refer to plan at left for distances between joists.)

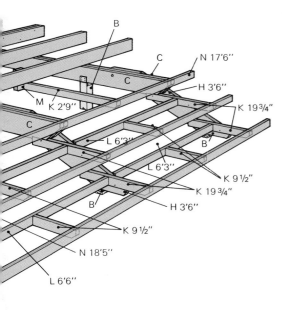

Parts list

Part	Name	Quantity	Thickness	Width	Length	Material
A	Ledger	1	1½"	7¼"	21'	2 x 8 redwood
B	Post	12	3½"	3½"	✳	4 x 4 pressure-treated pine
C	Long beam	6	1½"	7¼"	14' 4¾"	2 x 8 redwood
D	Short beam	2	1½"	7¼"	8' 3¾"	2 x 8 redwood
E	Long joist	5	1½"	5½"	23' 10"	2 x 6 redwood
F	Medium joist	7	1½"	5½"	16' 5"	2 x 6 redwood
G	Short joist	1	1½"	5½"	9' 5"	2 x 6 redwood
H	Stringer	4	1½"	7¼"	†	2 x 8 redwood
I	Corner stringer	1	1½"	11¼"	5' 9"	2 x 12 redwood
J	Wide step support	6	1½"	5½"	†	2 x 6 redwood
K	Narrow step support	22	1½"	3½"	†	2 x 4 redwood
L	Rear step support	8	1½"	3½"	†	2 x 4 redwood
M	Tie	16	1½"	3½"	✳	2 x 4 redwood
N	Skirt	12	1½"	3½"	†	2 x 4 redwood
O	Bridge	3	1½"	5½"	†	2 x 6 redwood
P	Module	24	3"	3'	3'	2 x 4 redwood
Q	Tread	42	1½"	3½"	✳	2 x 4 redwood

✳ To be determined during construction.
† See exploded view for dimensions.

Ledger (A), covered with flashing, is 8½ in. below deck top, which is located 1 in. below floor of house. Attach ledger to masonry, using ½-in. lag screws and lead expansion anchors placed at 16-in. intervals. Use bolts to attach ledger to wooden siding.

Installing posts, beams, and joists

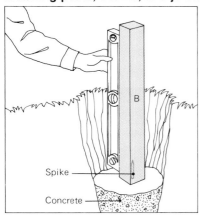

1. Using a plumb bob at post locations, place 8-in. spikes, heads down, in soft concrete. Make sure spikes are vertical and precisely below cord intersections. Drill centered holes in one end of each post (B). Set posts on spikes when concrete has dried. Plumb each post with a level held against adjacent sides. Fill holes with soil; tamp it down. Spread black plastic sheeting on ground to discourage weeds.

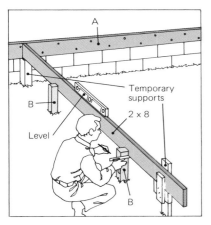

2. Select the four straightest pieces of 2 x 8 lumber. Align them against the posts that will support the main deck area, and support them at both ends at the height of bottom of ledger (A). Level lumber, and mark where it intersects posts. Saw off the posts at that line. The five posts that support steps will be cut off at or near ground level when you install stringers (Steps 5–10).

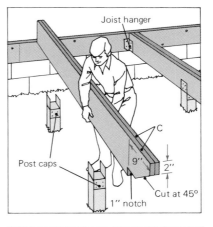

3. Saw off 1 in. from lower edges of long beams (C) 9 in. back from outer ends. Saw short beams (D) in same way but back 28 in., and saw one short beam 7 in. shorter than other. Miter outer ends of beams, leaving a 2-in. perpendicular face. Bolt pairs of beams at 3-ft. intervals with 4-in. carriage bolts. Rest beams on posts with ends butting ledger. Nail beams to posts, using post caps and 1¼-in. roofing nails. Nail joist hangers to ledger and beams.

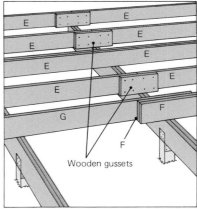

4. Toenail joists to beams with 10d grooved nails. Nail short joist (G) to house side of first medium joist (F). If you join two pieces of lumber to make a joist, as may be required for the long joists (E), locate the joint above a beam. Splice joists by nailing on wooden gussets—pieces of lumber that are the same width as the joists and that overlap the ends of the joist pieces.

Installing stringers and surrounding step supports

5.
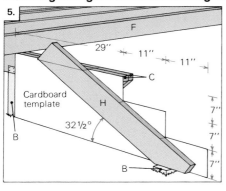

6.
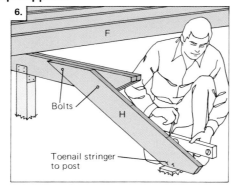

5. Make a cardboard template of steps; tack it to left beam (C). Cut three 4-ft. stringers (H). Saw their bottom edges to 32½°. Hold a stringer against template, and mark where corners of notches intersect it. Draw a line on stringer at top of beam; mark beam where stringer intersects it. Cut off post (B) so that stringer rests on it.

6. Remove stringer and saw top edge on line; reposition stringer on beam. Align level with notch marks, and draw lines across stringer. Fasten stringer to beam with 5½-in. carriage bolts and to post with nails. Nail step supports (K) to stringer along lines. (Miter ends of step supports as you did the beams.) Repeat Steps 5 and 6 for stringer on right side.

7. Clamp middle stringer to its beam; cut post. Rest a 2 x 4 across step supports; mark where 2 x 4 touches middle stringer. Saw top of stringer and fasten stringer to beam and post. Attach parts K.

8. Use same template for fourth stringer (H). Position template on outermost double joist (F); mark where it meets beam (C). Remove template and lay stringer on it. Mark critical points. Saw bottom edge of stringer at 19°, and notch top to fit beam; cut post. Nail stringer to joist, beam, and post. Hold template against stringer and extend line of wide step support (J) onto stringer. Mark lines for top and bottom step supports (K) with level; nail step supports to stringer. Nail tie (M) to top step support and J.

7.
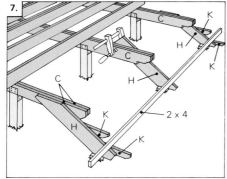

8.
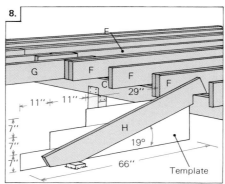

9. Saw upper end of 2 x 12 corner stringer (I) at 76°, then miter this cut so that stringer fits flush to beam (C) at 45° angle.

10. Saw stringer's bottom edge at 14°. Saw off post; position stringer with lower end on post and upper end at junction of second joist (F) and beam (C). Nail stringer to beam and post.

11. Nail bottom course of skirts (N) to ends of nearest step supports (K) already in place; tops of skirts should be 1½ in. above tops of K's.

12. Lay bottom course of rear step supports (L), making space between N's and L's 9½ in. Miter ends of L's where they meet at corner stringer, and cut other ends to length. Position L's so that their top edges are level with tops of K's (see exploded view, p.302); nail in place.

13. At end of stringer cut a 1½- x 3½-in. notch for narrow step support (K). Hold a 3-ft.-long 2 x 4 above notch, and mark where 2 x 4 meets skirts. Saw each end at 45° and undercut lower edge at 45° (a compound miter). Nail step support in place.

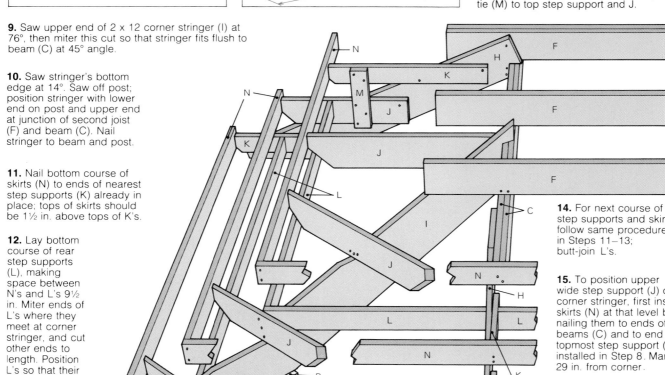

14. For next course of step supports and skirts, follow same procedure as in Steps 11–13; butt-join L's.

15. To position upper wide step support (J) on corner stringer, first install skirts (N) at that level by nailing them to ends of beams (C) and to end of topmost step support (K) installed in Step 8. Mark 29 in. from corner.

16. Hold wide step support across marks made in Step 15. Mark step support for end miter cuts, and measure down 7 in. from bottom of step support to mark stringer for back corner of notch. Cut out notch. Miter step support; nail it in place.

Completing substructure, steps, and decking

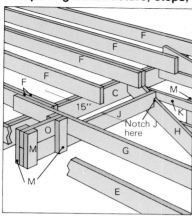

17. The shorter of two wide step supports (J) is 15 in. from the long beam (C). After marking J's position on joists (E and G), nail in bridge (O) and nail ties (M) on one side of bridge. Notch end of step support to fit stringer (H). Nail step support to stringer and to ties. Nail ties to other side of bridge and to part J.

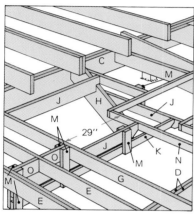

18. The other wide step support (J) is centered between short step support and short beams (D), its end 29 in. beyond short joist (G). Nail through joists (E and G) into bridges (O), then nail ties (M) to one side of bridges. Bolt or nail step support to ties; nail ties to other side of step support. Nail narrow step support (K) to ties so that its end butts the middle step support (J) on long stringer (H). Nail through middle step support into part K.

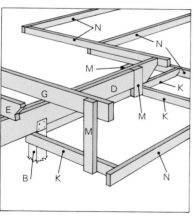

19. Nail two ties (M) at end of shorter beam (D) and one to short joist (G). Nail three step supports (K) to post (B) and to ties as shown. Nail skirts (N) across ends of step supports just installed. Cut remaining nine step supports (K) to length (see pp.302–303). End-nail seven of them between rear step supports (L) and skirts (N). Nail other two between uppermost step skirt and ties that are nailed to back of outermost joist (F).

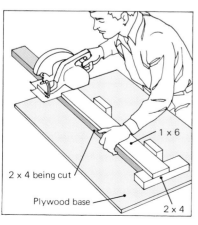

20. To cut 2 x 4's to 3 ft. for modules (P), make a jig of a 1 x 6 and a 2 x 4 as shown. The distance from the edge of the 2 x 4 to the end of the 1 x 6 should be 3 ft. minus the distance between edge of your saw guide and its blade. Butt jig against one end of lumber to be cut as shown; make the crosscut with the saw guide against the 1 x 6. Cut three hundred and twelve 2 x 4's 36 in. long.

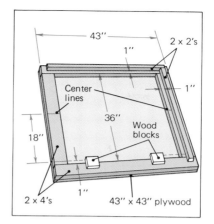

21. Make a jig for assembling the modules by nailing two 43-in. 2 x 4's and two 36-in. 2 x 4's to a 43-in. square of plywood as shown. Nail two 2 x 2's on top of 2 x 4's 1 in. from their inner edges. Nail two wood blocks on one 2 x 4, overhanging 2 x 4 by 1 in. Extend line of edge of blocks to 2 x 4's; measure in 18 in. along 2 x 4's from those lines. These points are center lines for lining up center crosspieces of modules.

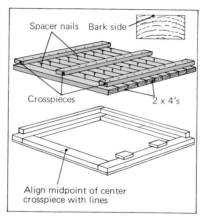

22. Lay ten 3-ft. 2 x 4's on the plywood, using nails to space them evenly. Lay three 3-ft. 2 x 4's as crosspieces with their ends butting against one 2 x 2. Lumber should be laid so that when module is right side up, bark side of grain faces up (inset). Drill slightly angled holes for 10d nails in staggered rows. Make two holes at crosspiece ends for each decking piece. Drive nails into holes.

23. Lay a module on joists at rear right corner of deck; nail with 16d nails through crosspieces. Lay adjoining modules at right angles so that their overhanging top boards cover the crosspieces of the first module; nail. Then lay modules next to house and work outward. When you reach outer edge, determine which modules will have crosspieces extending beyond decking; saw crosspieces even with decking. Nail the three remaining skirts (N) along outer edges.

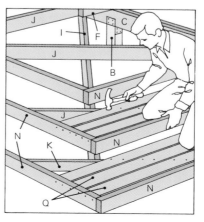

24. Starting in front at left corners, place 2 x 4's for treads (Q) on supporting members, spacing them evenly on each step. Predrill holes and drive two 12d grooved nails into each supporting member. Nail through skirts (N) into ends of treads, using two nails per tread. When piecing treads, do so where ends of boards can be nailed to a step support (J or K), but do not piece all boards of a step over same support.

BRICK DRIVEWAY, PATIO, OR WALK

Brick paving provides a rustic or colonial look that is not only more attractive than concrete but easier to build as well. This handsome brick driveway provides off-street parking and also serves as a pathway to the side entrance of the house. You can use the same construction methods to put in a brick patio or walk.

For the most part, the joints between the bricks are mortarless. Only the bricks around the perimeter of the walk are set in mortar in order to prevent the bricks within the perimeter from shifting. If the perimeter is edged with timbers or by bricks set on end and half-buried in the ground, it is not necessary to use mortar.

Mortarless, or flexible, construction offers easy installation (you do not have to fill and strike hundreds of joints), and it is easy to repair. If some bricks lift because of freezing weather conditions, it is a simple matter to pry up the mortarless bricks once the ground has thawed, tamp down the heaved earth, and reinstall the bricks.

In order to support heavy vehicles, a brick driveway requires at least a 4-inch base of gravel under a 2-inch bed of sand. A 2-inch bed of sand alone is usually sufficient for a patio that will not support heavy loads. In areas where the ground seldom freezes, a narrow path can be laid directly on the tamped earth.

Roofing felt placed between the sand or earth and the bricks discourages weeds from sprouting up between the bricks and prevents algae growth, caused by dampness, from "greening" the brick surface.

Ordering materials: Masonry industry organizations recommend the use of bricks that are graded SX for outside use. These bricks are called pavers, and they are available in several sizes. The pavers used in this project measure 1⅝ inches thick by 4 inches wide by 8 inches long. You will have to order four pallets to duplicate the 50-foot-long, 420-square-foot driveway shown here. Each pallet contains 500 bricks for a total of 2,000 bricks. Only 1,890 bricks are needed for this project; the extra 110 bricks allow for breakage and for bricks that must be cut where the drive way flares out from 8-12 feet wide at the street.

Since 2,000 bricks weigh 8,000 pounds, let the dealer deliver the bricks and the 11½ tons of sand and gravel.

When laying the bricks, do the three mortared edges first. The fourth edge is formed by the sidewalk or street and needs no mortar to prevent the bricks from shifting. Isolation joints should be placed between the bricks and the curb, sidewalk, and foundation (see *Index,* p.379). Before you finalize your plans, check your local building code to see if a permit is needed and if a private brick driveway may abut a public road.

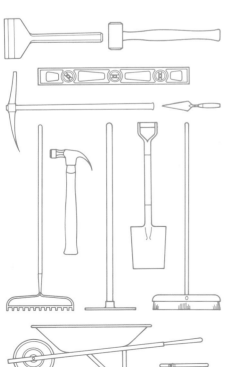

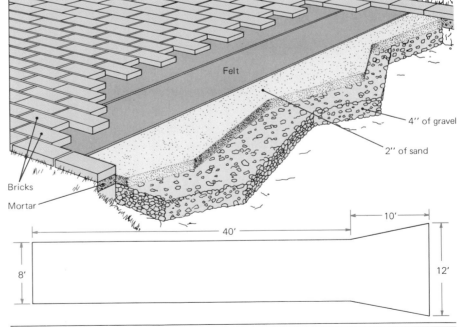

Felt

Bricks

Mortar

4'' of gravel

2'' of sand

40'

8'

10'

12'

Tools and materials: Shovel, pickax, commercial or homemade tamp (see Step 3). Hammer, rubber mallet, broad-blade brick chisel, mason's trowel. Wheelbarrow, broom, hoe or garden rake, garden hose. Carpenter's level, 100' of string. Screed of 2 x 6 lumber 14' long. Six or more wooden stakes. Four pallets of 1⅝" x 4" x 8" brick pavers (2,000 bricks). Three sacks of dry-mix mortar, 7½ tons of gravel ¾"–2¼" in dia., 4 tons of mason's sand, 850 sq. ft. of 15-lb. roofing felt.

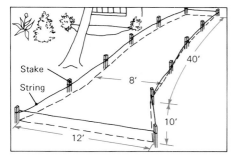

1. Mark the perimeter of the driveway with stakes and string. Then excavate the area to a depth of approximately 7½ in. (4 in. for gravel, 2 in. for sand, 1½ in. for the bricks, which should rise slightly above ground level).

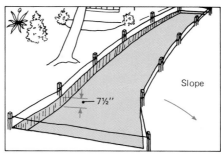

2. When excavating, provide for drainage by sloping the driveway bed away from the house ¼ in. for each foot of pavement width. Check slope by placing a straight board and a carpenter's level across excavation.

3. After the site is dug, spread a 4-in. base of gravel evenly and tamp it down firmly, using a commercial tamp. Or make a tamp by nailing a 4-ft. length of 2 x 2 lumber perpendicular to a 1-ft. length of a 2 x 6 or 2 x 8.

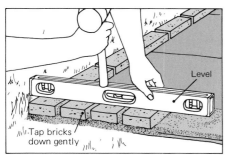

4. Next, spread a 2-in. bed of sand. Use a hoe or garden rake and the screed board to level the sand, then tamp it down firmly. Roll out two layers of roofing felt over the sand. Butt the edges of the felt, but stagger the joints.

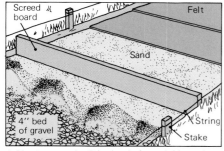

5. Mix mortar and water in a wheelbarrow until it is the consistency of soft mud, then lay a 2-in.-thick bed of mortar the width of one brick around the edges of the site. Mix only enough mortar to lay 10 ft. of edging at a time.

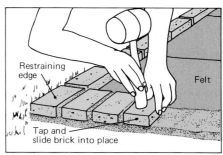

6. Lay bricks along edges of driveway. Place each brick into the mortar 2 in. away from the previous brick, then slide the new brick toward the other one until it is ⅜ in. away. This should cause mortar to fill the joint.

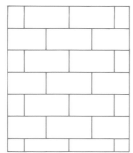

7. To lay bricks evenly, place a level across several bricks and tap down gently on the level with the wooden handle of a hammer or mallet until the bricks are even and level. Use a mason's trowel to remove excess mortar.

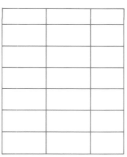
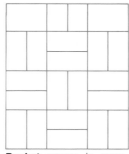

8. To cut a brick, score both faces with a broad-blade brick chisel. Place the end of the brick you want to keep on a hard surface, and strike the other end sharply with a hammer to snap the brick on the score marks.

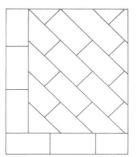

9. When the mortar is hard, lay bricks within the perimeter, spacing them evenly ⅜ in. apart. When all bricks are laid, spread sand over them and sweep it into the joints. Hose down driveway and add more sand.

Variations

Running bond pattern is the strongest arrangement for bricks that must support vehicles. Bricks must be parallel to length of vehicles.

Jack-on-Jack is a simple design for patios and walks that is easy to lay because no edges have to be cut if the project is sized evenly.

Basket weave is more interesting than Jack-on-Jack and involves no waste if patio or walk is sized according to brick dimensions.

Diagonal pattern is simply a running bond that is set at a 45° angle to its edging. Every brick that touches the edging must be cut to fit.

Herringbone pattern can be laid with bricks parallel to edging or at a 45° angle (shown). Angled pattern is pretty but calls for much cutting.

FLAGSTONE PATIO

Both esthetic and practical, a stone patio provides a bridge between your house and the outdoors. It is best built on a level or very gently sloping site. On a site with a severe slope a wooden deck may be a better outdoor living area.

Attractive touches in this 15- x 18½-foot patio are the flower beds, one 2 x 12½ feet under the window and the other 2½ x 3 feet in one corner. These are planted with annuals, but they could also be filled with low shrubs or ground cover. Your site may have different requirements as to size and shape. The materials listed below are sufficient for this patio; calculate your needs based on your design.

Location: In designing your patio, consider shade, privacy, the time of day you expect to use it most, and access from the house. Try to avoid placing it where an overhanging roof will drip water onto the patio; a heavy dousing each time it rains can cause the stones to settle unevenly.

The type of flagstone used here is called random rectangular bluestone. These flagstones come in many sizes, starting at a nominal 12-inch stone and increasing by 6-inch increments to 36 inches and occasionally 42 inches. In reality the stones are slightly smaller—about ½ inch each way—but use nominal sizes for drawing your patio to scale, since the ½ inch is accounted for by the spaces between the stones. Plan the patio so its length and width are divisible by six.

Although sold as 1½ inches thick, the flagstones actually range from 1¼–2 inches thick. You must compensate for the variety of thicknesses by putting more or less sand beneath each stone.

This patio is laid on 3 inches of sand over a 4-inch gravel base. The gravel pro-

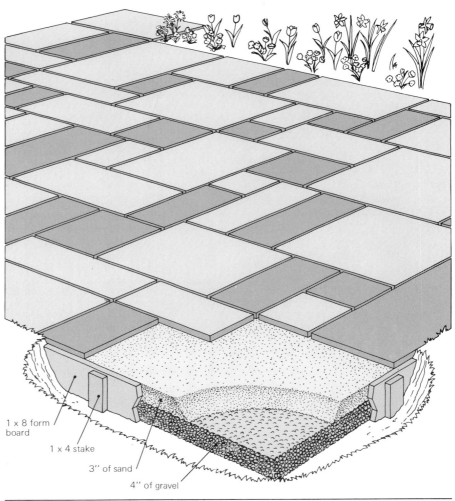

1 x 8 form board
1 x 4 stake
3'' of sand
4'' of gravel

Tools and materials: Spade, iron rake, wheelbarrow. Handcart (optional). Prybar or tire iron. Stonemason's chisel. Mason's hammer or steel mallet, hammer. Broom, garden hose, goggles, disposable paintbrush. Steel tape rule, graph paper, level, string, scissors, pencil. A 2 x 4 for leveling, a 2 x 4 or rubber mallet for tamping, 1 x 4 stakes 11"–12" long, 1 x 8 lumber as needed for form boards. One gal. creosote, 3 cu. yd. of crushed aggregate (gravel), 2⅓ cu. yd. of concrete sand, 250 sq. ft. of random rectangular bluestone. Box of 4d galvanized common nails.

vides drainage. In areas where the ground freezes, it is often recommended that a flagstone patio be laid on a reinforced concrete base. While concrete is more permanent, it is also more exacting and expensive and is best done by a contractor. A sand and gravel base is easier for the homeowner and, if done with care, reasonably permanent. After the first winter you may have to reset stones that have settled unevenly.

Ordering materials: When you call the stone supplier, specify the size of the patio minus any areas intended as flower beds. This patio contains 246½ square feet not including the flower beds; so 250 square feet of stone was ordered. The supplier will accept an order for exact stone sizes, but it is less expensive to order random rectangular bluestone. You will get an assortment of sizes. When

delivered, have them placed in the driveway or some place where they will not damage your lawn. Sort them by size and list the amount in each size.

Now make a scale drawing of the patio on graph paper with 1 inch equaling 1 foot. Cut out a shape representing each stone from another piece of graph paper, label each piece, and push the pieces around on the graph paper until you get a pleasing pattern. Try to avoid long, continuous lines between stones; if there is heaving from frost and thaw, it is likely to occur along such lines. Paste the shapes on the graph paper.

You can order the sand and gravel from the stone supplier or from a sand and gravel dealer. Buy crushed aggregate for the gravel (it shifts less than pea gravel) and concrete sand, which is coarser than mason's sand. Order them by the cubic

yard. To calculate the amounts needed for a layer, multiply thickness by width by length (in feet), then divide the total by 27. Remember to express the thickness by a fraction of a foot—that is, $\frac{1}{12}$ or $\frac{1}{3}$ for a 4-inch layer. With this formula, the patio shown requires 3 cubic yards of gravel and 2⅓ cubic yards of sand. Be sure not to include areas designated for flower beds in your calculations.

When the sand and gravel are to be delivered, have areas ready for their deposit. You will save an extra delivery charge if the supplier brings both in one truck that has a partition wall. If the truck can drive to the patio area, the gravel can be dumped directly into the excavation. However, the driver will not want to wait while you spread and level it, so have a place prepared for the sand where it will not damage your lawn.

1. Drive temporary stakes at the corners, allowing 1½ in. extra on each side for forms. Run string between the stakes to outline patio. Check that corners are square by measuring diagonally (see *Index*, p.379). Dig out soil to a depth of 8½ in. (You can hire someone with a backhoe to do this.) Save some of the turf and topsoil for use later. Check that the bottom of the excavation is level.

Temporary stake

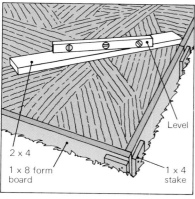

2. Prepare form boards of 1 x 8's and permanent stakes of 1 x 4's by painting them with creosote to prevent rot. Place the boards around the perimeter of the excavation. Drive permanent stakes at corners and additional stakes where ends of boards meet. Nail the stakes to the form boards with 4d galvanized nails.

Level

2 x 4

1 x 8 form board

1 x 4 stake

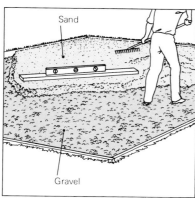

3. Spread the gravel in the excavated area to a depth of 4 in. Rake it smooth, and then level and pack it with a 2 x 4. Place a level on top of the 2 x 4 to check that the gravel is level. Cart the sand to the area. Spread the sand, level it, and pack it in the same way.

Sand

Gravel

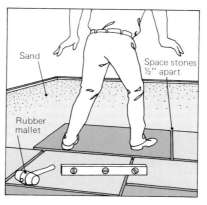

Sand

Rubber mallet

Space stones ½" apart

4. Begin laying stones, leaving ½ in. between the edges. (A handcart is useful for moving the stones.) Check each stone for levelness and make sure it does not teeter. A prybar or tire iron helps to raise one edge of a stone to shift its position or to add or remove sand beneath it to make it level with others. Tamp stones down with a rubber mallet or end of a 2 x 4.

5. Mix sand with some of the topsoil removed in excavating. Spread this mixture on the patio and sweep it into the spaces between stones. Water the surface to pack down the sand and soil mixture; let it dry. Repeat the process with more sand and soil until the joints are filled. Backfill edges of patio and cover with turf.

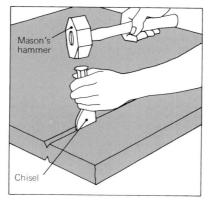

Mason's hammer

Chisel

6. Stones at perimeter may require cutting. Pencil a line where a piece is to be cut off. Wearing goggles to protect your eyes, score along line, using a stonemason's chisel and a mason's hammer or steel mallet. Score a line on opposite face. Place a board under the stone with the excess overhanging. Tap excess with the hammer or mallet until it breaks off.

BRICK SCREENING WALL

The solidity and texture of brick are enhanced by the airy design of this bracket-shaped wall. Ours is used to screen a carport. It could just as easily hide trash cans, a compost bin, or a tool shed. The instructions on the following pages are for building the wall alone and do not include the pillars that support the overhang of the carport.

The wall shown here is 12 feet long, with two perpendicular arms slightly longer than 4½ feet, and it stands 5½ feet high. Although the screening design makes it lighter, by almost half, than a solid wall of the same size, a firm foundation and solid footing are still needed. We have specified a minimum for a northerly area: a 4-inch-thick concrete slab, set deep enough to guard against frost heave, topped by seven courses of solid brick, all but one of which are underground. Before you start on the project, show the plan to your building inspector to be sure it conforms to local building codes and that the footing is below the frost line.

A large number of bricks must be cut in half for the wall. To cut them with a brick chisel and hammer is a skill worth acquiring; but until you become adept at it, you probably will not be able to salvage both halves of many bricks. It could be worth the investment to rent a heavy-duty brick-cutting saw for a day.

Another good investment might be the rental of a mixer, or you could order 8 cubic feet of ready-mixed air-entrained concrete for the foundation. As for the mortar, mix only as much as you can use in about an hour and a half. You can use dry mix (add only water) or masonry cement (add sand and water)—specify Type M. You can also mix your own from scratch (p.312, Step 1).

Hose down a pile of bricks about 15 minutes before laying them; they take mortar best when damp but not soaking.

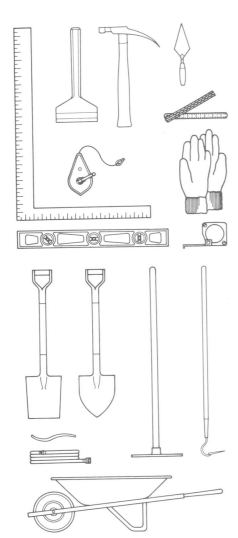

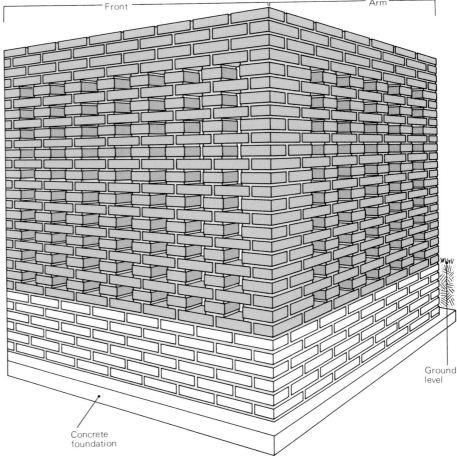

Front — Arm

Ground level

Concrete foundation

Tools and materials: Mason's hammer, brick chisel (or electric saw with masonry blade). Trowel, brick jointer. Spade, shovel, bull float, tamp. Wheelbarrow. Steel tape rule, framing square, torpedo level, 4' level. Chalk, chalk line, brick rule or story pole. String, burlap. Hoe, garden hose. Work gloves. Several short stakes, six batter boards (see p.311, Step 1), a 4' or 5' long 2 x 4. Six bags 1A portland cement, one bag hydrated lime, 16 cu. ft. mason's sand, 6 cu. ft. crushed stone or gravel, 890 SW solid bricks 2¼" x 3¾" x 8".

Laying the foundation

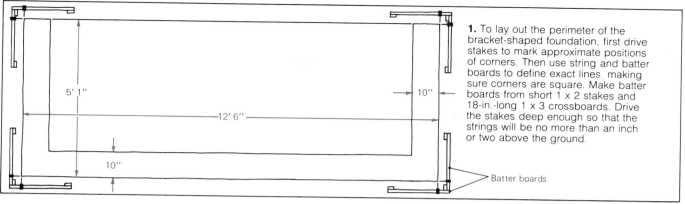

Batter boards

1. To lay out the perimeter of the bracket-shaped foundation, first drive stakes to mark approximate positions of corners. Then use string and batter boards to define exact lines, making sure corners are square. Make batter boards from short 1 x 2 stakes and 18-in.-long 1 x 3 crossboards. Drive the stakes deep enough so that the strings will be no more than an inch or two above the ground.

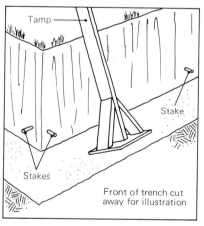

2. Dig a trench 10 in. wide and 20–22 in. deep within the defined perimeter. The walls must be straight and plumb, and the base level, even though the land may slope; use a straight 2 x 4 and a 4-ft. level to check. If you are building on a slight incline, make the deepest part of the trench 22 in. A steep incline may require a deeper trench to accommodate an extra course or two of bricks underground.

5. Use a long-handled bull float to produce a smooth and even surface. You can make a bull float by attaching an 8-in.-long piece of 1 x 8 to a 1-in. dowel handle. After bull-floating, wait until the concrete has lost its shine—that is, until the surface water has evaporated—then cover with burlap or straw. Allow concrete to cure for about 2 weeks, spraying the cover every day or two to keep it damp.

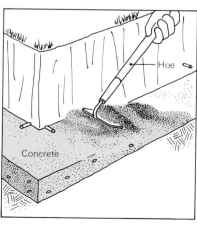

3. Tamp the earth down firmly. Near each corner, and at intervals of about 4 ft. along the front part of the trench, push small stakes into trench walls 4 in. from the base to guide you in spreading the concrete. Combine 4 parts portland cement (with an air-entraining agent), 9 parts mason's sand, and 12 parts crushed stone or gravel. Mix thoroughly with a garden hoe, then add enough water to produce a stiff but workable mix.

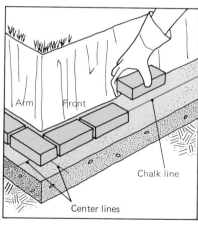

6. After concrete has been cured, remove the covering and snap a chalk line along the center of all three sections, checking both corner alignments with a framing square. Lay out the first course of bricks dry, centered along these lines, leaving ½ in. between bricks. Do not position end bricks of the two arms at this time.

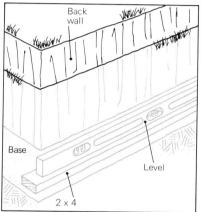

4. Dampen—but do not flood—the trench with a fine spray. Pour concrete to the level of the stakes in the walls. Do not pour all the concrete at one spot; rather, pour at three or four places, using a garden hoe to spread it evenly. Protect against the caustic effects of concrete by wearing gloves and clothing that protects the arms and legs. If concrete touches your skin, wash promptly with soap and lukewarm water.

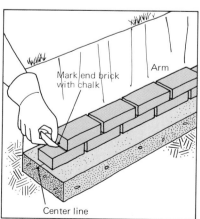

7. Lay out the second course dry, centering each brick on a joint of the first. Measure and cut end bricks for the first course so that they are even with the ends of the second course. You will need bricks of the same size at both ends of every odd-numbered course, including all the solid courses above the ground; for efficiency's sake, cut them all now (see p.313, Step 7). Trace outer face of the bottom course in chalk.

Building the wall

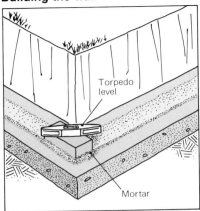

1. To make mortar, combine 4 parts portland cement, 1 part hydrated lime, and 12 parts mason's sand. Mix thoroughly and add enough water for a thick paste. Spread a ¾-in. bed of mortar over the chalk line to a distance of about 3 ft. in both directions from a corner. Position the corner brick carefully, pressing down so that mortar oozes out on all sides. Make sure brick is level in all directions.

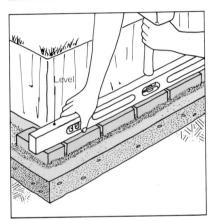

2. Butter the end of the brick that completes the corner and, while holding the first brick in place, push the buttered brick against it, leaving a ½-in. joint. Add a third and a fourth brick, clipping mortar from each joint—as though slicing with the trowel—to use in buttering the next brick. Place 4-ft. level on top of the row and tap as needed to level all bricks. Lay three bricks along the arm in the same way.

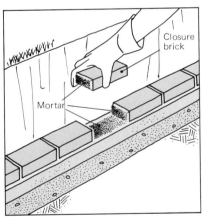

3. Lay in the other corner of the first course as in Step 2. Then complete and level the two arms, starting with the cut bricks at the ends. Finally, lay the center bricks along the front chalk line. To lay the last, or closure, brick in a row, butter both ends and butter the ends of the two bricks that will abut it. Lower closure brick without knocking off mortar, and tap into place.

4. Begin the second course at a corner, as you did the first, spreading a generous bed of mortar. Lay the corner brick across the joint below, pressing it down for a ½-in. joint. To ensure proper space between courses, use a brick rule—or make a story pole by marking a straight stick at 2¾-in. intervals. Level the corner brick, then lay three more bricks in each direction, being sure the faces are plumb and the tops level.

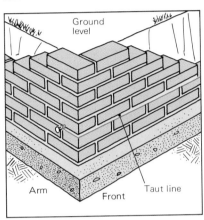

5. Continue building at the same corner, laying one less brick with each course until you have a pyramid seven courses high. The last course will be above ground level. Do the same thing at the other corner. Then fill in the front wall one course at a time, using a taut line as a guide. Check your work often with a level to keep the wall plumb and each course level.

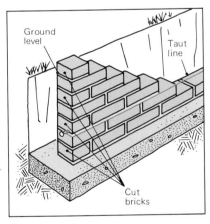

6. Build the two arms of the bracket similarly, beginning at the ends and working backward to create stairsteps of bricks. Alternate cut bricks with whole ones at the ends of the arms. Take special care in laying these end bricks; be sure they are even and plumb on all three open sides. Complete the arms with the help of the taut line as in Step 5. Point all joints that will be above the ground. Joints that will fall below the ground do not need to be pointed.

Bricklaying techniques

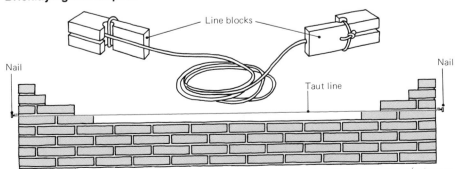

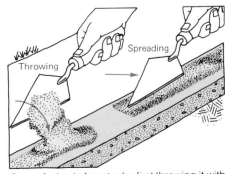

A taut line can be stretched between nails driven into the mortar separating courses or between plastic line blocks designed for the purpose. Attach the line so that it is flush with upper edge of corner bricks; lay intermediate bricks flush with, but not touching, the line.

Spread a bed of mortar by first throwing it with a short sweep of the trowel, then use the back of the trowel for spreading.

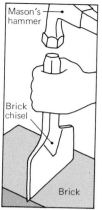

7. Every even-numbered course from the 8th through the 26th requires 23 half-bricks (4 in. long) and six bricks 6 in. long for a total of 230 half-bricks and sixty 6-in. bricks. To cut a brick, first score both faces with a brick chisel. Then, holding the usable end firmly on a hard surface, strike the waste end sharply with a mason's hammer. It is unlikely that you will be able to salvage both halves of the brick.

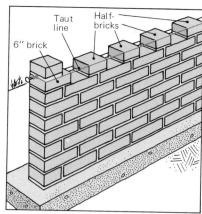

10. As each half-brick is leveled from side to side and front to back, clip the mortar all around. Point the joints as soon as the mortar is thumbprint hard. After the half-bricks have been laid all across the front wall, complete the eighth course along the arms in the same way, stretching the taut line between the corner bricks and the 6-in. end bricks.

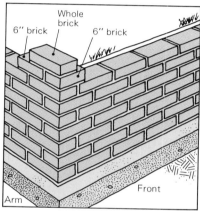

8. To start the eighth course, first lay two 6-in. bricks at each corner, the first aligned with the front wall and the second butting against it, aligned with the arm. Then lay a 6-in. brick on each end. Clip the mortar from the faces and exposed ends of all these bricks. Then lay a full-size brick across each corner joint and a half brick on top of each end. Level and plumb all bricks as they are laid.

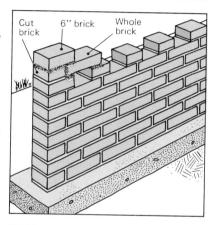

11. Begin the ninth course by laying a whole brick against each half brick, which is already in place. Spread mortar on the surfaces where a brick will rest; then butter the brick and position it, leveling it carefully. Lay a whole brick in each direction against the two corner bricks in the same way. Then lay the 6-in. end and corner bricks of the 10th course on top of them (see Step 8). Reset the taut line and complete the solid ninth course.

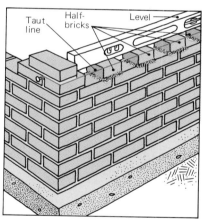

9. To complete the eighth course, first stretch the taut line across the front wall, flush with the upper edges of the 6-in. corner bricks. Then spread a short bed of mortar over each joint of the seventh course and press a half-brick into it until the front edge is almost even with the line. When several are positioned this way, place the 4-ft. level across them and tap it to force all the bricks down to the taut line.

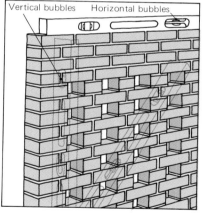

12. Continue alternating solid courses with open ones through the 26th course. Then lay four solid courses to the top, following the pattern used in laying the first seven courses. Use the 4-ft. level to check your work often as you build. Its bubbles will give you level readings vertically and horizontally; use it as a straightedge to check the face of the wall diagonally.

Bricklaying techniques

Butter a brick in four steps, first scraping mortar onto each long edge of the end of the brick, then onto each short edge.

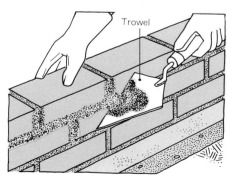

Clip excess mortar from joints with a slicing—not a scraping—motion, wielding the trowel as though it were a straight razor.

Point joints with a brick jointer or a short piece of metal rod to compress the surface of the mortar and seal out moisture.

BRICK BARBECUE

Whether built as a freestanding unit or as part of a brick wall bordering a patio, this handsome brick barbecue is designed to be the functional center of your outdoor patio and dining area. It stands 38½ inches high. Its exterior dimensions of 42 x 54¾ inches were determined from the measurements of available grill racks.

Our racks are 24 inches wide and 36 inches long; if you use racks of a different size, add 2–3 inches to each measurement to find the interior dimensions of your barbecue. The racks rest on ⅜-inch steel reinforcing rods, which project 2 inches from inside the front and rear walls of the barbecue. The six rods for the lower rack, on which hot coals are placed, are embedded 2 inches deep in the mortar between the eighth and ninth courses of brick. Those for the upper rack are between the 10th and 11th courses.

The damper for our barbecue is 10 inches square, determined by the size of available preformed damper doors. It is positioned in the front face, set on a ¾-inch bed of mortar on top of the third course of bricks. You will have to cut bricks in the fourth through the seventh courses to accommodate it.

Before beginning construction, it is a good idea to lay out a few courses dry, allowing ½ inch between bricks for mortar. Cut bricks wherever necessary at this time. Mark the corners of the foundation so that it will extend 2 inches beyond all sides of the barbecue. Then remove the bricks and excavate for the foundation.

Our barbecue was built in an area where frost heave can be a problem, so we used a slab/footing foundation, as shown on the opposite page. In warmer areas a solid 12-inch slab with steel reinforcing rods should be sufficient.

All bricks are laid on and separated by ½-inch thicknesses of mortar. Care must be taken to maintain the level line of each course as it is set. (For instructions on bricklaying, see pp.312–313.)

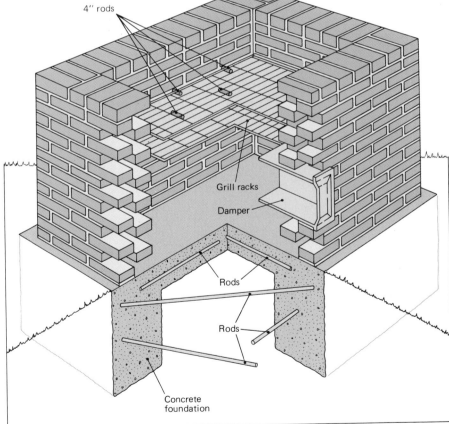

4" rods

Grill racks

Damper

Rods

Rods

Concrete foundation

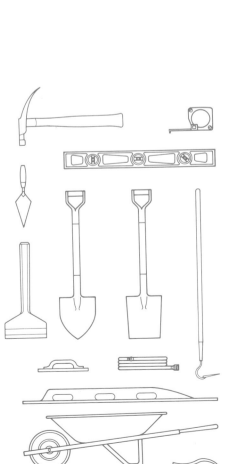

Tools and materials: Wheelbarrow. Spade, trowel, shovel. Hoe, garden hose. Hammer, brick chisel. Screed, bull float, wooden hand float. Steel tape rule, chalk, 3' level. Brick jointer. Plastic sheeting about 5' x 6'. Nine bags portland cement, two bags hydrated lime, 18 cu. ft. mason's sand, 17 cu. ft. crushed stone or gravel, 530 solid bricks 2¼" x 3¾" x 8". Two 24" x 36" grill racks. A 10" x 10" x 17" preformed damper and door. Steel reinforcing rods (⅜" dia.): twelve 4" lengths, eight 18" lengths, eight 24" lengths, and five 32" lengths.

Pouring the foundation

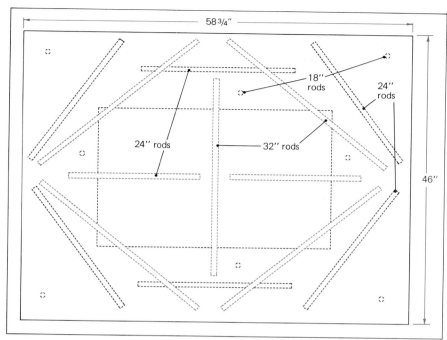

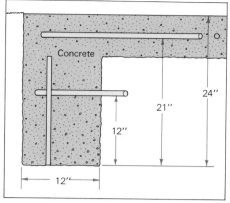

The slab/footing foundation provides a solid 2-ft.-deep base beneath the walls of the barbecue and a 6-in. slab in the center area. Steel reinforcing rods prevent concrete from cracking under the weight of the structure or from stresses caused by extreme temperatures. Drawings show how to place rods vertically and horizontally in the trench and horizontally across the slab.

1. Excavate the entire foundation area to a depth of 6 in.; then dig a trench 1 ft. wide to a depth of 24 in. all around the perimeter. Tamp the soil down firmly. If soil is too loose to maintain firm walls, make the trench large enough to accommodate stakes and boards for a wooden form around the outside (see *Index*, p.379). If a form is used, be sure to remove stakes and boards after concrete has set and fill around foundation with firmly packed soil.

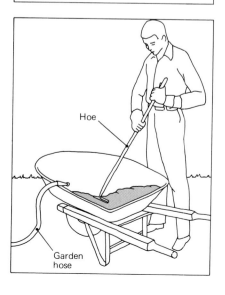

2. Make the concrete from 4 parts portland cement (with air-entraining agent), 9 parts mason's sand, and 12 parts crushed stone or gravel. Blend the mixture thoroughly with a garden hoe, then add only enough water to produce a stiff but workable mixture. As a rule of thumb, you should not add more than 6 gal. of water for each bag of cement. You can avoid mixing by ordering air-entrained ready-mixed concrete. You will need about 31 cu. ft.

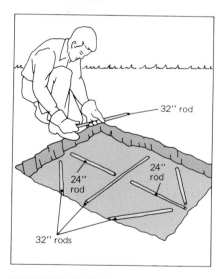

3. Pour concrete into the trench to a depth of about a foot. Then embed steel reinforcing rods as shown above. Finish pouring the concrete, making sure that the upright rods remain vertical. When the concrete is within 3 in. of the top of the excavation, place steel reinforcing rods horizontally across the center area. Then fill the excavation to the top with concrete.

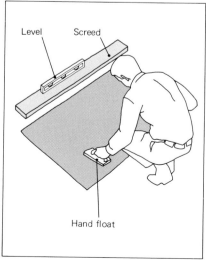

4. Use a long board as a screed to achieve a level surface, checking your work with a 3-ft. level. Then use a bull float to smooth out the rough places. (You can make your own from a piece of 1 x 8 with a 1-in. dowel as a handle.) Finally, finish the surface with sweeping arcs of a wooden hand float. Cover with plastic sheets weighted down with bricks, and allow the concrete to cure for at least 5 days before beginning work on the brick barbecue.

Laying the bricks

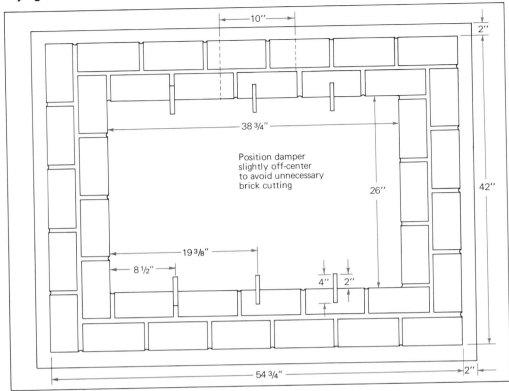

Position damper slightly off-center to avoid unnecessary brick cutting

Drawing shows pattern of first course of bricks for barbecue with 24- x 36-in. grill racks. Second course is a mirror image of the first so that all bricks are staggered, none lying directly on top of or beside another. If your racks are a different size, devise a pattern that will accomplish the same end with interior measurements 2–3 in. larger than those of the racks. Before mixing mortar, mark a chalk line 2 in. from the edges of the foundation and lay out the first two courses dry, spacing bricks ½ in. apart to be sure everything fits. If the resultant outline fails to coincide with the chalk line, make new lines to show the true placement. Position the damper door in the front wall and cut bricks as necessary (see *Index*, p.379), allowing ½ in. for mortar on both sides of the damper. Disassemble. Hose down bricks about 15 min. before use so that they will be damp but not wet when laid. (For detailed instructions on the bricklaying techniques mentioned below, see pp.312–313.)

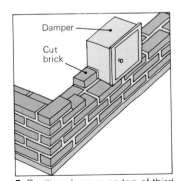

1. To mix mortar, combine 1 part portland cement, 1 part hydrated lime, and 6 parts mason's sand; add water for a thick paste. For ready-mixed mortar, order 6 cu. ft. of Type N mortar.

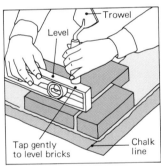

2. At each corner lay in bricks along chalk lines on ½-in. bed of mortar. Build the first course outward from the corners, buttering the bricks to achieve ½ in. of mortar at each joint.

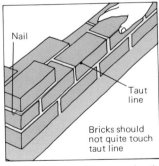

3. Build second course in the same way, spreading enough mortar on bricks of first course to provide a ½-in. bed. Keep courses level and plumb; clip off excess mortar as you work.

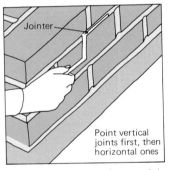

4. After third course is complete, use brick jointer to point (finish) the joints, making a smooth, concave surface to seal out moisture. Mortar should be thumbprint hard before pointing.

5. Position damper on top of third course on ¾-in. bed of mortar. Lay in precut bricks, abutting damper, and lay in corners of fourth course on a ½-in. bed; then complete fourth course.

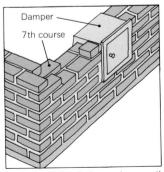

6. Build fifth, sixth, and seventh courses in the same manner, buttering precut bricks with ½ in. of mortar before abutting them to damper. Then point the joints of these courses.

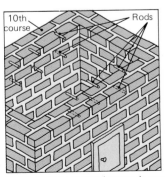

7. Be sure to spread enough mortar on top of damper to keep the eighth course level. While spreading mortar for 9th and 11th courses, insert the rods that will support the grill racks.

8. Point joints after 11th course. Continue to top, keeping courses level and plumb. Note that bricks of 14th course are laid side by side, perpendicular to those below. Point remaining courses.

BRICK-AND-WOOD STEPS

Redwood and brick have been combined in this unusual but attractive stairway that extends a brick walkway up a slope. Redwood is durable, resists rotting if treated with a preservative, and will take on a pleasant, weathered appearance in time. Cedar is a suitable substitute if the price of redwood is prohibitive.

The most difficult part of this project is the manual labor required to excavate the slope. You may want to hire a backhoe operator to do the job.

After the ground is prepared, you can install the steps in two ways. You can make concrete steps and let them serve as a foundation for the redwood and brick, or you can lay the redwood and brick on a bed of gravel and sand. The concrete foundation obviously provides greater stability. However, the project will take longer and will be costlier. (If you decide on the concrete foundation, see *Concrete Steps*, pp.320–322, for instructions.)

Construction: The first step and each alternate step thereafter are built using 2 x 4 redwood for the risers and restraining edges and 2 x 12 redwood for the treads. The second step and alternate suc-

ceeding steps are a combination of redwood and brick. Build each of these steps with 2 x 8 boards for the riser and restraining edges, a 2 x 4 board for the leading edge of the tread, and seven rows of 1½- x 3⅝- x 7⅝-inch SX brick pavers for the remainder of the tread. Since the actual thickness of the 2 x 4 part of the tread is 1½ inches, the board and the abutting bricks should line up evenly, leaving no protruding edges.

Alternate steps have different depths. The all-wood steps are 11½ inches deep (front to back), and the steps made of redwood and brick are 30½ inches deep. Lumberyards usually do not stock boards wider than a nominal 12 inches; if you want steps with a deeper tread, you will have to special-order wider boards. If you wish to shorten the depth of the combination redwood-and-brick steps, reduce the number of brick rows.

All treads and risers are 34½ inches wide. The height of the risers alternates between 3½ and 7½ inches.

The bricks do not have mortar joints. They are laid edge to edge and are kept firmly in place by the redwood restraining boards.

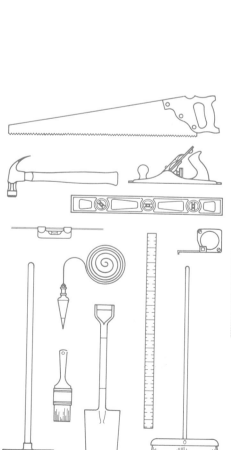

2 x 4
2 x 8
2 x 12
2 x 4
2 x 8
2 x 4
2 x 8
2 x 12
2 x 4

Tools and materials: Handsaw. Shovel or spade, tamp. Stiff-bristled broom. Hammer, plane. Plumb line, string level, torpedo level, carpenter's level, steel tape rule, straightedge, 15' of string. Redwood preservative, paintbrush. For six steps, 25 running ft. of 2 x 4 redwood, 24 running ft. of 2 x 8 redwood, and 9 running ft. of 2 x 12 redwood. About one hundred and five 1½" x 3⅝" x 7⅝" class SX brick pavers. Four pegs, 30 stakes 12" long, ten 3" x 3" wooden cleats. Mason's sand and gravel as required, 22 sq. ft. of 15-lb. roofing felt, 2 lb. of 10d annular ring nails. Concrete is optional (see text and following project, *Concrete Steps*, pp.320–322).

Laying out the site

Assuming that each step is 34½ inches wide, drive pegs into the ground along the path of the projected stairway and outline the site with string. To allow for the 1½-inch thickness of the stakes and boards you will use as restraining edges, make sure the pegs and string on each side of the site are 40½ inches apart (34½ inches + 4 × 1½ inches).

Refer to page 321 for instructions on how to determine the number of steps you will need for the particular slope on your property. Remember that the steps in this project are of two different depths, 11½ inches and 30½ inches, and that the risers alternate between 3½ inches and 7½ inches in height. Our slope is 126 inches in length, which will accommodate six

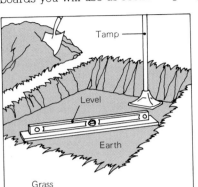

1. Excavate the site, digging well back into the slope. Remember that you have to lay in boards that are 33 in. long. Clear away rocks, grass, and roots from the bed of the site. Tamp down the earth to get a firm substratum. Using a 4-ft. level, make the bed as even as possible.

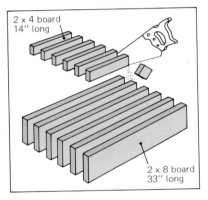

2. Cut redwood boards to the lengths required for the restraining edges, plus 2½ inches. Six 2 x 4's, each 14 in. long, and six 2 x 8's, each 33 in. long, were cut for the steps shown here.

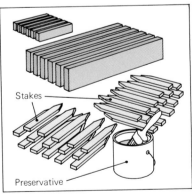

3. Give each board a liberal coating of redwood preservative and allow it to dry. Also apply preservative to the 1-ft. stakes. The number of stakes you will need depends on the number and the length of the restraining boards. In this case, 30 stakes were used. Place stakes 12–18 in. apart.

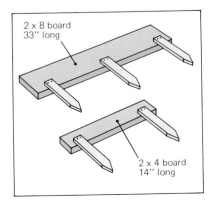

4. When boards and stakes are dry, nail stakes securely to boards with 10d nails as shown. Use two stakes for each 14-in. board and three stakes for each 33-in. board.

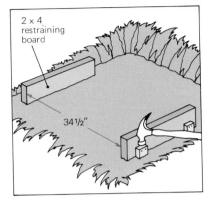

5. Install restraining boards for the first step, driving their stakes into the ground so that the bottom edges of the boards lie flush against the earth. Pitch the boards forward a bit (about ⅛ in. per foot) so that water will drain from the steps.

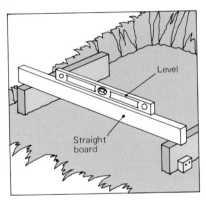

6. Make sure the restraining board on one side of the step lines up evenly with its counterpart on the other side. To do this, extend a straightedge across the step so it rests on top of the leading edge of each board. Use a level on the straightedge to help equalize the heights of the boards.

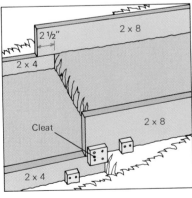

7. Install the restraining boards for the second step, overlapping the boards for the lower step by 2½ in. Drive the stakes holding the boards for the second step into the ground, and join the upper and lower restraining boards by nailing wooden cleats into the overlapping portions. Continue up the slope, installing all restraining boards in this manner.

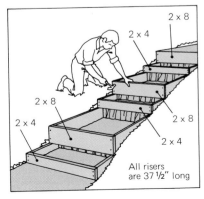

8. Cut 2 x 4 and 2 x 8 boards 37½ in. long for the risers of all steps. Apply preservative to all surfaces of these boards. When they are dry, nail them to the front edges of their restraining boards.

steps: three of them 11½ inches deep (3 x 11½ inches = 34½ inches) + three steps that are 30½ inches deep (3 x 30½ inches = 91½ inches) = 126 inches. The 33-inch height of the slope will also accommodate six alternating steps: (3 x 3½ inches = 10½ inches) + (3 x 7½ inches = 22½ inches) = 33 inches. It may take some mathematical juggling to figure out how many steps will fit your slope. Remember that all the risers can be made the same height (either 3½ inches or 7½ inches), if you prefer, and that the depths of the treads can be changed by using boards with different widths and by increasing or decreasing the number of brick rows. Plan your steps carefully on graph paper before you order materials or start to work.

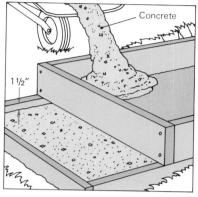

9. If you are going to lay a concrete foundation for the steps, see pp.320–322, then proceed. Otherwise, skip to Step 12. Do not pour in too much concrete; it should be 1½ in. below the top edges of the boards that are in place. In this way the boards and bricks that form the treads will lie flush with the top edges of the restraining boards and risers.

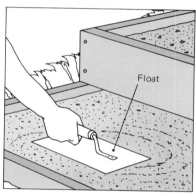

10. After pouring concrete, float it until it is level. Then follow the instructions given on page 322 (Step 8) for the proper curing of concrete.

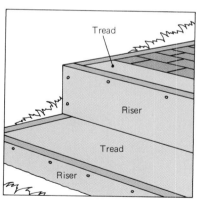

11. To complete the all-wood steps, lay redwood treads over the concrete and nail them to the edges of the boards already in place. To complete the combination redwood-and-brick steps, first lay the bricks in place, then position the treads so that their leading edges fit just inside the risers. If the treads are slightly high, trim them with a plane.

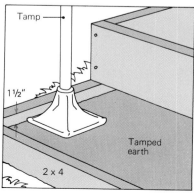

12. If you are not providing a concrete foundation, prepare the all-wood steps by sifting debris from a portion of the excavated earth. Fill each area that is outlined by 2 x 4's to within 1½ in. of the tops of the 2 x 4's after tamping down and leveling each bed. Nail the treads for these all-wood steps in place.

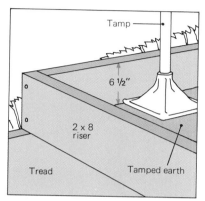

13. To prepare the combination redwood-and-brick steps, sift debris from some more of the excavated earth; then lay and tamp a 1-in.-thick bed of this earth in each area that is outlined by 2 x 8's. There should be a 6½-in. space between the tamped earth base and the tops of the 2 x 8's.

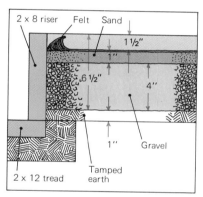

14. Fill this space with 4 in. of gravel and 1 in. of mason's sand, tamping down each layer. Place a single layer of 15-lb. roofing felt over the sand to prevent algae from attacking the brick and causing a "greening" effect. You should now have 1½ in. available in which to place the brick-and-redwood treads.

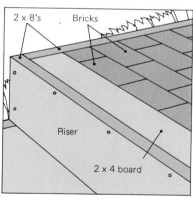

15. After checking to be sure that the roofing felt is both level and even, place the bricks edge to edge, beginning at the rear of the step. (It may be necessary to cut bricks; for instructions, see *Index*, p.379.) Finish the treads by installing the redwood boards even with the risers.

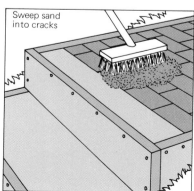

16. Backfill the site with more of the excavated earth after removing debris. Then spread some sand over the brick portions of the steps and sweep what you can into the cracks with a stiff broom; remove the excess sand. Restore the slope by planting grass or shrubs.

319

CONCRETE STEPS

If you have to walk up a sloping lawn to get to your house, consider building concrete steps. Properly laid out and constructed, they are maintenance free and have a look of permanence.

It could take 10 days or more to prepare the site and lay the concrete, so try to finish this project before the hot weather sets in. The best time to work with concrete is when the temperature is below 70°. Warmer than that, evaporation takes place and the concrete dries out. When setting, concrete goes through a chemical change involving the water content. It does not simply dry out. If too much of the water evaporates, the finished concrete will be weakened.

Local ordinances often restrict construction projects of this kind; consult your local building code and building inspector before starting any work.

When working with concrete, be sure to wear protective clothing, particularly gloves. Concrete is caustic, and any skin area that comes in contact with it should be washed with water immediately.

Layout: Measure the site carefully so that the steps are all the same size. Decide on the width you want, then add 4 inches on each side to allow for form boards and enough working room to remove the form. Use wooden stakes driven into the ground and tie string to mark the boundaries.

The steps shown here are 42 inches wide. Therefore, the width that was

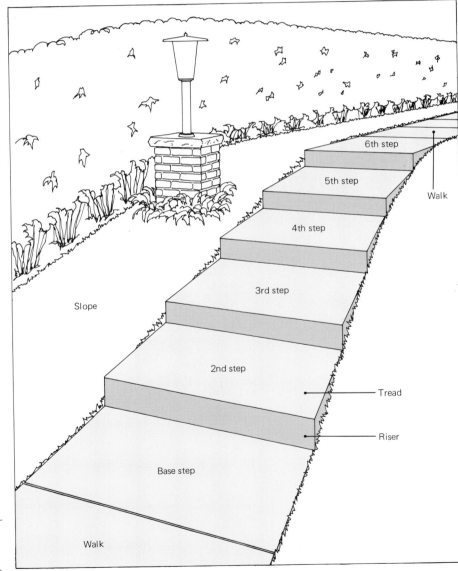

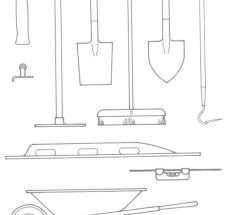

Tools and materials: Spade, wheelbarrow, tamp, shovel. Hoe, darby, edger, stiff-bristled broom. Garden hose. Hammer. Level, string, pencil. Work gloves. A screed of 2 x 4 lumber 4' long. Wooden stakes, lumber for form boards. Air-entrained portland cement, sand, crushed stone or gravel. Waterproof paper or opaque plastic sheeting for curing. Engine oil. 10d duplex-head nails.

marked off was 50 inches (42 inches + 4 inches + 4 inches).

Making forms: When buying lumber for forms, consider its actual rather than its nominal size, since the actual dimensions are usually ½ inch less. The variation between actual and nominal sizes depends on the lumber. Green (wet) lumber is best because it separates more readily from the concrete. It is closer to the nominal sizes than dressed lumber and should be less expensive. Your lumber dealer can tell you about the actual size and availability of the lumber you will need for the job.

Build a four-sided form to make steps two through six. In this project, the form's inner dimensions are 42 inches wide and 38 inches deep. This depth includes an extra 2 inches so you can overlap each step with the completed step below it. The step height is 6 inches.

Use duplex-head nails to build the form, and coat the boards with engine oil. Crankcase drainings will save you money. Duplex-head nails make it easier to dismantle the form; oil eases the separation of the boards and concrete.

About concrete: When you pour the concrete for each step and allow it to set before laying the next step, as suggested here, you will have to mix concrete yourself instead of ordering transit-mixed concrete, because suppliers are usually reluctant to deliver small amounts. While this method involves more time and work,

it is a better procedure for the amateur than trying to construct a one-piece form on the side of a slope.

To make concrete, put 4 parts air-entrained portland cement, 9 parts sand, and 12 parts crushed stone or washed gravel into a wheelbarrow. Use a hoe to mix the dry ingredients thoroughly, or rent a small concrete mixer by the day. Then add 6 gallons of water for each bag of cement and mix until you get firm, consistent concrete. Refer to the instructions on the package of cement, or consult your supplier, to determine how much concrete to mix each day until the job is completed. For general instructions on building forms and pouring concrete, see pages 268–269.

Planning the steps

All the steps should have the same tread depth (the front-to-back measurement) and riser height. To determine how many steps you will need in order to negotiate the slope you are working on, do the following:
1. Drive a long stake into the ground at the base of the slope. The stake should be taller than the height of the slope.

2. Drive a short stake or peg into the ground at the top of the slope and attach a line to it at ground level. Pull the line taut and tie it to the tall stake.
3. If you can reach a section of the line, hold a small level lightly against the line, or use a line level made to hang on a cord. Adjust the line up or down on the tall stake until the line is level. If you cannot reach the line, use visual reckoning and have another person check your observation.

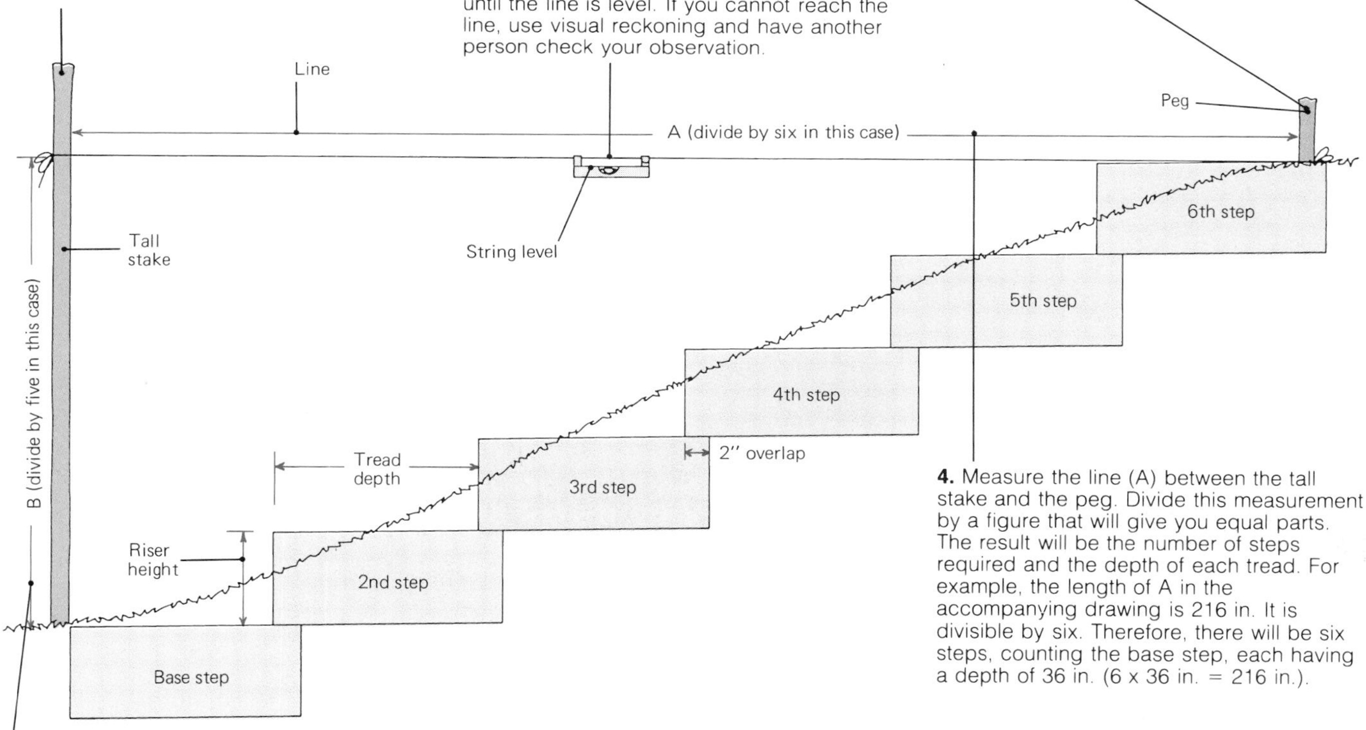

Line

Peg

A (divide by six in this case)

String level

Tall stake

B (divide by five in this case)

6th step

5th step

4th step

2″ overlap

Tread depth

3rd step

Riser height

2nd step

Base step

4. Measure the line (A) between the tall stake and the peg. Divide this measurement by a figure that will give you equal parts. The result will be the number of steps required and the depth of each tread. For example, the length of A in the accompanying drawing is 216 in. It is divisible by six. Therefore, there will be six steps, counting the base step, each having a depth of 36 in. (6 x 36 in. = 216 in.).

5. Now measure the tall stake from the ground up to line A. Divide this measurement (B) by the number of steps, minus the base step, to determine the height of each riser. For example, if B is 30 in. and is divided by five (the number of steps having risers), the height of each riser will be 6 in. Try to keep risers within a 4- to 8-in. height. Lower or higher steps are awkward to negotiate.

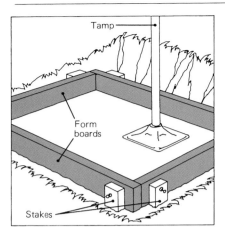

6. Use a spade to excavate the ground for the base step. Remove all grass, roots, and rocks. Mark the perimeter with stakes. For drainage, pitch the ground and form downward ¼ in. for each foot of tread depth. Tamp the earth to compact it, then nail form boards to the stakes. Since the base step need not be as thick as the others, use 2 x 3 lumber for the form.

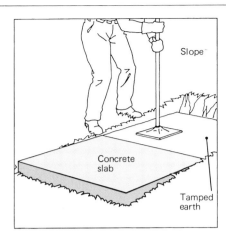

10. The next day run a small knife blade across an inch of the surface to test for hardness before beginning work on the next step. If the knife cannot penetrate the concrete, dismantle the form. Then excavate for the next step, digging into the slope to form the subsurface for the tread. Level the area, remembering to provide the ¼ in.-per-foot pitch. Then tamp down the earth.

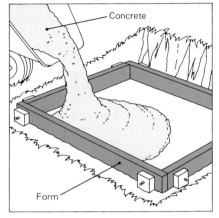

7. Make the two side boards of the form long enough so that a slab 2 in. deeper (front to back) than the desired depth of the tread can be laid. This extra depth will be overlapped by the step above to provide a firm bond between the two steps. Moisten the ground so that the earth will not draw water from the concrete. Fill the form with concrete.

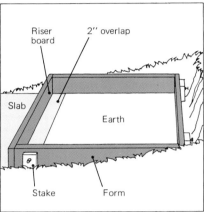

11. Drive stakes into the ground at the sides of the excavation. Place the form in position inside the stakes. See that the riser board overlaps the slab you built the day before. Allow for an overlap of 2 in. of concrete behind the riser board so that when you lay concrete for the next step a firm bond will be made with the slab below.

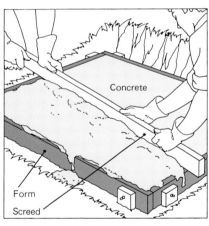

8. Run a square-ended shovel along the sides of the form and strike the sides of the form with a heavy hammer to settle the concrete. The concrete should be slightly higher than the top of the form. While the concrete is still wet, rest a screed across the top of the form. With a helper move the screed back and forth to strike off excess concrete and level the surface.

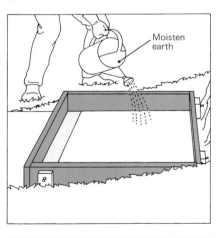

12. Nail stakes to the form. This will prevent the form from shifting as you pour and work with the concrete. Remember to moisten the ground as in Step 7 for the base slab. Build the remaining concrete steps by repeating Steps 7–11.

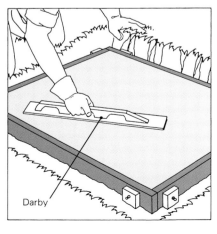

9. Work a darby across the surface with a sweeping motion to force stones or gravel below the surface of the concrete. Press the trailing edge of the darby down slightly as you move it in an arc across the surface. Use the edger to trim the edges of the slab. Cover with waterproof paper or plastic sheeting to minimize evaporation.

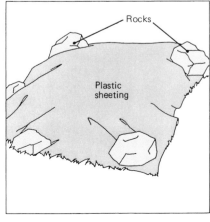

13. To ensure proper curing, moisten the concrete after it has hardened, then cover it with waterproof paper or opaque plastic sheeting. Weight down the edges of the cover with rocks to hold it in place. If the temperature remains between 50° and 70°, cure each step for 7 days. Cure each for 5 days if the temperature goes above 70°.

STAINED-GLASS LAMP

Stained-glass lamps were popularized by Louis Comfort Tiffany during the Art Nouveau period at the turn of the century. Tiffany's name became so closely associated with these lamps that many people refer to all stained-glass lamps as Tiffany lamps.

Although the lamps waned in popularity for many years, there has been a resurgence of interest in recent times. In fact, they have become so popular now that simple geometrical lamps (or plastic imitations) are even found in fast-food restaurants. But the proliferation of crudely built lamps and cheap imitations cannot dim the exquisite beauty of a well-designed, carefully executed lamp. A lamp like the one shown here will brighten any room with both its light and its beauty.

The basic pattern of this lamp is repeated three times. Begin the project by enlarging the pattern on the following page and making four copies of it—three on paper, one on cardboard (see p.48). Cut out the cardboard copy into glass patterns (templates used for cutting the glass), tape the other three copies of the pattern together to form the full "cartoon," and proceed to make the lamp.

The glazing method outlined in this chapter is the copper foil technique popularized by Tiffany. Basically, it consists of cutting the pieces of glass, wrapping their edges in copper foil, then soldering the strips of foil together and covering them with solder. The solder on the finished lamp is rubbed down with an antiquing solution to discolor the solder and give it the appearance of antique copper.

In the older lead-came method of glazing, the glass is slipped into cames (grooved lengths of lead) and the cames are soldered together. In the method used here, foil replaces the cames.

Cutting glass: Cutting a straight piece of glass is simple, but cutting curved pieces of glass to exact shapes and sizes can be tricky. If you have never cut glass before, practice on inexpensive window glass before beginning this project.

To cut glass, you must first score it with a glass cutter and then break it off with your hands or with pliers. Three types of pliers are used. The first type are breaking pliers, which have straight, wide, parallel jaws that help you break off narrow strips of glass; if necessary, you can substitute slip-joint pliers. The second kind, cut-running pliers, have curved jaws that exert pressure on both sides of a score, making it easier to break curves. The third, grozing pliers, have rough jaws for trimming rough edges. If you cannot find these, use needle-nose pliers instead.

Glass cutters must be kept lubricated. To do so, line the bottom of a small jar with a bit of soft cloth and add a thin layer of kerosene or light machine oil. Keep your cutters in this jar while you are working and dip the wheel of the cutter into the lubricant before making each cut.

Wrapping: After all the glass has been cut, each piece must be wrapped in copper foil and the edges of the foil crimped down over the front and back surfaces of the glass. The foil hugs the edges of the glass on all sides, making it possible to solder the pieces of glass together. Copper foil comes in rolls and has a paper backing that must be peeled off as you work with it.

When wrapping, be sure to get the foil on straight. Wrapping is easy, but there is

Parts list

Part	Name	Quantity	Total amount of glass	Materials
A	Background panel	21	8 sq. ft.	Purple opalescent glass
B	Leaf	24	2 sq. ft.	Green antique glass
C	Flower petal	48	2½ sq. ft.	Magenta antique glass
D	Flower center	12	½ sq. ft.	Yellow antique glass

Note: This chart gives the colors of the individual parts of the lamp and indicates the total amount of glass needed in each color. The sizes and shapes of each of the flowers, leaves, and background panels vary and must be taken from the cartoon on the next page. The amount of glass called for allows for waste in case you make bad cuts and have to repeat them.

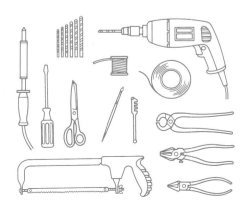

Tools and materials: Heavy-duty soldering iron with ⅜" plug-type tip, iron rest (or bent piece of metal secured to work surface). Several single-edged steel-wheel glass cutters. Breaking or slip-joint pliers, grozing or needle-nose pliers, cut-running pliers. Scissors. Wire stripper or sharp knife. Drill with ⅛" bit, hacksaw, screwdriver. Small wastepaper basket or cone made of stapled cardboard to hold lamp while working on it. Small brush, pencil, grease pencil, masking tape, transparent tape. Light cardboard, paper, carbon paper, tracing paper. Small jar, soft cloth, damp cellulose sponge, safety goggles, rubber gloves, work gloves. Antiquing solution (either copper sulfate or cupric nitrate), flux, kerosene or light machine oil, detergent. Roll of ¼" or ³⁄₁₆" copper foil, two 1-lb. rolls of 60/40 solid wire solder (60% tin and 40% lead). Glass (see above). Porcelain socket with threaded nipple. Brace bar, vase cap to fit upper opening of lamp, finial, two locknuts, chain for hanging lamp, spherical light bulb.

a strong tendency to work in a mechanical fashion; therefore, wrap carefully and always watch what you are doing.

Soldering: The wrapped pieces of glass must be brushed with flux and soldered together. Always brush a generous amount of flux onto the foil before applying the solder. Flux cleans the foil, prevents oxidation, and allows the molten solder to flow and adhere properly.

Soldering is done in three stages. First, all the pieces of wrapped glass are tacked together with drops of solder. Then a thin coat of solder is run along all visible lines of the copper foil. Finally, more solder is added on top of the first coat, and a bead is raised—that is, the solder is rounded off on top.

Beading can be tricky and may require practice to master. Be patient and work slowly, but do not hold the soldering iron too long in one place or the heat may crack the glass. Imperfect soldering can be reworked with a hot iron and small amounts of solder until smooth. If some solder flashes through (drips through to the other side of the lamp), let it cool before reworking the area. If solder lumps in one spot, apply flux to the spot, heat it with the iron, and push away the excess solder. Finally, if solder gets onto the glass while you are working, let it cool and then flick it off with your finger.

Solder solidifies almost instantly, but it cools slowly, so be careful not to touch a newly soldered surface. Keep a damp cellulose sponge nearby and use it to wipe the tip of the iron clean from time to time as you work.

Most soldering irons are not equipped with thermostats and can become too hot. You must keep unplugging your iron to maintain the proper temperature. You can only judge the temperature by the way the solder behaves. If the solder does not melt freely, the iron is too cool. If the iron smokes or the solder is runny, the iron is too hot.

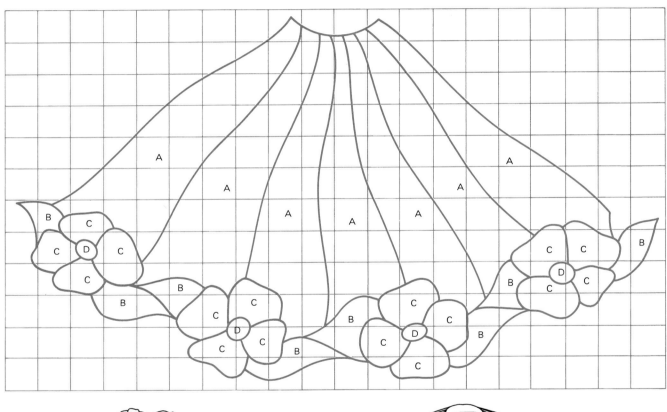

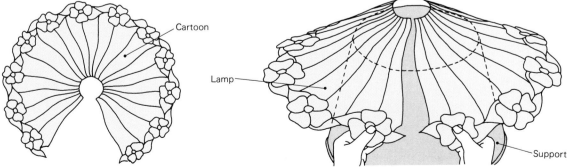

Preparing the cartoon: The first step in making the lamp is preparing the cartoon. Begin by enlarging the pattern at top (see p.48). Each square on the grid equals 1 sq. in. on the lamp. Be very careful to draw the sides of the pattern precisely, as the enlarged pattern will be duplicated and the sides of the copies must fit exactly into each other. To be sure you get your cartoon exact, draw all but the line on the right side of the pattern, then go over the line on the left side on tracing paper with a dark pencil. Place the traced line under the pattern so that this line is in the correct place for the line on the right side. Hold the assembly against a lighted window or a light box, and draw the line for the right side of the pattern by following the traced line. After you have enlarged the entire pattern, make three carbon copies of it on paper and one copy on light cardboard. Cut out the paper copies along their perimeters and tape them together with transparent tape to form the full cartoon as shown (above left). Make sure ends fit snugly (above right). Cut the cardboard copy along all lines to form the glass patterns.

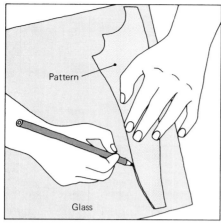

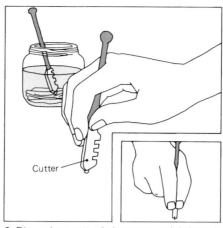

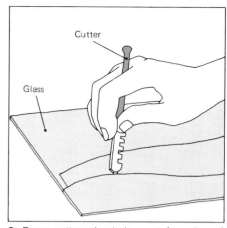

1. Prepare the cartoon and glass patterns, then get ready to cut the glass. Place the pattern for the first background piece near the edge of the smoother side of a sheet of glass. Trace the outline of the pattern onto the glass with a grease pencil.

2. Dip a glass cutter in kerosene to lubricate it. (Keep the cutter wheel in kerosene when not in use.) Hold the cutter between your index and middle fingers and brace it in back with your thumb. Stand up and lean over the glass for more freedom of movement.

3. Press cutter wheel down at far edge of glass and move cutter toward you along and just inside cutting line, applying firm, even pressure. (You should hear sound like radio static.) Score in a continuous motion, ending after cutter comes off near end of glass.

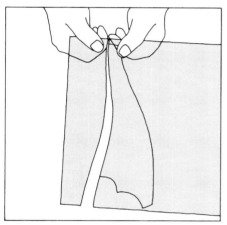

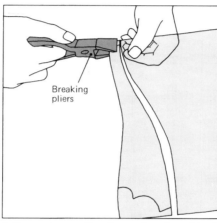

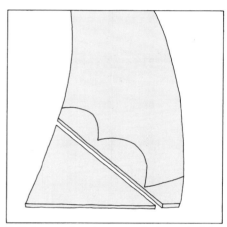

4. Pick up glass as shown with one hand on each side of score line and pointing in same direction as line. Gently push glass down and outward with your thumbs, using even pressure. Steadily increase pressure until glass snaps in two along cutting line.

5. Score along cutting line on the other side of the same piece. Swing your arm and body with the curve to ensure unimpaired movement of the cutter. If one side of glass is too narrow to break by hand, hold it with breaking pliers near score line and snap it off.

6. Before cutting the curves in the end of the piece, cut away as much of the excess as you can with a straight cut. Glass is basically brittle and inflexible and you cannot cut out sharp curves in one step. You must remove unwanted glass from inside of curve in stages.

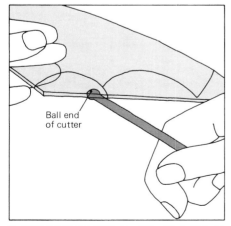

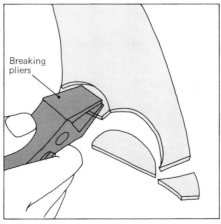

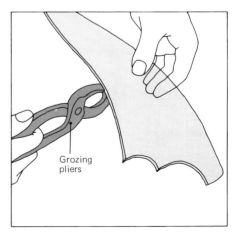

7. After removing what you can with a straight cut, score the curve you want in the end of the piece and tap the score gently on the back with the ball end of a glass cutter to keep the cut from breaking wild. Tapping will cause a partial break, but glass will not separate.

8. Divide glass to be removed from inside of curve into easy-to-cut sections. Score on dividing lines and snap off pieces with breaking pliers one at a time. Score in one unbroken motion. If you go over a score, you will get a bad cut and dull cutter.

9. Cut two more background sections like the first and put the three sections one on top of the other to make sure that they are exactly alike. Remove any rough edges with grozing pliers. Wear goggles while grozing. Put cut pieces in place on cartoon smooth side up.

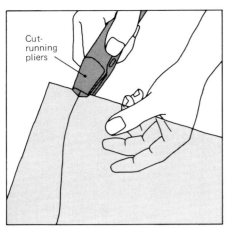

10. Cut all the remaining glass in the same way. When breaking a long curve, apply cut-running pliers across score line so that line on jaw of pliers runs in same direction as score line. Squeeze handles of pliers until you hear a snap. Complete break by hand.

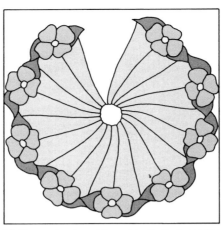

11. Remember to cut three identical pieces for each shape in lamp. After cutting each piece, put it into place on cartoon smooth side up. Continue cutting glass until all the pieces have been done. The next step is to wrap the edges of all the pieces with copper foil.

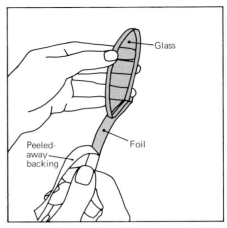

12. Peel off a section of the paper backing from the foil. Hold the foil in one hand and a piece of glass in the other. Center the end of the foil on the edge of the glass about ¼ in. from a corner or curve. Pull foil tightly around corner or curve, keeping it centered.

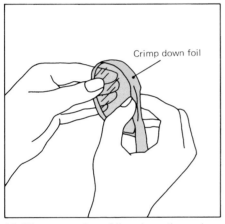

13. Wrap one edge of the glass, then crimp down the foil with your fingers so that it hugs both sides of the glass evenly. Wrap the other edges of the glass, being careful to keep foil centered on edge of glass. Keep your eye on the foil at all times to keep it straight.

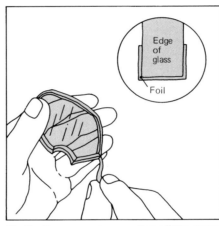

14. Continue wrapping, peeling off the paper backing as you proceed, until you reach the corner or curve where you began. Let ends of tape overlap slightly. Tear off foil by twisting it back and forth a few times. Crimp down foil on all edges of glass and at corners.

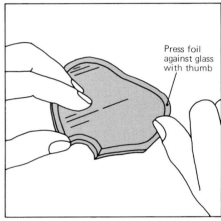

15. Go around the perimeter of each piece of glass, carefully pressing the foil against the glass. If the edges overlap at a slight angle, trim them with a razor blade. If the foil is very crooked, remove it and start over. Put the wrapped pieces on cartoon smooth side up.

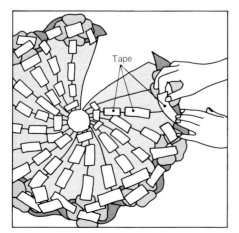

16. When wrapping a piece that will be at bottom edge of lamp, start on an edge that will butt against another piece. If ends of foil are left free, they may pull loose in time. When all pieces have been wrapped and placed on cartoon, connect them with masking tape.

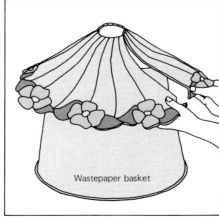

17. Place a wastepaper basket or cardboard cone on your workbench to support lamp while you work. Carefully pick up taped lamp by its ends and pull it up and around wastepaper basket or cone. Tape its ends together. Generously brush all foil with flux.

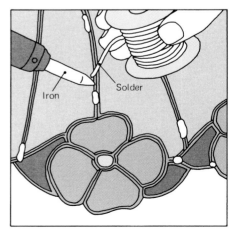

18. To tack each of the adjacent pieces together with solder, hold the end of the wire solder over the place where the strips of foil join, and touch a hot soldering iron to the solder until a large drop of it falls onto the joint. Use several drops of solder on long joints.

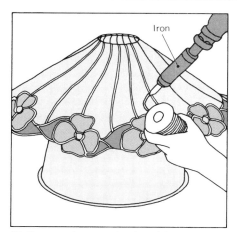

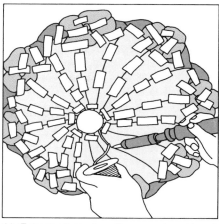

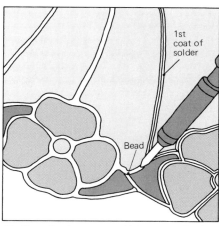

19. Remove the tape that is holding the ends together and brush the area with flux. Float a thin coat of solder over all the foil on the outside of lamp so that no foil remains visible. If there are small gaps between pieces due to imprecise cutting, fill them with solder.

20. Take the lamp from its support and turn it upside down. Add flux and a light coat of solder to the top and bottom rims. Remove the tape from one seam at a time, being careful not to pull up foil. Brush foil with flux and float a thin coat of solder over all foil.

21. Turn the lamp over. Using a cooler iron, slowly add more solder over top of first coat to raise a bead (rounded ribbon of solder) along all outside lines of lamp. Area being beaded must be level (horizontal to work surface); so prop up lamp while beading outside.

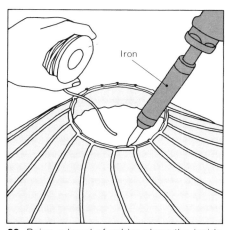

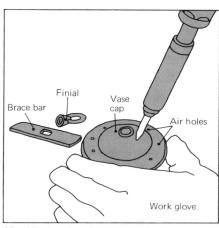

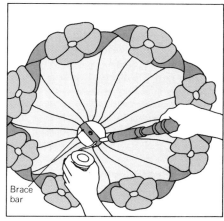

22. Raise a bead of solder along the inside lines of the lamp, then raise one along the top and bottom rims, being sure that the solder on the rims touches the solder on both the front and back of lamp. Do not leave iron in one place for too long or heat may crack glass.

23. Wash the lamp carefully in detergent and water, then rinse and dry it. Drill eight ⅛-in. holes through the vase cap to allow heat from the light bulb to escape. Coat the vase cap and the finial with solder to make them match the rest of metal on lamp.

24. Use a hacksaw to trim the brace bar to make it fit snugly across the top of the lamp on the inside. The bar must touch solder on both sides. Brush ends of bar and top rim of lamp with flux, and solder bar into place on lamp on both top and bottom.

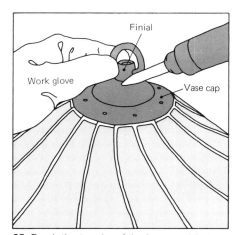

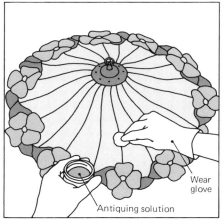

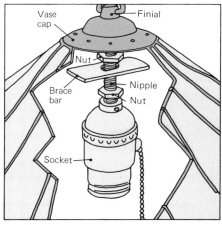

25. Brush the top rim of the lamp and bottom of vase cap and finial with flux. Solder the vase cap into place on the top of the lamp and then solder the finial onto the top of the vase cap. Be careful not to get solder into the hole in the finial, as the wire must fit through it.

26. Wearing rubber gloves, rub down all the metal on the lamp with an antiquing solution until it becomes a uniform antique copper color. Wash the lamp in detergent and water, then rinse and dry it. Attach chain to loop in finial and hang lamp where you want it.

27. Screw the nipple through the brace bar and into the finial with a nut above and below the brace bar. With the electricity turned off, pass electric wire through the finial and the nipple. Then screw on the socket and attach the wires to it. Screw in a spherical bulb.

GLASS-HOUSE TERRARIUM

Show off your plants to great advantage in this glass-house terrarium. The inside of the house can be used as a true terrarium for moisture-loving plants, or the top of the planter can be opened and the inside filled with other plants by swinging down the two hinged panels. In addition, small plants can be grown in the side flower pots and in the chimney.

Use the stained-glass techniques discussed in the preceding project to make this terrarium. Techniques not included in the preceding stained-glass lamp project are given on the following page.

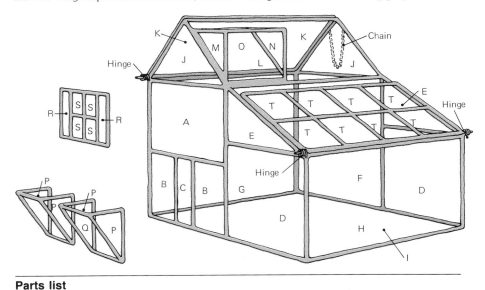

Parts list

Part	Name	Quantity	Shape	Width	Length	Material
A	Upper left wall	1	Rectangular	4″	5″	Clear glass
B	Flower pot backing	2	Rectangular	2″	4″	Clear glass
C	Flower pot divider	1	Rectangular	1″	4″	Opalescent glass
D	Side porch wall	2	Rectangular	4″	5″	Clear glass
E	Porch roof support	2	Triangular ✳	3″	4″	Clear glass
F	Right wall	1	Rectangular	5″	8″	Clear glass
G	Back wall	1	Rectangular	8″	10″	Clear glass
H	Front porch wall	1	Rectangular	5″	10″	Clear glass
I	Bottom	1	Rectangular	9″	10″	Clear glass
J	Main roof support	2	Triangular ✳	3½″	3½″	Clear glass
K	Main rooftop	2	Rectangular	3½″	10″	Clear glass
L	Chimney front	1	Rectangular	2″	3¾″	Clear glass
M	Left chimney side	1	Triangular ✳	2″	2¼″	Opalescent glass
N	Right chimney side	1	Triangular ✳	2″	2¼″	Clear glass
O	Chimney back	1	Rectangular	3″	3¾″	Clear glass
P	Flower pot side	4	Triangular ✳	2″	2¾″	Clear glass
Q	Flower pot front	2	Rectangular	2″	3½″	Clear glass
R	Side windowpane	2	Rectangular	½″	2½″	Opalescent glass
S	Center windowpane	4	Square	1¼″	1¼″	Opalescent glass
T	Porch roof shingle	8	Rectangular	2¼″	2½″	Clear glass

✳ Every triangular piece is a right triangle (one of its angles is 90°). To make a pattern for a right triangle, draw a square or rectangle as needed and divide it in half diagonally.

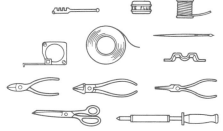

Tools and materials: Heavy-duty soldering iron, iron rest. Single-edged steel-wheel glass cutters. Needle-nose pliers, breaking or slip-joint pliers, wire cutters. Steel tape rule, pencil, grease pencil. Scissors, small brush. Masking tape, light cardboard, small jar, soft cloth, rubber gloves. Antiquing solution (either copper sulfate or cupric nitrate), flux, kerosene, clear silicone glue and seal. Four sq. ft. of clear glass, 1 sq. ft. of opalescent glass (clear glass can be substituted). Roll of ¼″ or ³⁄₁₆″ copper foil, 1-lb. roll 60/40 solid wire solder, 52″ of 18-gauge copper wire, 6″ copper chain.

1. Cut cardboard patterns for all the different parts of the terrarium except the bottom (I). Trace the shapes of the patterns onto the glass with a grease pencil, and cut all the glass called for in the chart except the bottom. Wrap each piece of glass with copper foil.

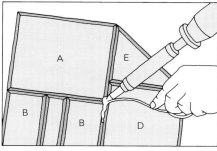

2. Assemble the upper left wall (A), flower pot backings (B), flower pot divider (C), one side porch wall (D), and one porch roof support (E). Generously brush flux over all the visible foil; then tack pieces together securely with several drops of solder along each joint.

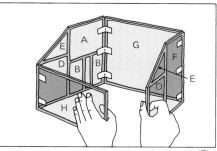

3. Use solder to tack together right wall (F), one side porch wall (D), and one porch roof support (E). Tape these pieces together with the back wall (G), the front porch wall (H), and the pieces assembled in Step 2. Carefully pull up taped pieces into a standing rectangle.

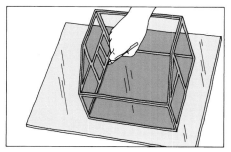

4. Tack the sections together with solder, using several drops of solder on each joint so that the sections will hold together while you work. Remove tape. Place structure on a sheet of glass and trace a line around inside perimeter of structure with a grease pencil.

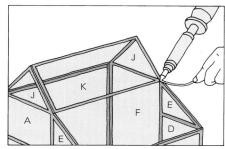

5. Cut the glass along the marks to form the bottom (I). Wrap the edges of the bottom with foil, brush the foil with flux, and tack the bottom to the terrarium with solder. Tack the main roof supports (J) and then the front section of the main rooftop (K) into place with solder.

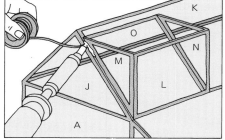

6. Tape together the chimney front (L), left chimney side (M), right chimney side (N), and chimney back (O). Pull the pieces up and around to form chimney. Tack pieces together with solder and remove tape. Tack chimney into place on roof with more solder.

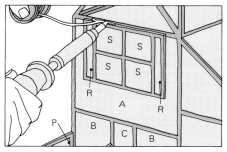

7. Tack the flower pot sides (P) into place and the flower pot fronts (Q) over them. Tack together the side and center windowpanes (R and S), and cover all the foil on the back of the window with solder. Solder the top of the window to the top of the upper left wall (A).

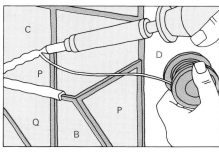

8. Float a coat of solder over all the foil on the outside of the structure except for the vertical lines of the outermost corners, where the hinges will go. Slowly add more solder to raise a bead. Repeat soldering and beading over all foil on inside and bottom of house.

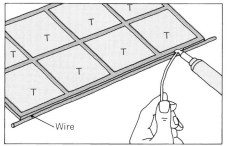

9. Solder together the porch roof shingles (T). Tack an 11-in. length of wire to one long side of porch roof and another to one long side of back section of the main rooftop (K) so that the ends of the wire protrude. Cut two 6-in. and two 9-in. lengths of wire for hinges.

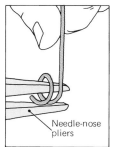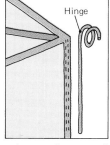

10. Form the hinges by using needle-nose pliers to twist two circles into one end of each of the four lengths of wire. Solder one long hinge to one back corner of house and one short hinge to one front corner of porch with their looped ends just above walls.

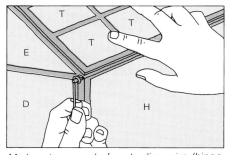

11. Insert one end of protruding wire (hinge pin) on one side of porch roof into hinge on porch corner. Fit the other short hinge over free end of hinge pin and solder the hinge into place. Add back section of main rooftop (K) in same way. Cut off excess wire.

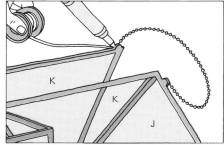

12. Solder one end of chain to a top corner of back section of main rooftop (K) and other end to main roof support (J). Cover all foil that is still showing with a bead of solder. Antique and wash metal. Apply silicone glue and seal to inside joints to waterproof them.

LOG TOTE AND CRADLE

The messy job of transporting firewood from outside and storing it indoors is simplified by this handsome log tote and cradle. The unit is constructed of copper water pipes and fittings and is assembled like a Tinkertoy project. Since the joints do not have to hold water, only a drop of solder is needed at each joint to lock the parts together.

The unit consists of the tote (two handles and a sling for carrying the logs) and a cradle for storing the log-filled tote. The sling is supported by resting the handles in the four U-shaped fittings (sawed-off Bull Head T's) at the top of the cradle.

A tubing cutter makes fast, straight, clean cuts in copper pipe. You may be able to rent one at a hardware or plumbing supply store. If not, you can make all the required cuts in the pipe with a hacksaw or with a saber saw.

The cradle and handles: Following the instructions on the facing page, cut all the metal, then clean the parts, apply flux to them, and assemble the cradle and handles. Align the assembled parts and apply a drop of solder to each joint. Polish the metal and attach the sling.

When soldering, apply the heat to the fittings, which warm slowly, to avoid overheating the pipes. Solder the joints that are facing up in order to keep the solder from running. When the metal has cooled sufficiently, turn the piece over and solder the remaining joints.

Test the alignment of the top fittings (K) by laying a scrap piece of pipe between them. Remove the scrap pipe and apply solder sparingly to the insides of the fittings. After soldering, use a strong detergent and water to scrub off any flux that has run out of the joints.

The sling: Make a pattern as shown on the following page. Cut two pieces of fabric to fit the pattern and lay them out, finished sides together. With a No. 18 needle and upholstery thread, sew the pieces together ¼ inch in from the edges on all sides, but leave a 6-inch opening along one edge of the main body.

Cut the outside corners, and slash the inside corners to keep them from binding when the fabric is turned inside out. Turn the sling inside out, straighten out its edges, and iron it flat. Run the fabric through the sewing machine again, using a contrasting thread, to create a border stitch ¼ inch from the edge, and close the 6-inch opening.

Test-fit the sling and adjust it so that it just touches the frame of the cradle when pressure is put on its center. Attach the sling to the handles as explained at the top of the following page.

Parts list

Part	Name	Quantity	Size	Length	Material
A	Close nipple	8	1"	2⅛"	Copper pipe
B	Cross-member nipple	8	1"	3½"	Copper pipe
C	Support-post nipple	8	1"	4½"	Copper pipe
D	Long pipe	7	¾"	20"	Copper pipe
E	End pipe for handle	4	¾"	8½"	Copper pipe
F	Center pipe for handle	2	¾"	6¼"	Copper pipe
G	Upright pipe for handle	4	½"	3"	Copper pipe
H	Grip pipe	2	½"	6½"	Copper pipe
I	Base T	4	1" x 1" x 1"	—	Copper T-fitting
J	Long-pipe T	14	1" x 1" x ¾"	—	Copper T-fitting
K	Top fitting	4	¾" x ¾" x 1"	—	Bull Head T-fitting
L	Foot cap	4	1"	—	Copper cap
M	Handle cap	4	¾"	—	Copper cap
N	Handle T	4	¾" x ¾" x ½"	—	Copper T-fitting
O	Handle elbow	4	½"	—	90° elbow
P	Sling	1	45"	2½ yd.	Canvas or denim

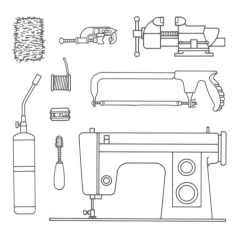

Tools and materials: Hacksaw or saber saw and carbide-tipped blade or tubing cutter. Drill with carbide cutoff wheel (optional). Sewing machine with No. 18 needle. Vise, propane torch, wire brush, scissors. Emery cloth, 000 steel wool, solid-core solder, paste flux, work gloves. Heavy upholstery thread, thread of contrasting color, 2½ yd. of 45" wide canvas or denim. Copper pipe fittings and caps (see I–O above) plus 3' of ½" copper pipe, 16' of ¾" copper pipe, 8' of 1" copper pipe.

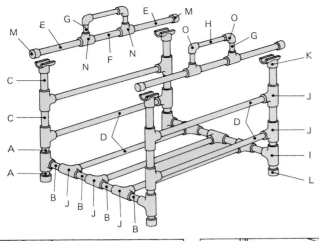

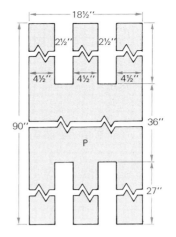

Attaching the sling: If you have access to a heavy-duty sewing machine, make the sling of canvas. Otherwise, use a lighter material, such as denim. Make the sling as described in the text. To attach the sling, pass its center fingers through the handles, and loop the outside fingers over the end pipes (E). Overlap the fingers and sew them to the main body of the fabric. If you want to remove the sling for washing, attach the fingers with buttons, hooks, or Velcro.

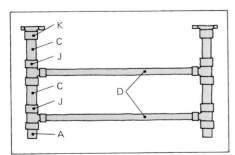

1. Rent a tubing cutter and cut all the pipes to the sizes indicated in the chart on the previous page. If a tubing cutter is not available, secure each pipe in a vise and cut it to size with a hacksaw or with a saber saw and a carbide-tipped blade.

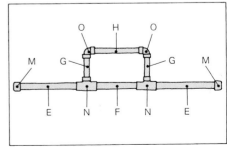

2. To make the top fittings (K), cut the Bull Head T's in half, using a hacksaw, a saber saw, or an electric drill with a cutoff wheel. Then cut one arm off of each T. Scribe the cutting lines on the T first and clamp the T securely in a vise before cutting it.

3. Clean all the copper pipes and fixtures; otherwise, the solder will not penetrate the metal and hold. Use strips of emery cloth to clean the outsides and a wire brush for cleaning the insides of the fittings and 1 in. into the insides of the pipes.

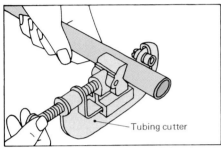

4. Apply a thin coat of flux to the inside edges of the fittings and the outside edges of the pipes before assembling. Keep the flux at least ½ in. from the ends or it will run out. Assemble a close nipple (A), base T (I), and foot cap (L) to make each foot.

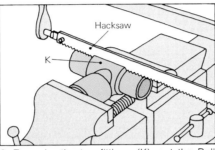

5. Assemble the cross-member nipples (B) and long-pipe T's (J) to form the cradle ends. Attach the feet to the cradle ends, insert the long pipes (D), and join the cradle ends together. Square up the cradle and tap all the fittings to securely seat the pipes.

6. Apply a torch flame to each fitting in turn. When the fitting is hot and the flux is boiling, apply the end of the wire solder to the joint. When a small amount of solder melts, remove the wire. Wear gloves and turn the assembly to keep the solder from running.

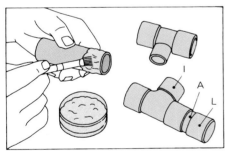

7. Make each of the four support posts with two support-post nipples (C), two long-pipe T's (J), one close nipple (A), and one top fitting (K). Connect each pair of posts with two long pipes (D), and fit the assemblies into the prepared base.

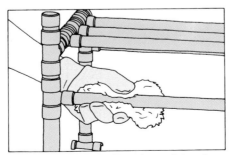

8. Let the cradle cool. Place it on a flat surface and square up, making sure all the pipes are fully seated in the fittings. Test the alignment of the top fittings (K) by placing a pipe across them. Wash off all flux and shine the metal with 000 steel wool.

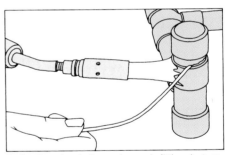

9. Assemble the tote handles, using two end pipes (E), two handle caps (M), two handle T's (N), one center pipe (F), two upright pipes (G), two elbows (O), and one grip pipe (H). Solder the joints, wash and shine the metal, and attach the sling (P) as described above.

STEEL WINE RACK

You can store up to 15 bottles of your favorite vintage in this modern-looking all-metal wine rack, which takes up very little space. Your bottles will be stored properly—tipped slightly downward to keep the corks moistened—and yet remain clearly visible for easy selection.

The lightweight rack is made of thin steel rods that are brazed together. To do the brazing, you will need a Mapp gas torch and some flux-coated nickel-silver filler rod. Be sure to use a Mapp gas torch with a capacity for brazing; an ordinary propane or butane torch will not provide enough heat to do the job.

Brazing is actually nothing more than high-temperature soldering. You need only clean and heat the pieces of metal to be joined and then apply the filler rod to the joint until the filler rod melts on con-

tact. The melted rod will flow toward the hottest point. To cover the joint completely, move the torch and the rod together over the area, keeping the tip of the flame just ahead of the melting filler rod. If the rod sticks or stops melting, you are not applying enough heat—heat the spot a bit longer and move the torch and rod along more slowly. Molten filler resembles mercury in appearance and behavior and produces a smooth finished braze. If you underheat the filler, it will be mushy—movable but not flowing—and its finished appearance grainy and rough.

To get an adequate supply of heat from the small Mapp gas torch recommended, you will have to set up a heat-reflecting shield of firebricks around the joint being brazed. Experiment with various setups until you find the one that works best.

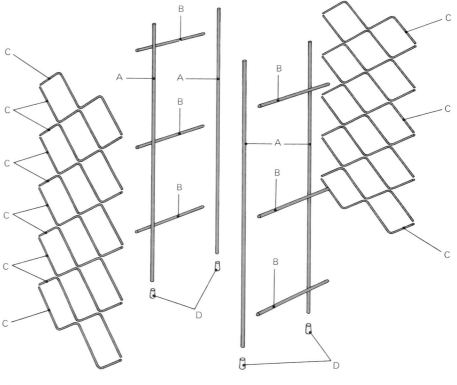

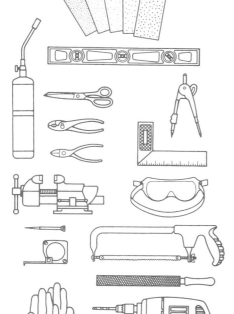

Parts list

Part	Name	Quantity	Diameter	Length	Material
A	Post	4	⅜″	36″	Steel rod
B	Rail	6	⅜″	10⅜″	Steel rod
C	Rib	20	³⁄₁₆″	18″	Steel rod
D	Cap	4	⅜″	—	Furniture leg cap

Tools and materials: Hacksaw. Electric drill with ³⁄₁₆″ twist bit. Mapp gas torch, safety goggles, welding gloves. Wire cutters, scissors, scribing tool, 8″ flat mill file, ⅜″ round bastard file 10″ long. Steel tape rule, compass, try square, level. Vise, wrench or pliers. Coarse and fine emery cloth, rustproof spray primer, spray enamel, lined notebook paper, pencil. Six to twelve 1″ x 4″ x 8″ firebricks. ⅜″ and ³⁄₁₆″ steel rods and furniture leg caps (see above). Two 1″ x 15″ and two 2″ x 15″ pieces of 20-gauge sheet steel scrap. A 3′ length of ⅛″ threaded steel rod and hex nuts to fit, a 2′ length of ¼″ pipe. Flux-coated nickel-silver filler rod, soft baling wire.

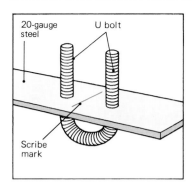

1. Make two jigs from 1- x 15-in. strips of 20-gauge sheet steel to hold posts while brazing. First, use a steel tape rule and try square to scribe parallel lines 9½ in. apart on each jig. On the first jig also scribe lines 13⅜ in. apart. Drill a ³⁄₁₆-in. hole on both sides of each line ½ in. apart. Bend six 3-in.-long sections of ⅛-in. threaded rod to form U bolts that will fit through pairs of holes.

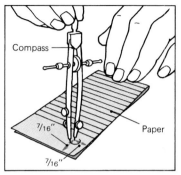

2. Make a template for scribing cutouts on rails by cutting a 3-in.-wide strip of lined paper 10⅜ in. long (the length of a rail). Fold strip in half (end to end). Mark a point ⁷⁄₁₆ in. from loose ends and one side edge, then use a compass to scribe a circle with a ⅜-in. diameter around the point. Cut out circle on doubled paper, then unfold the strip.

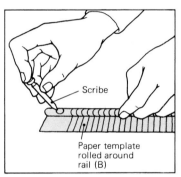

3. Align one rail (B) with long edge of template nearest circles. Roll template around rail so that lines on paper align. When circles cover rail, scribe their outlines onto metal. Unroll template and remove rail. (Darken scribed lines on rail with black India ink if you wish.) Repeat process for other five rails.

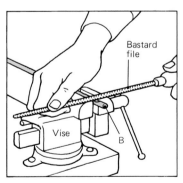

4. Clamp each scribed rail in a vise and remove the waste metal inside the scribed circles with a ⅜-in. round bastard file. Stop filing when metal is removed to scribed lines. The cutouts should be parallel to each other and of equal depth. Center line of each rail should bisect both cutouts at right angles.

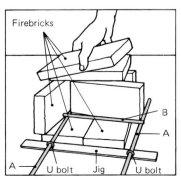

5. Mark posts (A) 4¾ in. from each end and at center. Clamp posts in place over lines on jigs that are 9½ in. apart, using U bolts and nuts. Lay hollowed-out rails over marks on posts. Arrange each post/rail assembly on firebricks for brazing. Stack more bricks around and over each joint area to create a heat-reflecting oven that will aid brazing.

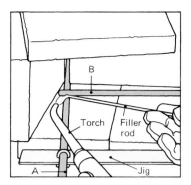

6. Wearing gloves and goggles, braze joints with torch by heating overlapping pieces cherry red and then rubbing flux-coated rod at point where flame tip contacts metal. Hot metal should melt rod and cause it to flow over entire joint (see text). When finished, quench joints in water, clean with flat file, then polish with emery cloth. (Joints must be cleaned thoroughly to remove oxides and flux residue.)

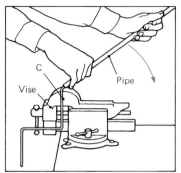

7. To form W-shaped rib (C), first mark an 18-in. length of ³⁄₁₆-in. rod at 4½-in. intervals. Then clamp rod in vise at marked points and slip length of ¼-in. pipe over rod and use pipe as a lever to make opposing 90° bends in rod. Stand in line with rod and push pipe away from you. File outside edges of rod ends to 45° angles. Repeat for other 19 ribs.

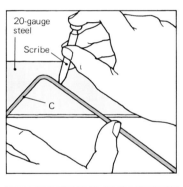

8. Make two more jigs from 2- x 15-in. strips of 20-gauge sheet steel to hold ribs to post/rail assemblies during brazing. Scribe parallel lines on each jig 13⅜ in. apart and drill holes for U bolts as in Step 1. Center ribs on jigs so that ends protrude 1½ in. beyond edges of jigs. Scribe around ribs, then drill holes in jigs on both sides of outlines.

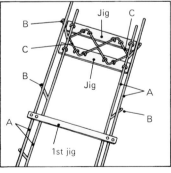

9. Use U bolts to clamp jigs made in Step 8 to both post/rail assemblies at one end. Mount ribs to jigs with U bolts or soft wire. Corners of ribs should touch; ends should meet at post/rail joints. Attach first jig made in Step 1 to opposite end of assembly. Arrange firebricks as in Step 5, then braze ribs to posts. Reposition jigs and braze ribs at opposite end, then at middle of assembly.

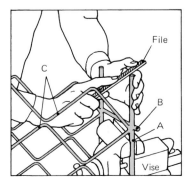

10. Keep repositioning jigs and brazing. Attach the remaining ribs. When finished, trim bottoms of posts so that rack stands level (some warpage may have occurred). Trim and bevel tops if desired. File all joints clean; finish with emery cloth. Spray rack with one coat of primer, then two coats of enamel. When enamel is dry, install caps (D) on bottoms of posts.

METAL JEWELRY

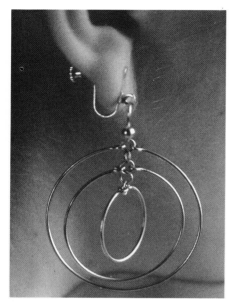

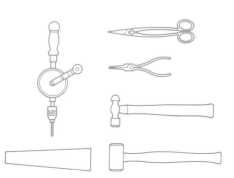

Wire earrings

While the skill of a master craftsman is required to create certain types of intricate jewelry, a great deal of fine jewelry can easily be made by a layman. By following the directions in this section, you can make a variety of handsome metal articles. (The instructions for these projects call for silver, but copper or brass can be substituted.)

Annealing metal: If the metal you are using is hard to work, make it more malleable by annealing it. To anneal a piece of metal, place it on asbestos and brush it with flux to prevent oxidation. Then move the flame of a propane torch over the metal until it begins to glow a dull red. Do not let the metal turn bright red or it may melt. Let the piece cool, then "pickle" it (see text on page 335).

The wire earrings: The loop earrings on this page are shaped on a mandrel and fitted with jump rings. A mandrel is a tapered metal rod for shaping bracelets or rings; the metal is pushed around it and hammered with a rawhide mallet to make it fit snugly against the mandrel. If you do not have a mandrel, use a dowel or wooden cylinder that is the desired size, and shape the metal with a ball peen hammer instead of a mallet. Jump rings are the most common type of findings (ready-made fasteners) and are available at most jewelry supply stores.

For the drop earrings, jeweler's pliers are used to shape the wire triangles, and pendants and beads are slipped onto the triangles. The pendants are made by flattening pieces of wire.

Tools and materials: *For both types of earrings:* two pairs of needle-nose or flat-nose jeweler's pliers, metal snips, silver polish. Jump rings, earring findings (either clip-on fasteners or type for pierced ears). *For loop earrings:* bracelet mandrel and/or ring mandrel (depends on size of loops), rawhide mallet, 19-gauge silver wire. *For drop earrings:* hand drill with ³⁄₁₆" bit, ball peen hammer, metal surface, 19-gauge silver wire 6" long, 18-gauge silver wire 8" long, six glass beads.

Loop earrings

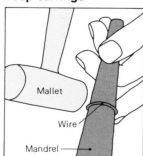

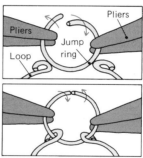

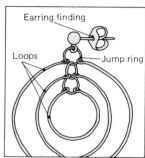

1. Form three pairs of different-sized loops by bending 19-gauge wire around a mandrel and tapping loops into shape with a mallet. Snip off wire, leaving ½-in. overlap.

2. Bend ends of each loop into circles and connect them with a jump ring. To open or close a jump ring, hold each side with pliers and twist in opposite directions at a slight angle.

3. Use jump rings to hook loops together to form each earring in the design of your choice. Attach each earring to an earring finding with another jump ring. Polish the earrings.

Drop earrings

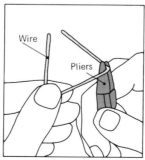

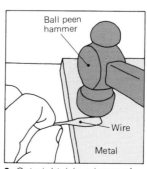

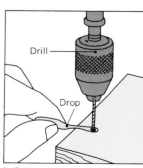

1. Use metal snips to cut two 3-in.-long pieces of 19-gauge wire. Use jeweler's pliers to bend each of the two pieces into a triangle. Leave the triangle slightly open at the top.

2. Cut eight 1-in. pieces of 18-gauge wire for drops. Flatten bottom two-thirds of each with a hammer on a metal surface. Taper and flatten tops of the drops at right angles to bottoms.

3. Drill a ³⁄₁₆-in. hole into the top of each drop. Slide drops, separated by beads, onto triangles. Make loops in ends of triangles and attach them to earring findings with jump rings.

Bangles and soldered ring

The attractive bangles shown at the left are easy to make. The directions for the swan-neck bangle can be used to create a ring instead; simply make the piece smaller and shape it on a ring mandrel.

A band of soldered jump rings can be shaped into a ring as described below or soldered together to form pendants like those shown (below left).

Soldering: This is a tricky process and takes practice. When soldering, be careful not to overheat the metal, or it might melt. If the metal turns red, remove the flame for a while and then continue. Never touch the metal during or just after soldering; it stays hot for a long time. If you must move a piece of metal during soldering, use a wire poker. (You can make a poker by filing the end of a length of coathanger wire to a point.)

Pickling: To clean a soldered piece and keep it from discoloring, pick it up with copper tongs and place it into a glass container of boiling-hot water mixed with pickling powder. Let it soak until it turns white. Rinse and dry it.

Tools and materials: *For all bangles:* bracelet mandrel, ball peen hammer, metal snips, silver polish. *For swan-neck bangle:* needle-nose jeweler's pliers, 14-gauge silver wire 13″ long. *For open-loop bangle:* 17-gauge silver wire 20″ long. *For braided-wire bangle:* flat-nose jeweler's pliers, vise, silver tubing ¼″ long, 19-gauge silver wire 48″ long. *For soldered ring:* propane torch, asbestos, metal surface, ball peen hammer, copper tongs, wire poker, tweezers for handling solder chips, small brush. Hard and medium silver solder, flux, commercial pickling powder, silver polish, flameproof glass container. Jump rings.

Bangles

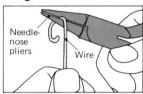

Swan-neck bangle: 1. Hold the end of the wire with needle-nose pliers and twist the wire into a large, loose coil. Make the same coil at the other end but in the opposite direction.

2. Place the center of the wire against a bracelet mandrel and use your thumbs to push the coiled ends of the wire around the mandrel until the bangle hugs the mandrel.

3. Leave the bangle on the mandrel and use the ball of hammer to pound it flat. This will strengthen the wire and improve the design. Take bangle off mandrel and polish it.

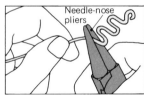

Open-loop bangle: Make open loops of equal size along the wire. Twist a small eye at each end to serve as a fastener. Form the bangle on a mandrel, flatten it, and polish it.

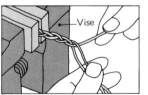

Braided-wire bangle: 1. Use snips to cut wire into six equal strands. Clamp the wires together in a vise and separate them into pairs. Braid the pairs together tightly.

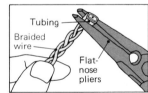

2. Snip silver tubing in half and push one piece of it over each end of braid. Crimp the tubing closed with flat-nose pliers. Form the bangle on a mandrel and then polish it.

Soldered ring

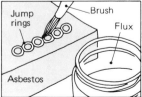

1. Place jump rings side by side on asbestos. Brush rings with flux, and pass a 3-in. flame from a propane torch over them until the flux dries and crystallizes.

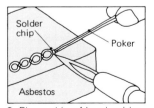

2. Place chip of hard solder over each joint and continuously pass a flame over it until the solder flows. Pickle the piece (see text above) and rinse it.

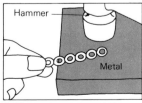

3. Place piece on metal surface and flatten it with hammer. Shape ring on mandrel. Solder ends together with medium solder; pickle and polish.

335

Ring with stone

Buy a polished stone and make your own setting. The setting is made up of a bezel (a band that surrounds the stone), a baseplate (a silver plate that fits under the bezel), and a shank (the finger band).

You must cut the silver for the shank and baseplate with a jeweler's saw. Since the saw should be held perpendicular to the metal being cut, place the silver over the slot in a bench pin (a piece of wood with a V-shaped slot that protrudes over the edge of a workbench).

Cut the ring shank to a length of ⅛ times the ring size needed plus 1 inch. Cut the baseplate and bezel to fit the stone. If the bezel or finished ring is too small, stretch it by putting it onto a ring mandrel and pounding it with a mallet toward the thick end of the mandrel.

Since this ring must be soldered three times, three different grades of solder are required. First, use hard solder, which has the highest melting point; then use medium solder and finally easy solder. If you are making a second bond on a piece and you use the same grade of solder (or one with a higher melting point), the first bond may melt under the heat.

Tools and materials: Propane torch, vise, ring mandrel, bench pin, jeweler's saw with No. 1 blade, asbestos. Ball peen hammer, rawhide mallet. Copper tongs, tweezers for handling solder chips. Small brush, No. 2 file, metal snips, poker, metal scribe or awl. Burnisher (knifelike tool with flat and rounded sides for closing bezel against stone). Setting nail (concrete nail with point ground and polished). Hard, medium, and easy silver solder. Flux, commercial pickling powder, silver polish, flameproof glass container. Polished cabochon (rounded) stone, 22-gauge sheet silver for baseplate, 16-gauge sheet silver for shank, and ⅛", ³⁄₁₆", or ¼" silver bezel wire.

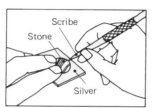

1. Place stone on 22-gauge silver for baseplate, and scribe shape of stone onto the metal or use a template the size of the stone and scribe into the metal along the inside of template.

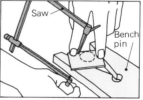

2. Position scribed metal on a bench pin. Using scribed line as a guide, carefully saw out baseplate, holding the saw perpendicular to the silver. Then file the baseplate smooth.

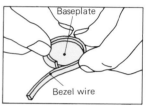

3. Wrap bezel wire around the baseplate and use a scribe to mark the place where it overlaps. Remove the baseplate and snip off the wire at the mark. Adjust fit of bezel if necessary.

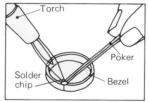

4. Place bezel on asbestos, brush with flux, and dry flux with torch. Place chip of hard solder over ends of bezel. Pass flame over bezel until solder flows. Pickle and wash (p.335).

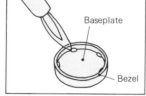

5. Test-fit stone in bezel. Flux baseplate and bezel. Dry flux. Attach bezel to baseplate with chips of medium solder around inside perimeter of bezel. Pickle and wash piece.

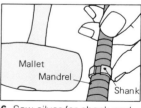

6. Saw silver for shank and shape it on mandrel. Center of shank should be at ring size. Pound shank with mallet, then turn it over and pound it again. File ends of shank flat.

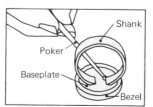

7. Apply flux to bottom of baseplate and ends of shank. Dry flux. Position shank on baseplate and place chip of easy solder at each corner. Heat solder until it flows. Pickle and wash.

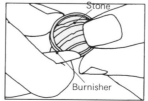

8. Place stone into bezel and push top edge of bezel down over stone with flat side of burnisher, using firm, even pressure. Turn ring over and press bezel from opposite direction.

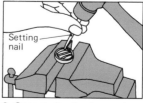

9. Secure ring in vise and gently tap around top of bezel with flat end of hammer. Hold point of setting nail against bezel and gently hammer nail until no gaps are left. Polish.

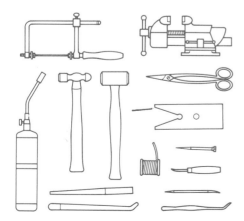

PLAYGROUND SET

Children love to be contrary. They may have worlds of fun at a distant playground, but they quickly tire of the slides and seesaws they have at home. However, if you build a playground with basic units like the ones described below, you can keep changing it to suit the whims of children. Build a tower with a slide, and when the novelty wears off, reassemble the parts and make a seesaw or a pickup truck. Reassemble the units again—perhaps add more units—and build a fort or whatever else your imagination can conjure up. Treat the units as pieces in a giant Tinkertoy set. You will have as much fun thinking up new projects as the children will have playing on them.

Directions for making the four basic units of the playground set are given below. Directions for making the tower and slide, seesaw, and pickup truck follow. The basic units are made of pressure-treated 2 x 6 pine (or any other wood), a few nails, and some glue. Special pieces call for extra 2 x 6's and a few odds and ends. All the projects can be built with simple hand tools. (For specific directions on the techniques called for here, such as crosscutting wood or countersinking screws, see the *Index,* p.379.)

Basic units

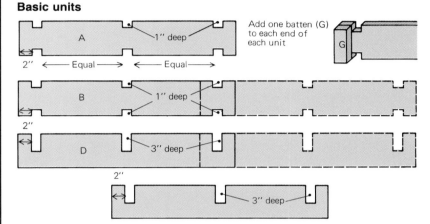

Making the basic units: 1. Use crosscut saw to cut wood for short units (A) 34 in. long. (You can cut four short units from a 12-ft. 2 x 6.) **2.** Use saw and chisel to cut notches into units, positioning notches as shown above. Each notch should be 1 in. deep and as wide as board is thick **3.** Overlap two short units so that notches on opposite ends are aligned. Use overlapped units as a template for cutting long units (B). (You can cut two long units from a 12-ft. 2 x 6.) **4.** Make short and long ties (C and D) as you did regular units, but cut notches only on one side and make them 3 in. deep. **5.** Cut 2-in. strips of wood (use scraps from units) for end battens (G). Place one batten at each end of a unit or tie, but be sure that it does not obstruct notches. To keep nails from splitting wood, blunt their ends with a hammer, and then glue and nail battens into place. **6.** Sand all finished units and ties, and paint them with wood preservative to protect them from bad weather.

Parts list for tower and slide

Part	Name	Quantity	Thickness	Width	Length	Material
A	Short unit	20	1½"	5½"	34"	2 x 6 pine
B	Long unit	3	1½"	5½"	61½" ✻	2 x 6 pine
C	Short tie	2	1½"	5½"	34"	2 x 6 pine
D	Long tie	2	1½"	5½"	61½" ✻	2 x 6 pine
E	Upright	8	1½"	2¾"	35"	2 x 6 pine
F	Plain board	6	1½"	5½"	27"	2 x 6 pine
G	End batten	54	1½"	5½"	2"	2 x 6 pine
H	Slide board	3	1½"	5½"	10'	2 x 6 pine
I	Slide support base	3	1½"	2¾"	15"	2 x 6 pine
J	Slide support side	6	1½"	2¾"	10½"	2 x 6 pine

✻ Lengths of parts B and D are approximate; measure and cut as shown above.

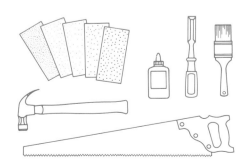

Tools and materials: Crosscut saw, ripsaw. Hammer, chisel. Paintbrush. Waterproof glue, Nos. 120 and 220 sandpaper, wood preservative. A 1½' x 10' strip of linoleum, fourteen 12' lengths of 2 x 6 pressure-treated pine or fir. One lb. 6d finishing nails.

Tower and slide

Children can climb this tower and slide back down to the ground. Besides the basic units, you will need four ladder frames and a slide to complete this project. After making the basic units, as described on page 337, build the ladder frames and slide as indicated below.

To construct the tower, fit the ladder frames together and into a base made by connecting two long ties (D) with one short unit (A). Build the tower higher by adding one short unit (A) to the front, back, and sides, then add one short unit to the front (the part with the opening) and one to the back. Add one short tie (C) to each of the two sides.

Make steps for the inside tower by laying three short units (A) across the inside of the tower at different levels and hooking them over the horizontal pieces. Create a half-roof with two short units (A). Nail the steps and half-roof into place. Make a floor with three long units (B). Finally, hook the top support of the slide over one of the top boards of the tower.

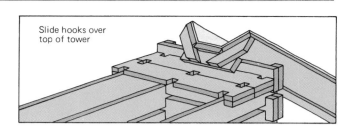

Slide hooks over top of tower

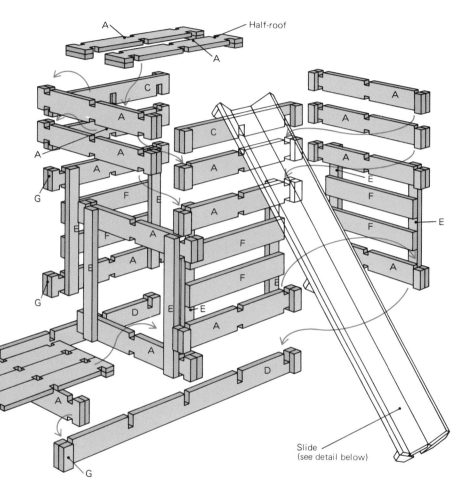

Half-roof

Slide (see detail below)

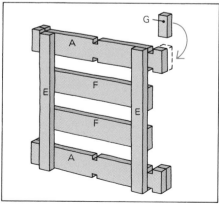

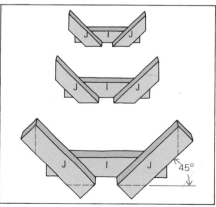

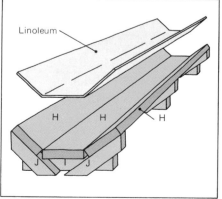

Linoleum

Ladder frames and slide. To make the first ladder frame (left), use a ripsaw to cut a 35-in. board down the center, creating two uprights (E). Glue and nail these to two short units (A) and two plain boards (F) in a ladder shape. Make two more identical frames and a fourth without the two plain boards—the opening will serve as an entrance to the tower. Next, make supports for the top, middle, and bottom of the slide (cen-

ter). Use a ripsaw to cut a strip of board 2¾ in. wide. For each support, cut one strip 15 in. long for the support base (I) and two strips 10½ in. long for the support sides (J). Glue and nail the two sides to the base at 45° angles. Saw off the projecting points of the sides (J). Glue and nail the three slide boards (H) to the insides of the supports to form a trough (right). Glue the linoleum to the slide surface.

Seesaw

Select a sound 2 x 6 for the seesaw board (K). Make the spine (L) from a 2 x 4 or use a ripsaw to cut it from a 2 x 6. After you have cut the spine, round off its upper corners with a wood file or a plane. Bore a hole in each end of the spine with a 1-inch spade bit. (Position the holes 2½ inches from each end and 1½ inches from the top.) Cut the handles (N) from the dowel and sand them down to fit tightly in the holes. Glue each handle into place and secure it from the top edge of the spine with a countersunk screw.

Center the spine (L) on the seesaw board (K), glue it down, and screw it into place from the underside of the seesaw board. Cut four seesaw battens (M) from a 2 x 6. Glue and screw one batten to the underside of each end of the seesaw board (K). Cut one edge of each of the remaining battens to a 45° bevel. Mark the center of the seesaw board on the underside, then try to balance it on the narrow edge of a 2 x 6. If necessary, move the seesaw back and forth to find its balance point. Use a pencil to trace the outline of the 2 x 6 onto the bottom of the seesaw. Glue and screw the beveled battens to the underside of the seesaw so that the beveled edge of each batten is flush with one of the balance lines.

Following the illustration, make the base for the seesaw with the short units (A) and short ties (C). Seat the seesaw board across the short tie on top.

Parts list for seesaw

Part	Name	Quantity	Thickness	Width	Length	Material
A	Short unit	4	1½"	5½"	34"	2 x 6 pine
C	Short tie	3	1½"	5½"	34"	2 x 6 pine
G	End batten	14	1½"	5½"	2"	2 x 6 pine
K	Seesaw board	1	1½"	5½"	10'	2 x 6 pine
L	Spine	1	1½"	3½"	6'	2 x 6 pine
M	Seesaw batten	4	1½"	5½"	3'	2 x 6 pine
N	Handle	2	1" dia.	—	7"	Dowel

Tools and materials: Crosscut saw, ripsaw. Drill with 1" bit. Screwdriver, hammer, chisel. Wood file or plane. Paintbrush, pencil. Waterproof glue, Nos. 120 and 220 sandpaper, wood preservative. A 1" dowel 14" long, four 12' lengths of 2 x 6 pressure-treated pine or fir. Fourteen 6d finishing nails, twenty 2½" No. 8 wood screws.

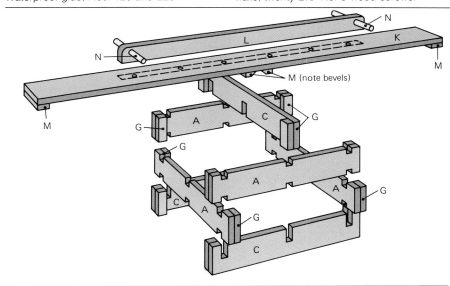

Pickup truck

Although this pickup truck has no wheels, a child's imagination can make it go. The truck is made up entirely of basic units. No extra parts are needed, and there is nothing to be screwed or nailed. To build the truck, just follow the drawing. Older children can build this project themselves with an ample supply of basic units, then they can disassemble it and build something else with the same units.

Tools and materials: Crosscut saw. Hammer, chisel. Paintbrush. Waterproof glue, Nos. 120 and 220 sandpaper, wood preservative. Six 12' lengths of 2 x 6 pressure-treated pine or fir. One-half lb. 6d finishing nails.

Parts list for pickup truck

Part	Name	Quantity	Thickness	Width	Length	Material
A	Short unit	13	1½"	5½"	34"	2 x 6 pine
B	Long unit	2	1½"	5½"	61½"✳	2 x 6 pine
C	Short tie	2	1½"	5½"	34"	2 x 6 pine
D	Long tie	2	1½"	5½"	61½"✳	2 x 6 pine
G	End batten	38	1½"	5½"	2"	2 x 6 pine

✳Lengths of parts B and D are approximate; measure and cut as shown on page 337.

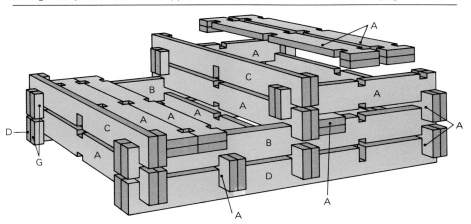

CHILD'S WORKBENCH AND TOOL CADDY

A sturdy workbench will keep a little carpenter busy for hours. Built of inexpensive pine, this bench has a pegboard for tool storage and a blackboard on the reverse side. The bench also has plastic tools, bought in a toy store, and stands 20 inches high at the work surface, 32½ inches high overall. You can scale the dimensions for any age child and equip the bench with real or play tools.

Construction: Use a table saw or a portable circular saw with a rip guide to cut the bench pieces to the lengths shown in the chart below. Rip a 10-foot length of 1 x 4 pine into a board 2¾ inches wide for the sides (B), front (C), center support (D), and leg supports (E). Then cut these parts to the specified lengths.

Cut a piece of 1 x 4 pine into two pieces 17½ inches long for the top and bottom of the bench back (F). Cut another piece of 1 x 4 pine 12¾ inches long for the sides of the bench back (G). Use a router with an edge guide or a table saw with a dado head to cut a rabbet ¾ inch wide and ¼ inch deep on both ends of the 12¾-inch length of 1 x 4. After the rabbets are cut, rip the piece in half lengthwise to form the two 1¾-inch-wide sides.

Cut the table top (H) and the ends of the tool caddy (I) from a piece of 1 x 10 pine.

The bench legs (J) should be cut about 21 inches long and then trimmed to the correct 15° angle.

Cut the hardboard for the blackboard (K) and the pegboard (L) into 17½- x 11¾-inch pieces. The blackboard should be painted with special blackboard paint or with flat black latex. Cut the bottom (N) and sides (M) of the tool caddy from ⅛-inch hardboard.

Sand all lumber with No. 120 sandpaper and carefully round off any sharp edges on the table top and bench back. You can finish the worktable with a clear coat of varnish, or you can paint it. It is easier to paint the legs and back pieces before assembly. Be careful not to get any paint into the glue joints, and leave the side of each leg bare where it will contact the sides of the table.

Finally, cut a 1-inch dowel into 3- or 4-inch pegs (A) and paint them in bright colors. Do the same with any leftover ¾-inch dowel from the caddy handle (O). Drill matching holes into the table top and front so that a child can hammer these pegs into and through the workbench.

Tool hangers designed to fit a ⅛-inch pegboard are used to display the toy tools. Get some chalk and an eraser for the blackboard to complete the project.

Parts list

Part	Name	Quantity	Thickness	Width	Length	Material
A	Peg stock	1	1" dia.	—	3'	Hardwood dowel
B	Table side	2	¾"	2¾"	8¾"	Rip from 1 x 4 pine
C	Table front	1	¾"	2¾"	18"	Rip from 1 x 4 pine
D	Table center support	1	¾"	2¾"	15"	Rip from 1 x 4 pine
E	Leg support	2	¾"	2¾"	16"	Rip from 1 x 4 pine
F	Top and bottom	2	¾"	3½"	17½"	1 x 4 pine
G	Side	2	¾"	1¾"	12¾"	Rip 1 x 4 pine in half
H	Table top	1	¾"	9½"	18"	Rip from 1 x 10 pine
I	Tool caddy end	2	¾"	6⅛"	6⅛"	Rip from 1 x 10 pine
J	Bench leg	4	1½"	2½"	21"	2 x 3 fir or pine
K	Blackboard	1	⅛"	11¾"	17½"	Hardboard
L	Pegboard tool holder	1	⅛"	11¾"	17½"	Pegboard
M	Tool caddy side	2	⅛"	3"	10½"	Hardboard
N	Tool caddy bottom	1	⅛"	6½"	10½"	Hardboard
O	Tool caddy handle	1	¾" dia.	—	10½"	Hardwood dowel

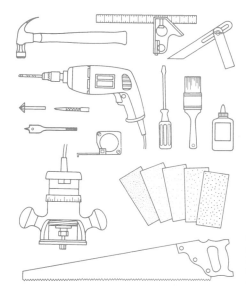

Tools and materials: Router with edge guide or table saw with dado head. Electric drill with set of twist bits, countersink, and ⅝" spade bit. Handsaw or portable circular saw with rip guide. Carpenter's bevel or protractor, steel tape rule, combination square, pencil. Hammer, nail set, screwdriver. Paintbrushes. No. 120 sandpaper, carpenter's glue, nontoxic paints in bright colors, flat black or special blackboard paint, polyurethane varnish (optional). A 3' length of 1 x 10 pine, 8' length of 2 x 3 fir or pine, two 6' lengths of 1 x 4 pine. A 2' x 2' piece of ⅛" hardboard, 1' x 2' piece of ⅛" pegboard. A ¾" hardwood dowel 1' long, 1" hardwood dowel 3' long. Sixteen 1½" No. 8 wood screws, twelve 1" No. 8 wood screws. Twelve finishing washers, two 3" stove bolts ³⁄₁₆"-20 with two hex nuts and four flat washers, two ³⁄₁₆" wing nuts. 4d and 6d finishing nails, ⅛" pegboard tool hangers to suit tools purchased for bench.

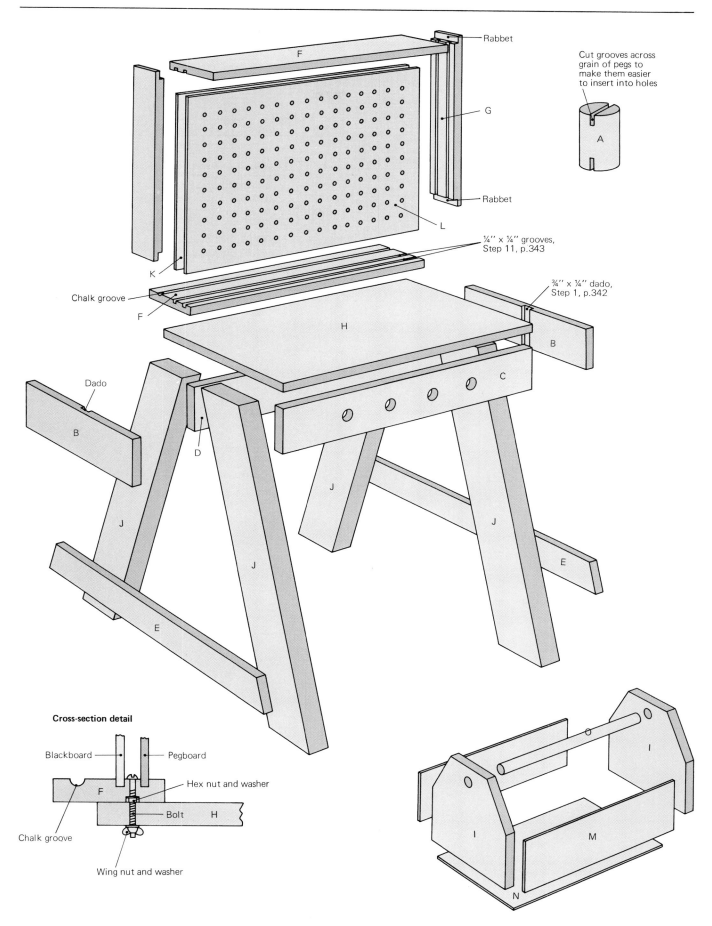

Rabbet

Cut grooves across grain of pegs to make them easier to insert into holes

F

G

A

Rabbet

L

¼'' x ¼'' grooves, Step 11, p.343

K

Chalk groove

F

¾'' x ¼'' dado, Step 1, p.342

H

B

Dado

C

B

D

J

J

J

J

E

J

E

Cross-section detail

Blackboard

Pegboard

Hex nut and washer

F

Bolt   H

Chalk groove

Wing nut and washer

O

I

I

I

M

N

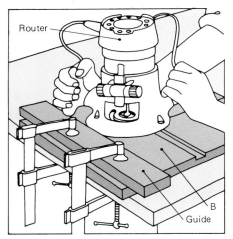

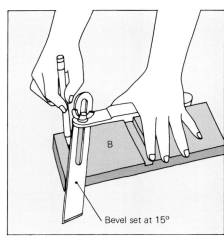

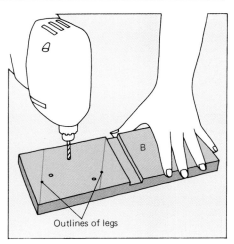

1. Cut side pieces (B) to proper length, then clamp them side by side to the worktable. Clamp a piece of scrap wood in place as a guide. Cut a dado ¾ in. wide x ¼ in. deep across the center of both pieces.

2. Using a protractor and carpenter's bevel, draw two lines along the side pieces (B) at a 15° angle. The lines should be on the same side as the dadoes and should start at the lower corners and slant inward.

3. Lay the legs (J) along the lines drawn in Step 2 and trace their outlines onto the side pieces (B). Drill three ³⁄₃₂-in. pilot holes for each leg in a diamond pattern so that they do not fall onto the same grain lines.

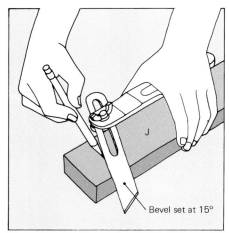

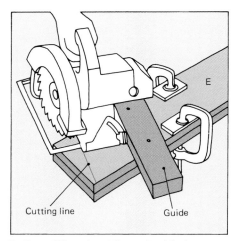

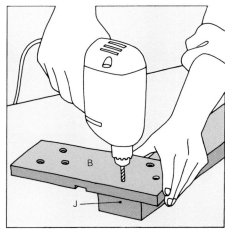

4. Use a protractor and carpenter's bevel to draw 15° angles on the top and bottom of one leg (J). The lines should be parallel. Cut off the ends of this leg along the lines and use this leg as a pattern to cut the remaining legs.

5. Draw 15° angles at the ends of the leg supports (E). These lines should intersect the corners of the supports and slant in toward one another, similar to those in Step 2. Clamp the two supports together and cut them at once.

6. Countersink the holes on the outside of the side pieces (B) so that the screwheads will lie flush with the wood surface. Carefully position the sides (B) over the legs (J) and drill pilot holes about halfway through the legs.

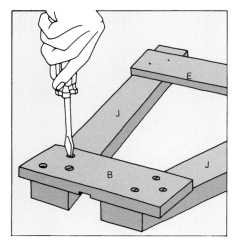

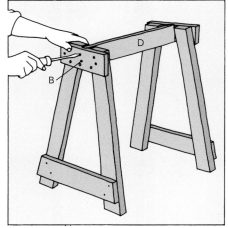

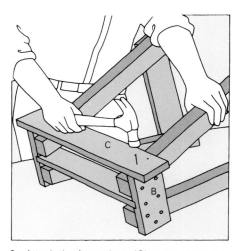

7. Fasten a pair of legs (J) to each side (B) using glue and 1½-in. wood screws. The tops of the legs should be even with the tops of the side pieces (B). Attach the leg supports (E) with glue and 4d finishing nails.

8. Drill and countersink two pilot holes into the dado in each side piece (B). Hold the center support (D) in position and drill pilot holes into its ends. Fill the dadoes with glue and screw the center support to the side pieces.

9. Attach the front piece (C) to the sides (B) with glue and 6d finishing nails. Align the tops of all three pieces and position the front so that it is centered with a ½-in. overhang at both sides. Use a nail set to set all nails.

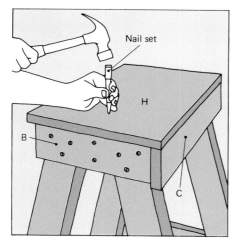

10. Attach the table top (H) to the front (C) and sides (B) with glue and 6d finishing nails. The edges of the top should be flush with the front and side pieces. Use a nail set to set all nails below surface of wood.

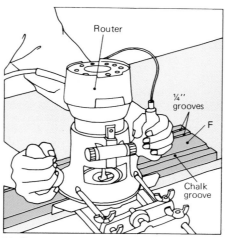

11. Cut two grooves ¼ in. deep x ¼ in. wide into the top and bottom (F) and sides (G) of bench back, ½ in. and 1¼ in. away from the same edge of each piece. Cut a semicircular chalk groove ½ in. from opposite edge of F.

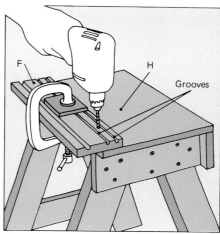

12. Cut a rabbet ¾ x ¼ in. deep at each end of the sides (G). Clamp the chalk ledge in position on the table top (H) and drill two ³⁄₁₆-in. holes through the ledge and into H. The holes must be between the grooves.

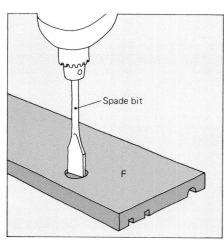

13. Turn the chalk ledge over and use a ⅝-in. spade bit to drill two recesses into the bottom so that the hex nuts and washers between the chalk ledge and table top will be flush (see detail in exploded view, p.341).

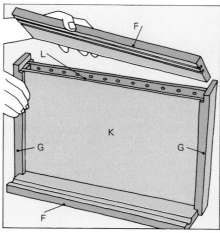

14. Sand and paint all parts. Place the bolts through the chalk ledge and secure them with hex nuts and washers. Assemble the sides (G) and bottom (F) with glue and 4d nails, then slide blackboard and pegboard into place.

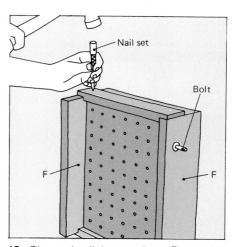

15. Glue and nail the top piece (F) onto the back assembly. Use a nail set to set all the nails in the back. Secure the bolts protruding from the chalk ledge to the table top with wing nuts and washers.

16. Lay out and drill ¾-in. and 1-in. peg holes into the top and front of the table. Clamp the ends of the tool caddy (I) together and drill a ¾-in. hole for the handle through both pieces at once.

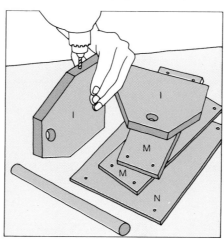

17. Drill four ³⁄₃₂-in. pilot holes into the bottom (N) and each side (M) of the tool caddy about ½ in. in from the edges. Use these pieces as patterns to mark and drill pilot holes into the ends (I) of the caddy.

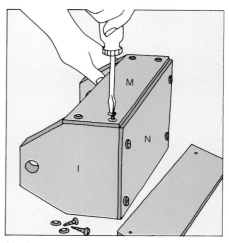

18. Assemble caddy with 1-in. wood screws and finishing washers. Slide ¾-in. dowel through the caddy ends (I); mark it and cut it flush with the ends of the caddy. Glue dowel in place. Cut leftover dowel into pegs.

MODULAR DOLLHOUSES

For centuries dollhouses have sparked the imaginations of little girls—and little boys too! The dollhouses shown here are made from two standard shapes: a box module and a roof module. If you put several boxes in a row, each with its own roof, you have built a single-story ranch house. If you stack up several boxes under a single roof, the result is a brownstone or town house. Many other variations are possible. The fronts of the boxes can be intricately decorated to resemble a particular house (perhaps your own). The boxes in the project have interchangeable fronts, held on by Velcro fasteners, so that several different houses can be created from a supply of four boxes and three roofs.

Construction: Cut the parts as indicated in the chart. Sand all the edges smooth and assemble the boxes as shown in the illustrations on the following page. Paint the outsides of the boxes dark gray and the insides white. Use nontoxic water-based paints. The optional false fronts can be cut from a 2- x 4-foot sheet of ⅛-inch hardboard. The rooftops and false fronts are covered with shingle and brick paper, available at model railroad shops. Doors and windows are drawn on unruled 3- x 5-inch file cards with India ink or felt-tipped pens, cut out, and glued to the shingle or brick paper with rubber cement. Velcro fastener (sold in sewing shops) is attached to the boxes and false fronts with contact cement. Use the Velcro only near the top of each false front so that the fronts can be peeled off without excessive force, which might upset the stack of boxes.

Arranging the boxes to build houses

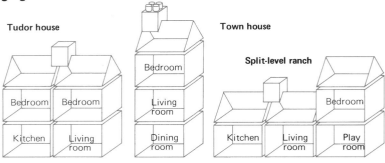

Parts list

Part	Name	Quantity	Thickness	Width	Length	Material
Boxes (4)						
A	Batten	8	¼"	1⅛"	11¼"	Lattice
B	Top and bottom	8	¼"	11⅜"	11½"	Sanded plywood
C	Front	4	¼"	7⅞"	11⅜"	Sanded plywood
D	Side	8	¼"	7⅞"	11⅝"	Sanded plywood
E	False front (optional)	11	⅛"	7⅞"	11⅞"	Hardboard
Roofs (3)						
F	Base	3	¼"	11⅜"	11⅜"	Sanded plywood
G	Batten	6	¼"	1⅛"	11¼"	Lattice
H	End		¼"	8¼"	8¼"	Cut from three squares of sanded plywood (see Step 6)
I	Top	6	¼"	8⅝"	11⅞"	Sanded plywood
Chimneys (2)						
J	Top	1	¼"	2"	2¾"	Sanded plywood
K	Pot	4	½" dia.	—	1"	Hardwood dowel
L	Side	4	¼"	2¾"	2⅞"	Sanded plywood
M	End	4	¼"	1½"	2⅞"	Sanded plywood

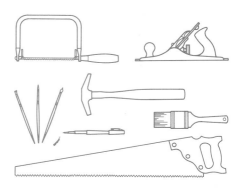

Tools and materials: Hand or power saw, coping saw. Tack hammer, plane. White glue, contact cement, rubber cement. No. 100 sandpaper, nontoxic paint, India ink and pens or felt-tipped pens, 3" paintbrush, artist's brushes. Shingle and brick paper, two dozen unruled 3" x 5" file cards. A 4' x 8' panel of ¼" sanded plywood, 2' x 4' piece of ⅛" hardboard, 14' length of ¼" x 1⅛" lattice, ½" dowel 4" long. Two small brass hinges or 5" length of silver duct tape, 2' Velcro. Box of ½" brads.

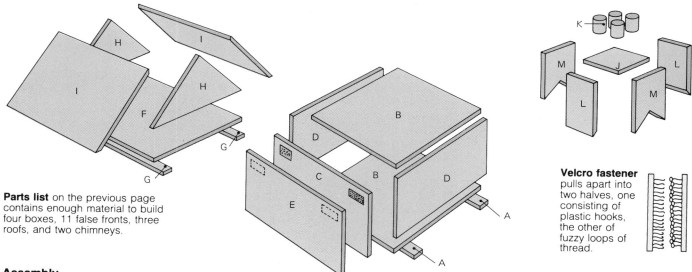

Parts list on the previous page contains enough material to build four boxes, 11 false fronts, three roofs, and two chimneys.

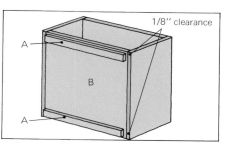

Velcro fastener pulls apart into two halves, one consisting of plastic hooks, the other of fuzzy loops of thread.

Assembly

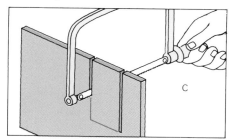

1. Use a coping saw to cut a 3- x 6-in. door 2 in. from the edge of one of the front pieces (C). Cut matching pieces from three of the false fronts (E). After painting the boxes and door, attach door with small hinges or tape.

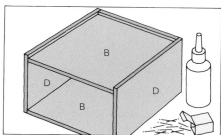

2. Assemble the basic boxes with white glue and ½-in. brads. The top of each box (B) should be about ¼ in. lower than the sides (D) and front (C), but the bottom (B) should be flush with the sides and front.

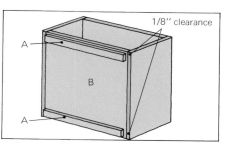

3. Glue and nail two battens (A) flush with the short edges of each of the four box bottoms (B). Allow ⅛ in. of clearance at each end of the batten so that the boxes will fit together without undue force.

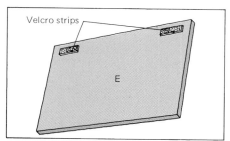

4. Cut Velcro into 22 strips 1 in. long. Use contact cement to attach hooked Velcro halves near upper corners of false fronts (E). Attach eight Velcro fuzzy halves to fronts (C) of the four boxes in corresponding positions.

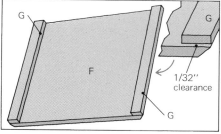

5. Plane a 45° bevel on two opposite edges of each roof base (F). Glue and nail two battens (G) underneath each base, flush with the sharp edges of the bevels and with about 1/32 in. of clearance at the unplaned edges.

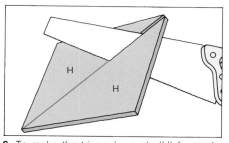

6. To make the triangular ends (H) for each roof, cut a piece of plywood 8¼ in. square. Draw a diagonal line across plywood square and cut square in half along this line. Smooth edges thoroughly with sandpaper.

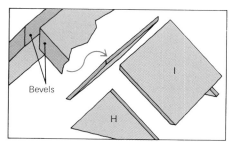

7. Glue and nail the six ends (H) of the roofs to the three bases (F). Plane a 45° bevel on each long edge of the six rooftops (I). Then glue and nail the tops on, matching the beveled edges along the roof ridge.

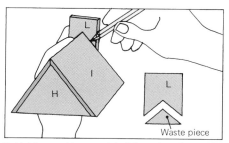

8. Hold one chimney side (L) against the peak of one roof and trace the peak's profile onto the side. Cut out a notch along the line with a coping saw, then use the cut piece as a pattern to mark and cut other three sides.

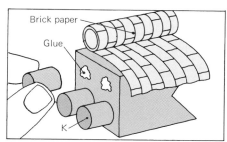

9. Assemble the two chimneys with white glue and cover them with brick paper. Glue the four chimney pots (K) to the top (J) about 1 in. from each corner. Glue this assembly to one of the chimneys. The other chimney is left open.

DOWNHILL RACER

Our downhill racer is a sturdy gravity go-cart meant for everyday fun. It was designed by racing driver Sam Posey, who has been building such racers since he was six. This model incorporates the sophisticated "ground effects" aerodynamics found on modern racing cars. The bottom of the car is curved in such a way that air passing under it creates a partial vacuum, sucking the car to the ground, which improves its handling and braking at speeds as low as 20 m.p.h.

The car is steered with the feet; the rubber tie-down straps give the steering a self-centering action. The hand brakes, though primitive looking, are highly effective. The rubber-tired wheels are standard 10-inch utility wheels that are sold in hardware stores; their metal centers have been painted to match the green and buff paint scheme of the car.

Construction: Most of the body parts can be cut from a single panel of ½-inch plywood. The belly pan, trunk, and hood (S, T, and U) are made from ¼-inch tempered hardboard, such as Masonite. (Untempered hardboard is not strong enough and may shatter if the racer strikes a stone.)

Make patterns for curved parts and lay out parts A–R on the single panel of plywood, as shown on the opposite page. Cut out the curved parts carefully with a saber saw and the straight parts with a circular saw. Start the assembly by aligning the curved lower edges of the outer hulls (M) and pontoons (N) and drilling the axle hole through all four of these parts at once. The rear axle keeps the parts in proper alignment during assembly. Drill pilot holes for all nails and screws to avoid splitting the wood.

Parts list

Part	Name	Quantity	Thickness	Width	Length	Material
A	Hull crossmember	1	½″	12″	8½″	B–C plywood
B	Hull crossmember	1	½″	12″	2⅞″	B–C plywood
C	Hull crossmember	1	½″	12″	5¾″	B–C plywood
D	Hull crossmember	1	½″	12″	11⅜″	B–C plywood
E	Steering platform	1	½″	11½″	✷	B–C plywood
F	Hull crossmember	1	½″	12″	7¼″	B–C plywood
G	Hull crossmember	1	½″	12″	21⅝″	B–C plywood
H	Dashboard	1	½″	12″	4¼″	B–C plywood
I	Hull crossmember	1	½″	12″	14½″	B–C plywood
J	Hull crossmember	1	½″	12″	4″	B–C plywood
K	Hull crossmember	1	½″	12″	4½″	B–C plywood
L	Hull crossmember	1	½″	12″	2½″†	B–C plywood
M	Outer hull	2	½″	✷	✷	B–C plywood
N	Outer pontoon	2	½″	✷	✷	B–C plywood
O	Brake tower	2	½″	7″	9″	B–C plywood
P	Brake tower	2	½″	7″	8¾″	B–C plywood
Q	Bottom pontoon	2	½″	7″	18¼″	B–C plywood
R	Brake tower	2	½″	7″	6½″	B–C plywood
S	Belly pan	1	¼″	12″	66¾″	Tempered hardboard
T	Trunk	1	¼″	13″	22¼″	Tempered hardboard
U	Hood	1	¼″	13″	26¼″	Tempered hardboard
V	Brake handle	2	1½″	1½″	20½″	2 x 2 pine or fir
W	Steering arm	1	1⅛″	5½″✷	32″✷	5/4 x 6 pine board
X	Seat back	1	¼″	11½″	12″	Plywood
Y	Seat	1	¼″	11½″	18″	Plywood

✷ See instructions on opposite page.
†Measurement is approximate and not critical.

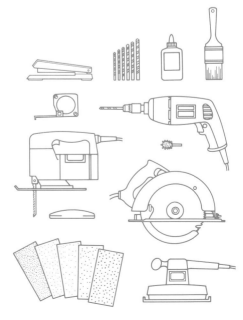

Tools and materials: Electric drill with twist bits and rotary rasp. Circular saw with plywood or combination blade, saber saw. Orbital sander with Nos. 100 and 180 sandpaper, a sanding block. Steel tape rule. Office stapler, staples. Carpenter's glue, paint, paintbrushes, paint thinner. A ½″ x 4′ x 8′ panel of B–C plywood, a ¼″ x 4′ x 8′ panel of tempered hardboard. A 4′ length of 2 x 2 fir or pine, a 3′ length of 5/4 x 6 pine board, a ¼″ x 1′ x 3′ piece of plywood. An 8′ length of ¼″ nylon rope, two 3″ snap rings, ⅔ yd. of 16″ wide canvas, ¾ yd. of 1″ thick foam rubber 24″ wide, 1½′ of Velcro fasteners. One pair of 3″ strap hinges, eighteen ½″ flat washers. Two 3′ lengths of ½″ threaded rod, a ½″ carriage bolt 6″ long. Four ½″ nuts and five ½″ locknuts to fit rods and bolt. Four 1″ screw eyes. Two 15″ rubber tie-down straps. Four 10″ semipneumatic wheels. Four 2″ dia. casters, two lock hasp and staple sets, four brass handrail brackets. Twenty ⅝″ and 120 1½″ No. 6 roundhead wood screws, sixteen 1″ No. 10 flathead wood screws. A box of ¾″ No. 18 brads.

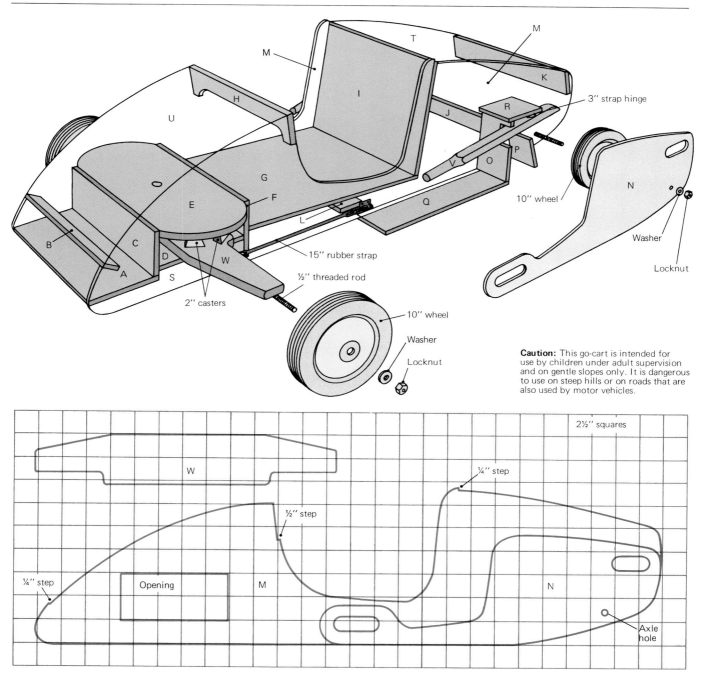

M

T

M

H

K

U

I

R

3" strap hinge

J

V

O

P

N

10" wheel

G

Washer

E

F

Q

Locknut

B

L

15" rubber strap

C

D

W

A

S

2" casters

½" threaded rod

10" wheel

Washer

Locknut

Caution: This go-cart is intended for use by children under adult supervision and on gentle slopes only. It is dangerous to use on steep hills or on roads that are also used by motor vehicles.

2½" squares

W

¼" step

½" step

¼" step

Opening

M

N

Axle hole

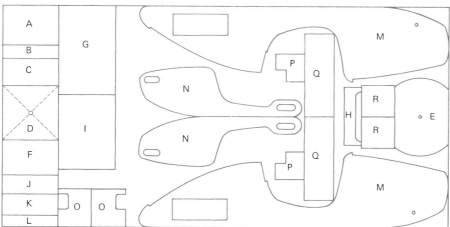

A

G

B

C

M

P

Q

N

D

I

R

R

H

E

F

N

Q

J

P

K

O   O

M

L

Enlarge pattern above (see p.48), using 2½-in. squares. Make separate patterns for the outer hulls and pontoons (M and N). Position the pattern for M, as shown at left, on a 4- x 8-ft. panel of plywood. Then reverse the pattern and trace its opposite side onto the panel. Do the same with N. Exact dimensions for the notches in the brake towers O and P are given on page 348, Step 10. Lay out an 11½- x 13-in. rectangle for the steering platform (E); then draw diagonal lines from corner to corner to locate its center. Use a compass or a length of string to draw the two curved sides of E, swinging arcs from corner to corner on the 11½-in. sides of the rectangle. The back edge of the steering arm (W) should be straight for shorter drivers so that their legs can reach it. For taller drivers indent the back edge as shown on the grid.

Cross-section view

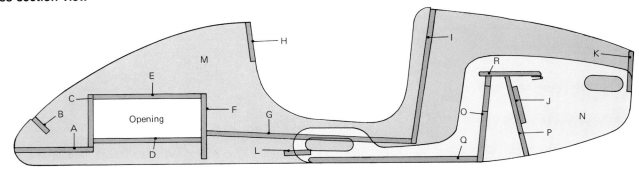

Use this view to position parts A through L and O through R (see Steps 4–6, 11, and 13–16).

Construction

1. Cut all wood and hardboard to the sizes given in the chart and diagrams on pages 346 and 347. The height of the rectangular openings in the outer hulls (M) must equal the combined heights of the steering arm (1⅛ in.), steering platform (½ in.), axle (½ in.), and casters (2⅝ in.), plus ⅛ in. for clearance. Adjust this dimension to suit height of casters you purchased.

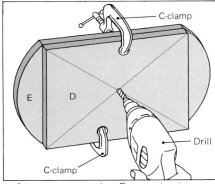

2. Center crossmember D over steering platform (E) and clamp the two parts together. Draw diagonal lines from corner to corner on D to locate its center, then drill a ½-in. hole for the carriage bolt through the centers of both parts at the same time.

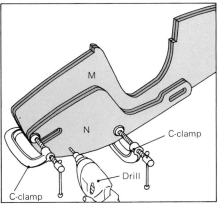

3. Clamp outer hulls (M) and pontoons (N) together so that curved bottom and rear portions of all four parts are aligned. Use pattern on preceding page to mark position of rear axle, then drill a ½-in. clearance hole for axle through all four pieces.

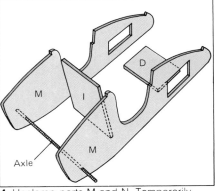

4. Unclamp parts M and N. Temporarily insert an axle through parts M in order to keep them in alignment, and attach crossmembers I and D between parts M, using glue and 1½-in. No. 6 screws.
5. Use a rotary rasp or file to round off the sharp corners on the bottom edge of crossmember B. Use a saber saw to cut the curve into the bottom of the dashboard (H). Then glue and screw parts A, B, C, F, G, H, J, and K between parts M, using 1½-in. screws.
6. Turn the hull upside down and center the steering platform (E) in the hull. Temporarily insert bolt through parts D and E to align them. Then glue and nail E into the hull. Remove bolt.

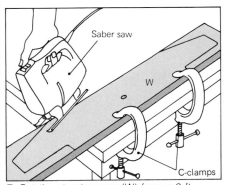

7. Cut the steering arm (W) from a 3-ft. length of ⁵⁄₄ x 6 pine board, using the pattern on page 347 and a saber saw. Use the rotary rasp to round the front edge of the arm for about 7 in. from each end. Drill a ½-in. hole for the carriage bolt in the exact center of the arm. Paint the arm.

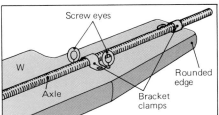

8. When the paint has dried, attach the front axle under the steering arm, just in front of the center hole, using screws and clamps from four brass handrail brackets. (Discard the brackets themselves.) Attach four screw eyes to the bottom of the steering arm in approximately the positions shown. Make sure that all clamps and screws are mounted on the narrow outer sections of the arm, leaving the center 18 in. clear.

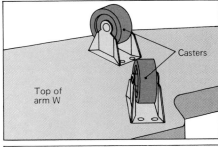

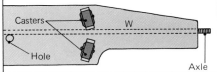

9. Turn steering arm right side up and attach four casters to the top of the arm with 1-in. No. 10 wood screws. Position casters as shown, two on each side of the arm.

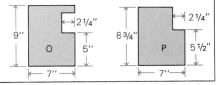

10. Use the saber saw to cut notches in the brake tower parts O and P to the dimensions shown above.

11. Attach parts O, P, and bottom pontoons (Q) to the outsides of the hull in the positions shown, using 1½-in. No. 6 wood screws and glue.

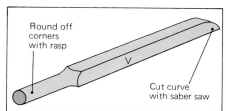

Round off corners with rasp

V

Cut curve with saber saw

12. Shape brake handles (V) from two 20½-in. lengths of 2 x 2 pine or fir. Use the saber saw to round off the top of the end that will contact the wheel. Use the rotary rasp to round off the sharp edges at the end that the driver will pull on.

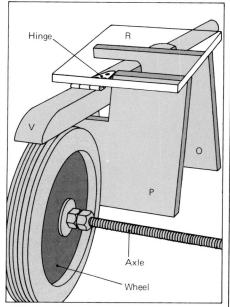

Hinge

R

V

O

P

Axle

Wheel

13. Temporarily tape a brake tower R in position on top of parts O and P. Position a brake handle so that its back end can touch the wheel and its front end extends forward through the hole in O. Mark the position of the hinge that will join parts R and V. Attach the hinge to the brake handle.

14. Untape part R from the brake tower and attach brake handle hinge to R. Position R on brake tower so handle will rub against the wheel when it is pulled up and fall away from the wheel when it is released. Reattach R with glue and 1½-in. screws. Repeat Steps 13 and 14 on opposite side.

15. Attach crossmember L to the hull with 1½-in. screws and glue. This part serves as a support for the belly pan (S) and should be positioned about halfway between parts F and I and 1 in. above the lower edge of parts M. Its forward edge should be about ½ in. lower than its rear edge.

16. Cut tempered hardboard to size for the belly pan (S), trunk (T), and hood (U). Cut a 4-in.-square opening in the center of the pan about 12 in. back from its front edge (for access to the carriage bolt and nut). Attach the pan to crossmembers A, F, I, J, K, and L with nails and glue. Attach the trunk to parts I, K, and M with nails and glue. Temporarily attach hood with ⅝-in. screws but no glue.

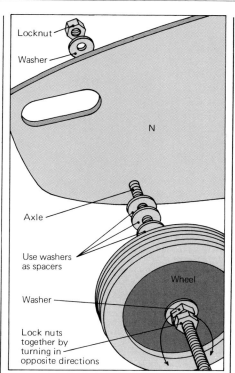

Locknut

Washer

N

Axle

Use washers as spacers

Washer

Wheel

Lock nuts together by turning in opposite directions

17. Position two nuts and one washer on each end of the rear axle to hold each rear wheel even with its brake handle. Turn the nuts in opposite directions to lock them together firmly. Slide each wheel onto the axle, then add enough flat washers to take up the space between each wheel and its outer pontoon (N).

18. Use the rotary rasp to round off all exposed corners on the car, then paint car to match our green and buff color scheme—or any colors you prefer.

19. Attach outer pontoons (N) to parts O, P, Q, and R with glue and 1½-in. screws, making sure that the space between the pontoons and the rear wheels is filled with flat washers. Place a washer and a locknut on each end of the axle and tighten them down onto the pontoons.

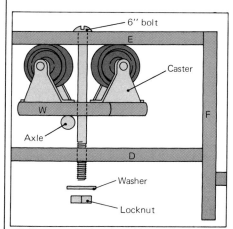

6" bolt

E

Caster

O

O

W

F

Axle

D

Washer

Locknut

20. Remove the hood and insert the front axle assembly through the hull with the axle under the arm. Secure the axle assembly with the 6-in. carriage bolt, a washer, and a locknut. Insert the bolt downward so that its head remains on top of the steering platform. Do not overtighten the nut or you will warp the plywood.

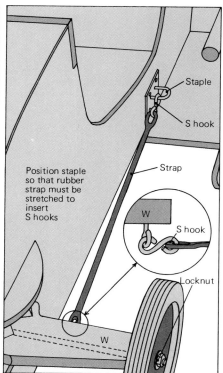

Staple

S hook

Position staple so that rubber strap must be stretched to insert S hooks

Strap

W

S hook

Locknut

W

21. Hook one end of each rubber tie-down strap to the inner screw eyes behind the front axle. Hook the other end of each strap to the staple portions of two lock hasp sets. Position the staples on the hull so that they will exert moderate tension on the straps when the axle is in the straight-ahead position; then attach the staples with screws. Discard the hasps. Use pliers to crimp shut the S hooks on the tie-down straps.

22. Reinstall the hood. Attach the front wheels to the axle, using a washer on each side of the wheels and a locknut at the ends of the axle.

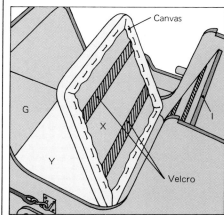

Canvas

I

G

X

Y

Velcro

23. Cut foam rubber ¼ in. oversize and glue it to the seat (Y) and seat back (X). Wrap canvas upholstery tightly around the foam and staple it to the backs of X and Y. Staple matching Velcro strips to the hull and to the backs of X and Y, and press the seat and seat back into place.

24. Attach snap rings to the ends of nylon rope. Clip rope to the outer screw eyes on the steering arm in order to pull the racer uphill. Unclip the rope and store it under the dashboard before coasting downhill.

CANDLE-POWERED BOATS

An invention of the 19th century, candle-powered toy boats operate on the same principle as jet-propelled airplanes. In an airplane air is pulled in and heated in a constricted space until it expands and pushes outward, driving the plane forward. In the boats water is the driving force: it is heated until it turns into steam. The pressure of the expanding steam out the tube propels the craft forward. At the same time, more water is sucked in.

The engine shown below is the same for both boats. When each boat is finished, dribble hot wax on the bottom of the engine housing beneath the coil, and anchor the candle stub in the wax.

To start the engine, place the flexible plastic tubing over one end of the copper tubing. Light the candle and put the boat in water. Wait a few minutes to give the tubing time to heat up. Then use the flexible tubing to suck just a bit of water into the engine; you may have to experiment to find the right amount of water. When the engine gurgles and shudders, it is ready to go. Carefully remove the flexible tubing and release the boat. Because the boats are so light, they work best in the calm waters of a bathtub or pool.

The windshield of the first boat is made from a small screw-top can. You can find such cans, containing rubber cement or the solvent used on PVC pipes, in art supply or hardware stores. Empty the contents of the can into a jar with a tight lid. Wash the can thoroughly in detergent, and let it dry overnight. Make sure no flammable material remains inside.

Making the engine

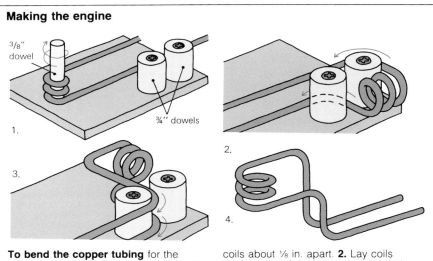

3/8" dowel

3/4" dowels

1.

2.

3.

4.

To bend the copper tubing for the engine, mount a 3/8-in. dowel and two 3/4-in. dowels on a board. The space between the two larger dowels should be equal to the diameter of the copper tubing. **1.** Bend the tubing three times around the smaller dowel, spacing the coils about 1/8 in. apart. **2.** Lay coils against one of the larger dowels, and bend each end around the dowels as shown. **3.** Insert the two tubes between the dowels; bend them as indicated. **4.** Completed engine should be about 2½ in. high.

Parts list for boat No. 1

Part	Name	Quantity	Size	Width	Length	Material
A	Hull	1	1"	4"	13"	Styrofoam
B	Engine housing	1	2⅝" dia.	See Step 2		12-oz. juice can
C	Deck and bottom	2	—	4"	13"	Oak tag
D	Side	2	—	1"	16"	Oak tag
E	Hole lining	1	—	1"	7"	Oak tag
F	Rudder	1	—	¾"	2½"	Metal from juice can
G	Rudder post	1	¼" dia.	—	2½"	Dowel
H	Windshield	1	2¼" dia.	—	—	Screw-cap can
I	Smokestack	1	✳	—	2½"	Light metal tubing
J	Engine	1	3/16" dia.	—	18"	Soft copper tubing

✳ Part I must fit over mouth of part H.

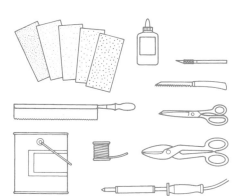

Tools and materials: Soldering iron or gun. Fine serrated-blade knife, tin snips, dovetail saw, scissors. Solder, waterproof glue, quick-set epoxy, No. 100 sandpaper. High-gloss paint, heat-resistant black paint, varnish. A screw-cap can, 12-oz. juice can, candle stub. A block of 1" Styrofoam 5" × 14", oak tag, 3/16" soft copper tubing 18" long, light metal tubing 2½" long (see I in chart above), flexible plastic tubing 2' long (see text), ¼", 3/8", and ¾" dowels. Two brads.

Boat No. 1

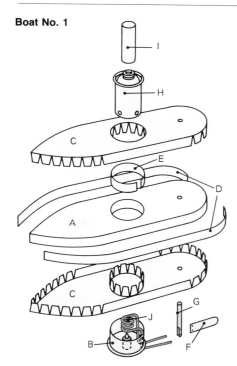

Templates for boat No. 2 Scale: actual size

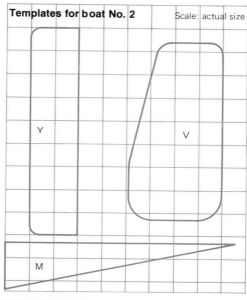

Y

V

M

D

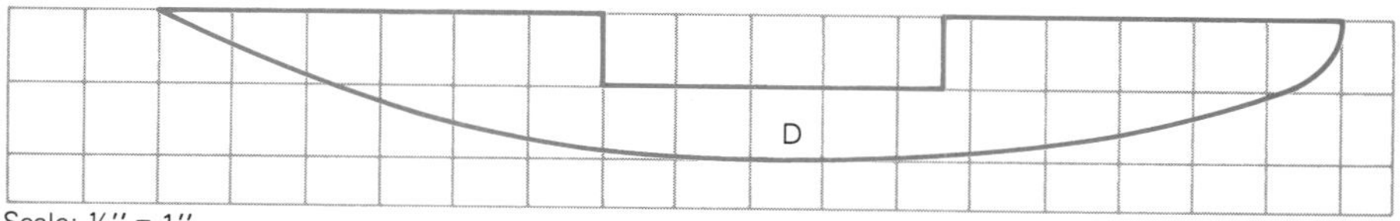

Scale: ¼'' = 1''

(Double D template to make A)

To assemble mast, bind spreader to mast with thread. Cut slits in mast and strut to let in a wedge of 1/16-in. balsa; glue it in place.

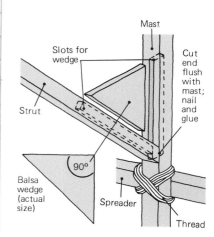

Mast

Slots for wedge

Cut end flush with mast; nail and glue

Strut

90°

Balsa wedge (actual size)

Spreader

Thread

Boat No. 2

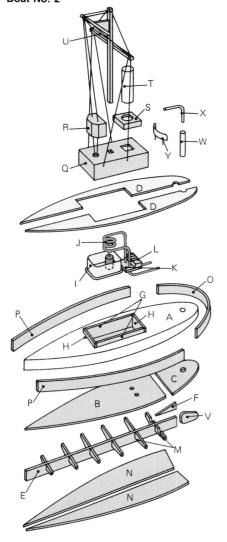

Parts list for boat No. 2

Part	Name	Quantity	Size	Width	Length	Material
A	Hull	1	1''	4''	16''	Styrofoam
B	Hull bottom	1	1/16''	4''	12''	Balsa
C	Hull bottom	1	1/16''	4''	4''	Balsa
D	Deck	2	1/16''	2''	16''	Balsa
E	Keel	1	1/8''	3/4''	14''	Balsa
F	Filler wedge	1	1/8''	3/16''✳	2''✳	Balsa
G	Engine well lining	2	1/8''	1¼''	5''✳	Balsa
H	Engine well lining	2	1/8''	1¼''	2⅜''✳	Balsa
I	Engine housing	1	—	1⅞''✳	3¾''✳	Luncheon-meat can
J	Engine	1	3/16'' dia.	—	18''	Soft copper tubing
K	Floor lining	1	1/8''	1¼''✳	2⅜''✳	Balsa
L	Engine support	1	1/4''	1/2''✳	2⅜''✳	Hardwood
M	Floor timber	12	1/8''	See pattern		Balsa
N	Bottom plank	2	1/16''	2½''✳	12''✳	Balsa
O	Transom	1	1/16''	1''✳	4''✳	Balsa
P	Topside	2	1/16''	1¼''✳	16''✳	Balsa
Q	Cabin	1	1½''✳	2½''✳	5⅛''✳	1/16'' balsa
R	Wheelhouse	1	1¼''✳	2''✳	3/4''✳	1/16'' balsa
S	Smokebox	1	1/2''✳	2''✳	2''✳	1/16'' balsa
T	Smokestack	1	3/4'' dia.	—	3''	Oak tag and foil
U	Mast assembly	1	3/16''	3''	5''	Balsa strips
V	Rudder	1		See pattern		Metal from can
W	Tiller sleeve	1	Size to fit tiller			Metal tubing
X	Tiller	1	1/8'' dia.	—	5''	Soft metal rod
Y	Tiller stay	1	—	See pattern		Metal from can

✳Measurement is approximate; cut to fit during construction.

Tools and materials: Soldering iron or gun. Fine-tooth hacksaw, tin snips. Fine serrated-blade knife, craft knife. Solder, waterproof glue, quick-set epoxy, No. 100 sandpaper, sanding sealer, paint, varnish. Heavy-duty thread, luncheon-meat can, candle stub, flag. Asbestos oven mat, aluminum foil. A block of 1'' Styrofoam 5'' x 17'', oak tag, 3/16'' balsa strip 36'' long, two 1/16'' x 6'' x 36'' balsa sheets, one 1/8'' x 2'' x 36'' balsa sheet, 1/2'' x 1¼'' x 2'' balsa block. Copper wire, 3/16'' soft copper tubing 18'' long, flexible plastic tubing 2' long (see text), 1/8'' soft metal rod 5'' long, metal tubing, 3/8'' and 3/4'' dowels. Three brads.

Boat No. 1

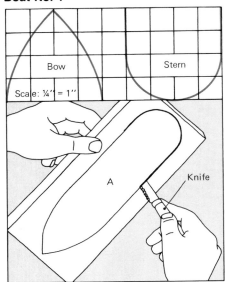

Bow   Stern

Scale: ¼" = 1"

A   Knife

1. Make a template for the hull (A) using the pattern above (see p.48); but add 5 in. more between bow and stern to make the overall length 13 in. Transfer to Styrofoam block; cut out with serrated-blade knife. Trim with sandpaper.

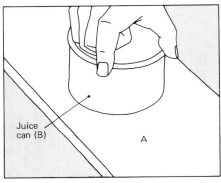

Juice can (B)   A

2. Use tin snips to cut a 12-oz. juice can in half. Use half of can to cut a hole in hull. This half becomes the engine housing (B). Save the other half for the rudder (F).

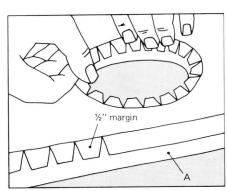

½" margin   A

3. Add ½ in. to edge of template for marking deck and bottom (C) on oak tag. Trace and cut out shapes. Cut circles to match hole in hull but 1 in. less in diameter. Snip triangles into ½-in. margins. Glue with waterproof glue to hull. Turn down and glue margins as shown. Glue oak-tag strips (D and E) on hull sides and opening. Apply three coats of high-gloss paint; varnish.

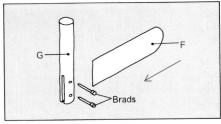

G   F

Brads

4. Use a dovetail saw to make a ¾-in. slot in rudder post (G). Insert rudder (F), and fasten it with two brads nailed all the way through post. Cut brads flush with post and file them smooth. Drill a hole for the post about 2 in. from edge of stern; post should fit tightly.

5. Bend the copper tubing to form engine (J) following instructions on page 350.

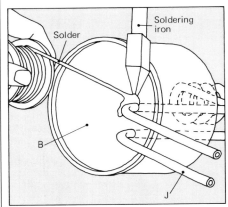

Solder   Soldering iron

B   J

6. Punch two holes the size of the copper tubing into bottom of engine housing (B) close to its rim; they should be positioned so the copper tubing will fit through. Push the free ends of tubing through the holes from inside housing. Hold the coiled part of tubing vertical to housing and solder the straight parts to housing.

7. Push can up through hull until it is flush with hull bottom. Trim top edge of can so that it rises only ½ in. above the deck.

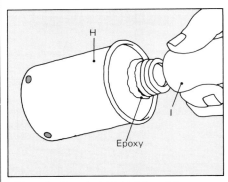

H

Epoxy   I

8. To make the windshield (H), cut the bottom from a screw-cap can and punch four or five holes around its bottom edge. Discard the cap. Glue the smokestack (I) to the windshield with epoxy.

9. Coat all metal parts with heat-resistant black paint. Push in the rudder post (G). Affix a candle stub in the engine assembly and insert the assembly in the hull. Drop the windshield assembly over the engine after lighting candle. (See text, p.350, for directions on starting the engine.)

Boat No. 2

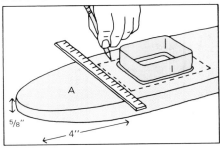

A

⅝"   4"

1. Enlarge the pattern (p.351) for the hull (A); transfer it to Styrofoam, cut it out with a serrated-blade knife, and trim it with sandpaper. Draw a line across the bottom 4 in. from stern. Starting at the line, taper hull so that it is ⅝ in. thick at stern. Cut opening for engine 1¼ in. longer and ½ in. wider than can that will be used for engine housing (I). Cut can 1 in. high.

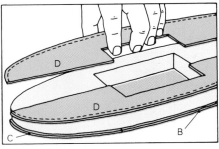

D   D   B   C

2. Using waterproof glue, attach the deck pieces (D) to top of hull and the bottom pieces (B and C) to the underside. Sand all edges flush with hull and opening.

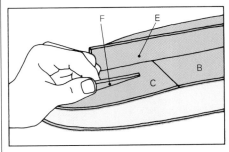

F   E   B   C

3. Glue the keel (E) to the hull bottom, one end aligned with the bow. Cut a wedge (F) to fit the gap between the stern end of the keel and the hull bottom. Glue it in place.

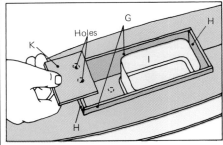

G   H   Holes   K   I   H

4. Glue engine well lining (G and H) inside well; it should rise ¼ in. above deck (D). Place engine housing (I) toward front of well. Cut floor lining (K) to fit behind housing, and glue in place. Shape copper tubing for engine (see p.350). Drill two holes through floor about ½ in. behind housing.

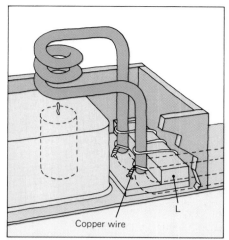

Copper wire

5. Cut engine support (L) to fit snugly across back of well. Bind the tubing to it with copper wire and reinforce with epoxy. Glue the support in place behind the engine housing. Remove the housing. Cut pieces of asbestos to fit the walls near the engine. Glue them in with epoxy. Put engine housing back in the well.

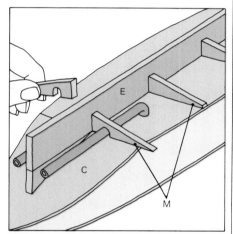

6. Starting 1¾ in. from the bow, glue five pairs of floor timbers (M) along keel, each pair 2 in. apart. File a groove in the remaining pair to clear the tubing; glue them in place. Trim off any protruding ends.
7. Glue on bottom planks (N), first trimming floor timbers if necessary. Seal seams with epoxy, and seal holes around tubing.

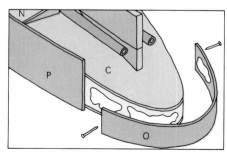

8. Glue on the topsides (P). Cut the transom (O) across the grain so that it can be bent; glue it to the stern, pinning it in place until the glue has set. Trim or sand all parts flush with the hull. Seal all seams with epoxy so they are watertight.

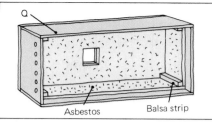

Asbestos · Balsa strip

9. Build three bottomless boxes (Q, R, and S), strengthening their corners by gluing in strips of balsa. Strips in cabin must stop ¼ in. short of bottom of box to allow it to fit over the engine well lining. Line cabin (Q) and smokebox (S) with asbestos. Make six small holes on rear of cabin. Position smokebox on cabin so it will be above candle, and mark its position. Cut hole in cabin roof half the size of the smokebox.

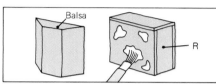

Balsa

10. Shape front of wheelhouse (R) by gluing on a piece of balsa beveled at the ends. Mark position of wheelhouse on cabin.

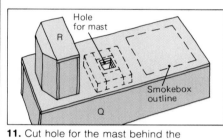

Hole for mast · Smokebox outline

11. Cut hole for the mast behind the wheelhouse in the cabin roof. Glue strips of wood inside cabin around edges of hole as support for mast (use same wood as for mast). Glue the wheelhouse in position.
12. Make a smokestack (T) by wrapping aluminum foil six times around a ¾-in. dowel; glue with epoxy after the first and final wraps. Glue on several layers of oak tag with waterproof glue. Remove dowel and let smokestack dry overnight.

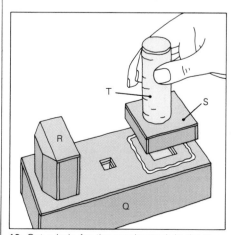

13. Cut a hole for the smokestack in the top of smokebox (S). Glue the stack in place with epoxy. Glue smokebox to cabin.

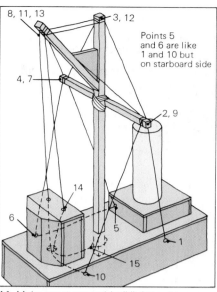

Points 5 and 6 are like 1 and 10 but on starboard side

14. Make mast assembly (U) (see diagram, p.351). Bind parts together by wrapping them with thread and covering with glue. Use a needle to pierce holes in cabin (Q) and wheelhouse (R) for rigging. Glue mast in place and rig it in sequence indicated. Knot inside point 1, tie to mast at point 15, and glue at each point in between.

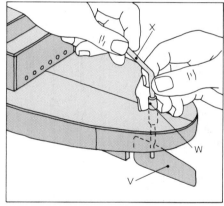

15. Drill a hole near the stern for the tiller (X) and fit the hole with a metal or plastic tube to serve as a tiller sleeve (W). Cut rudder (V) from leftover metal can. Make a slot in tiller with a fine-tooth hacksaw. Solder the rudder into slot. Insert tiller in sleeve and bend it parallel with deck.

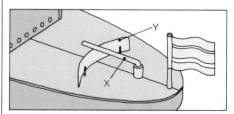

16. Cut the tiller stay (Y) wide enough to hold the tiller stationary. Solder a brad near each end. Bend the stay into an arc and push the brads into the deck. Mount a flag at the stern. Apply two coats of sanding sealer to all balsa surfaces, then paint and varnish them. Make windows of aluminum foil and use epoxy to secure them in place.

BUNK BEDS

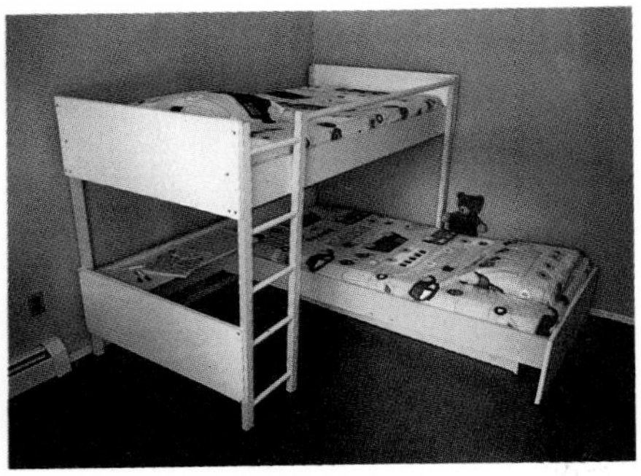

If you have the space, these bunk beds are an interesting alternative to the usual parallel arrangement and include a child's desk beneath the top bed. The unit is made of hardwood posts and dowels, with wood frames that can be cut from three 4- x 8-foot panels of plywood. Relatively expensive lumber-core plywood must be used because screws do not hold well enough in common veneer plywood.

The two beds are assembled separately and are attached to the corner posts and ladder through their rails and headboards. The frames will accept 4- x 30- x 75-inch mattresses.

The unit can be painted or stained and varnished if you choose a plywood veneer that complements the hardwood.

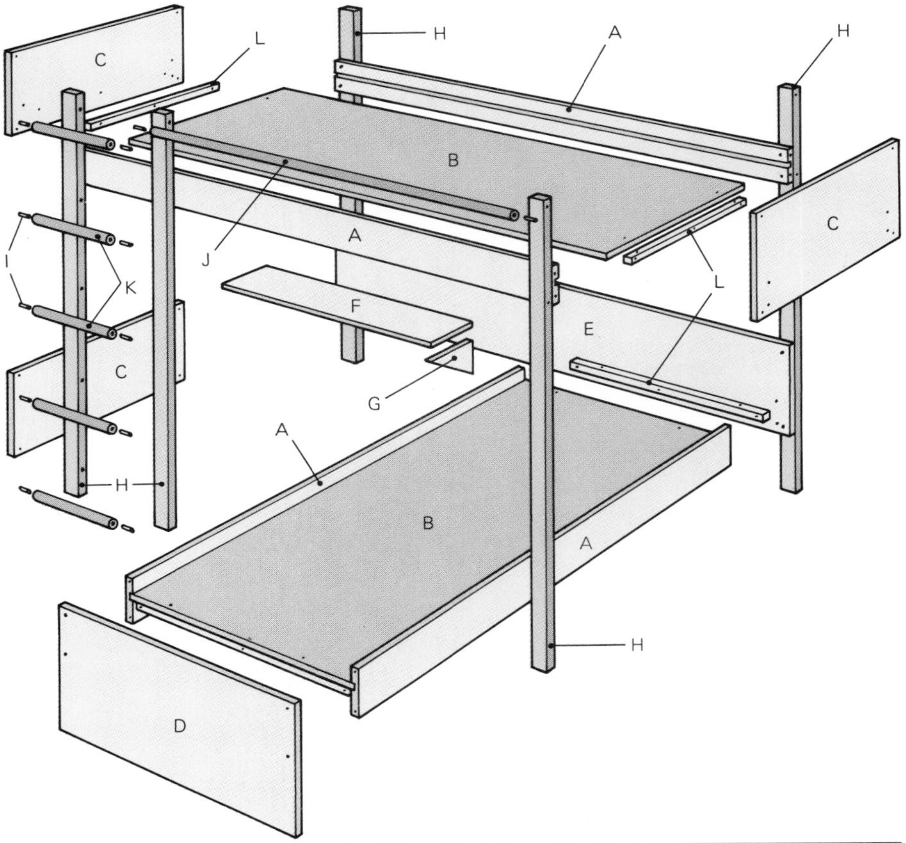

Parts list

Part	Name	Quantity	Thickness	Width	Length	Material
A	Bedrail	4	¾″	6″	76″	Lumber-core plywood
B	Base	2	¾″	31¾″	76″	Lumber-core plywood
C	Headboard	3	¾″	14″	35″	Lumber-core plywood
D	Footboard	1	¾″	14″	32½″	Lumber-core plywood
E	Backboard	1	¾″	14″	76″	Lumber-core plywood
F	Desk	1	¾″	11″	39″	Lumber-core plywood
G	Desk support	1	¾″	6″	11″	Lumber-core plywood
H	Post	5	1⅛″	2″	53″	5/4 x 12 hardwood
I	Peg	12	½″ dia.	—	1¾″	Hardwood dowel
J	Guardrail	1	1⅜″ dia.	—	59″*	Hardwood dowel
K	Ladder rung	5	1⅛″ dia.	—	12″	Hardwood dowel
L	Cleat	4	1⅛″	1¼″	31½″	5/4 x 6 hardwood

*Length is approximate; cut guardrail after measuring precise distance between posts.

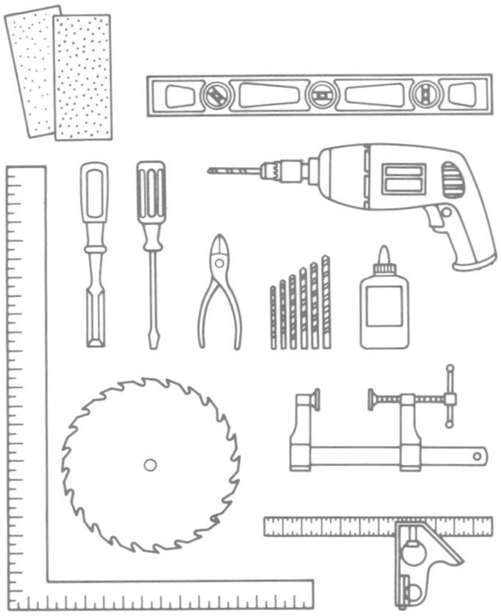

Tools and materials: Radial arm saw, circular saw, or table saw. Electric drill with 7/64″, ⅛″, and ½″ twist bits and No. 10 Screwmate bit. Vise and workbench. Combination square, framing square, level, pencil. Two quick-action clamps. Screwdriver. Wire cutters. Small chisel or knife. Wood glue, wood putty. Nos. 100 and 150 sandpaper. Three 4′ x 8′ panels of ¾″ lumber-core plywood, one 5′ length of 5/4 x 12 hardwood board (for posts), one 3′ length of 5/4 x 6 hardwood board (for cleats). Hardwood dowels: ½″ x 3′, 1⅛″ x 6′, 1⅜″ x 6′. Twenty-six 1¾″ No. 10 flathead wood screws, thirty-four 2½″ No. 12 brass ovalhead screws with brass countersunk washers. Four 4d wire brads.

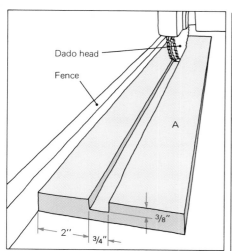

Dado head

Fence

A

3/8"

2"

3/4"

1. Cut plywood to sizes shown in chart (see cutting plans below). Rip 5/4 hardwood boards into 2-in.-wide posts and 1¼-in.-wide cleats (see *Index,* p.379). Cut posts (H), cleats (L), and dowels (I, J, and K) to required lengths. Label all parts. Fit the radial arm saw with a ¾-in. dado head, and position it 3/8 in. above the saw table. Cut through a scrap of ¾-in.-thick wood and make adjustments, if necessary, until the cut is 3/8 in. deep and a piece of ¾-in. plywood will fit snugly into it. Use this setup to cut dadoes down the length of each of the four rails (A) 2 in. from one edge. Dadoes can also be made with a router, circular saw, or table saw (see *Index*, p.379).

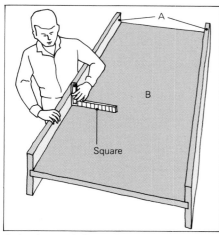

A

B

Square

2. Apply wood glue to the dadoes and fit a pair of rails to each of the bases (B). Though you do not have to clamp these joints, you must be sure that they are square. After you set the pieces aside to dry, check each joint with a square.

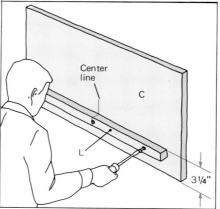

Center line

C

L

3¼"

3. Mark center lines on the cleats (L), headboards (C), footboard (D), and bases. Draw a line parallel to one long edge of each headboard 3¼ in. up from the bottom. Align the top edge of a cleat with the 3¼-in. line and align their center lines too; then clamp the cleat to the headboard. Use a No. 10 Screwmate bit to drill three equally spaced holes through the cleat into the headboard. Attach the cleat with 1¾-in. No. 10 flathead wood screws. Repeat on second headboard.

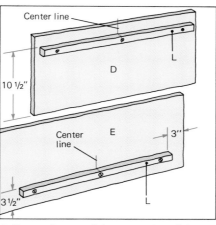

Center line

D

L

10 1/2"

Center line

E

3"

3½"

L

4. Draw a line parallel to one edge of the footboard (D) 10½ in. up from its bottom. Place a cleat below this line, center it, clamp it, drill holes, and attach the cleat with No. 10 screws, as in Step 3. Draw a line parallel to the long edge of the backboard (E) 3½ in. up from its bottom. Clamp a cleat below this line so that its end is 3 in. from the edge of the backboard. Then drill and attach the cleat in the same way. Fill exposed plywood edges with wood putty. Sand all parts with Nos. 100 and 150 sandpaper. Paint headboards yellow, all other parts white.

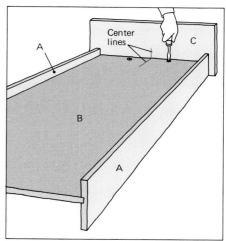

Center lines

A

C

B

A

5. Put one of the headboards at the end of one of the beds you assembled in Step 2 so that the base rests on the cleat and the center lines on B and C are aligned. Use the No. 10 Screwmate bit to drill two holes, one 10 in. from each rail, through the base and into the cleat. Repeat for the headboard at the other end of the bed. Attach the base to the cleats with four No. 10 screws. Carefully put this bed aside.

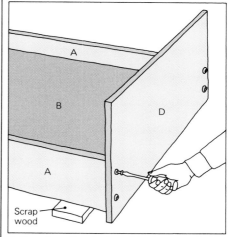

A

B

D

A

Scrap wood

6. Turn the other bed upside down, and set it on top of scrap wood ¾ in. thick so that the end of bed is exactly ¾ in. off the floor. Place the footboard on the floor and against the end of the bed; the cleat should rest on the base of the bed. Center the bed on the footboard. Use a ⅛-in. bit to drill two pilot holes through the footboard and into each rail 1¼ in. and 4¾ in. from the bottom of the footboard. Slip countersunk washers over No. 12 brass ovalhead screws and screw the footboard to the rails.

Plywood cutting plans

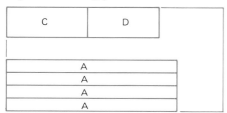

| C | D |

| A |
| A |
| A |
| A |

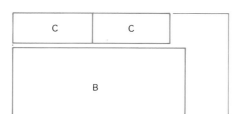

| C | C |

| B |

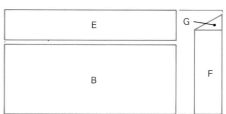

| E | G |

| B | F |

Lay out parts A–G on three 4- x 8-ft. panels of plywood as shown above. Dimensions for these parts are in the chart.

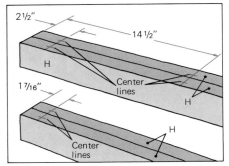

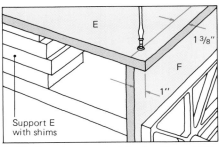

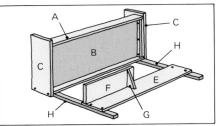

7. Choose two of the posts (H) for the ladder and place them side by side with their 1⅛-in. faces up. Measure and mark one post 2½ in., 14½ in., 26½ in., 38½ in., and 50½ in. from one end for peg holes for attaching rungs. Use a combination square to draw lines from these marks across both posts. Draw a center line perpendicular to each of these lines down the length of each post. Use a drill stop and drill ½-in. holes 1 in. deep into the posts at each of the 10 crossmarks. Select one of the ladder posts plus another post; lay them side by side with the peg holes on the ladder post facing down. Mark each post 1⁷⁄₁₆ in. from its top end and drill ½-in. holes 1 in. deep for pegs (I).

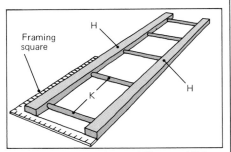

8. Using the same bit and drill stop, drill into the center of both ends of each of the five ladder rungs (K). Apply wood glue to these holes and to those in the posts. Slip the pegs halfway into each of the post holes and assemble the ladder. Check it with the framing square when you set it aside to dry.

9. Starting at one end of the backboard (E), draw a line 39 in. long and 1 in. down from the top edge of E. Turn the backboard over and draw a second line 1⅜ in. from the top edge. Place desk (F) in a vise so that its long edge barely protrudes from the jaws. Set the backboard on top of desk so that the top edge of desk is aligned with the 1-in. line. Shim the other edge of the backboard to make it perpendicular to the desk. Use the ⅛-in. bit to drill four evenly spaced pilot holes through the 1⅜-in. line and into the desk. Drive a No. 12 brass ovalhead screw with a countersunk washer into each hole before drilling the next one.

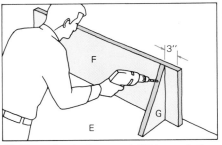

10. Place the desk support (G) beneath the desk and against the backboard 3 in. from the end of the desk. Drill one ⅛-in. hole through the backboard into the support, and fasten with a No. 12 screw and countersunk washer. Use the No. 10 Screwmate bit to drill a second hole at a slight angle through the bottom of the support and into the desk at a point where their combined thickness just exceeds 1¾ in. Attach the support to the desk with a No. 10 flathead wood screw.

11. Lay two of the remaining posts (H) on the floor on their 2-in.-wide faces about 70 in. apart. Lay the upper bunk bed on its side on top of them. Adjust posts so that they fit snugly into the corners formed by the rear bedrail and the headboards and protrude ¾ in. past the tops of the headboards. Check for squareness. Then use the Screwmate bit to drill two holes through the rail, 1 in. from its top and bottom, and into each post. Attach the rail and posts with No. 10 screws. Put backboard on top of posts so that its lower edge is 7¼ in. from the bottoms of the posts. Use the Screwmate bit to drill two pilot holes through the backboard into each post, and drive No. 10 screws into them. Use the ⅛-in. bit to drill holes 1½ in. from the top and bottom of each headboard and centered on the posts. Then secure the headboards to the posts with No. 12 screws and countersunk washers.

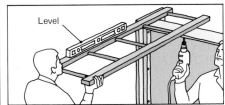

12. Lay the ladder on the front rail of the upper bed so that the corner post of the ladder rests against the headboard and bedrail and extends ¾ in. above the headboard. Have a helper hold the ladder level. Use the Screwmate bit to drill two holes through the rail and into each post of the ladder 1 in. from the top and bottom of rail. Attach ladder with No. 10 screws.

Construction details

Overhead and side views show how the guardrail and upper bed are attached to the corner post (see Steps 14–16).

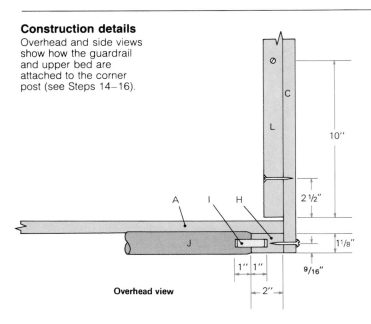

Overhead view

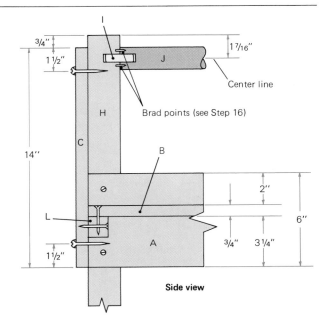

Side view

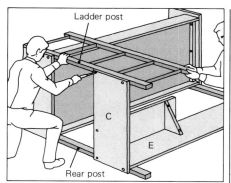

Ladder post

C

E

Rear post

13. Place the lower headboard on its edge on the floor, between the rear post and the ladder post, so that it meets the backboard at the rear post. Make sure the headboard is square. Use the ⅛-in. bit to drill two holes through the headboard into the rear post and two holes into the ladder post 1½ in. from the top and bottom of the headboard. Drill one more hole through the headboard into the desk 2 in. back from its front edge. Insert five No. 12 screws and countersunk washers. Drill two holes through the other headboard for the upper bed and screw it to its post similarly.

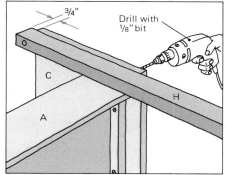

3/4"

Drill with ⅛" bit

C

H

A

14. Position the last post against its headboard and bedrail so that it extends ¾ in. above the headboard. Drill two holes through the headboard, 1½ in. from its top and bottom, into the post, using the ⅛-in. bit. Do not insert the screws until Step 16.

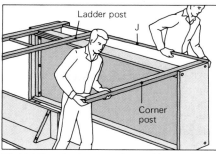

Ladder post

J

Corner post

15. Holding the last post in position and level, rest the guardrail (J) against the corner post and ladder post, mark the exact distance between them, and saw off the rail at this mark. Use the ½-in. bit with its tape marker (see Step 7) to drill 1-in.-deep holes into the center of both ends of the rail.

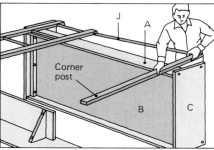

J

A

Corner post

B

C

16. Use an ¹¹⁄₆₄-in: bit to drill two holes 1 in. deep into each end of the guardrail beside each center hole. Snip the heads off four 4d brads and fit them shaft first into the holes. Apply wood glue to the ½-in. holes in the rail and the posts. Slide the pegs (I) halfway into the holes in the rail and insert the rail between the posts, pushing in the pegs and setting the brad points into the posts. Put the corner post back into position and insert two No. 12 screws with countersunk washers through the holes in the headboard and into the post. Use the Screwmate bit to drill two more holes through the bedrail and into each post, one above and one below the base (B). Insert No. 10 screws into these holes.

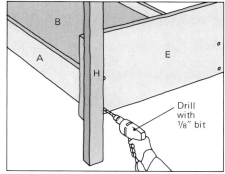

B

A

H

E

Drill with ⅛" bit

17. Turn the unit right side up. Position the lower bed so that its base rests on the cleat attached to the backboard. Using the ⅛-in. bit, drill two holes through the backboard into each rail of the bed. The post at the corner may prevent you from drilling all the way into the outside rail; drill as far as you can, then remove the bed from the cleat and finish the drilling. Reposition the bed and attach the backboard to the rails with No. 12 screws and countersunk washers. Use the Screwmate bit to drill two holes through the outside bedrail into the front corner post, and attach them with No. 10 screws. Use the Screwmate to drill two holes through the base into the cleat and secure with No. 10 screws.

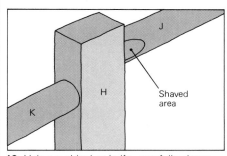

J

H

K

Shaved area

18. Using a chisel or knife, carefully shave down the ends of the guardrail so that they do not extend beyond the edges of the posts. Sand the ends smooth with Nos. 100 and 150 sandpaper.

Variation

This design can be adapted to make the more conventional parallel bunk beds. Both beds are built in the same way as the top bed (see Steps 1–5, p.355). Dadoes are cut in the bedrails and the bases are installed. Cleats are attached to the four headboards, and the bases are screwed to these cleats, securing the headboards to the beds. When the posts are laid flat, both beds are attached to them with No. 10 screws driven through the rails into the posts and No. 12 screws driven through the headboards into the posts. The ladder is attached to the outside rails of both beds. Attach guardrail to upper bed only. The desk, footboard, and backboard are eliminated.

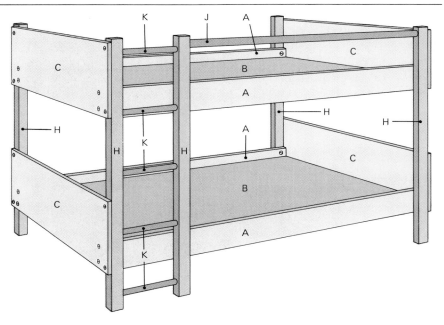

K J A

C

C

B

A

H

A

H

H K H

C

B

A

K

ROCKER AND SEESAW

If you have young children, or grandchildren, you can keep them happily and safely occupied for hours on end with this easy-to-construct combination rocker and seesaw. This project actually gives you two fun toys in one: a wooden rocker, or rocking boat, and a seesaw that is as much fun as a bucking bronco—and far easier to control. The rocking boat will hold two small children, and there are stops to keep it from rocking too far and tipping over. For extra safety, be sure the children climb into the rocker at one end and not over the side.

When the kids get tired of playing in the rocking boat, you can turn it into a seesaw in a few seconds. Merely fit the slots in the seesaw spine (H) into the slots in the tops of the back rests (E).

The rocker and seesaw can be used in any backyard, on a deck, or even indoors. It is also easy to store when not in use if you remove the seesaw attachment. The seesaw can be stored flat against a garage or closet wall, and the rocker will take up only a little additional space.

You can make the rocking boat without the seesaw. If you do this, do not cut slots in the tops of the back rests, as instructed in Step 5, and of course eliminate the final step, "Making the seesaw."

To build this project, you need only a few simple hand tools, assorted wood screws, a small amount of wood, and materials for finishing the piece. As shown, the sides of the rocker and the supporting rails are stained and varnished and the other parts are painted. If you prefer, you can stain and varnish the entire assembly or paint it all in the color of your choice. If the rocker and seesaw are to be left outdoors, be sure to cover all parts of the wood with paint or varnish to protect it from the weather.

To make the rocker and seesaw, cut out all the parts except the sides to the specifications given in the chart, then follow the step-by-step instructions. (For more complete information on finishing wood, see the *Index,* p.379.)

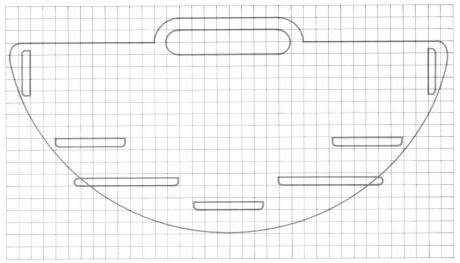

When copying pattern for rocker sides enlarge each square on grid to 2 in. (see p.48).

Parts list

Part	Name	Quantity	Thickness	Width	Length	Material
A	Side	2	½″	18″	35½″	Plywood
B	Back rail	4	¾″	¾″	3¾″	1 x 1 softwood
C	Seat-and-foot rail	6	¾″	¾″	5¾″	1 x 1 softwood
D	Stop rail	4	¾″	¾″	8½″	1 x 1 softwood
E	Back rest	2	¾″	3½″	15¾″	1 x 4 softwood
F	Seat-and-foot board	5	¾″	5½″	15¾″	1 x 6 softwood
G	Seesaw board	1	¾″	7¼″	8′	1 x 8 softwood
H	Seesaw spine	1	¾″	1½″	8′	1 x 2 softwood

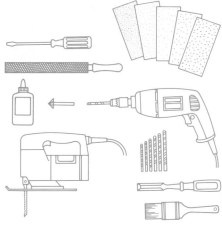

Tools and materials: Electric or hand drill with set of twist bits, countersink bit. Saber saw. Backsaw or other fine-tooth saw. Wood file, chisel, screwdriver. Paintbrush, waterproof glue. Nos. 120 and 220 sandpaper, wood stain, polyurethane varnish, nontoxic paint, turpentine, soft cloths. Lumber (see above). Sixteen 1″, twenty-one 1¼″, and eleven 1½″ No. 8 wood screws.

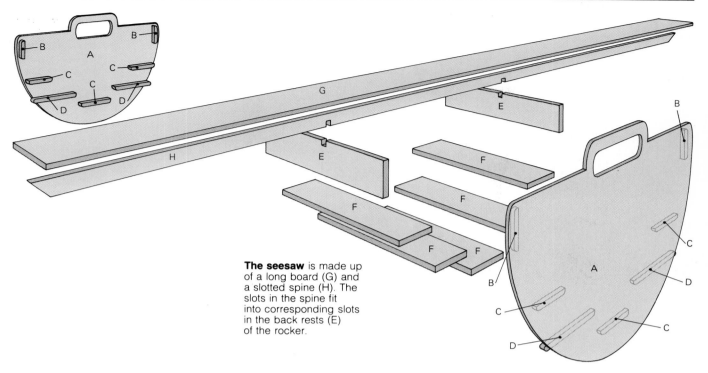

The seesaw is made up of a long board (G) and a slotted spine (H). The slots in the spine fit into corresponding slots in the back rests (E) of the rocker.

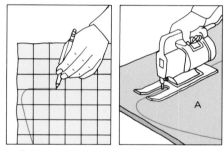

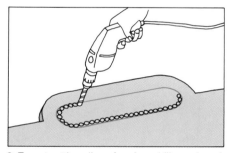

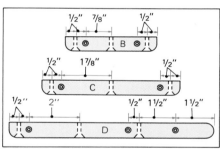

1. Enlarge the design given on the facing page for the rocker sides (A), transfer the outline of the enlarged design onto plywood (leaving out the rail placements), and cut out two matching sides with a saber saw.

2. To cut out handles of rocker, drill a series of holes around perimeter of area to be cut out. Remove excess wood with chisel or jigsaw. Sand all surfaces of cutout sides with No. 120 and then No. 220 sandpaper.

3. Use an ¹¹⁄₆₄-in. bit to drill pilot holes for the screws in the rails. Drill two holes in each back rail (B), two in each seat-and-foot rail (C), and three in each stop rail (D), placing the holes as shown above.

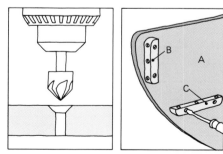

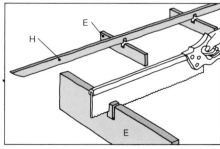

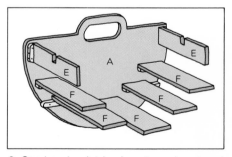

4. Counterbore the pilot holes with a ³⁄₈-in. bit or a countersink. Round off the rail edges with a file, then glue and screw the rails to the sides (A) with 1-in. screws. Stain and varnish the assembled sides.

5. Use a wood file to round off longer edges of back rests (E) and seat-and-foot boards (F) to eliminate sharp edges. Cut a slot the thickness of seesaw spine (H) into center of top edge of each back rest (E).

6. Sand and paint back rests and seat-and-foot boards. When paint is dry, attach back rests and center F board to appropriate rails with 1¼-in. screws. Screw on remaining seat-and-foot boards.

Making the seesaw: Drill and counterbore screw holes in seesaw board (G) as shown at right. Round off edges of board and sand it. Cut slots into spine (H) to match slots in back rests (E) and bevel its ends. Glue and screw spine to seesaw board with 1½-in. screws. Paint assembly.

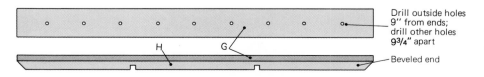

Drill outside holes 9″ from ends; drill other holes 9¾″ apart

Beveled end

JUNGLE GYM

You can make your children the envy of their friends by building this sturdy, fun-packed jungle gym. The structure consists of a central two-story house with ladders for walls, a fireman's pole, a rope for climbing, and a long unit made up of horizontal and diagonal ladders and three swings. The entire gym is nearly 10 feet high, 8 feet wide, and 25 feet long.

Although the jungle gym is not particularly difficult to build, it requires a lot of careful measuring, cutting, and drilling, and you will need good power tools to do the job. The directions that follow do not explain certain basic techniques, such as cutting dadoes and rabbets or laminating. To find directions for these and other techniques, see the *Index,* p.379.

Begin the project by building the platform (second-story floor), then prepare the house posts. When cutting the posts, use a radial arm saw and cut through 2 inches from one side, then the remainder from the opposite side. Drill the needed bolt and nut holes into the platform, then erect the house and add on the slide and swing assembly.

To prevent rust and rot, use only galvanized or stainless steel hardware and pressure-treated lumber wherever possible. As you work, sand the wood to prevent splinters. Varnish the rungs, and stain the other wooden parts before assembling them. If you do not use pressure-treated lumber, finish the gym with weatherproof paint instead of stain and varnish. You can purchase a ready-made baby swing in a toy store and aluminum tubing for the fireman's pole from an electrical supply house.

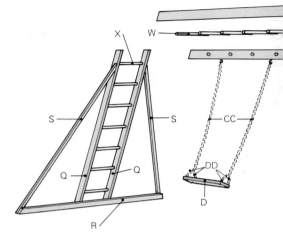

Caution: As the lumber used in this jungle gym ages, it will shrink and the fasteners may loosen. Retighten the nuts and bolts periodically for about 6 months, then apply a liquid thread-locking compound, such as Locktite, to all nuts and bolts.

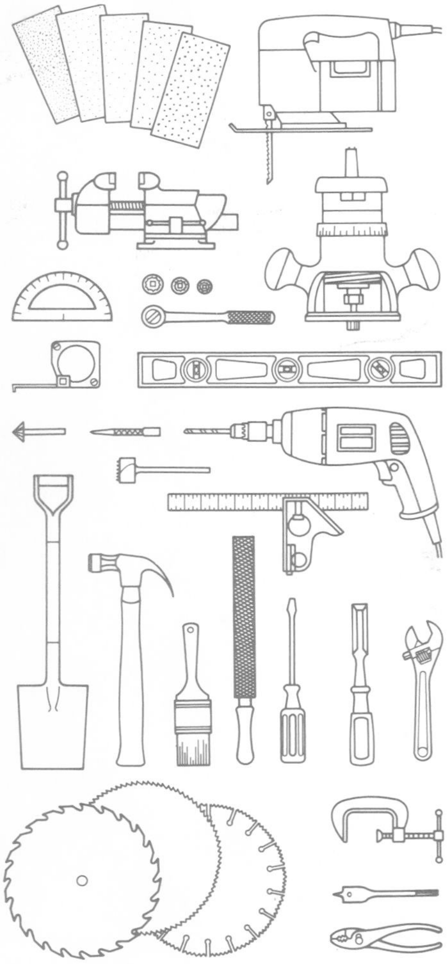

Parts list

Part	Name	Quantity	Thickness	Width	Length	Material
A	Corner post	4	3½″	3½″	96″	4 x 4 pine ✵
B	Short center post	2	3½″	3½″	96″	4 x 4 pine ✵
C	Long center post	2	3½″	3½″	114″	4 x 4 pine ✵
D	Swing seat	2	1½″	7¼″	20¾″	2 x 8 pine ✵
E	Floorboard	9	1½″	5½″	50⅞″	2 x 6 pine ✵
F	Long ridgepole	1	1½″	5½″	86⅜″	2 x 6 pine ✵
G	Short ridgepole	1	1½″	5½″	71⅞″	2 x 6 pine ✵
H	Overhead rail	2	1½″	5½″	142″	2 x 6 pine ✵
I	Slide rail	2	1½″	5½″	89¼″	2 x 6 pine ✵
J	Slide foot	2	1½″	5½″	17½″	2 x 6 pine ✵
K	Slide foot base	1	1½″	5½″	15¾″†	2 x 6 pine ✵
L	Fireman's pole base	1	1½″	5½″	18″	2 x 6 pine ✵
M	Long platform beam	2	1½″	3½″	50⅞″	2 x 4 pine ✵
N	Short platform beam	3	1½″	3½″	48⅜″	2 x 4 pine ✵
O	Roof rail	2	1½″	3½″	54⅜″†	2 x 4 pine ✵
P	Rafter	4	1½″	3½″	37½″	2 x 4 pine ✵

✵Use pressure-treated pine for protection against bad weather.

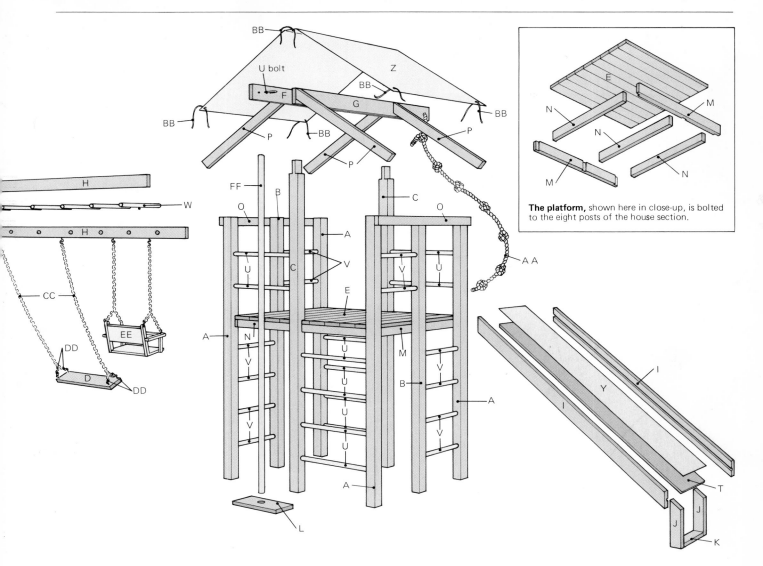

The platform, shown here in close-up, is bolted to the eight posts of the house section.

Parts list

Part	Name	Quantity	Thickness	Width	Length	Material
Q	End-ladder rail	2	1½"	3½"	99⅝"	2 x 4 pine ✳
R	Ground support	1	1½"	3½"	75"	2 x 4 pine ✳
S	End-ladder brace	2	1½"	1½"	88"	2 x 2 pine ✳
T	Slide board	1	¾"	21"	84¹³/₁₆"	Exterior fir plywood
U	Long house rung	12	1⅜" dia.	—	25¾"†	Hardwood dowel
V	Short house rung	12	1⅜" dia.	—	24"†	Hardwood dowel
W	Overhead rung	11	1⅜" dia.	—	20⅞"†	Hardwood dowel
X	End-ladder rung	7	1⅜" dia.	—	17⅞"†	Hardwood dowel
Y	Slide covering	1	—	20¾"†	85½"	Plastic laminate
Z	Roof cover	1	—	60"	83"	Awning canvas
AA	Rope	1	—	—	15'	Manila rope
BB	Roof tie	6	—	—	12"	Lightweight nylon rope
CC	Long chain	4	—	—	52"	2/0 bowtye chain
DD	Short chain	8	—	—	6"	2/0 bowtye chain
EE	Baby swing	1	—	—	—	Ready-made baby swing
FF	Fireman's pole	1	2" dia.	—	10'	Aluminum tubing

†Measurement is approximate; cut to fit during construction.

Tools and materials: Electric drill with twist, spade, multispur, and countersink bits. Radial arm saw with dado blade, circular saw, saber saw. Router with laminate cutting bits. Wood chisel, wood file. Vise, eight 6" C-clamps. Socket wrench, adjustable wrench, pliers, screwdriver. Shovel. Hammer, nail set. Level, combination square, protractor, steel tape rule, pencil. Paintbrush. Waterproof cement, waterproof glue, No. 80 sandpaper. Semitransparent exterior wood stain, exterior polyurethane varnish. Short piece of scrap pipe. Sixteen ¼" plywood scraps. Twine, grommet kit with grommets large enough to accept the lightweight nylon rope used for roof ties (BB). The following ⅜" bolts: twelve 3½" long, eight 4" long, four 5" long, thirty 5½" long, and eight 6" long. One ⅜" U bolt long enough to go around 2" pipe and through 1½" wood. Six ½" eyebolts 6" long and eight ⅜" eyebolts 2" long. Double washers and nuts to fit all bolts. Twelve .177 and six .250 S hooks for connecting swing chains. Sixty-two 2", six 2½", and twenty-two 3½" No. 8 flathead wood screws. Four 3" and fifty-four 3½" No. 10 flathead wood screws. 6d and 10d finishing nails. (For protection against rust use only galvanized or stainless steel hardware.) For all other materials, see chart at left.

Building the platform

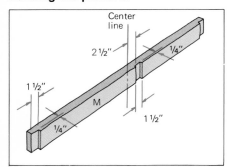

1. Cut the long and short platform beams (M and N) to the lengths shown in the chart, then cut a ¼-in.-deep rabbet 1½ in. wide on each end of the two long beams. On each long beam also cut a ¼-in. dado 1½ in. wide with its closest edge 2½ in. from the center of the beam. (The dadoes must clear the center posts in the completed structure.)

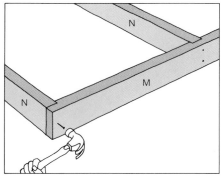

2. Fit the ends of the short platform beams (N) into the dadoes and rabbets of the long platform beams (M). Drive one 10d finishing nail into each corner of the frame, centering the nail in the beam. Drive two nails into each end of the center beam.
3. Cut the platform floorboards (E) to length, then arrange them on top of the platform frame with ¼-in. plywood spacers between them. The outside floorboards should be flush with the sides of the platform. If they are not, adjust the spacing between the boards or rip one of the end boards down to adjust the fit.

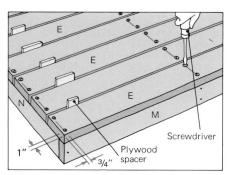

4. Draw a line across all the floorboards ¾ in. from each end. Draw a parallel line to indicate the location of the center beam. On each floorboard drill ¹³⁄₆₄-in. screw holes along these lines 1 in. from each edge. Countersink the holes. Check the frame for squareness, then screw the floorboards down with 3-in. No. 10 screws. Be careful to maintain the proper spacing. Remove the plywood spacers.

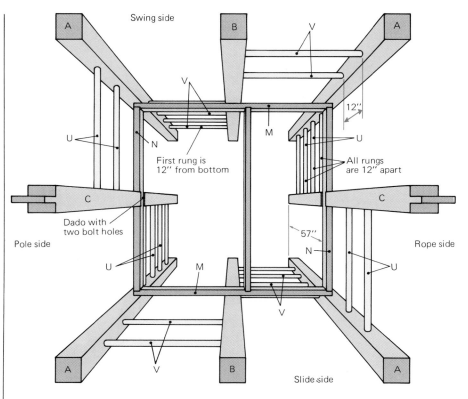

Preparing the posts

1. Cut each of the eight posts (A, B, and C) to the lengths shown in the chart. Mark each post to identify its location in the completed structure, and mark each side of each post to show its orientation—slide side, swing side, pole side, and rope side. If you fail to mark all the posts, you risk cutting or drilling them in the wrong places.
2. Place all the marked posts together with the sides that will touch the platform facing up. Square off the bottoms of the posts by pushing a piece of wood against them.
3. Draw a line across each post 57 in. from its bottom. Draw a second line at a distance above the first line equal to the thickness of the platform. (The platform will be bolted on between these lines.) Cut dadoes between the lines on the two long posts (C) half as deep as the posts are thick.

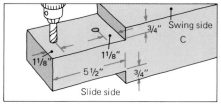

4. Cut rabbets for the ridgepoles (F and G) into the tops of the long posts on their slide and swing sides 5½ in. wide and ¾ in. deep. Drill two ²⁵⁄₆₄-in. bolt holes through the center of each rabbet 1⅛ in. from the top and bottom of the rabbet.
5. Drill two ²⁵⁄₆₄-in. bolt holes into the centers of the dadoes on each long post ¹⁵⁄₁₆ in. up from the bottom of the dado and 2⁷⁄₁₆ in. from the top. These bolt holes will be used for fastening the platform to the posts.

6. Drill two ²⁵⁄₆₄-in. bolt holes into each of the two short center posts (B) between the lines drawn in Step 3. Drill holes ¹⁵⁄₁₆ in. from the bottom line and 2⁷⁄₁₆ in. from the top line.

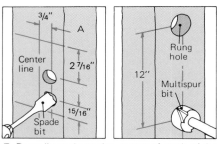

7. Draw lines down the center of each of the corner posts (A) between the lines drawn in Step 3. Draw a parallel line on each post ¾ in. from the center line toward what will be the inside of the house. Mark each of these lines ¹⁵⁄₁₆ in. from the bottom and 2⁷⁄₁₆ in. from the top. Use a ⅞-in. spade bit to counterbore a ⅜-in.-deep hole at each mark. Drill ²⁵⁄₆₄-in. bolt holes through the first holes and completely through the posts.
8. Study the drawing at the top for the placement of the rung holes. Each post gets two holes on the upper half of one side and four on the lower half of another side. On each post draw a line down the center of each side that will receive rung holes. Mark the rung hole locations along these center lines. The lowest ones should be 12 in. from the bottom of the post and the highest 84 in. from the bottom. The other rungs should be 12 in. apart. Use a multispur bit with the same diameter as your dowel (measure it) to drill the rung holes 1 in. deep.

Preparing the platform for bolting

1. Find the exact center of each platform side. Mark off a distance equal to half the thickness of the posts to each side of the center. Extend these marks up and down the entire thickness of the platform to guide the placement of the center posts.

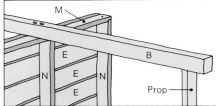

2. Stand the platform on its side and position the first short center post (B) between the guidelines just drawn. Be sure the lines on the post marking the position of the platform are lined up with the top and bottom of the platform. Prop up the bottom of the post and make sure that the post is perfectly perpendicular to the platform.
3. Insert a drill with a ²⁵⁄₆₄-in. bit into the bolt holes in the post and drill into the platform. Remove the post to complete the drilling. Repeat for the other short center post and the two long center posts (C). When positioning the long posts for drilling, fit their dadoes over the edges of the platform.
4. Mark the position of each corner post (A) on the side of the platform it will be bolted to by marking off a distance from the corner equal to half the thickness of the post. (Unlike the center posts, only half of each corner post touches the platform.)

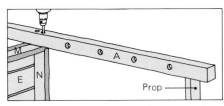

5. Position each corner post, in turn, on the platform, using the marks made in Step 4. Prop up the bottom of each post and make sure that the post is perfectly perpendicular to the platform. Drill through the bolt holes in the post as far into the platform as you can with a ²⁵⁄₆₄-in. bit. Remove the post and continue to drill into the platform to a depth of 3½ in. Be sure to keep drill straight.

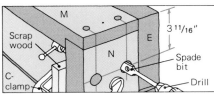

6. Draw lines across the centers of the newly drilled holes to the corners of the platform. Use a combination square to extend these lines around to the other side of each platform corner for 4 in. Draw lines intersecting these lines 3¹¹⁄₁₆ in. from and parallel to each corner edge. Use a ⅞-in. spade bit to drill holes completely through the platform where these lines intersect. When drilling, clamp scrap wood behind beams to keep them from splitting. These new holes will house the nuts and washers that screw onto the bolts.

Erecting the house

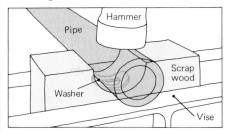

1. Drill a ⅞-in. hole in a piece of scrap wood and cut the wood across the center of the hole. Clamp the wood into a vise with the half-hole facing up. Place a washer that fits a ⅜-in. bolt into the half-hole, hold a piece of pipe over the washer, and hammer the pipe until the washer bends into a curve. Repeat with 11 more washers.
2. Measure the distance between the posts on each side of the platform, and add 2 in. to each measurement to get the lengths for the house rungs (U and V). Cut the rungs.
3. Have two helpers hold up the platform while you put the long center posts (C) into place on it, fitting the dadoes on the posts over the edges of the platform. Fasten these posts into place with 4-in. bolts, flat washers, and nuts. Attach the short center posts (B), using 5½-in. bolts.
4. Use a level to plumb each post in both directions. Straighten the posts if necessary, then level the platform on all four sides by sinking or cutting one or more posts as needed. Position the first corner post (A) and insert the house rungs into their holes in the corner post and adjacent center posts (B and C), tipping the corner post as necessary to fit the rungs in. Slip 6-in. bolts with washers into the corner post.

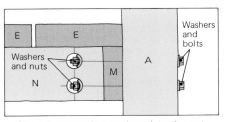

5. Slip a bent washer and nut into the nut holes in the platform and onto the ends of the bolts. Start tightening the nuts with your fingers and finish with a wrench. Plumb the post and level the platform again. Attach the other posts and rungs in the same way.

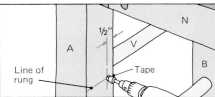

6. Extend the line of each rung onto the adjacent side of the post facing the inside of the house. Mark a point on this line ½ in. from the edge of the post nearest the rung. Drill a ³⁄₁₆-in. shank hole ¹⁵⁄₁₆ in. into the post at this point, holding the drill at a slight angle and pointing toward the edge of the post. (Put tape on the bit to act as a depth gauge.) Countersink the hole. Drill a ⅛-in. pilot hole through the shank hole and into the rung. Drive a 2-in. No. 8 screw into each end of every rung.

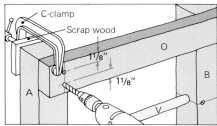

7. Measure the width of the entire house at platform level and cut the roof rails (O) to this length. Clamp the rails into place, making sure that the center posts are at the exact centers of the rails. Hold a piece of scrap wood against the inside of each post, in turn, and drill two ²⁵⁄₆₄-in. bolt holes through each rail and post 1⅛ in. from both the top and bottom of the rail. Fasten the rails to the posts with 5½-in. bolts, washers, and nuts. Remove the clamps.
8. Cut the ridgepoles (F and G) and clamp them into position on the long center posts one at a time, making sure that the distance between the tops of the posts is the same as it is at platform level. Both ridgepoles should extend 16 in. beyond the post on the rope side of the house. Hold a piece of scrap wood behind the ridgepole at each post. Use a ²⁵⁄₆₄-in. bit to drill through the holes in the posts and completely through the ridgepole. Draw a line down the ridgepole along the outside edge of each post, then take the ridgepole down.
9. Drill a ²⁵⁄₆₄-in. bolt hole into each end of each ridgepole 2⅞ in. from the top of the ridgepole and ¾ in. out (toward the end) from the post lines drawn in Step 8.
10. Drill a 1-in. hole for the rope (AA) through each ridgepole 1½ in. from its rope end and 1½ in. from its top.

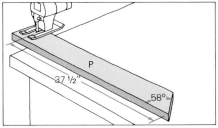

11. Cut the rafters (P) to length by cutting one end of each at a 58° angle and squaring off the other end 37½ in. from the longest point of the angled end.

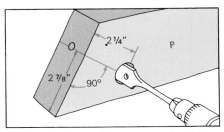

12. Draw a line across the end grain of the angled end of each rafter 2⅞ in. from its longest point. Drill a ²⁵⁄₆₄-in. bolt hole at the center of this line, holding the drill at a 90° angle to the end and drilling to a depth of 2¾ in. Along the same line and 2¼ in. from the angled end, drill a ⅞-in. nut hole through the side of the rafter.

Erecting the house (continued)

13. Fasten the angled ends of the rafters to the ridgepoles with 4-in. bolts, bent washers, and nuts. (Put bolts through the outermost bolt holes in the ridgepoles.)

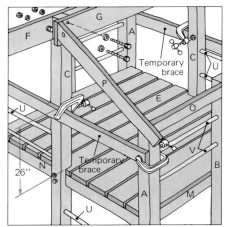

14. Measure the width of the entire house at platform level on the rope and pole sides, cut two temporary braces from scrap 2 x 4's to those measurements, and mark the positions of the center posts (at platform level) on them. Clamp the temporary braces to the posts about 26 in. above the platform with the ends of the braces flush with the outer edges of the corner posts and the center posts at the center post marks. Braces will keep post tops the proper distance apart while you work. Fasten ridepoles with their rafters to the long posts with 5½-in. bolts, washers, and nuts.

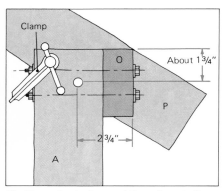

15. Clamp the bottoms of the rafters to the posts flush with the ends of the roof rails (O). Holding a piece of scrap wood behind each post, in turn, use a ⅜-in. spade bit to drill a bolt hole through the rafter and post near the square end of each rafter. The hole should fall between the two bolts in the top of the corner post to which it will be attached and 2¾ in. from the outside edge of the rail. Fasten the bottoms of the rafters to the posts with 5½-in. bolts, washers, and nuts. Remove the clamps and the temporary braces from the structure.

16. Cut the pole base (L) to size and cut a 2-in. hole through its center. Do it by drilling a hole for a saber saw blade, then cutting out the rest of the hole with the saber saw. Fit the bottom of the pole (FF) into the hole and sink the base into the ground so that the top of the pole rests against the long ridgepole 4 in. from its end. Use a level to make sure gym pole is absolutely vertical.

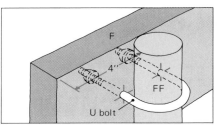

17. Slip a U bolt around the pole and mark where its ends hit the ridgepole. Drill ⅜-in. holes at these marks and then fasten the pole to the ridgepole with the U bolt, washers, and nuts.

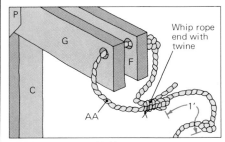

18. Knot the rope (AA) every foot, leaving the top 3 ft. knot free. Pass the top end of the rope through the 1-in. holes in the ridgepoles and knot it to keep it from slipping back through. Whip the loose end at the top to the body of the rope with twine.
19. Follow the instructions in a grommet kit to install grommets in the canvas roof cover (Z) at each of its four corners and at the center of each long edge.
20. Add on the slide and swing assembly, as described in the folliwing steps, then position the cover over the top of the roof. Thread 12-in. lengths of nylon rope (BB) through the grommets and tie them around the ridgepoles and rafters.

Making the slide

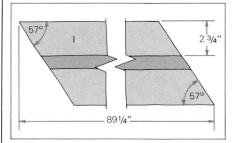

1. Cut the slide rails (I) with a 57° angle at each end so that the ends are parallel. The length of each rail should be 89¼ in. from point to point. Sand the rails thoroughly to guard against splinters. Cut a ¹³/₁₆-in.-wide, ¾-in.-deep dado into the inside face of each rail 2¾ in. from the top of the rail and running along its entire length.
2. Find the width of the slide board (T) by measuring the distance between the posts the slide will be attached to, subtracting the combined thicknesses of the slide rails, and adding 1½ in. (the depth of the dadoes in the rails). Cut board to correct width, square off the bottom, then use a circular saw to cut a 57° bevel into the top edge so that the board is 85⁹/₁₆ in. long on top.

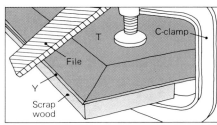

3. Cut the slide covering (Y) ¼ in. larger all around than the slide board. Laminate the covering and slide board with waterproof cement. Use a router to trim the plastic even with the wood. When trimming the beveled edge, clamp wood along its top and trim the plastic from the bottom. File an angle into the top edge of the plastic to match the angle in top of slide board.
4. Slip the slide board into the dadoes in the slide rails and screw it into place from the bottoms of the rails ⅜ in. from the inside edge. (Use three 2½-in. No. 8 screws per side and drill ³/₁₆-in. holes for them.)

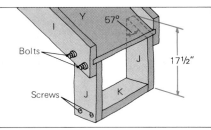

5. Cut each slide foot (J) with one end at a 57° angle and the other squared off 17½ in. from the point in the angled end. (If the ground is uneven, this measurement may vary; clamp the slide into place—see Step 6—and check the measurement before cutting.) Measure the distance between the slide rails and cut the base (K) 3 in. shorter. Fasten the base between the squared ends of the feet with 3½-in. No. 10 screws. (Use two screws for each foot and drill ¹³/₆₄-in. holes for them.) Hold the angled ends of the feet against the lower inside faces of the slide rails and flush with the bottom of the slide. Drill two ²⁵/₆₄-in. bolt holes through each foot and rail. Attach the feet with 3½-in. bolts, washers, and nuts.

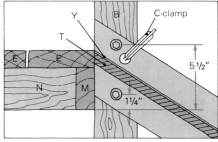

6. Clamp the top of the slide to the insides of the two appropriate house posts so that the plastic is flush with the tops of the platform floorboards. Use a ⅞-in. spade bit to counterbore two ¼-in.-deep holes into each slide rail. Position one hole 1¼ in. from the bottom of the house platform and the other 5½ in. up. Drill ²⁵/₆₄-in. bolt holes through these holes and completely through the posts behind them. Fasten the slide into place with 5-in. bolts, washers, and nuts.

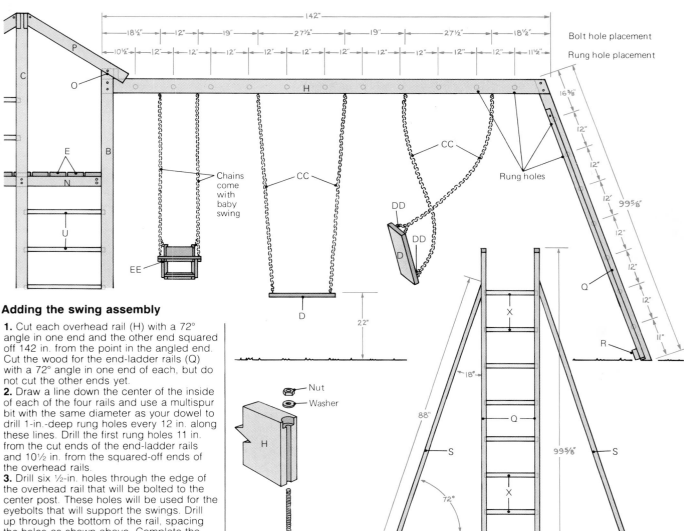

Adding the swing assembly

1. Cut each overhead rail (H) with a 72° angle in one end and the other end squared off 142 in. from the point in the angled end. Cut the wood for the end-ladder rails (Q) with a 72° angle in one end of each, but do not cut the other ends yet.

2. Draw a line down the center of the inside of each of the four rails and use a multispur bit with the same diameter as your dowel to drill 1-in.-deep rung holes every 12 in. along these lines. Drill the first rung holes 11 in. from the cut ends of the end-ladder rails and 10½ in. from the squared-off ends of the overhead rails.

3. Drill six ½-in. holes through the edge of the overhead rail that will be bolted to the center post. These holes will be used for the eyebolts that will support the swings. Drill up through the bottom of the rail, spacing the holes as shown above. Complete the holes by drilling from the top of the rail.

4. Determine the length of the overhead rungs (W) by measuring the distance between the posts the overhead ladder will fit between, subtracting the combined thicknesses of the overhead rails, and adding 2 in. (to allow for the depths of the rung holes). Determine the length of the end-ladder rungs (X) by subtracting combined thicknesses of the end-ladder rails from the length of the overhead rungs. Cut all the rungs to the proper lengths.

5. Drill ³/₁₆-in. shank holes for the rung reinforcement screws through the tops of the overhead rails and at a slight angle through the backs of the end-ladder rails into the dowel holes. Countersink the holes. Insert the rungs into the rung holes. Drill ⅛-in. pilot holes through the shank holes and into the rungs. Put 2-in. No. 8 screws into the end-ladder rungs and 3½-in. No. 8 screws into the overhead rungs.

6. Clamp the overhead ladder into place just under the roof rail (O) on the swing side with the squared ends of the rails flush with the inside edges of the house posts and the opposite ends of the rails propped up with lengths of wood that are clamped on. Make sure that the ladder is perfectly level. Drill ²⁵/₆₄-in. bolt holes through the rails and posts 1⅛ in. from both the top and bottom of each rail. Fasten the overhead ladder into place with 5½-in. bolts, washers, and nuts.

7. Position the end ladder between the ends of the overhead rails with the uncut ladder ends sticking up above the overhead rails and flush with their ends. Cut the ends of the end-ladder rails to make them flush with the tops of the overhead rails. Drill ²⁵/₆₄-in. bolt holes through the overhead and end-ladder rails 1⅛ in. from both the top and bottom of each overhead rail. Fasten the ladders together with 3½-in. bolts, washers, and nuts. Remove the props.

8. Cut the ground support (R) and clamp it to the end ladder at ground level so that the ladder is centered on it. Drill a ²⁵/₆₄-in. bolt hole through each end-ladder rail and the ground support.

9. Cut each of the end-ladder braces (S) with an 18° angle in one end and the other end squared off 88 in. from the point in the angled end. Position the braces with their angled ends against the end-ladder rails and their squared ends overlapping the ends of the ground support. Use a 1-in. spade bit to counterbore a hole ½ in. deep into the top of each brace. Then drill a ²⁵/₆₄-in. hole through this hole and into each end-ladder rail. Mark the ground support to show exactly how the braces fit against it. Take down the braces and support.

10. Using the marks as guides, clamp each end-ladder brace into position over the ground support and drill a ²⁵/₆₄-in. bolt hole through the overlapping brace and ground support 2¼ in. above the bottom of the brace. Cut off the upper corners of the ground support to make them flush with the outer sides of the braces.

11. Fasten the ground support to the end-ladder rails with 5½-in. bolts, washers, and nuts. Fasten the end-ladder braces to the ground support and end-ladder rails with 3½-in. bolts, washers, and nuts.

12. Cut each swing seat (D) to size and drill a ⁹/₃₂-in. hole at each corner. Slip a 2-in. eyebolt into each hole with washers, and fasten it into place with a nut. Use .177 S hooks to connect these eyebolts to the short chains (DD). Connect the loose ends of the two short chains on each side of each swing to a long chain (CC) with more .177 S hooks. Connect the loose ends of the long chains to the 6-in. eyebolts with .250 S hooks. Squeeze all S hooks closed with a vise. Slip the ends of the 6-in. eyebolts with washers through the holes in the overhead rail and fasten them into place with nuts. Attach baby swing (EE) with .250 S hooks and 6-in. eyebolts.

GRANDFATHER CLOCK KIT

Tall case, or grandfather, clocks have graced American homes since colonial times, and they will probably continue to do so far into the future because of their beauty and elegance. You can make your own grandfather clock from a kit for half the cost of buying the same clock fully finished. The mahogany clock shown here is Model No. 110 from the Emperor Clock Company (see p.377 for the address). It is 72 inches high, 16¾ inches wide, and 10 inches deep.

The clock is sold in three sections: the clock-case kit, the clockworks, and a finishing kit. All the materials you will need are supplied except for glue, wood filler,

sandpaper, and glass for the two doors. It is a good idea to have a glazier cut and install the glass for you.

The cabinet parts are all precut, but a few pieces will require trimming and some dadoes may have to be adjusted. Consequently, you will need a few tools that are not included (see below).

When you get the kit, check the parts supplied against the parts lists in the instruction booklets to be sure that nothing has been left out. The clock-case booklet has a separate parts list for each section of the case (the base, waist, and hood) and another for the hardware. The clockworks booklet has its own list.

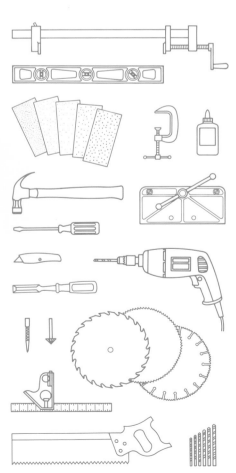

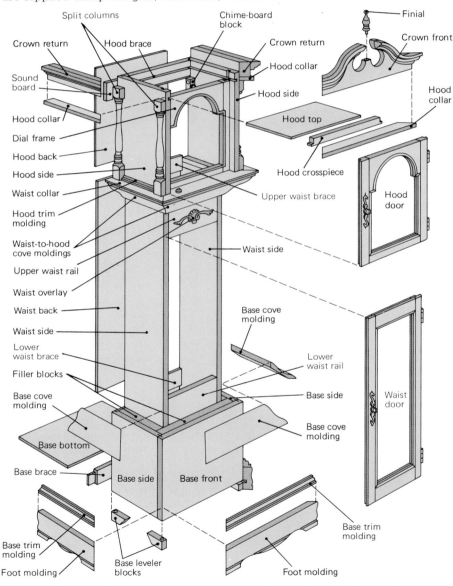

Tools and materials supplied with kit: Precut wood for case, all required hardware, clockworks, finishing kit.
Not supplied with kit: Drill with set of twist bits and countersink. Backsaw. Table saw (optional). Utility knife. Wood chisel, hammer, nail set, Phillips screwdriver,

standard screwdriver. Small vise, several 6″ C-clamps, and 4′ pipe or bar clamps (optional). Level, combination square. Nos. 100, 150, and 220 sandpaper. White glue, wood filler (manufacturer suggests Wood Dough). Glass cut to fit hood and waist doors.

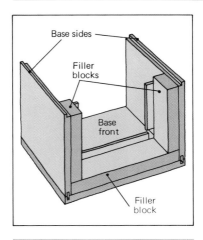

1. Before assembling each section of the clock case (base, waist, and hood), test-fit all pieces and sand them. Use Nos. 100 and 150 paper, then finish with No. 220 paper. Remember to sand all visible interior surfaces. Begin assembly with the base, following the assembly sequence in the manufacturer's instruction booklet. Position base sides and filler blocks on back of base front as shown, trimming blocks to fit if necessary. Set any nails used, fill holes, and sand filler flush with wood.

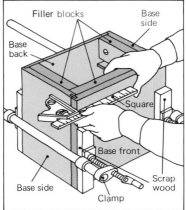

2. Drill ⅛-in. pilot holes through filler blocks into base front and sides, and countersink the holes. Attach the blocks to the base front and sides with glue and 1½-in. screws. Attach the base sides to the base front with glue and clamp nails as instructed. Then put the base back temporarily in place to help you square the unit, and close any gaps by applying pipe or bar clamps if you have them. Check the alignment with a square. Attach the base brace as instructed.

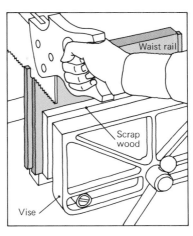

3. Trim waist sides to uniform size if necessary. Check fit of tenons on waist rails in waist sides and trim ends of tenons to get a snug fit. (To trim tenons, clamp each rail in a vise with scrap wood between rail and vise jaws. Saw off most of excess, then saw or chisel off remainder, cutting with grain.) Glue rails in place with waist back temporarily in position to help you square unit. Tack on waist braces and screw down rails as instructed.

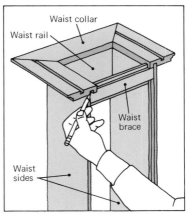

4. Test-fit the preassembled waist collar over the waist by pushing dadoes on underside of collar over top edges of waist. If collar does not fit snugly, adjust the dadoes by removing obstructing wood with a small chisel. (Adjust the rabbets that receive the waist, base, and hood backs in same way if the backs do not fit flush.) Mark and trim the back ends of the waist collar to make them flush with the backs of the waist sides. Remove the waist collar.

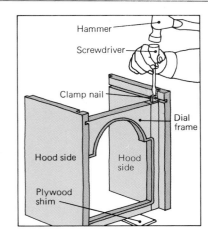

5. Test-fit hood sides in grooves on top of waist collar. Position and square up dial frame. Trim if necessary, then glue together hood sides and dial frame as instructed. Use screwdriver to drive clamp nails home without damaging the machining in tops of hood sides. Attach the hood crosspiece, tack on hood brace, and glue and screw on waist collar as instructed. (Drill ⅛-in. pilot holes for screws and countersink them.)

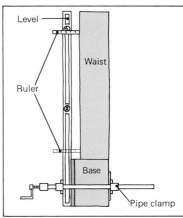

6. Test-fit waist in base. Base sides must be parallel to waist sides, and base front must be parallel to waist rails. Check by clamping a long level to base and measuring distance between level and waist at several points. Adjust by placing shims under waist if necessary. Mark position of waist on base, then glue it in place. Drill ⅛-in. pilot holes, countersink holes, and screw waist to base. Permanently attach waist braces and trim rabbets in waist sides as instructed.

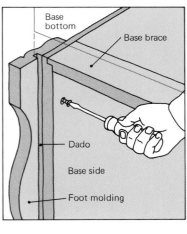

7. Glue and nail on foot moldings, making sure tops of dadoes in moldings are flush with bottoms of base sides so that you can slide the base bottom in place. (When driving nails near the end of a piece, remember to predrill ⅟₁₆-in. pilot holes for nails to keep wood from splitting.) Drill ⅛-in. pilot holes and drive screws through base (from inside) into foot moldings. Slide in base bottom and install base leveler blocks as instructed. Test-fit, trim, and install base trim moldings.

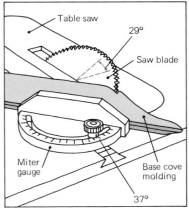

8. Test-fit base cove moldings and trim side ones flush with back of case. If front cove molding must be trimmed, make a compound cut (a miter plus a bevel cut). To do this on a table saw, set the blade at 29° and miter gauge at 37°, then run molding through on large flat section of its back side. Drill ⅟₁₆-in. pilot holes and glue and nail base cove moldings in place.

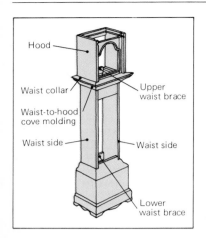

9. Test-fit assembled hood and waist collar on waist sides. Check for alignment and squareness, then glue and screw hood and waist collar to waist as instructed. Remove nails from waist braces, and trim and notch rear of collar to accept upper brace. Attach braces with glue and one ¾-in. screw in each end. Turn case upside down and attach waist-to-hood cove moldings as you did base cove moldings.

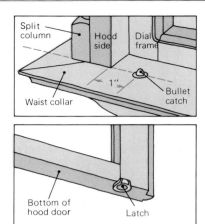

13. Instead of locating bullet catch according to instructions, mark center of bullet on waist collar on a line with and 1 in. from front edge of left hood side. Drill a small hole, then a ⅜-in. hole deep enough to hold bullet housing flush with surface. Mark outline of bullet on bottom edge of hood door. Drill into center of bullet outline and use utility knife to carve out enough waste to hold latch flush. Use a small brass brad to attach latch to bottom of door.

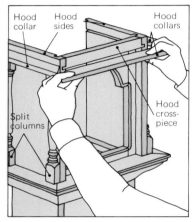

10. Trim split columns to fit, then glue and nail them in place as instructed. Position three-piece hood collar and check miters for neat fit. Trim excess from back ends of collar sides. Glue and nail collar in place and clamp until glue dries. Position crown front and crown returns and check fit of miters. Trim off excess from back ends of returns. Glue and screw crown front and returns in place as instructed.

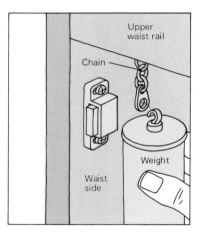

14. Remove doors and their hardware. Attach overlay to upper waist rail with glue and brads. Push plastic inserts for levelers into holes in base leveler blocks. Screw levelers into inserts. Install clock movement as instructed. Screw chimes to sound board and attach sound board to chime-board blocks in clock case. Install weights and pendulum. Remove hood top and brace to adjust chime hammers with small pliers. Adjust levelers to make clock case plumb.

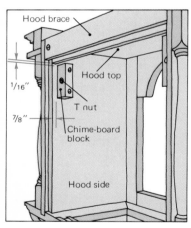

11. Insert hood top and screw in, but do not glue, hood brace. Cut hood trim moldings to fit between front and rear columns. Glue and tack moldings in place. Install T nuts in single holes in backs of chime-board blocks. Using remaining predrilled holes, screw, but do not glue, blocks in place ⅞ in. from shoulders of rabbets on hood sides and 1/16 in. below front edge of bottom of hood brace. Insert finial into hole in crown front.

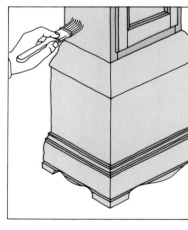

15. After a day or so, remove chimes, movement, weights, and pendulum. Set any nails not yet set and fill all nail holes and cracks. Give case a final sanding. Wipe away all dust and apply stain, then varnish interior and exterior of case according to directions on container. Let varnish dry thoroughly. Take doors to glazier and have him install glass, or install it yourself according to instructions in clock-case booklet.

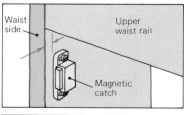

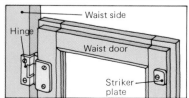

12. Test-fit and trim hood and waist doors. Install door pulls and their backplates. Attach doors to case with hinges as instructed. Attach magnetic catches to inside face of left waist side 7/16 in. from front edge of side with screws positioned in centers of slots in catches. Place striker plates on magnets and press door firmly against them to mark their locations. Install the plates over marks in door. Adjust magnet positions to engage striker plates.

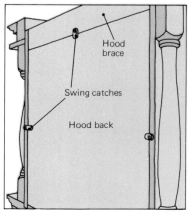

16. Place clock in its permanent location and readjust levelers so that both front and sides of clock are plumb. Put the doors and their hardware and the movement, chimes, weights, and pendulum back in place. Adjust moon dial disc, set clock, and start it as instructed. Attach base back and waist back with brads. Attach hood back with swing catches.

LOW BED AND TRUNDLE BED KITS

As in earlier times, today's bedrooms may be just a bit too small to accommodate two beds—especially when the second bed is needed only occasionally. This low bed and its accompanying trundle bed are great space savers in such a situation. They come in two separate kits from Cohasset Colonials.

The 19th-century original of the low bed, owned by New York's Metropolitan Museum of Art, has holes in all the rails for a woven rope mattress, but these holes are copied in the kit's footrail only. The rest of the underpinnings, as well as the dimensions of this reproduction, have been altered to hold a modern box spring and mattress. The low bed is available in both twin and full sizes, measuring overall 44 x 80 inches and 59 x 80 inches, respectively. For a modest extra charge you can get either one 6 inches longer. The smaller trundle bed (34 x 74½ inches) rolls on hard maple rollers and fits beneath the low bed when not in use. You can order a cloth-covered foam mattress to fit the trundle bed from Cohasset Colonials or buy a piece of foam rubber and cover it yourself.

The kits contain all the necessary hardware. All you do is glue a few joints, insert screws and bolts in predrilled holes, and sand and finish the wood. If you have a bar or pipe clamp, use it when installing the panels in the bottom of the trundle bed instead of the rope-and-stick tourniquet suggested in the instructions.

When you open the kits, check for missing parts and inspect each piece of wood carefully. The insides of the mortises may still contain bits of wood left when the mortises were bored out. Use a chisel to remove these chips and to ensure that the corners of the mortises are perfectly square; otherwise, the tenons will not fit properly.

Sand the ends of the tenons so that they will slide smoothly into the mortises. Test-fit all parts before gluing, then take everything apart and sand any tenons where the fit is tight (remember that the glue needs a little space). The edges of the headboard have been coated with a protective sealer; sand this off, first with medium sandpaper, then fine, so that the edges will take the stain.

Finishing: The stain included in the kits—a blend of boiled linseed oil, driers, and Gilsonite—may be all you need. Test it on the underside of a part; if it is not dark enough, add a coat of Stain Tone, a product you must order separately. If you want a water-resistant finish, add a coat of another product called Clear Coat. This is a "long oil" varnish, which is flexible when dry, allowing the wood to shrink or expand with changes in humidity.

Parts list for low bed (dimensions below are for a twin-size bed)

Part	Name	Quantity	Thickness	Width	Length	Material
A	Footpost	2	2⅝"	2⅝"	24½"	Maple
B	Headpost	2	2⅝"	2⅝"	33"	Maple
C	Footrail	1	2⅝"	2⅝"	42¼" ✷	Maple
D	Headrail	1	1½"	3½"	42¼" ✷	Laminated maple
E	Headboard	1	⅝"	11¾"	40¾" ✷	Pine
F	Side rail	2	1½"	3½"	76¾"	Laminated maple
G	Slat	1	¾"	1½"	36¼" ✷	Pine

✷ For a full-size bed, dimension is 15" longer.

Parts list for trundle bed

Part	Name	Quantity	Thickness	Width	Length	Material
A	Post	4	2⅝"	2⅝"	8¾"	Maple
B	End rail	2	1½"	3½"	31½"	Laminated maple
C	Side rail	2	1½"	3½"	69¾"	Laminated maple
D	Bottom panel	2	⅜"	29¾"	27½"	Birch plywood
E	Bottom panel	1	⅜"	29¾"	13¾"	Birch plywood

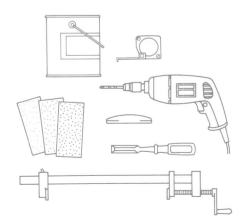

Tools and materials for low bed supplied with kit: Wood parts (see above). Wrench. Glue, medium and fine sandpaper, stain. Four large bolts and nuts, six angle irons, two wing nuts and bolts, 12 flathead wood screws.
Not supplied with kit: Orbital sander or sanding block. Steel tape rule, ½" or ⅝" chisel. Clear Coat or carnauba wax. Wood stabilizer (optional), Stain Tone (optional). Soft cloths.

Tools and materials for trundle bed supplied with kit: Wood parts (see above). Rope. Wrench. Glue, medium and fine sandpaper, stain. Four bolts and nuts, 30 flathead wood screws.
Not supplied with kit: Orbital sander or sanding block. Steel tape rule, ½" or ⅝" chisel. Awl or drill and ⅛" bit. A 4' bar or pipe clamp (optional). Clear Coat or carnauba wax. Wood stabilizer (optional), Stain Tone (optional). Soft cloths.

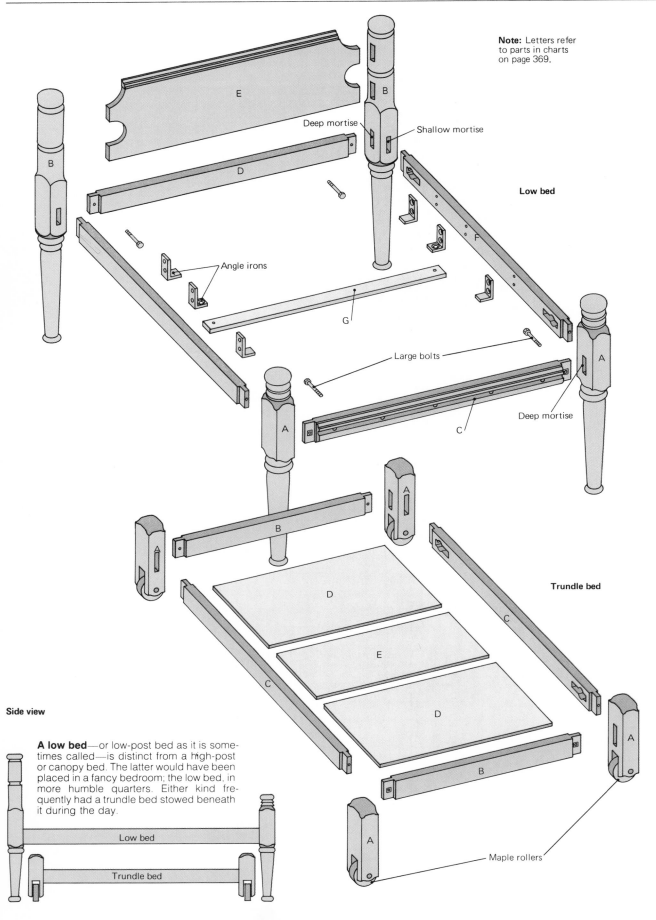

Note: Letters refer to parts in charts on page 369.

Deep mortise

Shallow mortise

Low bed

Angle irons

G

Large bolts

A

Deep mortise

C

B

A

Trundle bed

D

E

C

C

D

B

A

A

Side view

A low bed—or low-post bed as it is sometimes called—is distinct from a high-post or canopy bed. The latter would have been placed in a fancy bedroom; the low bed, in more humble quarters. Either kind frequently had a trundle bed stowed beneath it during the day.

Low bed

Trundle bed

A

Maple rollers

Low bed

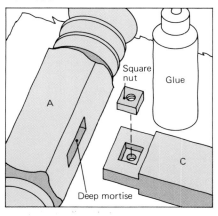

1. Spread newspaper on floor to catch any glue that may drip. Lay footposts (A) on paper with shallow mortises facing down, deep mortises facing each other. Spread a thin coat of glue on walls of deep mortises and on sides of tenons (not on ends). Fit square nuts into holes in tenons of footrail (C) and push tenons into deep mortises.

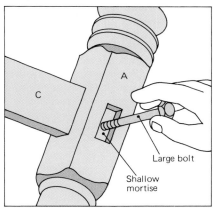

2. Turn the assembly over. Insert large bolts in the shallow mortises, and screw bolts into the nuts temporarily. Measure the distance between posts at the tops and bottoms; if it is the same, posts are parallel. Adjust posts if distance is not the same. Allow glue to dry at least 4 hr. before taking out the bolts, which will be reinserted in Step 5.

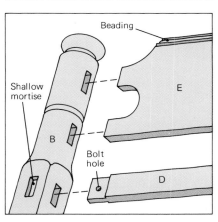

3. Follow the same method in assembling the headposts (B), headrail (D), and headboard (E). Make sure that the beading located on top of the headboard faces the same direction as the shallow mortises in the headposts.

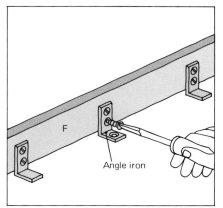

4. The side rails (F) have predrilled holes for attaching the six angle irons. Screw a three-holed angle iron to the center of each side rail and screw remaining angle irons to each side of center ones. Angle irons will support box spring. (The slat, installed in Step 6, prevents the side rails from twisting from the weight of the bedding.)

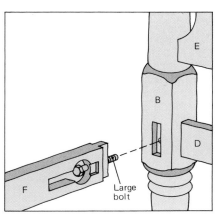

5. Lean headboard assembly against wall. Fit the side rails into the shallow mortises, but do not glue them. Insert large bolts through slots in the side rails into the nuts. Tighten the bolts with the wrench provided in the kit until the shoulders of the tenons fit against the posts. Attach the foot assembly in the same manner.

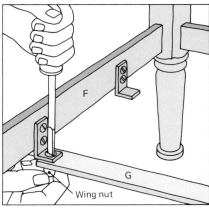

6. Place the slat (G) under center angle irons, and bolt slat in place, using wing nuts and bolts. Sand wood surfaces lightly with fine sandpaper to remove glue residue and dirt. Round all edges with medium and fine sandpaper. Using soft cloths, apply stain in the same direction as the grain. After 5 min. wipe off the excess.

Trundle bed

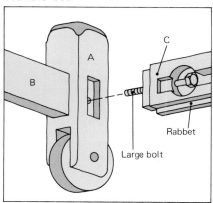

1. The end rails (B) and side rails (C) of the trundle bed are joined to the posts (A) in the same way as those of the low bed (Steps 1–2 and 5 above). The rabbets in the edges of the side rails should face inward and downward. Do not glue the side rails into the posts but simply bolt them as you did in the low bed.

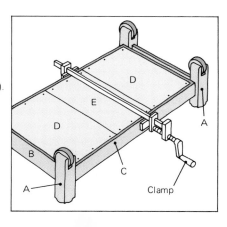

2. Place frame on floor with rollers up. Spread a bead of glue on rabbets. Place panels (D and E) in rabbets with countersunk parts of predrilled holes facing up. Hold side rails parallel with a 4-ft. bar or pipe clamp. Make starter holes in side rails through predrilled holes in plywood with an awl or drill and ⅛-in. twist bit. Insert wood screws.

371

BUTLER'S TABLE KIT

Classic simplicity marks this butler's table kit from the Heath Company (see p.377 for address). The table is made of solid mahogany with a top of inlaid veneer. The four hinged leaves can lie flat or be folded upward. In former times a servant carried the top part as a tray and placed it on a stand in the drawing room. Today most butler trays are firmly anchored to their stands, as this one is.

The table measures 43⅞ inches long, 33¹⁵⁄₁₆ inches wide, and 17 inches high when the leaves are flat. When the leaves are folded upward, the table measures 34 inches long and 24¼ inches wide. The owner's manual and work sheets that accompany the kit give detailed instructions on how to assemble the table. The work sheets can be tacked to a wall for quick referral. Putting the parts together will pose no difficulty for anyone who has basic cabinetry skills.

You will need a clean work area about 5 feet x 10 feet and a raised, level work surface slightly larger than a card table;

do not use a card table, however, unless it is a very steady one. Spread wax paper on the work surface to protect it from glue and stains, and cover the floor with newspaper or plastic sheets.

The mortises and tenons that join the legs and rails are precut, as are the notches for the hinges that hold the leaves. Once you have determined that the joints fit snugly (Step 1) and that the notches are level and the correct depth (Step 3), all that remains is to glue the assembly, mark and drill holes for the screws, and sand and finish the wood.

The paste stain and clear paste varnish that come with the kit are easy to apply. As with any finish, its final appearance is to a great extent the result of the care taken in sanding the wood. Sanding instructions are given in the work sheets. It is best to do the sanding, staining, and varnishing before attaching the leaves to the table top so that you can reach all surfaces. Use turpentine or baby oil to clean the finishing materials from your hands.

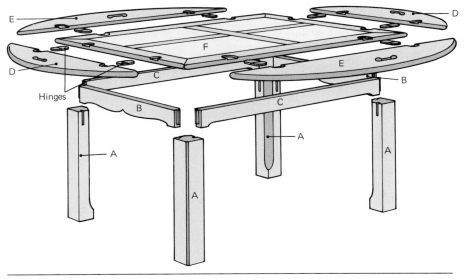

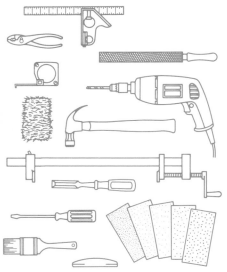

Parts list

Part	Name	Quantity	Thickness	Width	Length	Material
A	Leg	4	2¼″	2¼″	16¼″	Mahogany
B	Short rail	2	¾″	3¼″	16¾″	Mahogany
C	Long rail	2	¾″	3¼″	26¾″	Mahogany
D	Short leaf	2	¾″	5⅝″	22¾″	Mahogany
E	Long leaf	2	¾″	5¾″	32½″	Mahogany
F	Top	1	¾″	22¾″	32½″	Inlaid mahogany veneer

Tools and materials supplied with kit:
Wood parts (see above). Eight hinges, fifty ⅝″ No. 5 brass flathead wood screws, eight 1¾″ No. 8 flathead wood screws. Depth gauge for drill, ⁵⁄₆₄″ and ³⁄₃₂″ bits. Scribe (nail). Glue, Nos. 150, 220, and 280 sandpaper. Paste wood stain, clear paste varnish. Owner's manual and work sheets.
Not supplied with kit: Electric or hand drill. Standard screwdriver with ¼″ blade, No. 1

or No. 2 Phillips screwdriver. Hammer, pliers. Two 3′ bar or pipe clamps or one web clamp. Combination square, steel tape rule. Bevel-edged chisel, rasp. Sanding block or straight-line electric sander, 0000 steel wool. Lint-free cloths. Tack cloth or vacuum cleaner with extension tool. Paste filler, paintbrush, and rough cloths such as burlap (optional). Turpentine or baby oil.

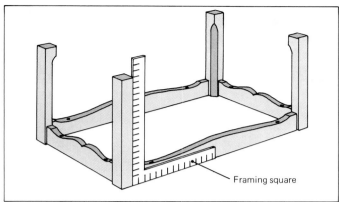

Framing square

1. Assemble the parts without glue to make sure that the joints fit and that all the parts are square. Use a combination or framing square to check that the legs are perpendicular to the table top. Also measure the distances between legs at several points along their lengths—these distances should be the same. During this trial run practice the clamping arrangement described in Step 2. If you are using bar or pipe clamps, prepare pieces of scrap wood and tape them to the jaws of the clamps to protect the mahogany.

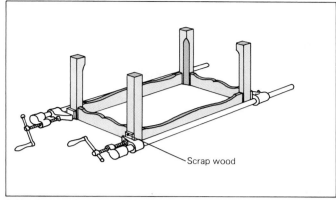

Scrap wood

2. Use bar or pipe clamps to help align the legs. Then glue and clamp the long rails into the legs as directed in the work sheets. To hold the assembly while the glue dries, you can fit the short rails into their mortises without glue. As soon as the clamps are on (do not overtighten them), check that the parts are square as you did in the trial run. Adjust parts that are not square with your hands or by shifting clamps. You have about 10 min. before the glue sets. After several hours glue short rails into their mortises.

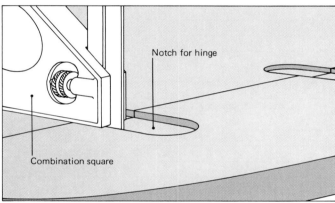

Notch for hinge

Combination square

3. Hinges must sit flush with the table top and leaves, and their bottoms must be level (except for the parts cut to receive the hinge knuckles). Test-fit the hinges; if bottoms seem irregular, extend the blade of the combination square to the depth of each notch and move blade across notch. Resistance indicates a high spot. Chisel such spots level. If a hinge sits lower than the table top or leaf, place a thin shim of cardboard beneath it to bring it to the required level. Do this before drilling screw holes and finishing wood.

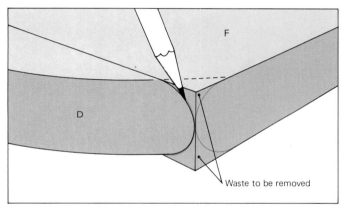

F

D

Waste to be removed

4. To round the table-top corners to match the contours of the leaves, mark the outlines of the leaves on the table top. Use a rasp for fast removal of wood. Hold the rasp at a 45° angle to the wood with the rasp's flat side against the wood. Move the rasp back and forth, changing the angle frequently so that you cut a series of narrow, flat areas that give the appearance of being rounded. When you have cut almost to the marked line, switch to No. 150 sandpaper, and do the final rounding and smoothing.

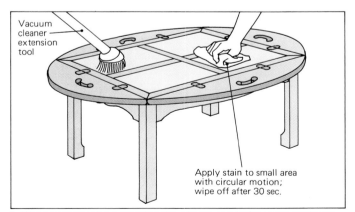

Vacuum cleaner extension tool

Apply stain to small area with circular motion; wipe off after 30 sec.

5. When you are done sanding the pieces but before you apply the finish, remove dust from surfaces with the extension tool of a vacuum cleaner, or wipe the surfaces with a tack cloth, which you can buy in a hardware store. (Keep the cloth in a covered jar so it does not dry out.) The paste stain and varnish supplied with the kit give the wood a natural look. One coat of stain is sufficient, but apply several coats of varnish to protect the table from stains and wet glasses. Rub table with 0000 steel wool between coats.

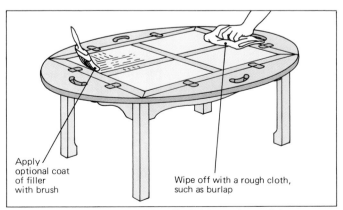

Apply optional coat of filler with brush

Wipe off with a rough cloth, such as burlap

6. If you want a shinier, more mirrorlike finish, apply an oil-base paste wood filler before staining the wood. Test the filler on the bottom of the table first to be sure it will accept stain. As purchased, the filler will be too thick; so thin it with turpentine to the consistency of thick paint. Then brush it on, first across the grain, then with the grain. When it has lost its shiny look (10–15 min.), wipe off the filler, using a rough cloth such as burlap. Again, wipe across the grain first, then with the grain. Stain and varnish as indicated in Step 5.

CHEST OF DRAWERS KIT

It is beyond the skill of most home carpenters to reproduce the intricate carving and meticulous joinery that distinguish the Chippendale block-front chest of drawers, built sometime between 1760 and 1780, that is on display at the Henry Ford Museum in Dearborn, Michigan. With a kit from the Bartley Collection, however, anyone with a working knowledge of basic carpentry can assemble a copy of this fine piece, either in Honduras mahogany or in Pennsylvania cherry.

The kit comes in three sections, shipped at intervals of about a week. Each includes assembly instructions and helpful drawings. Section 1 (A–K) is for the case, Section 2 (AA–QQ) is for the drawers, and Section 3 (RR–VV) is for the legs. All parts are precut and shaped, including mortise-and-tenon joints, tongues and grooves, dovetails, and miters. Screws, nails, and other necessary hardware are included, as are glue, finishing materials, and two band clamps.

Parts list for Section 1

Part	Name	Quantity	Thickness	Width	Length	Material
A	Top	1	³⁄₄″	21″	36″	Mahogany or cherry
B	Side	2	³⁄₄″	19¼″	24″	Mahogany or cherry
C	Front base rail	1	1½″	2½″	33⅝″	Mahogany or cherry
D	Side base rail	2	1½″	2½″	20¹⁄₃₂″	Mahogany or cherry
E	Back base rail	1	1½″	1½″	29⅛″	Mahogany or cherry
F	Front rail	3	³⁄₄″	2¾″	31⁵⁄₁₆″	Mahogany or cherry
G	Short frame rail	9	³⁄₄″	1¾″	15¹³⁄₁₆″	Mahogany or cherry
H	Back rail	3	³⁄₄″	1½″	31⁵⁄₁₆″	Mahogany or cherry
I	Lower back panel	1	¼″	19⅞″	31¹⁄₁₆″	Lauan plywood
J	Upper back panel	1	¼″	4¹¹⁄₁₆″	31¹⁄₁₆″	Lauan plywood
K	Corner block	2	³⁄₄″	1½″	1½″	Mahogany or cherry

Parts list for Section 2

Part	Name	Quantity	Thickness	Width	Length	Material
AA	Top drawer front	1	1⅞″	3⅞″	30¼″	Mahogany or cherry
BB	Top drawer side	2	⁷⁄₁₆″	3¹³⁄₁₆″	16⅛″	Oak
CC	Top drawer back	1	⁷⁄₁₆″	3¹³⁄₁₆″	29½″	Mahogany or cherry
DD	2nd drawer front	1	1⅞″	4⅝″	30¼″	Mahogany or cherry
EE	2nd drawer side	2	⁷⁄₁₆″	4⁹⁄₁₆″	16⅛″	Oak
FF	2nd drawer back	1	⁷⁄₁₆″	4⁹⁄₁₆″	29½″	Mahogany or cherry
GG	3rd drawer front	1	1⅞″	5⅝″	30¼″	Mahogany or cherry
HH	3rd drawer side	2	⁷⁄₁₆″	5⁹⁄₁₆″	16⅛″	Oak
II	3rd drawer back	1	⁷⁄₁₆″	5⁹⁄₁₆″	29½″	Mahogany or cherry
JJ	Bottom drawer front	1	1⅞″	6¹¹⁄₁₆″	30¼″	Mahogany or cherry
KK	Bottom drawer side	2	⁷⁄₁₆″	6⁹⁄₁₆″	16⅛	Oak
LL	Bottom drawer back	1	⁷⁄₁₆″	6⁹⁄₁₆″	29½″	Mahogany or cherry
MM	Drawer bottom	4	¼″	15⅞″	29″	Oak plywood
NN	Rub blocks	40	½″	½″	2″	Mahogany or cherry
OO	Guide track	4	½″	2″	16³⁄₁₆″	Mahogany or cherry
PP	Guide strip	4	⅜″	¹¹⁄₁₆″	16½″	Mahogany or cherry
QQ	Base cleat	1	³⁄₄″	³⁄₄″	3½″	Mahogany or cherry

Parts list for Section 3

Part	Name	Quantity	Thickness	Width	Length	Material
RR	Leg front	2	1⅜″	5³⁄₁₆″	6⅞″	Mahogany or cherry
SS	Leg side	6	³⁄₄″	5³⁄₁₆″	6⅞″	Mahogany or cherry
TT	Leg cleat	8	³⁄₄″	³⁄₄″	3″	Mahogany or cherry
UU	Base trim	2	1⅜″	1½″	9¼″	Mahogany or cherry
VV	Drawer stop	8	³⁄₄″	³⁄₄″	1½″	Mahogany or cherry

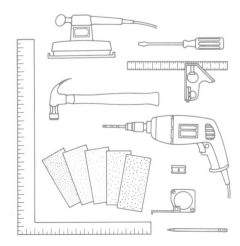

Tools and materials supplied with kit:
Wood parts (see above). A ⁷⁄₆₄″ twist bit with stop. Two band clamps. Eight brass drawer pulls, four brass key escutcheons. Sixteen ⅝″ No. 7 flathead wood screws, fifty-four 1¼″ and four 1¾″ No. 8 flathead wood screws. Twelve ⅝″ No. 9 clamp nails, twenty-two ¾″ wire nails. Eight ½″ drawer-guide tacks. Nos. 120 and 150 sandpaper. Glue. Two finishing kits.
Not supplied with kit: Drill. Orbital sander or sanding block. Steel tape rule, combination square, framing square, pencil. Razor blade. Hammer, screwdriver. No. 80 sandpaper. Soft cloths. Four 4′ bar or pipe clamps (optional instead of band clamps).

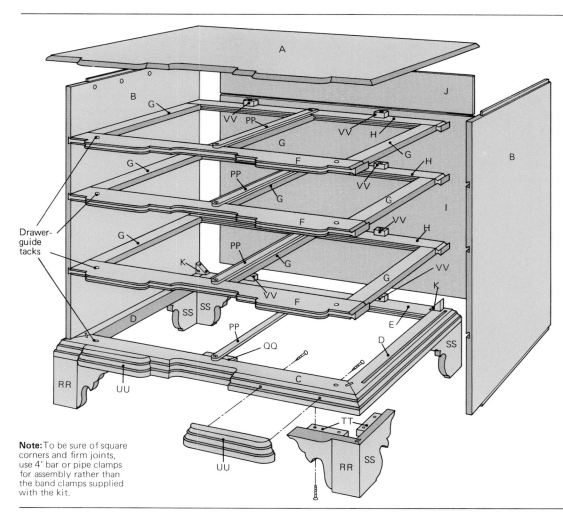

Exploded view shows how parts fit together. Before joining with glue, assemble each section dry to be sure no pieces are missing and all fit properly. Use Nos. 80 and 120 sandpaper to make adjustments. Then disassemble and sand all external surfaces with Nos. 120 and 150 paper, using orbital sander or sanding block on flat surfaces. During final assembly allow excess glue to dry, then remove with razor blade and sand well—glue that is left on or merely wiped off will cause light spots in finish. Two finishing kits are provided, each containing ½ pt. paste stain, ½ pt. paste varnish, a special filler, and sandpaper. You may choose one of eight different stains, ranging from rich cherry, through several tones of mahogany, to deep walnut. After assembly, fill any spaces, then sand once again with No. 150 paper. Stain and varnish according to instructions in the finishing kits.

Drawer-guide tacks

Note: To be sure of square corners and firm joints, use 4' bar or pipe clamps for assembly rather than the band clamps supplied with the kit.

Assembling the drawers

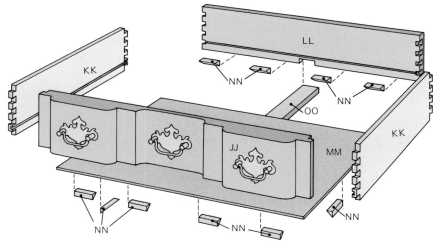

Drawers are included in Section 2. Check dovetail joints immediately; sand tails, if needed, for snug but not tight fit. To assemble bottom drawer (shown), glue dovetails of one side (KK) into slots of front and back (JJ and LL). Slide bottom (MM) into its grooves without glue, then glue the other side (KK) in place. Measure drawer diagonally in both directions to ensure squareness (the measurements should match), and apply clamps. Assemble the other three drawers in the same way.

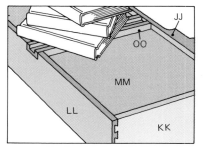

1. After glue is dry, turn drawers upside down and glue tenons of guide tracks (OO) into mortises of drawer fronts (AA, DD, GG, and JJ); center and glue backs of guide tracks in notches of drawer backs (CC, FF, II, and LL). Place weights, such as books, on guide tracks until glue dries.

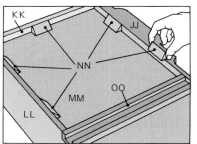

2. To attach rub blocks (NN), apply glue to the two squared surfaces of each, and press against drawer bottom (MM) and adjoining surface, using a rubbing motion to force out excess glue. Each drawer receives four blocks against front and back and one against each side.

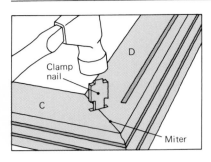

1. Join the front corners of base one at a time by applying glue to mitered end of a side base rail (D) and one end of front base rail (C). Then drive clamp nails into top and bottom of kerf that crosses each miter. Use framing square to be sure that both corners are true.

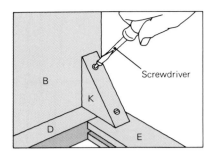

7. Drill ⁷⁄₆₄-in. pilot holes and secure corner blocks (K) to sides (B) with 1¼-in. No. 8 screws. Secure top (A) with glue in front 2 in. of joint and with 1¼-in. No. 8 screws. Then drill pilot holes up through countersunk holes in side base rails (D) and drive 1¼-in. No. 8 screws into sides.

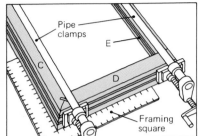

2. Glue tenons on ends of back base rail (E) into mortises of side base rails (D) so that groove in back base rail faces forward and rabbeted edge is up. Square up base structure and apply bar or pipe clamps from side to side, using scrap wood to protect surfaces of side base rails.

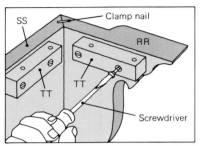

8. To assemble front legs, glue miters of leg fronts (RR) and leg sides (SS), and drive clamp nails into kerfs at tops and bottoms. Assemble rear legs the same way, using leg sides (SS) only. Glue leg cleats (TT) inside legs, ¹⁄₃₂ in. from top edges, and secure cleats with 1¼-in. No. 8 screws.

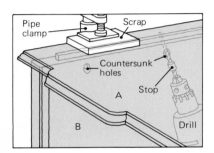

3. Insert tongues of sides (B) into grooves of side base rails (D) and top (A) without glue; square up and apply clamps from top to base. Drill ⁷⁄₆₄-in. holes into top through countersunk holes in sides, using plastic stop in kit to be sure bit does not go through top.

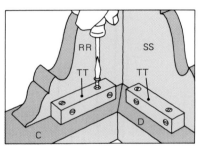

9. Turn chest upside down and position legs at corners, set ¹⁄₁₆ in. back from edges. Drill ⁷⁄₆₄-in. pilot holes into base through countersunk holes in leg cleats (TT). To secure each leg, apply glue to top edge and drive 1¼-in. No. 8 screws through cleats only until joint is firm.

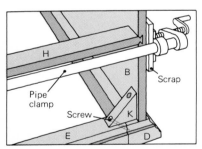

4. Place corner blocks (K) against sides (B) ³⁄₁₆ in. from rabbet. Drill ⁷⁄₆₄-in. pilot holes into back base rail (E) through countersunk holes in blocks, and drive in 1¼-in. No. 8 screws. Glue dovetails of back rails (H) into slots in sides. Transfer clamps to back, keeping structure square.

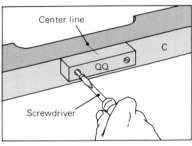

10. Glue and screw base cleat (QQ) to back of front base rail (C), centered and flush at the top, with 1¼-in. No. 8 screws. Push drawer-guide tacks into front rails (C and F) so that drawer sides will ride on them. Position drawers so that their fronts are flush and centered.

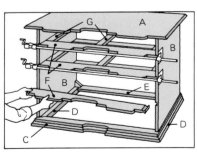

5. Insert dovetails of all front rails (F) partway into slots in sides (B). Then remove one front rail at a time to glue three short frame rails (G) in place, centering the middle one. Secure each front rail with glue and clamp it before going on to the next (see Step 6, below).

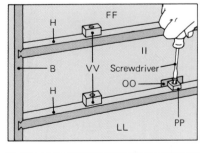

11. Slide guide strips (PP) into guide tracks (OO) from the back without pushing drawers forward; position drawer stops (VV). Secure stops and backs of guide strips with ⅝-in. No. 7 screws. Remove drawers carefully and secure fronts of guide strips with No. 7 screws.

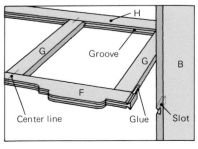

6. To secure front rails (F), apply glue to slots in sides (B) and a little glue to the front 2 in. of the outer short frame rails (G). Insert dovetails in slots so all front surfaces are flush, while guiding tenons at rear of short frame rails—without glue—into grooves in back rails (H).

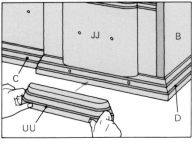

12. Put bottom drawer back in place and mark positions of base trim (UU) to align with curvature of drawer front (JJ). Secure trim with glue and 1¾-in. screws. Attach panels (I and J) with glue and wire nails. Sand and finish unit, following instructions in kit, and attach drawer hardware.

WHERE-TO-BUY-IT GUIDE

Most of the tools and materials used to build the projects in this book are readily available across the nation. They were supplied by the firms listed on page 5 or were purchased at local hardware stores, lumberyards, or home centers. In a few cases, it was necessary to use unusual tools and materials that may be difficult to obtain. Offered as a service to our readers, the list below contains the names and addresses of companies that supplied these hard-to-find tools and materials. This list in no way constitutes a testimonial or recommendation by Reader's Digest.

You may be able to buy similar items at lower cost elsewhere. Your best bet is to attempt to purchase such items locally. Remember that many stores can order items that they do not have in stock from a nearby distributor.

Lumberyards often specialize in certain types of wood. A yard that sells mostly building materials may not be interested in special-ordering a small amount of hardwood or veneered plywood, while a yard that deals in hardwood might not be the best place to shop for green boards to use as cement forms.

Phone a few lumberyards to get an idea of the products they specialize in.

If you cannot obtain an item locally, you can contact one of the sources listed below. Some are dealers who are willing to accept mail orders. Others are manufacturers, distributors, or importers who should be able to supply the address of a retail outlet near you. Many have mail-order catalogs that are available for a few dollars. Reader's Digest cannot guarantee the quality or availability of any item ordered from the companies listed below.

PAGE(S)	DESCRIPTION/SOURCE
52	**Dowel centers:** Garrett Wade Co., Inc. 161 Ave. of the Americas New York, N.Y. 10013
72	**Dovetail saw:** Garrett Wade Co., Inc. 161 Ave. of the Americas New York, N.Y. 10013
80, 94	**Rabbet plane:** Garrett Wade Co., Inc. 161 Ave. of the Americas New York, N.Y. 10013
100, 206	**Veneer saw:** Garrett Wade Co., Inc. 161 Ave. of the Americas New York, N.Y. 10013
128	**Casters:** Bassick Div. Stewart-Warner Corp. 960 Atlantic Ave. Bridgeport, Conn. 06602
128	**Rack-Sack garbage bag holder:** Extrufix P.O. Box 366 Wilmington, N.C. 28402
128	**D81-6 Wilsonart laminate:** Ralph Wilson Plastics Co. Div. of Wilsonart 600 S. General Bruce Dr. Temple, Tex. 76501
128, 198, 224	**Pilasters and shelf supports:** Grant Hardware Co. Div. of Buildex, Inc. 10 High St. West Nyack, N.Y. 10994
132, 156, 214, 234	**Electronic stud finder:** The Brookstone Co. 127 Vose Farm Rd. Peterborough, N.H. 03458
139, 150	**Makita model 1100 portable power plane:** Fine Tools Shops 20 Backus Ave. Danbury, Conn. 06810

PAGE(S)	DESCRIPTION/SOURCE
150	**Dead-blow hammer:** Garrett Wade Co., Inc. 161 Ave. of the Americas New York, N.Y. 10013
166	**Metal drawer pulls:** Amerock Corp. 4000 Auburn St. Rockford, Ill. 61101
176	**Accent Art stenciling kit (Pennsylvania Dutch design):** Hunt Mfg. Co. 1405 Locust St. Philadelphia, Pa. 19102
180, 185	**Walnut drawer pulls:** Simon's Hardware, Inc. 421 Third Ave. New York, N.Y. 10016
180, 185, 206	**Grant slides and Grass hinges:** Dave Sanders Hardware 107 Bowery New York, N.Y. 10002 or Simon's Hardware, Inc. 421 Third Ave. New York, N.Y. 10016
180, 194, 214	**Doweling jig:** Garrett Wade Co., Inc. 161 Ave. of the Americas New York, N.Y. 10013
194	**Vises and bench dogs:** Garrett Wade Co., Inc. 161 Ave. of the Americas New York, N.Y. 10013
198	**Selby hardware:** Albert Constantine & Son, Inc. 2050 Eastchester Rd. Bronx, N.Y. 10461
198, 206	**Multispur and Forstner bits:** Garrett Wade Co., Inc. 161 Ave. of the Americas New York, N.Y. 10013
214, 242	**Corner clamps:** Garrett Wade Co., Inc. 161 Ave. of the Americas New York, N.Y. 10013

PAGE(S)	DESCRIPTION/SOURCE
228	**Heatilator Advantage fireplace:** Heatilator, Inc. Div. of HON Industries 1915 West Saunders Rd. Mt. Pleasant, Iowa 52641
234	**Shenandoah FP-S freestanding fireplace:** Shenandoah Mfg. Co., Inc. P.O. Box 839 Harrisburg, Va. 22801
258	**SAR (super-abrasion-resistant) Lucite:** E.I. du Pont de Nemours & Co. 1007 Market St. Wilmington, Del. 19898
258	**Natural Desert Shade 4" x 8" quarry tiles:** American Olean Tile 1000 Cannon Ave. Lansdale, Pa. 19446
258	**Surpoxy 111 epoxy mortar and grout:** L & M Surco Mfg., Inc. P.O. Box 105 South River, N.J. 08882
258	**Kitchen exhaust fan No. 9870:** Sears, Roebuck and Co. Sears Tower Chicago, Ill. 60684
258	**Tongue-and-groove redwood paneling:** California Redwood Assn. 1 Lombard St. San Francisco, Calif. 94111
294	**Adhesive syringe:** Garrett Wade Co., Inc. 161 Ave. of the Americas New York, N.Y. 10013
323, 328	**Stained-glass tools and supplies:** Glass Masters Guild 621 Ave. of the Americas New York, N.Y. 10013 or S.A. Bendheim Co., Inc. 122 Hudson St. New York, N.Y. 10013

PAGE(S)	DESCRIPTION/SOURCE
334	**Metal jewelry tools and supplies:** Allcraft Tool & Supply Co., Inc. 100 Frank Rd. Hicksville, N.Y. 11801
344	**Brick paper:** Town of Yorktown Museum 1974 Commerce St. Yorktown Heights, N.Y. 10598
366	**Grandfather clock kit:** Emperor Clock Co. Emperor Industrial Pk. Fairhope, Ala. 36532
369	**Low bed and trundle bed kits:** Cohasset Colonials 603 JX Ship St. Cohasset, Mass. 02025
372	**Butler's table kit:** Heath Craft Woodworks Heath Co. Benton Harbor, Mich. 49022
374	**Chest of drawers kit:** The Bartley Collection, Ltd. 747 Oakwood Ave., Dept. RD1 Lake Forest, Ill. 60045
	Hardwoods and veneers: Albert Constantine & Son, Inc. 2050 Eastchester Rd. Bronx, N.Y. 10461
	Paste stains and varnishes: The Bartley Collection, Ltd. 747 Oakwood Ave., Dept. RD1 Lake Forest, Ill. 60045 or Heath Craft Woodworks Heath Co. Benton Harbor, Mich. 49022

CREDITS AND ACKNOWLEDGMENTS

Illustrations

Renderings on pages 8, 13 (window seat), 26 (chess set), 31 (fence), 37 (steps), 45 (desks), 49, 52, 106, 240, 266, 290, and 320 by Ray Skibinski.

Photography

Photos on pages 9 (plant stand and coat tree), 12 (serving cart), 16 (spice rack), 17 (storage rack), 18 (message board and knife block), 19 (globe lamp), 22, 24 (prep center and stool), 28 (planter and light), 29 (table), 30 (refuse locker), 39 (log tote), 40 (workbench), 58, 60, 112, 148, 156, 158, 160, 168, 192, 194, 218, 220, 236, 252, 254, 256, 298, 330, and 340 by Gene Hamilton.

Photos on pages 9 (Early American bookcase), 44 (Early American bookcase), and 62 by Ernest Coppolino.

Photos on pages 10 (bookcase), 11, 12 (end table and couch), 13 (coffee table), 14, 15 (breakfast bar), 19 (night table), 20, 21, 23 (entertainment center), 27 (picture frame), 30 (tie garden), 31 (rock garden), 32 (storage shed), 38 (lamp), 43 (butler's table), 44 (modern bookcase), 68, 72, 80, 88, 94, 108, 115, 120, 136, 166, 176, 180, 185, 188, 190, 206, 242, 264, 272, 278, 323, and 372 by Morris Karol.

Photos on pages 10 (bench), 16 (table), 17 (table), 18 (vanity), 25 (freestanding fireplace), 34 (cart), 86, 139, 150, 162, 234, and 288 by Harry Lawton.

Photos on pages 10 (coffee table), 27 (chess board), 33 (bike rack and chair), 37 (patio), 38 (wine rack), 41 (jungle gym), 76, 238, 274, 276, 308, 332, and 360 by Joel Musler.

Photos on pages 13 (cabinet), 28 (table), 100, and 247 by Joseph Barnell.

Photos on pages 15 (cupboard and work island), 16 (menu center), 17 (storage bins), 23 (sewing center), 25 (bar), 27 (room divider), 30 (greenhouse), 43 (clock), 124, 128, 144, 152, 198, 202, 224, 258, and 366 by Wayne Bukevicz.

Photos on pages 15 (work center), 24 (bookcase), 26 (wall unit), 39 (jewelry), 40 (dollhouses and playground set), 41 (seesaw and boats), 132, 214, 244, 334, 337, 344, 350, and 358 © 1976, 1977 The Reader's Digest Association Ltd., London.

Photos on pages 19 (chest) and 170 © 1981 Shopsmith, Inc., reprinted from *Hands On! The Home Workshop Magazine* by permission.

Photos on pages 25 (built-in fireplace), 29 (deck), 31 (trellis), 32 (birdhouse), 33 (doghouse), 42 (bunk beds), 45 (fireplaces), 228, 270, 284, 286, 301, and 354 by Wade Hoyt.

Photos on pages 32 (bird feeder) and 282 by Paul Lewis.

Photos on pages 34 (compost bin), 35 (window greenhouse), 292, and 294 by Robert G. Beason.

Photos on pages 34 (fountain) and 296 by Barbara Murphy.

Photos on pages 36, 37 (barbecue), 306, 310, 314, and 317 courtesy the Brick Institute of America.

Photos on pages 37 (concrete driveway) and 268 courtesy the Portland Cement Assn.

Photos on pages 38 (terrarium) and 328 by William Sonntag.

Photos on pages 42 (downhill racer) and 346 by Ellen Greisedieck.

Photos on pages 43 (beds) and 369 courtesy Cohasset Colonials.

Photos on pages 43 (chest of drawers) and 374 courtesy The Bartley Collection, Ltd.

Project designs

Shaker plant stand (58–59), Coat tree (60–61), Serving cart (112–114), Spice rack (148–149), Hanging storage rack (156–157), Cork message board (158–159), Knife storage block (160–161), Globe lamp (168–169), Jewelry box (192–193), Old-world workbench (194–197), Kitchen or bar stool (218–219), Prep and serve center (220–223), Folding screen (236–237), Outdoor table and bench (252–253), Outdoor lighting fixture (254–255), Deck or patio planter (256–257), Refuse locker (298–300), Log tote and cradle (330–331), and Child's workbench and tool caddy (340–343) designed by Katie and Gene Hamilton.

Plywood desk (49–51), Rolltop desk (52–57), Window seat (106–107), Basket-weave garden fence (266–267), Trellis (270–271), and Picket fence and gate (290–291) designed by Gordon Chapman.

Early American bookcase (62–67), Dining table (80–85), Modular couch (94–99), TV and stereo cabinet (100–105), Platform bed (180–184), Cabinet headboard unit (185–187), Entertainment center (206–213), Picnic or patio table (247–251), and Jungle gym (360–365) designed by Joseph Dross.

Jointed hardwood bookcase (68–71), Trestle coffee table (72–75), and Cherry end table (108–111) designed by Maurice Fraser.

Pegged coffee table (76–79) and Inlaid checker or chess board (238–239) designed by Frances Cohen.

Foyer bench (86–87), Cafe table and chairs (139–143), Butcher-block table (150–151), Bathroom vanity (162–165), Mission-style headboard (188–189), Freestanding fireplace (234–235), and Potting cart (288–289) designed by Harry Lawton.

Vinyl-covered couch (88–93), Breakfast bar (136–138), Reading lamp (190–191), Compost bin (292–293), and Window greenhouse (294–295) designed by Robert G. Beason.

Kitchen cabinets (115–123) designed by architect Kenneth J. McGahren, RA, and executed by cabinetmaker Rudd Rowen.

Kitchen cupboard (124–127), Mobile work island (128–131), Menu-planning center (144–147), Storage bins (152–155), Room divider (198–201), Sewing center (202–205), Mobile dry bar (224–227), and Greenhouse (258–263) designed by Bernard Price.

Peninsula work center (132–135) designed by Douglas Donaldson, AIPD.

Chest of drawers (170–175) © 1981 Shopsmith, Inc., reprinted with adaptations from *Hands On! The Home Workshop Magazine.*

Stencil designs for Stenciled blanket chest (176–179) designed by Wendy Everett for Hunt Mfg. Co. Stencil arrangement (178) executed by Wendy Everett.

Built-in bookcase (214–217) designed by Derek Hall, MSAAT.

Built-in fireplace (228–233) and Wooden deck (301–305) designed by Wade Hoyt.

Acrylic chess set (240–241) © 1976 The Reader's Digest Association Ltd., London.

Picture frame (242–243) designed by Edward R. Lipinski.

Chinese boxes wall unit (244–246) designed by Graham Henderson.

Tie garden (264–265) and Rock garden (272–273) designed by Andrew Beason.

PVC and canvas chair (274–275) and PVC bicycle rack (276–277) designed by Joel Musler.

Storage shed (278–281) designed by Mario Ferro.

Bird feeder (282–283) design © 1980 Verlag Das Beste GmbH, Stuttgart, adapted by Paul Lewis.

Birdhouse (284–285) designed by William Blanco.

A-frame doghouse (286–287) © 1980 Verlag Das Beste GmbH, Stuttgart, adapted by Wade Hoyt.

Garden fountain (296–297) designed by Barbara Murphy.

Flagstone patio (308–309) designed by Henry S. Orr.

Stained-glass lamp (323–327) designed by Thomas D. Garcia.

Steel wine rack (332–333) designed by John Maury Warde.

Metal jewelry (334–336) designed by Kevin McGlue.

Playground set (337–339) and Modular dollhouses (344–345) designed by Jackson Day Designs.

Downhill racer (346–349) designed by Sam Posey.

Candle-powered boats (350–353) designed by Ron Fuller.

Rocker and seesaw (358–359) designed by Peter Cannings.

GENERAL INDEX

Page numbers in **bold** type refer to color illustrations.

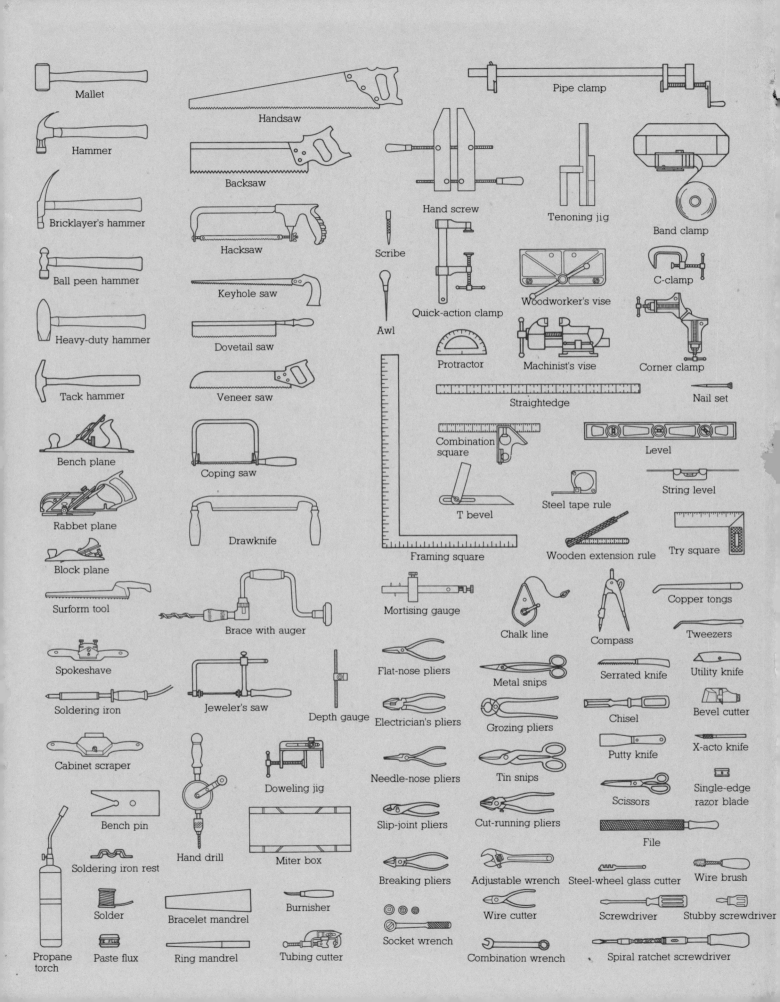

Mallet

Hammer

Bricklayer's hammer

Ball peen hammer

Heavy-duty hammer

Tack hammer

Bench plane

Rabbet plane

Block plane

Surform tool

Spokeshave

Soldering iron

Cabinet scraper

Bench pin

Soldering iron rest

Solder

Propane torch

Paste flux

Handsaw

Backsaw

Hacksaw

Keyhole saw

Dovetail saw

Veneer saw

Coping saw

Drawknife

Brace with auger

Jeweler's saw

Depth gauge

Doweling jig

Hand drill

Miter box

Bracelet mandrel

Ring mandrel

Burnisher

Tubing cutter

Scribe

Awl

Quick-action clamp

Protractor

Hand screw

Tenoning jig

Woodworker's vise

Machinist's vise

Pipe clamp

Band clamp

C-clamp

Corner clamp

Straightedge

Nail set

Combination square

Level

T bevel

Steel tape rule

String level

Framing square

Wooden extension rule

Try square

Mortising gauge

Chalk line

Compass

Copper tongs

Tweezers

Flat-nose pliers

Metal snips

Serrated knife

Utility knife

Electrician's pliers

Grozing pliers

Chisel

Bevel cutter

Needle-nose pliers

Tin snips

Putty knife

X-acto knife

Slip-joint pliers

Cut-running pliers

Scissors

Single-edge razor blade

File

Breaking pliers

Adjustable wrench

Steel-wheel glass cutter

Wire brush

Wire cutter

Screwdriver

Stubby screwdriver

Socket wrench

Combination wrench

Spiral ratchet screwdriver